REPORT

OF THE

COMMISSIONERS

APPOINTED TO INVESTIGATE THE CAUSE AND MANAGEMENT

OF

THE GREAT FIRE IN BOSTON.

BOSTON:
ROCKWELL & CHURCHILL, CITY PRINTERS,
122 Washington Street.
1873.

CITY OF BOSTON.

In Board of Aldermen, Nov. 15, 1872.

Ordered, That His Honor the Mayor be requested to appoint a scientific commission, consisting of five persons, to investigate the cause of the recent fire and the efforts made for its suppression, and report to the City Council in print; the expense attending such investigation to be charged to the appropriation for Incidentals.

Passed in Common Council. Came up for concurrence. Read and concurred. Approved by the Mayor, November 15, 1872.

A true copy.

Attest: S. F. McCLEARY,
City Clerk.

REPORT OF THE FIRE COMMISSION.

To the Honorable the City Council: —

The Commissioners appointed to investigate the cause of the recent fire, and the efforts made for its suppression, respectfully submit their Report.

The fact is painfully familiar, that on the 9th of November last, on a calm and mild evening, a fire broke out in the building numbered 83 and 85 Summer Street, and raged without control till the afternoon of the following day, spreading through the best business portions of Boston, covering sixty-five acres with ruins, destroying 776 buildings, assessed at the value of $13,500,000, and consuming merchandise and other personal property estimated at more than sixty millions of dollars.

This Commission, appointed on November 26th, was organized on the next day, and entered at once upon its duties. We have held forty-two sessions, and summoned about two hundred witnesses, including every one whose name was suggested, or of whom we could hear in any way, and giving public notice, inviting all, who had any facts to communicate. Some of the witnesses failed to appear, and we had no power to compel their appearance; nor could we insist upon having a reply to any question which the witness was reluctant to answer. Much of the testimony has been immaterial, irrelevant, and hearsay. But this was unavoidable, as our duty was, first, to make a thorough investigation, and, second, to satisfy the public that it was thorough. For the same reasons we have published a mass of testimony, some of which is of little value, preferring to let each witness tell his story to the community in his own way, rather than appear to suppress any material portion of the evidence. We regret that the time necessarily consumed in printing this testimony has so long delayed our report.

ORIGIN OF THE FIRE.

It is conclusively proved that the fire began near the elevator in the rear of the basement of the building, and passed with great rapidity up the elevator to the upper stories. The positive testimony of the many witnesses who distinctly saw the fire in the basement first, and then saw it, in the language of one of them, "roaring up the elevator," is not controlled by the negative testimony of those who from their position failed to see the flames in the lower part of the building, or of those who did not see the fire at all until it had mounted to the upper stories and the roof. The condition of the floor, after the ruin, shows that it probably began near the ceiling.

To the more important question how the fire began, no answer can be given. There is no evidence whatever criminating any of the occupants of the building, nor is there anything to show that it caught from the furnace or the boiler, except the fact that it began in that portion of the building. And the condition of the boiler and its surroundings, after the fire and the excavations, as described by witnesses, and as observed by members of the Commission, seem to show that it did not take from the heating apparatus, unless it took from some flue. Of this there is no evidence.

We would also say that there is no reason to believe that there was any incendiarism during the progress of the fire. The only witness who expressed his suspicion on this point admitted that showers of sparks were falling upon the building of which he spoke; and he did not know whether the windows were open or closed.

Nor, during the ten days following the fire, was there one case of incendiarism in the city, notwithstanding the sensational reports prevailing at the time. Owing to the strict precautions taken, and especially to the closing of the liquor saloons, the city was unusually free from crime and disturbance during this period.

The fire was first seen at 7.08 or 7.10 P. M. The first alarm was given at 7.24. The second alarm was at 7.29, followed by alarms at 7.34, 7.45, and at 8 P. M. When first seen, the fire had made great headway, and yet there was a disastrous and strange delay of quarter of an hour in giving the alarm. We would call especial attention to the evidence of Messrs. Sargent and Brown, policemen of Charlestown, who saw the fire from Prison Point Bridge. We refer to their testimony, because they fix the time by a clock, and by a depot clock, which may well be supposed to have been accurate.

Their statement is, in general, confirmed by many persons present in Summer and Kingston Streets, and it leaves no doubt that, for fifteen minutes after the fire had become visible, even in a neighboring city, no steps were taken to call out the Fire Department of Boston.

Yet there is no evidence of fault on the part of our police. Each man in the neighborhood was on his beat, and engaged in the discharge of his duty. At ten minutes before seven an officer had passed the building, and observed nothing. Several of them, on seeing the fire, started at once; and officer Page, happening to stand by a box, when he saw it, lost not a second in sounding the alarm.

The rear of the building where the fire began was on an alley, not frequented, and not likely to be observed. It is, of course, always a matter of chance how soon an officer shall see a fire in any portion of his beat. The probability of seeing it early would be increased, if there were more officers and less extensive beats.

It is a remarkable fact that so little was done by the neighbors and bystanders towards giving the alarm. Some of them testify that they were criticising the Fire Department, and wondering at their delay, while they, themselves, were neglecting to take the only means for calling them out. In this connection, we shall inquire, in another portion of our report, whether the city does not need more fire-boxes, freer access to them by the citizens, and a more general knowledge as to the places where keys are deposited. The annoyance of an occasional false alarm is not to be weighed against the dangers of delay.

The rapid spread of the fire in the building first consumed was chiefly owing to this delay, and to the faulty construction of the elevator, which, like most other elevators in Boston, was sheathed with wood, and destitute of self-closing hatchways. If the proprietors of the building had procured automatic hatchways, such as are generally used in factories, and one of which was in use in a neighbor's warehouse, our city would probably have escape this calamity, as the fire would not have reached the roof before the engines arrived.

DANGEROUS ARCHITECTURE.

The uncontrolled spread of the conflagration from the first building through the great district swept by the flames, was principally owing to the delay of the apparatus in arriving, and to the general faulty construction of the buildings, and especially to the exposure of timber to the flames at a height which could not be reached by water, — an exposure which would deserve condemnation, even at a lower level. The dangers arising from this mode of building were greatly aggravated by the narrowness of the streets, and by the great height of the buildings.

This danger had been foreseen, and our calamity had been foretold both here and abroad. There is sad interest in the statements of our State Insurance Commissioner, who tells us that just before the fire, English underwriters spoke to him, at Liverpool and London, of the probable fate of Franklin Street, Winthrop Square, and their surroundings, and proposed to cancel their policies, and to cease insuring in our city. While some of us were justly priding ourselves on the elegant architecture of this district, and boasting that it was practically fire-proof, English insurers were dreading a conflagration on this very spot, and preparing to withdraw their agencies from our city.

These dangers had been brought to the attention of the public, and of our municipal authorities. The remarkable warning of Mr. Joseph Bird was given through the press in November, 1871. The members of the Fire Department protested in vain against the style of building; and the Chief Engineer, especially, declared, after the Chicago fire, that a similar disaster might occur in our own city, and on this very spot. It was plain to him and his associates that our style of building required larger provision for the extinction of fire than we had made.

With this knowledge, the department should have taken all possible precautions, so that every fire might be met at the earliest moment. Seeing that our only salvation lay in confining every fire to the building where it began, no time should have been lost by the department in bringing all its available force to the scene of each fire.

DELAY FROM WANT OF HORSES.

Unfortunately this was not done. During the prevalence of the horse distemper, the department relied upon hand-power to bring up the apparatus; and this error was one great cause of the terrible calamity that befell us on November ninth. It is no less our duty to censure this error, because rumor has greatly exaggerated the delays caused by it. We know that many witnesses of the fire confounded the time that elapsed before the alarm with the time that elapsed after the alarm and before the arrival of the apparatus; and many added these two periods together in making up their charge against the department. We know that there is some difficulty in using untried horses in drawing steamers, but it was a difficulty which could be overcome, which has been overcome in other cases, and was overcome in some instances on that very night. The testimony shows that volunteers were enrolled in order to facilitate the arrival of engines, and that an order had been given to the police, designed to secure a more prompt alarm during the prevalence of the disease. We admit also that the difference of speed between horse-power and hand-power is less than the general public suppose. But, with all these reasons for mitigating censure, the great fact remains; time was invaluable, and time was lost.

The first piece of apparatus, Hose 2, came as soon as it could have come by horse-power. So did the first engine, No. 7. These were from the immediate vicinity. Engine 15 came as fast as it could have come by horse-power. Three engines were drawn by horses. But all the other Boston apparatus was delayed from three or five minutes for the nearest, to forty minutes for the most distant. No one can tell what was the cost of these minutes to our city.

It will not be supposed that the horses were dispensed with from motives of humanity. It is not denied by any one, however humane, that man has a right to overwork a beast in case of necessity, or to work a beast to death, if the need be sufficiently great. The horses of the department were not used, because they were generally unfit to be used, and could not have gone as fast as the men did. Excepting, perhaps, a few that were convalescent, and excepting a few that were employed, they were rightly left in the stable or the hospital. The fatal error lay in not having supplied their places with others able to do the work. The evidence shows that at that time the disease had greatly abated; that horses were freely used on the omnibus and horse-railroad lines, and were in general use in the city, and before this time might readily have been obtained for the use of the Fire Department. There is no evidence that this occurred to any one, but it ought to have occurred to those whose especial duty it was to guard the community from the perils of fire.

The fact that there was loss of time appears from the table of time (approximate) made by each piece of apparatus, printed in Appendix, and from the testimony of the officers who were all examined on this point. It is the testimony of honest and heroic men, whose desires and feelings and prejudices would all lead them to uphold their department, and to protect their Chief, but who state facts as they occurred.

We cannot but feel that the earlier arrival of aid, between 7.30 and 8 P.M., might perhaps have prevented the flames from crossing from Summer to Otis Street, both by throwing streams on the northerly side of Summer street, and by reducing the heat on the southerly side, which prevented such streams from being thrown on the opposite buildings. This was the "key of the fire" at its outset; and when it was lost, the flames became almost uncontrollable. But even then, a larger force might, possibly, have checked the fire before it had crossed Franklin street. Whether the employment of horses would alone have achieved success at either of these points, it is impossible to form a definite opinion.

WANT OF WATER IN THE BURNT DISTRICT.

The efforts of the firemen were greatly impeded by the want of water, especially in Summer street. The demands of the Chief Engineer for larger mains, for more hydrants, and for the more efficient Lowry hydrant, had been unsuccessful. He had especially called attention to the exposed condition of this district; and his forebodings were fully realized. The insufficient supply of water was felt at the outset, and was, without doubt, one cause of the conflagration.

WANT OF FUEL.

There is proof that some of the engines early on the ground were not properly supplied with coal; but there is no proof that there was any loss of power from that cause, at that time of the evening. The place of coal was filled by broken boxes and by other wood; and although this is not the proper fuel for our fire engines, it does make steam as quickly as coal. Later in the night, when the fire had gained proportions altogether beyond the preparations made by the department, there was, in some cases, an entire lack of fuel. In one case it was reported that an engine had come upon the ground early in the night without fuel, but this was proved by overwhelming evidence to have been a mistake of the witnesses.

THE FIRE DEPARTMENT.

The engines were generally in good order, and they continued to be so throughout the fire; the hose was generally excellent. Some difficulty arose in coupling, as the hydrant-couplings of different towns differ in size. This is not strange, and can only be remedied by a general law; but it does seem strange that Boston hydrant-couplings differ from each other, being of two sizes. Some of the Commission were surprised to learn that we have no engine of the largest size in Boston. We need larger steamers, and in the city proper we need a larger number. In the city proper we have but six engines. There are the same number in Ward 16. The assessed value of the property of the city proper is $514,697,450.00. The assessed value of property taxed in Ward 16 is $31,395,300.00.

In the most important element of a Fire Department — in its men — Boston has the best material. Words fail to describe the courage and devotion of our firemen. No battle-field ever witnessed nobler heroism than was seen in our streets. The story of the fire, as told simply and truthfully by the engineers, is a story of hardships endured and dangers braved in obedience to duty. More than one of our firemen has literally proved "faithful unto death." We know that the whole community join in the praise recently bestowed by our Mayor on the members of the department, and in the thanks which he renders to the authorities and citizens of other places, far and near, who so promptly furnished aid in our time of need.

The successful resistance of the firemen on the southern boundary of the district, and again in preventing the fire from crossing Washington Street, and finally on the northern line, when it was conquered, has left in the scorched and half-burned buildings now standing indisputable proofs of their great service.

THE CHIEF ENGINEER.

The Chief Engineer deserves all praise for his courage. He shrank from no exertion, and from no danger. Indeed, he sometimes exposed his life when it ought not to have been risked. He manifestly intended to do all that he could to subdue the flames. He is described as being cool, and, with perhaps one exception, as master of himself, of his temper, and of his faculties. But while seeing this, and while admiring his many good qualities, we cannot fail to see that there was a want of preparation for so great an emergency, a want of system when the emergency came, and especially the want of a leader capable of grasping the details of a great plan adapted to the terrible occasion. The fire was attacked piecemeal, as chances occurred. The heroism of individuals was too often wasted, because it was not directed by a master-mind.

The Chief seems to have performed the duties of a fireman from time to time, now placing a ladder, now performing some act of humanity, now applying fire to a mine. In a word, he tried to unite the services of a private with those of a commander-in-chief. It seems to us that, at such a time, the Head of the Force should remain for the most part in some accessible place where he could command a view of the conflagration — a place known to his subordinates, where he could receive reports from them, and send them his orders. This would prevent much confusion; and orders would be issued more wisely and carried out more effectually than when the Chief is actually engaged in fighting the fire from place to place. For example, when aid from abroad was telegraphed for, the Superintendents of Railroads were not generally informed of this, nor were they requested to "give the track" to the coming engines. This necessarily delayed the coming of the desired aid. It is not strange that this did not occur to one who was risking his life in actual warfare with the flames. It would have occurred to one who was directing the contest, as a commander directs an army.

Again: Mr. Damrell gave an excellent order to the Deputy Chief of Police, that a hundred officers should be detailed to combat the fire with wet carpets, or other woollen fabrics. This order was wholly ineffectual, because there were no men who could be so detailed. But there were thousands of good citizens in the streets — longing to be of some service — who would gladly have performed this duty under proper leaders. These would have been found if the Chief had allowed himself leisure to superintend the whole work, instead of spending his time and power in attending personally to details. For the same reason, there was great lack of attention to the reception and disposition of engines from other towns. They were, no doubt, desirous of being directed by our Chief; and the law gave him nearly absolute power over all persons present. This power was by no means fully exercised.

Great complaint has been made, that hose were not in more instances carried to the roofs, or upper stories of buildings, where water could be more effectually used. It is replied, that this was done more frequently than is supposed. For instance, at the corner of Otis and Summer Streets, where it has been said that no hose was carried up, it was done, bravely, and, for a time, with good prospects of success. It is further said, that the great heat made it unsafe, and often impossible, so to use the hose. When this is said by brave and skilful firemen, no member of the Commission can deny it; and the most critical of the witnesses admit that they may have erred in preferring their judgment on such a point to the opinion of veterans. It is certain that this desirable way of applying water was rendered much more dangerous and difficult by the absence of fire-escapes on the buildings, which would have provided a way of retreat, and which would, therefore, have given confidence to the firemen.

It is said, also, that great quantities of water were wasted by being thrown ineffectually against closed windows and granite fronts at the second and third stories, while the upper stories of the building were consumed by the flames, and reached by no streams. This, undoubtedly, did occur, both early in the fire and afterward, when, from causes just mentioned, the roofs could not be reached by the men, who still desired to make some use, however slight, of the water and of the apparatus. A more thorough supervision of these men would have employed them and the engines in some better service.

Ill feeling must often arise at large fires from suspicion that favor is shown in directing the efforts of firemen. The commission have carefully examined one such charge; and we find that the Chief Engineer acted with great discretion in withdrawing a stream of water from a house which probably could not have been saved, and in ordering it to be used in Oliver Street, where, with the aid of other streams, and by personal efforts by the occupants of the buildings, the lower side of Oliver Street was saved from destruction, and the fire was prevented from spreading to the varnish, oil, and paint stores in the rear.

EFFORTS OF CITIZENS TO SAVE THEIR OWN BUILDINGS.

The occupants of some of these buildings on Oliver Street have been summoned by the Commission, and have told their story modestly. Enough appears to show that they fought back the fire by their personal exertions, and put heart into the firemen by their example. If the flames had passed this point, it is difficult to say where they could have been stayed. Thus a great service was rendered to the public. Like remarks apply to the owner and occupants of the store of Messrs. Hovey & Co., on Summer street. The story of their co-operation with the firemen, both at the great fire and at the renewal of that fire on Monday morning, deserves to be carefully read and remembered. The same building had been saved by like means, on a former occasion, — when the Adelphi Theatre was burned. It now stands a monument to the value of substantial construction, and to the worth of energy, of common sense and of hopeful courage.

Mr. Freeland also rendered invaluable service by directing the efforts of the firemen on the City Exchange. The occupants of the buildings on the west side of Washington street were equally efficient in protecting their buildings with wet cloths and carpets. Similar efforts on the part of others would have saved much property from destruction. It was one misfortune of the night that owners and occupants were generally absent, and therefore the firemen were unable to obtain information as to gas, water, the construction of buildings, and other important particulars.

The conduct of the gentlemen to whom we have referred as aiding the firemen by their personal exertions, was in marked contrast with the thoughtlessness of many spectators who crowded the streets, and greatly impeded the efforts of the department. In some cases violence was necessarily used toward these persons. Yet, many of them would have gladly joined in efforts to save property, if more well-directed efforts had been made to that end.

We have received, and are compelled to publish, some evidence of misconduct by a few firemen, and by men who wore the badges of firemen. The instances were rare. We are glad to believe that much of the wrong-doing was by men who falsely represented themselves as belonging to the honorable body of firemen. And we feel bound to condemn the grave mistake of those who gave away their stocks of goods when it was impossible to save them. The motive was amiable, but the practice tended to demoralize firemen and other citizens, to encourage theft by confounding thieves with honest men, and to bring about a time of plunder and confusion.

POLICE AND MILITARY.

This was one of the greatest troubles with which the police were obliged to contend, as it became impossible for them to distinguish the guilty from the innocent. The conduct of the police officers was exemplary; and their services, considering their limited number, were very efficient. They were reinforced by the Marines from Charlestown Navy Yard; by regular soldiers from the forts, and by the Volunteer Militia of the State. Thanks are due, and thanks have been rendered to those bodies, for their effective aid. At every great fire in a large city, military assistance in preserving order has become a recognized necessity. Fortunately, we have in our Volunteer Militia an armed police, of whose aid no citizen need be jealous. It is desirable that some signal should be fixed, by which in like emergencies, or in any emergency, they may be called into immediate service.

DANGERS FROM GAS.

The fire, like all great city conflagrations, was greatly aggravated by the escape of gas from the burning buildings. The fall of heavy warehouses broke the main pipes, and on Monday morning, the escaped gas in the sewers exploded, and caused another fire, which destroyed a million of property, and cost two lives. The officers of the Gas Company believed that their water-valves were sufficiently powerful to cut off the supply of gas, as they had proved to be hitherto, but found that the belief was an error.

The lack of valves properly constructed, and so placed as to isolate the burnt district, led to terrible loss, exposed us to the inconvenience and peril of total darkness during two nights, and endangered the whole city. The company have undertaken to repair this error by providing sliding-valves. The risk arising from the impossibility of isolating a burning district should never be incurred again.

GUNPOWDER.

The peril from the combustion of gas was increased by the manner of using gunpowder. And this is only one of many dangers incurred by the unscientific use of explosives.

The law governing the demolition of buildings by gunpowder, or otherwise, during a fire, is fixed by the statutes of the Commonwealth, and has been explained in several decisions. The power is given to three firewards, and in their absence, to other civil or military officers. In Boston, the power of firewards is given by statute to the Engineers; and the City Ordinance provides, that if the Chief is present, he must be one of the three Engineers consenting to the demolition of a building. When three firewards, or in Boston three Engineers, are present, no one else has by statute the right to destroy a building, in order to stay a fire. One fireward has no more right to do this than any other person, even when it is impossible, by reason of the fire, for three to be present; nor has one fireward a right to act, even when the Board has voted to grant the power to one, in case of an exigency. It is not enough, that three firewards concur that gunpowder must be used in general. No building can be destroyed, until it has been specially adjudged by the three there present, that the particular building must be destroyed. As the power to select a building for destruction cannot be delegated to one fireward, of course it cannot be delegated to any other person. It is necessary to state the law so far, in order to appreciate the action of various parties at this fire. For this reason we give in the appendix a statement of the laws and of the decisions in this Commonwealth.

The common-law right, which exists independently of legislation, and which prevails everywhere, to destroy a structure, in order to suppress a fire, is not taken away or superseded by the statutes of this state.

There is a conflict of testimony as to the balance of good or evil arising from the use of gunpowder on November 9 and 10. It is less necessary to strike that balance accurately, because all witnesses agree, and all sane people will agree, that explosives never should be used again, as they were at that time, and that, if used at all, we should be prepared to employ them skilfully, carefully, and by a fixed plan. We have no word of censure for the citizens who volunteered to risk their lives in brave and energetic attempts to save the city. But they will all admit that the only justification for employing powder, as it was employed, is the fact that no proper provision had been made for the use of explosives; and they will concur with us, that the greatest wonder of that night was, that no life was lost, and no personal injury was incurred from the use of gunpowder.

The Chief and his associates did not believe in explosives. They had studied the matter to some extent, and generally agree in condemning this method of attempting to check fires. This is one reason why no preparation had been made by storing a magazine, nor by providing means for confining powder when used, nor by drilling persons for its use. We were left to the chances of obtaining an inadequate supply at the shops, or of sending to a distant magazine, or of taking it from the powder boats. We were, also, left to the chances of finding skill and discretion to apply this dangerous remedy. Yet history had told us that gunpowder had often been used with good effect in staying great conflagrations. The story of the Fire in London was in the books of children. After the great Boston fire in 1678, the town was divided into four districts, each of which was provided with four barrels of gunpowder for use in case of fire. And in our own day the town of Nantucket had been saved from destruction, by the foresight and courage of one man, who prepared in advance to use gunpowder in the day of need, and who dared to use it when the day came.

When it was at last decided to use powder, it was done by the Chief Engineer giving written authority to several public-spirited gentlemen to remove goods and demolish buildings. Some slight attempt at organization was made, but no proper system of action was devised; and in a short time the different parties were in confusion and at variance. Instead of three Engineers designating the buildings to be demolished, each man was left to act as he pleased. The Chief Engineer now heartily condemns his error in this respect, and we agree with him. It is evident that he was still unconvinced of the wisdom of using powder, and that he yielded to the pressing demands made by many of our best citizens.

The course actually pursued was objectionable, not because it was illegal, but because it was dangerous and inefficient. The action of the parties was not such as is provided by statute, nor such as is necessary to make the city liable for the property destroyed. But it by no means follows that it was unlawful. The courts of our own state and country, and of other states and countries have always held that, in case of necessity, it is lawful to demolish buildings, in order to stay the spread of a fire. And in our own state it has been distinctly declared that this right is not taken away by the statutes regulating Fire Departments. It was impossible to obtain the adjudication of three engineers, including the Chief, on each building selected for demolition. The assistant engineers could not be constantly withdrawn from their other duties without great injury to their work, nor was it possible for the Chief to be present at each building proposed to be destroyed. But it is to be deeply regretted that there was not a more thorough organization of the parties engaged in this service.

The dangers of using gunpowder at a fire hardly need to be stated.

It demolishes the gas pipes, and thus creates a fierce fire when the gas is not shut off; it tends to scatter the flames; it drives back and discourages the firemen; and, above all, it causes long delay in attempting to quench a fire, when delay is ruinous. Added to this is the danger of premature and accidental explosions, especially when powder is carried in open kegs, as it was, at least in one case, at our fire.

RECOMMENDATIONS.

Dangerous as explosives are, they must sometimes be used, and we suggest, as our first recommendation, that preparation be made for the future, for using a far more powerful and less dangerous explosive, and for training a number of men to use it skilfully. The best explosive now known for this purpose is Dynamite, sometimes known as Giant Powder. It is ten times as powerful as gunpowder. Its force as an explosive is so directed as to bring down a building, rather than to scatter its materials. It does not, of itself, kindle any fire when exploded, nor does it explode when brought into contact with fire. It may be dropped, or jarred in any way without danger; and cartridges containing it may be safely cut or broken; so that it is free from the peculiar perils that attend the use of other explosives, and especially of gunpowder. It may be safely stored and conveyed to the midst of a fire. Some better article may be furnished by science; but, at present, this is clearly the best known material for the purpose under consideration.

A quantity of this material should be kept constantly in proper places.

A portion of the force belonging to the Fire Department should be instructed in the use of it, and especially in the proper manner of using it at fires. These men might do other and ordinary work in the department; for it probably will not be thought expedient to keep a body of men exclusively for a service which may not be required for many years, and which we hope will never be required. They would act, of course, under the orders of the Chief Engineer, and the Chief, with some, or all of his assistants, should be trained in the use of explosives.

It seems to us that the law on this subject needs careful revision; and if general legislation is not desired, that a special Act should regulate the demolition of buildings in Boston in cases of fire, so as to secure more prompt action.

MORE ENGINES.

We need more fire apparatus, more men, and more powerful engines. It would probably be wise to procure a few larger steamers, and reserve them for great emergencies, as the lighter ones are more easily handled. We gladly record the construction of a powerful fire boat; and one member of the Commission has witnessed its successful use. The feasibility of using a self-propelling engine with advantage in our streets perhaps needs to be tested further. In this connection we call attention to Richard's Hose Elevator and Fire Escape, a sample of which is now attached to the Lawrence building, at West street. The new engines, or some of them, should be placed in the large districts still exposed and unprotected.

WATER SUPPLY.

The city needs a better distribution of water, especially in the burned district. The six-inch pipe in Summer street was entirely inadequate to the needs of a street, which has changed its character, from a place of private dwellings to a street of great warehouses. Nor is this the only district where such a need exists.

We also want more hydrants, and hydrants better adapted to the use of firemen. The Lowry hydrant, which is used in the neighboring towns, in the Highlands, in Ward 16, and in East Boston, is quite as necessary in the city proper. The evidence shows that while it is less liable to freeze than our hydrant, it will furnish four engines with two streams each. Such was the operation of the Lowry hydrant which was tried for a short time in Winthrop Square, in 1862, and its success then led to its adoption by Charlestown. This style of hydrant is attached to the main pipe, while ours are attached to four-inch branch pipes. It gives five times the supply of the Boston hydrant, which was fit only for the hand engines. Abundant evidence has long shown that little or no trouble arises from the use of these hydrants during the season of snow, or at any time.

MISCELLANEOUS.

The supply of fuel for the steamers should be more methodical. A want of system prevails as to the duty of shutting off the water at the reservoirs, and this leads to waste. This duty should be provided for by a fixed rule. The overflow from the reservoir should not be allowed to pass into the sewers. If it flowed into the street, the water would be made visible.

Bridges are needed for the protection of hose. We have already called attention to the need of more fire-boxes, and to the question whether they should not be made more accessible. The Mayor has recommended that the police force should be enlarged. We heartily indorse the recommendation, with a view to security from fire, while the increase is needed for other purposes as well. The police is our chief reliance for giving early alarms.

The Chief Engineer suggests that a large fire-bell be placed on the City Hall, to supersede the various bells in the city proper which now give the alarm, with the idea that one bell would give it more clearly. We commend the suggestion to your consideration.

We call attention to an extract from a letter of Prof. Tyndall, as to Respirators, which we are permitted to print in the Appendix.

It seems to us that the Committee on the Fire Department should have a wider jurisdiction, including all means of subduing and preventing fires. At present, another committee has charge of the location and construction of engine houses; a third committee takes charge of fire alarms, while a distinct department places or removes the hydrants. Thus, the means of extinguishing fires are parcelled out among four bodies of officials. Unity of action, rather than division of labor, would seem desirable in this matter. We would, also, respectfully suggest, that if the Engineers were nominated by the Mayor and confirmed by the City Council, it would be one step toward the establishment of a more responsible rule than we now have. The appointment of a competent Fire Inspector appears to be desirable.

THE BUILDING ACT.

The Building Act passed at the extra session of the Legislature seems to us to need careful revision, aided by the testimony of skilful architects. It is especially desirable that ELEVATORS in warehouses should be forbidden, except such as are constructed with self-closing hatchways. Experience has shown that these can be made with little cost, and used without any inconvenience. They are not only a safeguard against the spread of fire, but they are of great value in preventing loss of life by accident. If the existing law relative to FIRE-ESCAPES could be extended to all warehouses, or, better still, to all buildings of a certain size, it would tend to save life, and to encourage firemen in their work. It is well to consider whether every high warehouse ought not to have a permanent stand-pipe of iron capable of having hose attached to it.

GAS.

Proper sliding valves should be placed on the gas-mains and distributing pipes as soon as possible, and the districts capable of being isolated by each valve should be small. The Gas Light Company will be obliged to replace all the gas mains in the burnt district, and expect to take this opportunity to supply a sufficient number of valves. It would be well to have this, and other similar work, done under the supervision of some competent person in the interests of the city. The Fire Department should attend to the shutting off of gas more systematically and thoroughly than they now do; or the Gas Company should be represented at every fire by one or more persons detailed for this service.

PORTABLE APPARATUS.

We would earnestly recommend the general use of Fire Extinguishers and Hand Pumps in every building. These would prevent many fires from becoming serious, and they would inspire confidence in cases of alarm of fire.

FINALLY.

The Commission are unanimous in the opinion that His Honor Mayor Gaston intended to do his full duty, and labored faithfully to that end. But Messrs. Philbrick and Firth hold that he failed to give that guidance, unity and efficiency to the efforts made to stay the fire, which the occasion required, and which the public had a right to expect from their Mayor.

The majority had not supposed that a criticism of the Mayor, favorable or otherwise, was expected from a Commission appointed by the Mayor to consider the cause of the fire, and the efforts made to suppress it. One of their number is certain that he would not have been appointed as member of a Court of Inquiry on Mayor Gaston, and if appointed, he would not have served.

We find no evidence that the Mayor failed of any duty in regard to the efforts for suppressing the fire. That duty belonged to the Chief Engineer and his associates. They were not subordinate to the Mayor in this respect, but were by law his superiors. Nor does the Mayor have, officially, any especial knowledge as to fires, or the art of suppressing them. The increase of a fire to the proportions of a great conflagration, does not, by law, transfer the charge of its suppression from the skilled official to the unskilled, nor does it, in fact, confer experience upon him. We think the Mayor properly left the service of subduing the fire to those whose duty it was to perform it, and who were best qualified for the work. And, since it has become necessary to speak on the subject, we thank him for the coolness, intelligence and firmness which he displayed in the performance of his duties at a most trying time, and especially for the firmness with which he withstood the solicitation of many eminent citizens, who, in the excitement of the moment, demanded of him an unlawful and disastrous course of action.

We repeat our regret that the time required for printing the testimony has so long delayed the presentation of our report, and that we are now obliged to present it without the printed evidence. We regret, also, that it was impossible to arrange more conveniently the order of the witnesses. We heard them in such order as we could find them, and as it suited their convenience to attend. And their testimony was reported, and necessarily printed in the order in which it was given. We have tried to deal with it fairly, and now submit to your honorable bodies the result of our careful consideration.

THOMAS RUSSELL,
CHARLES G. GREENE,
SAMUEL C. COBB,
A. FIRTH,
E. S. PHILBRICK.

APPENDIX A.

SOME LAWS AND DECISIONS IN MASSACHUSETTS AS TO FIRES.

The General Statutes, Chapter 24, Secs. 4, 5, 6, 7, are as follows:

SECT. 4. The firewards, or any three of them, present at a place in immediate danger from a fire, and where no firewards are appointed, the Selectmen, or Mayor and Aldermen present, or in their absence, two or more of the civil officers present, or in their absence two or more of the chief military officers of the place present, may direct any house or building to be pulled down or demolished when they judge the same to be necessary in order to prevent the spreading of the fire.

SECT. 5. If such pulling-down or demolishing of a house or building is the means of stopping the fire, or if the fire stops before it comes to the same, the owner shall be entitled to recover a reasonable compensation from the city or town; but when such building is that in which the fire first broke out, the owner shall receive no compensation.

SECT. 6. Such firewards or other officers may, during the continuance of a fire, require assistance for extinguishing the same, and removing furniture, goods, or merchandise from a building on fire or in danger thereof; and may appoint guards to secure the same. They may also require assistance for pulling down or demolishing any house or building, when they judge it necessary; and may suppress all tumults and disorders at such fires.

SECT. 7. They may direct the stations and operations of the engine-men with their engines, and of all other persons for the purpose of extinguishing the fire; and whoever refuses or neglects to obey such orders shall forfeit for each offence a sum not exceeding ten dollars.

Act of 1850, Chapter 262, gives Boston power to establish a Fire Department; and in Sect. 3 confers on the Engineers thereof the same power that was given by the Revised Statutes to firewards. The General Statutes are on this point a re-enactment of the Revised Statutes.

City Fire Ordinance, Sect. 11. "Whenever it is adjudged at any fire, by any three or more of the Engineers present, of whom the Chief Engineer, if present, shall be one, to be necessary in order to prevent the further spreading of the fire to pull down or otherwise demolish any building, the same may be done by their joint order."

The statute provision making compensation does not apply to a building which is pulled down after it is so far burnt that it is impossible to save it from destruction by fire. (Taylor *vs.* Plymouth, 8 Metcalf, 462.)

In this case, page 465, Chief Justice Shaw says: "In order to charge the town, the remedy being given by statute, the case must clearly be brought within the statute. Independently of the statute, the pulling down of a building in a city or compact town in time of fire is justified upon the great doctrine of public safety, when it is necessary. (Mouse's case, 12 Coke, 63.)"

In Coffin *vs.* Nantucket, 5 Cushing, 269, it was held, that the town was not liable, where one fireward gave the order to demolish a building, under the supposed authority of a by-law delegating the power to one, in urgent cases.

In Ruggles *vs.* Nantucket, 11 Cushing, 433, it was decided that in order to maintain an action against a town for property destroyed to prevent the further spread of a fire, it must be shown by the owner of a house, that the destruction of his house was ordered by three firewards, and not merely that they agreed generally that some houses must be demolished, and that the plaintiff's house was selected by one of them. "The plain intent of the statute is, that no house or building shall be demolished, unless it shall be judged necessary by three firewards, or by other officers authorized to act, in their absence, or where no firewards have been appointed." "They must determine upon the particular house or building, which they shall adjudge necessary to be destroyed."

In Power *vs.* Pettengill, 11 Allen, 507, it is decided, that one fireward acting alone has no more authority than any other man to direct the destruction of a house, although it may be impossible for the other firewards or officers named to get to the place when the occasion for their action arises.

In this case, which grew out of the great fire in Gloucester, it was also held that the plaintiff could only recover the value of his property at the time of its destruction, taking into account the risk from the fire.

In Metallic Compression Casting Company *vs.* Fitchburg Railroad Company, argued with Middlesex cases, 1872, Chief Justice Chapman repeats the statement that the common-law right to use or destroy property to check a fire is not superseded by the statute on the subject.

The duty of extinguishing fires and of keeping engines in repair and ready for use is imposed not upon towns or cities, but upon firewards, engineers and other officers, chosen either by the inhabitants or by the selectmen, or Mayor and Aldermen. (Fisher *vs.* Boston, 104 Allen, 87.)

Insurance against loss or damage by fire covers a loss arising in part from explosion and in part from combustion of gunpowder on the premises. (Scripture *vs.* Lowell Mutual Fire Ins. Co., 10 Cushing, 356.)

EVIDENCE.

ALEXANDER K. YOUNG, *Sworn.*

Q. (By Mr. Russell.) Where do you live?

A. In Chelsea.

Q. Of what store were you the occupant?

A. I was the occupant of the third and fourth stories, and part of the fifth story of the building on Summer street, entrance No. 87. I was the lessee of the fifth story, and occupied a portion of it.

Q. For what purpose did you occupy it?

A. The manufacture and sale of hoop-skirts and bustles, and the sale of corsets; not the manufacture of corsets.

Q. How many persons did you employ?

A. Usually, about two hundred and fifty. When we paid off, the last pay-day, we paid off one hundred and sixty hands — since the fire. Since the horse disease, the trade has dropped off some.

Q. How many of those were employed on the premises?

A. About two hundred and thirty, probably; two hundred and twenty-five or two hundred and thirty.

Q. Any machinery on the premises?

A. Nothing but sewing machines and eyelet presses, — such machinery as is used in the manufacture of hoop-skirts, operated by the foot; nothing run by steam.

Q. Was there any steam used in the building?

A. There was; for heating and hoisting.

Q. Where was the steam engine?

A. In the basement.

Q. Directly under your premises?

A. Well, my premises covered the whole estate. It was in the basement of the same building.

Q. Anything else in the basement?

A. Well, yes, Tebbetts, Baldwin & Davis occupied it and the first floor; and they hired, I should judge, about seven-eighths of the fifth floor, for storing, and used it for a packing-room for shipping.

Q. (By Mr. FIRTH.) What was their business?

A. Dry goods and merchandise, wholesale.

Q. (By Mr. RUSSELL.) How much stock had you there?

A. We have just returned our proof of loss to the insurance companies, which amounts to $50,746.63.

Q. Where were you insured?

A. I don't know, sir. I can give you the amount of insurance,—$17,600.

Q. Do you know how the offices stand as to solvency?

A. My impression is that they are good, with the exception of one, which offers eighty cents. The amount of that is $2,300.

Q. When were you on the premises last before the fire?

A. About half-past five o'clock on that Saturday evening, as near as I can judge. It might have varied five minutes, one way or the other.

Q. How many persons did you leave there?

A. I was the last, with two others; I locked the store myself.

Q. Who were the others?

A. One was Patrick Cotter; the other's name is Boyd K. Bullock, our bookkeeper; and my wife — I forgot her.

Q. Where does Cotter live?

A. In Charlestown.

Q. Do you know his address?

A. No, sir, I don't. He is down at our temporary place at the present time.

Q. Bullock, I suppose, is with you, of course?

A. Yes, sir.

Q. Did Cotter lock the door?

A. I locked it myself, sir.

Q. When did you first hear of the fire?

A. I don't know what the hour was. I should judge it was after eight o'clock. I was visiting a friend. I was in the house of Capt. A. J. Hilborn, in Chelsea,—Mr. Klous's partner, the owner of the building.

Q. I suppose you know nothing about the cause of the fire?

A. No, sir.

Q. Any suspicions?

A. Well, I have not had any suspicions of anybody. There were some circumstances which looked rather strange to me. The grounds of suspicion would be so very slight that I should not like to volunteer to state them. I don't want to say that I suspect any one.

Q. You have been burned out once or twice before?

A. Never but once.

Q. When was that?

A. That was, I should judge, in 1864 — No. 65 Hanover street.

Q. In the same business?

A. Yes, sir.

Q. What was supposed to be the cause of that fire?

A. Well, if I remember correctly, there were some parties who had recently moved into the place below, who had been burned out several times before, and some people suspected them. They did not get their insurance. They had a very light stock.

Q. Who were they?

A. I don't remember. In fact, the whole thing had gone from my mind. Our insurance was very light — six thousand dollars. Our loss was considerably in excess of that.

Q. Is that the only time?

A. That is the only time. I was a member of a New York firm, that is, I had an interest in it, but gave no personal attention to it, and had been there but very seldom. They were the agents for the sale of Samuel Williston's spool thread. At the time they got burned out, the fire originated above them, in a hoop-skirt factory, and damaged them with water.

Q. That was in New York?

A. Yes, sir, on Chambers street.

Q. You were never burned out in Boston at any other time than you have stated?

A. There was a slight fire in Sudbury street, where the damage was about a hundred dollars. I didn't consider that of any account. I hire the building and sub-let it to mechanics. The engine belongs to me.

Q. Did it take in your room?

A. No, sir. I will give a statement of my progress. I went away at twelve o'clock to collect some rents from the tenants on Sudbury street, and went back and wrote some letters, and went downstairs and locked up. I did not go into the room upstairs, which I can prove by a great many witnesses.

Q. Had there been any fire on your premises that day?

A. No, sir, nothing but gas in the counting-room; we did not light up upstairs.

Q. You know nothing about the origin of this fire?

A. No, sir. There were steam pipes on the premises.

Q. (By Mr. Greene.) As I understand it, there was no fire in the apartments you occupied, save the gas light?

A. Not to my knowledge. I was not there that afternoon. I made an attempt to go upstairs, but the young man said, "They have all gone out," and I went out and locked the door. The reason why I locked up, the two previous nights the book-keeper locked up and took the key, but over Sundays, my partner requires me to keep the key, and the man who has been in the habit of locking up lives close by me, — he is a carpenter, and was making some stalls in my stable, — and the book-keeper locked up and took the key, except Saturday night, when I took it home with me. I went down with my wife to the stable to get my horse, and Capt. Hilborn came across the street and asked me to come to his house that evening; we were talking about selecting a candidate for Mayor and ward officers. I told him I would, and went down directly to the stable and got my carriage and drove home, and met Mr. French, of Chelsea, going in the same direction, and soon after seven o'clock I got home, read the paper, got my supper, and was in Capt. Hilborn's house, — it could not have been more than ten or fifteen minutes past seven, — with several other citizens of Chelsea.

Q. (By Mr. FIRTH.) Was there any fire in the engine that had been used that day?

A. I don't think that I have been in the engine room for more than a year. That was in the basement. That belonged to the landlord. I have learned since that the engineer was in the habit of drawing out his fires Saturday nights; other nights he banked them and kept them over, so as to have steam the next day. But that night he drew his fires, and stayed there until seven o'clock.

Q. What is his name?

A. I don't know that.

Q. You had nothing to do with that?

A. Nothing at all, except that I very often smelt liquor in his breath, and I did not like that in a man holding a responsible position.

Q. (By Mr. GREENE.) Who employs that man?

A. Mr. Daggett, agent for S. Klous. I don't think I was in the building an hour that afternoon. I came back and wrote three letters, had two of them copied, and locked up and went away. The first I heard, a carriage came to the door, and Mr. Hilborn informed me that our store was on fire. Five minutes before that, somebody said there was a great fire in Boston, at the corner of Summer and Bedford streets. I did not go out, but our overseer got a hack and came over after me, and I went back with her, and when I got there, everything was in ashes, and the fire was in the vicinity of Winthrop Square. The first knowledge I had of the fire was when the overseer came.

Q. (By Mr. RUSSELL.) What is the name of your overseer?

A. Kate McCauley.

Q. She was the person who told you it was your store?

A. Yes, sir.

Q. Do you know where she lives?

A. No. 11 Oak street; but I understand she is stopping with her sister in Lynn, since the fire.

Q. Have you heard anything about a cigar being thrown into the elevator, which it was supposed caused the fire?

A. No, sir.

Q. (By Mr. GREENE.) What is your idea about the origin of the fire?

A. Well, my opinion is, that the engineer must have raked out his fires, and the coals came into connection with some wood work. There was a wood partition close to the boiler.

Q. That is, you think it commenced in the basement?

A. Yes, sir, that is my opinion.

Q. And went up the elevator?

A. Yes, sir, there was a draft going up the elevator; there wouldn't be likely to be one coming down.

Q. Was not the fire first discovered coming from an upper room?

A. No, sir, it was not. Here is a list of persons who saw the fire when it first broke out: Mr. and Mrs. Chester D. Pratt; Louisa P. Pratt; Mr and Mrs. Alonzo C. Pratt; Mrs. Clara Pratt; Mrs. Abby F. Pratt, residing at No. 17 Kingston street; and Mr. and Mrs. Halsall, who have moved since the fire to No. 5 Cambridge street. I never saw either of them. Our Mr. Reed learned that they had seen the origin of the fire.

Q. What is the man's name who first saw the fire below?

A. All these parties saw it from the house directly opposite. They were going out on some visit. Their house is not more than fifty or sixty feet from the building; it may be a longer distance, but it is almost directly opposite this alley-way. These parties were going out, or this Mr. Halsall and wife were going out, on a visit, somewhere, and he came down and was waiting for his wife, and saw the light and went over, called them, and they all went over, and looked at it, before there was any alarm given, and watched its progress.

Q. (By Mr. COBB.) How long had you been in that building?

A. About five years. We had just taken another lease for three years longer. The five years would expire the first of January; but I went in there before the first of January, I should think about a month.

[Mr. YOUNG sent to the commission, the day following his examination, a letter, touching some points in regard to which he was unable to give the details when he testified, from which the following extract is taken: —

"I take the liberty to present a few facts for your consideration of which I shall take pleasure in giving you ample proofs.

In the first place our assets were at time of fire more than ten dollars to one of indebtedness.

Secondly, our business was very profitable; our profits up to time of fire this year exceeded thirty thousand dollars.

Thirdly, our books and accounts, all evidence of bills receivable, computed at about fifty thousand dollars, was placed in our safe by our bookkeeper, he as well as ourselves knowing that the safe was out of order and could not be locked; we were well aware that in the event of a fire our books could not be saved, but we had no apprehension of a fire and took our chances.

Fourthly, our schedule of stock on hand, made out by the parties I this day send you, and sworn to by Mr. Loomis and myself, show a stock on hand exceeding fifty thousand dollars, on which the total amount of insurance was $17,600.

Fifthly, on or about October 20, 1872, insurance on the burned property, amounting to $2,320, expired, and on application for renewal of the same by Mr. Stoddard, of the firm of Brown, Pope & Co., I declined, against his remonstrances, to renew or increase our insurance on that property, and assigned reasons which he will give.

Sixthly, we propose to pay our indebtedness as it matures, asking no favor of any, and demanding simple justice of all. Very respectfully yours,

A. K. YOUNG."

Subsequently, another communication was received from Mr. Young, in which he says: —

"I would like to correct a statement made before your committee by myself, namely, that the fire on Hanover street did not occur on our premises. On inquiry, I learn that it did occur in our place; but I had forgotten all about the affair. That fire was the only one that ever occurred in premises occupied by me during my life, to my knowledge. The fire in New York occurred over the store and damaged the stock by smoke and water. The stock was the property of Samuel Williston, of East Hampton, Mass., and insured on his behalf; the only interest of the firm of which I was partner — Howell, Colby & Co. — was a commission on sales effected, as they were the agents of Samuel Williston."]

AUGUSTINE SANDERSON, *Sworn.*

Q. (By Mr. Russell.) Will you state what you know about the fire of November ninth?

A. The ninth of November (I recollect the time very distinctly, because I was a little disappointed in the matter) I went up to Small's boot and shoe store, in Bromfield street, to get my boots, which were not done, and I left there between five and ten minutes past seven. I went straight down Bromfield street, and up Washington street as far as the corner of Winter street, and there I met Mr. John S. Holmes. No alarm had then been given of this fire; there was nobody halloing fire. I immediately started down Summer street, and halloed fire from the time I crossed Washington street, until I reached Kingston street. When I arrived at Kingston street, I should say there were not more than a dozen persons in Kingston street, and then the fire was coming out through the roof of the building occupied by Tebbetts, Baldwin & Davis; there was no fire in the upper story. The first party I met there was a boy, and I asked him where the box was; and he told me there was a box up on the corner of Bedford and Washington streets. I asked him why they had not given the alarm; and he said he didn't know. In the mean time, a policeman came through Kingston street from Summer street, and I asked him why he did not give the alarm. He said that he had given the alarm. Said I, "There has no alarm been struck, not a sound;" and said I, "Why don't you go and give the alarm?" Then he remarked to me that he had been at the box, and he could not get any answer. In the mean time, two other officers came through from Summer street into Kingston street, and I started those two officers and this other officer, and they started through Kingston street, into Summer, and down Summer street. They were gone perhaps half a minute, and in a minute or two after they got back, the alarm struck.

Q. Who was the officer you first met?

A. I don't know. Then the fire had crossed the passage-way in the rear of this building, and ignited the other building on the opposite side of the passage-way on Kingston street. I think all those buildings were on fire. The coving had caught fire on the buildings on the opposite side of the passage-way on Kingston street. They were all on fire, I think, when the alarm was struck.

Q. (By Mr. Cobb.) Outside?

A. Outside.

Q. (By Mr. Russell.) Wooden coving?

A. Yes, sir. The fire seemed to be in the upper story of this building occupied by Tebbetts, Baldwin & Davis, and burning furiously through the roof and through the skylights. I stayed in Kingston street until after the fire had come down and come out through the upper story and burst out through those windows, and was coming down into the next story below, before any fireman arrived there at all.

Q. Did you see any fire in the lower stories, or basement?

A. No, sir.

Q. Have you any doubt you should have seen it, if there had been any?

A. I think I should. I stood there until I thought it was dangerous standing there.

Q. Did you fix your attention on the question whether the lower part of the building was on fire or not?

A. I looked at the building, and the fire seemed to me to be, and always has seemed to me to be, in the upper stories of the building. I should say the first hose carriage came in ten minutes after I arrived there, drawn by hand. The next apparatus that came there was a hook and ladder company. That came in about five or six minutes after the hose carriage arrived. The next thing that came after that, I should say, to the best of my knowledge and belief, was a steamer drawn by hand, which took the hydrant on the corner of Kingston and Summer streets.

Q. How much of a team of men was there on it?

A. I should say there might have been on that one perhaps twenty-five or thirty.

Q. Men or boys?

A. Men and boys together.

Q. Did they come up fast or slow?

A. Well, they didn't come up very fast.

Q. (By Mr. COBB.) Did you make any note of time? consult your watch at all?

A. I looked at my watch, and I should say, to the best of my knowledge and belief, if my watch was right, that the alarm was struck between a quarter and twenty minutes past seven.

Q. (By Mr. GREENE.) How long was it before any engine arrived?

A. I should say it was twelve or fifteen minutes before any engine arrived there.

Q. (By Mr. RUSSELL.) How long was it from the time of the alarm before the first stream was thrown on the fire?

A. I think that before the first stream that took upon that fire that I saw, it was good thirty minutes.

Q. From the alarm?

A. From the time at which I arrived there, I should say it was thirty minutes.

Q. How long was it from the time when the fire-alarm was given before the stream struck it?

A. I should say it was from twenty to twenty-five minutes.

Q. Do you know anything about a want of fuel?

A. I do not. I saw no want. I have heard people say that the fire was built of boxes. I did not see it, because I stayed there until I had my eye hurt, and then I went up to Mr. Tompkins' apothecary shop, and from there to Jordan & Marsh's building, and remained there until half-past seven o'clock.

Q. Was the stream of water effective?

A. No, sir.

Q. Did it hit the place where the fire was?

A. No, sir. They placed a ladder against the block where Tebbetts, Baldwin & Davis's store was, but the ladder caught fire before they got any water up to it.

Q. Did they take the hose up the ladder?

A. They undertook to take it up, but the ladder caught fire.

Q. (By Mr. FIRTH.) In regard to the alarm; you say you went down to Summer street. How long do you think you were going down there?

A. I should not say I was more than five minutes from the time I left Bromfield street, until I was in Kingston street.

Q. Did you hear no alarm?

A. I did not. I heard nobody halloing fire, or anything of the kind.

Q. Was anything being done when you got there?

A. There was nobody there but strangers, nobody who had any authority, more than I had; people simply standing there and seeing it burn.

Q. (By Mr. Cobb.) Were you there when the first engineer arrived?

A. I was.

Q. Who was it?

A. The first man I recognized was a brother-in-law or cousin of Alderman Pope, Capt. Jacobs; and I assisted Lieut. Childs in putting a rope from the corner of Kingston street across Summer street, to keep the crowd back.

Q. Did the streams seem to have any effect?

A. No, sir. The two streams, in my opinion, which they played from the opposite side of Summer street, did not seem to amount to anything. The building was all on fire, up to the coving, and the water did not reach beyond the second story.

Q. (By Mr. Firth.) Did you notice the time of the arrival of the second engine?

A. I did not.

Q. Had it come in when you left?

A. Oh, yes, sir. It came up the other way; I did not notice the time.

Q. Do you speak of the time that elapsed between the alarm and the arrival of the first engine, from actual knowledge?

A. Yes, sir, I do. There was another gentleman, who is in the Assessors' department, who came after I got there, and stayed there after I went away, and saw the whole thing. That is Mr. Richardson. I told him then that they had got more of a fire than they could handle. We talked the thing over, and I made up my mind, the way they were going at it, they would never stop the fire in that block. I have had some conversation with Lieut. Childs (if you have not sent for him, I think it would be well to do so) on the point of carrying streams into the stores in the block beyond the store that was on fire, and putting those streams on the roof. I think that would have been the most effectual way of reaching that fire, because a stream would not reach it, or, if they got a stream up to it, it would spread, and the fire was so intense that it would evaporate, and have no effect at all.

Q. (By Mr. Russell.) You thought the best way was to carry the stream on to the roof?

A. Yes, sir, and pour it down. You could reach the fire in no other way. I have been on the police four years and three months, and I have been to fires with the Boston Fire Department in years gone by, when a young man.

Q. Were you a member?

A. No, sir, only a volunteer.

Q. (By Mr. FIRTH.) How could the hose have been carried up on the roof?

A. By going beyond. Suppose you could not get on top of the building occupied by Tebbetts, Baldwin & Davis, by going two doors below, you could carry the hose on to the roof, and pour the water into the burning building. That was the way the fire in the State Street Block was controlled. I was at that fire. They carried the hose through the buildings, and got the water down upon the fire.

Q. (By Mr. COBB.) Did you see the Chief Engineer that evening?

A. I saw the Chief when he came there.

Q. About what time was that?

A. He did not arrive there until after an engine had come, a hook-and-ladder company, and a hose-carriage. I saw him there just after they had all got there. The hook-and-ladder came up through the street directly opposite Kingston street, on Summer street.

Q. Did you hear him give any orders?

A. I did not. Lieut. Childs went and took a rope from the hook-and-ladder company, and I assisted him in putting it across the street, to keep the crowd back.

JOHN M. PAGE, *Sworn.*

Q. (By Mr. RUSSELL.) You are an officer of Station No. 4?

A. Yes, sir.

Q. Will you state all you know about the fire of November 9th?

A. Well, the most I know about it, I was the first officer to get to the box and give the alarm.

Q. What was the first thing you knew about the fire? Where were you when you saw it?

A. Well, as near as I can place it, — I did not look at my watch, — I should call it not far from quarter-past seven. I was on Lincoln street, going towards Summer, and when I got up to the corner of Summer and Bedford, I saw the fire streaming up from the top of the building. I was right at the alarm box, and I stopped right there, opened the box, and gave the alarm. I did not go round to see what building was on fire, or what part of the building was on fire.

Q. When you give an alarm, do you know whether you have succeeded? Is there a response?

A. Yes, sir, there is a ticking in the box. I heard the ticking in the box.

Q. (By Mr. FIRTH.) What was the number of this box?

A. No. 52.

Q. (By Mr. RUSSELL.) I suppose there were no circumstances which you noted that seemed suspicious?

A. I did not see anything of the kind. From where I stood, I could not see the building that was on fire, because of some other high buildings that interfered.

Q. Do you know anything else about it?

A. Nothing material that I know of.

Q. (By Mr. FIRTH.) Did you hear anybody give any alarm?

A. I heard boys halloing fire before I saw it.

Q. Before you reached the box?

A. Yes, sir. I stood right at the box until I had given the third alarm.

Q. (By Mr. COBB.) What did you do then?

A. I went up Bedford street, where the hose run through a yard where there were some old people living — old lady Foster and Capen. I went in and got on to their shed, and drove a lot of boys out of their yard, and I stayed there for an hour.

Q. (By Mr. FIRTH.) Who gave the second alarm?

A. I did.

Q. How long after the first?

A. Well, I couldn't hear the bells at all, there was so much confusion and noise, and there is no bell near there. I gave it when I thought the first alarm had had time to get through striking.

Q. How long was that?

A. Probably five minutes or eight minutes.

Q. Then in regard to the third alarm?

A. I gave the third alarm when there was word brought to me by another officer from an engineer, to give the third alarm.

Q. Then the third alarm was given by the order of some engineer?

A. Yes, sir. That is, I did not get the order direct from him; it came through some other officer.

Q. How long was that after the second?

A. I should not think it was more than ten minutes, probably.

Q. (By Mr. COBB.) You don't know what time the Fire Department got to the building?

A. No, sir, I can't tell. I was not at the building until after the fire was well under way. Finally, I was not round in front of the building for an hour.

(*Subsequently recalled.*)

CHARLES A. STEARNS, *Sworn.*

Q. (By Mr. RUSSELL.) On the ninth of November you were the officer on duty at the fire alarm, were you not?

A. I was, sir.

Q. Will you state what took place in regard to the alarm?

A. Well, sir, I was sitting at the window which faces in the direction of Summer street, reading a newspaper. I looked up and saw a light; got up out of my chair and looked for a few seconds, and my instruments to give an alarm of fire commenced giving the number. I had to walk across the room, perhaps twenty feet from where I sat. I took the number, read it on the paper twice, turned to my other instruments, and got ready as soon as possible to strike the bells. That was the first alarm, and after getting through with the first alarm, which was box 52, twice repeated, I waited, I can't say how long, but only a short time, and another alarm came in. I struck the second alarm, and so on with the third and fourth alarms. The general alarm was telegraphed in by one of our men who goes to fires by order of the chief.

Q. What was the time?

A. After I had taken the alarm, which takes, I judge, twenty seconds, set my apparatus to strike, and had started the instruments to strike the bells. I then looked at the clock, and as near as I could judge it was twenty-four minutes past seven. The clock was at the farther end of the room, perhaps twenty-five feet off, but as near as I could see, it was twenty-four minutes past seven. That was about the time the first blow was struck.

Q. What does the second alarm mean?

A. It means ten blows from the same box. Instead of striking the same number of blows, they strike ten.

Q. Does that give any additional force?

A. Yes, sir. That the Fire Department regulates; I know nothing about it.

Q. (By Mr. COBB.) What time did you give the second alarm?

A. I could not swear from memory the time, but I recorded it immediately after striking, and it is recorded 7.29. The third alarm is recorded 7.34; the fourth alarm, 7.45.

Q. (By Mr. RUSSELL.) Was there any further alarm?

A. Yes, sir, a fifth alarm, which is not an alarm; but we struck it at eight o'clock.

Q. (By Mr. COBB.) What does that fourth alarm mean?

A. Three times twelve. First, the number of the box; second, ten blows; third, twelve blows, once repeated; fourth, twelve blows, twice repeated, making three times twelve.

Q. (By Mr. FIRTH.) What is the meaning of the fifth alarm?

A. There is no such thing as the fifth alarm; everything is supposed to be at the fire, as I understand it, after the fourth alarm; but then, it was a big fire, and we struck the bells again. We thought, if they wanted another alarm, we would keep striking.

Q. (By Mr. RUSSELL.) Do you know anything further about the matter?

A. No, sir; I did not leave the room for twenty-four hours.

Q. (By Mr. FIRTH.) Have you, in any other instances, sounded a fifth alarm?

A. Yes, sir; at the time of the great fire we had in East Boston, and quite a number of those large fires. We keep striking — fifth, sixth, seventh. It is nothing, except, perhaps, to call out-of-town engines.

Q. That is usual?

A. It is usual to do so, when we have a great fire.

CLARENCE A. DORR, *Sworn.*

Q. (By Mr. RUSSELL.) You are a banker?

A. Yes, sir, banker and broker.

Q. On the ninth of November, where were you when you noticed the fire alarm?

A. I was at the corner of Kingston and Summer streets when I noticed what I did notice. I did not expect a big fire. I left the Merchants' Exchange Reading Room at a quarter after seven, exactly, by their clock, and proceeded by the way of Washington street to the Old Colony station, where I was to take the half-past seven train. I was accustomed to going there every day, back and forth, and generally allowed myself just about time enough to go there. When I got to the corner of Kingston and Summer streets, I looked to see if I had plenty of time to get there by the way of Kingston street, and it was exactly twenty-one minutes past seven by my watch, which I think was one minute fast by the clock inside the Old Colony station, which I believe they keep regulated by standard time. While I was looking at it, there was no one in the street, and I heard a big noise over my head. I looked up and I saw what seemed to be steam escaping; and my first impression was, that there was a printing-press there; that there might be a newspaper office there, and it was accompanied by a noise very similar to that of a printing-press. In fact, the impression was very much as it is when passing by the "Post" building in Devonshire street; if you look up, you will see the steam escaping from the roof. That was exactly what it reminded me of, and I thought to myself whether there was a newspaper office there. While I was looking, I looked up and down the street to see if any one was coming that I could say something to, and did not see a soul; and while I stood there, which was perhaps ten or fifteen seconds in all, I saw it was accompanied by a little smoke. That immediately started my suspicions, and I ran to the back part of the building, — I did not observe any light in the front of the building, — as near as I could get to it; there was an old-fashioned house between me and the building, — and I looked up, and there I saw the flames. I did not see any light in the lower part of the building at all; I think I should have noticed it, if there had been any there; and I immediately made the remark to one or two that came running up, that the fire took in the upper story. That was the conclusion I immediately arrived at. By the way, I did not speak of one other thing. On my way round there, after I first noticed it, there was no cry of fire, or any alarm in any shape or manner; but when I was running round, I am sure I heard some children's voices, — it sounded like boys and girls, — crying fire. I did not hear a man's voice at all. Just at that stage of the proceedings, or when I got fairly round, I asked the people there if anybody was attending to the alarm, and they said yes, that was looked after; and by that time the cry became general. The fire spread very rapidly, when it started, into the various rooms. I was looking at it, and listening very closely for the alarm, bnt did not hear it. Time went on, and the first alarm I heard, I looked at my watch, and it was exactly thirty minutes past seven. But I was assured by the people round there that it had been sounded before; but I did not hear it. I think I should have noticed it, if it had been. I have been through that street very often, and very often at that time; it is usual for me to go home about that time, and I think I should have noticed if there had been any light in the lower part of the building. A gentleman said to me afterwards that he thought it took below; and I told him I did not see how it could be so. I was rather anxious for a hose-carriage to arrive, and I did not see one arrive there until about the time I heard the alarm myself, which was the second alarm, I was told, that was sounded. I supposed it was the first alarm; but since then I have heard others say that the alarm was sounded at an earlier stage of the proceedings. In regard to time, I feel very sure I am right, because at half-past seven I stood on the corner of South street and looked towards the Old Colony illuminated clock, and I even thought then of running and taking the train, but I found I did not have time; and about two or three minutes after that, as I stood there, a hose-carriage came up that street.

Q. How soon did the hose throw water?

A. It seemed to me only two minutes after I saw it go by. I think they must have thrown water by twenty-five minutes of eight. I know it was very quickly done.

Q. When did a steamer arrive?

A. I heard a steamer, but I did not see it. I was on the other side when the steamer arrived. It came from the direction of Washington street, I think.

Q. Can you tell the time when you heard it?

A. I should think it was almost exactly upon the striking of what I thought was the first alarm, and it struck me as peculiar; that is, 7.30; my watch, by the way, being one minute fast. The hose-carriage came very near on that hour, and I think (I would not swear to it) that I heard another one approaching, on the other side, about the same time. I ran round the building several times to see the progress of the fire; after I had been to the back side, I went round to the front, and there I saw the glass melt down and fall into the street. There were very few people there, and it seemed a long time before people arrived.

Q. In what story did the fire first show itself?

A. It showed itself from the very upper story, the highest part of the building. The back side of it was different in construction, looked different from the front.

Q. What was the front?

A. The front was covered more by the Mansard roof. I saw the fire coming out of the upper windows in the Mansard roof.

Q. Did you notice whether the building back of that was on fire or not when the water was first thrown on?

A. I think it was not. I watched very closely to see if any other building caught fire, and I did not see that. I went round the building several times.

Q. (By Mr. Cobb.) Could you see the water thrown on the fire?

A. Yes, sir; and one of the first things I noted, and what made me think it would be a bad fire, was the fact that the water did not seem to make any impression on it.

Q. Did the water reach it, apparently?

A. It reached it sometimes, but it had the appearance to me — I did not feel right; I had seen a great many fires break out, and I remained there for that reason, because I felt it was to be a bad fire; otherwise, I should have got to my home as quick as I could. The water did not seem to make any impression; it seemed to be turned into steam. I talked with several men about it, and they said it looked bad, and we made the remark that we were afraid it would go across the street, it was so hot; it was very hot indeed.

Q. You say the flames were coming out of the upper windows of the Mansard roof before water reached that portion of the building?

A. I should say they did. I should say the upper part of the stream did reach it, but it did not seem to have any effect.

Q. (By Mr. RUSSELL.) Was the hose carried up a ladder?

A. They carried it up a ladder and stood on the roof, as near as they could. The firemen stood on the top of the roof. The first thing I noticed was that.

Q. (By Mr. COBB.) The roof of the building that was burning?

A. Yes, sir. I made the remark, "What brave fellows those firemen are to go at this thing right off!" They went so close to it, that when the upper part gave way, I thought they must have fallen through at one time; but when the smoke and flame cleared there they were standing at their posts, holding up something as a screen before them.

Q. (By Mr. RUSSELL.) How long was that after the alarm you heard?

A. That might have been five minutes after the alarm I heard when I saw them on that roof; certainly not over ten.

Q. From 7.35 to 7.40?

A. Yes, sir. It struck me, that considering they could not use horses, they got to work there remarkably quick. That was the impression I had at the time. They seemed to be very active and very quiet about it. I was close to them at first, while they were making ready, and it struck me that they went to work very rapidly, and how quick they got on the roof, and how quick they got to work.

Q. (By Mr. FIRTH.) Do you know how they got on the roof?

A. I think the first ascent to the roof must have been made through the building; at any rate, I did not see any ladders in the first of it. I think I saw people on the roof before I saw ladders put up, and then I did see ladders.

Q. (By Mr. GREENE.) Did you notice whether the ladder took fire?

A. I did not see it take fire. I think I should have noticed it, if it had taken fire.

Q. (By Mr. FIRTH.) Did you notice what engine it was that first arrived?

A. No, sir; I did not.

Q. Or the hose?

A. I did not notice it. My impression is that the hose carriage that arrived on Summer street, while I was standing there, was the East street hose-carriage; but I do not know positively that it was. I took it for granted it was, because it came from that direction.

FREDERICK U. TRACY, *sworn.*

Q. (By Mr. RUSSELL.) You are the City Treasurer of Boston?

A. Yes, sir.

Q. Will you tell us when and where you first noticed the fire on November 9th?

A. I came up on the Old Colony road, and went from there to the Albany depot, and just as I turned the corner into Beach street, I noticed some boys crying fire, and running across Kingston street, and I followed them up to the corner of Kingston and Bedford.

Q. What was the time?

A. I am not certain about the time. I looked at my watch in South Boston, when we stopped there, and it was about five minutes past seven. But I stopped some time at the Old Colony depot, trying to get a carriage there to ride home, but did not succeed, and then walked up. It may have been twenty or twenty-five minutes past seven.

Q. Do you know when the alarm was given?

A. I did not hear any alarm given. There was a great noise of boys shouting "Fire;" but I don't think the alarm was given until after I arrived at the corner of Kingston and Bedford streets.

Q. How long after that did any hose come?

A. I did not see any hose come, sir.

Q. Or any engine?

A. An engine came, probably, I think, in quarter of an hour after I got there.

Q. Did you notice how long it was after the engine came before any water was put on the fire?

A. I should think, from the time I first heard the boys' cry until the engines began to play, it was three quarters of an hour. Of course, I cannot judge exactly; I have no means of judging, only time passes quickly at such times. An engine (I think it was No. 3) came down dragged by hand; they had no fuel, — evidently waited for fuel, — and when the fire was got up, they used something besides coal for firing, the smoke was so dense; I supposed it was petroleum, or something of that kind.

Q. Where was that stationed?

A. About the centre of Kingston street, then.

Q. Did you notice that they had no coal, except from seeing the smoke?

A. I did not notice that they had no coal; I noticed that it took them some time before they got fire up, and when they did fire up, I noticed the dense smoke, because I could not see directly in front of me. I could only see the buildings on each side of the street; I could not see the building on Summer street, in front, on the corner.

Q. You don't know about any other engine?

A. I don't. I don't know of any streams except two hose streams, I presume, from the force with which the water was thrown. I could see that there were two streams of water, which apparently were wasted entirely.

Q. (By Mr. Cobb.) Where was the fire when you got there?

A. When I first arrived there, the attic of the store on the corner was apparently in a blaze throughout. I don't know, but I am pretty sure, that it broke through the roof before I got there, before I supposed any alarm had been given. It seemed as if the whole interior of the building was on fire. There was no light in any of the stories except in the attic; that is, I could not see any light; but it was not long before every window, I suppose, in the second and third stories of the building was thrown out, and a blaze of fire followed. I did not see a sign of fire there before.

Q. (By Mr. Greene.) Do you understand the signal for coal?

A. No, sir, I do not. I could not have heard the signal. There was so much noise it would have been impossible for me to have heard it. There seemed to be some trouble about getting up steam.

Q. (By Mr. Cobb.) These two streams that you say did not touch the fire, did they reach up to the place?

A. Oh, no.

Q. Where did they strike?

A. About the third story, I should think. The fire was two stories above.

Q. (By Mr. Russell.) How was it with the water from the steamer?

A. That had force enough. The very moment they got up steam, the steam dissipated the smoke, and I could see the whole of the upper story of this corner building and the dormer window, and I could see (even when the smoke was there) that there was a place on fire just round the top of the dormer window. They would throw a stream and strike that, and it would go entirely out, but it would light up again very soon; and then they would throw another dash of water at it; but I can't say where the stream from the hose went to.

Q. (By Mr. Greene.) Did you see any hosemen on top of the building?

A. No, sir; no hoseman could live there. But there were men on the next building to it, whether firemen or people in charge of the store, I don't know. There seemed to be a passage-way between the two buildings, — the one on Kingston street, and the one on Summer street, — and they were protected there by a high brick wall, and stayed a long time after the fire began, and after it was in full blaze, and the blaze going directly towards Columbia street. There is where I supposed the fire was going when I left it. I must have stayed there nearly an hour, but the building that was first on fire, after this blaze came out of the second story, seemed to fall in from that story up. The whole of the stone work seemed to fall in; evidently a very intense heat.

Q. (By Mr. Cobb.) You are sure there was no one on the roof of the building?

A. No, sir, I can't say that. I am sure I saw no one; but I don't think any one could have stood there.

Q. (By Mr. Greene.) The people on the adjoining building were spectators, were they?

A. I am not sure. I heard them call out to the men below, and I supposed they were connected with the Fire Department. They were evidently not engineers; that is, they had not engineers' caps on.

Q. (By Mr. Russell.) This building was five stories high, including the Mansard roof?

A. Yes, sir.

Q. (By Mr. Firth.) Did you see the second engine arrive?

A. I did not see any other engine come there. I could see only directly on Kingston street; I could not see what was doing on Summer street at all. No second one came for a long, long time, I think. I stayed there some time, still supposing that the fire was going the other way. There seemed to be an unaccountable delay in getting water; I did not understand it.

Q. (By Mr. Greene.) I understood you to say that you thought it was fifteen minutes after the alarm before you saw an engine?

A. I did not hear the alarm at all. After the boys cried "Fire," I think it was three-quarters of an hour before this engine got up its stream and began to play. When it did play, there was plenty of power to throw the water anywhere on the building, because it threw it up to this upper dormer window, and put the fire out.

Q. (By Mr. Cobb.) Did you see either of the engineers come?

A. I did not see either of the engineers come. The hose were playing on Summer street. There might have been an engineer connected with the engine, but I did not know him.

A. C. MARTIN, *sworn.*

Q. (By Mr. RUSSELL.) You are an architect?

A. Yes,.sir.

Q. You live in Boston?

A. Yes, sir.

Q. Will you state when and where you first noticed the fire on the 9th of November?

A. I had been to Concord, N. H., on Saturday, Nov. 9th, and first saw the light of the fire about twenty miles from Boston, coming down in the train; followed it, of course, all the way to Boston, and as soon as I got to the depot, I inquired about it, learned the extent of it, and immediately went up to Franklin street, and first saw the fire between ten and eleven o'clock, — very near eleven o'clock.

Q. Will you state anything that you know about the fire that you think will be of value?

A. I was particularly interested, as a spectator, in observing how the fire took, and watching its progress, speculating on the best way of stopping it, and all that sort of thing.

Q. How long have you been an architect?

A. I have been an architect since 1859. I first established myself then.

Q. Go on and state anything you noticed.

A. I first saw the fire on Franklin street, and watched its progress from building to building, and I made up my mind, from what I saw, that the principal reason why the fire spread with such rapidity was owing to the fact that the buildings were all much higher than the height to which the steamers could throw their water. They did not work from the tops of the buildings in fighting it at that time. I thought it would have been much better to have gone to the top of a building, the second, third, or fourth away from the one on fire, and fight the fire from above, rather than stand in the street, as they did, and fight it from there. I noticed that in some buildings the fire seemed to catch along the wooden cornices and wooden finish around the Mansard roofs; in other cases, the fire would appear inside the building, and the building would be wholly lighted up before the fire attacked the roof at all. From that I made up my mind that the partition walls were not thick enough; that the fire went directly through the brick work and communicated with the floor timbers let into the walls. But the wooden cornices and Mansard roofs, and the entire lack of party walls extending up to the roofs, account, in a great measure, for the fire extending as it did.

Q. Did you see any of the firemen standing on the roofs of the houses?

A. I did not see any of the firemen standing on the roofs in the early part of the fire. They did not seem to make any effort to get on the roofs and fight it from the roofs. I noticed particularly Hovey's employees, — I supposed, of course, they were not firemen, because they did not have firemen's hats on. I noticed that they put blankets on the roof and over the windows, and threw water on them, fighting it in the best possible way. I have no doubt that that saved the roof from taking fire, and probably saved the building, although the rear wall was very thick — 24 to 28 inches.

Q. (By Mr. Greene.) You say the fire ignited beneath the roofs in several instances?

A. Yes, sir, I saw it in several instances. It would get into a building without attacking the outside. It would be inside and get well going, then the glass would crash, and the flames would belch out. I understand that that was caused by the bricks getting so hot that they ignited the wood work inside. There is no question, I believe, that that is the fact. It is the practice in Boston to build the floor timbers into the walls, and in an ordinary brick wall, if the floor timbers are let in the usual length, there would be but four inches of brick work between the ends of the floor timbers. Of course, the wall will get very hot, the ends of the floor timbers will be burned off, and they will fall out, and, the fire continuing to burn, in a short time that four inches will be red-hot. I have no doubt that in many instances the fire went right through walls, on account of their not being thick enough.

Q. (By Mr. Russell.) Did you watch the fire on other streets?

A. Yes, sir. I went nearly round the fire. Later in the evening, it made its way down to the water, and it was not so easy to pass in that direction, and I skirted down through Pearl street, and Oliver street way.

Q. (By Mr. Firth.) Were those walls you speak of stone or brick?

A. They were brick between the buildings.

Q. Did you see any case where the fire went through stone walls?

A. There are no party walls between buildings of stone; they are always brick. In many cases, the fire would communicate across a street from the heat.

Q. In cases where the buildings were stone?

A. Yes, sir, very frequently. That did not seem to make any special difference, but the fire would go across the street, and catch any wooden finish there was about the roof. There is where the wooden finish on a roof was more dangerous than stone or brick. For instance, I was down in Congress street at one time, and there seemed to be a complete mass of flames across the street, so that there was no space between them.

Q. (By Mr. RUSSELL.) Will you give us your opinion of the Mansard roof, as constructed in Boston?

A. The Mansard roof, as constructed in Boston, if it is constructed out of the reach of water, is a very dangerous feature in a building.

Q. Suppose it is within reach of water?

A. If it is within reach of water, and the walls are carried up through, it could very easily be made comparatively safe. If the roof is properly constructed, with no wooden finish about it, it is as safe as any roof.

Q. (By Mr. GREENE.) The trouble is, there is a great deal of wood about it?

A. That is the trouble. You may say our architecture here in Boston has sprung from foreign architecture, which was carried out in stone; but it is so much easier to make a showy window in wood, and so much cheaper, that the owners were willing to do it, and architects, of course, were willing to produce an effect; so that, instead of the stone constructions which they have abroad on their roofs, and nothing else, we have great masses of wood, which become, in case of fire, very objectionable features.

Q. (By Mr. RUSSELL.) Is there any trouble with the Mansard roof in itself, if the materials are proper?

A. I do not see any objection to the Mansard roof, if the materials are proper, and the work put together in a proper way.

Q. (By Mr. COBB.) What do you think of copper?

A. Copper is the best roof covering we have, and the most expensive. Then I think another reason why fire spreads so rapidly in our cities — I do not know that Boston is peculiar in that respect — is that we have timber very plenty. We put in our heavy floor timbers, three, four and five inches thick, and fourteen or sixteen inches deep, and from six to twelve inches apart, as the case may be; then comes the under floor on top of these timbers, and the upper floor on top of that; then the walls are furred, and lathed and plastered, making all the floors and the furring on the walls open, so that the air passes freely through; and in case of fire, these spaces become conductors; the currents pass through very freely, and fire is communicated very rapidly, especially in an upper direction. There seems to have been an utter absence of any legal provision in the direction of guarding against fire, until within the last two years. Two years ago, we got a Building Act passed, and that had certain restrictions; but even those were opposed by certain parties in the city government, and we had to make a fight last year before the

Legislature to retain those restrictions. There seemed to be an unwillingness on the part of the public to submit to any limits to their individual ideas of what they wanted and what they should build.

Q. (By Mr. RUSSELL.) Were the architects generally desirous of having the Act?

A. Yes, sir, the Society of Architects drew up the Act. I drew up the Act, or compiled it from the London, New York, Philadelphia, and Baltimore fire laws; and after I had gone as far as I could with it, the Society passed it in review, amended some of the provisions, and then it was handed over to the city government, and they further amended it, changed quite a number of the provisions to suit their own views, and then it was put into the hands of a committee at the State House, and after a number of hearings, it finally became a law.

Q. (By Mr. FIRTH.) What are its main features as passed?

A. The main feature of the Act is to provide, to a certain extent, against the abuses in building, which have been very prevalent in Boston. I think the law stands something like this: Buildings 35 feet in height shall have walls not less than 12 inches thick up to the top of the upper floor, and not less than eight inches thick above that; and all buildings over 35 feet in height, and not exceeding 50 feet, shall have walls 16 inches thick, and the party walls shall be carried up through the building to the roof. We could not get a provision to have the party walls carried up through the Mansard roofs; somebody objected to it. Then there were some other things, such as the security of foundation walls; and there was a clause forbidding any one to cut an opening from one warehouse to another without a permit, and providing double iron doors, and a provision against hatchways. There was also a clause providing for the appointment of inspectors to visit all fires, and inquire into their origin and cause, and report to the Fire Department the peculiarities of construction of buildings. The idea, in general, was to keep the Fire Department well posted upon the construction of all buildings in Boston, so that they should know if there was any peculiarity about a building, which, in case of fire, would render it unsafe for the firemen to go upon the roof.

Q. (By Mr. GREENE.) Have these restrictions been observed?

A. The Act was only passed two years ago. There is an inspector of buildings now, with two assistants, and the provisions of the law have been carried out, to a certain extent. If such a law had been in existence ten years ago, those buildings would have been in a much better condition than they were.

Q. (By Mr. COBB.) Could such a fire have occurred?

A. I don't think it could. The law is not sufficiently stringent. It requires to be considerably more stringent. I think there should be a limit to the height of buildings as compared with the width of the street. Of course, there is more risk in having a high building on a narrow than on a wide street, but I doubt if the city would be willing, even now, to place any such restrictions upon the desire of people to build whatever they have a mind to.

Q. (By Mr. Russell.) Have you seen the Building Act that is now pending?

A. I have seen it reported in the newspapers; I have not seen the whole thing.

Q. Was not High street built subsequently to the time the Building Act went into effect?

A. I think some of the stores were, sir.

Q. (By Mr. Firth.) Do you understand why there should be any objection at City Hall?

A. I don't know why there should be; but we were obliged to go up to the Legislature the year after the Act was passed and oppose an attempt to repeal a certain portion of the Act. Then we tried to get a prohibition of Mansard roofs more than one story high, and bay windows more than a certain height above the street, and certain other things, which were defeated, I don't know why. I did not follow it up myself, but I know they did not get the amendments to the Act which they tried to get.

Q. How long were you present at the fire?

A. All night, sir. I got there about eleven o'clock. I worked part of the time helping a friend move books. I was there all night, until eight o'clock in the morning, before I got home.

Q. (By Mr. Firth.) Did you at any time see any firemen on a roof, anywhere?

A. I did not. They were on the roof of the building opposite to the "Post" building, I was told, but I did not see them there. But on Franklin street and Summer street I did not see anybody on the roof except the employees of Hovey & Co., on their own building.

Q. What seemed to you, towards morning, after the fire had grown to such proportions, was the thing to be done?

A. I kept watching all the time to see some preparations made to blow up buildings, but I did not seem to see anything started in that direction until along about three o'clock, when there seemed to be indications that they were going to blow up buildings. I saw one building blown up, and saw one building that they attempted to blow up where it was a failure, and after that, they blew up quite a number of buildings. But I should say, also, that one great difficulty that night was the crowd in the streets. It was difficult for the firemen to get round; it was difficult for them to handle their engines and handle their hose. What was needed was perhaps a regiment of soldiers to clear the streets and keep them clear in the immediate vicinity of the fire. I noticed that particularly in cases of fire abroad. I happened to be in a German town, Mannheim, when they had the largest fire they had had for a great many years, and I got to the place as soon as possible, but before I got there, they had a batallion of soldiers on the ground to clear the streets, and nobody was allowed to come within a certain distance, and then parties were pressed in to assist them, if they were needed. Everything seemed to be under the control of one leading mind. That did not seem to me to be the case at our fire. Of course I could not tell. I did not see the chief engineer or anybody else, but everybody seemed to be in despair and hopeless. There did not seem to be anything doing, or anything that could be done.

Q. (By Mr. Greene.) Panic-stricken?

A. Yes, sir, panic-stricken. That is the feeling I had.

Q. (By Mr. Cobb.) Were there any buildings that succumbed to the fire, that you know of, where the walls were twenty inches thick?

A. I think I saw quite a number of cases where the walls were twenty inches thick; some of those buildings on Pearl street, and other places I have noticed. I don't think, in case of a fire like that, after the fire gets well going, as that fire did, it would make any difference how thick the walls were, as long as there was so much timber to burn. I do not see any reason why the same thing should not occur in other places in Boston, or New York, or any other city. There is so much to burn in any particular building, that if a fire gets well going, there will be such an amount of heat, that the adjoining buildings and all about it will be placed in a dangerous position.

DANIEL F. MARDEN, *sworn.*

Q. (By Mr. Russell.) You are foreman of Engine No. 7?

A. Yes, sir.

Q. Where is Engine No. 7 stationed?

A. On East street.

Q. At what time did you hear the alarm on the 9th?

A. I didn't notice the clock, but it was on the first stroke of the bell, about quarter past seven.

Q. What did you do then?

A. We were on our way to the fire at that time.

Q. You were on your way to the fire before you heard the alarm?

A. Yes, sir.

Q. How did you get notice of the fire?

A. Some one came and tolled our door-bell and halloed, "Fire in Bedford street!" and we started our hose-carriage; our hose-carriage was just outside the door when the bell first struck.

Q. Did you go with the hose-carriage?

A. I went as far as South street, about four or five rods.

Q. Then what did you do?

A. I turned back and got all the crowd I could to bring the engine to the fire.

Q. Where did you get the men for the engine? — from the crowd?

A. From the crowd in the street.

Q. How much of a team did you get?

A. I should think there were over a hundred men and boys.

Q. What proportion of them men?

A. I should say about one-half of them.

Q. At what rate did they go to the fire — fast or slow?

A. They ran all the way.

Q. How long were they in getting to the fire with the engine?

A. I should say they were inside of two minutes. It couldn't possibly have been more than that.

Q. How long before you threw water on the fire?

A. Well, I will set that at two minutes more, which I consider outside of the limits. In four minutes from the time the bell struck we played water with the steamer.

Q. Was that played from the street, or was the hose carried up on a ladder, or how was it?

A. We took our hose in the rear of this building that caught fire, to keep it from going into the rear. We went to the rear of the building from Bedford street.

Q. Was that building on fire when you got there?

A. It was smoking, and there was danger of its catching fire, and my object in playing there was to try to stop the fire from spreading, instead of putting our water directly on the fire.

Q. So that you didn't play directly on the fire?

A. We didn't play directly on the fire in the building which first caught.

Q. What was done with the hose at that time? Where was that placed?

A. That is where we played our steamer; the hose-carriage and steamer usually are connected, but they ran separately that night.

Q. I thought there was also a hose screwed to the hydrant — that was not yours, if there was any?

A. Our line from the hose-carriage was laid from the hydrant, but when they brought the steamer to the hydrant, we immediately connected that with the steamer.

Q. (By Mr. COBB.) All the water you threw was from the steamer?

A. Yes, sir.

Q. (By Mr. RUSSELL.) There was only one stream from your engine?

A. Only one stream.

Q. What engine came next?

A. I don't know.

Q. Did the water you threw reach the top of the building?

A. It did at times.

Q. Where was the fire in the first building which caught?

A. It appeared to be from top to bottom. I didn't stop to examine it closely, but I should say that the fire was all through the building. I hardly ever stop to look at a fire, but my object is to get to work as quick as possible.

Q. Did you have plenty of fuel?

A. That is something I don't know anything about; I don't have anything to do with it.

Q. I suppose that would follow, if you threw water in four minutes?

A. We have warm water in our boilers always. We have a heater connected with the steamer which keeps the water hot.

Q. Do you know whether it was hot that night or not?

A. I don't recollect, but I think it was. I have nothing to do with the fires in the engine myself; it is not my business to attend to that.

Q. Do you know whether there was any failure of fuel at any time that evening?

A. I don't know as there was.

Q. Would you not have known it if there had been?

A. I think I should, up to the time when I left. I received a sprained ankle the first part of the evening, but I kept around with the engine until half past two o'clock, when I had to leave; I couldn't stand it any longer.

Q. Where was the engine then?

A. On Federal street. It fell back a little from the Hartford & Erie depot, towards South Boston.

Q. As a general thing, were the engines supplied with fuel properly?

A. They were, so far as I know.

Q. (By Mr. FIRTH.) Is there some sort of signal by which you know whether they need fuel or not?

A. When they need fuel, the engineers blow their whistles.

Q. (By Mr. Russell.) Whose duty is it then to bring it to them?

A. Whose duty it is I don't know, but it is usually done by one of the drivers, who takes his pair of horses and goes to the fuel wagon by order of the engineer.

Q. Where is the fuel wagon kept, — in the engine house?

A. I don't know.

Q. At this time, had you had instructions about using horses or otherwise?

A. I received instructions from the district engineer to double the men in my company, and run the hose carriage by hand to certain sections of the city on the first alarm, and on the second alarm I think the instructions were to bring the engine.

Q. By hand?

A. By hand.

Q. You were not to use horses at any time?

A. Not to use horses at that time — while they were sick.

Q. How did those instructions come to you?

A. Verbally, from our district engineer. He came to the engine-house and sent for me to come there, and gave me these instructions.

Q. Could there be much difference in the time of reaching the fire whether the engine was drawn by men or horses?

A. I don't think it would make ten seconds' difference either way. I don't think whether we had horses or not would have made ten seconds' difference.

Q. (By Mr. Greene.) Is No. 7 very near where the fire broke out?

A. I think I could run there in one minute. I think I could run from the engine house to the fire in about one minute. I have stated that it took two minutes with the steamer, and I consider that outside the limits.

Q. (By Mr. Russell.) Who was at the engine house when the alarm was given besides you?

A. I can't say whether there was any other hoseman in the house, but two of the steamer's men were in the house; whether a third was there or gone to supper, I can't say.

Q. What is the rule about having anybody in the house?

A. That I have nothing to do with; I know nothing about it.

Q. Are there any orders to you?

A. There are no orders to me.

Q. You are not bound to be at the engine house?

A. No, sir. The hosemen or foreman, as I understand it, have no business at the engine house, or with anything in the engine house.

Q. What, in your opinion, was the cause of the fire getting beyond control so soon?

A. Well, that is a very hard question for me to answer. The fire was burning furiously, and the building was very high, and the buildings connected with it, and those Mansard roofs, I think, helped it along. In regard to the steamers coming in, whether they had steam enough to put their streams to the top of those buildings, or anything of the kind, I don't know anything about it.

Q. You know about your own stream?

A. Our steamer gave us a good stream of water.

Q. (By Mr. Cobb.) Are you foreman of the steamer?

A. There is no foreman connected with an engine company. The man is sometimes called foreman of the company, and sometimes called foreman of the hose, but I have nothing to do, according to the city ordinances, with the men or apparatus in the engine house, or anything in the engine house; I have no business there. When the engine goes out, I have the placing of her at any place to get a supply of water, and have charge of the hose and hosemen connected with the company.

Q. (By Mr. Russell.) You direct where the water shall be thrown?

A. Well, I should take that responsibility; of course, that is my place, unless I have orders from an engineer, which I am bound to obey.

Q. (By Mr. Firth.) Until he arrives, you give directions?

A. Until he arrives, I use my own judgment. After that, I must obey his orders.

Q. (By Mr. Russell.) Where was your engine stationed next after you left that spot?

A. We went to the hydrant opposite the Hartford & Erie Depot, corner of Federal and Broad streets.

Q. Was there any trouble there about water or steam?

A. No trouble about steam or water.

Q. Where did you go next?

A. They fell back from there to the reservoir, perhaps three hundred feet along Federal street, towards South Boston. We were driven away from that corner and had to fall back to the next place, and there we did the best we could to stop the fire, and, with others, we did stop it on Federal street. I couldn't stand the pain in my ankle any longer; I felt as though I must get home.

Q. There you say the fire was stopped?

A. The fire was stopped.

Q. Can you tell just where it was?

A. I can't tell exactly where it was, but it will show for itself.

Q. (By Mr. Cobb.) Did it go any further afterwards?

A. No, sir. At the time I left, they had stopped the fire there.

Q. How many streams were playing there?

A. There were two in sight, besides ours, that I could see.

Q. (By Mr. RUSSELL.) Do you know what engines they were?

A. I think one was from Hyde Park, and one from South Boston.

Q. You do not know anything about the use of gunpowder at this fire?

A. No, sir, I know nothing about it.

Q. (By Mr. COBB.) You say that when you went to this fire, you played upon the building in the rear; what building was that?

A. It was the building fronting Kingston street, right in the rear.

Q. And the building on the corner was apparently on fire from top to bottom?

A. Yes, sir.

Q. How soon after you got there did you see an engineer?

A. Well, I don't think it was over five minutes.

Q. Who was that?

A. Capt. Regan, our district engineer, who lives near by. In setting this time, I judge of it by others who have held watches when we have gone to other places and gone to work. Of course, we are very busy getting to work, and we can't tell the time; but I judge from the distance and our time of getting to work, that we played water inside of four minutes from the time the alarm struck.

Q. (By Mr. FIRTH.) Can you tell when the second engine arrived there?

A. No, sir, I can't tell anything about it.

Q. (By Mr. COBB.) Did you see the Chief Engineer?

A. I saw the Chief Engineer, I should think, from seven to nine or ten minutes after I got there.

Q. (By Mr. FIRTH.) About when did you leave that place to go down to the Hartford & Erie Depot?

A. Well, I can't tell; I couldn't state the time within an hour and a half, and I can't tell, as time goes very quick in such cases.

Q. How many men have you?

A. There are eleven men, all told, in the company. There are seven men under me.

Q. (By Mr. GREENE.) Was there any deficiency in the power of your stream?

A. I don't think there was; I think we had our usual good stream.

Q. (By Mr. RUSSELL.) I understand you to say that that was the case until you left?

A. That was the case all the time I was with the engine.

Q. (By Mr. COBB.) There was no want of water or otherwise?

A. There was no want of water or anything of the kind with our engine.

Q. (By Mr. Firth.) Who were the three men not under you?

A. The engineer, fireman, and driver, who are permanently employed. All the others are under my direction.

Q. Who directs those three?

A. I don't know anything about it. They are not beholden to me.

NATHAN S. BROWN, *sworn.*

Q. (By Mr. Russell.) You are foreman of Hose Co. No. 2?

A. Yes, sir.

Q. Where is Hose 2 situated?

A. On Hudson street, sir.

Q. What time did you first know of the fire on the 9th of November?

A. I can't state exactly, but I think between quarter and half-past 7.

Q. (By Mr. Cobb.) How did you know? By the alarm?

A. By the alarm, sir.

Q. (By Mr. Russell.) Where were you?

A. Standing in my shop door at the foot of Pine street, on Harrison avenue.

Q. How soon did you get to the engine-house?

A. I started on the first blow of the bell, for the reason of not being able to haul the apparatus with horses, and special orders from our chief to be on hand. When I got to the hose-house, the carriage had gone, started by volunteers.

Q. What did you do?

A. I immediately kept on. Seeing the light of the fire, I didn't need to count the box. We always have to count the box to find out whether it is in our circuit or not; but seeing the light, I kept on and arrived at the hydrant at the corner of Bedford and Kingston streets, just as the carriage got there. I immediately attached to the hydrant, and ran up to the rear of the building by an alley-way, put on my pipe, and passed the word to get water, and put the pipe right into the flame in the cellar window. At the same time, the burning *débris* and stuff were flying from the upper windows down on to us. The reason I know that fact is because I had to take the pipe out of the cellar window and play on the hose behind me to prevent its burning, being new hose, and not wanting, of course, to have my hose burst right there at that critical moment. Likewise, there was a large piece of burning stuff came and struck one of my men, and knocked his hat off.

Q. The building was on fire from top to bottom when you got there?

A. Yes, sir. I saw it coming out of the roof when I turned the corner of Oak and Hudson streets. That is about one minute's run from my shop.

Q. Was anything else playing on that fire when you got there?

A. No, sir; ours was the first water put on. I held the pipe myself, and put on the first water.

Q. How high would that throw water?

A. At that time that hydrant ought to throw a stream thirty feet, at the least calculation. There was no other hose, of course, tapping it at that time, and the force of the water was as powerful as it ever is.

Q. When did you see the first steamer come?

A. I should judge we had played there about five minutes. Amid the excitement of the moment, I can't state the time exactly, but it didn't seem longer than five minutes before I saw No. 4 drive up, and take the hydrant on the corner of Kingston and Summer streets. But previous to that, steamer No. 7 must have been at work, though I didn't see them, because they are the nearest steamer; but while we were playing in the alley-way, a line of hose from No. 7 came through the fence, and they passed the word. That is where I met the Chief. He asked me where I was stationed, and I told him, and he said, "Take your line right out, and take it into the adjoining building." The fire was then catching on the upper windows. This alley-way is not, I should judge, more than ten or a dozen feet wide.

Q. (By Mr. Firth.) How long had you been there when you saw the Chief?

A. I had not been there over five or eight minutes; about eight minutes, I think. I took the line right out of the alley-way, under the Chief's directions, never stopped the water at all, because I knew if I stopped the water, the chances were a steamer might come up and take the hydrant, and that would be a delay of perhaps three minutes, and at that time we needed the water; so I roused the hose up three flights with the water on into a room, and found the window-sills and frames going. I threw one of the windows right up, and jumped at the window-curtains, and, with the rest of the men, tore all the curtains down. Then we tipped the cases over that stood upright, so that they would not draw the fire, and played there until our water was cut off, in consequence of No. 3 coming up and taking the hydrant; and then word came to me to come out of the building immediately, in consequence of the wall of the building that first caught being liable to topple over on this building. Not immediately crediting the order, because I didn't receive it from an engineer, I went into the street to find out the truth of the report, and there I met an engineer, who told me, " Capt. Brown, take your line right out ; " and then I gave orders to have the line taken out, and I stood in the street and played with a powerful steamer stream, for No. 3 had then got to work, and was playing two streams — their own, and supplying us.

Q. What building did you get into?

A. It formed the south-east corner of the alley-way.

Q. (By Mr. Cobb.) That was in the rear of the building where the fire caught?

A. Yes, sir, directly in the rear, fronting on Kingston street.

Q. (By Mr. Russell.) The second building that caught?

A. Yes, sir.

Q. Did the walls fall?

A. Yes, sir, the walls of that building fell; but the wall of the one that caught first fell first.

Q. How soon after you came out?

A. I shouldn't judge it was more than ten or fifteen minutes. The rapidity of the fire was beyond anything I have ever seen. I have been connected with the Fire Department eleven or twelve years; been foreman of the company three years. The fire seemed to leap, as it were, almost ran like lightning from window to window.

Q. Was that so at the first?

A. Yes, sir, at the first of it.

Q. To what do you attribute that?

A. I attribute that to the heat being so intense amongst the dry goods, that it was undoubtedly creating a draught of itself, that would force the fire on. The place was reported as used as a hoop-skirt factory, and the articles are very combustible, and they blazed right up, and burned very freely.

Q. Was there any want of water at that time?

A. No, sir. At that time there was water in plenty. Those two streams, the steamer's and ours, rendered service there all the time. We didn't have to move, because we happened to be to the leeward of the fire; but steamer 4, I guess, didn't keep that hydrant more than twenty minutes, when they had to leave with suctions and all left at the hydrant, I believe; they didn't have time to take them off, because the fire had then reached such a pass that it was dangerous to subject the men, or the steamer either, to that position. But of course I can't say anything about this thing for certain, only by seeing them myself, you know, and knowing the facts of the case, being right there.

Q. Do you know anything of any steamers being short of fuel?

A. Not at that time, the first of the fire; but I guess, after the fire, the fuel got rather low, because I know that steamer 3's men had to break up boxes and one thing and another.

Q. What time of the night was that?

A. I should think that might have been about one o'clock in the morning. The fire in that locality was then under control, and the engineers and what available force was coming in on the alarm from out of town was immediately despatched down town to go to work there, because it didn't look as if the fire was going to spread any further that way; so of course they paid attention to other parts.

Q. Did you stay in that neighborhood through the fire?

A. No, sir.

Q. Where did you play next?

A. We played there until about twelve o'clock on top of the new building now in process of finishing very near the corner of Summer and Kingston streets; played over the roof of that building into the building occupied by Klous & Co., and in fact, all around us where we could make a stream available, we played. We had that order. I superintended the stream myself.

Q. You carried the hose on to the top of the building, and from there played on to the other buildings?

A. Yes, sir.

Q. (By Mr. Cobb.) That new building in Kingston street?

A. Yes, sir.

Q. Did you carry it up by a ladder, or the stairs?

A. Carried it by the stairs. That was a dwelling-house, and the fire, when we went up, was burning the blinds and windows. We went up through that house, and then from the top of the dwelling-house, we got on to the roof of the new building. Then I had orders from an engineer to take our line down, and run it through Bedford to Columbia street, and through the Columbia building, to check the fire on Lincoln street. We played there on the dwelling-house that fronted on Bedford street, and the dwelling-house that fronts on Lincoln street, forming the corner. After playing there awhile, we deadened the fire down, and then we took our hose up to the second-story windows of the building fronting on Lincoln street, and played across the street on to the corner of Lincoln and Summer street. We worked there, I guess, until about two o'clock in the morning, and then steamer 3 made up, and I had no special orders from any engineer to make up, but I knew the hydrant stream wouldn't be available, and as long as the fire was checked in that locality, I thought best to follow them, which we did as lively as we could, to the corner of Water and Washington streets. There we attached, and both companies ran a line of hose, and we passed the word to play; but when the water came, the stream was so small that it was ineffectual to do any good at all. We couldn't play more than fifteen feet from the pipe, because the hydrant above where the steamer was stationed was tapped so that we couldn't get water to furnish two streams, and the steam company having precedence, I made up my hose. But previous to that, I took the Captain of the steamer, Mr. Hine, and we made a circuit of the fire clear down to the Sailors' Home, to find an available spot to get to work with our apparatus, and not finding any, we came back, and Captain Hine concluded he would stay there until he got orders, and I took my company and carriage, and went down through, and tried every steamer as we went along to get to work, but they were all throwing two streams of water, and those draughting from the reservoirs were throwing two streams, and there was no chance for a hydrant company to get to work until I reached the corner of Milk and Kilby, or Water and Kilby, I am not certain which. There I met a steamer called Navy Yard 2 of Charlestown, waiting for reducing couplings, in order to connect with the hydrant. I immediately furnished them with the requisite couplings, and they connected with the hydrant, and we connected with the steamer, and ran off and went to work under the direction of Captain Jacobs. We worked there about an hour in the street doing the best we could, and then Captain Jacobs said we must try to stop the fire by going on the roofs. We told him we were perfectly willing. I broke open the doors of a building that was just finished, and took the tackle and falls and put it on my pipe, and sent part of my men to the loft, and put the rest of the men on the falls, and we hauled the pipe up into the loft and gave them orders to close the rear shutters and wet down everything, and just as soon as the fire made its appearance anywhere to go for it. We stayed there as long as we could, but the smoke was so dense, and the heat so fierce from the opposite buildings, which were some of them five stories high, that we couldn't live there. The men reported that fact to me, and I went up and found it to be as they said, so I ordered the line down and we took the very next building and served it the same process; went up there and wet everything down, and hung to it just as long as we possibly could. At that time, the Type Foundry was on fire on the opposite side of the street, a building seven stories high, I should judge, with a Mansard roof and very tall chimneys, and when that got to going, the heat was overpowering, and, fearful that the men might be cut off, I ordered the line down into the street again. When we stood in the street playing, there came an explosion directly opposite to us, caused by the heat coming into the building, and blew the shutters and windows out, prostrated two men, and almost knocked me over; but I managed to right myself, being pretty solid, and we stayed there and fought the fire until we stopped it on that street. It finally stopped at the stone building which is right exactly opposite the Fairbanks' scales warehouse, and there is a sign up which says "Dry Salters," or something like that. That is where the fire was stopped; but we still kept to work on that side of the street, and when we got pretty well down to the corner, there was a factory where they have imported pickles and preserves, and the next building to that was full of paints and oils; but we mounted the roof of the corner building, and went along the ridge-pole until we came to a chimney, where we made the hose fast, and passed the word for water, and got a powerful stream and played directly over this establishment, where they have pickles and preserves, to the roof of the building on fire; and that stream, with a couple more streams from the alley-way on the other side, checked the fire on that street.

Q. The fire stopped there?

A. Yes, sir.

Q. (By Mr. Cobb.) What time did you get through there?

A. That was about three o'clock Sunday afternoon, and by that time, we were pretty well tuckered out.

Q. (By Mr. Greene.) Were those operations obstructed by the crowds of people, materially?

A. No, sir, the crowd was kept back very well indeed; more so than I have seen them at a great many fires. One reason was, that the fire covered so wide a range that it would take a pretty good crowd to fill all the avenues, and then lines were drawn, and teams prohibited, although the first part of Sunday morning the teams came up there, loaded up with goods, and carried them off. But we had no bursted hose from that cause. I tried to be careful of my hose. I have orders not to allow any wagon to go over a line of hose, and that order is rigidly enforced, but in such a time I thought we would do the best we could, and I told my men, "If there is any way that you can let those teams get over to pass goods, give them all the show in the world." We played there until about five o'clock on Sunday afternoon, and then we got relieved until five o'clock Monday morning. That is, relieved from that fire, but not relieved from an alarm of fire, and I took the men up to the Sherman House, but there was nothing to eat, and I told them they had better go home and get their supper and get their rest, because there would be a hard day's work on Monday.

Q. How long were you on duty?

A. We were on duty from the time the bell struck, until five o'clock Sunday night. We were relieved by Providence 6 steamer.

Q. Did you have anything to eat during that time?

A. Some of the men got a little refreshment. I didn't have anything to eat, and some of the rest didn't have anything to eat. There was a report along in the afternoon that there was something to eat at Young's Hotel, and I sent a man up there to find out the truth of it, and he came back with the report that everything was eaten up, and there was no use for the men to trail up there, because they were tired, and I thought it was no use to let them go. We were relieved at five o'clock, and at twelve o'clock there came an alarm from box 42, and I dressed and started down, and on the way down another alarm was sounded, and the third alarm was struck; when I got there, and after I got there, the fourth alarm was struck. When I got there, I found that the apparatus was left with a line of hose down at the recent fire. Of course, we had nothing to work with; I looked round for a sight, told the men to keep right together, and finally I found that Fall River Co. No. 4 had gone to work with two lines of hose, but being short-handed they were only working one line of hose; the other line was run off, but there was no pipe on it. I discovered it merely by accident; gave that in charge of the company; found a pipe, and asked the engineer of the steamer if he would give us water, and he said, "Yes, all we wanted." We went over a small shed on the corner of the alley-way that runs by Jordan & Marsh's, and played there, I guess an hour, and then the Fall River folks got reinforcements, and they saw we had a good stream and wanted it, and by courtesy it belonged to them, and I gave it up and reported to Capt. Shaw, and he told me to take charge of a line of hose there was running from steamer 4, that had then gone up on a spliced ladder on Stevenson's building on Washington street. I sent two men up there to relieve the pipe men, because I knew it was cold and wet. I told two men to relieve them, and I would be right up directly and relieve them. They went up there, and I stood round on the ground for a while superintending putting in a couple of pieces of hose where they burst, and finally I went up on the spliced ladder and found that the men had gone across the roof and were playing directly into the flame in Shreve, Crump & Low's building. That stream, with the steamer on Washington street, opposite Shreve, Crump & Low's, which was playing a powerful stream into the Luthern windows, did more to stop the fire there than anything else, I think. Every drop of water I put into that building told directly on the flame. I relieved the men on the pipe, because I knew they were tired, and stayed there until seven o'clock. The fire had then got pretty well deadened down, and I got an order from an engineer to take the line down from there. I stood there and lowered the line myself and came down through the scuttle into the street, met my men, and had orders to take them down to the United States Hotel and give them some breakfast. So we went down there, but we couldn't get anything to eat, there were so many out-of-town firemen there in a hurry to get home, who had worked hard, and I told the engineer in charge, that I thought the Boston firemen could get served better down town, and give all the show in the world to the out-of-town firemen. He happened to think the same as I did, and two or three companies, with my own, went down to North Market street, where we had our breakfast; then I went back to the place where we left our reel and line of hose, made it up, came up to Broad street, and went to work on the coal that was burning there. I worked there about an hour, and Capt. Brown, assistant engineer, came along and told me he wanted me give all the show in the world to those men who had safes, wet them down and cool them off as fast as it could be done. I immediately put on three lines of hose, detailed two men to take charge of them, and then took a hose-carriage we have and went back to Oliver street, rolled on a full reel of hose, and came back and peddled it out in one length and two lengths, to merchants and others who had safes, who could not get any companies handy, and couldn't get any hose. I did everything I could to accommodate them, because I thought they were the sufferers, and because I thought they should be accommodated.

Q. (By Mr. Russell.) When you first went to the fire, while the first buildings were burning, was there anybody on the roof of the building where the fire caught?

A. No, sir.

Q. Was there not at any time?

A. No, sir, because it was impossible for anybody to get there. We were the first company there, and we reeled off a line of hose.

Q. Would it have been possible to carry it through the first building?

A. No, I don't think it would, but we went right up three flights in the second building.

Q. You didn't get up as far as the roof?

A. No, but there was a line above us. I think steamer 4 was above us.

Q. How high were they?

A. They must have been up four flights.

Q. They were not on the roof?

A. No, sir. I don't think they were on the roof at all. I think they were up in the attic story.

Q. You speak of the explosions having been caused by gas?

A. It might have been gas, or it might have been hot air, because the rear of this building was burning furiously, three or four stories down, where it would not show in front at all. It was burning down in the rear where the front was comparatively not burning at all.

Q. Did you see any trouble from burning of gas any more than usual at a fire?

A. No, I didn't see anything that night at the fire. It all worked well, as far as I know. The houses that we carried our line of hose up through in Kingston street were all lighted with gas, and were all right, and they were pretty near the fire; but the next night, Sunday night, the gas went out at my residence twice, and I told parties then I guessed they were shutting off the gas, because I thought it was necessary it should be done, knowing the vast amount of gas pipes that were out of order, and leaking gas and everything.

Q. (By Mr. COBB.) How long did you work upon the first building when you got there?

A. I think we worked there about ten minutes.

Q. The building where the fire began?

A. Yes, sir. I am liable, of course, to make misstatements in regard to the exact time; because we were all laboring under some excitement at that time, but some parties more than others. The hosemen, for instance, were of course laboring under excitement; but then it is the business of a foreman to keep cool; and it is the business of an engineer also. I know that I had to take the pipe right out of the hands of the man who was with me when it was in that cellar, by main force, and play on the hose behind me to keep it from burning. He was kind of excited, and would not give ear to an order.

Q. (By Mr. RUSSELL.) How much delay do you suppose there was in getting the hose-carriage to the fire in consequence of using men?

A. In regard to our hose-carriage, I think we arrived at the scene of the fire even sooner than we should if we had had a horse, and for this reason: being early in the evening, and Saturday evening, when there is not a great deal of business done, and there are always more or less hangers-on, you know, calling into the house, and one thing and another, the light of the fire was discovered before the alarm was given, the doors were flung open, and the carriage started. My shop is about one minute's run from the house, and when I went to the house on a run, the carriage was rattling over the pavements on Kneeland street. Hudson street is not paved; Kneeland street is. I very often notice it in the night time, when I am chasing the carriage. I can tell where she is by her rattling over the pavements on Kneeland street. I know then that she is crossing that street.

Q. What, in your opinion, made the fire so uncontrollable in the first place?

A. I don't know as I can offer an opinion on that subject. It got to going, and there didn't seem to be any stop to it. I never saw the like of it. I can hardly explain how it got to going so; it created a draught of itself. When we were on top of that new building, the breeze blew a perfect gale; blew fearfully; but parties have since told me that it was rather a calm night — not much wind outside.

Q. Did you see or know anything of the use of gunpowder that night?

A. No, sir, only by hearing the explosions, and the reports that they were using gunpowder. I saw one building blown up.

Q. Where was that?

A. That was in Liberty Square.

Q. What was the effect?

A. The effect was very bad for the fire, and didn't do the building any hurt at all. I stood and watched the building some little time before the explosion came, and it simply blew out all the glass, and unhung the doors, and blew them down; but so far as shattering the wall, or breaking the wall or roof, or even the chimneys, I couldn't see that it did.

Q. (By Mr. Greene.) It didn't stop the fire at all?

A. No, sir, it didn't; in fact, it created more fuel for the fire, for it would not only blow all the glass out of the building that was blown up, but it would blow the glass out of the surrounding buildings, as in the case of the building that was blown up on the corner of Water and Congress streets, near the new Post-Office. I was not there; but when we arrived down there, the sidewalk was strown with glass clear up to Devonshire street. There was thick plate glass all over the sidewalk, where it had been blown out of the windows.

Q. Was that from Simmons' block?

A. Yes, sir, that was Simmons' building.

Q. (By Mr. Russell.) Didn't it bring the floors down in that building in Liberty Square?

A. No, sir, I don't think it did; but I was not a very full observer. I had a direct view of the whole of the front of the building, but all I could see was glass flying, and doors, and some little confusion and racket. But it didn't seem to materially injure the walls, or settle the floors, or anything of that kind.

Q. (By Mr. Firth.) Were you aware that they were going to blow up the building?

A. Yes, sir; at that time the street was roped off. The insurance companies' men were the parties who were used to warn the firemen and crowd back.

Q. Were you all watching that?

A. No, sir, not all of us. We were at work at that time on the fire, but two or three stood looking at it.

Q. How many men have you?

A. We have nine men with the two substitutes that are furnished us.

Q. Were they all on duty that night?

A. Yes, sir, every man of them. There were only eight available hosemen; the ninth man is driver and steward of the company; his business is to take care of the apparatus and drive to fires. That is all that is expected or required of him, because we have to have some one to look after the horse.

JOSEPH PIERCE, *sworn.*

Q. (By Mr. RUSSELL.) Are you foreman of engine No. 4?

A. I am not foreman now. I was last year. The foreman is sick, and I acted as foreman on the 9th of November.

Q. Where is engine No. 4 stationed?

A. Brattle Square.

Q. What was the first knowledge you had of the fire?

A. I was called by the alarm.

Q. Where were you?

A. Coming down Anderson street.

Q. Did you go down to the engine-house?

A. No, sir.

Q. Did you come to the fire?

A. Yes, sir.

Q. I suppose you went pretty quick?

A. Just as soon as I could get there, right up over the hill.

Q. Did you find the engine there?

A. No, sir.

Q. How soon did the engine come?

A. The hose-carriage was there, but not the engine.

Q. Where was the hose-carriage?

A. Attached to the hydrant, and the line run off.

Q. Did you start as soon as you heard the alarm?

A. Just as soon as I got the box, No. 52, to know where I had got to go to.

Q. What was done there with the hose?

A. It was taken into the building. It was in the building when I got there.

Q. Into what part of the building?

A. The building on Kingston street, back of the one where the fire originated.

Q. Was it carried up?

A. Yes, sir, up through the building into the upper room.

Q. The building was four stories high, wasn't it?

A. Four or five. I can't say which with certainty.

Q. It was not carried to the roof?

A. No, sir.

Q. Were they throwing water when you got there?

A. Yes, sir, they were playing when I got there.

Q. When did the engine come?

A. I should say the engine came in five or six minutes afterwards.

Q. How soon were they throwing water?

A. Well, it couldn't have been more than two or three minutes; long enough to take our hose off from the hydrant and then attach to the suction, which didn't take more than three minutes.

Q. Where then did they play?

A. They draughted from the hydrant on the corner of Kingston and Summer streets.

Q. Where did they throw water?

A. That was our steamer we were playing with, from the building on Kingston street, on the attic floor, to save it from going south down Kingston street, on the roof.

Q. That engine was drawn by men, I suppose?

A. Yes, sir.

Q. Did you see it when it came?

A. I saw it when it came; I was looking out of the window.

Q. How did it come, fast or slow?

A. It came on what I should call a good trot.

Q. Was there any want of water while you were there?

A. Yes, sir.

Q. You mean there was not water enough?

A. We couldn't get force enough to do that execution which we had at times preceding, and have since.

Q. What was the difference?

A. It seemed to me that the engine, as engine men call it, was running away from its water. I presume that the meaning of that is, that they cannot get enough water.

Q. The water don't flow fast enough — don't feed it?

A. That is the meaning I should put on it. I am not an engineer.

Q. Was there any want of fuel?

A. Not that I know of.

Q. Do you know of any that night?

A. No, sir.

Q. Do you know of their having to use broken boxes instead of coal?

A. I saw them using boxes in the morning, round at different places.

Q. How late?

A. I should say eight or nine o'clock in the morning, — I don't know what engine it was, — when I went down to take a look of the fire on Liberty square side.

Q. Did you see the Chief Engineer there?

A. Yes, sir.

Q. What time did you see him? How soon after you got there?

A. Well, I should think the Chief got there close on to me; or, in other words, he might have been there, and I not have seen him until afterwards, after I got into the building.

Q. Where did you go from there?

A. Our line was ordered down out of the building into Kingston street.

Q. Did the same difficulty continue about water?

A. No, sir.

Q. You had plenty of water then?

A. Yes, sir; afterwards.

Q. Where did you go from there?

A. When the walls of the building fell, they cut our line, and then we had to take our line, what we could get of it, and carry it round on the Summer street side — round up Bedford street, up through Chauncey and down on to Summer street, and connect on the other side, because we couldn't get through Kingston street to Summer street, on account of the walls having fallen into the street; we couldn't get through that way; it was not possible, the heat was so strong and intense.

Q. How late did you stay at the fire?

A. Until five o'clock Sunday night.

Q. Where were you last?

A. Down at Liberty square, playing at the junction of Liberty square and Water street, I guess.

Q. Playing on the building where the fire stopped in that direction?

A. Yes, sir.

Q. Were you on the roof of a building at any time?

A. Yes, sir.

Q. Where was that?

A. That was between Arch and Otis streets, on the left going down Summer street.

Q. How long were you there playing?

A. I think I was at a Luthern window six or seven stories high; I won't say for certain. I should think I was standing there for fifteen minutes.

Q. Was there any chance to stand on the roof of the first building that burned, or the second one?

A. No, sir, I should say not, by what I saw when I got there.

Q. It was too late?

A. Yes, sir; nor the one adjoining on Summer street.

Q. What in your opinion made the fire get beyond control so quick?

A. Well, I think by its being such a high building, and the heat being so intense, it was impossible for us to get up into it, and fight it as we would if the building had been lower.

Q. (By Mr. Firth.) With regard to the time that your engine took to reach the fire, what is your opinion as to whether any time was lost by its being drawn by men instead of horses? if so, how much?

A. I shouldn't say it would make more than three minutes' difference, because the horses have to be hitched, harnessed, — what I mean is, they have to be taken out of the stalls, backed on to the pole and harnessed, and such as that, and during that time, fifty or a hundred men could take an engine and run quite a piece.

Q. (By Mr. Russell.) When you first gave up horses, was your attention called to the question how much longer it took to get to a fire?

A. No, sir; I made no particular point of it.

Q. (By Mr. Firth.) What orders had you in regard to running with your engine at this time? Did you answer at the first alarm with the engine?

A. Answered with the hose-carriage at the first alarm. The orders were given, as I have understood, whoever the officer was, he should give the alarm, if he saw a fire in the third, fourth or fifth story, and just as soon as he rung the alarm into the City Hall, give it again for a second alarm, just as soon as possible, and that would fetch the engines.

Q. Is that order in writing to you?

A. Oh, no, sir, not to me.

Q. How did it reach you?

A. I have heard it by hearsay, and saw it in the papers, I think, that the notification had been sent to the Chief of Police for the officers to do so, or a request, as you might say, from Chief Damrell to the Chief of Police, asking that favor.

Q. In what way did the order come to you not to have the engine answer the first alarm?

A. I heard it as I would be likely to hear anything around the engine house.

Q. Did it come to you as an order?

A. No, sir, not to me.

Q. Would it come to you if intended for your engine?

A. No, sir.

Q. To whom would it come?

A. It would be likely to come to the engine man, to take the engine out.

Q. (By Mr. RUSSELL.) You go to a fire, if there is only one alarm, don't you?

A. Yes, sir.

Q. (By Mr. FIRTH.) So as to be there with your hose?

A. Yes, sir; for instance, if I was disengaged now, and an alarm should be struck, and I had to respond to it, for instance, 41 or 56, I should go right to that box.

Q. Can you tell about the date that order was given, that the engines should answer the second alarm?

A. No, sir, I cannot.

WM. A. GREEN, *sworn.*

Q. (By Mr. RUSSELL.) You are assistant engineer of the Fire Department?

A. Yes, sir.

Q. Will you tell the first you knew of the fire on the 9th of November?

A. I will state that I answered an alarm of fire from box 52 on the evening of the 9th. I was at that time at my residence in Montgomery Place, No. 8. I was at the door, waiting until the alarm struck 52, and then proceeded as fast as I could to the fire.

Q. At the first alarm?

A. At the first alarm.

Q. Do you know the time?

A. I don't know; I didn't look. It was a little past 7, I should judge. There was a clock right in the room, but I didn't notice it.

Q. State what you found when you reached the spot.

A. As I was going down Summer street, it was a little ways from the corner of Washington street, I saw a bright light. I hurried down as expeditiously as I could, and when I got to the corner of Kingston and Summer streets, but previous to that, when I got where I could see it, I saw that the upper part of this building was all one mass of fire; the upper story was all one mass of fire. As I went down Kingston street, I saw the fire down in the lower part; the building seemed to be on fire from top to bottom. The building south of that was taking fire in the Mansard roof.

Q. (By Mr. GREENE.) Did the fire appear to be working down or up?

A. I can't tell you; there was a large body of fire rolling out of the upper windows, and appeared to be on the roof; and the door on the southerly end down Kingston street was very much on fire; that is, through the door, the lower part of the building.

Q. (By Mr. RUSSELL.) What engines and hose were there at that time?

A. I did not see any engines at that time. There was a hose there, but I didn't stop to look to see whose, nor what line of hose it was.

Q. What did you do?

A. I saw the fire was going into this next building, over across a passage-way twelve or fifteen feet wide, probably. I then sung out for an axe, and a man speaks up and says, "The axes are not here." I looked at him, and saw it was a man I knew, and says I, "Go into that next building and get a joist or something to batter the door with." He did so, and got a stone or rock, and we opened the door and went up into the top of this building, clear up into the attic. The window-frames and window-sash in the upper story were more or less on fire. I think all of them. I am certain that four of them were more or less on fire. There was a lot of sewing-machines lying there; and I told the men who went up with me, Mr. Randall, and two young men, I don't know who they were, to take the sewing-machines back, and I looked round and found a sink there was there, and we went to drawing water and wetting it. Then I sent down word to have a line of hose brought right up. In a very short time there was a line of hose brought up into the building. In the mean time I had sent for an axe, and we had cut the plastering all off on the Mansard, and raked it right down between the windows, as I was certain the fire was going to work in under the casing of the windows, and so on; and when the stream came up there, I directed them to wash right backwards and forwards the whole length of that side of the building. Captain Regan, the gentleman who has just gone out of the room, came in with the line, and I says to him, "Captain Regan, can you hold this now?" and he says, "I think I can." I left then and came out of the building.

Q. Where did you go next?

A. I saw that the next building, right directly opposite this building, which was not finished, — that is, there were no windows or doors in it, although the roof was on, and it was furred more or less, and like enough part of it was plastered; the mechanics had been at work, because the shavings and lumber were lying round there, — I saw it was catching fire, and I took engine 3's stream up there, and got up on the other floor and called for water; but the fire was so intense, so hot, that it burned our hose off. I think four or five of No. 3's men went in with the hose. I said to one of them, "We may be cut off; see what chance of retreat there is." We could not get any water; they sung out that the hose was burst. The fire was very intense, and we were obliged to leave, and when we went out, we had to go out the back way, on some lumber that he had piled across into another new building that came in from Chauncey street.

Q. Was there any want of water at the outset?

A. I should judge not. We didn't get any water in this line of hose; we got water in the first building I went into.

Q. Were the engines delayed in getting there by the want of horses?

A. That is a question I cannot answer.

Q. Did you see some of them come up?

A. No, I did not. I was in the buildings all the time; I didn't see the engines roll in, not one.

Q. Where did you go after that?

A. I came up Chauncey street and went down Summer street to the fire.

Q. How soon did you see the Chief; when did you see him first?

A. I can't give you the time. At a fire I can't tell you whether it was fifteen minutes, or half an hour, or still longer. Really, I cannot give you an idea; but I should judge it was in about twenty minutes; it may have been sooner, and may have been longer.

Q. Was there any chance to get on the roof of the house with the hose when you first got there?

A. No, sir.

Q. The fire had got along too far?

A. It was all one mass of fire; it was rolling right out of the windows; it was so hot you couldn't live there, sir.

Q. How was it on the other building?

A. On the other building, when we raised up those windows to throw the water out — we didn't dare to throw it against the glass — we couldn't find any pail; we had nothing but dippers, that would probably hold a quart or so, that the girls used for their coffee or something; as we raised the windows up, it was so hot, it would almost blister us. I thought we could hold it until the line came up, and we should probably save it; that was our intention. The fire had not got inside then, but it was burning around the windows.

Q. Did you see anything of the use of gunpowder that night?

A. I saw some gunpowder about there.

Q. Did you see any building blown up?

A. I did, sir.

Q. Where?

A. I can't give you a correct statement where, with the exception of one or two instances. I saw it in a number of instances; the first time I saw any powder burned was in Federal street; but to designate the building, I cannot.

Q. What was the effect on the building?

A. It blew the windows and doors out; it didn't bring the building down.

Q. Didn't it bring the floors down?

A. No, sir; that is, at the time that powder was burned, the fire was coming down so rapidly in front of it, that I didn't go very near it, and didn't desire to, because that was the first powder I saw burned, and I didn't know what the effect was going to be.

Q. Did it do any good?

A. My impression is, that it did not.

Q. Did it do any harm?

A. No, sir, I don't think it did.

Q. Did you see it used in any other instance?

A. Yes, sir.

Q. Where was that?

A. The next place I think was near the corner of Congress and Water streets.

Q. What was the effect there?

A. About the same.

Q. Did you see it used anywhere where it had any effect in bringing the building down?

A. Yes, sir.

Q. Where was that?

A. In what I term the Merchants' Insurance Building. I don't know as that is the name of the building, but it is close to the new post-office. It blew the building down; blew it down handsomely, I think; that is my judgment of it.

Q. What street was that on?

A. That was on the corner of Congress and Water streets. That is my recollection of it.

Q. That fell in such a way as to be of some service?

A. Yes, sir.

Q. (By Mr. GREENE.) The walls fell in?

A. I happened to be by that building a great many times when it was being raised up and altered, and I was always a little fearful of it. There were two partition walls running through the centre of it, if I recollect, and there were arches through those walls, to go into the different rooms. The powder was placed right under one of the arches, and we happened to find a plank there; and after the fuse was put in, we put the plank over the powder, and the doors were taken out and put over the arch, which made a sort of Λ that confined the powder, and when the explosion took place, the building was lifted up and came down.

To go back to Summer street; I fought the fire on Summer street for a long while; I should judge until about nine o'clock. I went into a building, I think on the corner of Otis and Summer street. There is where I received my first order from the Chief that I remember now. I saw that the fire was getting into the upper part of the building, and likewise going into the windows across the streets. There was a line in the building, on the third floor, I think, and I ran up stairs and saw the fire was getting into the upper part. I ordered them to take it up stairs, and the Chief came to me and said, "Green, can you hold this building? can you stop it?" Says I, "If you will give me plenty of water, I think I can;" but before we got up there, the fire was so intense, and it went so rapidly, that it drove us down; went right over us, almost instantly. Then we kept fighting back, fighting back, until I got on top of Mercantile Hall building. I then was determined to make a strenuous fight there; I thought there was a chance to make a strenuous fight there. Or, before we got on the Mercantile Hall building, we went into the next store this side of the one where the heat drove us out. I then made up my mind that I would go right up into the upper part of that store and keep the fire out. There was a blank wall there, and I went up there and saw that the fire was working in under the Mansard roof, and I ripped the sheathing all down and got a pipe in there. I felt we could make a stand at that time, but come to look out back, there was a narrow passage-way that led from Otis street, and the first I knew, the flames got into the third story below me, and they went across that room nearly as quick as I could, and we hurried to get out, and did get out, that is all I can say. The next stand I made was in the Mercantile Hall building, and after I got my lines laid, a gentleman came to me and said that the Chief Engineer sent him to me to tell me to take my wagon — that is, there is a wagon that carries clothes, and they call it mine — and go into Dock square and get powder, and meet him at the corner of Milk and Congress streets. I did so, and there is where I received orders to use this gunpowder.

Q. How much did you get?

A. I got five magazines full.

Q. How much is that?

A. I can't tell you, because they keep it in quarter casks, and eighths and flasks. I went to Mr. Lovell's store, on Washington street, and took a magazine from there; and then I went to Reed & Son's and took theirs; to Mr. Walker's, and took his; to Mr. Smith's, on Central Wharf, and took his; to Mr. Mahan's, on Long Wharf, and took his, and carried them up there.

Q. How did you get into these places?

A. Used an axe.

Q. What were those magazines?

A. Copper.

Q. Can't you give us any idea as to how much there was?

A. They are supposed to hold about a hundred pounds, but whether they were all full or not I can't tell.

Q. (By Mr. FIRTH.) Why was the powder at those places?

A. They are licensed to keep and sell gunpowder.

Q. And you as an Engineer knew where it was kept?

A. Yes, sir.

Q. Where was it used first under your supervision?

A. In Federal street.

Q. (By Mr. COBB.) And the next place was where?

A. Corner of Congress and Milk streets.

Q. Was it effectual there?

A. It didn't bring the building down.

Q. (By Mr. RUSSELL.) Was it confined in either of those places?

A. We could not find any lumber to confine it until we got into this building, where we used the doors. The building that is owned by the Merchants' Insurance Co. was the first one where we had any effectual operation, in my judgment. I don't profess to be competent to judge.

Q. You used one magazine there?

A. No, sir; at that time, the team had been sent to Chelsea, and we put in there four hundred pounds — got four of those barrels — and we confined it.

Q. How did you touch it off?

A. With a match.

Q. With a fuse?

A. Yes, sir.

Q. How long a fuse did you have?

A. Probably rather longer than we needed, for the reason that we wanted to know that everybody was out of the way.

Q. How did you put the fuse into the barrels?

A. Into the bungs.

Q. Into each bung?

A. In most of those barrels that came from the Navy Yard there were wooden taps that could be turned out; there were two or three of those that came from the Navy Yard, that didn't have the taps, and those we took a weight — it was rather hazardous, rather risky — and knocked the heads in.

Q. When did you first get an order to use powder?

A. To the best of my judgment, it was about 11 o'clock. It may have been before or later.

Q. What time was it first used, to your knowledge?

A. I can't tell you. At a fire, it is hard for me to tell time. That is, I have been with the department a great many years, and after I have been to a fire, somebody will say, "It is 4 o'clock, or 3 o'clock," and really I didn't think it was 12. I don't have any idea of time.

Q. (By Mr. Greene.) You think the powder was ineffectual, because the arrangements were not properly made? The powder was all right?

A. We hadn't the materials; the powder was all right enough, but in order to use powder, we want a lumber team, just as much as we want powder.

Q. Therefore, the powder would have been a good agent, if properly applied?

A. That is my judgment.

Q. (By Mr. Russell.) You say you wanted a lumber team?

A. Yes, sir; we want lumber to confine it.

Q. Did you see it used effectually anywhere else besides in that building?

A. There was a building on the corner of Lindall and Kilby streets, where it was used pretty effectually, sir.

Q. Was that done by the Fire Department?

A. Well, I suppose I could name the parties who did it. It took us some time to get this powder confined. We could find nothing to confine it. We took the doors, and anything we could get hold of in that shop. That building was quite narrow, and what we intended to do was to confine the powder so that it would throw the front right out, and that would let the rest of the building down, and we blocked up with books, and I don't know what not, to confine the powder.

Q. How large a charge was used there?

A. I think two barrels, about a hundred pounds; I am not positive about that, but that is my impression.

Q. That building came down pretty thoroughly, didn't it?

A. Yes, sir.

Q. Where was that powder placed?

A. In the second story.

Q. (By Mr. FIRTH.) In what story was the powder placed in the other building, where it was used so effectually?

A. That would be the second story, counting the basement; that was a half-basement.

Q. (By Mr. RUSSELL.) Did the fire stop there?

A. The Post Office was right opposite.

Q. Did it cross the street?

A. I think it came up on the other side; it did not cross

Q. On Kilby street, it was checked just there?

A. I think it extended a little there.

Q. The fire burned a little there, but it was stopped by water?

A. Yes, sir.

Q. Could that have been done, if that tall building had not come down?

A. That would be a matter of opinion with me. It wouldn't amount to much, any way.

Q. The building opposite is there now, partly burned, isn't it?

A. Yes, sir.

Q. Did you see any other effectual use of powder?

A. I don't know that I did.

Q. (By Mr. COBB.) What time was it when that building was blown up, on the corner of Lindall and Kilby streets?

A. It was a little after daylight.

Q. (By Mr. RUSSELL.) Was there any trouble from the crowd of people?

A. There was a very great crowd of people.

Q. Were they much in the way of the firemen?

A. They didn't happen to be, on Summer street, so far as I could see, that is, I was right down by the fire, and had no occasion to go up in the crowd, but it would have been considerable of a task for a fireman to go through.

Q. Did you see any trouble that night from gas explosions?

A. Not on Saturday night.

Q. How was it on Sunday night? How much do you know about that fire?

A. I never left this fire until between eight and nine o'clock Sunday night. The detail was made for me to relieve Capt. Smith at one o'clock on State street. I went home, but didn't go to bed at all. I laid down upon the lounge, and when the alarm of fire was sounded, I was very tired and sleepy; not being in my usual sleeping room, with the gas lit,

I could hardly wake myself up to find my way out of the room; when I went down the steps, into Province street, another gentleman being with me, we discovered that the man-hole was up. Really, I didn't sense it; I took it that some desperado had taken it up for somebody to run or fall into. I stopped and put it on, and then ran to the fire, and when we got there, the building below the corner building, a large stone building, was on fire. There were two or three quite large explosions after I arrived there.

Q. Do you know the time?

A. No, I do not.

Q. How long after you heard the alarm was that, probably?

A. I should suppose it would take me like enough five minutes to stop and put on those covers and get to the fire.

Q. What box did that alarm come from?

A. Box forty-three, I think.

Q. Anything about that fire that is worth mentioning?

A. No, sir; I don't know of anything.

Q. Did you happen to see the way in which Hovey's building was saved?

A. I did not. I was then in Congress street.

Q. (By Mr. Firth.) Had you ever had any experience in the use of powder?

A. No, sir; not in blowing up buildings.

Q. (By Mr. Russell.) Was it ever used in Boston before?

A. Not to my knowledge.

Q. (By Mr. Firth.) Had the question ever been debated in the Board, in your hearing, in regard to what was to be done in a certain contingency?

A. I have been an Engineer since 1858, and in every instance where powder has been used in any city in this country, the Board of Engineers have taken measures to ascertain, either by sending some one personally or writing to the Chief Engineer, the facts in regard to the use of powder in blowing up buildings, and it has been discussed and talked over a great deal in the Board.

Q. Well, what was the general testimony on that subject that came to your knowledge?

A. The impression that I have always received from personal observation and from letters that we have received is, that it has never resulted in much good.

Q. (By Mr. Greene.) This powder, where it was placed in a building and proved ineffectual, was not confined at all?

A. Well, it would be confined temporarily. In some places, we would find the truckman's skids, and endeavor to get them under a girder, or something of that kind, but we couldn't make them stay; they would be either too long or too short. That was the grand trouble we had to contend with, as far as my experience went.

Q. (By Mr. Cobb.) Do you know anything about powder being put into the building on the corner of State and Congress streets, where the Webster Bank is?

A. No, sir.

Q. You were not there?

A. I was not present. I know the building, but I have no idea there was any powder put into it.

Q. (By Mr. Firth.) May I inquire what is your present view about the use of powder, after seeing what you saw that night?

A. My present view would be, in a city like Boston, I don't think I should ever use it, unless we were deprived of water, and had no other resource.

Q. Should you, or not, think it desirable to be prepared for that emergency?

A. I certainly do. If I had a voice, I would recommend that certain parties be drilled or disciplined, in case of emergency, because we are liable to have our water cut off, and then we should have no other resource. This fire happened in a bad locality; if it had been in any other part of the city, powder, in my judgment, might have been much more beneficially used than it was in this locality. You take a storehouse with merchandise in it, and if you blow it up, and blow it up effectually, you don't blow the building down, you don't lower it but very little, and you expose the surroundings of that building more than they were exposed when the building was in its natural state. That is my judgment. You blow the walls down, and the gas-pipes are broken and you have that to contend with. That sets the building on fire almost immediately. I saw quite a number of instances of that kind.

Q. (By Mr. Russell.) Did you see any that night, where gunpowder was used?

A. Yes, sir; that is, the building took fire almost immediately after the explosion, and I say that was the cause of its taking fire.

Q. (By Mr. Firth.) Were the buildings you have in your mind so near to the fire as to have the gas set on fire by the flames?

A. No, sir; it must have come from the explosion of the powder.

Q. Can you specify any building where that took place?

A. I think one was on the corner of Milk and Federal streets, or just above the corner.

Q. (By Mr. Russell.) Do you know of any accident caused that night by the use of powder?

A. No, sir.

Q. No person was injured to your knowledge?

A. No, sir.

Q. Have you ever heard of any?

A. No, sir.

Q. (By Mr. Firth.) Did anything fly?

A. No, sir.

Q. Was that due to the precautions which you took?

A. I know of no person being injured in the least — not a scratch on any person.

Q. (By Mr. Russell.) People didn't go very far out of the way, did they?

A. When those last charges were put in, they stepped back one hundred or one hundred and fifty feet.

Q. (By Mr. Firth.) You had ropes stretched across the street?

A. We had, in some instances; I don't think we had in all instances.

Q. (By Mr. Russell.) There were no ropes in Kilby street, were there?

A. I don't remember that there were; everybody stepped back.

Q. (By Mr. Firth.) Word was passed along?

A. Yes, sir; we had quite a strong force of police.

Q. (By Mr. Cobb.) How long a time elapsed from the time you lighted the fuse before the explosion?

A. From eight to twelve minutes, probably. We probably cut them longer than we need to. We thought that would be the proper way, sir

Adjourned to Saturday, at 3 o'clock.

SECOND DAY.

SATURDAY, NOV. 30, 1872.

GEORGE P. BALDWIN, *sworn.*

Q. (By Mr. RUSSELL.) What part of the building that was first burned did you occupy?

A. We occupied the two lower stories and part of the upper loft, except that in that loft there was a temporary scaffolding or floor, which made another floor in that loft.

Q. Was that for storage?

A. It was.

Q. How long had you occupied that building?

A. I think it would have been a year the first of January following. We occupied a portion, by the way, a year previous, but we took the whole of it with the exception of a passage-way which Mr. Young reserved for the purpose of getting access to the scaffolding which I spoke of; with that exception, we had the whole of it last year.

Q. What was your opinion of the engineer of the building?

A. I think the engineer is a remarkably faithful and careful person, and competent.

Q. Sober or otherwise?

A. Temperate, decidedly, I should say.

Q. If you know anything further, I should like to have you state it.

A. Of course you don't desire that I should state anything except what I know positively of my own knowledge. I have no question myself, that the theory of the fire starting in the basement is a simple fallacy. The engineer, I have no doubt, will testify that he doesn't draw his fires in any way, and that at the time he left the building there was simply about a bushel of embers, almost entirely burned out.

Q. (By Mr. COBB.) How long have you occupied the premises?

A. I think three years the coming first of January.

Q. (By Mr. FIRTH.) What are your numbers?

A. 84 and 85 on Summer street, and my impression is, that the upstairs door was No. 87.

Q. (By Mr. GREENE.) Mr. Young leased of you?

A. No, sir, we leased the premises of Mr. Klous, as also did Mr. Young, and the portion of the loft which we occupied he leased from Mr. Klous; that went with his lease.

KATE McCAULEY, *sworn.*

Q. (By Mr. RUSSELL.) What was your position in Mr. Young's store?

A. Overseer, sir.

Q. How long had you been there in that position?

A. Five years next February.

Q. On the evening of the ninth of November, did you leave the store with Mr. Young?

A. No, sir.

Q. When did you first know of the fire?

A. At about quarter-past seven, when the alarm was given.

Q. Where were you?

A. On Washington street.

Q. What did you do?

A. I went as far as the corner of Tremont Row to meet a young lady friend of mine, and met the engine coming along; and to get out of the crowd I came back again, and came down as far as Winter street, and then didn't know that it was our place that was on fire, and I walked part of the way up Washington street again, in hopes of meeting my friend. When I got to the corner of Summer street, I looked down the street and then I saw the fire. I thought it was the corner of Chauncey street and Summer. There were two brass signs; Damon & Temple had one, and there was a brass sign at the corner of Chauncey street, of a new firm that had gone in there, and I thought I saw the fire coming out over that brass sign; then I thought the fire was in the building occupied by the new firm at the corner of Chauncey and Summer streets. I stood there a while, and finally saw where it was.

Q. What did you do then?

A. I then went down to the Boston Post Office to get Mr. Young's address to telegraph for him, and they couldn't find it. They told me that nobody knew the number of his box except the gentleman himself. I then went down to try to telegraph, and they told me the Chelsea office would be closed.

Q. What time did you go there?

A. I can't tell you. I did it all and got back again by quarter-past or half-past nine.

Q. What did Mr. Young say when you told him?

A. Mr. Young was not there when I got there, and then I went up to another house in the hack that I went over in after him.

Q. You don't know anything about the fire except this?

A. No, sir.

Q. (By Mr. Cobb.) In what part of the building was the fire when you saw it first?

A. It was coming out over this brass sign. It was Damon & Temple's window, I should say; but I can't say for certain, I was no nearer than the corner of Summer street.

Q. (By Mr. Greene.) Which story was that of the building?

A. That was the second story.

Q. Did you see Mr. Young when you went to Chelsea?

A. Yes, sir.

Q. Did he make any remark about the fire?

A. He didn't think it was as bad as I said it was. He wanted to know if I thought it had reached the upper story. I told him I thought it had by that time.

Q. Had there been any fire on the premises that day?

A. We didn't light up the gas at all that night. We usually do on Saturday afternoon, but we didn't that day.

Q. The building was heated with steam, I believe?

A. Yes, sir.

Q. (By Mr. Russell.) What time did you leave the building?

A. I think it was a few minutes after five.

Q. What did you tell Mr. Young about the fire being in the upper stories when you left?

A. I told him that the fire was coming out over Damon & Temple's window, over the brass sign, and then he said if that was the case that our books were gone. That was on the bridge coming over.

Q. Where were the books kept?

A. In the third story. Our salesrooms were up two flights, and the work-rooms up three and four.

Q. (By Mr. Cobb.) When you left the store in the afternoon, whom did you leave there?

A. There was Mrs. Young — I couldn't see who was in the private office, I could see her face, and there were three of the boys; this book-keeper, Judson Coffin, and Patrick Cotter; and Mr. Taggert, I suppose, was there, for he always closed up, but I didn't see him when he came down stairs through the sales-room.

Q. Was Mr. Young there?

A. No, sir, I didn't see him.

Q. (By Mr. Philbrick.) In which story did you work?

A. In the two upper stories.

JUDSON COFFIN, *sworn.*

Q. (By Mr. Russell.) How were you employed?

A. I was employed by A. K. Young & Co. I was clerk there; attended to customers, examined goods, and received goods, and had charge of the stock. I looked after the stock in the stock-room and saw that it was kept up,— the materials for manufacturing.

Q. Were you there on the night of the ninth?

A. Yes, sir, I was.

Q. How late?

A. It was between twenty and twenty-five minutes of six when I left.

Q. Did you leave at the same time with Mr. Young?

A. No, sir; there were four there when I left.

Q. Who were they?

A. Mr. and Mrs. Young, Mr. Bullock, and Mr. Cotter. They were all ready to go out as I came out.

Q. When did you hear of the fire?

A. I heard the alarm; that was the first I heard of it.

Q. How soon did you get there?

A. I didn't start until the third alarm sounded. I was at the South End. I got into a horse car and came down and saw the top of the building was on fire. I came down Bedford and went up Kingston street as near as I could get to the building, and saw the fire was all in the back part and in the top. I was there when the back wall fell in; that fell in first.

Q. Was there any fire in the lower part at that time?

A. The fire was all in the back part of the building. I could see fire in the windows there, and in the upper stories, too. The building seemed to be nearly all on fire inside.

Q. (By Mr. PHILBRICK.) Did you see any fire in the lower story?

A. The fire seemed to be in the lower story, in the back part of the building, more than in the front part.

Q. (By Mr. COBB.) What time was it when you got there?

A. I can't say.

Q. Were there any engines there?

A. Oh, yes, sir, they were playing when I got there.

Q. The building was all on fire?

A. It seemed to be mostly, inside.

PATRICK W. COTTER, *sworn.*

Q. (By Mr. RUSSELL.) You are employed by Mr. Young?

A. Yes, sir.

Q. What time did you leave the store on the night of November ninth?

A. I think it was between twenty-five and twenty minutes of six.

Q. Who left with you?

A. Mr. and Mrs. Young came down stairs with me. The book-keeper left about two or three minutes before.

Q. Everything was all right when you left?

A. Yes, sir, everything was perfectly right.

Q. Where were you when you heard the alarm of fire?

A. I didn't hear any alarm. I live in Charlestown, and went up Main street a little ways, and the first I heard of the fire was on Main street, about quarter-past eight, I think.

Q. Did you ever see any one smoking in that building?

A. Yes, sir, I have.

Q. Any parties in the habit of smoking there?

A. The only person I ever saw smoking, except one or two customers who came in, was Mr. Young.

Q. Did you ever see him smoking in the loft?

A. No, sir, I never did.

Q. Do you know that his safe was out of order? — wouldn't lock?

A. I don't know that it was out of order; I know that it wasn't locked. We had a new book-keeper, Mr. Bullock, and he couldn't lock it. I could lock it, but it might take me half an hour to unlock it. I used to lock it some years ago. It is my impression that it wasn't locked that night, because it hadn't been before for some time.

Q. (By Mr. COBB.) Had there been any fire used about the premises that day?

A. No, sir.

Q. (By Mr. GREENE.) Were Mr. Young's books burned?

A. I understand that they were. Mr. Young carried them over to the house, but they were so charred that he couldn't make anything out of them.

BOYD BULLOCK, *sworn.*

Q. (By Mr. RUSSELL.) Were you a clerk for Mr. Young?
A. I was A. K. Young's book-keeper.
Q. What time did you leave, Nov. ninth?
A. It was about twenty-five minutes to six.
Q. Did you leave at the same time Mr. and Mrs. Young left?
A. Yes, sir, I left at the same time.
Q. Was everything all right at the time you left, so far as you knew?
A. Everything, so far as I saw.
Q.. Was there any fire in the building?
A. None that I know of; not that I am aware of.
Q. Any used there?
A. I never saw any.
Q. How was it with the engine?
A. The engine was below in the basement.
Q. Do you know how that was that night?
A. I don't; I wasn't down there.
Q. Any gas used there that night?
A. Yes, sir, I had the gas lit in my office.
Q. Where is the office?
A. It is on the third floor, I think they called it, near the middle of the room.
Q. Did you turn that out?
A. Yes, sir, I turned that out myself.
Q. What is the condition of the safe?
A. The safe has not been locked since I went there. I think it was an old safe; at least, I could never lock it. The book-keeper who was there before me, left before I came there. I told Mr. Young a short time after I went there I couldn't lock it, and it was open that night when I left.
Q. (By Mr. COBB.) How long have you been employed there?
A. Six months and a half.
Q. (By Mr. RUSSELL.) How early did you go to the fire?
A. As near as I could say, I was there at twenty or twenty-five minutes past seven.
Q. What was the condition of the fire then?
A. The fire was coming out of the corner of the building, near the top, near Bedford street.
Q. Was there any fire in the basement at the time?
A. I didn't look; when I saw it was there, I ran round to the store door, 87 Summer street, thinking I could get in there, and save the books.
Q. Did you see any fire in the lower stories?
A. I never looked. I saw it in the upper stories, just bursting out. I didn't look at all below.
Q. I suppose you would have seen it if there had been a great light there, wouldn't you?
A. I suppose I would, but the blaze was coming right from the top, and my anxiety was to save the books, and I never looked below at all — it never crossed my thought.
Q. How long after you got there did any engine begin to throw water?
A. I believe it was more than ten minutes before I saw an engine. The

first thing I saw was a ladder company, coming from Franklin street, I think is the name of the street, right opposite.

Q. How long was that after you got there?

A. That was more than ten minutes, as near as I can tell.

Q. At what rate was that coming, fast or slow?

A. It was coming slow. I don't remember whether there were horses or men on it.

Q. Did you notice the rate at which the steamer came?

A. I didn't see a steamer for twenty-five minutes after that, until I was driven from the door by a policeman. After that, there was a man came with an axe, and smashed open the door, and I went to help them pull down the door, and I made a rush to go upstairs, and a policeman caught me here [by the collar], and drove me back; I said, "I am A. K. Young's book-keeper," and he said, "I don't care; go out;" and he drove me down again.

Q. Did he give any reasons?

A. No, sir, he gave no reasons at all.

Q. Do you know who he was?

A. No, I don't at all, anything further, only that he was a big man.

Q. You were on Summer street?

A. Yes, sir, in the door.

Q. (By Mr. Greene.) Were you attempting to get at the books when you were rushing up stairs?

A. Yes, sir. I wanted to go up stairs at the same time with this policeman who had an axe, but he drove me down.

Q. (By Mr. Firth.) Do you think you could have reached the story where the books were, if you had gone on?

A. I think I could, if I had been in time. I saw a great light in all parts of the house; I didn't see any smoke or anything like that, and I supposed it was the reflection of the light from the top of the building.

Q. Did the fire seem to be above you, or below you?

A. No, it seemed above.

Q. (By Mr. Russell.) There was nothing to prevent your getting to the books, except the police officer?

A. I don't think there was. I ran up about six steps, I think. There are about six steps from the door, and then I made a rush up about six steps inside, and then he stopped me. I stood so close to him that he hit me with the axe. I wanted to be as close to him as I could, to get up.

Q. (By Mr. Philbrick.) What did he do with the axe?

A. He smashed open the door.

Q. (By Mr. Firth.) Did he go up himself?

A. Yes, sir.

Q. (By Mr. Greene.) The policeman went where you were attempting to go?

A. Yes, sir, and I made a rush up, and he pushed me down.

Q. Then if he had made an attempt to get the books, he could have recovered them?

A. I think he could, if he had had some person there to show him where the safe was.

Q. (By Mr. Firth.) Did anybody go up besides the policeman?

A. Well, I saw two men around there; they were firemen.

Q. How many went up?

A. Three or four men; I can't exactly say, but there seemed to be a rush.

Q. (By Mr. PHILBBICK.) About what time was this that you attempted to make a rush upstairs?

A. I suppose it was twenty-five minutes past seven when I arrived, and I suppose it was ten minutes after that. I didn't notice particuticularly the time, but I guess it was about that.

Q. About what time was it when you saw the first engine come?

A. It was about twenty minutes to eight; the first engine I saw was coming up from the Hartford and Erie Railway. I didn't go round on to the Franklin street side.

HENRY A. PIPER, *sworn.*

Q. (By Mr. RUSSELL.) You are a member of the firm of Tebbetts, Baldwin & Davis?

A. Yes, sir.

Q. How late were you at the building on the night of Nov. 9th?

A. I left the building at five minutes past six.

Q. Did you go into the basement shortly before?

A. Yes, sir, I did.

Q. Did you go to wash your hands?

A. Yes, sir.

Q. Was there any gas lighted in the basement?

A. No, sir.

Q. You washed your hands in the dark?

A. I did, sir.

Q. There is a door from your basement to the engine room?

A. Yes, sir.

Q. Did you see any light there?

A. No, sir.

Q. Notice any smoke?

A. No, sir.

Q, You were in a dark room and saw no light there?

A. Yes, sir.

Q. Who left the store with you?

A. Mr. Tebbetts.

Q. You locked the door, I believe?

A. I locked the door.

Q. And walked off with Mr. Tebbetts?

A. Yes, sir; we went up the street together.

Q. What is your engineer's name?

A. Wm. Blaney. We have no control over that; he is engaged by Mr. Klous, and that is something we have nothing to do with, except we ha.e to pay our portion of the expense.

Q. What sort of a man is he?

A. I always esteemed him an honest man. I think him to be one of the most capable men we have ever had in the building; we have only had two, though.

Q. Is he a sober man?

A. Yes, sir, to the best of my knowledge and belief.

Q. Does he draw the fire Saturday nights?

A. I don't think it was his custom to draw the fires Saturday nights; I think he used to draw them on Monday morning.

Q. Have you had any talk with Mr. Young's partner about the case?

A. No, sir, I have had no talk with him; but Sunday morning after the fire, he came to the ruins. I was standing there looking after our safe, and he made the remark to me, why we were there so late Saturday night, being Saturday afternoon; he said, when they left the building, it was all lighted up. He said he left at half-past five.

Q. (By Mr. GREENE.) You didn't light up at all?

A. Oh, yes, sir; on the first floor. Mr. Tebbetts, Mr. Davis and myself sat there in the counting room while the boy was sweeping out, — we were only waiting for him to get through, — and at twenty minutes to six I left the two there, Mr. Tebbetts and Mr. Davis, and went down stairs and washed my hands. I then went up stairs, and Mr. Davis made the remark, "I guess I will go home;" and he left Mr. Tebbetts and myself there, and we sat there talking until five minutes past six. I then said, "I guess it is time we were going, for I have got to take the train," and we came right out together.

Q. Have you heard anything from Mr. Young or his partner about where the fire originated?

A. No, sir.

WM. F. HALSALL, *sworn*.

Q. (By Mr. RUSSELL.) Where do you live?

A. I reside at 5 Cambridge street. I did reside at number 17 Kingston street, at the time of the fire.

Q. How early did you see the fire?

A. I saw the fire when it was in the basement; that was about twenty minutes past seven.

Q. Was that before the alarm, or after?

A. It was before the alarm.

Q. Did you see the fire before you heard any alarm?

A. Yes, sir.

Q Hear any people crying fire?

A. No, sir. I saw the fire through my chamber window. I didn't see any one on the street when I went myself on the street and cried fire.

Q. Where was the fire?

A. It was in the basement of Tebbetts, Baldwin & Davis' store.

Q. Did you see it in any other room?

A. No, sir, not until it went up the elevator; then I saw it in their rooms.

Q. Could you see it go up the elevator?

A. Yes, sir; I saw it go up the elevator.

Q. Where did you see it then? Where did it break out?

A. It went up the elevator very rapidly, and broke out of the windows and went right up to the roof, and seemed to enter the chambers.

Q. (By Mr. Philbrick.) Did the elevator passage have any windows in it?

A. Yes, sir; on the alley-way between Hatch's store and Tebbetts, Baldwin & Davis'.

Q. Was it through those windows that you saw the fire go up the elevator?

A. Yes, sir; when I saw it in the basement from my chamber window, I immediately ran down stairs, and ran on the street and cried "Fire." I didn't know where the box was to give an alarm, because I hadn't lived there a great while, and I went into the alley-way and saw the fire going up the elevator. It went very rapidly, the same as a blast would.

Q. Burning the sides of the elevator as it went up?

A. Yes, sir.

Q. How long after you saw the fire was the alarm given?

A. That I can't say. I don't remember.

Q. How long after you saw the fire was it before this hose-carriage or engine came?

A. I can't say positively, but it was a very long time. When I went down stairs, I noticed by my clock in the chamber that it was twenty-four minutes past seven. The clock was about five minutes fast, my wife said. After being in the street and running round considerable — I was very much excited — I went into my chamber and looked out of the window, and when I saw a stream play, it was quarter of eight by our clock.

Q. Do you know that that was the first stream?

A. It was the first stream that I saw.

Q. (By Mr. Cobb.) From what side was that stream?

A. That was from the Kingston street side.

Q. Do you mean by that that it was twenty minutes to eight?

A. Yes, sir; I should think it was that time before a stream was put on the fire.

Q. (By Mr. Philbrick.) Where was that stream played from?

A. I can't tell where it was played from. It looked to me like a hydrant stream, the way they were playing it. It didn't seem like a steamer's stream, but at that time, I was very busily engaged in getting men to save some of my things.

Q. From what street did they appear to play from?

A. They played from Kingston street, between our house and Mr. Hatch's store.

Q. (By Mr. Firth.) At that time when you saw the stream play, was the fire through the roof?

A. Yes, sir. The whole building was enveloped in flames; it went up the elevator and it seemed to go into each chamber as it went up the elevator. It went very rapidly up the elevator, and went into each chamber; it seemed to me as though the elevator doors were open, and it went into the chambers. That is, I could see it through the basement windows from my chamber windows, and I made the remark to my wife, "That place is on fire," and ran down stairs.

Q. (By Mr. Philbrick.) You are sure there was no fire above that?

A. Yes, sir; I am positive of it.

Q. (By Mr. Russell.) Was it checked at any time when it went through the elevator?

A. It seemed to hesitate about the third story, but it went very rapidly. It didn't seem more than a minute from the time it was in the basement before it went up; if it had been saturated with something inflammable, it couldn't have burned quicker.

Q. Had you any business in this building?

A. No, sir.

Q. What is your occupation?

A. I am a sign-painter, on Kilby street. I was burned out with the rest.

Q. (By Mr. FIRTH.) Did you know any of the parties in that building?

A. No, sir.

Q. (By Mr. PHILBRICK.) Did you board in Kingston street?

A. Yes, sir; we occupied the two front rooms in the second story.

Q. (By Mr. RUSSELL.) Have you anything to say about the management of the fire at that point as it came towards Kingston street?

A. No, sir. I was very busy at the time, and I suppose they did all they could. It seemed to me they were not there soon enough.

Q. Did you notice the rate at which they came? Was it slow or fast?

A. They seemed to me very slow; the men seemed to be very tired. I saw three of them who were used up completely.

Q. On their arrival?

A. Soon after their arrival two of them were brought into the house; one man was so bad, we had to give him a great deal of water and some brandy.

Q. (By Mr. COBB.) What did he say the trouble was? Did he say he was used up by drawing the engine?

A. He didn't say it was drawing the engine, or whether it was the heat, or what it was. It was very warm between the buildings.

Q. This was after he had been at work upon the fire?

A. Yes, sir; a short time afterwards.

Q. (By Mr. RUSSELL.) Do you know what engine he was connected with?

A. No, sir, I don't remember.

Q. (By Mr. PHILBRICK.) How long was it before the fire reached your house?

A. Well, it reached it very soon, but we put it out with water; we passed water and put it out.

Q. Was your house burned finally?

A. No, sir. My place of business was burned. There was a building which was partly finished, and there was a new brick wall which separated it from the dwelling-house. The Luthern window caught fire two or three times, but we put it out with pails of water. It was a flat roof and we passed up water and put it out.

Q. (By Mr. FIRTH.) You think you saved it by the application of water?

A. Yes, sir, because at that time we couldn't get any stream.

Q. (By Mr. PHILBRICK.) How long did you have to fight the fire on the building?

A. Until about ten o'clock. I left about ten o'clock to go and secure my books on Kilby street. I saw how far the fire had got, and was considerably excited at the time.

Q. (By Mr. FIRTH.) Were you in time for that?

A. Oh, yes, sir, I saved my books.

Q. (By Mr. PHILBRICK.) Was the very next building to the one you were in burned?

A. No, sir; the next building to me is a dwelling-house, and the next building to that is a new store, or store partly finished. That store was partly burned, but the wall was new and it saved our dwelling. The roof caught fire, but we put it out by throwing water on it. They did eventually get a stream on, and they threw a stream on the dwelling-house.

CHARLES B. PRATT, *sworn.*

Q. (By Mr. RUSSELL.) Did you see this fire before the alarm or after?

A. I saw it before the alarm.

Q. At what time?

A. It was somewhere about quarter-past seven; within a minute or two of that time.

Q. Where was the fire when you saw it?

A. The fire was in the basement of Tebbetts, Baldwin & Davis' store. It shone over the alley. The alley leads right into the rear of their store, and what first attracted our attention we heard the cracking of glass. I went from my parlor up into the second story to see some gentlemen who were there, who were going to the theatre. The wife of the gentleman who just went out was just putting on her bonnet, so that I know very accurately what time it was, and we heard this cracking, and we went to the window and saw a bright light from those two windows that were grated up, the basement windows, and Mr. Halsall and my son immediately went down below and went out and went into the court. I stepped up one flight further, — there were quite a number of ladies looking out of the window, — so as to give me a better view. I remained there and saw the fire go from story to story until it got to the attic; when it got to the third story, it didn't spread into the room so rapidly as it did into the others, and I attributed that to the elevator doors being closed. It spread rapidly after it got to the attic, and it spread rapidly in the lower floors.

Q. Do you know when the engines arrived?

A. Well, I was on top of my house; I immediately went and got pails, and filled them, and carried them on top of my house. I was on top of my house when the first engine came, and when the first water was thrown on the fire; I should think it must have been twenty minutes or more before there was any water thrown. I heard the engine when it came up. I was on top of my house, and saw the first stream that was played.

Q. That you say was about twenty minutes after you saw the fire?

A. I should think it was as much as twenty minutes, if not more.

Q. How long after you saw the fire was the alarm given?

A. Well, they hallo d "Fire" instantly, as soon as they went out, and they spoke to some one who said he knew where the box was and he would give the alarm. I don't know who the person was, and can't tell. I should think it was within a minute or two afterwards I heard the first alarm struck, but I was going up and down from the roof of my house to my tank filling pails, and getting them in readiness in case I needed them.

Q. Did you notice whether the steamer came slow or fast?

A. I didn't. I wasn't where I could see.

Q. Were you at work packing goods?

A. No, sir, I didn't pack up any; that is not my motto. I had rather put out a fire than pack up my goods; I never packed, nor took a thing out of my house, although I hadn't a cent of insurance. I stood on top of my house and put out the fire by the use of pails, probably twenty times, when it caught on top; if it hadn't been for that, I probably shouldn't have had a home there now.

Q. Did you see the firemen do anything in your house that you objected to?

A. I saw a fireman that I moved from his quarters, I didn't like to have him where he was sitting. He had been sitting there some time.

ALONZO PRATT, *sworn.*

Q. (By Mr. Russell.) You are a salesman of Burr, Taft & Co., on Franklin street?

A. Yes, sir.

Q. What is your father's business?

A. He is overseer in a manufacturing establishment.

Q. About what time did you first see the fire?

A. As near as I could judge, it was quarter-past seven. It may have been a minute before or a minute after.

Q. Were you getting ready to go to the play?

A. No, sir, but I was in the room with Mr. Halsall and his wife, who were getting ready to go. He looked out of the window and saw the fire, or his wife, I don't remember which it was, but I know Mr. Halsall and myself started and went into the alley-way between the two stores.

Q. Where was the fire when you first saw it?

A. In the basement near the elevator, just a little towards Kingston street from the elevator.

Q. Did you look down through the grating?

A. Yes, sir, through the grated window on the side.

Q. As you looked through the grated window, what did you see?

A. Well, the bulk of the fire, that is, the heaviest part of the fire, seemed to be right near the window, within a few feet, in the basement.

Q. Was there any fire in the stories above?

A. No, sir.

Q. Then what did you see after that?

A. Within a minute or two — you know how excited a person gets, he can't tell hardly about time — but within a few minutes, the fire broke through the elevator wall. Mr. Halsall and myself were in the alley-way, and as it started and went up the elevator we backed out and went across the street and went into our house.

Q. When did the first steamer come?

A. I should think it was about half-past seven, from that to twenty-five minutes to eight, before any steamer got there.

Q. Through what street?

A. It came up Kingston and Bedford.

Q. Did you notice whether it came fast or slow?

A. No, sir, I didn't notice particularly about that.

Q. How soon did they get the first water on the fire?

A. I should think it was twenty minutes or quarter to eight; it seemed a very long time.

Q. How long after you saw the fire was the first alarm given?

A. I can't tell you anything about that, because I didn't hear it.

Q. You cried "Fire"?

A. We cried "Fire;" if I had known how to give the alarm, I should have gone off myself and given one.

Q. State anything you saw the firemen do in your house.

A. When I came down into the parlors, — all our ladies had left the house and there was no one but myself and father in the house. — I saw two firemen, or men who had firemen's badges on, who had a box out of a bureau in the back parlor, and I took a silver fruit knife away from one of them, and it seems we lost a gold pen during the evening, but I don't know whether they took it or not. It was in the bureau before the fire; that was the place where it was usually kept.

Q. Do you know what company they belonged to?

A. I don't. I just told them to drop that, and took this knife from them, and shut the drawer up, and ordered them out of the house. I didn't notice particularly what badge they had on, and don't remember what it was; that is what I should have done.

Q. (By Mr. Philbrick.) What time was that?

A. It was some time after midnight.

Q. (By Mr. Russell.) That was when your house was out of danger?

A. Well, partially so, although the fire had worked around through Mr. Klous' store, and we apprehended some danger from there.

Q. What was the box they had?

A. It was an ordinary pasteboard box, taken out of a bureau drawer.

Q. (By Mr. Greene.) What did they say when you took the things away from them?

A. They didn't say anything.

Q. Gave them up?

A. Yes, sir.

Q. (By Mr. Firth.) Did they leave the house when you told them to go?

A. Yes, sir.

Q. How near were you when you looked into the basement?

A. Within three feet of the flames; standing as near to the window as I dared to go.

Q. (By Mr. Philbrick.) Did the flames come out through the window?

A. No, sir, not while we were there. It seemed to be working towards the alley-way; there seemed to be a strong draught that way. The instant it went into the elevator, it ran up as though there had been a train of powder laid there. I suppose on account of the elevator being well greased or oiled.

DANIEL W. CHILDS, *sworn.*

Q. (By Mr. Russell.) On the night of Nov. 9th, you were on outside duty, weren't you?
A. Yes, sir.
Q. What time did you hear the alarm?
A. It was about twenty minutes past seven.
Q. Were you then at the station house number 2?
A. I was, sir.
Q. Did you look at the clock?
A. Yes, sir, I looked at the clock.
Q. Did you go to the fire immediately?
A. Yes, sir.
Q. When you got there what did you see?
A. I got there just as the insurance wagon drove into Summer street, and immediately afterwards came through Otis street into Summer, hook and ladder company No. 1. I went immediately to the insurance wagon, and asked the driver for a line, took it out, called some officers of our own station who were there, and roped off Summer street, and drove the crowd back.
Q. Did you have officers there to man the ropes?
A. I did, sir. I then went to the end of the hook and ladder carriage and took one of their ladder ropes, and roped off Otis street.
Q. Did you send any message to your station?
A. As soon as I got Otis street and Summer street roped off, I sent an officer to the station to ask Lieut. Burleigh if he wouldn't send me all the officers he could.
Q. How soon did you send that message?
A. Within ten minutes after I got there, and then I don't think it was five minutes after that, I sent Sergeant Bates to Lieut. Burleigh, to ask him if he wouldn't telegraph the different stations to send me all the help they could; it might have been five minutes afterwards, but I don't think it was over that, and I got help very promptly.
Q. How many men did you get?
A. I can't tell you the exact number. In less than three-quarters of an hour after that, I had sixty men.
Q. Where were the men under your immediate charge?
A. They were in Summer street and in Otis street, and through Franklin and Devonshire streets.
Q. Where were Sergeant Foster's gang?
A. Sergeant Foster had a gang on the lower side of Summer street, and followed the fire back down through Federal and High streets, and that vicinity.
Q. And Sergeant Bates?
A. Sergeant Bates followed up Summer street until along in the morning, after it got to be nearly two o'clock, and then he took the north side of Water street.
Q. How long were you there?

A. I was there until five o'clock Sunday afternoon.

Q. You had no relief until then?

A. I had no relief until the fire was out.

Q. Did you get anything to eat in that time?

A. Yes, sir, I did.

Q. The police officers didn't suffer for want of food?

A. I relieved them as much as I could, through orders from the Chief, and directed them to go to the Parker House and get what they could to eat; relieved them part at a time.

Q. Did you notice whether the steamers came up fast or slow?

A. They came slow. There was but one steamer that I saw, when I got there. I understand there was one on the lower side, but that is where I didn't go. There was one below me, down on the corner of Bedford and Kingston streets. That was No. 7, I think. I can't say whether there were any others there or not.

Q. How long before any other came up, so that you could see it?

A. I think it was five minutes before I saw the second steamer on this side.

Q. What sort of a gang did they have — men or boys?

A. Men and boys together.

Q. Were they running?

A. They were on a slow run; about a trot. The hook and ladder carriage was dragged by men. That was the second thing I saw there besides steamer 4. I think that was there, and just getting to work when I got there.

FREDERICK HOFFMAN, *sworn.*

Q. (By Mr. Russell.) You are an officer of what station?

A. Station 4.

Q. What time did you hear the alarm of this fire?

A. I didn't hear any alarm at all that night.

Q. What do you know about the fire?

A. I was standing at the corner of Essex and Lincoln streets, and saw officer Page, who gave the alarm, on the opposite corner with officer Farwell. I was talking with a man and left him to go down Lincoln street towards officer Page, when this man I had been talking with called out to me and attracted my attention, and I looked round and saw there was a fire. At that time I heard some boys up the street halloing "Fire," and I ran up, and when I got to the corner of Summer and Bedford streets, officer Page was there, and had just closed the box after giving the alarm. Then I ran round the Freeman's Bank at the corner of Kingston street, and saw the fire was above the second story, and came back and told them to ring the second alarm. I went back and met engineer Regan there, and the driver of the insurance wagon. They were cutting away the front door. Engineer Regan told me to go round and ring in the second alarm. I went round and told officer Page to ring the alarm, and then I went back to the fire and helped clear Kingston street.

Q. How late did you stay?

A. I stayed until two o'clock; then I went to the station-house.

Q. (By Mr. PHILBRICK.) What time did you see them breaking the door down?

A. I should think it was about twenty minutes past seven. It might have been twenty-five, I can't say, because everything was excitement there. I didn't look at my watch.

Q. What door was it they broke down?

A. It was the front door of the building the fire broke out in. They gave up trying to cut in the front door and went round to the rear, right in the alley-way from Kingston street.

Q. Did you see any fire in Summer street?

A. Yes, sir, I could see the fire through the basement windows.

Q. (By Mr. FIRTH.) Was there any fire above the basement?

A. There was fire above the basement in the rear. I couldn't see it through the front part of the building. When I got back there from the box, before there was any answer on the bells at all, I could see the flames coming out of the second and third story windows in the rear.

Q. At your first view of the building, where was the fire?

A. The fire was in the rear of the building, coming out of the windows. When I got to the corner of Lincoln and Bedford streets, there was a low house, and I could look right across to the building, and there was where I saw the flames breaking out through the windows.

Q. From what stories?

A. From the second and third stories.

Q. (By Mr. PHILBRICK.) Was there any fire above?

A. Not at that time; very shortly after that it came out of the roof.

Q. Then, I understand you, when you got there on Summer street you could see no fire except through the basement windows?

A. No, sir.

MOSES S. MOULTON, *sworn.*

Q. (By Mr. RUSSELL.) You are an officer at station 4?

A. Yes, sir.

Q. Give us an outline of your beat.

A. Commencing at the corner of Washington street and Harvard street, running on the south side of Harvard street to South street, thence by South street to the Boston & Albany Railroad track to the corner of Washington and Indiana street, and then from the corner of Indiana street and Washington street, by Washington street to the corner of Harvard street, the first starting-point.

Q. Where were you when the fire first broke out?

A. I was sitting in my kitchen, taking my tea.

Q. (By Mr. COBB.) Where do you live?

A. No. 2 Columbia street. I heard the outcry of "Fire," and stepped to the door, and saw it, as soon as I stepped to the front door, bursting out of the building.

Q. What part of the building?

A. On the south side of the building, this building being on the corner of Kingston and Summer streets.

Q. The upper stories or lower?

A. I can't exactly say, but I should say it seemed to be about half-way up. The body of the fire seemed to be about half-way from the top of the building to the bottom.

Q. Did you notice whether there was any fire in the basement or not?

A. I can't tell, I didn't go near it. I ran without hat or coat to box 52, at the corner of Kingston and Bedford, and there found three officers who had just arrived there, giving the alarm. Then I went back to the house and looked out for my own things.

Q. How soon after that did you see any engines?

A. I can't say. I was considerably alarmed about my people in the house. I had twenty families in the house that I seemed to be responsible for. They came to me for advice, and I had them there from that time until twelve o'clock asking me questions, what I thought it would be best for them to do, and I told them I thought it would be best for them to pack up in case the house was likely to go.

BENJAMIN F. FARWELL, *sworn*.

Q. (By Mr. Russell.) You are an officer of the 4th station?

A. Yes, sir.

Q. The boundaries of your beat are Lincoln, Essex, Kingston, Summer, Chauncey, and Harrison avenue?

A. Yes, sir.

Q. What time did you pass Kingston street on the night of the fire?

A. I went through Kingston street about a quarter or twenty minutes past six o'clock, to the best of my judgment.

Q. You were distributing letters, weren't you?

A. I managed to distribute at different places.

Q. When did you pass Kingston street again?

A. About five minutes past seven; five to ten minutes, I should think. I came through Edinborough street, and from Edinborough into Essex and down Kingston street, a little past seven o'clock.

Q. Did you see any trouble then?

A. I saw nothing then. I stopped on the corner and saw nothing then.

Q. Were you on Lincoln street when you saw the fire?

A. I was.

Q. What were you doing then?

A. There was a crowd of boys; it was Saturday night, and from the "Palace" as it is called, or Lincoln block, there was a crowd of quite large boys running through the street, and I went into the middle of the street and dispersed them. There were some dozen or fifteen, more or less. I saw the fire when I got into the middle of the street.

Q. What did you do then?

A. I went as quick as I could to the box at the corner of Bedford and Lincoln streets.

Q. Whom did you find at the box?

A. John M. Page.

Q. Giving the alarm?

A. Yes, sir.
Q. What time was that?
A. Between fifteen and twenty minutes past seven, as near as I can judge.

EUGENE McCARTY, *sworn.*

Q. (By Mr. Russell.) You are an officer of the 4th station?
A. Yes, sir.
Q. You were on patrol on the night of the 9th of November?
A. Yes, sir, I was on duty that night; at six o'clock I went on.
Q. Where were you when you heard the alarm?
A. I was standing on the corner of South and Kneeland streets.
Q. What time?
A. Set it at fifteen or twenty minutes past seven.
Q. Did you run to the fire?
A. I did.
Q. How long did it take you?
A. I should think all of three to five minutes.
Q. Where was the fire when you got to the building?
A. The fire was breaking out of the upper story and roof on the corner of the passage-way running from Kingston street, and coming out of the side windows.
Q. Was there any fire below?
A. In the rear there was. You could look through and see the fire, but it didn't seem to break out there.
Q. Were there any firemen there?
A. The firemen were laying the hose through Kingston street. Shortly after I arrived, I saw the hose in the street; there was no water in the hose.
Q. You went to work keeping the people back?
A. I went to work to clear the street. I got some officers and cleared the street.
Q. Do you know when the engines came?
A. I drove the people back as far as Bedford street, and there was a steamer at the corner of Bedford and Kingston street.
Q. What time was that?
A. Perhaps that was ten minutes after I arrived at the fire.

JAMES QUINN, *sworn.*

Q. (By Mr. Russell.) You are Deputy Chief of Police?
A. Yes, sir.
Q. Tell us all you know of the beginning of this fire — the first thing you know about it, and what you did.
A. The first of my getting to the fire, I think it was a few minutes past eight o'clock. I didn't go down until the general alarm was given. The fire was then in Tebbetts & Baldwin's. I remained there until I saw the fire cross to Otis street, on the corner of Otis and Summer.
Q. Will you tell us what the police detail was?

A. I then sent immediately to the office and requested them to telegraph to the stations to send all the available men they could spare to meet me at the corner of Devonshire and Franklin streets. I went immediately there, and then we commenced to rope in to press the people back, and we roped in at Arch street and Franklin; we roped in Devonshire and Franklin, and roped in afterwards at the end of Franklin on that side. The men were round on the south side previous to that. We have a certain number of officers who are detailed to attend fires at the first alarm, and they were at the south side attending to their duty. We then had a few men to spare, and I threw them out as scouts, from the fact that I was satisfied, being a large fire, there would be more or less pilfering, with directions to take any man they caught with property, and if he couldn't give an account of himself, lock him up; and that order was carried out very faithfully. We locked up some four hundred and fifty, and there were some three hundred more arrested who were released on their giving the account, which most of them gave that night, that the goods were given to them.

Q. Were there any convictions?

A. I think there were, in the Highlands; I think some of them were arraigned at the Highlands. I shouldn't want to say certain; but my impression is that they were.

Q. Was the police line held?

A. It wasn't broken during the time I was there. I got wet there and went home to make a change, and returned. I got badly wet in Summer street, but I went on making these arrangements. I assisted in getting along the hose, the hose burst, and I got pretty well wet.

Q. Can you tell what detachments were made from the several stations?

A. I can't, but the Chief can; I think the Chief has the list, sir.

Q. Have you anything further that you can tell about the management of the fire while you were there?

A. Well, gentlemen, when I first got there, I found the buildings were pretty well enveloped in flames. I was with an old friend, Joseph L. Drew, one of the Assessors; he was my third officer in the department for some years, and we got into position in front of Otis street for a full survey, and returned back to the building of Tebbetts, Baldwin & Davis. I kept my eye upon that corner, for I was satisfied in my own mind that if the fire reached that roof, it would be almost impossible for them to check it. When the fire took upon that roof, I made the remark to Mr. Drew, said I, "You will see the largest fire Boston has ever witnessed to-night. It has got into that roof, and I don't see any possible means now of their checking it." That was a point that I think above all others should have been secured. I remained until the fire (and it was very rapid in its course) passed over and came up into Devonshire street; that is, after I had made this allusion to him, that this fire would be the largest fire Boston had ever seen; then I passed down and saw that it had crossed Devonshire street. I then went round to Summer street. There were four engines stationed then at the reservoir on Summer street. I then passed round and went up to High street, stopped at Stedman's crockery store, and saw there were parties in their store. I continued round and went down Federal street; the fire was then going to the leeward very rapidly. I saw it from Milton place, and also from Sullivan place. When I struck Franklin street, there were four engines there. I have no doubt (I speak very candidly, gentlemen), I have no doubt that Capt. Damrell did everything he could do, under the circumstances, but men have different views in regard to contending against a fire to prevent its spreading. In Franklin street, my idea would have been to establish a base of operations. There should have been a flanking movement made. There is a reservoir at the head of Franklin; passing down Franklin three hundred feet, there is another at the corner of Hawley street; and passing down Franklin until you get to the corner of Devonshire, there is another; passing round the end of Franklin to the corner of Channing street, you find another. These reservoirs will hold about four hundred hogsheads of water each. I am not taking into consideration the hydrants. I think the one on the corner of Franklin and Hawley streets is smaller than the others, but they are all fed by the same main. I recollect when the reservoirs were located, for I went round with Capt. Barnicoat, and I know that when the question came up about locating them, it was an immense number to be located in one street, but on account of the large property in that neighborhood, they thought it was a very important matter. I think there should have been a constant pressure of the force in Franklin street, with five engines to each reservoir, fed by a four-inch main from the Cochituate, together with the hydrants. I consider that there would have been a good chance to check the fire there in that way. That point passed, there was not so good an opportunity, the streets being narrow. Franklin street, you recollect, was very wide, and on the north side, the roofs were not very high; but I think a concentration could have been accomplished at that time, when the fire reached there, because we had additional force all around, and I was in hopes that something of the kind would be done. Capt. Damrell spoke to me at the time I was there, and asked me if I would look round and see if there wasn't some place that it would be advisable for us to blow up, and I told him I didn't know of a place in that locality where it would be convenient to do it.

Q. At what time did he ask you that question?

A. I can't say definitely, but I think it must have been somewhere between nine and ten o'clock. It must have been probably half-past nine, as near as I can guess. I took no note of the time, particularly.

Q. You thought then there was no place where gunpowder could be used to advantage?

A. I didn't, after you passed that point.

Q. Your opinion is the same now, is it?

A. It is. With regard to the means of extinguishing fires, — I make an allusion to it; I don't know as it will be of any consequence, — if a fire should take place in a certain locality, we have not the means to-day of reaching it, if it should break out in the top of a building. We are deficient in that respect. For years, the highest ladder was sixty feet, and, with the additional splice that is now used, it does not extend over seventy feet. If a fire took place in the Parker House, for instance, there is no possible means of reaching the top of the building, or even its coving. I saw them raise a spliced ladder at the State street fire, and I think it fell short of the coving. When I was in the Board of

Engineers — I was in the department some twenty-five years — I saw they were building houses five, six, and seven stories high, and I said to Capt. Barnicoat, at the time, that I thought we ought to keep up with the times; that people were building very high, and that our means were not sufficient to meet it. I said, "This is a progressive age in which we live, and we should keep up with the times. If they build these six, seven, and eight story buildings, we have no means of reaching the top in case of fire;" but the old gentleman's idea was, that if they were too high, they would burn down so low that we could reach them. I said I would not put any man in a place I wouldn't be willing to go in myself. You can't control a fire by getting under it, any way; to make water effective, you have got to get above the fire, and had there been any means of going above that State street block, that fire would have been subdued in a very short time.

Q. (By Mr. Cobb.) Your idea would be to throw the water down?

A. To pour it right down on the fire.

Q. (By Mr. Russell.) Do you think that was done in the case of the fire on the 9th, as far as it could be? Was anything wanting in the department in regard to going on the roofs of buildings and throwing water down?

A. That was not of much use after the fire crossed Otis street, in that direction.

Q. (By Mr. Philbrick.) What effort did you see made to stop the fire in the building at the corner of Otis and Summer streets?

A. I saw two streams raised from the reservoir. There were two engines stationed there, but neither of the streams went above the third story.

Q. There was no hose carried up?

A. I saw none carried up.

Q. Was there any effort made to carry the hose up to stop that building from burning, by wetting the top of it?

A. Well, sir; we ought to have a class of engines that would throw the water to the roof of that building without much trouble. I was somewhat surprised that the water wasn't more effective that night; that the streams didn't go up to the top of the building; I was quite surprised. I thought, when they first raised the stream, that it would accomplish the object and extinguish the fire, but I found it didn't go above the third story.

Q. Was there any opportunity to carry the hose up?

A. Certainly; break the door open and carry the hose up to the top.

Q. Was there time and opportunity to have done that?

A. Yes, sir, plenty of time.

Q. Didn't it occur to you at the time that it ought to have been done?

A. To tell you the truth, gentlemen, my idea always in fighting a fire was to get into the building; to get up to the top of it; that was my rule always; never to fight a fire from the street. You must get inside of the building, if you want to be effective.

Q. (By Mr. Cobb.) Go where the fire is?

A. Go into the building to get at it.

Q. (By Mr. Russell.) Could that have been done that night, without too great risk of human life?

A. I think it could on the corner of Otis street. I didn't get there till after the general alarm was given, a few minutes past eight. The first alarm was given somewhere about twenty-five minutes past seven.

Q. (By Mr. PHILBRICK.) About what time was it you saw the fire cross Summer street?

A. I can't tell the time, because I took no note of time; but I had been there some little time before it crossed Summer street.

Q. (By Mr. FIRTH.) You speak of a certain class of engines which we ought to have, to throw water to the top of a high building — what are they?

A. The engines didn't work so well as I have usually seen them; that is, they didn't throw a stream up to that height which I have been accustomed to see them throw.

Q. What was the cause of that?

A. Probably the wind might have deflected the stream; then the question is, whether they had steam enough to carry the stream to that position. That is a question that I can't answer, for I didn't examine the engines; the wind might have broke down its force.

Q. Then it was not another class of engines you had in your mind?

A. Not at all.

Q. (By Mr. RUSSELL.) Do you know anything about the use of gunpowder that night?

A. I know it was used.

Q. Did you see it used?

A. I was down on Congress street, when Mr. George O. Carpenter told me he was using it, and that he had a charge then in the building on the corner of Bath and Water streets.

Q. Did you see any buildings blown up?

A. I didn't see any blown up.

Q. Have you had any experience in the use of gunpowder at fires?

A. I have not; but I was in Chicago shortly after that fire, four days afterwards, and I made some inquiry there about the manner of blowing up buildings, among the officers of the army, and I have also read other statements in connection with it, but I never have seen it used.

Q. How many years were you on the Board of Engineers?

A. I think I was in the Board about two years only. I was in the department about twenty-five years. I was foreman of the Old North three years, I was foreman of No. 13 three years, and No. 10 seven years, and an active member of the department about twenty-five years.

Q. (By Mr. PHILBRICK.) Did you see the fire spread down Summer street?

A. No, sir, I didn't; I was on this side; after that, I was at the office when the inquiry came for powder, and by request of the Chief, I went to Mr. Reed's, Mr. Brown's, and other places. As I said, there was an application made for powder, and it was said they were going to try the experiment of blowing up; and I then spoke of taking one of the powder-boats and bringing her to Central wharf, as the best movement that could be made. I was kept pretty busy at the different points.

Q. (By Mr. COBB.) Did Mr. Carpenter tell you under whose orders he was acting?

A. He told me that he was acting under the orders of the Chief.

Q. (By Mr. FIRTH.) Were you aware of anything in regard to the failure of the supply of water which prevented the streams going so high as you anticipated?

A. I didn't look into that matter. I attributed it at that time to the wind, more than anything else. When I was at my house, Capt. Damrell sent an officer there for me to take a hundred policemen (that was after I went home to make a shift), and open the first carpet store in the neighborhood of the fire, and take carpets and go on top of the roofs and keep them wet. I had, as I stated to Mr. Hersey, no authority to control the department; the Chief of the department was the man through whom the order should come, and especially in an order of that kind, I should want the authority. In fact, I had no authority to do it; the order should have gone to the Chief, and the order should have been a written order, as it was one of some moment. In regard to taking off a hundred men, our department is divided into three parts; one division goes on duty at eight o'clock in the morning, and is relieved at six o'clock by the second division, and they are on duty until one o'clock, when they are relieved by the third division, and the third division remain on duty until eight o'clock in the morning, when they are relieved by the first division. It would have been impossible, as I stated to him, for me to have collected that number of men at the fire without completely throwing everything open; in fact, the men were scattered in every direction, and it would have been impossible to get one hundred men, or even fifty, for that purpose. The area that they covered in their line of duty was such, that they would have had to abandon it. They were constantly at work pressing the people back, to give the firemen an opportunity to work, and also protecting the lives of people. I myself was obliged to take one man in Franklin street by the collar and bring him back. He was foolhardy, as some men are apt to be in cases of that kind. The men were kept very busy, and it would have been impossible to comply with that order. Mr. Hersey was the party who brought the order to my house.

Q. (By Mr. RUSSELL.) Nothing was done in pursuance of that order?

A. No, sir, not in that direction. I couldn't have accomplished it even if I had had the authority.

Q. (By Mr. FIRTH.) To what conclusion did you come, from what you learned at Chicago, in regard to the use of powder?

A. To tell you the truth, I didn't come to any definite conclusion with regard to it, for it is one of those questions where a great many things have to be considered. There are certain buildings which are blown up where the ingredients they contain are such, as, for instance, phosphorus, as would be quickly ignited. It is one of those subjects that I should want to give considerable attention to before forming an opinion. Then, again, there are buildings where cotton would be exposed. I have seen a building take fire by falling in, in consequence of the contents being exposed to the air. For instance, there was the store of Lewis Bros., in Broad street. I was in the department when that fell, and from the nature of the stock, I felt very certain that we should have a fire, and told Capt. Barnicoat so. A portion of the department was called out, and in some twenty minutes after the building fell, the ruins were in flames. and we were kept at work there for two nights. There was a large quantity of phosphorus, and other inflammable material, which ignited spontaneously. I have no doubt that Capt. Damrell did the best he could, under the circumstances.

SEMAN KLOUS, *sworn.*

Q. (By Mr. RUSSELL.) You owned this building in which the fire took place?

A. Yes, sir.

Q. Did you the land?

A. I own the land.

Q. What were the dimensions of this building?

A. Fifty feet on Summer street by one hundred in depth. I have the dimensions here: "Store corner of Summer and Kingston streets:—Lot, 50 × 100 feet; square feet 5,021⅚, four stories attic; outside wall next to street, 2½ feet; foundation under stone and iron columns of block granite, 4 × 5 feet, and 20 inches thick; foundation under partition walls of granite, 3 × 4, and 20 inches thick; stone posts for iron columns, 2 × 1½; outside walls, 20 inches thick; brick partition wall, 20 inches in basement, 16 inches to top of second chamber floor, 12 inches for the balance to roof; iron columns in basement 10 inches diameter, 1½ inches shell, in stone 9 inches, 1½ shell; first chamber 8 inches, 1¼ shell; second chamber 8 in, 1¼ shell; outside columns 12 inches square, 1¼ shell; in the three first stories the timbers were 3 × 14 inch, balance 3 × 12; trimmers, 8 × 14; all floors and walls, well tied together; Mansard roof, covered with tar and gravel. Mr. Blaney, engineer, resides in Charlestown; been employed about three years, very industrious, careful man. Occupants, Tebbetts, Baldwin & Davis, dry goods; Damon Temple and Co. neck ties; Alex. K. Young and Co. hoop skirts." I have a diagram of the lot. [*See Diagram, page* 81.]

Q Does that show where the boiler and engine were?

A. Yes, sir, everything is marked down.

Q. (By Mr. PHILBRICK.) Were there any partitions in the basement?

A. That I don't know. I don't remember I had my book-keeper go through with all the dimensions originally.

Q. Who was the architect?

A. John R. Hall, of Boston.

Q. When was it built?

A. I think in 1866. That is my impression.

Q. You know the character of the engineer, Mr. Blaney, personally?

A. I don't know so much as Mr. Daggett. He speaks of him in the very highest terms, as being a sober, honest, and upright man, and I should say he is all that, because Mr. Daggett would not keep him unless he was strictly temperate.

LYMAN DAGGETT, *sworn.*

Q. (By Mr. RUSSELL.) You had charge of this building?

A. Yes, sir.

Q. Will you give us the character of the engineer?

A. I consider him a very careful, very industrious, watchful man.

Q. Was he a sober man or otherwise?

A. Sober.

Q. You wouldn't be likely to keep him, if he wasn't?

A. No, sir.

Q. Was he in the habit of drawing his fires on Saturday night?

A. I can only give his own answer in regard to that. He says he has not drawn his fires since last August.

Q. You have seen this account of the building that Mr. Klous brought in — is that all correct?

A. Well, I made it myself.

Q. (By Mr. PHILBRICK.) Were there any partitions in the basement story?

A. Nothing only what is represented here, except a partition here that was as high, perhaps, as this [referring to the one in the room]; and then glass over that; what they used for a packing-room.

Q. A half-high partition, with a glass top?

A. Yes, sir.

Q. How was that used?

A. Tebbetts, Baldwin & Davis used it as a packing-room.

Q. How were the contents generally left? What was the appearance of the room — packing-boxes and material scattered about?

A. Yes, sir, but usually kept in very good order; that is my recollection of it.

Q. (By Mr. FIRTH.) Was there anything about the engine-room that would be likely to take fire?

A. I never saw anything; I never apprehended any danger, because I was there frequently, and sometimes just at night, and in the morning, and all times of day, and at night; and there was nothing there to take fire that I could see in any way or shape. On the outside, the boiler was brick, and around the boiler there was a space just wide enough for the engineer to get through, and get round the back side of the boiler. There was a brick floor front of the boiler, and a brick partition-wall next the engine-room; there was a wooden step next the packing-room.

Q. Where was the fire-door?

A. At the end of the boiler next the engine.

Q. Where did you keep the fuel?

A. The coal was kept on the brick floor, and the wood and fuel for firing up during the day, by the side of the boiler.

Q. How was it brought in there?

A. By a wheelbarrow, through the passage-way from under the sidewalk.

Q. Was the floor brick all the way through there?

A. No, sir, that was a wooden floor through there; there was a brick floor underneath the elevator.

Q. What goods did they keep there?

A. Dry goods.

Q. They were manufacturers?

A. No, sir, they were jobbers.

Q. (By Mr. COBB.) Then the goods were lowered down and there put into cases?

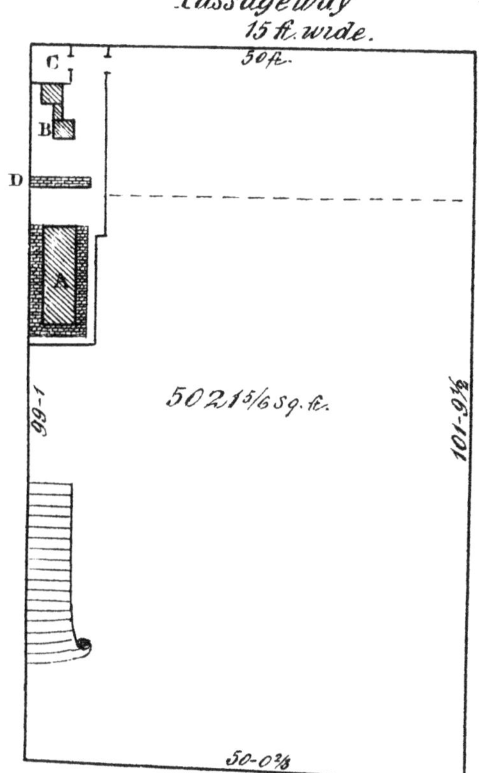

Nos. 83, 85 & 87.
SUMMER STREET

A Boiler. 48 in. × 14 ft. Inspected July 19th, 1867.
B Engine.
C Elevator, about 5 ft. 6 in. square.
D 8 in. Brick Wall. Large window for light.
Distance from head of boiler to brick wall, about 10 ft.
" " brick wall to Elevator, about 15 ft.
Brick floor in Boiler and Engine room.
Width of Boiler room, about 6 ft.
" " passageway, " 3 "

A. At that time I think they didn't occupy anything but these two floors, the basement and the first floor.

Q. How was the front portion of the basement occupied?

A. Dry goods laid out on the counters.

Q. (By Mr. FIRTH.) What was the lining of the elevator?

A. Wood — pine, or spruce, perhaps.

Q. (By Mr. PHILBRICK.) How were the sides of this packing-room finished?

A. Ceiled with wood?

Q. And a wood floor?

A. Yes, sir.

Q. (By Mr. COBB.) Was there any sub-cellar there?

A. No, sir; this boiler-room was about eight or ten inches below the engine-room.

Q. About a step?

A. Yes, sir. This engineer was always in the habit of sweeping up every particle of coal, or anything of that kind, after raking the fire, and then he had the water-pipes come in here, and when he shut off the water at night from going up stairs, the outlet would overflow, and run all over this part of the boiler-room; the bricks were lower here, and there would be perhaps two or three quarts of water that would run right on to those bricks, so that in case any fire should be left here, it would be put out by that water.

Q. Where did the fire-flue pass up from the boiler?

A. It went up against the party-wall side, and into the chimney near the engine-room.

Q. Was there any smoke-pipe, or was it all a brick flue?

A. A brick flue.

Q. Did the chimney-flue pass through that partition-wall to the roof?

A. Yes, sir; about three or four feet from the floor of the boiler-room, there was a window cut through for light and air, into the engine-room.

Q. Did they get daylight into the fire-room?

A. Oh, yes, sir.

Q. Through the elevator?

A. Through the elevator; the sheathing went up about five feet, and then glass windows at the top.

Q. Could they use this room through the whole day without gas-light?

A. Yes, sir; there were side lights under every window, and then Hyatt lights in the sidewalk, which made this very light, and then there were two windows in the rear besides.

Q. I suppose there were gas-burners there?

A. Yes, sir.

Q. Where were they, in the ceiling or on the side?

A. In the ceiling.

Q. (By Mr. COBB.) Did you see anything of the fire?

A. I didn't see it until the roof was pretty well burned.

Q. At the time you saw it, was the fire confined to the upper portion or was it all over the building?

A. I came down Summer street; I didn't stay a great while. I saw I couldn't do anything there, and I went round to Mr. Klous' store, at the corner of Devonshire street, and let this go. I couldn't get near the building.

Q. (By Mr. PHILBRICK.) Had any mechanics been at work in that basement recently?

A. Not that I know of.

Q. (By Mr. FIRTH.) When you came in sight of it, was the whole building on fire?

A. All the upper part.

Q. How was it below?

A. It seemed to be entirely dark in the basement and store.

Q. On what side of the building were you?

A. I was coming down Summer street.

Q. There was no light shining out of the Summer street basement?

A. No, sir.

Q. (By Mr. FIRTH.) If there had been any fire below there, do you think it could have escaped your notice?

A. I don't know that I should have seen it; my attention was directed to the upper part of the building more than the lower.

Q. How much of a basement window was there in front on Summer street?

A. All glass.

Q. How high?

A. About twenty inches, perhaps more. I think it was twenty-four inches, and glass all the way round, except for the doors and stair-ways.

Q. Where was the entrance from Summer street?

A. There was an entrance for the chambers, and then two doors on the lower floor to the store.

Q. Were those doors open when you arrived there that night?

A. I can't say.

JOHN S. DAMRELL, *sworn*.

Q. (By Mr. RUSSELL.) You are Chief Engineer?

A. Yes, sir.

Q. How long have you been so?

A. It will be seven years the 1st of April next, — six years and nine months.

Q. How long have you been in the department?

A. I joined the department in 1846, remained about five months, and took hold again some two years subsequently.

Q. Were you Assistant Engineer?

A. I was elected to the office of Assistant Engineer in February, 1858.

Q. Did you continue to hold that office until you were elected Chief Engineer?

A. Yes, sir.

Q. At what time did you first go to this fire on the 9th of November?

A. I was at my residence, No. 60 Temple street, when the alarm came in. I partially clothed myself — not as fully as I frequently do, knowing it to be, as we term it, a very bad box. On counting the box, and ascertaining what it was, I started for the fire. I got the second alarm when I had made the point on the corner of Park and Beacon streets. As near as I can judge in time, it might have been eight or ten minutes from the time that the alarm was first given, when I arrived on the fire ground.

Q. What was the condition of the fire when you arrived?

A. Well, sir, I have no language that I could describe it, really; suffice it to say, that the building was on fire from the basement to the top, presenting, as it were, one vast furnace. The heat was so intense on my arriving there that it was impossible to get within fifty or seventy-five feet of the building. The material of the building being granite, its explosive properties were shown very conclusively by the shower of granite that was flying in every direction, from pieces weighing one pound to ten and twenty.

Q. When you arrived?

A. When I arrived. Engine No. 4 was at the hydrant on the corner of Kingston and Summer streets. Hose No. 2, I can't state the hydrant that they took at that time, but their line was in the passage-way between the brick building and the large granite building that was on fire, — having a stream up that passage-way.

Q. (By Mr. PHILBRICK.) The passage-way leading from Kingston street?

A. Yes, sir. I found Engineer Regan in command of that stream.

Q. Was there anything else there?

A. Yes, sir. Engine No. 7 was located farther down, towards South street. The exact position of the hydrant that they had I cannot designate. But their stream was over the sheds, playing into the rear of the main building itself that was on fire.

I don't know that I located No. 4's stream; but they were at the hydrant. Their stream was down Kingston street and up in the attic or in the Mansard of the brick building on Kingston street, just below the granite building, which building was on fire, and burning very rapidly at that time. That stream was in command of Engineer Green. That comprises, so far as I know, the apparatus that was at the fire when I got in. In coming out and coming from the building up, Hook and Ladder 7 came in to the fire.

Q. (By Mr. RUSSELL.) Now we would like to have you go on and tell all you saw, and all you did, and all the orders you gave.

A. Well, sir, the next move that I made, I went on to Summer street, and met No. 8. The thought occurred to me then and there that I did not hear the third alarm. I spoke to an officer, and told him to go and turn in the alarms. He said that they had been turned in by order of Captain Regan. I told him to go to the box and ascertain, and to turn in a general alarm, whether it had been two or six, it made no odds which, but to give a general alarm. I sent a courier to meet No. 8 and to bring her into Winthrop Square, to locate at that hydrant. I then ordered a spliced ladder on to the building on the corner, on the opposite side, and for the ladder-men to scale those roofs. While that was being done, I was informed that the third building on Summer street on the opposite side, back of the sky-lights, was all on fire in the roof. I crossed the street as quick as possible, and ascertained that such was the fact, and went and took Capt. Regan from the passage-way and pointed out to him the duty that I desired to be done — the extinguishment of that, and to bend his energies in that direction.

I then met the Chief Engineer of Charlestown, and he asked me if he could be of any service. I says, " Yes, I want your entire department." He said I should have it; and I asked him to mass his force in Winthrop square, and take water from the reservoir on Franklin street, and to hold the building on the left of Bebee's building by massing his force there, as that was the key to the fire at that time.

The Inspector of Buildings, Captain Chamberlain, came up at that time, and asked if he could be of any service. I told him that he could be of great service, and for him to bend his energies, in conjunction with the Chief of the Charlestown department, to holding that point, if it was possible for man to do it. He said that he would do his best, and I believe that he did.

At this point, the Chief Engineer of Cambridge, through his First Assistant, reported to me. I massed his department on the right of Devonshire street, to command that point and stop the fire from crossing through in that direction. That was the point that Engine 8 was stationed at, for that very purpose at that time, and for which I had sent for them.

I then went to Summer street and asked Captain Green to hold the building on the corner of Devonshire and Summer streets at all hazards; or rather, I used these words to him: "For God's sake, hold this corner." He replied to me that he would if I would give him the water. I would have been most happy to do it, but I had not the water to give him. I did, however, shut off all the streams on that line but the one that he was using then on the roof of the building, which enabled him to accomplish the work for the time being.

I then sent a courier to State street to telegraph to every town and city within fifty miles of Boston.

Q. Can you tell what time it was that you did that?

A. I should judge that this must have been about five or ten minutes past eight; *i. e.*, I sent the courier at that time. He came back and stated that the telegraphs were all closed on the Worcester road at Newton, Framingham, and all those places. I then sent the same messenger to the Worcester depot to find the Superintendent, and asked him to say to the Superintendent to send a special train to Worcester and bring all the men and apparatus possible from all the towns on that line of the road.

The members of the Hook and Ladder Company that I had sent out previous to this as scouts and pickets, to look after the roofs and windows, reported to me that the fire was burning briskly in Purchase street, and in some sheds on the wharf near the Hartford and Erie Railroad. Learning that, I started in that direction, for the fire in that vicinity. But the thought struck me that I could get an additional auxiliary, and I immediately returned and sent an order for the "Lewis Osborne," a tug-boat that was supplied with Blake's pumps, I think; but I may be mistaken. They are forcing pumps. The order I gave was to bring that boat up to the wharf at the foot of Summer street, and to press into service on the boat the members of Hook and Ladder "5;" and to say to them, that it was my order that they obey the orders of this man, Mr. Scott, as though he were an engineer. I then came back to the place where the fire commenced and ordered a member of Hook and

Ladder Company No. 3 (his name I cannot give), to take the Insurance patrol-wagon and go to the store-room at City Hall and take every piece of spare hose on storage, and bring it to the fire-ground.

I was then notified by an engine-man of No. 4, that he could not remain in his position longer, on account of the intensity of the heat and the missiles that were being thrown. I told him to put on another piece of suction and swing his engine farther around on the corner, and to remain there until he burned the gauge-cocks off his engine, and for the hose-men to put streams on the engine-men and firemen alternately, so that they could stay at their posts. He replied that he would stay until he got orders to leave.

I then gave an order to No. 4's men to take their line (the building on the opposite side being abandoned for the time being) into the roof of that building. They started to accomplish that work; but before they completed it, the coving of the building on this side, from the heat, came down and cut the suctions right down at the engine. That necessitated making the engine up and going to another place, and procuring a new outfit for it.

Just before, or just at this time, I am not positive, gentlemen, which, the operator at the fire-alarm, whose duty it is to report to the Chief on the fire-ground at all times, came to me and asked me if I had any orders. I gave him an order to strike an alarm of fire from South Boston, and to follow it up with a general alarm. The object in doing that was, that by previous orders one engine was to stay at South Boston to cover that territory, unless specially sent for by an Engineer. The reason why I caused the alarm to be given was in order to bring that engine, so that I might have every piece of apparatus. I went to Purchase street at this time.

Q. About what time was this?

A. Well, it might have been quarter or half-past nine. It would be impossible for me, gentlemen, to fix the time. I will simply say, that the reason why I think that it was about this time is, that at this time I had a report that the boat was in service at the foot of Summer street.

I have omitted one thing; previous to this, Alderman Jenks came to me on Summer street, and asked me if there was anything that he could do to assist me. I said "Yes. Go to the telegraph office and ascertain for a dead certainty whether my telegrams have gone or not. You can serve me better in that way than in any way that I know of. If they have, all right. If they have not, see to it that they do go." There was something at this time said by Alderman Jenks to me about powder, but I am unable to state what that was; but I made a reply to it. Then I started for another scene, of which notice had come to me. I was told that the people in the tenement houses refused to leave, and that they were so eager to get their household goods, that unless I gave special orders and authorized different means from what were then employed, there would be many lives lost; and I then went and gave my immediate attention to that in person.

Q. (By Mr. Firth.) The tenement houses in what street?

A. I think they were on Oliver place, but I cannot name the street. They were down in that vicinity. I followed at that time the lead of those who came to give me the information. The first that I met was a little lad about twelve years of age, who came up and took me by the hand, and asked me to get his father and mother. I endeavored to do so; took him by the hand and asked him to point out where they were. But it was too late. It was impossible for me to get into the building. I got into one story, but to get to the other I could not. I then took him away safe, and turned him over to some others, and went into another building. They were tumbling down goods and the stairs were blocked. I gave orders to the men to lift the windows and put them out just as fast as possible.

In going down to Pearl street and Oliver street with those men, I called for a police officer and one responded to me. I told him to go to the Deputy Chief of Police at City Hall, and say to him that I wanted the Deputy Chief with fifty policemen; to say to him that he had authority from the Chief Engineer to go into any gentleman's house or carpet store, wherever goods of that kind might be found, and press into service any team or men, and to cover the roofs and windows of every building that it was possible to cover, with carpets, and to say to any engineer or fireman, that any engine that he needed was to be taken for the purpose of wetting those roofs. I did not hear any word until I met the Deputy sometime after that. I asked him if he got my order, and he said that he did. The man found him at his house, but he could not comply with my request, because he had no men; otherwise, he should have done it.

Q. (By Mr. Russell.) He gave no other reason, did he?

A. No, sir. Only that he had no men; that they were engaged.

Q. What messenger did you send?

A. It was a police officer, I cannot tell who. I sent him to the Deputy Chief at City Hall, and he went from City Hall to the Deputy's house, and found him at his house.

I then went to Milk street and took an axe and a lantern and opened a door and went up to the top of the building, on the roof. I took a survey then of the entire fire. My object was, to ascertain, if possible, the point where I could make a more successful attack, either by gunpowder or by water. I surveyed it carefully, and after looking Franklin street through, and other streets, I could not satisfy my mind that I could use gunpowder with any sort of success. The reason suggested to my mind was this: "If Franklin street presents no width in which I may successfully battle and meet the flames, where can I make a breach in this district, as it is now seen, that would give me a greater width than I have on Franklin street?"

Q. What building was that?

A. It was a large building, and, as near as I could judge, it was used for wooden wares.

Q. How many stories high?

A. I should judge that that building was six stories.

Q. (By Mr. Firth.) Could you see the whole fire there?

A. I could see every corner, I think, of the fire. I could not look at the different buildings abstractly, but I could see the fire as it came up from the different directions. I then went to the corner of Bedford and Chauncey streets, I think, and called for an engineer at that point. I found Captain Colligan. I asked him to cover that section well, for unless he held that the fire would certainly work back on to Washington street the other way. He said that he would; and I told him to cover Hovey's store on the rear and save that as a key and battlement to fight all other points from.

At that time, I sent Captain Monroe to Church Green to hold the Freeman's Bank building, if possible. I left the order with Captain Colligan, that the moment he could accomplish that, and it was safe, to mass his entire force to the leeward of the fire, as quick as this point could be held, and to keep in constant communication with South Boston and Boston wharf, as there was my greatest trouble. It gave me, I presume, as much uneasiness as anything I had to contend with during the time.

Q. (By Mr. Russell.) You mean, for fear of the fire crossing?

A. For fear of the fire crossing to South Boston, there being not a single piece of apparatus there to protect it, and knowing that there was but a single outlet, and that through Washington Village, and Adams's sugar house and all the oil mills, and Boston wharf, with an innumerable number of stables, cooper-shops, etc. Had the fire reached there from the cinders, South Boston would have been consumed, in my judgment, and the loss would have been terrible beyond description.

At this point I went down into Federal street (I think it was Federal or Congress; I am not positive which, but it was one or the other), and I asked the Chief of Lynn if he would hold that corner — bring up his force in that direction and hold that corner. He told me he would do his best.

At this point I met His Honor the Mayor.

Q. What time was that?

A. I should judge that to be somewhere in the vicinity of half-past eleven o'clock. With him were Alderman Woolley, Chairman of the Committee on Fire Department, Alderman Jenks, and Councilman Jones. I had then sent (but they had not reported to me) for Captain Green, Captain Smith and Captain Regan. I ordered Captain Green to take the patrol-wagon, and to detail such force as was necessary to open the store of Mr. Lovell, Mr. Reed and others, and secure such quantity of powder as would enable him to operate; Captain Smith to go to the Magazine at Chelsea, get a load of powder, and report to me at that place — corner of Congress and Federal streets (that was previous to my seeing the Mayor, that I had sent these men); Captain Regan to go to Mr. Boyd's store, open it, and take out every piece of hose there was in the place and bring it on to the fire ground. I then sent — almost simultaneously with the orders to these men — for the other engineers to meet me for consultation. It took some thirty minutes, I should judge, before I could get my engineers. They were making a hard fight at their points and they were very loath to leave them. I stated in brief that I believed the demand would be made for a trial of powder, to stay this conflagration by the use of that, if possible. There was some expression of doubt as to the expediency of so doing, but they were willing to use it, if by so doing any good could possibly be accomplished.

That reminds me, gentlemen, that I omitted one matter, in connection with the powder. Previous to this, some thirty minutes or even an hour,

Captain Chamberlain met me very near this point and asked me if I had farther service for him. I said "Yes, sir. If you will take the South-west District of this fire, and report to me at the earliest possible moment any place where, in your judgment, powder can be used with success in staying this conflagration."

Q. You say this was about half an hour before you met the Mayor?

A. Yes, sir. It might have been a little longer than that. I should say that it was all of that, certainly.

Some fifteen minutes after I dispatched Captain Chamberlain on that mission, I met Deputy Chief Quinn. I stated to him that Captain Chamberlain had taken that position, and asked him if he would oblige me by taking the other, and report to me at the earliest possible moment, if he could find the point in that line where gunpowder could be used.

Q. In what direction was that?

A. On the other side, towards State street.

Q. North-east?

A. Yes, sir. Captain Chamberlain reported to me that he could not find that point. I did not get the report from Captain Quinn, as I missed him. I understood that he was there to report (but I don't know the fact) that he found no place to use it. I am not clear in my mind as to whether he reported to me or not. It is one of those points that do not seem to be so clear as I should wish, in order to make a statement of the fact, under oath.

The members of the Board and His Honor the Mayor went into a building that was then on fire. The exact words of the Mayor, as near as I can repeat them, gentlemen, were: "Mr. Chief, what are your plans and purposes for the staying of this fire?" I told him, in as brief a manner as possible. I asked him if he had any objections to the following out of that plan, and if he had any suggestions to make. He said that he was satisfied that the plan I was pursuing was the best, under the circumstances, and that he saw no reason why he should interfere.

I must say, gentlemen, that the presence of His Honor, the coolness and calmness that he manifested, did a great deal to strengthen and encourage me, and for it I shall feel that he will command my respect as long as I live. While others came up blustering, and suggesting some of the most wild suggestions that were ever made, His Honor was cool, calm, deliberate, and exact. I then stated to His Honor that the Board had voted to use gunpowder as an additional means to stay this conflagration. I told him that I proposed to give him my opinions in regard to its use, in brief, and what I thought would be the result. I then said: "Mr. Mayor, in using gunpowder, I should have at my command a battery of water which would enable me to deluge the *débris* that might be levelled by any blasting that could be made, but I am unable to find that building, as yet, which warrants to my mind any sort of success in its use." They were mostly large warehouses, filled with merchandise from cellar to roof; the use of gunpowder would shatter the walls and lift the roof; but on account of the merchandise, it would be impossible to drop it any distance; and in addition to throwing out the walls and opening out all the windows (which would make it more ready to ignite) I should destroy every gas-pipe in every building, and open the gas-mains, and a perfect flood of gas would permeate every part of the *débris*, which would make it inflammable to an extent that it otherwise would not have, in the absence of that agency. In addition to that, I should shatter every window within four rods of the building that might be blown up, and open it as a conduit for cinders, flame and heated air. That was my conviction of the result of its use, and it was also the best information that I have been able to obtain wherever it has been tried as an experiment in like cases.

The Mayor says: "I sanction any effort you may make reasonably, for the suppression of this fire; but, in doing it, I charge you that you exercise a due regard for human life." At this point I left His Honor, and proceeded about my duty. We were then so contracting the fire that I was drawing in the lines very rapidly. The apparatus arriving from out of town was being put into service as rapidly as possible under the circumstances. There were many difficulties to surmount, which caused considerable delay and a great deal of vexation. One difficulty was owing to the peculiarity of the couplings; the want of a perfect system in the size and kind; some using the Bliss, and some using one kind and some another. We continued to draw the lines in, and to mass the force on the south-west and north-east sections of the fire.

Q. When you say south-west, don't you mean south?

A. When I say south-west, I take Washington street at right angles with Summer street.

During the evening, many suggestions were made to me as to what I ought to do and might do; and I assure you some of them were very wild, — such as getting out a park of artillery and battering down Milk street, sending to the Navy Yard for shells and exploding them in the buildings to tear them to pieces. I continued to draw in the lines from that time until Sunday afternoon, at one o'clock, and then I am very happy to say that the fire was completely under control, and in the hands of the department.

Q. Did you report that at that time?

A. I reported at City Hall at one o'clock.

But I have omitted to say, that I received, about an hour and a half after His Honor the Mayor left me — I don't know as it was quite as long as that, but I can't measure time — an order from City Hall, which at first I did not obey, because circumstances seemed to demand my attention more upon the ground, to report at City Hall to His Honor the Mayor. I had, I confess, when the message first came, some doubts whether it came from His Honor, because I had left him upon the fire-ground, submitted my plans (which he had approved), and I was then prosecuting them, and I felt that to take me away would be, in a measure, at least, quite disastrous. But feeling that the executive had a right to my presence, I obeyed, and went to the Hall.

Q. (By Mr. Cobb.) What time was that?

A. I should say that it must have been nearly one o'clock. It might have been past one.

Q. At that time did you consider the fire under your control?

A. No, sir; I did not consider it under my control. I will say to you candidly, gentlemen, that I had formed opinions as to the boundaries of the fire, and I have had no reason to change my opinion from that time to the present.

Q. What was done at City Hall when you reported there?

A. Well, sir, I met the Mayor and an innumerable number of the members of the City Government, and some of our most eminent citizens there. I could not designate them all now. I recognized quite a number — Ex-Mayor Rice, Ex-Mayor Norcross, Gen. Burt, and, if my memory serves me right, and I think it does, Judge Abbott, Mr. Carpenter, Alderman Cutter, Alderman Jenks, Alderman Woolley, Alderman Ricker; I am not positive as to other Aldermen, but I am under the impression that an Alderman from South Boston, Mr. Powers, was there. Mr. Bicknell of the Council, was there, Mr. Page of the Council, Mr. Shepard of the Council; Mr. Dickinson, President of the Council, I think was there, but I cannot positively state that. I believe that the Hon. Mr. Cobb was present, but I am not certain as to that. Judge Russell, I think, was present, though I am not positive as to that. So far as I can, gentlemen, I have named those who, if my memory serves me right, were present.

Q. What was said there?

A. Well, sir, I think it would be impossible for me to repeat the words of the gentlemen correctly; but, if my memory serves me right, I listened to some remarks from Mr. Burt, who went on to say that he wanted the gates of the Common opened that goods might be carried there. He wanted the militia turned out, and wanted somebody sent to the Navy Yard to get powder. He wanted the Mayor or Chief Engineer, to organize parties of gentlemen, composed of one hundred citizens, who should have authority to remove goods and to blow up buildings. I think that was the extent of the work that he wished done. I notified him that I was ready to receive the assistance of any gentlemen, and would authorize them to remove goods, or to do such other work as the exigency of the case might demand, even to the blowing up of buildings, and as the Board of Engineers had authorized me to blow up buildings, I cheerfully would receive any aid that they might offer in that direction. I believe that is about all. I then sat down at the table and wrote that A, B, and C, or the gentlemen who were there — Mr. Burt, I think, was one; Gen. Benham was another; the Hon. George O. Carpenter another; Colonel Shepard another; Alderman Jenks another; Mr. Allen, President of the Water Board, another; and L. Foster Morse, another.

Q. (By Mr. GREENE.) They were all authorized to blow up?

A. They were authorized to aid and assist in removing goods and to blow up buildings. I think I expressed myself then very clearly — the same to be executed under the direction of an engineer. I don't think that upon the note that I gave them, I put the word "engineer," but that was the express term that I used to them.

Q (By Mr. RUSSELL.) You gave each one a note, didn't you?

A. Yes, sir.

I then sent for the Chief of Police and requested him to make a detail of four officers to aid and assist the gentlemen named in the execution of such work as would be to the best interests of the city. I then left the Hall. But on leaving, I was requested by some gentlemen to go on to the top of the City Hall. They thought that by so doing I might get a better view of the extent of the fire, and it might be of some service in the further staying of it. I did so.

But one thing I have omitted; previous to my going, General Benham said to me that I should not go back to the fire ground; that I was the Chief Director and I should have my head-quarters where I could be found. I said to him, I think, "That will do, General, for the field, but it will not do in this case." Orders were then sent, when I left the Hall, in addition to the powder from the magazine, which I had ordered Captain Smith to get, to bring up the powder-boat to the end of Central wharf. I confined myself, gentlemen, then, to the bringing in and contracting of the lines, from the time that I left City Hall until I reported again at one o'clock Sunday afternoon.

Q. (By Mr. Russell.) Did you see any of the explosions?

A. Only those that I exploded myself.

Q. What ones were those?

A. One was in Milk street and there was a corner building, I think, on Batterymarch street. They were two very near together.

Q. Can you describe the building on Milk street?

A. The building on Milk street was a low, three-story building, and I brought up a stream of water. I think there was an oil store, I am pretty positive there was, the other side of it, down towards the water. That I blew up, with Engineer Jacobs.

Q. What charge did you use?

A. I put in ten twenty-five pound kegs of powder.

Q. That came from the powder-boat, I suppose?

A. Yes, sir.

Q. Did you have any way of confining it?

A. The only way I had of confining it was to put it under the stairs, and the stairs being in the centre of the building, I used the skids as a purchase on the top of the powder.

The fire was coming through in the second story and the cinders were flying around so that I could not possibly get up there with it or I should have put it in the second story. I put it in the first story above the street. The cinders were flying like the flakes in a driving snow-storm.

Q. Did you put the fuse into the bung-hole of each keg?

A. I put the fuse into the bung-hole of four of the kegs. In fact, I could not get it into the others, because I did not have the time, for we were obliged to brush the sparks and cinders off of the kegs while we were accomplishing it. I cut the fuse off within three feet of the keg. I said to my comrade, Mr. Jacobs, "If we go up, we will go together; but we will make a clean thing of this."

Q. How many minutes will such a fuse burn?

A. I calculated it would burn from a minute to a minute and a half.

Q. (By Mr. Firth.) What notice did you give there?

A. The street was cleared before I went in. I gave the order to have the street cleared, and the streams were waiting, under cover, to come up immediately.

Q. What was the effect of that explosion?

A. It lifted the roof and dropped it on to the first floor and threw out the basement story where the powder was, and broke the glass all around everywhere within two rods of it.

Q. (By Mr. PHILBRICK.) Did you light all those fuses?

A. I cut the fuses off, all four of them; and then I took a match and took a newspaper and took them into my hand *that* way (illustrating) and lit them together.

Q. That is, all in a bunch.

A. Yes, sir; all in a bunch.

Q. (By Mr. RUSSELL.) How long did they burn?

A. I did not get more than twice the length of this room before the explosion; but I got far enough away on the side of the building to be all right.

Q. Was the effect of that explosion beneficial?

A. Not at all, sir.

Q. Was it injurious?

A. I can't say that it was very injurious, from the location. I had a blank, dead wall above me, and I wanted to level that building, so that I might sweep through from street to street with my streams, and having my water there, I felt that I might do that and stop the fire getting into that oil-building.

Q. The fire was prevented from getting into the oil-building?

A. No, sir. It swept right square through it, quicker than I am talking about it.

Q. How was the other explosion on Batterymarch street?

A. That was a building which did not seem to have much in it, and it dropped right down.

Q. What charge was used there?

A. About the same amount.

Q. Confined in the same way?

A. No, sir. That was put into a closet. That I did alone. There was nobody with me.

Q. That dropped the building, you say?

A. That dropped the building down.

Q. How many stories were there?

A. That was a three and a half-story building with a pitched roof, as near as I can recollect. I don't know any more than this; that there were three corners, and there was a chance to make a square where I could have room to fight the fire as it came up.

Q. (By Mr. FIRTH.) Did you consider the effect beneficial?

A. Under some circumstances, I might. But I think not, from the fact that the withdrawal of the streams from other points for the purpose of that explosion proved, I think, more disastrous and more detrimental than it would have been to have maintained our position.

Q. (By Mr. RUSSELL.) About the other explosions, you know nothing, except what you have been told?

A. Simply, sir, that I came upon an explosion, in passing through, very quickly, from point to point, that was made. I think it was in the building below the new Post Office, on the corner of Congress and Water streets, where there were offices and bay-windows. That building was admirably adapted for an explosion, being occupied as offices, and there being nothing to hinder its being dropped right down.

Q. Was that the fact?

A. It was. That was the observation that I made while passing, that that was successfully done, let it be done by whom it might.

Q. Do you know who did it?

A. I do not.

Q. Did you notice any effect of the gas from the explosions which you conducted?

A. Yes, sir. Simply, that at first there was a very strong odor of gas that manifested itself at once. That was evident all through the district, after the fire commenced, so that it would be almost impossible to say where it was or where it was not. In consequence of the falling of walls and the melting of the supply pipes from the gas-meters, the whole atmosphere was thoroughly permeated with gas.

Q. Did you happen to hear any violent explosions of gas, or see any violent flame from gas?

A. There were a great many explosions. They were so numerous, in fact, that to designate any one would be almost impossible. In consultation with Captain Smith, Captain Green and others, they were of the opinion, early Sunday forenoon, that the further use of gunpowder would be terribly disastrous, and appealed to me to stop it. I sent word to Capt. Smith, by one of the firemen (I can't designate him; I can't tell whether he was an out-of-town man or an in-town man, as his face was besmeared and blackened, but he was a fireman), to use no more gunpowder in that section.

Q. About what time should you think that that consultation was on Sunday morning?

A. Well, it was not a general consultation between us, but they came to me personally, following right along, in regard to it; not that we were together or that we came together, but speaking of the use of gunpowder in the line, as I was going from point to point, as fast as I could, covering this place and the other, word would come to me, "We have no fuel, Captain," and I had to issue orders to provide for it. Questions would be asked which it seems to me, if the person had had his thoughts about him, he would not have asked. My orders were: "If the coal don't come as quick as you need it, you have shutters on that store and blinds on that, and a building here, or materials there. Use it!"

Q. What time did you say this was that they spoke to you?

A. I should judge that it might have been very near twelve o'clock — between eleven and twelve. I don't know that it was as late as that, Sunday morning; I can't mark the time.

Q. You say you sent word to Mr. Smith to tell him to use no more powder in that section?

A. To have no more used in that section.

Q. That included what part?

A. I understood from the courier who came to me that he was on Devonshire street, running from State street, near the "Post" building, in that direction. That was the understanding that I got from the courier who came to me, — that he was in there, and that unless the gunpowder was stopped, the fire would go back of them into Washington street, that way, and sweep through that way before they could get control of it, if their force was to be withdrawn to provide for the use of gunpowder.

And one appeal that the courier made to me was that parties had attempted to explode the powder, and it didn't explode, i. e., that some casks did not explode, and as for going up and fighting it under those circumstances, they could not. I understood that four or five casks were taken out of a building, with the hoops all burned off, that had not exploded. That was the reason of my imperative order to stop it at all hazards.

Q. (By Mr. Cobb.) You only know by hearsay. You did not see anything of the kind?

A. That was from the courier who came to me. That was the reason of that order emanating from me. And word came down, following that immediately, from Alderman Woolley, that the parties did not and would not respect Capt. Smith's order.

Q. (By Mr. Philbrick.) The parties who were using gunpowder?

A. Yes, sir. I sent word back by the same party, to Alderman Woolley, to say, "Arrest the man and lock him up until I get there, if he resists, and take the police to do it." I then succeeded in stopping the fire at that point where I was, and started for this place myself; and in going I met another courier, who said that Engineers Jacobs and Shaw wished to see me at another point. I went there and listened to what they had to say. They asked if there was not a deposit of dualin, I think it was, in a store. They said they had been informed that there was. I asked them where they got their information. They pointed to a gentleman on the sidewalk. I asked him what he knew about it, and he said he knew nothing, "only, can't you read?" and he pointed to a sign on the store. I replied to him that I could read, and that if he didn't move I would read a lesson to him that he would not want to listen to.

Q. (By Mr. Russell.) What was the sign?

A. Well, sir, it was some chemicals, or something or other, but I could not make out that there was anything in the nature of dualin about it, and I ordered the attack, and they made it and made a very handsome and successful one, and the fire was stopped before it got there.

I started to go towards State street, and a young man met me and said the Mayor desired to see me at 42 State street, at once. I went there and asked for the Mayor, and they said he had not been there; and General Benham (I took it to be Gen. Benham, a stout, red-faced man) said, "We propose to mine State street, but not to fire the mine, Mr. Chief." I emphatically said, "No, sir," and left him. That, gentlemen, ends my knowledge of powder, and all that matter.

I retired then to the Post Office, and went into the building and asked a young gentleman whom I met if he could show me the nearest way to the roof of that building. He said, "Yes, I am familiar with it; follow me." He took me by the hand. I confess I was terribly fatigued, and it was quite an effort to get up there, I assure you. My lungs were very sore from being burned. But I succeeded, and found, on arriving at the top of the building, a stream of water over the door from Lindall street. I asked the fireman if he could hold it, and he said he would try. I asked him, "Under whose orders are you working?" He told me, "Under Engineer Farrar's." I said, "All right." I went to the window and saw Captain Green on the opposite side towards Water street, and told him to bring his streams across, and on to the Post Office building. I passed down, and went on to State street and ordered a spliced ladder to be thrown on the building above the Post Office, and two lines of hose to be taken through that building and on to the roof to command the building in the rear, that went down nearly to the entrance of the Post Office, and also directly into the angle of the Post Office. Those three streams were placed there, and left in charge of Captain Hebard, of the Dorchester district. I then went up on to Congress street, I think, on to a building there, and found Mr. Jones of the City Council. I said, "I have got no man to take charge of this stream. Here is an axe-man and a stream. Will you hold this fire at this point, and do me service here?" He says, "I will do anything you say, Mr. Chief." I got that stream to work and remained with him until I saw the fire held in check at that point.

Q. (By Mr. Cobb.) Let me ask you just here: Do you know anything about any gunpowder being put into the brown stone building at the corner of State and Congress streets?

A. I don't know that there was. There might have been and might not have been. I can't answer correctly in regard to the powder that was used in all these places. I am simply satisfied in my own mind that with my knowledge of the city, and that particular place, never again would I use gunpowder.

Q. (By Mr. Philbrick.) In that class of buildings?

A. In that class of buildings. I would use it in dwellings, and where there were squares running parallel, where a breach could be made, but never in a body of warehouses where there were neither angles nor squares, but one continuous circle within circle.

Now, if you will allow me, gentlemen, in regard to this powder, to say a few words. They may not bear directly upon this case, but I have endeavored for the past ten years to obtain every particle of information possible upon the use of gunpowder, wherever it has been used for the purpose of staying a fire. I had written, or opened communication, through the Clerk, with Buffalo, Portland, New York, Charleston, S. C., Sacramento and also San Francisco. In every one of those places, and especially in San Francisco, was its use deplored, as being a means of spreading to a great extent the fire.

Q. (By Mr. Russell.) Was Chicago one of those places?

A. Learning that gunpowder was used in Chicago, and used successfully by General Sheridan, I went to His Honor the Mayor and got a letter of introduction, and started for Chicago in company with Mr. Ryan, a member of the City Council. I called upon the General on my arrival, Thursday evening, at his head-quarters on Wabash Avenue and presented my letter, and he said he was pleased to meet any gentleman from the East, and was ready and willing to give them all the information he possessed, which was very little. I said, "The papers of the East, General, give glowing accounts of your success in staying the conflagration in Chicago, and that only through the medium of gunpowder was any part of the city saved that was saved." He said it was erroneous and false in every particular, if I would let him make one exception, viz.: that he blew up one building, or attempted to blow up one, on Wabash Avenue; that it was a signal failure, and the gunpowder was used by an ex-Alderman of the City of Chicago, assisted by firemen and policemen, and that the result of their effort was of no advantage; for, in the first place. they blew down buildings that would have been burned up, and that they burned quicker by being blown up; and on the other hand they blew up buildings where the fire was, to use his expression, eating up to the windward, where one steam fire engine would be of more service and save more property than all the gunpowder that was used during that night and day. That was the opinion I got from Gen. Sheridan himself.

Q. (By Mr. Russell.) You understood him that he only tried to blow up one building?

A. Only one; and he would not recommend it under any circumstances; that it could only be used, in his judgment, successfully, at a sufficient distance from the scene of devastation, from the fire, where a whole square could be leveled, and the *débris* be removed, and a sufficient amount of water could be brought up there to cover that, and advance from that as you would advance upon an enemy, under cover.

Q. (By Mr. Firth.) In the inquiries that you made at New York, did you refer to the great fire of 1835?

A. Yes, sir.

Q. What did you learn about that?

A. That it was quite disastrous. But in regard to that, the information I got was not as definite as I could wish, because I could not get hold of the parties. It was merely a matter of record, which they could not say positively was correct in every particular.

But at Charleston, S. C., Gen. Ripley came in and took possession of the city, and blew up indiscriminately, and carried the fire nearly a mile towards King street, which, in the opinion of those who had charge, would not have occurred, if he had not blown up. Of course, in regard to that, I cannot speak definitely, but that was the report I got. The matter was debated by our Board of Engineers from time to time. The map of the city was consulted, and the use of gunpowder taken into consideration, and the Board were unanimous all the way through, and have been for years, that it could not be resorted to in this city with any sort of success, except in the more southerly sections of our city, or at the extreme north end.

Q. (By Mr. Russell.) I suppose those views were not recorded? They were informal?

A. They were informal. The matter of using gunpowder I laid before the Board, stating how it was used in other places most successfully, so that the gentlemen of the Board had knowledge of the most successful explosions that had been made, in case they should be called upon to make them. Also, they knew where to get powder, because each gentleman had a list of the powder magazines in Boston, in his pocket, so that he could refer to it at any time.

Q. When is that given to them?

A. That is given to them every year, on the organization of the Board.

Q. (By Mr. Firth.) Had any arrangement ever been made, or any permission ever asked, in advance, of the authorities, to get the powder from Chelsea?

A. No, sir. I probably, in giving my orders, overstepped the bounds of propriety. "Get the powder at all hazards! Open the doors and take it, regardless of consequences!" But the Engineer didn't proceed in that way. More discreet, probably, in that than I was, he went to the Commander at the Navy-Yard and got permission, so that the powder was delivered in a proper manner; but it certainly was not by my order, for I ordered him to get it.

Adjourned to Tuesday, Dec. 3, at 3 o'clock P. M.

THIRD DAY.

TUESDAY, Dec. 3, 1872.

TESTIMONY OF JOHN S. DAMRELL, *continued.*

Q. (By Mr. RUSSELL.) State what in your judgment was the cause of this fire becoming uncontrollable.

A. It was uncontrollable from the fact that there was no alarm given until the building in which the fire originated was literally consumed; a matter which I think needs the most thorough and rigid examination.

Q. The other causes?

A. The other causes which made it unmanageable were the scarcity of water and the extreme height of the buildings.

Q. What was the reason of the scarcity of water?

A. The inadequate size of the pipes to give the supply.

Q. The street mains?

A. Yes, sir.

Q. Have you thought of any way of supplying that except by increasing the size of the mains?

A. I have thought of other ways which I have suggested to individual members of the government from time to time, which in my judgment would be a great auxiliary in cases of emergency.

Q. What are those means?

A. I suggested to Mr. Stone of the Council, about a year ago, and also to Mr. Webster of Ward Six, of the Council, that I thought a main should run from the salt water directly through the city, and that a stand-pipe should be erected at each end of the main with an engine and force pump, using Holly's pumps, and that upon that main there should be erected hydrants every hundred feet. The pumps named would if required give a pressure on the main of 400 lbs. to the square inch and would, from each hydrant, through a 1¼ inch pipe, throw a stream over the highest building. In this connection, I have thought of using water-wheels, taking the tide-water for power, by constructing a reservoir. I entertain no doubts of its entire feasibility.

Q. Is salt water much more valuable than fresh for extinguishing fires?

A. Very much so, because it is very much heavier, and its properties for extinguishing fire are very much better than fresh water.

Q. Was it used at all that night?

A. Yes, sir.

Q. Used on the wharves?

A. Used on the wharves.

Q. Do you desire to say anything about the construction of the buildings?

A. About the construction of the buildings and the height of them, I would like to say this: I have for quite a number of years regarded the buildings that have been constructed in Boston, especially the large warehouses, as being the instrument which would eventually destroy

Boston; on account of the vast amount of wood used and the inferior manner of their construction, and their inaccessibility on account of the height. So much was I impressed with this that I have labored for the last five years, of which I have a record here, to bring the matter directly before the City Council and also our State Legislature. Two years ago I succeeded in getting a bill (of which I have a copy with me), which I presented to the City Council, accepted by them.

[The witness here produced a copy of the Ordinance in relation to the "Regulation and Inspection of Buildings" (City Doc. No. 55, 1871), appended to which was the following certificate: —]

"CITY HALL, BOSTON, Nov. 30, 1872.

"Sections 1, 2, 3 and 4 of the foregoing ordinance, reported by the Committee on Ordinances, June 26, 1871, were based upon the recommendations made by the Board of Engineers as presented by the Chief Engineer of the Fire Department.

"Attest:

"JAMES M. BUGBEE, *Clerk Committee*."

Q. Was this adopted?

A. Yes, sir. In connection with that, sir, in the report I made to the Fire Department on my return from Chicago, will be found these words: —

"All of the large buildings of the city had what is known as the French or Mansard roof, with a superabundance of woodwork. These fired from the top, and were one of the great causes of the destruction of the eastern part of Chicago, which with a few additional dollars in its original construction, in placing corrugated iron cornices and mouldings in the finishing of those roofs, would have prevented their destruction by the cinders. I hope that our recently appointed Inspector of Buildings, with his long experience in this department as an engineer, will vehemently urge, and not only urge, but demand, that all Mansard or French roofs shall be so finished as to afford us protection from any serious conflagration from that cause."

I would also call your attention to the clause recommending an additional steam engine and a steam floating fire engine:

"Now, gentlemen, in conclusion, I shall deem it my duty to urge the government to add to this department an additional steam Fire Engine, to be located on Atlantic avenue, near the foot of State street. Also a steam Floating Fire Engine which shall in its pumps be equal to any three first-class Amoskeag steamers; believing that the cheapest and most economical Fire Department that can be maintained, is one so strong and effective in all its appointments, that its expense shall be large in its maintenance, rather than large in its losses, for the want of being fully equipped."

I also desire to call your attention to the remarks of General Sheridan in regard to the use of powder:

"He gave us a cordial greeting, and assured us that it would give him great pleasure to do anything he could for the citizens of Boston; but as to the matter of blowing up buildings in Chicago, *he* had nothing to do with it, nor did he possess any knowledge of the work. He supposed, however, that the powder was placed in the basement of the buildings by the parties who accomplished the work. I said, 'Is it true, General, that you did not blow up any buildings at this fire?' — 'Yes, if you allow this exception, that I attempted to blow one up on Wabash avenue, but it was a failure; so I stopped my efforts in that direction.' — 'Well, now, General, what is your opinion as to the success of blowing up buildings at this fire?' — 'Four-fifths of the efforts to blow up buildings were failures; the other fifth, on Harrison street and Wabash avenue, under the circumstances, were successful.' — 'Why here, General, more than in other places?' — 'Simply from the fact that the fire was burning up against the wind, and it left nothing for it to feed upon. I think one steam fire engine at this point would have done it better.' — 'Now, General, can you tell me who did this work?' — 'Yes, the firemen, the policemen, and a member of the City Government, or an ex-member.' — 'Now, General, would you be kind enough to give me the substance of what you have stated to me in writing?' — 'This, gentlemen, I shall have to decline, because I do not propose to enter into any controversy here or elsewhere, upon such matter.'"

In connection with the matter of water, not only in this district, but in other sections of the city, here is a copy of an order which was passed by the City Council, in accordance with a request which I presented, asking that greater protection might be afforded by the city in the re-laying of pipes in the Church-street district, which has never been done, I am sorry to say, although it was passed by the City Council.

Q. The order has never been carried into effect?

A. No, sir.

"CITY OF BOSTON, April 5, 1869.

"*Ordered*, That the Cochituate Water Board be requested to attach the Lowry hydrants to the pipes which are being laid down in the Church-street district at such points at the intersection of streets as they deem practicable and expedient. Passed in Common Council. Came up for concurrence. Read and concurred. Approved by the Mayor, April 7, 1869.

"A true copy,

"Attest, S. F. McCLEARY, *City Clerk*."

In connection with that, that I might be thoroughly posted, I applied to the City Engineer as to the cost, and here is his reply: —

"BOSTON, March 13, 1869.

"JOHN S. DAMRELL, ESQ., *Chief Engineer Fire Department*:—

"DEAR SIR:—The following is a statement of the comparative cost of the sidewalk and the Lowry Hydrants, made from data furnished by E. R. Jones, Supt. Eastern Division B. W. W.

Sidewalk Hydrant.

Cost of Hydrant	$35 00
" " Branch	12 00
" " 6-inch pipe from main	24 00
" " Hydrant bend	9 50
Incidentals, cartage, etc.	5 00
	$85 50

Lowry Hydrant.

Cost of Hydrant	$85 00
Difference in cover	5 00
Incidentals, etc.	5 00
	$95 00

Labor and boxes would be the same in each. Respectfully,

"N. HENRY CRAFTS, *City Engineer*."

Q. (By Mr. FIRTH.) In this connection will you give your views about the Lowry hydrants as compared with the common hydrants?

A. The advantage I have stated very clearly in a report I made to the City Council, and if you will allow me to read it, it will perhaps be better than for me to state it: —

"During the past three years, at large fires, much difficulty has been experienced for the want of an adequate supply of water for our steam fire engines. The immediate cause of failure is this: —

"The hydrants, in every instance, are placed upon branch pipes, the diameters of which vary from three to four inches; while the mains themselves, in almost every instance, are but four inches in diameter, that supply them.

"In case of fire, the hydrant upon these branch pipes will afford a supply to only one steamer; all others on the line are useless: the steamer being at work, makes a vacuum in the pipe by drawing the water to the hydrant first tapped. The result of this difficulty is, that much time is consumed in shifting the apparatus to lines of pipe in other streets; by reason of which long continuous lines of hose have to be used to convey the water to the scene of conflagration; and by this operation the amount of friction to overcome is very great, requiring oftentimes a water pressure from one hundred and eighty to two hundred pounds to the square inch, to be effectual in our high buildings.

"To overcome this evil, I would suggest that, upon our main thoroughfares, hydrants be connected with the main pipes, of size not less than eight inches in diameter, with a proper outlet, which would give us a supply of water fully equal, if not more than we now get from six of the ordinary hydrants.

"One of these hydrants would afford a supply for three of our engines, with one-third the amount of those now used to reach the fire. The pressure upon the hose would be reduced thirty per cent. and the bursting correspondingly decreased.

"As the city have adopted the 'Lowry Hydrant' in the Highland District, I would recommend that, when any additional hydrants are needed in the city proper, South or East Boston, the Lowry hydrant be adopted, instead of those now in use."

In that connection, I have a plan which I desire to call attention to. I became so intensely interested in this burnt district, on account of the scarcity of water to meet an emergency with, that I caused a plan to be made, showing Franklin street, Devonshire street, Hawley street and Morton place. Upon this plan is marked the different places where water could be obtained, showing the scarcity of water in case of fire in those streets.

Q. (BY Mr. RUSSELL.) When was that plan made?

A. In 1869, under the City Engineer.

Q. Have there been any changes in that?

A. None, except that the Water Board did run a 4-inch pipe with a dead end into Morton Place, giving one hydrant there. You will see that the length of Morton Place on a line with Devonshire street is 625 feet: on a line with Franklin street, 220 feet; from the corner of Morton Place and Hawley street to the reservoir on the corner of Hawley street and Franklin street, 130 feet; making 975 feet where you could not get water in case of fire. If the commissioners will cast their eye over the plan, they will see that I had a hydrant on the corner of Milk and Devonshire, and another on the corner of Franklin and Devonshire, a distance of 425 feet. There was that line of buildings, 425 feet on Devonshire street, and only those two points where I could get a stream of water; and in the rear, on Morton Place, in the rear of almost this entire line of buildings, not a place where I could get water.

Q. You called the attention of the City Government to that?

A. Of the Chairman of the Fire Committee. I believe the Chairman of the Committee went before the Water Board; but I am not able to say. A hydrant was at this time located on the corner of Franklin and Hawley streets, in front of the Pilot Building, but was removed at the request of Mr. Donahoe, the removal of which I protested against. [The witness pointed out upon the plan the location of the other hydrants in the section represented, and continued.] These hydrants are all marked out on the insurance maps (which I think the commission should put themselves in possession of), setting forth where water could be supplied. The engines were compelled to run long lines of hose, and the amount of friction we had to overcome to get the water up into the high buildings rendered our efforts, in some instances, futile.

Q. Are there any other districts in Boston to-day, as thickly inhabited, where the supply of water is no better than there?

A. Yes, sir, but not where the buildings are so high. The pipes were placed there when that territory was covered by dwellings. They have never been changed, while the buildings have been changing constantly; high stores have taken the place of the dwellings, but no attention has been given to the new wants caused by the changes. I sent a written communication to the President of the Water-Board upon this subject. He did not answer my communication in writing, but sent one of his clerks to me, saying, when they were in want of any suggestions from the Chief Engineer of the Fire Department, he would let me know. I sent him a communication suggesting certain improvements for the Fire Department.

Q. Was it about that time in 1869?

A. It was just previous to that.

Q. To Mr. Allen?

A. No, sir. Mr. Thorndike, I think, was the gentleman.

Q. Do I understand you to say the hydrants are the same now as when the territory was occupied by dwellings?

A. The same, sir, precisely. Then we have in addition, two sizes of hydrants, known as 2-in. and 2½-in. hydrants, which require extra couplings to connect to, called reducers and enlargers; this is annoying, and at times causes delay, as on the night of the 9th of Nov., in putting to work out-of-town steamers.

Q. How was it in regard to a want of fuel?

A. Each engine carries fuel enough to last from three-quarters of an hour to an hour. A second alarm of fire being given, the driver of the engine in the district where the fire is located, takes his horses and brings the coal-wagon upon the ground to supply the engines. That is his duty in case of a second alarm.

Q. How much does the wagon bring?

A. The wagon brings two tons at a time.

Q. How long will that last?

A. It will generally last about fifteen or twenty minutes, according to the fire that we have, and the amount of steam we are running.

Q. For one engine, is that?

A. No, sir, for the engines that are in the service. They go round to the different engines, and drop so much at each engine. Sometimes there is one engine, and sometimes half-a-dozen. They go from one to another. If an engine is in want of fuel, they blow their whistle. Three sharp whistles call for fuel. They go round, drop all the fuel, and go to the wharf and get another load, and so keep going.

Q. How many engines would two tons supply for fifteen minutes?

A. Probably thirty minutes all the engines right round. The coal-wagon starts before they consume the original amount they carry. They go round and dump the coal down.

Q. How many steamers are there in the city?

A. Six.

Q. It would supply six?

A. Yes, sir.

Q. How many in South Boston?

A. Three.

Q. East Boston?

A. Three.

Q. Roxbury?

A. Three.

Q. Dorchester?

A. Six. Twenty-one engines in all. If you will pardon me, I wish to state that I had brought the matter to the attention (probably you must be familiar with the fact) of the citizens and of the city, that this entire district, comprising nearly all the wealth of Boston, has been entirely destitute of steam fire engines; and no amount of influence that I could bring to bear has remedied the evil.

Q. When did you bring that to the attention of the city?

A. I have been constantly doing it for the last four or five years. I have called their attention to the fact that there was not a single steam fire engine in this entire district; taking a line from Prince street, on the north, to the water, and from East street, south, to the water (that being located very near Federal street), taking Prince street round to the Revere House and along to Boylston and Essex streets, taking Tremont street on one side as the boundary, and the water on the other, Prince street at the North End, and East street and Essex street at the South End, — that entire section was left without a single piece of steam fire apparatus.

Q. That includes all this burned district?

A. Every part of it, and more.

Q. Have you ever alluded to it in your reports?

A. No, sir; but I have called the attention of the committee to it. I labored earnestly to get an engine at the foot of State street; or at Milk street; or at the Court House. In my statement to the committee I stated that eighty per cent. of all the expenditures of the department is in its running; that eight-tenths of all the fires are in the territory where I asked that an engine might be located. We are constantly running into this district to do duty, instead of having the engines in the places where the fires are located.

Q. Where shall we get the testimony to that effect?

A. I think I have, in one of my reports, set forth this fact, — that eighty per cent. of the expenditures of the department were incurred in running expenses; I don't know that I have gone into the matter in my reports. These were my statements to the committee, and I shall be glad to present evidence bearing upon this from Hon. Avery Plummer, ex-Alderman Gibson, who was a member, and also Mr. Flanders of the City Council, whom I took into the district, with that plan in my hands, and pointed out the situation. In this connection, I would like to call attention to other sections of the city; for instance, between Dover street on one side, and Warren on the other. We have not a single steam fire engine in that entire section, it being a mile and three-eighths between Dover street and Warren street in Roxbury — between these streets and the water line on one side, and Beacon street on the other. I would like to have this commission visit the house and see how the apparatus is located. In the business section of our city bounded by Beach street, South and Blackstone street, north, the Fire Apparatus, with one exception, viz., Engine No. 4, is located on the outskirts, viz., Engine 8 and Hose 1, Engine 6 and Hose 3, and Engine 10.

Q. Why is it you have not stated these facts in your reports?

A. I have, sir. I have stated all the facts in regard to the want of apparatus to my committee.

Q. Have you stated to the City Council what you have stated here?

A. I have called the attention of the Committee on Fire Department to the territory unprotected by Fire Apparatus; but when in their judgment the city demanded additional Engines, Hose or Hook and Ladder Carriages, and they have presented the necessary orders to the City Council, there has been a reluctance to augment this department by the members of the government on account of its size as compared with other cities.

Q. Do you in your reports discuss the subject, or simply state what the facts are?

A. No, sir; whenever I have said much about this matter I have been met with the reply, "Don't try to magnify the wants of your department or of your office so much."

Q. The idea of the CityGovernment has been, that they employed you to do a piece of work, not to tell them what should be done?

A. Yes, sir. They did not consider my judgment worth entertaining; it went for what it was worth. For instance, upon this matter of inspection of buildings, I followed it up year after year, and the City Council through its counsel reported to me that they had no authority in the premises, and dropped it right there; but I kept pushing it, and finally carried it before the Board of Underwriters, and asked them to aid me in securing the law.

Q. Was it done?

A. With the change of the government it was. Mr. Drake was chairman of the Committee on Legislative Matters, and he, as a Boston merchant, took an interest in the matter, and succeeded in getting it before the House of Representatives, and it passed in the shape of a bill.

Q. Why is it that these engines are stationed in such bad places?

A. Simply from the fact, that at the introduction of "steam," they occupied the houses of the Hand Department under the old organization.

Q. Do you know anything about the scarcity of fuel?

A. I have no doubt, at times, there was a scarcity of fuel, but it ought not to have operated for one moment, because fuel was accessible at every point in an emergency. There were over one hundred tons of fuel carried upon that ground between half-past seven that night and ten o'clock the next morning.

Q. What kind of fuel?

A. English cannel coal, for which the bills have been presented to the city.

Q. How much stock do you keep on hand in the engine-houses?

A. About a ton and a half, to two tons, in each engine-house.

Q. Is that all carried with the engine at the time it starts?

A. No, sir. We carry about a quarter of a ton of coal, calculating it will last an hour on each engine.

Q. This statement in regard to the exact location of the engines you will give in your written account, so that we can have it to refer to?

A. Yes, sir.

Q. Did you observe the first engine that got there, whether they had sufficient fuel?

A. I didn't observe them, but I have no reason to doubt it, — not the slightest reason to doubt it, because the men who came on to the fire-ground with any want of fuel, if it was known, would be immediately discharged.

Q. You remark, that if they had not the coal, they had the means at hand. What do you mean by this?

A. Yes, sir. I was told by a man connected with an engine from out of of town that they had no fuel. I said, "You see those blinds? and those shutters? and that fence? Where is your axe?" The coal-wagon failed to supply one of our engines and the men obtained fuel by tearing out portions of an adjacent building.

Q. Anthracite is too slow?

A. Yes, sir. Wood will make the quickest fire.

Q. You begin with that?

A. Yes, sir, but we use cannel coal; it lasts longer and we can keep up our steam with it as easily.

Q. Do you know of any engine that used benzine, or any such substitute for ordinary fuel?

A. No, sir. Three or four years ago I attempted the use of petroleum as fuel, and fitted up an engine for the use of petroleum or gas;

but that is done away with. We carry a quantity of benzine — a small bottle — and sometimes, when the fire is slow and they want to quicken it, and sometimes in starting the fire, they throw that in.

Q. Does that make a great smoke?

A. It does make considerable smoke, but it is seldom resorted to. When an engine starts, they measure the distance they have to run before reaching the signal-box, and calculating from five to eight minutes for producing steam, they light the fire according to the distance they have to go. In this connection, you will allow me to say that we have in our engine-houses what is called a "Circulating Heater," where we keep from one to five pounds of steam on our boilers constantly.

Q. You mean with an outside fire?

A. Yes, sir.

Q. Is that provided in all your engine-houses?

A. No, sir, that is applied at the present time to engines seven, one, two, eight, nine, eleven, five, twelve, thirteen, twenty-one; the other engines are located where we could not build them, or are outside of the city, and it has not been considered really necessary to apply it to them.

Q. What term do you apply to this arrangement?

A. It is what we call a "Circulating Heater." It consists of a boiler with a coil of pipe with the necessary check-valves, supplied from a cistern, so that by making a fire under this small boiler we can keep up a circulation of water just the same as you would from the water-back in a range into a boiler, and from there force it over the house.

Q. You have to uncouple that when you start?

A. Yes, sir; we slip the joint.

Q. Does it uncouple quickly?

A. It uncouples itself.

Q. Now will you tell us what orders were given about using horses?

A. Shall I read the action of the Board?

[Witness read the vote passed at the special meeting of the Board of Engineers, held October 26th, 1872, and continued.]

This was Saturday afternoon, and raining very hard. We convened to take into consideration, as our horses were all prostrated, what we should do, and we resolved to double the department up, and the Chief authorized the Assistant Engineers to offer one dollar per alarm to all the veteran members, or ex-members, or persons who could be employed, to double the force of the department; drag-ropes were then procured, and there being no other conveyance, the Board of Engineers, at ten o'clock that night, took them upon their backs and distributed them through the different engine-houses in the entire city. Following that the following communication was sent to the Chief of Police.

[The witness read the communication appended to the vote before alluded to.]

Q. I would like to inquire if you got a sufficient number of volunteers; if the force was actually doubled?

A. Yes, sir; and trebled.

Q. You had the names?

A. Yes, sir. I have no hesitancy in saying that all the apparatus in the city proper which responded to this alarm, came in as promptly and responded with as much alacrity as if they had had the horses, and I am the more persuaded of this from the fact that they came in at a gait at which you could not have expected the horses to be driven at that time. I have evidence, from the several companies who responded, which will show conclusively that such was the fact. I will say that I did not wait a single moment, and I don't know of a single Engineer that did wait a single moment, at that fire, or any fire that preceded it, for apparatus to come in; of course the out-lying districts would consume more time. I have no doubt about that.

Q. Were any of your horses used that night?

A. Yes, sir. In this connection I would add, that each Engineer was to exercise his own good judgment, and if any of the horses, in case of an emergency, should have so far recovered that they could be possibly used, he had authority to cause them to be used, from the fact that he had supervision of the apparatus under his charge.

Q. Does that appear in your orders?

A. The apparatus is entirely, by the ordinances, under the Board of Engineers; they have full control of it.

Q. Whether the Engineers, in any order they issued, drew attention to the fact that each man was to use his own judgment as to the use of horses?

A. The Engineers have had that instruction.

Q. I ask if that is in writing?

A. No, sir. It was stated, — the Chief expects that every Engineer will use his discretion as to when the horses get so they can be used; and they were authorized to press, or hire, horses if an emergency required.

Q. In what form was that communicated to them?

A. Verbally, at this meeting.

Q. There was no vote, and no writing directing them not to use horses?

A. No, sir. That I might be better understood in this connection, it has been the rule with me, which has been adopted all through, that any foreman of a company, feeling or seeing that he could be of any service in any section, was authorized to use his judgment and respond without waiting to receive an order from the Engineer, and I have used language like this, which can be verified by every one of them, that I would not give one single cent for a member of the Boston Fire Department who was not willing to assume responsibility in case of emergency.

I don't hold them to any general order or rule to wait for an Engineer to give them an order to go, for instance, to Cambridge or Charlestown. If an engine got down to the city limits, and there was no Engineer there to give them directions, they were to proceed at once, and the Engineer would follow, and if they were not wanted, would send them back. I had made arrangements with Cambridge to help take care of the lower end of the city for me, and with Chelsea to help at East Boston, and so on.

Q. Do you remember any engine that was drawn in by horses?

A. Number sixteen was drawn in by horses, having four horses.

Q. Where is that from?

A. Sixteen is at Milton village.

Number nineteen came in by hand, and I am informed, credibly, although it is a mere matter of information to me, I do not know the fact, that, clear to the Four Corners, they were neck and tie with the engine that had the four horses on, and were into the fire with the men in less than four minutes after the time they got in with the horses. That was from Mattapan, the same distance that they came with the other. That is told me; I don't vouch for its correctness any further than it was told to me.

Q. There were no horses used in the city proper?

A. No, sir; there were none, only, after the alarm, we used them in drawing coal.

Q. How many of your horses did you use that night?

A. I used hook and ladder 5's horses, at South Boston. I used engine 7's horses; they run right out of their engine-house, being near to the fire; if it had been to any other section of the city, they probably would have used these horses. 4 had no horses to use. They were in the hospital; they were taken to the hospital that day, the doctor ordering them there, and they were not in condition, having the lung fever in addition to the horse disease; number 6's horses were recovering, and we were in hopes they could be used, and should have used them, probably, in a day or two; they were brought into service to haul coal with that night. 17's horses, at Dorchester, were used and are now dead from the effects of the use.

Q. Were there any horses able to work that were not used that night?

A. I don't know of a single one that was able to work that was not used. Of course, if I had known on that morning that a big fire was to take place (or an hour before) I should have made an effort to get other horses, but to have attempted to use our horses, I think, would have been terribly destructive; for if the horses could not have got to the fire, as the doctor assures me they could not, I should have had no preparation for bringing the engines to the fire, and the delay would have been such that it would have been terrible in the extreme. I should be pleased to have Doctor Very summoned. I had him in charge of the horses; and he is able to give their condition better than I can, from his skill and knowledge of their condition. I certainly was travelling, night after night, with him, looking at and watching the condition of the horses. I had employed Mr. Mahan. His horses were to convey engine 13 and hose 7, in case of an emergency, from the Roxbury district; and when the alarm struck, he reported, with his horses. He did not get to the engine-house until after the engine had started; he did not overtake them, and did not get in until after they did, although, I believe, he brought them in afterwards.

Q. Did you notice on that night any explosion of gas, or any trouble caused by the blowing up of gas-pipes?

A. There were constant explosions through the district. What it resulted from, I am not able to say. Whether it was gas, or not, I don't know; but this much I know, a building would be burning, and, from experience as a mechanic and as an engineer, I had no reason to feel or believe that the building would fall, and immediately it would go down and an explosion would follow very quickly. Whether it resulted from an explosion of gas in the pipes, I am not able to say.

Q. What can you tell about the fire on Monday morning?

A. That was caused by three distinct explosions of gas, which were tremendous.

Q. That was the jewelry store?

A. Yes, sir. I was in the cellar of the corner store when one explosion took place.

Q. How do you account for the gas getting out of the pipes there?

A. By working through the drains, round and back, and into the sewers.

Q. It got into the sewers from burning buildings?

A. Yes, sir; and from other leaks it may be. The pipe runs through the wall, and the gas which has escaped flows back into the drain, following it along into the main sewer, and there explodes. I think it was that which caused the cesspool cover in Washington street, which is a large iron cover, to be carried up one hundred feet into the air, as it was, by the explosion.

Q. How does the gas get into the sewer?

A. The pipes may be in the vicinity of a drain that runs into the sewer; for instance, it is not an infrequent case that we will see a fire burning forty or fifty feet along a stone building — burning through the crevices — burning out at a distance of three feet — a gas fire, the whole earth being permeated with the gas. We sometimes have a fire in a building, and the first thing you know there will be an explosion in the street at some distance from the burning building. For instance, down on Salem street and Hanover street; we went into a store there, and the moment the fire got there, so as to attack the gas, there was an explosion, and it followed up on Blackstone street and lifted and threw up a sidewalk that was eighteen inches thick, throwing it up like so many shavings.

Q. Can you suggest any method of remedying that evil?

A. Yes, sir; what should have been done years ago. At every corner of every street there should be a check-valve, which would enable the gas company to shut off the gas from one street without interfering with any other street. There is no reason in the world why it should not have been done.

Q. How is it in other cities?

A. I don't know; I believe in the suburban cities about Boston this protection is taken; I believe it is so in Jamaica Plains and in the Highland district, and all around; but in Boston, you never could touch the Boston gas-company anywhere with anything.

Q. How is that in Charlestown?

A. I think that is true there, but I am not positive as to that; but I do know it is true in some other sections of the city.

Q. Do you know how many stop-cocks they have?

A. No, sir; but I know that when there is a fire, we have to run round and hunt up their workmen to get them to shut it off from the building.

Q. Do you know how it is in large cities, — New York, Philadelphia?

A. In New York, particularly, they have certain sections divided up into parallels, where they can shut off certain squares. Since this fire, I have not been able to think about these things. I had previous to this matter. I prepared a communication some six months ago to send to the City Council upon this very point, but, from some reason or other, I omitted to do it.

Q. Has that ever been brought before the City Council or Legislature?

A. I don't know that it has. As to the inefficiency of the water-pipes and the likelihood of burning the city up by constructing such buildings, I have worked on these things, and it has been pretty hard to get them before the government, and get them adopted.

Q. Would the second fire have taken place if you had had those stop-cocks and checks?

A. No, sir. In my judgment it would not.

Q. You propose to have them where you could use them?

A. Yes, sir. I have a man in each ladder company whose duty it is, with a wrench, to go into cellars and shut off the gas. That is his duty. He is assigned to that particular duty; but that does not cut off the street mains; we cannot meddle with them.

Q. Do you happen to know, of your own knowledge, how Hovey's building was saved?

A. Yes, sir; that is, in part.

Q. State what was done there.

A. Whoever was in charge of Hovey's building so organized his forces, that, by the use of blankets, keeping them wet, he did a great and Herculean labor in saving the building; in which he was seconded by Engineer Colligan, who had one stream of water. I considered that a key to the fire which would prevent it stretching over that section of the city, and instructed him to keep that point, which he did.

Q. On the second night, do you know about turning off the gas?

A. I know I sent to the gas company to shut off the gas. I am not able to say whether they did or not. I sent an order. I don't know whether it was executed.

Q. Do you know about what time that order was sent by you?

A. It was after the striking of the third alarm for the fire. I cannot designate the time. I sent the man directly up there to do it.

Q. Were you down there at the time of the first alarm?

A. No, sir; nor the second. I came there between the second and the striking of the third.

Q. At the first fire, what time did you get home?

A. Sunday afternoon, at 4.45 o'clock, I went home and remained about twenty minutes to change my clothing, and then went to So. Boston for the purpose of supplying the engine houses with hose in that section of the city. The next time, Monday, at 3.15 P. M., and remained about one hour. I next went home Tuesday night, and remained until Wednesday morning. I next went home on Friday night.

Q. And on duty all the time?

A. Yes, sir.

Q. Where were you when the first alarm sounded on Sunday morning?

A. I was at the City Hall, in the Mayor's office. The Mayor was present.

Q. In general what was the behavior of the Fire Department?

A. Never better. Never did a body of men work more heroically or better. I have no language to express my gratitude to those men.

Q. Were there any exceptions?

A. Not any. I am indebted to them for the alacrity with which they responded to me. I am under obligations, which I can never repay, to the out-of-town companies.

Q. What is your opinion as to the behavior of the police, and the co-operation of the police?

A. I have nothing but universal commendation, sir.

Q. What do you think of the project of having an alarm to call out the military; or having it understood, that, on a certain signal, the soldiers should come to your aid?

A. I should say, that never before did I realize the real benefit that they could afford, in case of emergency, in driving back the crowd, and giving us room to work. That was one of the greatest obstacles we had during the fire, — the pressure of the crowd in upon us, keeping us from the performance of our work, and requiring a great deal of extra labor.

Q. You say the soldiers were very efficient?

A. Very, indeed. Very efficient, and very gentlemanly.

Q. When were they first on the ground?

A. The first I saw of them, I should say, was about four o'clock, or five. At five o'clock I saw a company, I think, of Marines. That was Sunday morning. It might have been later and might not have been as late. Time is entirely out of the question with me. One thing I do want to say: One of the worst things that ever was done, was done by the Boston merchants in giving their goods away.

Q. Was it better to let them burn?

A. Twenty-five times, — yes, a hundred times over. It was one of the greatest elements of disorganizing a regular force that could be resorted to, and one of the worst things I had to contend with, — disorganizing all that were engaged — out-of-town companies, as well as some of my own, I am sorry to say; but it was rarely; it was an exception. It was thoroughly disgraceful; and I am sorry to say that any Boston gentleman would have resorted to it for a single moment. It was the worst thing we could possibly have to contend with. There were whole blocks of stores that were completely filled with the greatest number of thieves I ever saw. I never saw anything like it. I went into one building, and took my fire-hat, and beat out fifty to sixty people. The awnings were all burning, and they never touched an awning; so eager were they to plunder, that they never attempted to save property. I am not certain that they did not set fire to get an additional amount of plunder. I am not sure of it in my own mind, for I feel that some of the fires were in very strange places.

Q. Were those firemen?

A. No, sir; they were not. But let me say, that from the ladder-carriages, where we had coats and extra sets of fire-hats, nearly all of them were stolen, and put on to the heads of parties to enable them to get access to the buildings. The rear wall of a store on Washington street had fallen in by the explosion of gas, and parties in there were cut off by the falling of the wall, and cried for help; members of the Boston Fire Department and the Charlestown Fire Department ran to their rescue, and before they could extricate them, the wall on the opposite side came in and killed the whole of them; consequently they lost their lives in the endeavor to save the lives of those who were in there when no legitimate business called them there.

Q. Was that in Bradford & Anthony's place?

A. It was along in that vicinity.

Q. Did they give any such authority?

A. I could not answer that question. The only instance of the kind, where the party was a fireman, was on Summer street. I met a fireman with a suit of clothes, and I immediately took him by the throat, and saw he was an out-of-town man, and spoke very strongly to him. I gave the suit of clothes to one of my own men, whom I could trust, and told him to carry it and put it in a proper place, and bring it to my office at a proper time; and it is in my office now. I don't know who it belongs to. That is the only case I saw of a member of the Fire Department taking what didn't belong to him.

Q. Were the firemen furnished with food and refreshment that night and the next morning? Was there any trouble about the want of proper food and refreshment?

A. I don't know of anything. I was so thoroughly occupied that I said to some gentlemen, "If you will relieve me from the care of these firemen, you will confer a great favor." Alderman Powers, by suggestion of the Mayor, went to the United States Hotel, and made arrangements for them there; and Councilmen Flanders and Jones took it upon themselves to provide refreshments at other places; so I was relieved entirely from that.

Q. So far as you know there was no trouble on that account?

A. I heard no complaint, neither at that time, nor have I since; but there might have been.

Q. To go back to the origin of this fire, you say that the alarm was not sounded until that building was a mass of flames?

A. I say this, and wish to be distinctly understood, that in my experience in the Boston Fire Department, covering twenty-five years, I never saw such a sight as was presented that night; within eight minutes from the time the alarm sounded, I was on the ground, and the building was literally consumed. I don't understand it to-day. It is a phenomenon which I cannot possibly fathom. With all the fires we have had in that district and other sections of the city, for the past twenty-five years that I have been connected with the Fire Department, I never saw the time, no matter how inflammable the building was, whether it contained oils or any other inflammable material, but what we could enter the building itself; but here was a case where you could not get near the building. On each side it was all on fire, through the Mansard roof, within eight minutes of the time that the alarm was given, — a sight I never beheld before in this city or in any other where I have happened to be when there have been large fires.

Q. About what time was it when you arrived on the ground?

A. It was probably half-past seven. I don't think it could possibly have been after half-past seven. It was not more than one or two minutes, either way, from that time.

Q. It was about fifteen minutes after what we hear was the first sight of the fire?

A. I don't know when that was. I simply say the alarm was sounded, and eight minutes after the alarm I was on the ground; I think sooner than that; but, in order that there may be a leeway, I say I don't think it could have been more than eight minutes. I think I could get from-my house to the fire, at the gait at which I went, in eight minutes.

Q. From the testimony we had at the beginning, it appears that the building was pretty well on fire before the alarm was given?

A. It must have been.

Q. I didn't know but, from the manner in which you spoke, you had some suspicion of wrong somewhere?

A. It is simply this: I don't understand to-day, and cannot comprehend, how this building, all the rooms up and down, in every part of the building, could be one perfect furnace in itself in so short a time. I never experienced such a result. Whether it be liquor, oil, japan, or varnish, I never experienced such a result before that night.

Q. May it not be partially explained upon the theory that it took in the basement and went up the elevator?

A. No, sir; you could not explain it to my satisfaction in such a way. If the fire had originated in any one part of that building, it would have burned a long time among the merchandise before there would have been a sufficient amount of heat generated to have ignited it in every part and to have made it present the appearance which it did present upon my arrival. It had thrown out every pane of glass in that building; the fire was on the top floor the very moment it was on the basement floor; and it was in the front part of the room at the same moment it was in the rear of the room; the basement, and the several stories, and every part of that building, were on fire at the same time. That is my opinion about it. Whether it is worth anything or not, I don't know. There was a fire in another building in that vicinity, some years ago, and the fire was in every story, and the whole building was one perfect sheet of flame, one small dash of water put out every mite of the flames; but there was not a single piece of goods in that part of the building that was scorched; and, to my mind, it indicated that they had been covered with alcohol. I don't know how you could get fire enough to consume a building in so short a time. Spontaneous combustion never would do it. I don't know how a fire would ignite at a furnace and go up a hatchway or stairway, I don't care how wide it may be, and produce the effect that was apparent here. I don't see how the flame going up through that hatchway could drive the fire each way at the same time, and literally burn up everything in so short a space of time. If the fire commenced in the basement and burned up through this hatchway, the extreme height of this building would have caused, in my judgment, a draft so strong in itself that the flame would have ascended, as in the case of a tall chimney. And this elevator or hatchway would be to that building the same as that chimney, and the spreading of the fire on the different floors would be caused by the intense heat, and not by the flame, as that would rush to the highest point. I never saw any such thing before, and I have had some considerable experience in this city. I have been to oakum fires, and oil fires, and lead fires, and fires of flour mills, and everything of the kind, — cotton fires, but I never saw anything like this; and I don't think there is a man in the Fire Department who ever did.

Q. After leaving the spot where the fire broke out, how long was it before it crossed the street, at the corner of Otis street, after you got there?

A. Within three minutes (I think it was) after I got there, I observed the fire across Summer street; the third store on Devonshire street was on fire on the roof, and I called the attention of Engineer Regan to the fact, and gave him orders to take his stream and attack the fire there; and sent a messenger for Engine 8 and located her there to meet that emergency, on the leeward of the fire.

Q. Did you get any water up there?

A. I am sorry to say, I could not.

Q. Was that the building where you put up your spliced ladder?

A. No, sir; I put that up on Devonshire street. I don't know but that there was one put up by some engineer below. There might have been and there might not. The first principle, in fighting a fire, is to make as direct and as close an application of the water as possible. It has been a great study with the members of the Board of Engineers how to direct our water upon the burning mass itself in the building and not to waste one drop of water. In eighteen cases out of twenty our efforts have been directed to the saving of property from destruction by water, as well as to putting out the fire. It is not an unusual thing when we have a fire in such a building, to make an opening in the roof to let out the heated air and smoke so that we can advance on the side, using our cloths to cover up goods, as the greater damage is usually by water instead of fire. In all our experience in this district, we have never had a fire get out of the building, and seldom out of the flat on which it took; but in this case, the building in which the fire originated was all on fire. There was one building on Otis street that was burning upon the inside before it was burning upon the outside, showing that the skylights must have been broken by some cinders falling upon them, and going down, and setting fire on the inside.

Q. If the fire had not crossed Summer street at that point do you think it would have spread?

A. No, sir; if we could have held it on the key, on Devonshire street and Otis street, I have no doubt we could have kept it there. I think we could have held the fire on the corner of Devonshire and Summer streets and it would not have gone further up than Mercantile Hall, if we had had a sufficient supply of water. Captain Green was in there, and I have no doubt he could have held that point if he could have had water enough.

Q. You comprehended that that was the key of the situation at that moment?

A. I did, most fully. If I had not, I should not have said to Mr. Delano, of Charlestown, "This is the key of the fire, and if you hold it here, we are safe; if you keep it out of Cathedral building, I have sufficient force to stop it the other way, if I can get the water;" but just at the time I got the Boston and Charlestown departments massed, the water gave out and we could not hold it. Whether we could have accomplished it, I cannot say positively, and I will not say so; but I will say this: it is terribly disheartening to a man, when he gets into such a position, to find that his water has gone.

Q. Did you have all the appliances you wanted if you had the water?

A. Yes, sir. The difficulty was, the hydrants were so far apart, and we had no other water supply; with these hydrants, in an ordinary fire, we should have had all we wanted, but in a large fire, the distance was so far, and it took so much time before we could get long continuous lines of hose to bear, the fire had gone by us. If we had had a line of Lowry hydrants down Summer street, we could have made a fight which we did not make and could not make under such circumstances.

Q. In other words, if you had all the water you wanted, with these Lowry hydrants, do you think you could have stopped the fire there?

A. I think we could have done a good deal towards it, if we did not stop it. I will not say we could stop it, but I think we could have done a good deal towards it. I don't want to say positively that, if I had this or that, I could have done differently, or cast any blame about it upon anybody. I simply say, we used the appliances we had in the best possible way we could. I have felt the inadequacy of the thing for the last three or four years, and have not failed to inform the proper parties of the fact. It was known by me and by every member of the Board of Engineers, and every one who had anything to do with the Fire Department. And I will say here, that when the Superintendent of the Salem Water Works came to see me about his water-pipes, I told him about this district, and my fears relative to it, and begged him not to get into the difficulty that we were in, in Boston; that it was much easier to put down large pipes while about it, than to have to turn up the streets and put in new ones. And I should like to have him summoned here to testify to that effect.

Q. Have you none of the Lowry hydrants?

A. We have them in Dorchester, and in East Boston, but we did not get them in East Boston until we sent a communication to the City Government, stating that we declined to take the responsibility of extinguishing fires in East Boston unless they furnished us with the means. We stated the fact; we knew that East Boston was doomed unless something was done. We lived in hopes that the good judgment of those who were deeply interested would put this section of the city into a proper condition. I have labored in regard to Boston Wharf, saying there was eight million dollars of property exposed there, and not a single particle of water accessible by land engines, and have asked for a boat. I got a vote passed authorizing the construction of a boat, and a contract was made, and the next City Government came in and revoked it, and gave the contracting parties a large sum of money to revoke it.

Q. How is it now about Boston Wharf?

A. It remains in just the same condition without that boat to-day, and I have only just one pipe running down there with a hydrant which would not supply the boilers of my engines without throwing my water. A boat has now been contracted for, and is nearly finished.

Q. When will that be ready?

A. In about three weeks.

Q. When was that ordered?

A. I think it was the last act of the Council of '71.

Q. Didn't you use her the other night?

A. No, sir. I sent and pressed into the service one of the T wharf tug-boats, and used her all the time. I sent for her before nine o'clock that night.

Q. What sort of water-pumps do the boats carry?

A. The boat building is having the Amoskeag pump.

Q. What kind of pumps did this one have that you happened to find?

A. The Blaikie pump, I believe it is called.

Q. They are put in for just such emergencies?

A. For wrecking purposes — pumping out ships that have been scuttled; but they are not what we want to use for fire purposes.

Q. Did the Lewis Osborn put out the fire on the Hartford and Erie R. R. bridge?

A. Yes, sir; and saved more than a million of dollars to the City of Boston.

Q. Do you know how long that was burning before she got there?

A. No, sir: I can't say. There are a great many things I could express with a good deal of vigor. You don't know the amount of opposition I have met in all these things. One member of my committee would say, "We will give you the boat, but as for any other engine, we will wait. We think you have got enough now." It is an unpleasant thing for an Engineer of the Fire Department, when we have a committee that don't see fit to endorse his recommendations, to push it over their heads. One point in this connection is this: The success which attended us in this very district gave us hope and encouragement that we never should have this thing to contend with. I had endeavored to make each man feel a personal responsibility in this matter, so that they might vie, one with another, in their interest and alacrity, and we relied upon, and felt such a deep interest in our organization, that we hoped and prayed we never should have to meet a calamity of this kind. We have been successful and would have been this night had we had the alarm when we should have had it. The night was nothing near so terrible as when the Adelphi Theatre was burned. If the great fire had come then, Boston would have been burnt to Chelsea Ferry. That was a very cold night; and water froze in the couplings; and I had to have a line of men bringing hot water from the hotels, to keep them from freezing. We had men all along the lines of the houses in the vicinity brushing off the cinders. I have published pieces in the papers in reference to this matter, and have sent them out to the citizens; for I think you will understand that it became my duty to prevent, as well as extinguish, fires; and with that object I have been publishing these facts, and sending them out constantly.

Q. You mentioned the dilatoriness of the alarm, as in your opinion one of the principal causes, or the secondary cause; would you also name, in that connection, the extraordinary rapidity with which the fire burned?

A. I don't know whether it was the rapidity with which the building burned, or the manner in which it was fired; but one thing I am certain of; I never experienced anything like it before. In regard to the matter of giving alarms: I went from the City Hall to the burning of the Chamberlain stables. I saw a large smoke, and went down to Haymarket square, and when I got there, there was no apparatus. I met Captain Green and I said "Where is the department? Where are the engines? What does this mean?" He said, "I don't know. I was so and so;" and it finally turned out that everybody was so engaged in taking out horses, and saving property (there were forty-eight or fifty horses in the stables) that nobody had given the alarm. They were so bent on doing what they were doing that nobody had thought to give the alarm. It might have been so in this case. I don't know how it was. In this place, unless it was very quiet, you couldn't hear the bells and would not know whether an alarm was given or not.

Q. Do you mean at Chamberlain's, or here?

A. Either one of these places.

Q. Where is the nearest bell to this place?

A. Boylston Market and East street; but you might be walking through here and the Faneuil-Hall bell might strike, and you would not know anything about it. You might be coming up Washington street, and the bell strike on the Old South, and the rattling of the carriages and the noise in the street would prevent your getting the alarm. I think Alderman Cobb was in the government when I brought that matter before the government, in regard to the alarm. I wanted a very large bell on City Hall, and do away with all the other bells. I urged, with a good deal of vehemence, that the bells all run into one sound. There is a box numbered 72, for instance, at one section of the city. The missing of one blow puts us off the track and sends us in the wrong direction, whereas, if we could put our ear on one bell, and allow the sound of no others to intercept it, there would hardly be any possibility of mistake. I urged that a steam-whistle sufficient in itself to indicate the number of the box could be used at the City Hall where they run steam nine months in the year, without any additional expense whatever.

Q. Could you hear a large bell all round in every section of the city?

A. There are bells which could be heard all over the city. I think a bell of the size I recommended, like the bell in Montreal, being struck by a person at City Hall with a very heavy sledge, there would be no difficulty in hearing. So many bells tend to confusion. I have also called the attention of the government to the fact that there was no water in other sections of the city. For instance, on Federal street (which was remedied afterwards), there were no hydrants except on this side of the street. If there was a fire on the other side of the street, all our lines of hose had to be crossed over the street, blocking up one of the most important thoroughfares, when hydrants on the other side of the street would have obviated the difficulty. I called the attention of the Water Board to the fact that Lawrence street, at the South End, where there was a continuous line of buildings, some forty buildings in the block, was without a single hydrant. I am not able to say whether that has been remedied at the present time, because I have not been up there to see whether one has been put in. I don't know upon what principle the Board acts in regard to putting in water for fire purposes. I am not posted on that. I called the attention of the Committee on Fire Department, and got a special committee to go out to the Highland District on Parker street, west of Tremont street, where there is no Cochituate water at all, and not a drop of water anywhere, unless the tide is up, all through that wooden district. The sub-committee reported in favor of attaching the hydrants to the Jamaica Pond pipes; but the Committee on Fire Department, after consultation with the Chairman of the Committee on Water, said they could not connect the hydrants; they were not Cochituate water-pipes, and so they remain to-day.

Q. What water have you there?

A. Not any for fire purposes, when the tide is out. For years we constantly put the matter of East Boston before them, showing that there was an entire destitution of water for fire purposes, and that when the engines were put at the hydrants they ran right away from the water, which only indicated five pounds to the square inch, and it was not until after the big conflagration that it was remedied. The Board of Engineers, previous to the large fire, said they would not be responsible. Then came the fire, then the action of the Water Board, putting in the large main with the hydrants.

Q. Whether, after you became impressed with the fact that that part of the city was not properly protected, you gave special attention to the question of some other agent in case water should fail — water, or anything else?

A. The matter of powder I have given special attention to for the last six or seven years.

Q. So I understand; but now I am asking whether you gave any definite directions to your thought as to what you would do in a certain emergency likely to occur?

A. In the use of powder?

Q. Anything that you would do in case water failed to control a fire. Suppose water failed entirely, as it may by the breaking of pipes?

A. In case the water had failed us by the breaking of the pipes, then we had the Frog-Pond on the Common. We have means of connecting our engines and bringing water from a distance to replenish our reservoirs. We have borne in mind and frequently discussed the subject what we should do in an emergency. We have discussed the plan of bringing tide-water into our reservoirs by connecting our engines. We can take one engine and play through a thousand feet of hose right into another steamer, if we keep the stroke about the same, so the hose will not collapse. We could carry water the same as we did when the arsenal was on fire. Then I took water nearly a mile.

Q. In the emergency which did occur, and which was always among the possibilities in your own mind, what had been your thought of the mode of proceeding? Had you marked it out in your mind?

A. In the absolute destitution of water, do you mean?

Q. I mean from the progress of the flames, from the fire becoming unmanageable from the height and peculiar construction of the buildings?

A. The best of protection that I could possibly think of under the circumstances was the use of woollens in covering up the buildings. It had occurred to me; and I had thought of it before, to immediately despatch a corps of men to board with the greenest kind of lumber every window and door. That had occurred to me, but I thought the most feasible way would be to take carpets and cover the windows and roofs, keeping them wet. The steam from them would do much to diminish the conflagration. I relied, in case that was to be done, on the police, who would be the men to do a work of that kind. We have but eight men connected with our steam companies, outside of the permanent force, Engineer and foreman. We have but eight men to manage a line of hose that may be from 800 to 1,000 feet in length. Each section weighs from 65 to 80 pounds, and you can imagine the strength that has to be put upon that line of hose to get it up into a building. We really have a minimum force all the time, and it often happens that we are one man short by sickness. We have but one man to drive a ladder carriage. We have got along well enough, but if one of these men was taken sick, a ladder carriage or a hose carriage might stay behind, because there is only one man. If he should die in the night, nobody would know anything about it. The fact of it is we have endeavored to get along economically. The Fire Department is an expensive department, at any rate, and we have endeavored to run it as economically as we could any way in the world and give a fair and equitable protection to our city. It is very delicate machinery that we run; it is liable to get out of repair constantly, and in order to keep it up to its maximum strength after every fire, there is a great deal of labor for somebody to do.

Q. Suppose the supply of hydrants to be what it should be, would you or would you not think it desirable to have some organization in addition to what now exists, under the control of the Chief Engineer, for the purpose of checking a fire which required something more than water to control it?

A. Yes, sir, but if explosives are to be used (I disapprove of gunpowder in every way), I believe that dualin should be used, or some other form of nitro-glycerine; something that is quicker than the coarse grains of gunpowder. I believe also that it should be employed in such a way, by undermining the walls, that it would not only have a lifting force, but that it would cut or break off the main pieces or supports of the building, and throw it down in that way.

Q. In what way would you propose to use the best explosive which is known, speaking in the light of your past experience?

A. My judgment is there should be an alarm which should call out an efficient corps of military to give ample protection to the city, and at the head of that military should be an experienced gentleman, who would be able to use just that corps to do just the work that was necessary to be done.

Q. There must be unity of action in deciding what line to blow up?

A. It should be an experienced man, whose judgment should be brought into requisition in consultation with others as to what they could do, who would draw his defensive line and act upon it; of course he would be liable to fail.

Q. Suppose the law to be as it is now, that experienced military gentleman would act under the direction of the Engineer? The Engineer would decide where to blow?

A. The Chief Engineer cannot do it himself, except with the aid of his Firewards, who must be there in number, and consequently in using the powder that night, knowing the statute, I did consult them.

Q. Why did you consult the Assistant Engineer about using powder?

A. The law requires it, and knowing the statute, I called my men together because I knew I had no more authority to use gunpowder than any one of you, notwithstanding they thought the Chief could blow up or tear down anything. The Chief Engineer must act in consultation with his assistants, and three of them must agree before he can blow up any buildings.

Q. When you were called to the City Hall in the early morning, on Sunday, after you had held conversation with the Mayor, when there were many people present at the City Hall, did you have any further conversation then with his Honor the Mayor?

A. Yes, sir; in this connection. I thought it very strange that gentlemen should come to the City Hall and then send for me to come there, and ask permission to remove goods, or aid or assist me. I was easily found, and they could have found me or one of my assistants, and they would have found co-operation in removing goods without taking up my valuable time. I felt a little hurt and cross, because I had made my arrangements, and the Mayor had approved of my plan, which was also understood between me and my committee; and then to take me away just as I had commenced this operation, I felt a little hurt, and perhaps I was a little abrupt when I came into the hall, I confess. When it was said, "We want the Common unlocked," I said, "Take an axe and knock the gates down." I like the spirit of a member of the City Council who came upon the fire ground that night, and said, "Your horses are sick; I have a good horse; use him if you kill him." That was Mr. Moulton, of Ward Nine. I feel that that is the way that kind of work ought to be accomplished, without so much formality or going through so many forms.

Q. After the authority was given for the blowing up of buildings, what arrangements were made for any definite plan of action? Was there any unity of action between these men? There were several men to whom you delegated authority?

A. I confess to a weakness of which I am ashamed, that, pressed as I was, I gave authority to certain men to do certain work without saying to them, "You may do it under my command," or my Engineers'. The idea I had was, under the Engineers' authority, but I left them to use their discretion in removing goods or blowing up when the blowing up would tend in any way to extinguish the fire. I feel very much grieved that I should have been so far persuaded as to allow any gentleman to do a work of that kind, because I was engaged in the work myself when sent for to go to City Hall. I had formed my line, but I say to you I had no confidence in the work. I deprecated the use of powder, but felt that the experiment must be tried, or the citizens would never feel satisfied if it was not done; consequently I was willing to take the responsibility, although it was against my better judgment that I acted, and I confess it.

Q. There were some buildings, one or more, blown up on the south side of Water street, near Congress street. Do you know whether there was any concerted action to destroy that line of buildings?

A. I don't think there was; I have no way of getting information, unless General Benham or General Burt, who have said they did a certain amount of work, should point out on the plan that they did blow up buildings, and exercise that judgment which we should expect gentlemen of that character to exercise in doing a work of that kind.

Q. Whether you urged any work for them to carry out?

A. No, sir; because I did not see them. I did not suppose any line of action would be followed, only what General Benham, from the Navy Yard (as I supposed when I was in the hall), as a leading man, would designate. I supposed he would designate that particular work, and would form the base and would make the line upon which all other parties would act. I had reason to suppose that would be the course.

Q. Did you say to him, "Now, General, take charge of this matter"?

A. No, sir; no more than I said, "I will give you authority to use gunpowder, as Chief, by vote of the assistants, wherever it can be used in staying this conflagration."

Q. Was there any organization among these men; or any subordination?

A. I cannot say that there was, or not. I don't know of any. I don't know whether they organized before they went into it. They had the authority, and I sent for the Chief of Police to give them police to aid them in the work.

Q. Did any of them come to you after that for counsel?

A. None of them came; they only sent to me, informing me that they were going to blow up State street.

Q. Did any of them come to you for counsel?

A. No, sir.

Q. (By Mr. COBB.) I would like to ask you a single question. I have on my notes, "When the Mayor came on the fire ground, the Mayor said, 'Mr. Chief, what are your plans or purposes for staying this fire'?" "I told him in as brief a manner as possible." What did you tell him?

A. Simply that I was on the south line, drawing in my forces. That I proposed to make a cordon, and bring up my batteries at that point. It was so far suspended the other way that I could do that. I in general terms stated where we were stationed, what we were doing, and what we hoped to do, and that I proposed to bring gunpowder to my aid. It would be impossible for me to give the words. My general plans were formed in studying and observing the fire, and drawing in the lines with the intention of closing up the fight as close as we could.

Q. What is your opinion now, as to the use of gunpowder that night? Was the fire stopped?

A. Not at all; but in every instance, in my judgment, it was extended beyond what it would have been if gunpowder had not been used. Central street would not have been burned, nor the post-office building been burned or injured, in my judgment. I think that is the judgment of the members of the Board of Engineers, and the members of the Fire Department, who were actually engaged in putting out the fire. I don't hold my judgment to be prominent above all others, but that is my judgment.

Q. You stated that Monday forenoon, in consultation with your Engineers, you decided that the further use of gunpowder would be disastrous?

A. Yes, sir.

Q. You say the same thing now?

A. I have seen no reason to change it at all.

Q. Do you know of General Benham disobeying any orders of yours?

A. I do not, any more than what was told me.

Q. Do you know of his accepting the responsibility you put upon him?

A. No, sir; I don't know that any one did so. I have my doubts whether any one of them accepted it.

Q. Didn't General Burt?

A. I have no knowledge of his accepting anything. They desired to organize one hundred men, under the command of six, or eight, or ten gentlemen, for the sole purpose of the removal of goods, and saving property, and, I supposed, to do what other work could be done, even to the use of gunpowder to stay the conflagration. I availed myself of their assistance very readily, but I am sorry that I gave that discretion into anybody's hands.

Q. If you were to be called to go through this same experience, wherein would you change your plan?

A. I have thought the matter over; have gone over the ground,—and have fought it over in my mind, again and again, and I say, candidly, that I know of no place where I could change my tactics, in any way, shape, or manner, with the exception of the use of gunpowder, and that I would not do. If I were to fight that over again in other sections, I probably should use gunpowder under other circumstances, but in this district I would not change my tactics.

Q. You made the best fight you could and did all you could at the corner of Otis street?

A. Yes, sir.

Q. Whether you can now see that anything further could have been done there?

A. No, sir; I don't see how there could have been anything more done. I formed the opinion that that was the key, and acted upon that, and brought to my aid all the help that I could get to carry that point, and I failed in carrying that from want of water, and the high buildings, and the inacessibility of them. All that I can say is, that I have the inward satisfaction of knowing that I gave to the city the best ability that I possessed with an experience of twenty-five years in the department. I did my best, and I don't know how I could do any better now.

Q. A person might have done his best and yet be able to do better another time?

A. I don't know any place where I could have done better. If I had known there was going to be such a fire, I should have gone to New York, and had the horses and all the paraphernalia.

Q. If you had known there was going to be such a fire, you would have had the apparatus on hand at its commencement?

A. I should have been on the spot. I should have acted as I have done in Boston, when there have been large snow-storms, when I have sat all night in my sleigh and have had the drivers sitting on their engines, and had men out shovelling and clearing away hydrants.

Q. It was a very favorable condition, added to the real danger, because you did not see the necessity?

A. I did not really apprehend it. It did not occur to me. We had met fire in that district successfully, and I was in hopes that we should still meet it successfully. I relied on that idea, of course, supposing that we could at any time grasp the situation.

Q. Did you attend the fire on Washington street, at the foot of Cornhill?

A. No, sir; I did not get off my bed.

Q. You don't know anything about that?

A. No, sir. I know the building. It is a splendid building. One of the buildings where you could make a very successful and easy fight. For instance, we had a splendid reservoir at Scollay's building; another at Brattle square; another in Dock square, with hydrants all the way up and down. Other Engineers who were at that fire can give those points more to the purpose than if I should state them. We met the fire at Houghton's, under the Pavilion. The whole floor of the Pavilion was on fire, but we met it, and kept the fire within and all round it, and there was no trouble in doing it. There was plenty of water there, and everything went on smoothly, and we have met every other fire as smoothly. I call the best fire outside of the present fire, that was ever handled by the Fire Department, the South Boston fire, where we had twenty buildings on fire at a time, and but one building out of the whole number was burned to the ground; the houses covered from forty to sixty rods of land. I don't hesitate to say, that for management and splendid victory, there was no fire in the City of Boston, or any other city, that was ever handled better in my judgment, or a better fight and victory ever won, than by the Boston Fire Department and those who came to there assistance at this fire; and I think the ruins will show it. I am willing to base my reputation upon it, as a man who has been striving for the last twenty-five years to make a reputation in that line; and if I have so signally failed this time, I am perfectly willing to rest there.

Q. Do you know whether anybody was in the building where a boy came and said his father and mother were in a burning building?

A. A little fellow came to me, crying, and said that his father and mother were in the building.

Q. Do you understand that his father and mother were in the building?

A. I don't know.

Q. You never knew?

A. No, sir. I got in as far as the first story, but it was impossible to go further. He said his father and mother were in there and could not get out, but I never knew whether they were or not. I led him to a place of safety at that time, and proceeded to clear the buildings the other way.

DEXTER R. DEARING, *sworn*.

Q. (By Mr. Russell.) What is your position in the Fire Department?

A. I am engineer of Steamer No. 4.

Q. Tell us all that happened on the night of the 9th, and the first thing you knew about the fire.

A. The first thing I knew about the fire was as I was sitting in my house. I got the alarm in the usual way.

Q. Where is your house?

A. It is in Brattle square.

Q. How soon did you start?

A. I started right off. I started the hose carriage first.

Q. Did you have enough to draw it?

A. I had a hundred men on the carriage.

Q. Did you go as fast as if you had had horses?

A. Yes, sir, fully as fast. It was as fast as I wanted to run. There were plenty of volunteers.

I went as far as the corner of Exchange street with the carriage. I could see the light from there.

There were men enough there to take hold of the engine. If we had had horses we would not have had steam when we got there. But when we got there, we did have steam. I was playing two streams inside of ten minutes from the time the bell struck — from the time I left the engine-house.

Q. Where were you stationed?

A. At the corner of Kingston and Summer streets, until the fire drove me out.

Q. How high could you throw water?

A. At the first start, I did not get a good stream. I did not get more than from ten to fifteen pounds of steam. The hydrant was not very effective. But we had to get out of that place. The wall fell over and buried the suction. We had to call on help to get the engine out.

Q. Do you know where No. 7 was?

A. I could not tell you. They started before the bell struck.

Q. Did you get more steam after a while?

A. Yes, sir. I could throw two streams, with the supply of water, over that building, twenty or thirty feet.

Q. Did you have a supply of water and steam that enabled you to do that?

A. Not until I got steam. Then the fire got such headway that the wall was coming over and I had to get out of that. Then I shifted and went around on to Chauncey street, where I got plenty of water. There were two engines with me, No. 20 and No. 18. They could not get any water at all. My suction was the longest and I took all the water.

Q. How long before you were obliged to move?

A. I should say it was not over thirty-five minutes after I arrived there, before the wall came over and buried our suction.

Q. How much of the building was burning when you got there?

A. When I arrived there, the whole rear of the building was on fire, and the upper stories both front and rear. The flames were coming right out fifteen feet. They would almost go across the street. I stayed there as long as I could. The Chief told me to stay there until it burned the gauge-cocks off, and I stayed as long as I could stand it.

Q. How soon did you see the Chief?

A. I saw the Chief right away after I got there — the minute I got my connection.

Q. Where did you go from Chauncey street?

A. Down to Batterymarch street. I stayed all night there at Chauncey street. I was on Hovey's building.

Q. How was Hovey's building saved?

A. It was saved by fighting the fire with the streams. There were men on the roofs with blankets.

Q. What part did the men on the building have in this saving?

A. That I could not tell. They would come out once in a while on the edge. I had all I could attend to with the engine.

Q. Did you have plenty of fuel all the time?

A. Yes, sir, except that after being on Kingston street a spell, I had to burn boxes.

Q. Did you lose any power, at any time, for want of fuel?

A. No, sir.

We used boxes and cases thrown out of the stores. We used coal while it lasted. Then there would be three-quarters of an hour when we did not have any coal, and we would use boxes. They came to us with the coal carts a dozen times during the night. Forrestall called out his teams and they drew coal to us. I don't think I stopped the engine once during the whole night. I would shut off one line, but keep the engine running all the time.

Q. Were you short of water when in Kingston street?

A. No, sir; short of steam. It was before I got it up.

Q. How long did it take to get the full head of steam?

A. If I was going in for fancy playing, or was out on trial, I could get up steam in from two to three minutes. When I go to a fire, I generally have three gauges of water, and it generally takes from five to six minutes.

Q. How long did it take you to get up the full head of steam to the maximum that you used?

A. After she gets five pounds, it don't take but a very few minutes to run it up. It might have taken fifteen minutes to get up to one hundred pounds and blow off.

Q. How long were you in coming down there?

A. Inside of ten minutes, I should say, to the best of my knowledge. In five minutes after our arrival, we could play the water over the building in one line. We could not play in two, because she uses steam so quick in playing two streams. When I went down on the low lands I got water enough on Broad street.

Q. Are boxes as good as coal?

A. Yes sir, — when the water is all hot in her. I had no trouble in regard to steam during the whole night. I did have trouble in getting water, when I worked smart. The draught of water ran so low that it would play air half of the time.

Q. That was at the reservoir?

A. The other Engineers would come to me and ask if I could not shut down one of my lines so that they could get water. I would shift it and then they would get water.

Q. (By Mr. Cobb.) How did the hose work?

A. Very well. We lost two hundred feet there, right on the start, when I first got there. We got the hose up into the granite building, and the fire came out from under the stairs and we had to get out of the way. The hosemen left the line right there and came out. Our hose burned up on Kingston street side. I know we lost two hundred feet before the building fell at all. I think we carried four hundred feet on the carriage.

Q. Did you have any trouble with bursting hose?

A. I didn't burst but two pieces that night, and that was after I got on to Chauncey street. It was leather hose.

Q. Did you have any trouble from wagons passing over the hose?

A. We did along in the first of it. We stopped that by having a man stationed right over the line, to stop the wagons from doing it.

Q. Didn't you use bridges?

A. When we went into Broad street, I laid joist along there by the side of the hose, so that the wagons could jump right over the joist. We did not have any other contrivance except a "jack" for horse-cars.

Q. Did you have any experience with gunpowder?

A. We were not in that section of the city. They did not use it where we were at all.

Q. You don't know what other engines were doing?

A. No, sir. I had all that I could attend to.

Q. Was there fire in the building from top to bottom, where you were?

A. You could see it come up the rear, and the two upper stories were all of a light blaze.

Q. How was it below?

A. It had not got down. I could not see it below. Seven minutes after I made my connections it began to fall. Then I disconnected and stood around the corner. The Chief came to me and called me by name and told me to stick to the engines until I burned the gauges off.

Q. How late did you work before you were relieved?

A. I worked until Monday afternoon. I have a fireman who can run in ordinary times, when everything is going on smooth; in fact, the engines are all situated in that way. I lay down in a doorway and got asleep in that way. They played on me and wet my clothes to protect me from the heat, and I went home Sunday morning and shifted my clothes, and was gone probably an hour.

Q. Was it in your first position that you were played on?

A. Yes, sir. That was with a little small hose that I have. I had the driver playing on me.

Q. Could you have lived without it?

A. No, sir. I could not have stayed there any time at all. I burned my coat as it was, and I was wet through all the time. I have been up three nights and three days, and run the engine all the time. I did not consider the labor of running the engine anything.

Q. Was there any trouble at your engine from want of proper refreshments?

A. No, sir. J. B. Smith furnished us with refreshments. There were plenty of neighbors around there that kept fetching us coffee and the like, and Sunday the Chief ordered refreshments, and they brought them around there.

Q. How did the men of that company behave?

A. They behaved well. They fought the fire as well as men could, like all the rest. We calculate that we have got as good hosemen as there are in the department. Our men fought as well as any men could fight. I had been on the hose eight years myself. I have been fireman ten years on the steamer, and engineer two years.

RUSSELL WHITE, *sworn.*

Q. (By Mr. Russell.) What position do you hold in the Fire Department?

A. I am driver of No. 4.

Q. Where were you when the alarm was given?

A. I was in the engine-house.

Q. How soon did you get the engine out of the house after the alarm?

A. I went out just as soon as I could. We counted the bell the first round. The carriage went out ahead of the engine and the engine followed as soon as the carriage got out of the way. I should say perhaps it might have been two or three minutes.

Q. How large a gang had hold of the engine?

A. I could not say. I should think that the ropes are fifty feet long — two of them; and I should say that there were fifty or sixty and perhaps seventy men on.

Q. Did they walk or run?

A. They went at a very quick run, most of the way. I got on to the seat of the engine and stopped its progress down by the City Hotel. We have to use a brake there. Horses would hold it back, but men could not hold it because you could not get enough of them on to the pole. The brake would keep it from going down on to them, until you struck Exchange street.

Q. How long were you in getting to the fire?

A. I should think we were there in perhaps eight minutes.

Q. Could you have got there faster if you had had horses?

A. No, sir, not the way we were situated. We have to go down Brattle street through this descent, and then the horses can't get their headway again until we get up into Chauncey street or State street. The stone flagging slips badly, and you can't force them. You can't get any headway until you get into Chauncey street. We went, I think, quicker through Exchange street and up State street than if we had had horses on.

Q. When you reached the fire, did you have steam up?

A. I should think not, because it takes ten minutes to get steam, so far as I know.

Q. What did you do when you got there?

A. We always drive to a hydrant, throw the reins down, jump off, and take the small suction. Every one has his part. I pull out the short suction, if the hydrant is within six feet of the inlet of the engine. If it is farther, we take one of the large ones off of the side of the engine. By that time the goose-neck that goes down into the sidewalk is on. The fireman takes that. As soon as that is connected, I get the hydrant-wrench and turn on the water. That is what I did.

After we get the engine connected, then I take my horses and blanket them, if it is cold, and either let them stand (if there is no one there) or there is a negro that runs on purpose to take care of the horses. When he is there by the time we get there, I always give them to him. He gets on to their backs and exercises them around a small circle to keep them warm. Then I go to doing anything about the engine that I can.

That night we connected, and we found it was so hot that we could not hold the hydrant. It was so hot in making the connections that we had to turn our backs to the fire. Then the Chief halloed, I think, "Move that engine around the corner, or something." We moved it so as to use our long suction. We tried the short ones at first, and it was so hot that we could not hold them. By his orders we drew around the corner, and used two lengths, the short piece, and a twelve-foot length on the end of that, which would make it perhaps eighteen feet from the hydrant.

Q. (By Mr. Cobb.) What was the condition of the fire when you got there? What part of the building was it in?

A. It was in the farther part. A very dense smoke was coming out all over the upper floors. Before we got connected, it burst out so, and the heat came down on us so severe, that we could not have held the hydrant where we were.

Then, after we moved around the corner, the heat was so intense that I got out the small hose from under the tank, used for putting out the body of coal under the engine, lest it should burn the wheels. I took that out and put it on the connection, and lay down beside the suction, and kept wetting it to keep it from melting. It would have melted it if we had not done that. A little time after that the building fell, and a stone that would weigh a ton came down on top of the hydrant, and we lost our water. We saw it coming, and jumped out of the way.

Q. How long was that after you got there?

A. I should not think it was twenty minutes, to the best of my judgment.

Q. (By Mr. Philbrick.) That was after you moved around and spliced out that suction?

A. Yes, sir.

WILLIAM T. CHESWELL, *sworn.*

Q. (By Mr. Russell.) What position do you hold in the Fire Department?

A. I am fireman of No. 4.

Q. Where were you when you first heard of the fire?

A. I was at home when the alarm was given — at No. 8 Maple place. I had just finished supper. I got up from the table and ran into Harrison avenue. I distinctly saw the fire when I arrived in the avenue. I could see the light of it, not the blaze. I then went through Harrison avenue into Kingston street, up Kingston and to Summer street. As I went across, Hose 2's hose coupled to the hydrant, and the word was given, "Play away, Hose 2!" I kept on and ran the engine as quick as possible to assist in getting at the fire; and I ran to the corner of Summer and Kingston streets, and there hesitated over the hydrant. I only stopped a minute, and then started. The reason I hesitated was that I wanted to mark that place for our engine as soon as she came. I started on through Otis place and found our hose-carriage at Bebee's building. I caught right hold of the rope, pulled the hose-carriage, and sung out to the men at the head to stop at the corner. They stopped there. I then started to assist in getting the engine there. I ran back and met the engine between Franklin and Milk streets, on Devonshire street, and I assisted in getting her to that hydrant, corner of Kingston and Summer streets. The engine was going very fast indeed. It was in a place on Devonshire street where there was a down grade from Milk street towards Franklin street. There was not a place on the rope for me to get hold of. Each rope was fifty feet long and was chock full of men. They were crowded. I went to the back part of the engine and pushed. There was a chance, as the hose-carriage was off.

Q. How long after you got to the corner was it before there was a stream on the building from your engine?

A. Not over three minutes at the farthest. When we got there, we did not have steam enough to run the engine. We let the hydrant stream run right through the engine, which we can do when necessary.

Q. How long after you arrived was it before you got to playing with a full head of steam?

A. Not over six minutes.

Q. How high did you throw water then?

A. We threw water over either of the buildings on Summer street— the one that was on fire and the one opposite.

Q. Were the hose carried into the burning building?

A. I don't know anything about that. It is not my business.

Q. What was the condition of the building when you came?

A. When I came through Kingston, street the whole rear part of that building was on fire.

Q. Was it in all the stories?

A. I would not say as to that, but in coming by in a hurry I saw the building burning apparently from cellar to attic. The windows were broken out. That was in the passage-alley.

Q. How long did your engine stay there playing on that building?

A. Until the wall fell and cut our water off. It broke the goose-neck so that it cut the water off from our engine.

Q. Up to that time did you have plenty of water?

A. No, sir. The engine ran away from the water. The hydrant didn't supply the engine. We draft from all hydrants. Most hydrants in the city don't give us over forty pounds. It is a very good hydrant that does that. We played two streams and we ran from one hundred to one hundred and twenty pounds' pressure, on two lines of hose from our engine. The hydrant only supplied forty pounds; consequently the engine ran away from the water. We could not get it from the hydrant.

Q. Was that because the pipes were too small?

A. Yes, sir.

Q. Where did you go next?

A. As soon as we lost the water at the hydrant, we went immediately to Chauncey street and connected, and put our suctions into a reservoir.

Q. Did you have any trouble there about water?

A. Yes, sir. Once I remember that there was no water in the reservoir; *i. e.*, our suctions would not reach water, and ours were the longest suctions there were. Two engines were at the reservoir — No. 20 and No. 18. The reservoir would only supply our engine, our suction being the longest. There was once, I know, that we shut down on account of the want of water.

Q. Did you have fuel enough all the time?

A. No, sir. After we went to the reservoir in Chauncey street, we had fuel there all of two hours, I think. We commenced to whistle for coal, but none came, and we went into Lewis Coleman's and asked if they had any old cases or boxes to let us have. The porter took our men right down cellar and told them, "There is the pile. Go at it!" I used it about as fast as three men could split it up. We kept steam up first-rate with it. It was the first time that we ever attempted it. They were dry-goods boxes broken up. We did not suffer from the want of fuel the least during the whole fire, though we certainly would have done so if it had not been for those boxes.

At the first of the fire, I saw the Chief there giving orders. In the morning he wanted to get an engine on Broad street, and we went there. We took the hydrant and ran a line of hose off through Broad street into Water street, and stopped the fire at the corner of Broad street and Liberty square.

Q. About what time did you get control of the fire in that spot?

A. We got home about six o'clock. The Chief told us to go, and we went. (The men were pretty well tuckered out.) He told us to stay there until twelve or one o'clock and then come out and he would set us at work again. I heard that. His idea was to keep the out-of-town engines at work a little while and then have his own department come in and let the out-of-town engines go as quick as possible.

Q. At what time were you liberated by his order?

A. The order came in this way: that the Chief says for us to go home. We got home just at six o'clock Sunday afternoon. I was there all day Sunday. I did not go home.

Q. When did you feel that that fire was under your control down at that point?

A. It did not burn very furiously there, and we knew when we got at work that we could stop it, with no breakage. Downer's was the next building to it, and the men knew they could stop it there. They were confident the moment they got there.

Q. Did you have any trouble that night from the hose bursting or being run over?

A. No, sir. I don't remember of bursting but one piece, and that was on Engine No. 1. It was the second stream. It was a piece of leather hose.

Q. What has been your experience in running to other fires?

A. I ran to two other fires. Once we ran with the hose-carriage and not the engine. The other time we went with both. The time that we ran with the engine was down in North street, where a member of No. 6 was killed a short time ago.

We went down to this fire just as fast as if we had had horses. I know that the men spread out and got the other side of the railroad track, for fear the engine would run into them. The engine runs as easy as a car. It is gauged to the track.

Q. Do all engines fit the tracks?

A. Yes, sir. All but one or two in the department fit the track of the railroad. The most of them fit inside; some one wheel inside and the other on top of the rail. These last are the best by a great deal, because they can turn out so easy.

Q. When you speak of meeting other engines, had they got to work or just arrived?

A. I could not say. We went down Sunday morning about half-past eight. Engine No. 7's horses pulled us there.

Q. Did you start from your engine house to the fire before you heard the second alarm?

A. I was at home when I heard of the fire.

GEORGE W. CLARK, *sworn.*

Q. (By Mr. Russell.) What position do you hold in the Fire Department?

A. I am Assistant Engineer.

Q. Where were you at the time of the alarm?

A. I was on Hanover street, corner of Elm.

Q. How soon did you go after you heard the alarm?

A. It was immediately.

Q. When you arrived there what was the condition of the fire?

A. The building was on fire in the two upper stories, the fire coming, as near as I can recollect, from nearly all of the windows in the two upper stories.

Q. Was it front or rear?

A. It was on both sides of Chauncey street, and the other street.

Q. Were any engines there when you arrived?

A. I found Hose Co. No. 2, and I think Hose Co. No. 8. The first had a stream on to the next building and were playing on to the building in which the fire originated. I went into the next building. I will not be positive about No. 8, but I think they were there at that time. I know that I saw them within a few minutes at any rate. I then came down stairs and went to the rear of the building, where I found Engine Company No. 7. By "the rear" I mean around on Bedford street. We reached the rear of the building by some sheds attached to a house on Bedford street which runs parallel on Summer. The front of this building was on Summer and Kingston, and the back was on a little passage running up from Kingston. That would make the other side. I don't know which you would call the rear. They are the sheds from Bedford street, on the South-east corner.

Q. What was done there, and how did those engines play on to the fire?

A. I left Engine Company No. 7 in charge of Assistant Engineer Regan. I then went around on to Summer street, and went on to the roof of the building on the side on which the fire originated first. I then came down across the street and went on to the roof of the building opposite, to see if there was any opportunity to put water on there to advantage. I then came down, and Hose Co. No. 5 put their water on the fire from the opposite side. By that time it had caught on the Mansard roofs on the opposite side of Summer street. I assisted in getting No. 5 to work, and also in getting Hose Co. No. 3 to work on the same roof, and went twice to get more hose to enable them to get nearer the fire. I waited until they got water on the fire. The Chief came up and ordered me to get streams on the roof of the block opposite the block in which the fire originated.

Q. Was there any hose carried up, to your knowledge, into the buildings on the north side of Summer street — corner of Summer and Otis?

A. I could not say whether there was in that building on the corner of Summer; but I know that there were streams carried through that building or the two near it, and over the roof on to the fire corner of Summer and Otis streets. I believe Otis street is nearly opposite Kingston street.

Q. What appeared to you to be the reason that the fire was not stopped in crossing Summer street? Under ordinary circumstances would you have stopped it at an early stage of the fire?

A. I should think not, — not with the water facilities in that neighborhood. We were short of water. It was almost impossible to force water from that side on to the fire. It takes time to get it through the hose. The hose went up through the buildings.

Q. In your judgment was it too late to do that when you arrived?

A. Yes, sir, — in the building that was then on fire, because the two upper stories were thoroughly burned out.

Q. What time was it when you got to the scene of the fire?

A. I could not say, because I don't know exactly what time the alarm was given. It was as soon as I could get there from the corner of Elm and Hanover streets. There was so much noise on Hanover street that I could not count the alarm then.

Q. How did the engines come in, fast or slow?

A. That I could not say. I was engaged from the time I got there. I was in the building trying to find an opportunity to put water on to the fire. It is customary for Assistant Engineers to look out for that.

Q. Was everything done opposite to the building that took fire, to stop the fire there?

A. Everything was done that could be done. The men stayed there until they were fairly driven from the roofs.

Q. Were you short of water?

A. Yes, sir. The streams from the pipes would not reach over fifteen or twenty feet at the most. I could not see whether they were hydrant or engine streams. The buildings were on fire on the edges of the roofs. The only way we could get water on to that fire was by throwing it on to the roof and letting it run over the edge. They were also troubled there with hose bursting. In forcing water to that height it is not an uncommon occurrence for hose to burst several times.

Q. At that place was there much bursting of the hose?

A. There was considerable, sir, on the start. The water would not play then within more than twenty feet of the roof, not any that I saw.

Q. If you had had plenty of water, what would have been the usual force under such circumstances?

A. With some hydrants, we could have played twice that distance. If the steamers had all the water they could use, they could play thirty or forty feet, and without lifting the hose up either. Still the water, after having been forced to the height of forty feet, would not be very effective.

The roofs were flat, and we could walk from one roof to the other direct. The firemen remained there until they were driven down by the heat. Engine Company No. 10, and I believe Hose Company No. 3, remained there until they were obliged to leave with their hose to save themselves. I will not be sure as to the former. That was on the north side.

Q. When you first arrived, did it occur to you that the fire was extraordinarily advanced in the building, considering the time that had elapsed since the alarm?

A. Yes, sir, it did.

Q. Did you see anything to satisfy your own mind, or what explanation did suggest itself to your mind as to the cause of the fire being so far advanced?

A. I don't know as I gave thought to the cause, only I know that the fire was rather farther advanced than we usually find it so soon after the alarm was given.

Q. Have you not often put out fires which you found as far advanced as that, when there was no wind?

A. No, sir, I don't remember ever seeing a building where the fire had got so far along.

Q. Can you now, in looking back upon it, suggest any further explanation of the fact of the fire's having made so much progress?

A. Only that there was some unaccountable delay in giving the alarm.

Q. Where did you go next from that place?

A. I remained on the roof on the south side of Summer street, and in the building for some time, assisting the company in getting their hose on to the roof. I found one stream on the roof on the south side of Summer street. When I was ordered there by the Chief, I succeeded after some time in getting another line, No. 17's, I think, on to the roof; and while waiting for another, I met Engineer Monroe getting another up the stairs, which made three on that roof.

Q. Was there much water thrown upon this fire from the roofs of the different buildings? Did the firemen get on many of the roofs?

A. Yes, sir, from both sides of the street. Later in the night, there were several other streams, though I will not state positively as to the north side. I think that they had five streams on the roofs on the south side of Summer street. I was part of the time on the north side of Summer street and the latter part of the time on the south side. There were streams of water on each one.

Q. Where did you go from that point?

A. I went and tried to find more streams to get on to the roof. I did not find them. I could not get hose enough to get the lines on to the roofs without breaking up several lines to make one. By that time those on the roofs were coming down. They had stayed as long as they could possibly live there.

Q. Was there a scarcity of hose, do you say?

A. Yes, sir.

Q. (By Mr. Cobb.) At what time was this scarcity of hose?

A. I could not tell you that. It was when the fire had advanced nearly through the block on the south side of Summer street. Perhaps it had worked half or two-thirds of the way down.

Q. If you had had more hose, would you have had water with which to use it?

A. If we had had more hose, I could have got streams on to the roofs. It required very long lines of hose after the first hydrants were connected.

Q. Where would you have gone for the water to attach this hose to, if you had had the hose?

A. Whatever engines were there at work, they all had lines on to the fire, some playing from the streets and some from the roofs. In order to get their streams upon the roofs, we would have required hose enough to reach from the engines to the roofs of the buildings again.

Q. Did you use all your hose at that time?

A. I could not say as to that. I presume that we did, except the spare hose in the houses, which would have to be sent for to get it on to the ground.

Q. Where did you go next?

A. After we were obliged to abandon the building on the south side of Summer street, I noticed that the sparks and embers were flying very freely in the direction of the water. It occurred to me that it might possibly be as well to take a look at Broad street and see if any farther fires had caught there. I did so. I found the sheds and the small wooden buildings on Broad street, and also a schooner, on fire in a dozen or fifteen different places. I came back to Summer street and got the insurance-wagon, with about two hundred feet of hose which I had picked up, and drove down there, took a hydrant, and got a stream with the assistance of laborers and men in that neighborhood, on to the buildings on Broad street. We put out the fire as fast as we could find it there; — I mean the wooden buildings, the sheds and the schooner. It seemed so necessary to me at that time to prevent the fire from extending there, that the alarm was rung from box 58, hoping that perhaps there might be some force spared from the fire elsewhere whom they would send down there. But there was no response to the alarm. I went back, and succeeded at last in picking up two hundred and fifty feet more hose that kept those buildings from taking fire until the horses were removed, also to put out the fire in one of them, and also the sheds upon the water front.

We remained until the main fire came to us, and then we had to retire. The buildings we put out were afterwards burned. After we were driven from there, or before the Engine 7 came down from that corner, I threw one stream into the Hartford & Erie freight depot. I ran a second line and kept it on until we were obliged to move. We retreated steadily before the fire until it destroyed the Hartford & Erie depot, and at last, with the assistance of Assistant Engineer Brown, several companies, and among them the Hyde Park engine, succeeded in stopping the fire two or three wharves below the Hartford & Erie R. R. depot, which I then left in charge of the Engineer from Hyde Park.

Q. Do you know what time it was that the fire was stopped there — what time you left there?

A. It was my impression that it was somewhere in the vicinity of one o'clock Sunday morning.

Q. Where did you go then?

A. I went across the line of fire on the south side, and found an Assistant Engineer in charge of every point until I got around to the corner of Milk and Washington streets, I think; but I am not certain whether that was where I brought up first, or whether it was at the "Post" building.

Q. What was done there?

A. I was there accosted by Councilman Bicknell, who informed me that he was about to blow up the building on the corner of Milk and Washington streets. I inquired his authority for so doing, and he produced a document authorizing him to blow up buildings wherever he deemed it expedient.

Q. Did you say anything farther to him?

A. I looked at the signature and found that it was signed, "John S. Damrell," the Chief Engineer — but not in the Chief's writing, I think. I did not dispute it, however; I told him if that was his authority I had nothing to say, and requested him to wait until I removed the engines on the corner of Washington and Milk streets. While I was doing so, the Chief himself came and inquired what I was doing. I told him, and he told me to hold on. I did so; and the Chief, I think, then had a consultation with Mr. Bicknell. But I am not certain. My recollection of that is not very distinct. At any rate, it resulted in our leaving the engines and putting seven kegs of powder into Currier & Trott's store.

Q. Did you have anything to do with the blowing up?

A. Yes, sir. I assisted.

Q. Did the Chief remain there at the time?

A. Yes, sir.

Q. What was the size of those kegs?

A. I don't think I can tell. There were either five or seven.

Q. In what position did you put them? Were they confined?

A. The only way we could confine them was to cover them with shutters. It was on the lower floor — the street floor. In fact, there was no time to do much of anything in the way of placing the powder there, for we were expecting every moment that a wall of fire would fall on us.

Q. How long were the fuses lighting?

A. Not a minute. We put the kegs just inside the door, so that we could light them and go. Probably it was twelve or fourteen feet.

Q. How long after you touched them off did the explosion occur?

A. It was some few seconds. It cracked the wall slightly and broke the glass on the opposite side of the street.

Q. Was any harm done, in the way of spreading the fire, — any harm except to window-glass?

A. No, sir.

Q. Did you see any other explosions that night?

A. No, sir. They had been made before I got around to that point.

Q. What time was that?

A. I could not say. It was daylight, I think. I should think it was somewhere between six and seven o'clock.

Q. Where did you go next?

A. I went then, I think, to the "Post" building, and assisted in getting two streams on to the roof of that.

Q. What do you think about the stopping of the fire at that point? Was it owing to the construction of the building?

A. There was no fire in the "Post" building itself. If there was, it was so slight that it was nothing to speak of. Our water was all put on to the building adjoining. Our hose were carried up over the "Post" building clear to the roof, and water used on the roof. We played from the roof.

Q. Was the fire stopped at that point by the water?

A. I should judge so. The building had partially fallen before I reached there.

Q. How long did you stay there?

A. It was but a few minutes; until I saw that there was no farther need of water on that building. I next went to Congress street. There was nothing to be done. Every stream that was on the ground was in use. There was nothing more that I could do.

Q. After that, what did you do?

A. I went to the Post Office, where I saw the same. Whatever streams there were were in good condition; and from there I went around to where they finally stopped it, at the other end of Broad street.

Q. Did you see any want of fuel that night for steam fire-engines?

A. I did not see anything of the kind, though I heard that one engine was short. I heard of that since, not at that time.

Q. (By Mr. Cobb.) Do you know anything about the fire Sunday night or Monday morning?

A. Yes, sir. I know that I was there at work until, perhaps, the middle of the next forenoon. I got there as soon as I could walk there after I heard the alarm. I was unable to run. I had been on duty then from the time the fire started on Saturday evening until within two and a-half hours from the time the alarm struck after the explosion Monday morning.

Q. What time did you go home Sunday night?

A. It was from eight o'clock to half-past eight, I believe. I will not say for certain.

Q. Were you present, at the fire at Rand & Avery's establishment?

A. Yes, sir.

Q. Was not that a very furious fire?

A. Yes, sir.

Q. Did it look as threatening when you first got there as this other fire?

A. No, sir.

Q. The building is higher than the other one, is it not?

A. I could not say, but I think not; not from the Cornhill side. It may be from the Brattle-street side.

Q. What was the difference between the fire here and down there, when you first got there?

A. They had got to work when I got to Rand & Avery's. No. 4 was there before the alarm was given. Their house is within a stone's throw — next to the old Brattle-street Church.

Q. Is there some difference in the supply of water there?

A. Yes, sir.

Q. Did it look as threatening at any time as the other?

A. That I could not say, because I immediately went into the building below, as I stated that I did at the other fire, to see whether water could be used to advantage.

Q. What in regard to the supply of water?

A. The supply was greater. It was sufficient to do good service.

Q. (By Mr. COBB.) Do you know what Engineer got to this fire at Rand & Avery's first?

A. Well, I don't know whether any one was there ahead of me or not. Engine Company No. 4 were there first; Hose Co. No. 1 should be the next, and I presume they were. Quite a number of soldiers were on duty there.

Q. (By Mr. COBB.) In the great fire, do you think that everything was done that could be done fight it?

A. So far as I could judge, yes, sir.

Q. Did the men behave well?

A. Yes, sir.

Q. Suppose the same thing were to happen again, do you think of anything which was here left undone, which you could do to stop the fire?

A. No, sir; not in the vicinity where I was most of the time. The other parts I could not say anything about.

Q. What do you think was the effect of that use of time, so far as it came under your observation?

A. I consider it worse than useless. We lost the time at any rate.

Adjourned to Wednesday, Dec. 4th, at three P. M.

FOURTH DAY.

WEDNESDAY, December 4th.

WILLIAM B. CLARK, *sworn.*

Q. (By Mr. RUSSELL.) Where do you live?

A. At No. 23 Kingston street.

Q. Tell us when you first saw this fire.

A. At ten minutes past seven o'clock, as near as I could tell. I was at home. All of the burning building that my window commanded a view of was the fourth and fifth stories. The fire was in every part of the building at once. I could not see the other stories which were in the same condition, nor could my room-mate. His name is Pierce. There was a building between me and the fire. My room-mate was inside of the room. I heard the disturbance in the street, jumped on a wash-stand and looked out of the window. I heard them apparently trying to break in a window. Then I looked out again and the flames came out like a flash from every window of the building. I heard the fire-alarm after I left the room, but it seemed an interminable length of time before it sounded. It seemed to me to be ten or twelve minutes after I saw the fire. It seemed as if I never saw an alarm so long in coming. I had no watch. I sat down to supper at ten minutes before seven o'clock, went up as soon after supper as may be, and had undressed myself ready to redress, which would have taken me about ten minutes.

Q. By "alarm" do you mean cry of fire or striking of the bell?

A. The fire-alarm must have been ten or fifteen minutes later, as near as I could tell. I had no intention of going until I saw how great the fire was going to be.

Q. Did you hear any crying out of "Fire"?

A. Yes, sir. I heard the yell "Fire" in the street, once or twice repeated.

Q. Did you see the engines coming to the fire?

A. I was the first one in the building, so that I did not see them as they arrived. I turned to my room-mate and said, "George, you had better go in and get your books out." I waited until the alarm sounded. I went with what clothes I had. I walked up and down the building four or five times and then turned to go up to the door again, and Mr. Damrell, the Chief Engineer, and an axe-man came up behind me, and the axe-man began breaking the door in. Mr. Damrell ordered the people out of the way of his axe. The axe-man went through and unbolted the door, and Mr. Damrell, two other men and myself, with considerable effort, pushed the door open. I stayed to clear away the litter, so that the door would open wide. I turned and looked up the stairs, and all up stairs was one mass of fire. I stepped into Damon, Temple & Co.'s, and that was one mass of flames the whole length of the building. All that time the hose was being brought into the building, and, there being an insufficiency of men to handle the hose, I took hold and helped bring it up. That was at the door that leads into Alexander K. Young's.

Q. Was there no fire in the basement?

A. I didn't see the basement, as I ran for the front door immediately. The whole of the Damon & Temple end was on fire, and of course the lower story must have been as fully and thoroughly on fire when I got to Damon & Temple's.

I turned and saw a crowd coming up Otis street, and they were dragging something; I can't tell whether it was a hook and ladder carriage or an engine; but the apparatus was there as soon as I have ever seen it in case of an alarm at box 52. Mr. Damrell was there when the door was broken in. I should think that he had come up with this apparatus, whatever it was; but he appeared at that time.

Q. When you say the apparatus was there as soon as you ever saw it after an alarm of fire at box 52, do you refer to the first carriage?

A. I stayed in the building ten minutes. When I came out it seemed to me that the steamers were all at their stations as quick as they ever were.

Q. Did you see any hose in Kingston street?

A. When I first went out I did not; but it was then that the alarm had just struck. I ran down from my room, which is at the top of the building.

Q. Have you often seen answers to box 52?

A. Not often. It is a box that very few alarms come from. I have sometimes seen them from box 43, which is as near to my house as box 52.

Q. You referred to box 52 as if it were usual to see the apparatus a little later when the alarm was from that box than when it was from others. Did you mean to say that?

A. No, sir. No more than that that was my box. I boarded first at 23 Lincoln street and then in Kingston street; so that I have been nearer to that box than to any other for three years.

The time seemed long, but of course the excitement was intense, and that would naturally have made it seem so. I don't speak of the time as taken from my watch.

I was in this house of Mr. Rogers's for some time. There did not seem to be a sufficient supply of water for the engine, and in the house after a while we could draw no water.

As soon as I found out how the fire was spreading, I took a squad of men and broke into the house of Mr. Henry M. Rogers, counsellor, and we worked together. Finally the house-water gave out altogether, and then it did not seem to come through the hose with the usual force. Mr. Rogers's is the only house left on this side of Kingston street. Next to that is a granite building, which has been partially taken down.

Q. On what floor did you try to draw water?

A. I should say the third floor; I had never been in the house before. I was in the back room. Then, at our own house, farther down, I heard them say that the water had given out.

Q. How did the Chief Engineer appear?

A. He appeared to understand what he was about thoroughly in every sense. Of course, there was a natural excitement, which I have always seen in him on his first appearance at a fire. I never was quite so near him before. But I have seen him arrive at fires several times.

Q. Do you think as well of him now, as an officer, as you did before that fire?

A. I do, fully. I have no reason to think otherwise.

DANIEL B. CLAFLIN, *sworn.*

Q. (By Mr. Russell.) Where is your place of business?

A. It is now No. 77 Lincoln street. Before the fire, it was at No. 94 Summer street, corner of Devonshire. My business is small wares.

Q. When did you first hear of the fire?

A. I was there at work with my partner. I was down stairs with him, blacking my boots at the time. I heard a noise — a sort of outbreak — and I supposed that it was a procession that was passing. I went on blacking my boots, and then looked over my linen stock. My partner was going to New York. We fixed up a memorandum of what we wanted. I then went into the other department, and there was a mass of jackets out of order. I went to work and put them in order. It took me some considerable time. I then looked out the shirts and drawers and put them in order. I went up-stairs and we lighted the gas in the other part of the store and opened some goods and my partner went to marking them. I still heard the noise, and I stepped out in front of the store and saw that there was a fire. The first apparatus that came was a hose-carriage and it hitched on to a hydrant in front of our door. I only give you these details in order to show you what length of time elapsed before I saw the fire. I cannot tell what the time was by the watch. This engine played on to the fire. It was my idea that it could not get the water up to where the fire was. When I first saw the fire, it was coming out of the eaves of Tebbetts, Baldwin & Davis's roof. In a very few minutes after I first saw it, it burst out. In a short time, I had a good view of the fire. I sat there right in my window and put the curtains up. Then there came an engine and hitched on to the hydrant.

Q. Which way did the engine come from?

A. I could not tell you that. I don't know what engine it was. We did not suppose that it was coming to our store, and we stayed there some time. Finally, both of the hosemen stood right in the middle of the street, and I saw those two streams of water going on to the fire. The hosemen could only throw the water to the second or third stories with the hose-carriage, and it did not do any good; but the engine could get a stream up on to the eaves. It was quite a while before they got those two streams on together. They would play, first one and then the other. They would first play into Mullen's and then on to the other corner on the other side of Otis street. After it burned down lower, on to two or three of the other flights, then the hose could get water on to it. Those were the only streams.

Q. Was it on fire in the lower story when you saw it?

A. No, sir. The first I saw of any fire was that it broke out under the eaves of Tebbetts, Baldwin & Davis's. It might have been burning in back and probably was, because it was some time before I got up there, I should say quite a little while.

Q. Did you see any fire on the north side of Summer street?

A. I did afterwards. I went to see whether we were in danger, and we were on fire then.

Q. Do you know what time it was when you first saw the fire on the north side of Summer street?

A. No, sir, I could not tell the time. I was too busy to look at my watch.

Q. Did you notice anything about the rate at which the engines came, whether fast or slow?

A. As I say, I did not see but two streams on that fire for some time. I was busy tying up goods after I found that it crossed over and did not notice so well. Before that, I didn't see any engine come but this one.

Q. Did that engine come slow or fast?

A. I would not say, — because, of course, my mind was taken up with the fire.

DR. HENRY J. BIGELOW, *sworn.*

Q. (By Mr. Russell.) Tell us what you know about this fire.

A. I should say that I knew nothing about this investigation until some ten minutes ago, and therefore my memory, probably, will not serve me as perfectly as if I had had time to reflect upon my testimony before giving it.

Q. Where were you when you first saw the fire?

A. I was down Summer street. I came from the South end. The alarm had then been given.

Q. Tell us anything that you think worthy of being stated to this commission.

A. The first obvious thing was, that the fire was sweeping up from the corner of Kingston street to the opposite or north-west corner, in spite of the firemen.

Q. Were the firemen there fighting it?

A. Yes, sir. I could see the streams. I got down as far as Trinity Church, and below there a little. But the great and obvious thing through the night was the utter inadequacy of the means to the end. The thing that I noticed, wherever I saw the engines and the fire was, that the streams failed to reach the upper story. They broke into spray and seemed wholly ineffective at that height. The second thing was that, I should say, half the time the streams seemed to be playing at the intervals between the windows, as if aimed at nothing; or, to give an illustration of it, as if the firemen were tired and had got to do something, and it did not seem to be of much use to play into a window; and so, as the water was coming, they just let it go. Occasionally there were spasmodic efforts to wet the opposite houses, but apparently they were soon abandoned. Occasionally hose was taken to the top of a store to play on the next store, but for some reason that was soon also abandoned. I suppose the firemen were roasted out. The radiated heat was immense at a distance, — I mean against the wind.

Another thing noticeable through the night was the number of unemployed engines to be seen standing at corners. Another thing I noticed was the way the fire caught from one building to another. A strong party-wall seemed to be the best protection. But when one store was pretty well burned, the upright roof of the next one (for they were most all of them French roofs) began to smoke at a dozen or so small points between the slates. After a while, a few little tongues of fire appeared here and there —

Q. Indicating that the timber had been roasted between the slates?

A. Yes. Before the slates gave way, these little tongues of fire were coming out between the slates; here fire, there smoke, and tongues of flame everywhere. Then came the flame, perhaps not larger than your finger or your wrist. Presently somewhere a place as big as your head was burned through, and then the whole roof was on fire. Within a very few minutes the story below the French roof showed fire at the windows. Then quite an interval elapsed, and the rest of the building seemed to catch a good deal at once in one or two instances. This was the course of the fire. The whole lower story perfectly dark until the fire broke out simultaneously from many windows at once, as if the ignition had been impossible from want of air, until the windows were broken, when the whole burst into flames.

The last half of the night, or as near as I can guess, from one to between four and five o'clock, I was on that large square in Oliver street, because it seemed to be the most comfortable place to look at the largest fire. The noticeable thing there was, the absence of firemen and engines. While at the head of Franklin street there was a crowd that broke your ribs, the people, at the height of the conflagration, were dotted about in this large square in groups of three or four or half a dozen, quietly sitting, with large spaces between them.

Q. Were those firemen that you speak of?

A. No, sir; — people. There were no firemen down there, or engines.

Q. Were there any in sight?

A. No, sir. I don't remember seeing an engine, and scarcely a stream. There was no attempt to save that large building where the Curriers were. The people were scattered over the place, walking about as they would do at a Fair.

Q. You spoke of seeing unoccupied engines standing at the corner of the streets; do you know why they were unoccupied?

A. I don't from my own knowledge. I inferred that it was from want of orders.

Q. You don't know whether it was from want of orders or from want of water?

A. No, sir; I have not the least idea.

Q. Were they from Boston, or elsewhere?

A. That I could not say. One that I noticed was an outside engine.

Q. When you saw that the streams failed to be effective, could you judge whether that was on account of want of water or want of steam?

A. It was want of steam, so far as I could judge. The full stream seemed to be directed upwards, but it broke into spray before it reached the place where the fire was. I am not an expert on this subject and cannot state with certainty what it was owing to.

Q. Did you notice any engines wanting fuel?

A. The engines were screaming about. They said it was for coal; and they were burning boxes.

Q. Where did you see that?

A. That I could not tell you. I was walking about the whole night backwards and forwards. I should say that it was not uncommon. But the coal-carts seemed active, and I came across one or more of them driving hard in all directions.

Q. Can you state the points where you saw engines idle?

A. No, sir, I cannot.

Q. Can you state the time when you saw them idle?

A. I could not. I don't think I looked at my watch the whole night.

Q. Were there points on Pearl and High streets where you thought engines could have been used to good advantage?

A. So far as I saw, I should say not.

Q. I suppose directly to the leeward of this fire there was no use in trying to play?

A. No, sir. The way I got at it was this (though this is perhaps not evidence): At the head of Franklin street and Summer street there was a dense crowd. It was impossible to move there. I followed down around the fire; went down first through Milk street and afterwards through State street, going backwards and forwards, and got down to where it was obviously to the leeward, directed at times by the light smoke high up in the air. Wherever I could get to the leeward of that smoke I found myself in the line of the conflagration, and knew that it was to come there. I went up Channing street and saw it come through those wool places there. That was in advance of the fire. I went down to Bebee's store and saw it come down there. Then I went down further to the leeward down towards Pearl street. Then I went down to this place in Oliver street, knowing that it was impossible to stop it to the leeward. I judged that that was the policy of the Fire Department; that they considered that it could go no further than the water and that they would let it go to the water, and would direct their attention to stopping it where their efforts might be of some avail. That was the general impression that I got of it. My father had a store in Summer street, and therefore I was interested there. You could not but feel, in standing at the head of Summer street, that if they would blow up a house or two as it came gradually to the windward, that the thing would have been stopped; or, if they did not blow up buildings, if they would wet them down, get on top of them and soak them through with a couple of streams, that the fire would have been prevented from coming up the street.

And then I remember that another thing that I remarked was that whoever was in command had a pretty hard battle, because he could not be on two sides of the fire at once. He must be either on the Milk-street or the State-street side, or else he had got to go up Tremont street in order to get down on the Beach-street side.

Q. So far as fighting the fire directly to the leeward went, should you make any criticism on the action of the Fire Department?

A. No, sir. I don't see what could have been done. The fire roared through there. I guess it took perhaps eight minutes from the time that it took hold of the top of those wool stores before it roared out at the bottom. The windows came out and it burst through. The sheets of flame were immense. They were exactly of the size of the smoke that rolled out, — just as you see in a coal fire where it is spitting. You see the gas now and then ignited in a place as large as a saucer and coming out again; so the flame ignited the smoke, ceased for a moment, and then took hold of it again.

The blowing up of a building was a new thing to me. I got to one place, I think at the corner of Congress and Water streets, where they said that they were blowing up a building. I turned and walked back, and while I was walking away it blew up, and I turned around and saw the building collapse. We turned from there up towards State street, and were astonished at the glass windows which seemed to be cracked for a space as large as from here down to State street, and the sidewalk was in some places an inch deep in fragments of glass. It was like walking upon a stony beach.

Q. That was in walking towards State street?

A. The concussion broke the glass in State street and in other neighborhoods. That building collapsed and fell successfully.

I don't see how that *débris* could have burned if it had been thoroughly wet. If you lower the height of what is in the path of the conflagration and deluge the *débris* with water, which is perfectly practicable, when you get the materials within the reach of your streams, I don't see why they should burn, as the Chief says "after being deluged."

Q. Was that the only blowing up that you saw?

A. Yes, sir. We were warned off from one or two places, and didn't stop.

Q. How near was the fire to that building when you saw it?

A. I could not tell you. I should say it was on the other side of the Post Office, a good way. John Sturgis was with me during all that time. He is an architect. Perhaps he would have some ideas to communicate if you were to summon him.

Here was one point to which my attention was directed: People seem to have asked, in other cities, how the fire could have crept to windward. It seemed to me that it was an eddy made by the curling around of the flame from that which struck the building next to windward. The flame would shoot out to the windward, and then the wind, coming from the top of a roof, would carry it in the opposite direction.

Q. Was there any considerable amount of wind, except the inward draft from all directions towards the fire?

A. That you could hardly tell. In Oliver street, we sat in the midst of a large empty square, dotted over with groups of people, with here and there heaps of boxes of all the colors of the rainbow, with this fire coming on, — the heavens full of flames. You walked about to find a place where you could get in a lee. There was so much wind as that. It was coming towards the fire in that case. It was off at right-angles with the wind. Wherever you were, of course you had the wind drawing in. That prevented you from knowing whether there was wind anywhere else.

ISAAC R. BARTON, *sworn.*

Q. (By Mr. RUSSELL.) Where was your place of business?

A. At No. 87 Summer street.

Q. When did you first notice the fire?

A. I room at 18 Temple place. I had gone home and just lighted my gas, and barely taken off my overcoat, when I heard the alarm. I always count all alarms from the fact that whenever an alarm rings near the store I go down. I heard fifty-two strike. There was one of the salesmen in the room who came there for his valise. I said, "Frank, our store is in that district; I must go down." I put my overcoat on and walked very rapidly down as far as Tompkins' store. He could scarcely keep up with me. I saw the smoke there very bright, and I ran from there down as far as our store, or as near as I could get to it; it was in Marr Brothers' door-way. I did not think of our store's burning, but wished to go and see where the fire was. I saw the fire even before it burst out of the windows, — inside of the building. It seemed to burst out almost simultaneously in A. K. Young's office and above the office.

Q. Where was the office?

A. The office is back of the front room on the first flight; and also they have another store-room in the rear of that. I could not see any farther back than that from the fact of my being on Summer street. I could not look around the corner any farther than that.

Q. Do you mean up one flight, or on the street floor?

A. I mean that it burst out on the third flight. It burst out there before it did from Damon & Temple's.

Q. How soon did you see any engines or hose-carriages there?

A. There was one engine there, but not playing when I got there.

Q. How soon did they play after you got there?

A. I should judge in fifteen minutes or so. There were other engines. I could not positively tell, from the fact that the crowd was accumulating so fast, whether there were two engines that came before this engine that was drawn by hand. I know that there were two following that, that were drawn there by hand fifteen or twenty minutes after I arrived there. That was before a very large crowd had gathered there, and the people cheered them very lustily from the fact of seeing the engines drawn by hand.

Q. At what speed did they come?

A. They were coming down the street quite lively, not nearly as fast as horses would draw a hose-carriage or engine, but coming on a moderate trot.

Q. Was there any hose-carriage playing when you got there?

A. No, sir.

Q. Did you go into Kingston street?

A. I could not get there, sir, although the store was at the corner of Kingston and Summer. They were very arbitrary about letting anybody pass, and not fearing the store's burning, I did not see fit to go in.

I was watching constantly for the boy that carries the key. It was impossible for him to get down to the store.

Q. Was there anything farther that you noticed specially?

A. No, sir.

Q. What time did you think it was when you reached this point?

A. It could not have been more than from five to seven minutes after the alarm — not to exceed that.

Q. Did you hear anything about there being any scarcity of water?

A. No, sir. There was no scarcity, seemingly, from the fact that the engines were playing with all the force they had.

Q. Did the streams reach up to the fire?

A. They did not, sir; our store was a very long time in catching. It caught on the left-hand side, going from Washington street, before it did on our corner, which was the nearest. I was on the opposite corner from Kingston street, and everybody following after the fire remarked that our store was a long time in catching, and seemingly a very small stream of water would have prevented its catching. I noticed, after it first caught on the roof, they commenced playing. From the fact of its catching on the opposite side of Summer street, they played on that and left ours.

Q. Did there appear to be apparatus enough to play on yours and the other too?

A. No, sir, there did not.

Q. Was your idea that they had better let the other burn and play on yours instead?

A. Yes, sir. They could have stopped it very easily; although, after those walls fell, there was no chance for our store, because the walls of that store crushed in. We had some side-lights on Kingston street, running clear down as far as that store ran, to the new building that is now being built, and the front window-lights — side-lights which you can observe now, even, through the bricks, inside of the building, and the heat, before those walls fell, broke the side-lights in our store. I saw the curtains burn and saw it well under way before I went to the telegraph office with a dispatch to Mr. Glazier, who was in Albany that night. There was no hope for our store after those walls fell. If they had kept it inside of the wall before that, they could easily have saved that side of the street. I don't think that playing on our building would have saved it after those walls fell. It drove the firemen away so that they could not play in from the side. It was impossible.

ALONZO HAMILTON, *sworn.*

Q. (By Mr. Russell.) What is your address?

A. 21 Kingston street.

Q. When did you first see or hear of this fire?

A. I saw it on the evening on which it occurred, after seven o'clock. I don't know the exact hour.

Q. Was it before the fire-alarm or after?

A. It was after the alarm. That is, I had heard the cry of fire.

Q. Were you then at home?

A. Yes, sir. I moved in town the day before and stayed at the store until, perhaps, about half-past six o'clock, and went home and took my tea, and then had occasion to go to a drug-store, and I went to Mr. Littlefield's, under the United States Hotel and came back. I was out perhaps eight or ten minutes. I came up Kingston street and went into the house and took off my boots and sat down at the table and read the evening paper. It was probably eight minutes from the time that I came into the house that I heard the cry of fire. The sitting-room that we make use of is in the second story. I looked out of the window of that room and saw the fire.

Q. In what part of the building was the fire then?

A. It was in the two upper stories, *i. e.* the Mansard story and the one below it. I saw no light in the lower stories whatever. I could have seen it if there had been a light there.

Q. What further did you notice about the fire?

A. The fire, at the time I first saw it, was clear fore and aft in those two upper stories.

Q. (By Mr. Philbrick.) Had it burst out of the windows?

A. No, sir, it had not.

Q. Had the bell then sounded the alarm?

A. No, sir; the bell had not sounded the alarm then.

Q. How soon after you first heard the cry of "Fire," did you hear the fire-alarm from the bell?

A. Well, I could not state the time, sir. It seemed a long while. It was probably three minutes, I should think. It seemed a much longer time than that.

Q. How long after the fire-alarm did you see any engine there, or any apparatus?

A. The first I saw was a hose, which was nearly opposite to my house. That was pretty soon after the alarm. It was but a few minutes.

Q. Did they play upon the building?

A. I did not notice that they did. It was a long while before the engine arrived — a very long while before there was water thrown from that street on to the fire.

Q. How long after you saw the hose should you think it was before the engine appeared?

A. I was not in a position to see the engine when it did appear; but it was a considerable length of time before there was any appearance of an engine or any throwing of water.

Q. Where were you at that time?

A. I was in my house, which is perhaps fifty feet below, on the opposite side from the fire — on Kingston street.

Q. As the engines came, did you notice whether they came fast or slow?

A. I did not. I did not notice the engines as they arrived. It was a very long time before they arrived.

Q. Did you notice any of the other engines when they came?

A. No, sir. I was not in a position to do so. The other engines came, I think, by the way of Summer street, and the engine that was in Kingston street was upon the same side of the street as my house, two hundred feet further down, and just in the turn of the street, so that it was not in a position where I could see it.

Q. Did you notice anything about the action of the firemen after they came, — whether they worked well or not?

A. I think they worked well after they got to work, but it was a very long while before they got to work.

Q. Can you give the time by the watch at which they got to work?

A. No, sir; I cannot.

Q. Do you mean that it was a long time after they got there before they got to work?

A. It was a long time before they got there, and a long time after they got there before they got to work.

Q. Did they carry hose into the burning building?

A. I don't think they did. I don't remember seeing any water reach the fire from Kingston street until it had burned down into the third story. The water did not reach the upper stories.

Q. Did you see it when it was thrown by the engine?

A. Yes, sir. It fell short. There was, it seemed to me, very great delay in getting the engines to work. They were short of fuel. They came to my house for it. A man came into my house and wanted to know if we had any wood. I said that we had plenty down cellar. He wanted to know if it was sawed. I said, "Yes." They came to my house three times to get wood; and as many as four, or six, or seven firemen came and took armfuls of wood.

Q. (By Mr. PHILBRICK.) Was that early?

A. The first was soon after the alarm was given. I cannot say how soon.

Q. Was it within half an hour?

A. I think it was. I can't say positively, because I can't remember taking out my watch through the whole night.

Q. Was it the first engine?

A. I suppose it was, but I can't say.

Q. Do you think it was some of the first that arrived?

A. Yes, sir. Not being in a position to see the engines when they did arrive, I could not say whether it was the first or second.

Q. Was that engine at work at that time, throwing water?

A. I can't say as to that.

Q. Did they say they were out of coal when they came, and asked for wood, or give any other reasons why they wanted wood?

A. They spoke of coal, and said that they could not get the coal, or that they had not got it.

Q. Did they take wood from your cellar?

A. Yes, sir. They took it three times.

Q. At what time in the progress of the fire did they take it for the second time, as near as you could tell? Was it early in the evening?

A. It was early in the evening, but I could not tell the precise time. The fire was all about me, and everything was excitement. I did not take out my watch to look at the time. I know that I went to the store, and the last time they came was immediately after my return; and some one in the house said that they had come for more wood, and asked if I would let them in. That was just after my return from the store.

Q. Did you notice anything else about the manner of conducting at the fire?

A. Well, sir, I don't know of anything special, more than what every one saw at the fire.

Q. Did you see the Chief Engineer of the Fire Department?

A. I did not. I don't know him. He was in my store during the evening, and said that the fire would not reach there. I went to the store, and they said that the Chief had been there, and that he said that the fire would not reach there, and that there was no necessity for packing goods. It was a very short time after that, that we were ordered out of the store, because they said that the store would be blown up. It was at the corner of Devonshire, Franklin and Federal streets, and ran through from Devonshire street to Federal. That was the order, viz.: that the store would be blown up; and we were ordered out of the store.

Q. Do you know about what time that was?

A. That, I think, must have been between eleven and twelve o'clock. I should think it was twelve o'clock, but I could not say about the time precisely.

Q. Your store was burned then, was it not?

A. Yes, sir.

ALDERMAN WILLIAM WOOLLEY, *sworn.*

Q. (By Mr. Russell.) What position do you hold in the City Government, in connection with the Fire Department?

A. I am at the head of the Committee on the Fire Department.

Q. How long have you occupied that position?

A. This is my third year.

Q. At what time did you first know of this fire?

A. I was in the city proper at the time the alarm was given, and I went down into the immediate vicinity of the fire. At that time the third alarm had been rung. I saw that there was to be quite a large fire and I started for East Boston in order to send over all the spare apparatus that we had over there. Being located in East Boston, I meant that we should not send everything. Naturally on the third or fourth alarm everything will leave, as the Engineers themselves come over. Feeling anxious for that section of the city, I went immediately to East Boston so as not to have all our force leave.

On getting to East Boston, there was an alarm of fire over there, and I stayed there until that fire was extinguished, and then came back to this city, getting back about ten o'clock.

Q. When you came back did you leave one engine there at East Boston?

A. I left one hose-carriage there. I left them playing on the fire there, with orders if there was no other alarm to come over to Boston. I reached the fire I should judge about ten o'clock.

Q. Where did you go?

A. I came into Winthrop square. The front part of Bebee's building fell just as I got on to the square.

Q. Tell us what you saw of the action of the Fire Department and of the conduct of the men and of the Chief Engineer.

A. On arriving in Winthrop square, I inquired for Capt. Damrell, and was informed that he was in that immediate vicinity, and found him perhaps in one or two minutes. I said to him, "We have got quite a large fire. What is the prospect of stopping it?" etc.

Q. What did he say?

A. I can hardly say now what his answer was. It was to the effect that he had got considerable of a fire to contend with. He said to me that he had telegraphed to all adjacent cities and towns for assistance. He requested me to pass down on to the other side of the fire and instruct the Engineers to put on the out-of-town apparatus and use it to the best advantage; and for me then to come back and report to him the condition of the fire on that side, i.e., the side towards Summer street. I passed around up Federal street and so around into Church Green square. When I got there, the Freeman's National Bank building was burning, and it fell a few minutes afterwards.

I met there Capt. Jacobs, and I think Capt. Brown and one other Engineer (I would not state now who it was); it was one of the Assistant Engineers. I saw what progress the fire was making and gave them my instructions which I had received from the Chief in regard to concentrating the force, if they could find any available point where they thought they could make a stand, and to be sure that all out-of-town apparatus, as soon as it arrived, was put in the best position for it to be of service.

I immediately returned back to Winthrop square. I met the Chief and reported to him, and he says to me, "I think it is my duty to go around on that side of the square and speak to one of the Assistants" (I could not say now which one it was; I did not take particular notice). There was one or more Assistant Engineers there. He gave that Assistant some orders, and we immediately started and went around into Church Green square. The fire seemed to be making the most progress in that direction. When we arrived there, the Freeman's National Bank building was entirely burned down, and the fire was raging in what is called "Webster's Home," and also at the south of Church Green square and the south of Summer street. We immediately went to work and got three streams upon the triangular building at that point — one upon the roof from a ladder on the opposite side and two on the side of the building, in hopes that we might stay the fire, or perhaps save that triangular building.

We did not have sufficient time, for the fire drove us away from there. It swept across the street and seemed to envelop the whole unburned side of that building. It was but a short time before the fire was in that building so as to drive the men out.

In the mean time, the ladder which had been put up to the top of the building had been removed, and after the firemen had been driven out of the building, we found that there was one hose-company on top of the building and no available ladder. I started and went down into Federal street and got the longest spliced ladder from the ladder cart there, and six of us, I think, took it up. We threw it up upon the building and the firemen came down at that time.

The building was then completely on fire from top to bottom. We had at that time three steamers, some playing two streams and some one, right there in Church Green square.

We found that the fire was getting around us, and that it was getting too hot, and we had of course to move the apparatus back again. I stayed at that point until this triangular building got well on fire, and then, at the Chief's request, I went down below, as the report had come to us that the wharves there were all on fire—that the cinders coming from over the buildings had set them on fire. I went down at his request to see if that was the case, and to see what force there was there, if any, and to come back and report to him, which I did. When I got around there, I found that there were one or two buildings or coal sheds on Prentice's wharf and Mr. Robbins' wharf and the Hartford & Erie Railroad freight depot, and all those wooden buildings there, were a-fire on the roof, with no really available force there, other than hand hose, etc., to protect them.

I came immediately back and reported to the Chief the condition. In the mean time he had sent one engine (I don't know which it was) around there in that vicinity and a hose carriage. I went back and we got some streams upon the fire in that direction.

We tried to make a stand, but the fire was setting down and the cinders were coming down like a heavy hailstorm, — whole shingles and pieces a yard square, — and we found it was impossible to make a stand and had to go back.

Seeing that the fire was sweeping down again, we all looked around to see what point there was where there was a chance to make a stand in that vicinity. I met Mr. Jones, who was superintendent of the eastern division of the Water Works, and asked him if his works were open, knowing that there was quite a yard in there. He said that he had men stationed at the gates, but that the gates were not open. I went in there and saw that there was a very good chance to make a stand in the back yards of several dwelling-houses, etc., adjoining it, I think on South-street place, which leads in from South street, where the Quincy school was, and also quite a yard of the Water Works.

I found Capt. Jacobs and Capt. Brown, of South Boston, and told them what my ideas were, and they coincided with them, after taking a hasty look at the place, viz.: — that we could make a stand and stop the fire there. I said, "Captains Brown and Jacobs, you do the best you can, and I will go around on South street, and see what they are doing there."

I went around and found on the farther side of South street that there were three swell-front houses that had had everything taken out of them except the floor timbers, and that there was a grand chance. I said to Capt. Colligan, "If you will take care of the fire here, I think we will take care of it back of us," and we did so, as you may see.

I was in hopes that we could save the Hartford & Erie R. R. passenger depot, but owing to the sparks and shingles lighting on it, we didn't save it. But we made out to make a stand there. I have no idea of the time, for I never looked at a watch. I don't know how long this occupied, or anything about it.

When I felt a full conviction that we had stopped the fire in that direction virtually, I immediately came round into Washington street and inquired all the way for the Chief. I understood that he was to be seen around in Congress street, and found the Chief and His Honor the Mayor, and Alderman Jenks, and I think Alderman Ricker and Councilman Jones. They were consulting in regard to the feasibility of using powder. I judged from the conversation that prominent citizens had been advising with the Mayor, and telling him that powder should be used. He was getting the Chief's opinion. I think that the Chief stated that he was willing to use it, and that he had convened his Board of Engineers as far as practicable, and taken them away from their several stations around the fire to advise with him. I understood that they gave their consent to its use, but doubted the practicability of it, as did the Chief. The idea that he conveyed was that we had not sufficient powder at command to make it practicable. He referred to me about it. I think my reply was that I did not believe in powder at all.

Q. Did the Chief make any other objection except that there was not powder enough, at that time?

A. I did not listen attentively to the conversation and did not hear it plainly amid the roar of the flames, etc. But what I understood from him was that he was generally opposed to the use of powder unless he had a sufficient quantity to make it available, and parties that were versed in the use of it.

Q. At what time was that, so far as you can tell?

A. I should judge that that was about eleven o'clock. It must have been somewhat past eleven o'clock.

Q. What did you do next?

A. The Mayor, Alderman Jenks, etc., started for City Hall. I think I went around and made a complte circuit of the fire and came back through Washington street and Summer street and then down Avon street and all through that vicinity, to see how well the parties had succeeded, down at the east corner of the fire, where I stated that I stood in the first place. I found that they had succeeded there in stopping the fire effectually, and I immediately came back and went up to City Hall.

On my way back, one of the Assistant Engineers stated that the Mayor had sent word that he would like to see me at City Hall. I went. The Mayor, the Chief Engineer, Genl. Burt, Alderman Jenks and several other citizens were there. Capt. Damrell was at a desk writing some passes or orders for parties to use powder. His Honor the Mayor said to me, "You are just the man we want to see; I want you to take charge of blowing up buildings in such a street" (I could not now say what street it was), "and to take such persons as you see fit to assist you."

My reply was, "Mr. Mayor, I don't believe in powder. I can fight fire better with water than with powder, and would rather that some other person would take this commission." I think he tendered the same position to Alderman Cutter. I would not say positively. I know that he stated so.

I don't think that I remained in the hall more than five minutes. I immediately went out and went down to the corner of Washington and Summer streets and down Summer street as far as Hovey's building. The fire then was raging in the building where Mercantile Hall was, and I found Capt. Shaw there in charge, and he was of the opinion that we should stop the fire there, that we should not let it into Trinity Church.

We worked quite hard there and tried to concentrate our force. We lacked for water. Sometimes one steamer would play a good stream and sometimes another. There was, so far as my observation went, a general lack of a supply of water all through that locality.

Q. (By Mr. PHILBRICK.) Is there not a very large main in Summer street?

A. I don't know but there is, but I have my doubts about it. My idea is that it never has been removed since it was put in there for dwelling-houses originally; and I know that all the hydrants in that district, or the most of them, are the old-fashioned hydrants, and are connected with the main pipes by only a four-inch pipe, whereas we connect our hydrants now with a six-inch pipe.

Q. When you say that there was a general lack of water through that district, what streets do you include?

A. I include Summer street and that immediate vicinity; I could not say much in regard to Franklin street, because I was not on it except the lower end of Winthrop square.

When I first arrived at the fire, and afterwards when the fire had got up very near to Washington street, later in the evening, I had no chance (not being in that immediate vicinity) of knowing and seeing whether there was really a leak there or not. But my impression is that there was only a six-inch pipe through Franklin street, and that the same pipe is there now that was laid at the time that Franklin square was occupied by dwelling-houses. I mean that over the district burned, as a general thing, there was not a sufficient supply of water to supply the large force that we had.

Q. Where did you go after the events of which you have spoken?

A. I stayed on Summer street, at the building where the Mercantile Hall was. I stayed there with Capt. Shaw and other parties, fighting the fire as best we could, and travelling back and forth from the head of Milk street around, taking general observations and assisting wherever I could, and consulting with the Engineers and doing the best I could to keep all parties supplied with coal, and to see that everything was working well, driving men out of stores where parties on Washington street would open doors and allow the crowd to come in and get goods. Their general reply was that they might as well have them as have them burned up. I told several parties that the fire would not cross Washington street. Goods were given away all along on Pearl street and Summer street — the west side.

In one hat-store under the Marlboro' Hotel, a gentleman opened his store and asked people to come and help themselves. I remonstrated and drove the crowd out, and said to him: "This is not only setting a bad example, but you are getting these parties into trouble, because the police will arrest all parties whom they meet supplied with goods. Although the goods have been given to these people, yet the police cannot take their word for it. It is my opinion that the fire will not cross Washington street. You had better keep your store closed." He seemed to be greatly excited. I don't know his name. He set out a whole box full of hats at the door. Then they pitched them out into the gutter. He seemed so excited that he didn't really know what he was doing.

I went up into two or three stores where people had been looking out, and I closed the windows which they had left open, so as to keep the sparks from going in. This was on the upper side of Washington street.

Q. Did you notice any want of fuel for the engines?

A. There was in some cases. We have our fuel wagons whose duty it is to supply the steamers.

It is the duty of No. 7's driver on arriving at a fire and immediately unhitching his horses, to go back with his horses and get the fuel wagon located there. Also on Salem street, it is the duty of driver No. 8 immediately to go back with his horses and get that fuel wagon. They drive in the vicinity of steamers which have a peculiar blow of the whistle which calls the coal wagon. On receiving notice that the steamer is out of coal, it is the duty of the driver to go there and supply it. They generally go over and dump some two hundred or three hundred weight of coal alongside of a steamer and then go to another one.

That night we kept our steamers playing on to the fires as long as we could — until we were fairly driven out. In many instances, we had to leave what little coal we had on the ground; we would not have time to shovel it up. Perhaps the steamer moving to a new locality might have but little coal in her tender, and would get out of coal in a short time. I noticed it several times in going around among them. Wherever I saw a steamer short of coal, I tried to find dry-goods' boxes or something to keep them a-going until we could find a coal wagon. I think there were one or two steamers that did stop for want of fuel.

Q. Where were they?

A. I think we had one steamer down by the Hartford and Erie depot that stopped from that cause. It was only for a few minutes, as I gave orders to them to go on to any wharf and get coal without consulting anybody. If there was no one there to deliver it to them, to take coal or fuel wherever they could find it, and not to let the steamers stay still.

Q. (By Mr. Cobb.) Where was the other instance?

A. That was later, Sunday morning, in Kilby street. One of the Salem steamers, not one of our own, lay still perhaps some ten or fifteen minutes from want of fuel. That was all that came under my observation, although several times during the night I heard parties inquiring for fuel, and Engineers stating that they were about out.

Q. (By Mr. Philbrick.) What stock of fuel had the department been in the habit of keeping in store?

A. In some of the houses we had facilities for keeping some five or six tons beside what was in the wagons. The wagons, to the best of my judgment, would carry from two to two and a half tons of coal. Some of our fuel wagons are larger than others. We keep them loaded, and then have a supply in the houses besides.

Q. Had that supply been run down in any case during the prevalence of the horse-disease?

A. Not that I know of. It is delivered to the houses by the party who has the contract to furnish city coal. During this night, the supply in the engine-houses gave out and we had to go elsewhere. The Chief has an understanding with a party to furnish coal for the city, and in case of the supply giving out some understanding in regard to getting it from the wharf, — so that the coal wagons drive right to the wharf and get it. That is also understood by the drivers.

Q. (By Mr. Russell.) How was it with the hose that night? Was there any extraordinary trouble by reason of the bursting of the hose?

A. No, sir. I don't know as there was anything more of that than is usual. Of course, that was a large fire, and buildings falling on to the hose would cut it.

Q. What hose do you use?

A. We use all kinds. I suppose there is a greater number of hose-manufacturers and more competition in that than in any other branch of business. Each party claims that his is the best, and we have in the office an innumerable number of samples. I always endeavor to buy the very best of hose.

Q. What proportion of leather hose do you use?

A. I think about one-half is leather, — I don't know but a little more than half.

Q. Whose make do you use?

A. Mostly Boyd's. We find that is superior to almost any other make.

Q. Do you use much cotton hose?

A. Very little cotton hose. We run a small-sized cotton hose on our extinguisher wagons. We have used it in the Department, but found that it was not good — that it was liable to rot out. That is the case with rubber hose. It apparently will look well, but will rot out by lying still in the houses quicker than it will by being used.

Q. How did the men work that night?

A. I saw no instance where the men did not work well. Every individual man appeared to try to do his duty, so far as came under my observation. I saw no man that showed a disposition to shirk; I mean, our own firemen. Of course. the firemen from out of town were not so much under the control of our own Engineers, or their own (they being away from home), as were our own men. But really I saw no disposition on the part of any fireman to shirk; although there were a great many in Boston whom we supposed to be firemen, who were not connected with any company that was here on duty. They had no apparatus, and merely came to see the fire. There were many men who had badges and fire-hats on who were not really firemen and never had been.

Q. Did you know of any Boston firemen being intoxicated that night?

A. No, sir; I didn't see one.

Q. Did you see any from out of town intoxicated?

A. I think I saw men with firemen's uniforms on, who were intoxicated.

Q. Where did they get their uniforms?

A. They may be connected with out-of-town apparatus. You would see men about the street with gaudy-looking firemen's uniforms on. That was a badge to pass them anywhere about the fire, and of course they put them on for that purpose. Most of the companies have some little badge or number of their own; and about all the companies have uniforms.

Q. What was the conduct of the Chief that night?

A. The Chief, as far as I saw him (and I saw him at all times,—I didn't leave the fire until Sunday afternoon about 5 o'clock), was perfectly cool, and at no time did I think that he was any way excited, or so but what he was perfectly master of himself all the time. I thought he was much cooler than what I should suppose he would be under the trying circumstances.

While speaking of the fire on Summer street, I would say that I stayed in Summer street until after Trinity Church was burned and Lovejoy's carpet store was well under way. At that time, the fire had extended through into Washington street, to Macullar, Williams & Parker's building, and, I think, all the way up almost to Milk street. Capt. Dunbar had charge from Milk street down to Franklin street.

We were doing good service there at that place. They had nine streams concentrated on Hovey's building, and Hovey's own folks were wetting the roof. They had blankets spread, which, had it been done by other parties, I have no doubt the fire would have been stopped in other localities where it was not.

I would state here that I heard the Chief say to a party (I could not say who it was), or give him orders, to go to the Chief of Police's office and ask Capt. Quinn if he could not detail a force of men to take blankets and sail-cloths and put them over the roofs of buildings to keep the fire from spreading.

I would state that I stayed there on Washington street, my principal aim being, with the assistance of Capt. Shaw and Capt. Dunbar, to keep the fire from spreading across Washington street. That was what we were working for, and what was finally accomplished. The fire had burned through Macullar, Williams & Parker's place and Copeland's confectionery store. If you will recollect, Mudge's store was a three-story old-fashioned brick building. It was the opinion of Capt. Shaw himself that we should stop the fire there, those buildings being low. If we could keep it from spreading across into the Marlboro' Hotel, our opinion was that there would be no doubt but what we would stop it when it got into those other brick buildings, if not save part of those buildings themselves. We were making for those, and in my opinion we should have saved them, if parties had not come there with powder. When the fire broke out of Macullar, Williams & Parker's store, and was in the rear of this brick block, a gentleman came there and said that he had orders to blow up the corner of Washington and Summer streets. I remonstrated with him, and so did Capt. Shaw. We told him that we were going to stop the fire there; that we had the fire under control; that it was not going to cross Summer street beyond Hovey's; that in our opinion we could stop it where it was, or at any rate that we could save Mudge's store. We explained to him that there were only two or three windows on that end, and that those had gratings, and that they only led into the stairway, where there was a fair chance to go right in and put out the fire if it should get in there; and that, on the other side, the back side next to these buildings, was a blank wall and a very stout one; that we thought it perfectly safe from Lovejoy's carpet store, and that we contemplated putting streams on top. We remonstrated with him, and finally he went away. In half an hour he came back and said that he had positive orders from the Mayor and Capt. Damrell to blow up that corner. Of course we had nothing else to do but call the firemen away. We limbered up, backed up the entire street, and I said, "If you are bound to blow it, then blow it." They put some powder into the farther end, where the Waltham Watch Company's store was, or the end next to Lovejoy's store on Summer street, and, after waiting some few minutes, it exploded. It did nothing but shatter the building and take the front windows out. I said, "I hope you are satisfied." He said that he was not. He got some more powder and broke in the front windows of Mudge's store on Summer street, got in there, put the powder in, set the fuse, and everybody ran back and waited. There was no explosion. We waited some four or five minutes. I thought it was a lack of good judgment for anybody to send orders down there unless they knew the situation of things. I immediately started and went up to City Hall and saw the Mayor. The Mayor says, "Woolley, I have issued no such orders. I do not intend to issue any such orders. I have no means of knowing whether it is right or not. I think my place is here in my office, where I can be found by all parties, and not at the fire. What do you think?" I said, "It seems to me in that way, viz.: that you should be where citizens can find you. Certainly they could not find you if you were about the fire." I immediately returned back to the corner of Washington and Summer streets. I found that their powder had not exploded even by that time, although three-quarters of an hour had expired. Two of the firemen volunteered to go and see what ailed it. I don't know what company they belonged to. They were not the men that put the powder there. They crawled into the window and said that the fuse had gone out. They removed the powder. Capt. Shaw, with my assistance and that of others, got the apparatus back into position again. In the mean time, these low buildings were completely burned out and there was no sign of saving any of them. We concentrated our forces on Mudge's building, and you see what condition it is in now. All the damage done to that building was done by powder. They put their powder in the lower or street floor, and it did not explode. There was certainly, to my knowledge, a delay of half or three-quarters of an hour, in the working of the apparatus, in which more property might have been saved.

Q. Do you know who that gentleman was?

A. Yes, sir.

Q. Who was it?

A. If I am not obliged to tell, I don't want to. It was ———, a member of the Common Council.

He said that he had authority. I did not feel that I had authority, nor did the Assistant Engineer Shaw feel that he had authority, in opposition to written authority signed by the Mayor.

I did not accept the position offered to me, of taking charge of blowing up buildings, feeling that I was not competent, even if I had believed in the use of powder at fires.

Q. Do you know how many kegs of powder they brought out of that building?

A. I think they brought out three or four. In my opinion, the quantity was not sufficient, provided there had been a necessity for blowing up the building. It was sporting-powder, and was in a keg of perhaps five pounds. They may have had a wooden keg that had more than that in it, but I saw some one who had two of these tin canisters. In my opinion, they might hold five pounds of powder.

Q. Tell what you did after that.

A. We got the force back there and put the fire out. We stopped the fire in that vicinity.

A. About what time was that?

Q. I could not tell you. I had no idea of the time. I never looked at my watch. I suppose I travelled back and forth from Milk street down to Summer street and Hovey's building, as many as a hundred times, taking general observations and looking out to do the best I could under the circumstances. It was before daylight. I immediately came around from there, when I found that we had stopped it at that point, and came around through Province street, and went into City Hall and saw the Mayor again, and spoke with him, and told him that the fire was stopped in that direction. I merely stopped a few minutes, and immediately went down to the head of Milk street, and they were using powder. I did not pass down through Milk street. I saw the Chief Engineer there, and Capt. Dunbar and others, and came from there and passed around to the other side of the fire, around Congress street into the vicinity of Simmons's block, which at that time was just commencing to burn. There was quite a force of the department in there. I found Capt. Hebard in charge, and the Chief Engineer of the Salem Department, with his assistant. I went with Capt. Hebard into the rear of Farwell's place, — what used to be the old "Transcript" building. We got some streams in there; went in and looked at it, and got streams in there, thinking to cut the fire off in there. It was raging quite strong in Simmons's building, and also in the new building between Simmons's block and the "Boston Post" building. We had got two available streams, as good as I had seen on the fire that night; one was from Engine No. 5, of South Boston; thought that we were doing good duty, and that we should save Farwell's building and stop the fire in that direction. Mr.Farwell spoke to me about it at the time, also ex-Mayor Wightman, and ex-Mayor ———— ; and I told them that I thought we should stop the fire there. We were doing good duty when a fireman came up, saying that they were going to blow up Farwell's building. I said, "It is not possible that they are going to do so, or they would notify us." He says, "They are." I says to Capt. Hebard, "Back your men, and I will go and see whether it is so or not." I got in through a window into a shed, and found that they had powder there, but that they had not put it into the building. I don't know the parties that had the powder, but I talked with them in regard to it, and they told me that they would not explode it without giving us notice. I told them that we had streams in the rear, and that it was outrageous, the manner in which they were running around with powder and exploding it without notifying the firemen. I passed back and told Capt. Hebard that I would look out for it, and told the firemen that there should be no powder exploded without their having sufficient notice.

In the mean time, Capt. Farrar had got another stream in there, making three. I saw that they were doing good service.

In the mean time, I think that the fire had got over on to the other corner, across from Simmons's block. There is the Hide and Leather

National Bank there. The fire had got over into that; and two of the Salem Department engines had streams up in the stone building where there was a little passage-way that led down, and they were playing on to this building with apparently a good prospect of stopping the fire there. I went from there around on to Liberty square and came up Water street as far as I could; found that the fire had got across into those varnish and paint-shops there. I had no idea that it was to go more than part of the way down Water street. When I came around back I found that the streams had been withdrawn, and that they had put powder into Farwell's building (it is what used to be the old "Transcript" building) and were trying to blow it up. They had withdrawn all the streams. In my opinion there was no necessity for it; and if that had not been done, it is simply my opinion that the fire never would have gone into Lindall street, — if they had not withdrawn their force at that particular point, on account of the putting in of that powder. It may be that I am prejudiced. I am against the use of powder unless it can be used in sufficient quantities to have the desired effect, and then be used by men who are trained to it. There was the trouble on the night of the fire. It was done by incompetent persons undertaking to blow up buildings.

After we had stopped the fire in that particular locality, Mr. ———, the member of the Common Council before referred to, said, "You were right."

I passed by George I. Robinson's store and I came across Alderman Ricker. Mr. Robinson called us in and asked our opinion in regard to the fire, and we stated to him that in our opinion his store was perfectly safe. At that time, I was not aware that the force had been withdrawn from Simmons's block and Farwell's building, and that powder had been put in there.

There was powder being exploded all around. We heard the reports so often that we didn't pay much attention to them.

When I got back there I said to Alderman Ricker, "I don't think that Mr. Robinson is safe. That fire will come through there." I stayed there in that vicinity giving advice, talking, etc., with the firemen and Engineers, and then passed around up into Congress square, and found the Chief there fighting the fire. I had some talk with him in regard to powder, and told him what I thought about it. He said that he thought the same thing and that he had stopped the use of it.

I went back and found the fire raging in Lindall street. The fire in the mean time had swept down into Kilby street. I went down there and found the Chief Engineer of the Salem Department had come around from Congress street in there and had made a stand there. I could not give the name of the Assistant Engineer who was there. Any gentleman who looks at the ruins will take notice that there are some old-fashioned, low-studded, low buildings in there. He said, "Mr. Woolley, we are going to stop this fire in there." I told him I thought the prospect was good; that all he wanted was a little more force.

I went and found Capt. Dunbar on State street. I told him that we ought to have another steamer in there, and that if we had, we could stop the fire there. They did send another steamer there. I don't know what it was. We were doing good and efficient duty and in my opinion would have stopped the fire along at the corner where Dodge & Gilbert's store was. But the first thing we knew, along came some men with more powder, and they were going to blow up No's 25 and 27 Kilby street. It was my general observation throughout the entire night that in selecting a place to blow up, they took a tall building where it overtopped a set of low buildings instead of taking the low buildings below it. The low buildings, were the ones to blow up, not the tall ones, in such a situation as that. (That is merely my opinion.) A hue and cry was raised that they had put the powder in there and touched it off, and that there had not been any explosion. I found that the force was withdrawn, and of course the fire had its own way then.

Finally, after waiting, I should think, some ten minutes, there was one very slight explosion which blew the windows out of No. 27, I think, and it was all done. Then there was quite a talk among these men that the ones who put the powder in there did not seem to have any heads. The firemen threatened to break their heads if they put any more powder in. There was quite a discussion as to whether the powder had all exploded. The firemen seized hold of one man and were going to force him into the building. I remonstrated with them, and finally one of the gentlemen says, "I will go and see whether it has exploded." If he did not go to see, they were going to make him. That was the force of their argument.

Finally, he went into the building, followed by one or two firemen, and they fetched away three kegs of powder which had not exploded. They said that was all there was. They had put in four and fetched away three, and yet they said that that was all there was. I said, "Are you sure of it? We don't want to get in there and be blown up. It is bad enough to have you fellows around here any way, and if I had my way, I would have you all arrested." I said to Assistant Engineer Smith, "If you see the Chief, you say to him that we can never stop this fire short of the North End, if he don't stop the use of powder." He gave me that as his opinion; and Capt. Green says, "We shall never accomplish anything with these men running around here in this way using powder, because it intimidates the firemen, and with good reason, too. It is bad enough for the firemen to risk their lives as they are doing and not be liable to be blown up all the time." They said that this powder was removed; they assured me that there was no more, and I said so to the firemen. I don't say that I had control of them. We got the streams well to work, and a fireman comes to me and says, "They are putting powder up into No. 5, which was well up above us, leading up one flight of stairs." He said, "Come with me." I found two police officers stationed at the door. They were East Boston officers. One was Mr. Thatcher, and the other Mr. Crandall. I spoke to Mr. Thatcher and said, "Are they putting powder in here?" And he says, "Yes, there are three men in there with powder." I went up to the head of the stairs and found three men there. I won't say how many kegs they had. They had a half-barrel of it and the head was nearly out, and as I went up the stairs I stepped on powder with my feet. I said, "What are you doing here?" They said, "We are going to blow up this building." I said, "By whose orders?" They said, "By General Benham's." I said, "You take this powder out of this building!" In the mean time

Capt. Smith had come around, and the officers told him where I was. He says, "Capt. Damrell says 'If anybody undertakes to blow up any more buildings, have them arrested, and if you can't arrest them, kill them.'" That was the way his orders came to me. I said to these men, "Do you take this powder out of here!" They said they would not; that they had orders to put it there. I said, "If you don't take it out of this building, I will have you arrested. It is perfectly outrageous for you to have this half-barrel of powder here with the head out of it." They would not take the powder away, and I undertook to remove it myself; and they took hold of me, and I called on the officers, and ordered them to arrest the three men. They did so. I called on the firemen and they came up, and we took the powder and carried it down on to the sidewalk. I said to one of the men, "Take your coat off and cover the powder up and take it away from here." These three men went away from the powder, and in fifteen minutes afterwards they came back headed by General Benham. He wanted to know by what authority I ordered that powder out of there. I told him I was Chairman of the Committee on Fire Department, and to my best judgment it was demoralizing the men, and I should take the responsibility as Chairman of the Committee on Fire Department and one of the members of the City Council, of arresting those men or ordering them to be arrested. Said he, "Do you know who I am?" I said, "I do not." Says he, "I am General Benham." I think I made the remark, "I don't care if you are General Damnation, that powder, is not going into this building, and if you attempt to have it put in, I will have these men arrested." He says, "You have not the power." I said to the officers, "If they undertake to put that powder in there, arrest them!" He remonstrated with the officers. But the officers said, "We know nobody but Alderman Woolley. We don't know you, and we shall have to do what Mr. Woolley tells us to do." General Benham took the men away and ordered the powder away. In a few minutes they came back with another General and an ex-alderman and wanted to know where Mr. Woolley was. In the mean time, the door had been closed. I had stationed men there with orders not to allow any man to come into the building. I came and showed myself. They wanted to know by what authority I resisted General Benham and their people. I told them. The ex-alderman says, "I have written authority from Capt. Damrell. Do you pretend to assume authority over Capt. Damrell?" There was quite a large crowd of firemen gathered around there that had left their apparatus and streams. The fire was raging and there was nobody to play water on it or do anything. There was a large crowd, and some talk of "Put them out. We will stand by you, Alderman Woolley," and such talk, which I did not pay a great deal of attention to. But I remonstrated with them, and had quite a talk. The ex-alderman insisted that he had authority, and showed it. I had nothing but verbal authority from the Chief, and of course his authority was superior to mine. I says, "You can do as you see fit, but, General, if this fire goes into State street you are responsible for it. You understand what I say, if this fire goes into State street, you are responsible for it." General Benham says, "Are you willing to take the responsibility of saying it will not go if we do not use the powder?" Says I, "I am. I am not afraid to take it. We have our force all concentrated here, and we can stop this fire here. It cannot go into State street." They insisted and did put the powder in there, but gave me their word of honor that the powder should not be exploded without giving me sufficient notice.

They put the powder up in there, and it hadn't been there but a few minutes before I came to Assistant Engineer Dunbar, and I said, "You have authority to order that powder out. The Chief is not here, and you are Chief here. The Chief is not on the ground, now do you order that powder out." He did order it out; and they took it out. When they did so, I went around into State street, and there I found a horse-wagon loaded with three tons of powder without any protection at all, and the tailboard out. I said to the ex-Alderman, "Do you know what you are doing? Do you realize what you are doing? Here is a team with three tons of powder standing right here in State street, and all these steamers in full blast, and all these men smoking right round it. Do you realize the situation?" Says he, "I didn't think of it." "Now," says I, "my advice is, if you can, that you get that load of powder away from this vicinity as quick as you can." That was at daylight Sunday morning. The powder was driven off immediately. Where it went to I don't know. I saw no more of that powder that day. In the mean time, the force went back to their work, and you see where the fire was stopped there. I saw that we were going to stop it in Kilby street. I went around into Kilby street, where I met General Burt. He had just come from the Post-Office Exchange. We had some conversation; and he wanted to know what I was trying to do, and I told him, "I am trying to stop this fire from going into State street, that is what I'm trying to do, and if I live I'm going to do it." I got along in front of the Post-Office entrance, and a gentleman says, "Alderman Woolley, the fire has got into the attic of the building here. If you will come with me, I think I can show you where you can bring a stream to stop it." The gentleman went up into the attic of the building, among the rubbish, and I saw that the fire had got into the attic. He explained to me that that part of the building was put in there by Mr. Dooley when he kept a hotel there, and at a certain place was a good strong wall, really fire-proof, and that the firemen need not be afraid of coming up in there. It was perfectly dark. I came down from the building and met Assistant Engineer Farrar, and told him what I wanted. There happened to be an available stream right there, and we shifted from Kilby street right up in there and took a line of hose up in there. In the mean time, Capt. John Regan had come from that vicinity, and the fire had gained some little headway. We fought the fire there with some indifferent success. The fire burned in through there. One of the steamers from Watertown came in and we got their stream in. I stayed by the fire there until we stopped it in that vicinity, and that is where we made the last stand, really, on the fire. Then it got to be along between four and five o'clock Sunday afternoon, and I had in the mean time passed down around Liberty square and round in that vicinity as far as Fort Hill District, and found that we had the fire under control all around that line, and could report from the other side that it was under control there. I came into Congress square and saw the Chief and other parties and saw that they had control of the fire there, and at the solicitation of the Chief I went up to the City Hall and reported to the Mayor that we had virtually stopped the progress of the fire.

Q. (By Mr. GREENE.) After General Burt met you and asked you what you were doing, what became of him?

A. I don't know; I did not see him again until the next day at City Hall.

I went up into the Post-Office building. He did not come up with me, nor did I see him in the building. He might have been there, but I was in the building from the time that we got the first line of hose in there; from the time the fire first took until it was stopped. I did not see General Burt to my knowledge afterwards. He might have been there, but I did not see him.

Q. Did you see him before that during the night?

A. Yes, sir. I did not see him but once before that. I saw him in the Mayor's office the first time when I went there, when they tendered me the commission to use the powder. He was there advising with the Mayor and talking with other citizens. There was quite a concourse of citizens and some of the Aldermen. I did not see him again until I saw him in Kilby street. He was one of the parties that insisted upon putting the powder into No. 5, where it was taken out so many times.

Q. Who were the other parties?

A. I could not tell. I will only mention General Benham, who seemed to be the man in charge, although I have learned since that he had no orders from the Chief to use powder; and I will further state that the Chief and the Mayor had both told me that they had never given any authority for the blowing up of the corner of Summer and Washington streets; that is, no special authority. I don't know who the gentleman was who took me into the Post Office; he informed me that he was employed in the office. He said that he knew all about it.

Q. (By Mr. COBB.) You said that when you got up into City Hall the Mayor says, "You are just the man I want to see. I want you to take charge of the use of powder"?

A. He gave me to understand that he wanted me to take charge of a particular street. The Chief was at the desk writing these commissions.

Q. (By Mr. RUSSELL.) Did you understand that you were to be one of these persons commissioned?

A. Yes, sir, and I declined to serve. I think Alderman Ricker stood there with a little paper in his hand; and Councilman Paige was there and Councilman Bicknell. It was understood that he was to take charge. He was calling for volunteers to go with him. I think perhaps the Mayor said, "Woolley, you are just the man we want to see."

Q. (By Mr. COBB.) You have stated the general lack of water through the fire district?

A. Yes, sir. It was, in my opinion, from the insufficient size of the pipes.

Q. How long has that been so?

A. I think the Chief has called the attention of the Committee on Fire Department to it, and they have given instructions to the Secretary to notify the Water Works as many as three or four times within as many years.

Q. Did you know that fact yourself?

A. I did not know it from the observance of it. I only knew it from what the Chief reported, that the pipes in that street were insufficient for the supply of water in case of a fire.

Q. Have you ever taken any action on that in your committee?

A. Yes, sir, to notify the Water Board.

Q. When did you do that?

A. I think our records will show, from the files.

Also, we have had petitions for additional apparatus in that vicinity. When the petitions came in, the Chief has laid them before the Committee on Fire Department for their action. They were endorsed by him, and it was considered that when we started the Fire Board, which Capt. Damrell has been at work upon ever since I have been connected with the committee, this additional apparatus would be secured. He has insisted upon it and tried to have it, and in my opinion would have had it, but for the opposition in the City Government to appropriating a sum of money.

Q. Are you now chairman for the second year?

A. Yes, sir.

Q. If you and your associates have known this matter and have not taken any steps, it is important for you to show where the responsibility rests.

A. It has come from the Chief that there was an insufficiency in the supply of water, in his opinion, and we have taken such action as we deemed proper to notify the Water Board, which we always do.

There is one thing which is a great detriment. The several engine houses, etc., should be in the hands of the Committee on the Fire Department. But they have not a word to say in regard to the location. It is referred to the Committee on Public Buildings. When the petition comes in for a new building for an engine-house it is in the hands of that committee. They will go and look for a lot, and find that the people charge a great price for the land, and instead of locating the engine-house where it should be, they go on the outskirts, where land is cheap. Therefore our apparatus, instead of being located in the centre of the city, where the large buildings are, is on the outskirts, where the land is a little cheap. That is one great trouble. Everything pertaining to the Fire Department should be in the hands of the Committee on the Fire Department. It was so formerly.

Q. As chairman of your committee, have you ever urged this matter upon the City Government, that the Committee on the Fire Department ought to be the best judges in regard to the location of engine-houses?

A. Not in any written report; but it has been urged and has been talked verbally that we should have that charge, and a verbal complaint has been made that we could not have it. If we wanted any repairs done we had no control at all — not to do the least thing, not even to put a screw into them.

Q. Have you, as a member of the committee, made any statement to the Board since you have been a member of it, that this district and other districts are uncovered, and that there is no apparatus in fifty or sixty acres?

A. I don't know that I have officially, but it has been discussed in the Committee on the Fire Department. The Chief has said that he did not feel that we were suitably protected in case of fire, and that we should have more apparatus in this immediate vicinity. There was a petition came in for the location of a steam-fire engine on Atlantic avenue. It was laid before the committee and discussed, and the general opinion seemed to be the same with all members of the committee — that we had apparatus enough, and that when we got a fire-boat on the water-front, that would be as good as two or three steamers; that there was no immediate necessity for more apparatus; that land was very high; that it cost too much, and that a fire-boat would answer the same purpose, which it would, to a certain extent. I don't want to throw any blame upon the department. Here is a street to be graded. The Paving Department go on and contract to raise the grade. They go right on and cover up our reservoirs. They re-lay sidewalks, raise the grade of them, cover up our hydrants, raise the grade around them, so that when snow comes in the winter-time they are covered up. They will put in new hydrants and remove old ones, and never to my knowledge did we have notice that such a thing had taken place. In my opinion, the hydrants and care of the hydrants and reservoirs should be in charge of the Fire Department. The reservoirs are in charge of the Chief Engineer, so far as keeping the snow removed in the winter-time is concerned; but they go to work and contract for grading the streets and cover up reservoirs and put in new hydrants and take out old ones, and do not notify us at all. In my opinion, the hydrants should be in charge of the Chief Engineer of the Fire Department. We pay the Water Department twelve dollars a year for each hydrant of which they have charge. It don't amount to anything. It is only the putting of a little salt-marsh hay around them in the fall and taking it away in the spring.

Q. Are you satisfied or dissatisfied with the conduct of the Chief Engineer at the fire?

A. I certainly am satisfied. I think he did all that any mortal man could do after I arrived at the fire. What the situation of the fire was at the start, I don't know, except what I hear from reports.

Q. Was there anything which should have been different except in regard to the use of powder and the withdrawing of the apparatus to make way for the powder? Was there anything else about the fire which you would criticise?

A. No, sir. There is no other thing which I should criticise.

Q. From what you have seen of this fire, what in your judgment would have been the issue of it if the water-pipes had been double and triple size, and they had had the Lowry hydrant?

A. The only opinion I should have would be that the fire would not have extended over one-twentieth part of the territory it did extend over. That is what I should judge from the situation it was in when I arrived on the ground.

Q. Were you at the fire in Cornhill?

A. Yes, sir.

Q. Were you there early?

A. Yes, sir.

Q. Tell us why it was easier to subdue that fire than it was this fire.

A. I should say that it was on account of the situation of the building. There was a chance to get at two sides of that building and play right through and through it, which there was not at this other fire. When this fire at Tebbetts, Baldwin & Co.'s store was first arrived at, there was no chance to get in at the rear of it. We had got to get in at the front. Where you can get in on two sides of a fire, you can make your streams meet right over the ground.

I was at the State-street fire before any water was put on at all. Capt. Dunbar had charge of both fires, and I was right with him all the time, helping to get the line and hose in. I was with Capt. Ricker, and helped to get the line of hose up upon that State-street block. It is a building where we have stopped a fire once or twice before.

Q. Does the power of your committee end when you have made representations to the Water Board?

A. Yes, sir, that is the end of our power. We have no control at all any further than that — only we recommend to them that certain things should be done. I know that after the great fire at East Boston, we labored hard and incessantly to get the pipes enlarged over there, and it was only by persistent efforts that we did get it. The effect of that large fire at East Boston was to direct attention to the insufficiency of the water supply. The pipes were eight-inch pipes. I think those pipes in Franklin street and also those in Summer street were only six-inch pipes, and they were clotted up so that they would be only equal to five-inch.

Q. Has your attention been called to the explosion of gas at fires?

A. Yes, sir. That is why I am opposed to blowing up buildings. It breaks up gas-pipes and the gas lights right off and the fire blazes right up fresh, unless you have force enough to wet those ruins down at once.

Q. Should there not something be devised to shut off the gas?

A. Yes, sir, there should be a stop cock at the corner of every street, so that they can shut the gas right off; it is done in other cities. I have understood that the Gas Company attempted to adopt that method, and will do so after this. I believe they do go round in case of fire and shut the gas off in the basement of buildings. But they can only shut it off from one building at a time in that way. They can only shut it off at the base of each building.

Q. How long have you been connected with the Boston Fire Department?

A. I have been a member of the Boston Fire Department, directly or indirectly, about twenty-three years.

Adjourned to Wednesday evening.

WEDNESDAY NIGHT.

RUFUS B. FARRAR, *sworn.*

Q. (By Mr. Russell.) What position do you hold in the Fire Department?

A. I am Assistant Engineer.

Q. Where were you when the fire broke out?

A. I think I was pretty near Doctor Boyden's, on Myrtle street. I might have been opposite Barnard's stable.

Q. Was your attention first called by the alarm?

A. Yes, sir.

Q. Did you go to the fire at once?

A. Yes, sir.

Q. How long did it take you to get there?

A. I should think I was inside of five minutes. I might have been four minutes; it was a short distance.

Q. What was the condition of the building when you got there?

A. The three principal stories were all going, and the back side.

Q. The whole of the back side?

A. Yes, sir; I should judge it was, by the looks of the light.

Q. Did it burst out?

A. I passed by the building, and the roof and windows fell in.

Q. Were any engines or hose carriages there?

A. Yes, sir; there were two streams on the fire, one of them, I think, was Engine 7; the other, Hose 2; I will not be sure.

Q. Were they at work then?

A. Yes, sir.

Q. Had Engine 7 got steam fully on?

A. I think she had. I didn't see her; she was round the corner; her stream came in the back way.

Q. Do you know how high the stream went?

A. I don't remember how high it did go. I don't know as I looked to see. I passed by the building.

Q. What did you do?

A. Went round up Kingston into Summer. I think the first apparatus I came across was Hose Engine 9, of South Boston, just drawing in, and I immediately got them at work.

Q. Where did they work?

A. They were attached to an engine in the Church Green; it was probably ten or fifteen minutes before we got them where we wanted to. I went up into a high building, — six or seven stories high, I should think, — and got a hose on to the roof.

Q. What building was that?

A. That was the building that faced Church Green.

Q. On the north side of Summer street?

A. As you go down Summer street, on the right-hand side, where the church used to stand.

Q. You got a hose on to the top of that?

A. Yes, sir.

Q. Where did you throw water?

A. Into the corner building; and as the fire increased it drove me back from time to time. I made a very good stand on the second building from the corner, because it was a little lower than the rest, and the brick wall came up there some eighteen inches; I should think this building was eighteen inches lower than the rest, so that the brick wall would be up eighteen inches. I was here reinforced by another stream, by Captain Clark, Assistant Engineer. He stayed there until the building on the opposite side got on fire; and I found the flames lapped round into the building I was on. I took the stream down and made the best fight I could, but was driven further along.

Q. What time was it when you withdrew?

A. I could not tell; I had no idea of time that night, more than a child.

Q. You kept falling back before the fire?

A. I made my last stand just below that long, low brick building on the corner of Pearl and Broad streets, — the lower street next the water. That is where the oil was kept. After I was driven down from this, some other engineer took the stream and went up to another place, and I went down a little further, and took No. 19 engine (she was just getting at work; she has to come nine miles), and made a very good stand in several places. I think six times I made her up, and at the foot of Pearl street she broke down. Her pump or something gave out. She is a small engine.

Q. Where did she come from?

A. She belongs out in Mattapan. It is a Boston engine. It caught from there on the oil store. Pearl street was on fire on both sides. As fast as the fire struck the buildings the stones began to fall, and we could not make any fight. I went down into Broad street and found Captain Scott, who said, "I have got a steam tug and I think I can cut the fire off here," and I made a good stand there at that time. Engine No. 2 of Cambridge came in — a splendid steamer with a splendid set of men. I took her, and got her at work, at the lower end of Oliver street. I thought I would make a good stand, there and I sent a man clear to Hose 2's hose, on Tyler street, to get a reducer. He was probably gone three quarters of an hour, or half an hour, before he came back. I then put No. 2 at work, and she took one side of the street, and the tug took the other side. The buildings were but one story high. This was on Broad street, and there we fought it for about four hours, and stopped it there, near the foot of Pearl street. As you go down Pearl street by turning to the left you will see where it was stopped. It is between Oliver and Pearl. That is where I made my stand. The oil store was full of oil, and of course you can never put oil out. The heat there was very severe, but we managed to stand it.

Q. For about an hour that Cambridge engine stood still for want of a reducer?

A. I should think for about three-quarters of an hour. I had to get a man, and send him up there. That was no fault of theirs, that their connections were not right. I had that company with me all the next day, and I don't want a better company, or a better-disciplined company.

Q. How did the men behave that night?

A. Splendidly, so far as they came under my observation.

Q. Were there any exceptions?

A. None that I knew of; none that came under my observation.

Q. Were any Boston firemen, that night, or the next morning, intoxicated?

A. No, sir.

Q. When did you see the Chief first that night?

A. I think he got there about the same time I did. I will not be certain. I think I heard his voice. I don't know that I saw him, but I heard his voice. I know him very well.

Q. Did you see anything more of him that night?

A. Once, when I was up in High street, putting No. 19 to work. The second time he came round, and asked me how I was getting along. I told him the best I could, being driven handsomely.

Q. What was his manner?

A. He was cool and collected, more so than I ever saw him at a fire.

Q. Was he hopeful when you saw him? What were his expectations?

A. He didn't state anything to me. He asked what I was doing; and I told him, "Doing the best I can."

Q. Did you have any trouble, that night, from want of water?

A. I did not.

Q. Or fuel?

A. We got out of fuel once or twice.

Q. Did you stop for want of it?

A. No, sir; we used boxes, or anything we could lay our hands on.

Q. You didn't suffer for want of fuel?

A. No, sir. When I was in Broad street, No. 2 was out of fuel, and I immediately stepped across the street, on the wharf, and took all I wanted. There was no trouble about fuel down that way.

Q. Did you see any gunpowder explosions that night?

A. No, sir.

Q. Was not the store next to the oil store blown up, on Broad street?

A. No, sir. I would not allow it to be done.

Q. Did anybody try it?

A. They wanted to, but I said, "I can stop the fire here. I have force enough."

Q. Who wanted to blow it up?

A. A gentleman belonging to the City Council.

Q. When did you see the Chief again?

A. I saw the Chief when I had got the fire almost out. He came down to see me.

Q. Did the person who wished to blow up the building show you his authority?

A. Yes, sir.

Q. Did you read it?

A. I saw the signature. I didn't look at it much, but I read it.

Q. The Chief's signature?

A. The Chief's signature was on it, and I think there was another one.

Q. Didn't it represent that it was to be done under the direction of the Engineer?

A. Yes, sir.
Q. You didn't see fit to give such directions?
A. I thought I could stop the fire. I had had no experience with gunpowder. I never fired a gun but once in my life.
Q. Did he ask your judgment?
A. Yes, sir. He put it in this form: He said he thought he could stop the fire by blowing up that building, and I said I thought I could stop it without.
Q. You spoke of the trouble with the granite. Describe the effect of the fire on the granite.
A. The moment the fire strikes the granite, it begins to crumble and fall off.
Q. How large pieces?
A. All the way from as big as your fist to pieces weighing one hundred and fifty to two hundred pounds, according to what the coping is made of, and how many projections there are under the caps.
Q. Does that happen when you don't throw on water?
A. Yes, sir.
Q. Of what size do you say?
A. From as big as your fist — small pieces — up to two or three hundred pounds. I saw it that night. I had seen it before, but that night it astonished me. I never saw so much of it before.
Q. Have you seen it in that way, to some extent, in other places?
A. It always does.
Q. You never saw so large pieces?
A. No, sir.
Q. Was there any more than the usual trouble about the hose?
A. No trouble at all about the hose.
Q. So far as you know, the hose behaved perfectly well?
A. It behaved splendidly. We have a splendid lot of hose.
Q. Whose leather hose is the best?
A. We get most of ours from Boyd — double riveted hose; tested, I think, at two hundred and eighty. I will not be sure. The Chief knows better than I do. It is all tested before we accept it.
Q. All kinds of hose?
A. Nothing but leather that ever I know.
Q. You were at the Cornhill fire?
A. Yes, sir.
Q. State why that was more controllable than this.
A. I can state what I did.
Q. I don't want to go into particulars.
A. When I got to the fire — I knew, very well, the building, and knew there was some heft in it, — I came across a gentleman who is foreman of the shop, down below the fire, and he says, "If you will take a stream up, I can show you a little hole in the last story where you can bear upon the fire, if you are quick." We had plenty of water, and I put a stream in there, and immediately got another one up; and we saved it. We had no stone to fall on the men on the back or front, and one hose was there before the alarm was given; it was No. 4. I had No. 8's stream.
Q. Water was plenty?

A. Water was plenty. There are a great many hydrants in that neighborhood.

Q. Did you have any scarcity of water in Summer street, before you were driven off?

A. No, sir. I went up into that building, — you probably remember how high it was — and I took No. 9's stream up certainly six flights; I should say that building was eighty-five feet high. I went up, and hauled it up four stories with a life-line, and then took it up two more flights, out of the scuttle and along one hundred and fifty feet to meet the fire, and I got a stream that played certainly fifty feet.

Q. Where did that stream draw from?

A. From an engine at the reservoir in Church Green. The reservoir was supplied with a four-inch pipe.

Q. How much does that reservoir hold?

A. It is full, always.

Q. What is its capacity?

A. I have forgotten the capacity of it. I don't know about all the reservoirs. It is quite a task to remember them all. It is a good-size reservoir, a little larger than the majority.

Q. Your engine was the only one drawing from that reservoir?

A. There were four drawing from that reservoir. You understand, the moment we set an engine at work, we turn a faucet and let the water in. We had five engines on the State-street reservoir without trouble.

Q. Will a four-inch pipe supply water as fast as four or five engines would use it?

A. Yes, sir; there is usually a good deal of holding on, and shifting hose; sometimes all the engines would hold on for five minutes.

Q. It depends a good deal upon the size of the street main from which it is drawn?

A. Yes, sir.

Q. You say in State street you had four engines on one reservoir?

A. Five; I put five engines to work.

Q. How long?

A. All day; I was in the Post Office all day.

Q. Is that reservoir any larger than the one in Summer street?

A. I think it is larger.

Q. You must have drawn it down if it had not been for the supply?

A. I shifted the streams often; and there were times when we were not playing. I was on the dome, part of the time. I had just crawled over the dome before it fell, and came very near going down with it.

Q. What dome was that?

A. The back part of the Merchants' Exchange.

Q. Engine No. 2 went round there with you?

A. Yes, sir.

Q. What time did you go home?

A. Sometime Monday forenoon. All the big fire was not anything to the Monday morning fire. I never went through anything like that, and don't want to again.

Q. At the head of Summer street, you mean?

A. Yes, sir. One of the buildings that had a granite front (the seven or eight country companies there, and they were not used to such things as that. I ran back into the centre of the street; at the corner of Washington and Summer streets the sewer cover went up and broke in two, but didn't happen to strike me; if it had, I guess I should have been gone now. I began to get a little grain shaky, and wished I was at home. We had the same trouble there in putting the country engines at work. For one hour I worked with Capt. Clark, and never worked so hard in my life. It was nothing but fight.

Q. Hadn't those companies been at work previously?

A. Some of them had. The New Haven company came in at about one o'clock and reported to me, with forty or fifty men, to go to work, and I put them to work. They happened to fit by taking a big wrench and making the connection. How they ever got it off, I don't know.

Q. The explosion made a cleaner sweep than you were used to?

A. A little cleaner than I ever saw; it left it a perfect shell.

Q. You have seen gas explosions?

A. Some.

Q. What did you do?

A. I went down to the Gas Company's office and ordered the gas shut off. Captain Green and I were of the same mind, and I went and ordered it shut off.

A. I do, considering the material we had to work with. If they had fitted the hydrants the same as we do, we should never have lost the corner building; but the delay in getting couplings prevented our stopping the fire. I had to go to the hose-carriages and find out if they had spare reducers; and it all took time.

Q. You consider that fight there a splendid achievement?

Q. Did you see the fire when it crossed Summer, on the corner of Otis, right opposite the building where it first took?

A. I was on top of the other building and could see it there.

Q. Was everything done to stay the progress of the fire there?

A. Everything was done that could be done. There were lines of hose on both sides of the building, and some in it; and the hose was lost. A splendid fight was made there.

Q. Did you consider that that might be the key to the fire?

A. That is what we considered. We thought we could stop it there.

Q. You think everything was done that could have been done?

A. I think everything was done that mortal man could do.

Q. What was your conclusion about that Monday-morning fire? Where was the mistake? Where was the omission there?

A. There was no mistake made.

Q. There was a mistake somewhere in letting the gas get in?

A. I don't know about that. I could not tell. I presume it slipped the mind of everybody. I did not think of it at the time.

Q. The only remedy would be to shut it off from Boston?

A. From the whole city. I ordered it shut off from the whole city. I smallest stones weighing three tons) was blown out clean. We had gave the order immediately after the third explosion, when the cesspool cover went up; I thought it was about time.

Q. Did you go to West street?

A. Yes, sir.

Q. Where did they have to go to do it?

A. I don't know, sir.

Q. Where were you when the alarm for Monday-morning's fire was given?

A. I was up this way somewhere. I think I was just coming out of the Post Office, or up Court street. I was going round that way. I think I had just seen the Chief and told him I would go home and get on a dry pair of boots — I was wet through. He said, "We will look around and see how things are going on, and if everything is right, you had better slip up and get some clothes" (I live in Revere street); but I didn't have an opportunity.

Q. How long were you in the Post Office?

A. All day, and part of the night.

Q. On Sunday?

A. Yes, sir. Captain Shaw was with me part of the time, — a good part of the time.

Q. Was General Burt there?

A. I don't know him. I saw no official there except one who was not going to let me in. I threw him about twenty feet.

Q. He declined to let you in?

A. I had considerable trouble in getting in. I didn't want to strike anybody, or shoot anybody, but I took him by the collar, finding I could harness him pretty well, and I got in and stayed there.

Q. You don't recollect that any of the gentlemen attached to the Post Office were there?

A. I know one gentleman, by the name of Appleton, who was there all day, and acted in a very gentlemanly manner; he showed me where I could get in through several places. He had the iron doors opened. They were not going to open the iron doors, but he got them open for us.

Q. He was the only one that belonged to the Post Office that you recognized?

A. Yes, sir; he worked very well all day long. By the way, in the forenoon, I had the Watertown Arsenal company there; they worked splendidly under the hands of a Lieutenant of the United States Army; they were all fresh and they did an immense deal of good.

Q. Did you have anything to do with any of the out-of-town companies except Cambridge?

A. On Monday morning, some seven or eight of them I got to work, and showed them where to find the hydrants.

Q. How was it with these as to behavior?

A. They behaved very well after we got them to work. They were a little afraid of the gas, and I had to tell them it was shut off from the city.

Q. Do you remember what companies they were?

A. No, sir; it was very dark, and I don't remember what companies they were.

Q. Did you see the men about Hovey's building at any time?

A. I saw some gentlemen up there.

Q. How do you suppose the gas got into that building to make that explosion?

A. I don't know. We have had several gas explosions that acted very queerly. I can tell of one that acted very queerly.

Q. That at the North End? The one that blew up in Blackstone street?

A. Yes, sir. That was the most singular thing I ever saw.

Q. What was the distance between the fire and the place of the explosion? As I understand it, you were fighting at one end, and it blew up at the other; what was the distance between the two ends?

A. It was across the street, certainly, fifty feet. At that distance, it lifted up a sidewalk stone that weighed three tons. I measured it.

JOSEPH DUNBAR, *sworn.*

Q. (By Mr. Russell.) You stand next to Captain Damrell?

A. Yes, sir.

Q. You take his place when he is absent?

A. Yes, sir.

Q. Where were you when the alarm was given?

A. In East Boston.

Q. At what time did you reach the fire?

A. I have no mode of fixing it exactly. I should judge about twenty or twenty-five minutes after the first alarm was given.

Q. What was the condition when you got there?

A. I found it was on Summer street, and had crossed over. It was on both sides of the street when I got there.

Q. Did the engines that came there, come fast or slow?

A. The engine I came with came very quickly.

Q. With horses?

A. No, sir.

Q. What engine was that?

A. Number 9.

Q. Where does that come from?

A. It is located in Paris street, East Boston.

Q. How much longer did it take than if it had had horses?

A. The way we started that evening, I think we were quicker than though we had horses. I should wish to explain that, however. If we had horses, we should not have started until the third alarm for that box, but I started on the second alarm — at twenty-nine minutes past seven. The third alarm would probably have come five minutes later; so I started five minutes sooner than if I had had horses.

Q. How long do you calculate it took you to reach the spot?

A. I should judge less than twenty minutes.

Q. Had the engine arrived when you got there?

A. I went with them. On the first alarm, I went to the engine-house, and we started on the second; and I should judge that from the time I started until I got there would be twenty minutes.

Q. Did your hose go on ahead of you?
A. No, sir, it was attached to the engine.
Q. You found the ferry-boat all ready to start?
A. They had the ferry-boat ready for us. We had no delay at all in getting over. We might have been sooner, but I have no particular means of knowing. We went as fast as we could run the whole distance.
Q. Did you notice any of the other engines as to whether they came fast or slow?
A. No, sir.
Q. What force had you on the engine? How many people?
A. I should judge there were fifty to seventy-five.
Q. Did the same ones run through with you?
A. Yes, sir.
Q. You got volunteers when the horses were given up?
A. Yes, sir.
Q. How many did you enroll?
A. About double the number of the company.
Q. How many would that be?
A. That would be twenty-two.
Q. Twenty-two more, or eleven more?
A. Eleven more.
Q. Where did the seventy-five come from?
A. It was generally understood there, — the state we were in; they seemed to be on the alert, everybody ready to give assistance.
Q. Did you see then that the fire was a threatening one?
A. I was in Mr. Seaver's store (having some business with him) when the alarm was given; I crossed over to the square and saw the light of the fire. The square is very wide there.
Q. What did you do when you got there? Where did you work?
A. I immediately went to work.
Q. Where?
A. On Summer street, and on Bedford street, and Winthrop square.
Q. Did you see any hose carried to the roofs of buildings?
A. I carried a number of lines of hose inside of buildings.
Q. Any of them up on to the roofs of houses?
A. I don't recollect, sir. I think not at that time.
Q. Did you use them from the windows across the street to other buildings?
A. Yes, sir.
Q. Did you have any trouble from the want of water that night?
A. I think it was not quite as good on Summer street.
Q. Did you have any trouble from want of fuel?
A. There might have been. I think there might have been at some parts of the fire, where there were boxes used.
Q. Did you see any lack of steam for want of fuel?
A. No, sir; I did not notice. There were boxes broken up. It is mighty apt to be the case in a fire of that kind, that you can't get round on the territory with your coal wagons.
Q. Did you ever know that to happen before at a fire in Boston since you have had steamers?

A. I don't know as I have. I have heard a great call sometimes for the fuel wagon. That oftentimes might be the case.

Q. You would not say there was much trouble from fuel as long as you had boxes to burn?

A. No, sir.

Q. There was no lack of steam?

A. No, sir; not to my knowledge. Sometimes the fuel wagon can't get around in season, although they do all they possibly can.

Q. Was there any trouble about hose that night?

A. No, sir; the department was well equipped with hose. I never saw it in better order than at that fire.

Q. How did the men behave?

A. Well; I never saw any drunkenness or anything of the kind during the fire. They were all prompt.

Q. Where did you first see the Chief that night?

A. I saw him on Winthrop square.

Q. How was he; cool, or otherwise?

A. He was very cool.

Q. Did you have any consultation with him that night, or at any time?

A. I did, on Otis street, I think.

Q. Can you tell about what time?

A. I can't recollect about the time. It must have been the first part of the evening. It might have been ten or eleven o'clock. I have not much recollection about the time.

Q. What was the amount of your consultation?

A. I think the fire was going through Otis street — if I recollect about the street — and I spoke to him about making a gap. What I meant was about blowing up the buildings.

Q. What did he say?

A. He said he had considered it, and thought of it, but didn't know where to strike — where to make a gap — to blow up; I suppose that is what he meant.

Q. Was not this the amount of what he said: "That he had considered it, but did not know where it could be done to advantage"?

A. I think about that; something of that kind.

Q. What did you say to that?

A. I told him I thought we could get our forces and make a battery. What I meant was to bring our engines together and make a battery down that street so as to keep the fire from crossing Pearl street; and I immediately went to work to do so; but everything failed and drove me along.

Q. Where did you go next?

A. My attention was then called to the fire crossing down Federal street, and that way; and I had orders then from the Chief that he wanted to see me.

Q. Did you see him?

A. I saw him after considerable time. I found him on Federal street, I think it was.

Q. Any one with him?

A. No, sir; he was alone.

Q. What consultation did you have there?

A. I spoke with him, and he said he was waiting for other members of the Board to come up to have a consultation about blowing up the buildings.

Q. Can you tell about what time that was?

A. No, sir, I could not.

Q. Did the other members come?

A. No, sir. I waited there some time, I could not tell how long; and I told him I thought my presence was needed on Washington street; and I went up to Washington street.

Q. What did you do there?

A. I went onto Franklin street, and found the firemen somewhere near the "Pilot" building. The fire was working its way on both sides of the street. I gave them my encouragement, and told them our greatest fight would be the Marlboro' Hotel. If it crossed there, it would take City Hall, and we must take our stand there and fight it; and we did so.

Q. At that time how many streams did you have?

A. I could not exactly say, but there might have been six. I could not say how many. We kept adding to them after a while.

Q. How long were you there?

A. I was there until I found everything was safe.

Q. When was that?

A. It must have been along towards daylight. After I found the Old South was safe, I left it and went into the "Boston Post" building and carried a stream of water in there.

Q. After the fire was stopped there, where did you go then?

A. I went on to Devonshire street.

Q. Was that the last place?

A. I think that was the last building I was in; that began to be along towards noon, I think, on Sunday.

Q. Did you have any experience with gunpowder, that night?

A. I was on Kilby street when one building was blown up — when they tried to blow it up, but it didn't amount to anything. I heard reports very often.

Q. Were you at the Monday-night fire?

A. No, sir.

Q. Were you at the State-street block fire and the Cornhill fire?

A. Yes, sir.

Q. What was the reason that those fires were controlled so much more easily than this?

A. The State-street block was a great deal better built than those on Summer street; or I consider it so.

Q. In what respect — party-walls?

A. Yes, sir. We had both sides of the building to work on, and we carried our lines of hose up, and through the scuttle, and could work on the building safer, and easier for the men.

Q. How was it at the Cornhill fire; how did that compare with this one.

A. At the Cornhill fire, we had both sides to work on.

Q. And had more water?

A. I think there was. I think there was a better supply.

Q. Did you see any engine that night out of employment?

A. Well, sir, I saw none of our engines out of employment; the engines that came from out of town would not connect, and that made some delay.

Q. None of the Boston engines?

A. Not to my knowledge; everything worked perfectly.

Q. When you first got on to the fire ground you say the fire was on both sides of the street. Did you notice the building at the corner of Otis and Summer streets, what the state of things there was?

A. I think the fire did not reach there for some time afterwards, if I recollect aright.

Q. Did you hear anything said about it, or think about it, whether or not that was the key to the fire; and that if you could stop it there, you could control the further spread of it?

A. When I first noticed the building particularly, I think the fire then was working down Winthrop street.

Q. Had it got past the corner?

A. Yes, sir. I recollect of telling Engineer 6 that they must look out well for the engine; that that building would soon go. I think I made that remark to him.

Q. Did it occur to you that a stand could be made in Franklin street, where the street is so wide, to prevent its crossing?

A. The fire then was working both ways; working up towards Washington street and towards South Boston.

Q. How did it get across the wide part of Franklin street, down in the square?

A. There were so many buildings there on fire I do declare I could not tell you how it worked.

Q. You don't know that it crossed the wide part?

A. I could not say. It worked in the rear, and down among the ells, and then along the fronts. I don't know but that I went into fifty buildings where we would have hard work to get out, the fire would get in so quick.

Q. Do you think the fire was controlled by the department as well as it could have been under the circumstances?

A. Yes, sir. I don't know of anything but that worked well.

Q. How did the Chief appear?

A. Whenever I saw the Chief he was not excited in the least; he was very calm; more than I should have been, I think, under the circumstances.

Q. You say you waited on Federal street with him for some one to come, and finally left him to attend to another matter; while you were standing with him did he consult with you about the use of gunpowder?

A. I told him I had come there at the request of the messenger to see him, and he said he wanted to call the Board together and consult about this matter of blowing up the buildings. I waited there as long as I could.

Q. While waiting there was there no conversation between you?

A. No, sir; he stood in front of those large buildings that were burning. He was very calm indeed.

Q. How long have you been connected with the Fire Department?

A. Thirty-two years, in the Boston and Charlestown Fire Departments.

ZENAS E. SMITH, *sworn.*

Q. (By Mr. Russell.) Where were you when you heard the alarm for the great fire?

A. I was at my shop, 65 Wareham street.

Q. How long did it take you to reach the fire?

A. At that box, I don't go until the second alarm.

Q. How long did it take you to reach the fire?

A. I was in my shop when the first alarm came, and had just got through my business. I put on my coat, went to the ladder-house at the corner of Harrison avenue and Wareham street, and just as I got there, the second alarm came in and we started.

Q. How long did it take you to get there?

A. I should think perhaps ten minutes from that time I was at the fire.

Q. What was the condition of the fire then?

A. The fire was coming out of all the windows on the Kingston-street side, I think, from the first story to the roof.

Q. Did you notice whether there were any engines there?

A. I could not say. There were none in Kingston street.

Q. If you saw the engines coming in, did they come fast or slow?

A. No. 3 came in right behind me, or perhaps a second later. I assisted them in connecting with the hydrant. I had great difficulty in keeping the people from the sidewalk enough for them to get their engine attached. I never had so much trouble, or came so near getting into a fight.

Q. Where did you connect it?

A. I connected it on the corner of Kingston and Bedford streets.

Q. Where does No. 3 come from?

A. From Washington street, just above Dover.

Q. At what rate did they come?

A. I don't know as I could tell you that. I didn't come in contact with them until I got there. I came from just above them. I was at the ladder-house just above them; and they came in just behind us.

Q. Did you come down on the trot yourself?

A. Yes, sir; a good smart trot.

Q. That engine got there very soon after you did?

A. Yes, sir. I was a little above them. I went down the street with them. There were about one hundred men on the truck.

Q. How did they travel?

A. It went very fast; full as fast as I could run.

Q. How much time do you suppose they lost from not taking horses on the ladder truck?

A. I don't know. I don't think there was more than four minutes' difference.

Q. What did you do after you got that engine at work?

A. I remained right there in the street with that stream on to the fire for a while, and then we found the building opposite was catching fire and we took a line into that building.

Q. On the other side of Summer street?

A. No, sir; on Kingston street. I did not go into Summer street until an hour and a half or two hours after, and when I went I went on at the head of Chauncey street. The fire was so hot soon after we got No. 3 into this building opposite, that it burned the hose, and it burst, and the men had to get out at the back of the building; they could not get out of the front, it was so hot.

Q. You lost your hose?

A. Yes, sir, a portion of it. I then went from there to Chauncey street to see what chance I could get in the rear, and I found there was a pretty good chance and came directly back and got some ladders, and went round right in the rear of this building, and put some ladders on the back of a Summer-street store, and took streams in from Chauncey street, and put out the fire in this building; then I took a stream right on top of a Summer-street store to cover the corner. There were two low buildings on the corner of Summer and Kingston, and I thought I could cover those and prevent its coming any further this way; and after we had worked there awhile we found the fire was opposite us, on Summer street, and it was setting the store on fire that we were on top of, and we had to let our hose down; then we thought we would make a fight on the third floor and keep it out; but it had got such a hold it drove us out and we had to jump out of the windows on to the back shed. They had thrown out a good many goods; some lit very easily. Then I changed this stream into the new building that ran from Chauncey street, and also went into Chauncey street and took a stream into the building opposite. Captain Green and myself went into the corner and took a line into the corner-store on Chauncey street, hoping we could keep it from getting a-fire. We went on to the roof with it, and I commenced in the attic and moved some cases of cloth back from the windows, thinking if I could keep them back a little ways we might possibly save them. I did that, and went on the next floor and did the same thing. In the mean time, the stream went down, and Captain Green says, "Who ordered the stream down?" I said, "I don't know." He said, "The men say an Engineer ordered the stream down." I said I did not know who it was. The fire got such a hold there we were obliged to go out. We put streams opposite, on what used to be the Post Office building [Mr. Capen's P. O.], and fought it the best we could. I could not tell what time it was; and then the Chief sent for me. A messenger came and wanted I should meet him in Federal street. I didn't take any notice of it. I don't remember who this person was — whether he was a fireman or a citizen. I felt my position was very important. It was something I had a great deal of interest in, and I was in hopes I could secure that point and prevent its going any further on Summer street, on that side, so I didn't heed the order immediately, and in about twenty minutes to half an hour one of the Engineers came and said, "The Chief said, 'Come immediately! and wait for nothing.'" I then started and went to the point ordered and met the Chief.

Q. What consultation did you have?

A. There were two or three others there and the Mayor. He called us into a store there, and said he had called us together to consider the matter of using powder. He said, "Captain Smith, what do you say?" Said I, "Mr. Chief, I think we must use it, or we shall be censured very much, I think;" and that seemed to be the opinion of all; and it was decided to use it, or allow its use. I said to him, as we came out, "I left a point that I hated to leave and I would like to return there. Shall I go?" He said, "I want you to remain here and assist here," and I remained there and assisted what I could; and in a very few minutes he came along and said, "I want you to go down on the wharf, and get a tug-boat and go on to the flat to the powder boat and get powder;" and I went as fast as I could to the end of the wharf, and there was a tug-boat passed just before I got to the end of the wharf; Captain Hebard was with me. We made out to make him hear us, and the tug-boat immediately stopped and came up alongside. We got on board and went down to the powder boat with the intention of raising the anchor, or unshipping it so we could take it right up, but we could do neither; but we took the hatches off, and got a quantity on board of the boat, and got it up, and some of the police came to the boat while we were there, and we worked in concert and got it up to the fire.

Q. How much did you bring up?

A. I think, twenty-five or thirty kegs.

Q. Twenty-five pound kegs?

A. Yes, sir.

Q. To what point did you carry it?

A. We brought it into Liberty square, I think, so far as my memory serves me. The police were with us. We put it into a wagon when we got to the wharf, and brought it up by hand.

Q. The wagon was drawn by men?

A. Yes, sir; the policemen and us. We drew it up.

Q. Did you have anything to cover it with?

A. We had not in the wagon, but we had on the boat.

Q. Were not the sparks flying about you?

A. I don't know. We didn't seem to fear it.

Q. Were the kegs tight?

A. I don't know whether they were or not; but I know two that were tight, on Kilby street, or that I guess were tight, because I saw them taken out whole from where they had been exploding, pretty well scorched about the chimes and hoops. After that, Mr. Carpenter, with some men who were said to be scientific men, said to the Chief, "This powder don't amount to anything. The place to get powder is at the Navy Yard." The Chief turned to me and said, "Captain Smith, take the first team you can get, go to the Navy Yard and get powder." I did so. It was a very long road. I hope I will never be sent on an errand there again in anything that is urgent. I got to the gate and rapped; a soldier on guard opened the gate and wanted to know what I wanted. I told him, and he told me to wait. After a while he went and called his officer. (I suppose he was a-bed and asleep, and he waited for him to dress.) Then I had to go with him up to the quarters in the centre of the yard, or wherever it was. The officer said he had no authority, but that we must go to the Commodore; the Commodore's house is right alongside of the gate. I had to go back to the gate with him and wait for him to report to his officer; and then we had to go to the Commodore's quarters. We went up there, to the Commodore's quarters, and found a watchman, and he took us into the house, and up stairs to the Commodore's room; woke him up and he came to the door. I told him my errand. He said, "I sent eight barrels at two o'clock." Said I, "They want more." "Well," he said, "take this man down to Capt. 'Somebody,' down to the lower end of the yard." And I had to go back to the gate to take my team in. They opened the gate, and I took the team in, and I supposed I was going to get the powder. We went to Capt. 'Somebody' and woke him up, and he came down and wrote me an order, and told me I would have to go over to Chelsea, to the magazine. I supposed, of course, I had got to go, and I did. I went over to Chelsea and banged away at the gate and woke another man up; he let us through the gate. We got through there in the course of twenty minutes, and then we went round to the magazine, and supposed he was going to open it; but he said, "I shall have to wait until the gunner comes." He said, "You saw him?" I said, "I saw a man that let us in at the gate, and that is all I have seen." "The devil!" said he; and he grabbed my paper (he was the only one that showed any disposition to move any faster than as though next week would do), and ran back for the gunner, and woke him up. He dressed and came out, and came along towards us, and the two men had got almost up to us, and I saw one of them start and run back again as fast as he could, and the other one came up and said the gunner got up, and dressed, and came out, and forgot to bring the keys of the house; however, he got there after a while, and we took eight barrels on to our wagon; and the Insurance Brigade wagon came there, in the mean time, and got six; and we came back.

Q. How large were those barrels?

A. One hundred pounds, I think.

Q. You took this wagon from Boston to start with?

A. Yes, sir. It proved to be a Chelsea man, or team.

Q. Had the insurance wagon followed you from Boston?

A. They didn't start for some time after we did, but they got along quicker after they got there; they found the road all broke.

Q. Have you any means of knowing how long it took you from the time you started until you got back?

A. I have no idea of the time. It went like lightning; still it seemed to me an age, waiting for them to move. From the time I went to that fire until eight o'clock Sunday morning, I saw no time, and I have no idea of it. There was a good deal of it that seems as though I did not know where I was; yet, from the time the Chief sent me, I was all the time until daylight after powder.

Q. You didn't get back with the load until daylight?

A. It was daylight and past, I think, when we got back. We came in then at the State-street end of Kilby street, I think it was, and stopped. I told the teamster to stop where he was. I didn't know where they wanted it. They had powder in the corner of Lindall and Kilby streets, and were telling them to stand back, and were waiting for an explosion; and directly they said they had better send the powder to the Custom House; and I think I told this man to take it down there. In the mean time this explosion occurred, but it did not throw the building down, only partially wrecked it; the front was tipped partly out, but did not fall; and in about five minutes, I should judge, the whole interior of the building was all a light flame. So it appeared to me that was pretty poor help. They went directly into the next building (it was an old brick building) and they put in, I would not say how many kegs, and fired that, and the hosemen didn't think, and Captain Green, who was present at the time, didn't think the powder had all exploded. The men said it had, and rather slurred us a little for being afraid to go in. Capt. Green said, "If you are sure it has exploded, you are not afraid to go in anyway." And finally two of them went in at the door. I don't know how far they went in; whether they went to where they put the powder or not, I don't know. They came out and said it was all right; and then the hosemen went in readily to put out the fire that had kindled, and as they came out they brought out two kegs of powder that had not exploded; and the chimes and hoops were considerably scorched; and the hairs on the firemen's heads were more like bristles than hair. I believe then these gentlemen, who were called scientific gentlemen, went away.

Q. Who were those people?

A. I knew Mr. Carpenter. The others I didn't know.

Q. Did Mr. Carpenter go into the building?

A. I think not. I think he stayed at the door; and those who were said to be scientific men, and who were to see to arranging it, and putting in the fuse, did the business so far as it was done. A short time after, twenty minutes or half an hour, some of the hosemen or firemen of one of the companies said to me, "Captain, they are going to blow up another building up above." Said I, "Where?" He said, "Up there, where the crowd is." That was a little this side of State street. I started and ran right up there. I saw Mr. Carpenter standing at the door. The door was open and the powder was in, and the man was about letting off his fuse. I said to Mr. Carpenter, "For God's sake, don't blow up any more buildings in this street! If you blow this building up, the fire will go to State street, just as true as you live. If you will go away, and let us alone, I will stop it where I am. I think it is pretty mean for you to come down here, and say nothing to us, and blow up buildings where you please." And I further said, "If that is the game, I think we had better go home." I didn't know I had any backers there until I got through saying that; but these men that brought the powder out just below were fully as much interested as I was; and the foreman of one of the companies speaks up to me and says, "Captain, if you say the word, the powder comes out." I said, "Hold on! I think I can get it out without any force or violence. I know Mr. Carpenter; and if he says he will take it out, I will trust him. He is a man of his word." And he said, "Captain, I will take it out!" And he did; and we went to work, then, with a relish, and stopped it below.

Q. Did you save that building?

A. Yes, sir.

Q. What building was that?

A. The one they were going to blow up?

Q. Yes, sir.

A. I don't know what door they went into. If you recollect, from the corner of State down to that freestone building, there is a building that has been built a good many years. It is a granite building; not very ornamental, on Kilby street, cornering on State street, and running down until it comes to this freestone building on the upper side. I was up on the tall building; I had three streams working on the Post Office. They were going to blow up the granite building that runs down to the freestone building.

Q. Do you know General Benham by sight?

A. No, sir; I don't. I suppose I saw him that night, but I don't think I should know him if I should see him now.

Q. Did you have any other experience with gunpowder?

A. I saw it used once or twice.

Q. Besides that?

A. I saw one or two explosions.

Q. Did they amount to anything?

A. No, sir.

Q. If you were to go into another fire of this kind would you advise the use of powder?

A. Not unless it was used differently from what it was used there. I will not say but what it may be used; but I do say all I saw used hurt us very much.

Q. Did it do more harm than good?

A. Yes, sir. It will take a good deal of time, in my judgment, and a good deal of labor, to do this thing effectually. To begin with, you want to have a large number of men; and you want lots of plank and joist; and then you want to shut the gas off. When you explode a building, you knock all the gas fixtures to pieces, and have the gas rushing in all on fire. I don't think, and I have heard other men say the same thing, after the explosion on the corner of Kilby and Lindall streets, that it was over five minutes before the whole material of that building was all in a blaze.

Q. Did that reduce the height of the building much? Did the roof come down?

A. I guess it broke the roof down. I think we could have covered that building. I think it would have been standing this minute unharmed if there had been no powder put in it.

Q. Did you see any lack of water that night?

A. I don't think I did, where I was.

Q. Did you see any of the steam engines — our engines — doing nothing? — disengaged?

A. No, sir; not any while I was there. I was away a good while, and I have felt a good many times since as though I had not done all I could, but still I did. Of course I had to go where I was sent.

Q. Did you see any want of fuel?

A. No, sir.

Q. How did the men behave?

A. Our own department I could not say a word against. I did not see one of our whole department that flinched or was intoxicated either; but I did see some others that were; and in Congress street, I guess it was sometime Sunday forenoon, I took three or four bottles away from an out-of-town fireman. I felt as though he was disgracing us as well as himself, and I went and spoke to him — he was staggering about with a bottle in his hand and others in his pocket — and I spoke to him pleasantly. I said, "My friend, throw that away. You are disgracing yourself and all your friends." He said he would not, and I finally took one out of his pocket, another one from another pocket, — took three out in all, — and I turned round and smashed them right before his eyes.

Q. Did you see the fire cross Summer street, to the corner of Otis?

A. No, sir.

Q. You don't know anything about what kind of a stand was made there?

A. I don't know anything that was done on Summer street. I was pretty busy trying to see what I could do in Kingston street. I then whipped round into Chauncey street, to see if I could head it off there.

Q. How long have you been a fireman?

A. I have been engaged in the department twenty-nine years; between fourteen and fifteen years as Assistant Engineer.

Q. What time did you go home on Sunday?

A. I didn't go home Sunday.

Q. Were you out on duty all through Sunday?

A. Yes, sir.

Q. Where were you during the Monday-morning fire?

A. I was on Kilby street when the alarm was given, about twelve o'clock Sunday night, and I did not see my home from Saturday until Monday morning at five o'clock; and I was really glad to get home then.

GEORGE BROWN, Assistant Engineer, *sworn.*

Q. (By Mr. Russell.) How long have you been connected with the Fire Department?

A. Twenty-five years.

Q. Where were you when the alarm was given?

A. South Boston.

Q. How soon did you come?

A. I probably arrived there within twelve or fifteen minutes after the first alarm was given.

Q. What was the condition of the fire when you came?

A. The fire then was raging very badly in the building that it took in, and also in the back part of the building or area. I suppose it went into the back area.

Q. What did you do?

A. I found three or four streams there and I conducted those to the best of my ability, as well as I could.

Q. Where did you go from there?

A. I went from there around on to Chauncey street. I stayed there a few moments, and I went back again; but we had to haul back from where we were playing, back to Church Green.

Q. With what engines?

A. There were three companies there then, 7, 1 and 9, I think they were.

Q. Were you there when the fire crossed Summer over towards Otis street?

A. Yes, sir.

Q. What sort of a fight was made there to prevent its crossing?

A. That was above me. I was below Church Green, and this was above.

Q. After you were driven away from this spot where did you fight next?

A. Down in Winthrop square. We took the next stand at Beebe's building.

Q. How many streams were there on that building?

A. After I shifted down there in the square?

Q. Yes, sir.

A. Really, I don't know as I could tell for a certainty. There must have been at that time, or at one time I think, we must have had six streams there, certainly.

Q. On Beebe's building?

A. Beebe's block and the adjoining building.

Q. Where did you go next?

A. Then I was up in the store which I think was occupied by Skinner & Co. I will not be sure. It was in the rear of the little building that was built in the square. There was a vacant lot there for several years; and they put up a three-cornered building there. I thought that would be a good shelter from the intense heat from Beebe's building; and I took two streams; one up on to the roof of that building, and one to the story below. That building sheltered us for some time. The building we were in was fired several times, but we succeeded in putting it out; and we stayed there until we were finally driven out; and then we hauled the hose down to Federal street through Franklin.

Q. Where did you go next?

A. Across Federal street. I met the Chief at Federal street, and he thought we would make a stand there; but it was impossible to get the force to make a stand there at that time — the force then had got separated.

Q. Where did you go next?

A. Then the Chief said we must make a stand up Pearl street. Capt. Dunbar was there with me, and he went one way and I went another. I then went down to the foot of Pearl street, and from that point I could not go back, and I made a stand there with the force I found there.

Q. How did you succeed there?

A. We stopped it there with the loss of the Hartford and Erie depot. It was a very great point to make; there were a lot of old stables and old wooden buildings in the rear which we were afraid would take fire.

Q. Where did you go after that?

A. After we got the fire checked there the Chief came round and requested me to go to Liberty square and that vicinity. I had to go up to Washington street to get down there.

Q. What did you do there?

A. There I went to work as usual.

Q. Where did you go next?

A. I stayed there until along Sunday forenoon, and checked the fire on Central street.

Q. What time did you go home?

A. I got home Sunday night about eleven o'clock.

Q. Was there any deficiency of water that night where you were?

A. Not that I noticed; no more than would naturally occur with so many hydrants and reservoirs being used.

Q. Was there any want of fuel?

A. Yes, sir; there was at times a want of fuel, for the reason the apparatus were so distributed about that it was almost impossible for the fuel wagon to get round.

Q. Did any of the engines stop for want of fuel; or did they make their fire from something else?

A. I don't know of any that stopped. They used old boxes or whatever they could find that would burn.

Q. How did the men behave?

A. Well.

Q. Did you have any trouble with them?

A. No, sir.

Q. Was there any cowardice?

A. No, sir. I never saw the men behave better; they could not behave better.

Q. Were any of them intoxicated?

A. I saw none of the Boston Department intoxicated.

Q. Did you see the Chief, and how many times? Did you see him that night?

A. I saw him, probably, a dozen times.

Q. Was he self-possessed?

A. Yes, sir, he appeared to be very much so, indeed.

Q. Did you have any consultation with him about gunpowder?

A. I did not.

Q. You did not have any experience with it?

A. I never had had any experience.

Q. Did you that night?

A. After I got round on that side of the fire, I saw one or two buildings that they were attempting to blow up.

Q. Did it do any good?

A. Not in my opinion.

Q. Did you see any building that actually fell?

A. I saw the building at the corner of Water and Congress streets.

Q. How much of a fall was that?

A. That took the whole upper part; probably three or four stories.

Q. Was not that serviceable in reducing the height so it could be reached?

A. It may have been, possibly, but it left a large mass of *débris* there ready to catch fire at once.

Q. So far as you know, was the use of gunpowder that night beneficial, or otherwise?

A. I think it was detrimental. I didn't see any reason, really, to use it.

Q. Did you notice, when the engines came, whether they came fast or slow?

A. I didn't have an opportunity to see many of them come in; I was busy around the fire.

Q. How was it with your South Boston engines?

A. Three of my apparatuses came by the aid of horses, and three by hand.

Q. Which made the best time?

A. The two hose-carriages came by hand, and one steamer. These were the nearest ones to the fire, so you could hardly draw a line between them.

Q. Could you judge whether they lost much time in coming by hand?

A. Perhaps they did not come over so quickly as they would if the horses had been well, but they came a good deal quicker than the horses could have brought them at that time.

Q. You mean, as fast as sick horses could have brought them?

A. Yes, sir.

Q. Were they in your stables at South Boston?

A. In the stables there. We used three pair of borrowed horses.

S. H. HEBARD, *sworn*.

Q. (By Mr. Russell.) How long have you been connected with the Fire Department?

A. Since the annexation of Dorchester to Boston.

Q. You were with the Dorchester Department before?

A. Yes, sir.

Q. When did you start to come in?

A. I started on the third alarm from my house.

Q. How long were you coming in?

A. I didn't look at my watch; somewhere from thirty to forty minutes.

Q. How did you come?

A. With a horse and buggy.

Q. Do you know about the engine from your neighborhood, when that came?

A. I don't know at what time she got in there. I had left before.

Q. What number is that?

A. Sixteen.

Q. You left before she came?

A. Yes, sir.

Q. What was the condition of the fire when you got there?

A. I came up Kingston street, and came on to it from there; and I met Captain Regan and Captain Smith. It was well burning, but I didn't take particular notice, because Captain Regan said, "You must go round on to Chauncey street and make an attempt to stop it there, if possible."

Q. That was where you made your first fight?

A. Yes, sir.

Q. What did you do?

A. We got three streams up in the rear of a clothing-store there. I don't know whose it was.

Q. On what street?

A. On Chauncey street. We first went into an unfinished building that faced on Kingston street, I think it was, and put the fire out in that building.

Q. You got your three streams where?

A. On that clothing-store, and fought it there until we were driven back, out into the street; then we went into another building, where we could be protected somewhat from the heat, and worked there until we were called out by Captain Smith sending word for us to come out; that there was danger of the walls falling, and it was not safe to stay there any longer.

Q. Where did you go next?

A. We went out into the street and put the streams on to the building adjoining; and when we came out I had not been on the street more than ten minutes before there was a messenger came and said the Chief wanted his Assistants in Federal street.

Q. Did you have a consultation with him there?

A. The consultation was had before I arrived. I saw him there.

Q. Did you have any talk with him?

A. I asked him if he was going to blow. He said, "Yes." That was the only conversation I had.

Q. Did he give you any directions about blowing; or about using gunpowder?

A. No, sir; he did not.

Q. Did you have any?

A. Yes, sir.

Q. From whom?

A. Captain Green.

Q. State what took place.

A. He said they must have more powder, and told Captain Smith and myself to go down to T wharf, — I think it was, — and take a tug boat and go down the harbor, and fetch up the powder boat.

Q. You went down with him?

A. Yes, sir.

Q. What did you do after you got back? After you got the powder to the fire?

A. We went into Congress street, I think, and there was a gentleman came up with a paper in his hand and said he had a document there from the Chief authorizing him to blow buildings. Captain Green looked at the paper and said that was all right. He was satisfied. I don't recollect of seeing any one carry powder in. I was back watching the fire, and trying to find an opportunity to make a stand against it.

Q. Do you know anything further about the use of powder?

A. No, sir.

Q. Was there any trouble from want of water that night, where you were?

A. Not in the immediate vicinity where I was.

Q. Was there any want of fuel?

A. Not that I know of.

Q. Was there any trouble about the hose?

A. Nothing more than usual.

Q. How did the men behave?

A. They behaved as well as I ever saw them at any fire.

Q. How long have you been a fireman?

A. I have belonged to the Fire Department over thirty years in Dorchester and Boston.

L. W. SHAW, Ass't Engineer, *sworn.*

Q. (By Mr. Russell.) How long have you been connected with the Fire Department?

A. I joined the Fire Department in 1852.

Q. Where were you when you heard the alarm?

A. I was directly opposite my house, 49 Winchester street.

Q. How long did it take you to get to the fire?

A. To the best of my judgment, about seven minutes and a half.

Q. What was the condition when you got there; and where was it?

A. According as it appeared to me, it was in a very far advanced state from what we usually find in anything of that description when we arrive on the ground.

Q. Was the building all on fire?

A. Yes, sir. The building the fire originated in was a mass of flames, and it had got into the next store south, and was smoking on the opposite side of the street.

Q. What did you do?

A. I took a point on the opposite side of the street and endeavored to prevent it from crossing.

Q. Opposite side of Summer, or Kingston street?

A. Kingston street.

Q. What success did you have?

A. I met with good success at that point. It was a dwelling-house. We used water in buckets, and anything we could carry it in, until I could get a line of hose in. A line of hose was on the opposite side when I got there; but when we had to abandon that, we took it into the dwelling-house, and succeeded in keeping it there.

Q. Was anything throwing water when you got their excepting the hose?

A. From the point where I went, I could not determine whether the engines were throwing water or not. I noticed there were engines there, but I was not in a position to see whether they were throwing water or not. Their lines were run.

Q. Where did you go next?

A. I went down into Bedford street and to Church Green.

Q. On what building did you work there?

A. The first building I went into there, was on the east side of a place. I don't know what the name of the place is. It was east of Devonshire street,— a place that run in from Summer street, north. There were some brands of fire that broke a window in the Mansard roof on the east side of that place, and I took a line of hose up there and put that out. The front room in that store was all on fire, and after putting that out, I put a line there on the rear with good hopes of stopping it from crossing at that point.

Q. Where did you go when you left there? You were driven from there?

A. I was not driven from that point, but I came out with the intention of sending in other streams to reinforce that, and I found the fire had driven round so furiously on the other side that there was an engine in danger of burning up; and I gave my attention to getting that away;

and when I came back, I found the stream had been driven from the point where I located it.

Q. Where did you go next?

A. We next attempted to make a stand at the corner of High and Summer and South and Summer — on those two points.

Q. Where did you go after that?

A. After we found we could not make a stand there, Captain Jacobs and myself consulted — we were the only members of the Board on that side — and we decided to take a stand further back from the fire, where we could man a battery, and command it when it came up; and we took a line right across from a point just south or south-east from the Hartford & Erie depot, right across to the Bowditch school. We cut down all the fences, and put lines of hose through, and wet everything down; and that is where we stopped the fire from going south.

Q. Then where did you go?

A. I then went down the line to report to the Chief, if I could find him, that the fire was stayed on that side. I went through into Chauncey street and found some of the Engineers there, but the Chief was not there, and I continued down the line until I got to Franklin street. I there found matters in such a condition that I abandoned my object of trying to find the Chief, and endeavored to make a stand at the corner of Franklin and Hawley streets.

Q. Which way was the fire going?

A. Up both sides of Franklin towards Washington.

Q. You don't know how it got across?

A. I have no means of knowing how it got across.

Q. How long did you hold that spot?

A. I had just got well to work there when I received an imperative order from the Chief, through his son, to meet him at the corner of Federal and Milk streets. I felt constrained to obey the order.

Q. What was the consultation?

A. The orders of the Chief were, to hunt up as many of the Engineers as I could find along the line, and send them to him at once; to tell them to go immediately, without any hesitation.

Q. And to go there yourself?

A. He didn't give me any order to return.

Q. Did you return?

A. I didn't. I found as much as I wanted to do to fight my way down through the crowd to find the others, and I thought enough had gone to him for the consultation he wished; and I found a point I considered was important, on my way back. I stopped where I found it.

Q. Where was that?

A. The line of Washington street from Winter to School, or Winter to Milk.

Q. How long did you stay there?

A. I was on that point, with one slight interruption — when I went from it to put a line into Hovey's store in Avon place — I was there from this time until the fire was successfully stopped on Washington street. I cannot tell how long it was.

Q. Did you have any experience with gunpowder that night?

A. My experience with gunpowder was very slight. There was one of the agents that were employed to use it, that came there and demanded of me to take my men away, and I refused, and commanded him not to use it at that point.

Q. Did he obey you?

A. He did temporarily; but when I was absent to get this line into Hovey's store, he put it into Mudge's store and attempted to explode it, and partially succeeded, as I understand.

Q. Was there any want of water that night?

A. Yes, sir; it was a very serious obstacle. One place was at the corner of Milk and Washington.

Q. How many engines were there there?

A. There were three.

Q. Could they not all get water?

A. They got it until they drew the reservoir dry.

Q. Was there any supply to the reservoir?

A. There was a gate into it; but the engines from other points were taking the water so fast it would not run in.

Q. Was there any other point where there was want of water?

A. Yes, sir; we got an inadequate supply on the corner of Kingston street, where I first went, after a certain length of time, after the other engines got to work.

Q. Corner of Kingston and what?

A. Bedford street.

Q. Was there any other point?

A. Well, there were other points; for instance, when I was in Water street, on the "Post" building, I was scant of water there, but really I can't tell you where the lines came from.

Q. Was there any trouble with fuel?

A. There was none under my immediate notice.

Q. Was there any trouble about the hose?

A. In what respect?

Q. In bursting any more than usual in a great fire?

A. No, sir; I didn't notice any.

Q. Was the hose in good condition?

A. So far as my knowledge was concerned.

Q. How did the men behave?

A. Splendidly; I never gave an order to a man that night, — that is, to our department, — but he sprang to it as though his life depended upon it.

Q. Were there any intoxicated men in the Boston Fire Department?

A. I didn't see one in my observation.

Q. Did you notice about the engines, whether they came fast or slow? Whether they lost time from having men instead of horses?

A. I didn't see any engine come in, except 3; 7 and 4 were there when I arrived on the ground.

Q. At what rate did 3 come?

A. I could not tell the rate she came, but I should judge from the time I was there, she was there very quick — almost as quick as if she had had horses, with the exception of the difference between one alarm and another, which would be five minutes behind.

Q. Where did she start from?

A. Opposite Williams market, on Washington street.

Q. What was the great trouble that made this fire uncontrollable?

A. Well, as far as my judgment goes, it had acquired a headway beyond what we are accustomed to have; and the buildings were very high. We find in all those buildings of that description that the upper part is built with combustible materials, and it went from one to another at a rate almost as fast as a man could go.

Q. Where did the buildings usually catch?

A. In the roofs.

Q. The wooden trimmings and wooden covings?

A. Yes, sir. Oftentimes it lodged on those Mansard roofs, round the windows, and caught in there. It did in this store on Summer street, that I spoke of — the first one that I went into after I went to Church Green.

Q. Was there anything that was done that was improper, or anything left undone, that night; or anything you could do better if it should happen again?

A. I have criticised my conduct as no other man could criticise it, and I don't know, so far as my duty was concerned, of one thing I could do differently if I should do it over again; which I consider very remarkable, as there is hardly a day passes but I see something that I can mend in my own business.

Q. In the general management of the fire, so far as you noticed, was there anything you could criticise?

A. I don't know of anything that could be done better, in regard to the general management, unless we could have prevented any powder from being used. I think we should have saved hundreds of thousands of dollars, if there had been no powder used at all. I don't know as there was any way to have prevented it.

Q. In what way do you think the powder did harm?

A. It did the harm of forcing our forces back every time, for fifteen or twenty minutes. We had to withdraw from every point where it was used. There is a sample of it in Washington street. If it had been used there, in spite of all we could have done, it would have crossed Washington street, if our forces had had to be withdrawn.

Q. You think the street was saved by keeping the powder away?

A. Exactly; I am just as confident of it as that I am sitting here.

Q. If there had been an abundant supply of water, and you had had the Lowry hydrants, in your judgment, what difference would it have made in the management of this fire?

A. If we had had the Lowry hydrants all over the city, or where it first started, I should have hardly said it would have gone beyond Summer street, and, perhaps, not on this side of Summer street at all.

Q. You are confident of that?

A. That is my feeling; and if it had got beyond that, if we had had a good supply of water, I should say it would never have passed Franklin street, certain.

Q. Was there not perhaps a defect in the size of the street mains, besides the want of the Lowry hydrants?

A. Yes, sir.

Q. The Lowry hydrants would not have brought the water?

A. No, sir; it would have been simple folly to put the Lowry hydrants on the pipes now in Franklin and Devonshire streets, because they are only four and six-inch pipes. That was just precisely what we needed, — larger pipes.

PHINEAS B. ALLEN, Civil Engineer, *sworn.*

Q. (By Mr. Russell.) How long have you been connected with the Fire Department?

A. Ever since Roxbury was annexed, 1868, I think.

Q. And before that?

A. Before that I belonged in Roxbury ever since 1850, and I belonged in Dorchester in 1848.

Q. What time did you start for the fire?

A. I started on the second alarm. I was in Hook and Ladder 4's house when the alarm was given. I was going home, and I stopped in there to see how things were; that is on Eustis street.

Q. How long were you in coming in?

A. I could not say exactly. I got into a car and came down as far as Worcester street, and Hose 7 came out of Worcester street; I think it was Worcester street; I will not be sure; but I got out of the car and run down with them.

Q. How much slower were they than if they had had horses?

A. I don't think any slower. They had a large team.

Q. When you reached the fire, what was the condition of things?

A. The first building, that is, the building the fire took in, was nearly consumed.

Q. What else was burning?

A. The building next to it on Kingston street was the one I went into first. I went in there with No. 13's line and stayed there until they said the building was not safe to stay in any longer, and we took the line out.

Q. Where did you go next?

A. I stopped there a few minutes; then I walked down to the end of Bedford street into Summer street. I stopped there until the engines were taken away from that reservoir.

Q. Why were they taken away?

A. The fire got down so close we considered them in danger, and they were ordered to move them as soon as they could.

Q. Where did you go then?

A. I went into Lincoln street. Then No. 17 went down to the corner of Lincoln and Essex streets to the hydrant there, and I went down that way with them. I then went back for the hose there was in the square, and got that back from the fire, and went to work there at that hydrant.

Q. Where did you go next?

A. After we got the fire stopped there, and supposed it was perfectly safe to leave, we came down to School street; and the orders came there to go down towards the Custom House as quick as possible; and we we went from there to Batterymarch street, and the engine went to work at the reservoir there; and the line was taken round into Milk street.

Q. What did you do next?

A. We stayed there until the fire was about stopped; when we were up there, No. 17 went home; and the Providence engine, — she had arrived here then or before; I had not seen her before, — she came in at Liberty square and went to work on that reservoir. The fire was about stopped then; some were confident it would not go further.

Q. Did you see the Chief that night?

A. I did.

Q. Where?

A. The last time I saw him was in Summer street.

Q. What time, about?

A. As near as I can judge, it was somewhere about twenty minutes or a quarter before eleven.

Q. Did you have any consultation with him?

A. A gentleman came to me and spoke about bringing engines from Worcester. He wanted to know if I would give him an order to send for the engines. The telegraph was broken down and they could not telegraph, and the gentlemen who had charge of the engines would not start unless they had a written order. I said, "I cannot give an order in writing. I have no pen, ink, or paper, and I am wet clear through, but," I said, "the Chief has just gone by, and if you will wait one moment, I think I can find him." I found him, and told him what the gentleman said, and he said, "Go to the depot with the gentleman and have an order sent." I went down and found the gentleman who had charge of the engines, and he said he would send one right of; and the way I came to know about the time, he said, "I will be back at half-past one." I looked at the clock and it was just eleven. I said, "You have got to work pretty lively to get back at half-past one." He said, "I will do it;" and a few minutes before that time he reported to me; he had arrived and wanted to know where to go. I said, "Go down Washington street, and you will find some one who will tell you where to go to work."

Q. Where did that engine come from?

A. Worcester. He went from here to Worcester and got his engine.

Q. The first engine that went out went to West Newton and got an engine?

A. That I don't know anything about.

Q. They had communicated by telegraph with Worcester?

A. They could not; the line was down. They didn't telegraph because the line was down. That is the reason I came to notice the time so exactly, because the man said, "I will be back at half-past one." I said, "You can't, you have only got two hours and a half." And he said, "I will do it." He did do it.

Q. Did you have any consultation with the Chief that night?

A. No, sir; I did not see him after that until Sunday sometime.

Q. Did you have any experience with gunpowder that night?

A. I did not.

Q. Was there any trouble about want of water that night?

A. We were short of water part of the time; the hydrants did not give us enough.

Q. Where was that?

A. Corner of Essex and Lincoln.

Q. Any other place?
A. That is the only place we were at until we came to the reservoir.
Q. When you got to the reservoir, did you have plenty of water?
A. We had plenty of it, I think, there.
Q. Was there any trouble from want of fuel that night?
A. We did not have coal all the time as freely as we do sometimes, although no engine stopped, because we procured wood and that like.
Q. How did the men work?
A. Every man did all he could, that I saw. I didn't see a man refuse to do anything from the time the fire began until it stopped.
Q. How came the fire to get beyond your control? What was the trouble that night that made it so great a fire?
A. I think the great trouble was, the fire was not discovered soon enough, and the alarm not given soon enough. I think the building had burned so far before it was discovered, it was impossible to stop it.
Q. What made it spread so fast?
A. The greatest trouble was in the high buildings, and the wood-work on top of them, the wooden covings, and wooden windows, and the like.
Q. Did the fire usually catch in the roof?
A. It did on Summer street. The fire came right down the coving, and you could see it.
Q. What, in your judgment, would have been the difference if you had had an abundance of water, and had had the Lowry hydrants?
A. I think if we had had the Lowry hydrants, we could have got some engines closer to the fire; it would not have required so much hose to play through. Some of the engines were playing through six or seven hundred feet of hose. With the Lowry hydrants, we should have had four engines on to one hydrant, and they would not have had to play through more than two or three hundred feet.
Q. Do you think the best use was made of the material you had?
A. Yes, sir. I think everything was done that could be with what we had to work with.
Q. Did the Chief seem to be cool?
A. Very cool, when I saw him. As cool as ever I saw him at a fire in my life.

JAMES MUNROE, Civil Engineer, *sworn.*

Q. (By Mr. Russell.) How long have you been in the Fire Department of Boston?
A. Since annexation.
Q. You were Chief Engineer of the Roxbury Department?
A. Yes, sir.
Q. How many years?
A. Nine.
Q. How long have you been a fireman?
A. Thirty-three years.
Q. What time did you start for the fire?
A. I started on the first alarm.
Q. From where?

A. From the Highlands.
Q. How did you come?
A. I ran part of the way, and part of the way in a car.
Q. What time did you arrive, as near as you can tell?
A. I should think within twenty-five minutes.
Q. What was the condition of the fire?
A. The fire was across Kingston street and into the building south of where it originated. I did not go on to Summer street. I came in on the south side and went to work on Bedford street.
Q. You cannot tell what was going on in Summer street?
A. No, sir.
Q. What fighting did you do there?
A. I fought it on the south side of Summer street, on the back side from Bedford street.
Q. Where did you go next?
A. I had an order from the Chief to report to him in Federal street.
Q. Did you go?
A. Yes, sir.
Q. What was the consultation?
A. In regard to using powder.
Q. What did the Chief say about it?
A. He said he proposed to use powder.
Q. Did he say where?
A. He did not then; he did after we had concluded to use it.
Q. What advice did you give, if any?
A. I advised him to use it, provided they went back far enough to get an opening before the fire would come up to it.
Q. About what time was this talk?
A. I don't have much idea of time. I should think it was pretty near twelve o'clock.
Q. Had he used any at that time, did you understand?
A. Not to my knowledge. He said he had sent for the powder.
Q. Were you there when it came?
A. Yes, sir.
Q. Did you take part in using it?
A. I did not.
Q. Did you see it used?
A. I did not.
Q. What did you do after that?
A. He gave me an order to go into Federal street. He said they were going to blow a building up on Federal street, on the left-hand side. He said they were going to blow that building, and ordered me to go to Congress street and clear the street. I went round there and did so, with the assistance of the police.
Q. Did the explosion take place while you were there?
A. No, sir.
Q. Where did you go next?
A. I went over on to Broad street, near the foot of Oliver street.
Q. Did you fight the fire there until it was stopped?
A. I stayed there until it was stopped.
Q. Where did you go next?

A. I then came down on to Oliver street, near Milk street, near the Boston Lead Company's store there, and the other stores in that block.

Q. You fought the fire there?

A. I stayed there until it was taken care of at that point.

Q. You had a Lynn company to help you?

A. I had one Roxbury engine, and there was a stream from one Boston engine, and two or three out-of-town companies; I don't know what they were.

Q. What time did you stop the fire there?

A. I think it was about noon; I don't know.

Q. Did you do any more that day?

A. We kept the engine there at work, and about three o'clock we got it under, and then came up town to get something to eat.

Q. How was the Chief when you saw him?

A. I never saw him any more cool and collected than he was at that time.

Q. How did the men generally behave?

A. Well, sir.

Q. Was there any intoxication on the part of the Boston Fire Department?

A. I didn't see any instance of the kind; not a man.

Q. Was there any want of water?

A. Yes, sir.

Q. Where was that?

A. On Lincoln street and on Oliver street; on that side of the fire. We had to run a line clear up through Broad street.

Q. Did the engines have to stand still for want of water?

A. Yes, sir; we could not get water enough to supply the engines.

Q. Were there any other points where you noticed that?

A. No, sir, not that I remember of.

Q. Was there any want of fuel?

A. Yes, sir.

Q. Did any of the engines stand still for want of fuel, or did they supply themselves?

A. They took boxes or anything they could get hold of.

Q. Did you lose any time for want of steam?

A. Yes, sir, I think there was one time.

Q. Where was that?

A. It was over on Broad street.

Q. Could they not get coal there?

A. I could not. I tried a number of wharves; they said they had no cannel coal, or anything that was suitable for us.

Q. You could not get fuel?

A. We could get wood there.

Q. Was there any trouble from hose that night?

A. No, sir, I didn't see any lack of hose where I was.

Q. Was there any difficulty from bursting of hose?

A. No, sir, very little of it.

Q. The hose was in good order and kept in good order?

A. All the hose I had anything to do with.

Q. What was the principal cause of the fire becoming uncontrollable?

A. It was a big fire before we got there.

Q. That is the first cause; what others?

A. I don't know as I could answer that.

Q. Did you notice where the fire generally caught; whether it was the roof?

A. The building was all on fire from cellar to attic.

Q. The first one?

A. Yes, sir, and the other buildings around it were on fire.

Q. What would have been the effect if you had had Lowry hydrants and plenty of water?

A. I think the fire would have been checked a good while before it was.

Q. Where do you think, to the best of your judgment, you could have checked the fire if you had had that?

A. I think if we had had plenty of water in Liberty square, we could have made a stand there and all along on that line.

Q. Suppose they had had it at the beginning of the fire?

A. I don't think it would have made any odds.

Q. You don't think you could have stopped it?

A. No, sir.

Q. At the time when the alarm was given, you don't think anything could have stopped that fire on the spot where it begun?

A. I could not tell what state it was in when the alarm was given, before the time I got there.

Q. You say it had crossed Summer street when you got there?

A. No, sir, it had crossed Kingston street.

Q. It may have crossed Summer street and you not have seen it?

A. Yes, sir, it might have been. I did not go on that side.

Q. You are an expert and an old hand at fires; was this a well-managed fire or otherwise?

A. I should say it was.

Q. Does anything occur to you now that could have been done that was not done?

A. No, sir.

Q. Suppose you had to do it over again, and you were Chief; do you see anything that you could do that was not done?

A. No, sir; I think that everything was done that night that men could do with what we had to do with.

JOHN COLLIGAN, *sworn.*

Q. (By Mr. RUSSELL.) How long have you been connected with the Fire Department of Boston and Roxbury?

A. Since 1843. I will say I ran two years on trial; then two years as a volunteer, from 1845 to 1847, and have been a regular member from that time to the present.

Q. Where were you when you heard the alarm?

A. At home.

Q. What street?

A. 1996 Washington street, Boston Highlands.

Q. How soon do you suppose you got in?

A. I should say less than thirty minutes. I ran part of the way and rode part of the way. From Dover street to Essex street, I think I came about as fast as most people want to ride.

Q. What was the condition of the fire when you reached it?

A. I got in in time to attack the building next to the one in which the fire originated. The apparatus of which I had charge in my district, — Hose No. 7 and Engine No. 13, — was coming down Essex street; I went to them and said to the engine man, " Are you all right?" He said he was. I went in the first place into a swell-front house on the left-hand side of Kingston street, and from there went into another building, on the opposite side, a dwelling-house altered over into a store, and got 13's line up to the attic, came down again to look at the building and found the fire was coming in under us. I said to Capt. Brown, " We will try to get another line to protect our folks up stairs, and try to stop it." I came down and met Capt. Brown, and we were going to get another line up there, and Capt. Chamberlain came along and said, " Have you got a line in that building?" I said, " I have." He said, " It is unsafe; every moment you keep the men there you keep them at their peril." I said, " I think we can stop it." He went on to describe the building quickly and said it was unsafe. I said, " I yield to your judgment," and I ordered the men out and we took our station in the street, immediately in front of the building and directly opposite the front entrance to the stairs. At that time, Capts. Munroe, Allen, Smith and myself were there. Then we separated. Somebody said, " The fire is working up Chauncey street." I said to Capt. Smith, " Shall I go, or will you go?" He said he would go, leaving me alone. I saw no other Engineer for some considerable time. Then Capt. Munroe came round and wanted to know if I could help him on Bedford street. I said I had only those lines, and I didn't think it was safe to leave. I said, " Look over the ground and see for yourself;" and he said that he didn't see that I could help him any. At this time I had 13's line in the street and a line from Hose 2 on the roof of the dwelling-house on the westerly side of Kingston street. I went up on the roof of that and put a ladder upon the new granite building facing on Kingston street, and had a line from Engine No. 13, manned by members of 15, through the swell-front house, cutting it off to protect the back part of the building on Chauncey street, and when I came down I relieved Engine No. 3 and sent them off to report to the back side of the fire. I remained there with two streams from Engine No. 13, 800 feet on one line and 600 feet on the other, until the order came to report on Federal street. I sent back word that I ought not to leave. I was alone some little time after that, and the order came back to me to report forthwith. I made the same reply, and was told the orders were imperative, and of course I obeyed them. I reported in Federal street. They asked what use they could make of gunpowder in Summer street. I said it was no use to use it, in my judgment; it would do no good at all. I said to Captain Dunbar, " It is wicked for me to stay here; I will go back to Summer street; if you want me, you will know where to find me." We stopped it on Kingston street, and I changed right round into Chauncey street, and kept the fire from working up Chauncey street to the South end. The fire at that time was in the second building on the westerly side of Chauncey and the southerly side of Summer, taking out that corner. Mr. Hovey wanted to know if I could save his building, and I said, "Yes; I didn't propose to let it go any further on that side." Meantime, I gave an order for Engine 2, which was stationed on Avon street, to take their line down, and saying that I would be back again, I went in with Mr. Hovey and took a survey of that building. Capt. Shaw then came round, and I asked him to give me a lift; I told him to take Engine No. 2's line into Hovey's attic and stop the fire on that side, and I would take care of it on the other side. He got the line up and reported back; and seeing that we were doing about what was right, let that remain until we could take care of it entirely on the Chauncey-street side, and sent them down to Sturgis street. In the mean time, Capt. Chamberlain had asked me to relieve some of the force. I said, "If you see any I can spare I will do it." He looked over the ground, and said he didn't think I could. The Chief came to me and said, "Can you stop the fire here?" I said, "Yes, sir, I propose to stop it here." He said, "Are you sure?" I said, "I am; I have looked over the ground and am sure." He gave me orders as fast as I could relieve any force to send it away. I told him with one engine disabled I didn't feel that I could at present, but would as soon as I could. Mudge, Sawyer & Co.'s store was packed with goods from cellar to attic, so we had to move several cases to get at the windows. There was no protection in the shape of shutters or anything of that kind. We located lines at the different stories, and put a man on top of the roof, and gave him notice if anything should occur there on the westerly side of Chauncey street to take care of it. We had stopped it part way through from Kingston-street side, so far as we could reach that way, and finally accomplished that purpose. I reported in State street with the apparatus, and some time in the course of the day, I think, but had been there but a few minutes before I had to go back. Before that time, however, the Chief came and said, "I want you to make up the force." I said, "The people are very much excited in this street, and want all the force you can spare." He looked over the ground and said, "You had better send it all." I sent off the apparatus and took a short cut to State street and reported to him. We had been there but a few moments when word came from Hovey's that they didn't consider themselves safe; that the fire was rekindling, and they thought it would get into the brick building there. It had been in it, in fact, while I was off on other business. We went back there again and finally cooled it down, and didn't go back there again until Monday; reported in State street, then went to Oliver street, and back to State street into the Post Office, and took a stream from the Navy Yard engine into part of the building, and cooled the stones of the building. I authorized the man who had command to use his judgment to stop the fire, if I should have to leave it, and then went into the rear of that freestone building on Devonshire street, — Congress square, I believe they call it. I went into the first story in the first place, and put out a little fire there. It came through very strong in the second and third stories, and we had quite a smart little fight there to stop it. Capt. Green came in with a line from No. 15, and we finally checked it. That was about ten or eleven o'clock. I had orders to go home. I did so, and had just got into bed when a policeman came and notified me the wires were down on the east side of the city, and I gave him the keys and ordered him to ring the church-bell for anything in Boston, no matter what it was. I don't know how long I had been in bed, — I had not had much sleep, but had got warm, — when I heard the bell. I got up and dressed as quick as I could and came into Summer street, and stayed there until Monday night, and got home at ten o'clock.

Q. When you were at work on Hovey's building, did they help you with blankets?

A. Yes, sir; they had no shutters on part of their building, sir, and of course the fire was very intense and very hot there. They did nobly themselves; did all they could do.

Q. How many of them were at work there?

A. I could not say. I only saw that they were doing all that lay in their power. I put a line in their upper story so we could reach into any part of the burning building. We had a good engine and a good line, so we could rely on it, and felt satisfied unless something unusual should occur we could control the fire.

Q. Was there any lack of water?

A. Not on my line.

Q. Was there any trouble from want of fuel?

A. I can only judge that there was. I saw the coal wagon there, and they said they were doing all they could.

Q. Do you know of boxes being used?

A. I saw boxes being used. I said, "If you get out of fuel, use any fuel you can get."

Q. Do you know of any engine that had to stop for want of fuel?

A. No, sir; I told them not to. The lines I had didn't stop.

Q. How did the men work?

A. Nobly.

Q. Have any trouble with them at all?

A. No, sir; I changed lines and broke up lines, and did many things that in ordinary cases would have occasioned murmuring, and there was none at all. They took hold very cheerfully. I worked the men so hard that I said to them, "I pity you, but you have got to do it."

Q. How was the Chief that night?

A. I saw nothing unusual with him. He discussed matters as he always does, in his quick way, but there was no excitement about him at all.

Q. Do you consider that the fire was well managed?

A. So far as I had opportunity to judge.

Q. Should you know how to do better if you had opportunity to do it again?

A. I have gone over it in my mind. I might have done differently in regard to leaving Hovey's. I felt satisfied we should be called back again. Still, on the whole, I did the best thing I could.

Q. That is the only thing you had any doubt about, — leaving there at the time you did?

A. Yes, sir. I wish to say one thing in regard to how our apparatus is divided, and what the duties of the Engineers are in their respective districts. Each Engineer has so much apparatus to look after. It is his duty to see that it is fit for service at all times, and at the breaking out of the horse-epidemic a meeting of the Board was called. I had notified all the principal establishments, like Day's factory, in my section of the city, that if there was a fire they must send men. In the mean time, I had given the driver of the engine orders to use horses to go to Day's factory. There we have no Cochituate water. We have no Cochituate water west of Tremont street. We have one reservoir between the railroad crossing and Parker street. I told him, "I want those horses put on any way." I gave that order to him on Monday night. We had the meeting Saturday night. He came or sent word to me, Tuesday, "I can't use my horses at all; can't get them out of the stable." I notified the Rubber Co. that I should call on their engines, and I wanted them to place at my disposal all the hose in their factory; and notified the carpet-factory and the paper-factory, and other large establishments; and they said they would keep their horses at my disposal. The paper-factory said they had no hose, and I said I would furnish them. Mr. Day and all the large establishments agreed to furnish men. I notified Hose 7 (they do not respond to any box north of Dover street until the general alarm) if they saw anything suspicious to start at once and I would take the responsibility. Engine No. 13 was not to start until the fourth alarm. I said, "Don't you wait if you see anything that looks suspicious." I secured horses of Mr. Mahan. His stable is about 450 to 500 feet away on Hampshire street. He agreed to furnish horses, and I gave him a list of the boxes we went to and the alarms. He didn't get his horses out in time. He started on the second alarm, but they had gone and he didn't overtake them. They came in by hand.

Q. How far did be come with his horses?

A. I don't know. He said he didn't see anything of them. Hose No. 7 started, and they got in, as near as I can learn, very promptly; and from the time the alarm was struck, until 13 was ready to work, did not exceed thirty minutes.

Q. What number was that where the horses did not overtake the engine?

A. 13, Boston Highlands, stationed on Cabot street; used to be Ruggles street. I should like to say one thing. We consider it a part of our duty, of course, to look out for our sections, and do what we can to prevent fires and facilitate putting them out. I have made two or three applications to the Water Board to lay a pipe from Washington street to Harrison avenue; and they said they would not lay a foot of pipe for fire purposes. West of Tremont street we have only one reservoir. The territory is composed of wooden buildings, some of them very large and very combustible. I waited upon Mr. Day and Mr. Rogers (they are large property-holders in that district) two years ago, and told them they must do something themselves; we could not do anything; we were powerless.

Q. Who did you apply to?

A. George Lewis. I told him the condition we were in.

Q. You made a verbal application?

A. Yes, sir. The territory I wished to protect was between Eustis street, Harrison avenue, and Hunneman streets. There is a large planing mill in that territory, engine shops, and dwellings. He said to me,

"It is no use; they will not lay one foot of pipe for fire purposes. I told him that on Harrison Avenue the pipe stopped dead end; that if an engine started at the end, she drew all the water away from the one behind, and *vice versa;* whichever starts first gets all the water and the other don't get any. He said, "We cannot help you any." I felt very anxious about that section.

Q. Have you made any representations since Mr. Lewis left?

A. Only through Mr. Day and Mr. Rogers. I told them to go to work, when we were powerless.

Q. Has there been any action taken in the Board upon this matter?

A. The matter has been talked over and my reply has been, "It is no use to try in our section of the city." I have said this in the Board: "The only way to do is to get the owners of property to move," and I told them what I had done, that I called upon Mr. Day and Mr. Rogers to get them to exert themselves to get water, that we were powerless, and it laid with them and the Water Board whether this section should be protected.

Q. It is more important now because there have been more buildings put up?

A. Yes, sir. It is increasing every day. Some are very high and some are of a very combustible nature. In the vicinity of the new planing-mill on what is now Parker street, we have no supply of water, and I told the owners when they first moved there it was their duty to look after it; that anything we could do in the shape of a recommendation we would do, but it belonged to them to get water. We must depend upon the high tide; the hydrants will hardly supply the boilers. If you felt as I do about it, you would not get many nights' sleep.

Q. Have they put in Lowry hydrants in their new work in Roxbury?

A. Everything there is Lowry, with the exception of where it runs down on the dead-end. There they have put in a Boston hydrant. The water before annexation was from reservoirs and from Jamaica Pond. The chief advantage of Jamaica Pond was supplying our reservoirs. While using that, we had gates within a reasonable distance, and since that time, at the expense of the Fire Department in Roxbury, we had pipes run up from the low land on Tremont street, up to the corner of Ruggles street. That gave us additional hydrants there, but they were Boston hydrants, and when the pipe was laid, it was in the charter that the City of Roxbury could have as many hydrants as they chose for fire purposes; we only had three or four on the entire line within the limits of Roxbury; but since that time, there is no section better protected than in the vicinity of Tremont and Ruggles street. We have in that section probably 60 lbs. pressure. It comes right from the main pipe. We have some hydrants on the sidewalk and some in the street. We prefer to have them in the sidewalk.

Adjourned to Thursday, at 3 P. M.

FIFTH DAY.

THURSDAY, Dec. 5th.

JOSEPH BARNES, *sworn.*

Q. (By Mr. RUSSELL.) Where do you live?

A. In East Boston.

Q. When did you go to the fire?

A. The fire had been burning perhaps forty minutes before I was there. We do not go at the first alarm from the city, from East Boston.

Q. Was this the third or the fourth alarm?

A. It was the fourth. We had four that night altogether. I went at the fourth. The other Engineer went at the second. Perhaps it would be necessary to state that we have rules and regulations in regard to that. We have certain boxes to go to, at the second alarm, in the city with our own apparatus, — box 2 to 23. Then we skip to 36, 37, and 41. We go at the second alarm, with one engine and one Engineer.

Q. What was the condition of things when you reached the fire?

A. The fire was going into Otis street, as you pass down there by Beebe's block, off from Summer street.

Q. What was done to prevent its getting into Otis street?

A. Everything that could be done in regard to playing on it.

Q. How many engines?

A. There were some three or four engines on Otis street and down by the front of Beebe's block when I got there.

Q. Were there any firemen on the roofs of buildings?

A. Yes, sir.

Q. On what buildings?

A. On the building on the right of Otis street, as you come from Summer down into Devonshire. I call it on the north side of Beebe's block.

Q. Where were they playing?

A. They were playing on to the fire on both sides of the street. Some of the streams were upon the sidewalks playing up upon the sides of buildings. Others were on top, playing across.

Q. Do you say that all was done that could be done there to prevent its crossing?

A. Yes, sir.

Q. Can you think of anything now that was not done that ought to have been done?

A. No, sir.

Q. (By Mr. PHILBRICK.) Did it look as though they could stop the fire in Otis street?

A. I didn't think so. I thought the fire had got the control.

Q. Where did you go after that?

A. I kept there until the fire drove me down Devonshire street, and had two engines that I shifted until we got down into Franklin street, and then I took a turn up Franklin street towards Washington, and fought the fire from Beebe's block down Devonshire to Franklin, and then up Franklin to Washington.

Q. Can you tell us how the fire got across Franklin street, whether in the wide or narrow part?

A. Yes, sir. I was there and saw the whole of it. The heat of the buildings on the upper side of Devonshire street, on both corners of Devonshire and Franklin streets, was very great. As we fought the fire, we kept all the streams on the opposite side of Franklin street, to prevent the fire from crossing over, and we held it there quite a while. But the heat was so intense that it finally caught.

Q. Where did it finally catch?

A. It caught on the upper part of the buildings — on the Mansard roofs. That was on the north side of Franklin, corner of Devonshire. I happened to be at that point.

Q. About how many buildings caught at once?

A. The signs on the buildings and the roofs caught about together, I should think, perhaps. We were playing there for two hundred feet. There were several streams. I was on the upper two streams. That is the nearest to Washington street. I should think there were some six or eight streams below me quite a distance — some one hundred and fifty to two hundred feet below me. The first place where the fire got fairly under way was nearly opposite the lower corner of Devonshire street. I think it crossed over first just opposite the lower corner. But there was not a great deal of difference between the upper and lower corner.

Q (By Mr. Greene.) That was Brewer's building?

A. I think so. Then it worked right up Franklin street against the wind, that is, the wind drew the other way, because on the south side of Franklin street the buildings were on fire in back up further than they were on Franklin street. The fire was some one hundred and fifty or two hundred feet further up on the south than on the north side of Franklin street, but still it was on the north side working up towards Washington very fast, and, of course, working towards the new Post Office, — working in that way down Devonshire.

Q. Can you think now of any way by which that could have been stopped?

A. No, sir.

Q. Do you think there was any chance to use gunpowder there?

A. Well, I don't think that there was.

Q. Why not?

A. Because I think that using gunpowder so near would only have shattered the building and let the fire in quicker than it would otherwise have gone in.

Q. Take that spot, Franklin street, right across, suppose those roofs had not been Mansard, with the customary wooden trimmings, do you think the fire could have been stopped there?

A. Well, I think it rather doubtful. There was such intense heat that it was almost impossible to stand there. In the first of it, of course we stood over on the north side of Franklin street, but the heat came so heavy on us that we had to back out each way — that is, down and up. I backed up towards Washington street.

Q. Was there any want of water there?

A. Yes, sir, there was.

Q. To what extent was there a want of water?

A. They could not play a very good stream. The streams were cut short some, on account of the want of water.

Q. (By Mr. PHILBRICK.) Where did you draw water from?

A. We drew it from the reservoir up on Franklin street. The want of water was not so great then as it was later at the fire on Washington street.

Q. (By Mr. PHILBRICK.) Did you draw the reservoir down below the suction?

A. Well, it was at some times. When we had but one engine at a hydrant, that worked very well.

Q. Was there any want of fuel there on Otis street or Franklin street?

A. Not at that time. I never heard anything about fuel or any call for it.

Q. You went into Washington street next?

A. Yes, sir.

Q. Where did you fight the fire then?

A. I fought it up on Franklin street until it came into Washington, there I fought it from the Old South down to below Franklin. Some part of the time it was on to Mudge's building — from there to the Old South.

Q. Did you play on to Mr. Donahoe's "Boston Pilot" building?

A. No, sir, I don't think I did.

Q. Was there any great trouble in Franklin street from the falling of granite?

A. Well, there was some. There were some tremendous heavy falls there.

Q. What luck did you have on Washington street?

A. We had very good luck when we arrived on Washington street. We had more help from engines coming from out of town; brought their streams down Bromfield and Winter streets, and then we had the reservoir from the Old South. We had two or three streams there from Charlestown, and we made a very good battery, and on the opposite side from the corner of Milk street and Washington street — the last building that burnt there opposite to the Old South. We had an engine in Province court, and took a stream on top of a building; and then the men that owned the buildings had got on to them and put on carpets and wet cloths, and kept their buildings wet on the eaves, and we played up with our streams on the front of the buildings on Washington street, and I took one stream up from Province court, which made a very good chance to work, and we wet those buildings down perhaps three hundred feet each way. These carpets and old rugs stopped the fire from crossing; otherwise I think it would have crossed Washington street, if they had not put out rugs and old sails and everything that they had. There was a flat-roofed building with a little summer-house on top of it. That caught right off. They had hard work to keep all those buildings from burning along there for two hundred or three hundred feet. It caught once at the corner of Bromfield and Washington streets. There is a low building there with roof windows. They have now repaired the windows by putting in new boards. Those caught and burned quite briskly, and we got a stream down Bromfield street. There was another engine that came up and played on them and put them out. These carpets and cloths were all together on the west side of Washington street on the fronts, and hung over the roofs. They kept them wet by putting water on them. We had a good chance with our stream to wet three hundred feet. They had blanketed that so that we could work along for four or five buildings each way. It was daylight when we calculated that Washington street was safe.

Then there was some one that came to me and stated that several engines in State street wanted to be set to work. We went round to Oliver and Batterymarch streets. They were mostly out-of-town engines. With the help of others, we set as many engines to work as we could and backed them up, that is, took the hydrants below. There were some of them that could not reach the hydrants at that time. Where the fire got down to the corner of Batterymarch street, you will see the last building that was burned. There was a very high building in front of it there that stopped the fire. We had some twelve or fourteen streams. We made a point to stop it there if possible, and we did. There were no blankets or carpets used there at all. It was an old-fashioned slated roofed building, rather low. We had a good chance to work upon it all around. There is a vacant lot on Fort Hill. We made a very good fight there and stopped the fire.

Q. Did you do anything after that?

A. No, sir. We stayed there until dark, but we calculated the fire was all safe after one o'clock.

Q. You say there was no want of fuel on Franklin street. Where was there a want of fuel?

A. On Washington street, the latter part of the night. They had three or four engines down to the reservoir, and the Charlestown suctions gave out. We waited ten or fifteen minutes and stopped two good streams on account of want of water. I took two streams up into a building before I got the one on Province court. I had one of the Assistant Engineers with me, and we got the two streams up, which was a great deal of trouble; and when we got them up, there was no water. There was no want of fuel where I was.

Q. How did the firemen behave?

A. The men behaved well. There was no exception to that in the Boston Fire Department.

Q. When did you see the Chief that night?

A. I saw him frequently. The first time I saw him was when I first arrived at the fire. He spoke to me and wanted to know what there was from East Boston. We were all there. Everything was there excepting one hose carriage. That is everything that we ever take off. There is one carriage that we have had there lately.

Q. How did the Chief appear?

A. He seemed to be cool and all right.

Q. How about your East Boston apparatus? Some of it came over before you did?

A. Yes, sir.

Q. At what rate did it come, fast or slow?

A. It came very fast. It came by hand, but very quick. When they went into the boat they had, I should think, thirty or forty men and two engines.

Q. When you came over did any apparatus come with you?

A. Yes, sir, No. 5; it came quick by hand. I should think they had forty men when they went off the other side.

Q. How many minutes were lost by having men instead of horses to draw the apparatus?

A. Well, I should think it would make some difference; I should think maybe it would make ten minutes' difference.

Q. What was the number of the engine you went with from East Boston?

A. No. 5.

Q. Did you have any experience with gunpowder?

A. I did not and never have had.

Q. Did you see anything done with it that night?

A. Something, not much.

Q. Were you there when they tried to blow up Currier & Trott's building?

A. No, sir. The only blowing up I saw was the first that was done; that was on Federal street.

Q. What was the effect there?

A. The effect was bad.

Q. How was it bad?

A. It shattered the building; and another thing was, that after they had put their powder in the building, they had to take their apparatus away from the fire and stop playing.

Q. Should you recommend the use of gunpowder in case of a similar fire?

A. No, sir; for the reasons I have already given, I should not.

Q. (By Mr. PHILBRICK.) Could not those reasons be obviated by having preparations made beforehand?

A. Yes, sir; I think they might. I think gunpowder might be effectually used if it was properly managed, and prepared beforehand in proper form, and there were regular men who understood the business.

Q. With the means and the preparation that the Fire Department had, could they have done better than they did?

A. I think they did everything that lay in their power, every man of them.

Q. How long have you been connected with the Fire Department?

A. Twenty-two years in succession.

Q. How did the hose behave that night?

A. Well, we had some burst, but where I was, it was no more than could be expected.

Q. As a general thing, was the behavior of the hose that night good or bad?

A. I think it was about as usual in such cases. Of course, it was a large fire, and there was more or less hose lost; but where I was, we didn't lose any of it. In coming from Franklin street, there was some of the hose that bursted, as is always the case at all fires.

Q. Did you consider the hose good, or bad?

A. I think the hose where I was was as good as it generally is. We always have more or less trouble with the hose, no matter what kind we have. It is nothing uncommon to go to a fire and when we first get a stream, some one will say, "Your hose has bursted."

Q. From what you know, do you think better hose could be got in Boston?

A. I don't think it could, not any hose that we have. I don't know but better hose could be made.

Q. Do you know of better hose?

A. No, sir.

Q. (By Mr. Cobb.) If there had been a better supply of water and the Lowry hydrants had been used, what difference would there have been in your fight with the fire?

A. Well, I don't think the fire could have been put out after it got the start. Taking the fire when I arrived at it, I don't think we could have put it out any way, with all the water that we could wish for.

Q. Could you have made a better fight if you had had more water?

A. I think we could not have put it out, the fire was working in so many different ways. In fact, there were four or five large fires at that time.

Q. Then what was it that enabled you to check it at all?

A. I tell you that on Washington street we had more force; we had some force from out of town, and then I think the wind rather died away, and that was one thing, and we had more streams combined together and more concentration on Washington street, and, somehow or other, the flames did not seem to work across so much as they did on Devonshire street when it crossed. On the opposite side of Franklin, there seemed to be a more intense heat and the fire was more spiteful than it was on Washington street.

GEORGE O. CARPENTER, *sworn.*

Q. (By Mr. Russell.) You are an ex-alderman of the city of Boston?

A. Yes, sir.

Q. What time did you go to the fire?

A. I should think it was about nine o'clock.

Q. When did you first go to the City Hall to meet the Mayor?

A. I did not see him that evening.

Q. Did you go to the City Hall that evening?

A. Yes, sir.

Q. Did you see the Chief there?

A. I saw the Chief of Police. I stopped at his door as I went up stairs.

Q. Did you see the Chief Engineer?

A. No, sir. I received something from him.

Q. Have you that document here?

A. Yes, sir. It is made out to Mr. Fabyan and reads as follows:— "Will blow up buildings or remove goods as his judgment directs." That was handed to me by a gentleman whom I did not know or could not see. I was with a crowd of gentlemen, pushed into the Chief of Police's office. I asked the Chief what it was. He said it meant to receive the men, whom he detailed at once.

Q. State anything that you did in pursuance of that authority.

A. The first thing I did was to request the patrolmen placed under my charge to meet me at the corner of State and Devonshire streets. My impression is, that four officers were placed under my charge by the Chief.

Q. At what time was this?

A. It was a long time after twelve o'clock. I should say about two o'clock.

Q. Did they meet you there?

A. Yes, sir, they met me there in a few minutes' time. The first inquiry as I left the Chief's office was, "Where can any people who understand the business and powder be obtained?" One of the patrolmen, then in the office, stated that he knew where powder could be obtained. Then the Chief said, "Very well, you know where to get it." He went then to Dock square. He came back in a few minutes and said that it was necessary for me to go there in person, as some one in authority must say say something about powder. I went down there and found Mr. Reed, the Engineer, of the firm of Wm. Reed & Son, sitting on a box, which he said had something which he did not want to put into any store, except by consent of a policeman, and he was ready to give me any information. I told him I had simply come down to ascertain where powder could be obtained in case it was wanted. He said it could be obtained, a certain portion, as it was wanted, in a store opposite, pointing out two or three places; and he placed certain quantities of powder in the carriage, which our men had then obtained.

Q. What quantity?

A. My impression would be two hundred pounds, in cans.

Q. What was done with that?

A. That was taken to the corner of Milk and Devonshire streets, where it was stated to us that General Burt would be found.

Q. What was done then?

A. At that time we waited for some one who knew about the business to appear. Who the parties were that appeared then, I am unable to say, except that two or three of my patrolmen stuck very close to me, to see that the powder was not delivered to the wrong parties. I cannot say who the parties were.

Q. What did they do?

A. Well, now, I must say right here, that of my own knowledge they did nothing, and that I know nothing.

Q. Pass over all that you don't know of your own knowledge. Do you know anything about any other powder that night? Do you know anything of your own knowledge of any incidents that occurred in the street?

A. I know that I entered no building to take charge of the matters inside, excepting in one case, in Congress street. I went into a building that was burning at the corner of Lindall and Congress streets, believing that they were preparing to blow it up. I wanted to see that there was no one hurt of a line of persons that were stationed at the stores; to see that the men were all called down before the powder was blown. We got them all out of the way.

Q. Was that building blown?

A. There was a loud noise came from it, sir, and I supposed something of that kind had happened.

Q. Did it fall?

A. I can't say. I was running for my own preservation.

Q. Did you see any building fall that night apparently from an explosion?

A. No, sir, I did not.

Q. (By Mr. PHILBRICK.) Was there any explosion at the corner of Milk and Devonshire streets after you had delivered the powder there?

A. Yes, sir. I heard an explosion, whether from falling walls or whatever it may be, I don't know.

Q. Did you remove or direct the removal of any gunpowder from any building that night?

A. Yes, sir.

Q. Where was that?

A. In the Mutual Insurance Co.'s building on Congress street. It was placed there temporarily, because the parties who brought it were determined to unload it there. It remained only a few minutes.

Q. Did you direct its removal?

A. I ordered a man placed there to assist in removing it, the instant some one appeared to take charge of it.

Q. Do you know where it was carried?

A. I do not know where it was carried.

Q. Was there any other instance in which you directed the removal of gunpowder from a building?

A. Not that I recollect at this moment.

Q. (By Mr. COBB.) You say you were told that General Burt could be found at the corner of Devonshire street. Did you find him?

A. No, sir: not until quite a while afterwards. He came to me afterwards and informed me of authority, which I think was similar to this, and showed me the paper.

Q. Was he acting under that authority?

A. Not at that time. He stated that he had that authority, and had been assisting some one in doing something, but I can't recollect just what the words were. My impression was that he was endeavoring to assist in saving the Government property.

Q. Did you notice anything special about the management of the fire which you think ought to be recorded or examined into?

A. No, sir, I did not.

Q. So far as you observed the working of the Fire Department, how were they working?

A. They were doing everything that was possible, after I reached it. I saw the Chief several times. He was very active indeed.

Q. (By Mr. FIRTH.) Was he cool?

A. No, sir; I can't say that he appeared to be cool, because it was a moment that required more than any human nature that I ever saw, to be strictly cool, and to be active. He seemed to understand what he was talking about most thoroughly, and in giving directions seemed to be acting on a plan which I thought he fully comprehended.

Q. Was he in possession of his faculties, apparently?

A. He was most decidedly in possession of his faculties. When he told me that he was determined that the fire should not reach State street, it seemed to me that he was carrying out a plan which he did carry out; and that although the fire was raging very fiercely, he was master of the situation. He had a general intelligent plan and was working upon it.

Q. Did he speak of powder?

A. Yes, sir.

Q. Did he favor it?

A. Yes, sir; he requested me verbally, and spoke to me like this: "George, I want those two buildings blown up at once. I want them blown simultaneously."

Q. What buildings were they?

A. One on the corner of Water and Congress streets, and the other on the corner of Water above Congress.

Q. Was there an explosion in those buildings?

A. Yes, sir.

Q. Both of them?

A. Yes, sir.

Q. How effectual was it?

A. In my judgment it was very effectual, and the fire was held in consequence at the corner of Water and Congress streets for several hours.

Q. It produced a good effect, then?

A. Yes, sir.

Q. How much of the building came down?

A. My impression is, that the Merchants' Insurance Building was almost a complete wreck.

Q. Did the roof fall?

A. The opportunity to see it was only for a moment. There was an immense hole made by the explosion, and the fire was kept in check in consequence. I knew from what he said, and the orders I heard him give, that his design was to have water placed upon these two buildings at once, he believing that a large area would be created at once. He then said, however, that State street was his line of the fire.

Q. (By Mr. FIRTH.) Was there any other explosion which seemed to you to be serviceable in staying the progress of the conflagration?

A. Yes, sir; the explosion of Leonard's eating-house, on Congress Water street. When that fell, I thought that was very excellent service. That was under the advice of Gen. Benham. I believe the fire did not go beyond it.

Q. Was there much fire coming out of these ruins after the explosion? Did the rubbish take fire immediately?

A. I observed no fire at the corner of Congress and Water streets until the fire spread across to Simmons's block.

Q. (By Mr. FIRTH.) How was it at the other place — the first blowing up? Did a fire spring up there?

A. My impression is, that the building was on fire before it exploded.

Q. Did you notice any want of water during the evening?

A. On Franklin street, I don't know that I noticed any want of water. On the northerly side of that street, the Engineers expressed themselves that it would not go across, but it did.

Q. Did you see it cross Franklin street?

A. Yes, sir.

Q. How was it done?

A. When the wool warehouse took fire, it was perfectly safe on the north side of Franklin street. Afterwards, Smith, Stebbins & Co's., Dudley, Poor & Co.'s, and Whiting, Frost & Co.'s warehouses took fire. Up to that time, there had no fire gone across.

Q. Did you notice it when it crossed, and where it crossed?

A. Yes, sir. It apparently crossed a little west of Isaac Fenno & Co's. That is on the south-east corner of Devonshire and Franklin streets, a little west of that corner.

Q. Where did you see the fire first?

A. I saw it on the eaves. The other side seemed to take from the wool of Harding's. It shot across the street as though it was an explosion. It sounded similar to what we heard in the latter part of the evening, from the blowing up of buildings.

Q. Did the firemen attack that corner vigorously?

A. I was up as far as Donahoe's block, and could not say. In the mean time, they had cleared the street.

JOHN S. HOLMES, *sworn*.

Q. (By Mr. Russell.) What is your occupation?

A. I am a member of the Boston bar.

Q. On the night of the great fire, how early did you go to it?

A. I was going down from my house, and stopped on the corner of Summer and Washington streets, about twenty minutes past seven, I should think (I took no absolute note of the time), meeting there Major Sanderson, of the Custom House. While standing and talking with him, I was looking down Summer street and saw a smoke going up over a building, and called his attention to it, saying that there must be a fire there. We at once started on the run, and when we got on the north side of Summer street, near Trinity Church, we both cried out, "Fire," and continued our way down to this building. At that time, no alarm had been given, at least not audible to me.

Q. What was the condition of the building?

A. As I came down towards the building, I saw, in the basement story, what at first looked like a large globe of fire. I saw it through the basement window as I came down. I looked across diagonally. I looked across and saw that the building and the windows were so situated that I could look the entire length of the basement, and in the Kingston-street end of the basement was, apparently, a large globe or ball of fire. It looked so to the eye.

Q. Was there any fire in the other stories?

A. There was no fire visible in the first story, or second story of the building. There was then breaking out in the third story on Kingston street a thick smoke, and that colored smoke which almost instantly precedes the bursting out of a fire; and there was, also, in the Mansard roof of the building the same kind of smoke in several places.

Q. How long after you first saw the fire was the alarm given, to your knowledge?

A. I did not hear the fire alarm at all. There was so much noise in a very few minutes that I paid no attention to any alarm.

Q. How soon did you see any apparatus for extinguishing the fire?

A. The first apparatus I saw was coming down through Otis place — a hook and ladder company.

Q. How soon after you got there?

A. I should say it seemed to be from ten to fifteen minutes, and a hose-carriage came along about that time. It was some minutes later before an engine came?

Q. Do you know the number of the hose company?

A. No, sir.

Q. Where did it station itself?

A. It ran down on Summer street, below the hook and ladder company. The hook and ladder company hurried directly out on Summer street, almost directly opposite the building that was then on fire, and they commenced breaking in the doors, or attempting to break in the doors. I did not see the hose attached to the hydrant, but I waited there until after they began to play. I was there two hours or more. The engine came up drawn by hand, and ran down and was stationed on the corner of Kingston street just below Summer.

Q. How soon did that begin to play after it got there?

A. It began to play within a very short time; but it played very imperfectly. I noticed that the jets of water did not strike the third story.

Q. When that engine passed, did there appear to be any fire in the engine?

A. I did not notice any; but I had the impression from the imperfectness of the jet that they had not steam up, or if they had started steam, that the coal had burned out.

Q. Did the playing of water from that engine improve?

A. Yes, sir, it did after a little time. It began to throw more distinctly.

Q. Did you see whether the hose-carriage or engine came fast or slow?

A. The first that I saw, the hose-carriage came with considerable rapidity, and also the hook and ladder came with considerable rapidity. On the steam fire-engine, I thought the men were tired out, as if they had been running hard. That engine came slowly through Otis street.

Q. Was there anything else about the fire that you observed that was worthy of notice?

A. Nothing except what was curious to me in the rapidity with which it worked through the Mansard roofing. I watched its working through the Mansard roofing of the first building; and then I got a position which enabled me to see how curiously it struck across the street and went down through Winthrop place. The flame, as I noticed it, went almost at right angles suddenly, as if by direction, human or divine. It crossed the street almost at right angles, and struck in, and the fire was continued on.

Q. Did you see it when it crossed to the corner of Otis street?

A. Yes, sir.

Q. Was there any effort made by the Fire Department to stay the fire there?

A. I didn't notice any particular effort there. I think the attention was then specially paid to the block on Summer street, because the fire was extending down through the various roofs of that large block on Summer street. I cannot say what people thought, but I did not see any particular attention paid to the building opposite, because I was a few minutes before standing just at the base of that building opposite, and I thought the fire was being confined entirely to that side of the street until I saw these rapid and angular movements of the flames.

Q. Did there appear to be much wind?

A. No, sir; the wind was exceedingly quiet and still at first; but there was suddenly a good deal of wind, and the upper currents of the air were very apparent, because this flame must have been carried by currents of air.

Q. What distance was it carried?

A. The whole width of the street. It seemed one whole tongue of flame. It was just as the roof was breaking out — the projections upon the window-frames and parts of the Mansard roofs began to peel off and fall, and that of course gave a larger space for the play of the fire in the roof.

Q. (By Mr. Cobb.) Did there appear to be a plentiful supply of water?

A. I could not judge, because my attention was called to this one engine which first came down, and which threw this imperfect stream. I watched that. Apparently, the diameter of the jet of water was large; but whether it was owing to the imperfectness of the engine or some other cause, why it did not throw higher I could not tell at the time.

Q. (By Mr. Firth.) Did you see any engines come later?

A. Yes, sir.

Q. How did they come as to speed?

A. I could scarcely tell, because the streets were so crowded in a moment, it being Saturday night, when people are all abroad. It took a very few moments to empty Washington street down to the bottom of the fire. The streets were so crowded that the engines had to come very slowly the last part of the way. They had to force their way through the crowd. The first engine that came that I noticed, there was no crowd to obstruct it. I did not notice what engine that was. I thought it might have been this engine here, because that was the nearest. The first engine that I saw came through Otis street.

Q. Did you see the Chief?

A. No, sir. In a few moments, Mr. Sanderson got hold of the rope and helped get it across to keep the crowd out. I thought the firemen seemed to attack the fire with great vigor.

Q. Did this crowd interfere with the working?

A. I thought they did at first, until they began to rope it off. I thought at first that the crowd was in the way.

Dr. T. S. PERRY, *sworn*.

Q. (By Mr. Russell.) What is your occupation?

A. Veterinary surgeon. I have charge of the horses of the Fire Department.

Q. What was the condition of the horses at the time of the fire?

A. Those that I had charge of were about recovering from the fever, a majority of them, but they were left prostrate and weak, which was the result of disease.

Q. In most of the cases where the horses have been sick, were they fit to be used?

A. No, sir.

Q. (By Mr. Firth.) What number do you speak of as not being fit for use?

A. Of all those that I had immediate charge of. There were some horses belonging to some engines that I did not go to see, because they were not severely ill. I had charge perhaps at that time of the horses of seven or eight engine companies and one or two hook and ladder companies — two I think, and perhaps five or six hose companies, and two extinguisher wagons.

Q. In their condition at that time could they have been used to advantage? Suppose you had been careless of the life of the horses, do you think they could have gone?

A. It was only with extreme difficulty that they could be taken out of the stalls, and one, that we were a little careless about, did fall down upon the hard pine floor. He backed out as sick horses would back out of the stall. They had almost all to be supported.

Q. Did this apply to one-half the horses of the department, or more?

A. Probably about one-half.

Q. What do you know about the condition of the other half?

A. The other half were ailing, and had been off their feed, all of them. I was unable to see the whole of them, because I was so busy attending to these, and the horses of the Health Department, and my outside practice, that I could only see extreme cases. I told Mr. Damrell, that if any horse was reported as being extremely ill, he should let me know, and I would go if I could go. Some I could attend to, and some I could not. But I furnished medicine for all of them, with directions for ts use, and the symptoms which would indicate its use.

ALBERT STANWARD, *sworn.*

Q. (By Mr. RUSSELL.) What position do you hold?

A. I am Superintendent of the Western Division of the Water Works.

Q. What is the Western Division?

A. It takes from the Brookline gate-house all west of that, the Chestnut Hill reservoir, and the works at Framingham.

Q. What map have you there?

A. I simply drew this off to show the distribution on the burnt district.

Q. Does it show all the hydrants?

A. I think not. I merely wanted the pipes; but I see he has got the most of the hydrants, and they average two hundred and fifty feet apart.

Q. Does it show the size of the pipe?

A. Yes, sir, the color indicates that. Here is Washington street, that shows the 24-inch pipe. Here is Bedford street, showing the 12-inch connection. There is Broad street, with the 12-inch. There is Pearl street. Follow this 12-inch pipe right round to State street, up State to Washington. This red line indicates the 16-inch pipe. There is Milk street. Summer street has 6-inch pipes.

Q. Is there anything else indicated on the map?

A. The small red lines show 4-inch pipes. There is a court called Milton place, which has 4-inch pipes, but the main distributing pipes are 6-inch.

Q. Are there any Lowry hydrants in that department?

A. No, sir. The only one set in the city proper was in Winthrop square, at the request of the Charlestown Water Board, to test the power of the hydrant. At that time, I had charge of the Eastern Division. I set it by consent of the Board, and the steamers went there and tested it, to see if it answered the requirements. It proved to be successful; and after the test was over, it remained there some little time, but as our steamers had nothing to attach to it, it was taken out, and there have been no Lowry hydrants since. That was in 1862. That was merely put in for the experiment. It worked well, so that the Charlestown authorities adopted it.

Q. Did you, as an expert, recommend its use at that time?

A. Yes, sir. I think I sent a testimonial to Mr. Lowry.

Q. Do you know why it has not been adopted by the Board?

A. No, sir.

Q. What is the comparative cost of that and of the old hydrant which you use?

A. That I could not give you. I have been upon this division since 1863. I resigned, and was gone three years, and then was recalled to the Chestnut Hill reservoir, so that the cost of those hydrants is something that I had nothing to do with. Mr. Jones, the Superintendent of that division, is now sick, and I am acting for him. I should think he would be able to be out in the course of a week.

Q. Is there anybody else who would know what he does about that?

A. No, sir. He is the man in regard to that, because he has furnished those hydrants for the Roxbury district and Dorchester district.

L. FOSTER MORSE, *sworn.*

Q. (By Mr. Russell.) What time did you go to the fire on the night of the ninth?

A. I could not tell what time. I did not leave Roxbury until the fourth alarm. I was in my office.

Q. Did you have anything to do with gunpowder that night?

A. I don't know that I did. I don't know that I should want to say anything about that.

Q. You are not bound to. Did you have any authority from the Chief Engineer that night?

A. No, sir, no authority from him.

Q. Did you receive any written paper from him?

A. No, sir.

Q. Or from any one?

A. No, sir.

Q. Did you see any explosions that night?

A. I heard some.

Q. Did you see the building fall at the time you heard the noise?

A. Yes, sir, I saw one building fall after the noise was made. That was next to the new Post Office on Water street, corner of Water and Congress street — the building with the high bay-windows.

Q. Did that fall completely?

A. It came very nearly down. It left one wall that stands there now. That was all that remained.

Q. Did the firemen play upon the ruins?

A. A short time afterwards they did. There was no occasion at that time. The fire was at the corner of Milk street at that time. There was no fire that originated in the ruins of that building until it caught from the building beyond.

Q. When it fell, they did not play on the ruins to soak them?

A. No, sir. The engines were there, but they did not play there because they kept playing farther up the street.

Q. Did you see any other building come down?

A. I did not see any come wholly down.

Q. Was there anything else worthy of notice that you saw at the fire, anything that you wish to state?

A. I don't know that there is. I should say that at the time that building fell down, or about that time, Capt. Damrell was in that vicinity. I heard him make a remark to Capt. Green which was a very good remark, viz.: to do all we could to keep the fire back until he could relieve some engines from Washington street, and as fast as he could relieve them, he would send them to him. I noticed that in particular, and saw that in an hour the different streams in that vicinity were as two would be to twenty.

Q. It improved?

A. Oh, certainly.

Q. How was the Chief at that time? Did he seem to be in possession of his faculties?

A. He certainly did, sir. I saw him almost every hour.

Q. (By Mr. PHILBRICK.) In the case of any other explosion, did you see any benefit resulting?

A. I think there was a benefit resulting from the explosion at the corner of Congress and Lindall streets. It was a granite building.

Q. Did you know of any powder being put into the New England Life office, at the corner of Congress and State street, that long building — any powder which did not burn?

A. No, sir. I saw them carrying powder in there after daylight. There was some powder on the sidewalk, and they set some of it in the doorway of that building, and covered it over with a rubber blanket — only for storage. I saw no parties attempting to touch it off after it was put there.

Q. (By Mr. COBB.) Did you notice any want of water that night?

A. I did not see any, because I was not around the steam engines close enough to see their gauges. That I suppose would be the only place to test it. I did not go near to any steam engine. There was not a sufficient supply for fire purposes. My impression is that there is not anywhere.

Q. How long have you been connected with the Fire Department?

A. I was attached to the Fire Department as a volunteer, from the time I was fourteen years old, twenty-three years ago.

I would say in regard to water, that the reason I spoke that way was, that I know when the water was being introduced into Roxbury, we wanted the Lowry hydrants to give us a better supply of water, and also larger pipes than we had.

Q. (By Mr. COBB.) You got them?

A. We got them through your instrumentality; and I have made the remark that we were better protected in Roxbury where the Cochituate ran than anywhere in the old city of Boston. It is so in New York. They have the same trouble that we have here. I heard a report last week in regard to this fire, from the New York engineers, and they said, "We want a new supply of water." And they have voted, and are now laying the large pipes, and the report is that the water is not to be tapped until it reaches below Chambers street. They are to have an independent supply for the whole lower part of the city.

Q. What have you to say about the conduct of the firemen?

A. The firemen fought the fire well. I saw them take doors and hold them up in front of them to keep the heat off, and play round the doors. I never saw them fight better. When the buildings were safe for them to be on the roofs, they went up on the roofs and stayed there.

Q. (By Mr. COBB.) What, in your opinion as an expert, would have been the difference if they had had a full supply of water, and the Lowry hydrants?

A. I was not there in the beginning.

Q. Have you any opinion about it?

A. I could only give a general opinion, that if they had had a better supply of water, they would have been better able to fight the fire. I have not heard any one say but what they did have water enough. This is only general impression. I know that when I was in the City Government, Mr. Damrell repeatedly called for more water and larger pipes. One case was after the fire at East Boston, two years ago. He wanted larger pipes down through that district. He was crying out for water all the time, and they did not give it to him. After the great fire, pipes were put there within a few months.

Q. What is your opinion of the general management of this fire?

A. So far as I saw it, I don't think it could have been better managed.

Q. Do you think of anything that could have been done better if you had had the charge of it?

A. No, sir.

Q. How about the use of powder? Could not that have been better?

A. No. I think those buildings that I saw blown up did good. I think the blowing up of the building on the corner of Congress and Water streets kept the fire from crossing to Simmons's Block for fifteen minutes, because the building was flat. It was easier for the fire to cross in the air than it was for it to go to the ground. The water could reach it more readily.

Q. Did you see any effect of the explosions on Washington street?

A. I just heard the explosion at Currier & Trott's building, and I said if that building comes down, it is the poorest thing that has been done this night. Then the Old South would have gone. There was space enough and a good wall to keep the fire back.

Q. (By Mr. PHILBRICK.) Did you see any effect of the explosion on Kilby street?

A. No, sir, I did not. What I saw was on Congress and Lindall. There was one building that I saw blown. There was no fire near it. It was a building occupied by Vincent & Hutchins for insurance. I think it is the corner of Kilby and Lindall streets. That did some good. It blew out the two upper stories and threw the balance into the street, so that when the firemen had a better chance to play on it, they stopped it. I heard other explosions, farther down the street, that I did not see any effect from, excepting the breaking of the windows, etc.

Q. (By Mr. FIRTH.) You said there was a call for water made in the City Council. Is it within your remembrance that a call was made by the Chief Engineer for this district that was burned?

A. In a general way; I think his report for, say 1868 or 1869, calls for a larger supply of water and a larger supply of pipes, and recommended the Lowry hydrants to be placed all over the city. I mean the Chief's Annual Report, which will speak for itself. So also in regard to the Mansard roofs. He spoke about them in his report; and he also recommended a steam fire-engine for Atlantic avenue, in his report for 1871.

With what experience I have had in the City Government, I know that it has generally been hard work to get anything for the Fire Department that might seem like going outside or increasing the force. You can see the same thing illustrated in Dorchester, after it was annexed. Dorchester had six engines. It was a long time before it was decided whether they should keep them or not. I think if their charter had been the same as others, Dorchester would have had but three engines, but they came in with six engines; and from the 1st of April, they had to make up their appropriation, and there was a strong effort made to take away two or three engines.

DAVID CHAMBERLAIN, *sworn.*

Q. (By Mr. Russell.) What is your position in the City Government?

A. I am Inspector of Buildings for the City of Boston.

Q. You had some consultations with the Chief Engineer on the night of the fire?

A. Yes, sir, I had conversations with him.

Q. What was your conversation?

A. My first conversation with him was to offer my services at any time or place that I could be of any service to him or to the department. He asked me then to take charge of a certain building and to prevent the fire from getting beyond it.

Q. Where was the building?

A. It was Beebe's building in Devonshire square, and all along that point.

Q. Was the Chief Engineer in possession of his faculties at that time?

A. Yes, sir.

Q. Was he cool or otherwise?

A. He was as cool as there was any need of.

Q. Did you meet him at other times during the night?

A. Yes, sir.

Q. Did you have any consultations with him as to the use of gunpowder?

A. Yes, sir, I met him, I should think, about eleven o'clock, — between eleven and twelve, I cannot tell the exact time. I met him on Federal street, and gave him the same proffers that I had an hour before. He said, "I want you to select some suitable locality in which the blowing up of buildings will have a tendency to stop the spread of the fire." I told him that was a very difficult operation for me to perform, but I would see what could be done. That was about the only conversation I had. He said if I would do it, he would take it as a great favor. I had but little faith in blowing up. I was Engineer in the Fire Department for seventeen years. The matter was always talked over. I had but little faith in it from previous information I had, and when I heard from the Chicago fire that was strengthened. I did not feel faith enough in the operation to select any place for blowing up.

Q. Did you do anything about blowing up?

A. No, sir.

Q. Did the Chief tell you at that time whether he had sent for powder?

A. He did, and said that it was ready at the end of Central wharf; that was between eleven and twelve o'clock. I should think it was nearer eleven than it was twelve.

Q. How long have you been Inspector of Buildings?

A. A little over a year.

Q. State what, in your judgment, were the causes of this fire being so uncontrollable?

A. Mansard roofs on high buildings.

Q. Where did the fire generally catch?

A. On the Mansard roofs generally.

Q. In what streets did you notice that?

A. On Summer street and Kingston street principally.

Q. Was there any deficiency of water that night?

A. Not at first. Afterwards, I saw engines playing streams of water that were of no use whatever, because they had not water enough.

Q. Where did you see that?

A. On Washington street, Water street, and Milk street.

Q. Was there any deficiency of fuel that night?

A. I think there was, because I saw them staving up and burning dry-goods boxes.

Q. Did you see any of the steamers that were idle for want of fuel, or did they supply the place of fuel with boxes?

A. They were all at work. I saw steamers that belonged out of town idle. I could not tell the cause of that. I saw Boston steamers waiting for want of fuel.

Q. How did the department work that night?

A. Admirably! Never better.

Q. As an expert, what is your opinion of the management of the fire?

A. I think it was as good as could be, under the circumstances.

Q. If there were to be such a fire again, and you were Chief Engineer, is there anything you would do that was not done?

A. I don't know that there was anything. I could not place my hand on a thing that the Chief Engineer fell short in. He seemed to be collected.

Q. Considering the extent of the fire, the character of the buildings, and all the circumstances, do you consider that his management of the fire was successful?

A. Yes, sir; I do. I think he did as well as could be done under the circumstances.

Q. Do you know anything about the supply of water for this district, where the fire originated?

A. When I was in the Board, there was always a complaint that there was a deficiency in that district. We always felt that there might be trouble there in the Board of Engineers I resigned a year ago to take this office which I now hold. I did some thirty years' duty as fireman, seventeen years of which was in the Board of Engineers.

Q. You had always feared a conflagration in this district?

A. Yes, sir; I feared that we should have trouble among those high buildings.

Q. Was it a matter of frequent discussion?

A. It was spoken of very often.

Q. Was it brought before the Committee on the Fire Department?

A. Not that I know of.

Q. Why not?

A. That belonged to the Chief Engineer. We knew that he had talked about it to the proper parties, or represented that he had done so.

Q. It was not your business to know what the Chief Engineer said to Fire Committees?

A. No, sir.

Q. Did not your Board, seeing the necessity which existed, pass a vote directing or requesting him?

A. I have no recollection of that. We often did pass votes requesting the Chief to ask the Water Board to put a Lowry hydrant here or there, but I don't recollect anything in that particular locality.

Q. What do you think about the desirability of having Lowry hydrants?

A. It is very important.

Q. (By Mr. Philbrick.) What do you think would have been the result if they had had them in this district?

A. I could not say, because the magnitude of the fire might have made it amount to nothing.

Q. I mean before the fire got so large?

A. It spread very rapidly. They had water enough at the first of it, two reservoirs and four or five hydrants. The water spread from these Mansard roofs so badly that the spray did not amount to anything. It went off in vapor before it reached the tops of those high buildings.

Q. Are there any suggestions you would like to make, except about Mansard roofs?

A. I think it is the duty of the City Government to get self-propellers for the Fire Department as quick as possible, and not depend upon horses that may be sick again. I also think it is their duty to enlarge their water-pipes. There are three grand points: they ought to stop Mansard roofs on high buildings, they ought to enlarge their water-pipes, they ought to procure self-propellers. There is where the fire had the advantage of us.

Q. Is there more legislation needed as to party walls?

A. I think there is, and that they should be carried up above the houses two or four feet. It has been suggested by builders. Six inches, as the law now reads, is some help, but where there is a large body of fire rolling up above the roof, it is but very little help.

Q. Have you seen the act now before the Legislature?

A. Yes, sir.

Q. Do you think it is adequate?

A. It is a great help. I don't know that I can suggest anything more than there is in that act.

Q. Does that make any provision about elevators?

A. I think that is struck out. They made a recommendation that elevators should be encased in brick walls. That was stricken out of the bill. I think it would be an excellent idea to have such a provision incorporated in it.

Q. Are there any such things as self-propellers?

A. Yes, sir. We sent to Manchester and got one. That has been making for us some time. They have been in use in New York for from five to eight years, to my knowledge.

Q. Suppose these Mansard roofs were made of different materials and did not display any wood on the outside?

A. That would have been very much in favor of the Fire Department's putting out the fire. As it was, all those mouldings and cornices were of wood.

Q. That is not a necessary arrangement for the roof at all?

A. No, sir; it is only a matter of cheapness.

Q. Your objection was only to wood Mansard roofs?

A. Yes, sir. Mansard roofs as they are constructed throughout that district and in Boston to-day. There may be a few exceptions. I don't know of any exception but that upon the Post Office.

Q. (By Mr. PHILBRICK.) There are some that show a good deal of finish?

A. Yes, sir; I have given permits in which I stated that all outside of the building should be of non-combustible material — galvanized iron and copper.

Q. Might they not add to this act the power to compel that?

A. Yes, sir. I had no power. I simply stipulated it because I thought I would bring them to it.

Q. (By Mr. FIRTH.) With your knowledge of the possible danger to the city, does it not seem that some preparation should be made for such an emergency as this?

A. It seems so. I thought so a year ago, when I appealed to the Legislature to make a law to that effect.

Q. (By Mr. FIRTH.) I mean as against fire — something besides water?

A. There ought to be some method by which fire could be stopped. Explosives that will level a building would be the desirable thing to have in the hands of proper parties. Since this fire, I have had instructions to level all dangerous walls in the district. At first I thought I would use some powder, but I was a little afraid of it, and a friend suggested that he had a method by which he could reduce buildings without any danger. He intimated that it was dualin or glycerine. He tried it on two buildings, and with two efforts on each, he levelled them to the ground, without endangering anybody, or doing anybody any damage. One was a pretty strong building. The material of the building was damaged, and it was of no value. It was the triangular building, with a circular front, at the corner of High and Summer streets. He tried, and threw it level with the ground at the second trial. The charge was placed right up against the building.

The explosive substance was in charges ten inches long, and as large as my wrist. He put a bushel of sand over the charge and ran a train to it by magnetic telegraph, and down the building came. The other building was the Episcopal Church on Purchase street. We tried the front of that and brought it down in two charges. At first it did not operate very well. The second trial brought the whole front down splendidly.

Q. Did it throw any rubbish to do any damage in any other direction?

A. A small stone might have peeled off here and there, but the whole thing seemed to drop in its tracks plump down.

Q. From what you have seen of this explosive do you think that it could be applied successfully in case of fire to level a building?

A. Unquestionably, because it does not carry fire with it as powder does.

Q. Is it not more sudden in its action?

A. There is nothing more sudden than powder. This substance men can carry in their arms right around the burning territory with safety.

Q. How would you use it in a building?

A. Pile it up against the principal foundation and apply the magnetic wire to it. It only wants to be covered with a bushel or a bushel and a half of sand, whereas in order to use powder that has got to be tamped. A barrel of powder has got to be held in some way in order to give force to the explosion, or else it will operate as I saw it do at that fire, — simply blow the windows out. I saw dualin cut a hole right through granite, — a hole seven or eight inches wide and twelve inches high, right through the solid granite, and it didn't disturb the next charge. It brought the building down.

Q. As an expert, don't you consider that there is great danger arising from the burning of illuminating gas at a fire and the impossibility of shutting the gas off?

A. Yes, sir, that was the great trouble, and one great cause of the conflagration spreading so fast during that night. Immense quantities of gas escaped and added to the heat.

Q. What would you recommend to prevent that?

A. I think that there should be gates at the corner of every principal street.

Q. Why not at every branch and every forking of the pipes?

A. I would recommend it at every branch of the gas-mains.

Q. Every time they fork or branch out in any way?

A. I don't know why not. It is important to isolate any particular portion of the city from the gas system. As I understand it, there was no opportunity to isolate in this case on that whole district. My recommendation is that every square should be so fixed that it can be isolated. We should not have had that disaster Sunday night if it had not been for the escape of gas.

Q. Did you go to the fire at Rand & Avery's Thursday night?

A. Yes, sir.

Q. Why was it that fire was subdued so quickly?

A. They had ample opportunity to play from the street and plenty of water. It was an easy fire to manage.

Q. Were not the brick walls calculated to give the firemen more confidence than stone walls would?

A. Not particularly that. The fire was early discovered, and they had an opportunity to get apparatus there and put it out. The fire was only in two stories. At the Summer-street fire, it was from cellar to attic all alive and as hot as blazes.

Q. What is the advantage of the Lowry hydrant?

A. The Lowry hydrant is equivalent to a reservoir. We have a great many reservoirs in Boston. A Lowry hydrant will allow three engines to come to it. I suppose it would not be worth much without a large pipe. You want a pipe of at least eight inches. It ought to be even larger than that.

OLIN D. PAINE, *sworn.*

Q. (By Mr. RUSSELL.) Where did you live before the fire?

A. No. 17 Kingston street, at the time of the fire.

Q. Did you see the fire before the alarm was given?

A. I did.

Q. At what time was this?

A. Well, sir, I am unable to state exactly. I should be willing to state, however, between fifteen and twenty minutes past seven.

Q. Where was the light? What part of the building?

A. Well, sir, the first I saw the light was reflected in a window of the third story of the building, in the elevator. This window opens right into the elevator of the building.

Q. On the passage?

A. Yes, sir. And at the same time, the light shone through the other windows on the same floor.

Q. Was there any light below that story?

A. Yes, sir. At the same time, there was a light in the basement window, a little, small, narrow window, perhaps three or four feet long, and wide in proportion. It looked like a living furnace. That was right under the elevator, exactly where that lets down into the basement. I looked down from the window where I stood right into that. I saw the fire when it burst through the window into the passage that leads from Kingston street, in the rear of the building that was occupied by Tebbetts, Baldwin & Davis.

Q. Did you give any alarm?

A. I gave no alarm at all.

Q. What did you do? Did you go out to the fire?

A. I was at the door a portion of the time, but I gave most of my attention to our affairs there, in the house.

Q. How soon after you saw the light was the fire-alarm given?

A. I can't tell you; I heard no alarm given.

Q. Was there anything special that you noticed?

A. Nothing special that I know of, except the very long time it took to get water on the fire. That was noticeable, and spoken of by all there.

Q. You heard no alarm, and don't know how long after the alarm was given before the water was on?

A. No, sir; but there were no people in the street when I looked out, except a few straggling persons. There was no crowd for several minutes; and it was a remarkably long time before anything like an engine or hose carriage appeared.

Q. How long, should you suppose, after you saw the fire?

A. Before the hose carriage came?

Q. Yes, sir.

A. I should set it, at the least, as twenty minutes. An engine didn't arrive until considerable time after that. We had about all we could attend to, the fire broke out so suddenly. We had to attend to our own house, and we gave less attention to the details than we otherwise would, perhaps.

Q. Where were you when you first saw the fire?

A. When I first saw the fire, I was looking from the second floor front window (that is, when I looked at the fire direct) of seventeen Kingston street, the house that I boarded in. That was directly opposite this passage-way where the fire, I supposed at the time, and always have supposed, originated.

Q. That is Mr. Pratt's house?

A. Yes, sir.

Q. Did you use a clock or watch in judging of the time from when you saw the fire, until when the hose-carriage came?

A. No, sir; that is mere supposition on my part.

Q. Was there any great crowd of people there before any carriage came?

A. Yes, sir. Before I saw any carriage, the street was full.

Q. What drew your attention first of all to the fire?

A. The first that drew my attention was the reflection on the wall back of our house. That runs very much higher than our house, and it flashed out in a second. I jumped from my chair (I was in the back of the house, on the second floor) and rushed through, the same as through this door, and looked out of the front window. Almost simultaneously with my looking out, it burst through the window. Then I looked down in the basement and it was on fire there.

Q. Did it look as if it was hotter in the basement?

A. It looked like a furnace; and another gentleman who boarded in the house and myself remarked that it looked as if the whole furnace had bursted. At the same time, there was a draught through the elevator, so we could hear the rushing and roaring of the fire like a steam engine. We supposed there was no way it could go down the elevator with such a draught as that. The conclusion we came to was, that it was going up instead of down. And I should say, the first point it burst through was the third-floor window. That was a pine wood elevator, sheathed with southern pine, very pitchy.

Q. Were you familiar with that fact?

A. Yes, sir; I have noticed it. That it is what I called it myself.

Q. You had noticed it before?

A. I had noticed that several times. I had noticed the color of the wood — a reddish wood, something of the color of sheepskin. It was inside of the house and running up perpendicularly with the walls inside.

I should be willing to stake my reputation that the fire started below the first floor, knowing the fact that there was such a draft in the elevator. It could not possibly come down. That is a fact that one can't well get over. We noticed the fact of the draught there the first thing, because what called my attention to it more distinctly was hearing the sound and roaring of the fire in the elevator.

Q. After the hose and engine came, did you notice anything remarkable about the management of the fire?

A. No, sir; I was attending to something else, trying to save the house we were in. It was on fire several times before twelve o'clock.

Q. Do you think the fire got into the upper stories any other way than through the elevator?

A. I saw no other way.

Q. You saw no fire above?

A. I saw no fire except in the elevator before it burst out. It seemed to draw everything in that vicinity, and burst through all the windows, and in a very few minutes the whole top of the building was on fire, you may say, in no time.

Q. How long?

A. I should say five minutes.

Q. You are confident there was no light there except at that one point?

A. That was the only point that I saw any light. I don't know but there were others, because the light might have been so intense there that I did not see any others; but it was very noticeable that that was the main point.

FRANK WORDELL, *sworn.*

Q. (By Mr. RUSSELL.) You live at Kingston street?

A. No. 17 Kingston street.

Q. What time did you see the fire?

A. I should think it was about twenty minutes past seven; somewhere in that neighborhood.

Q. Where were you?

A. At the time I heard of the fire, I was in the back part of the house, but I went through to the front part, to my room on the front side. By the time I got there, the fire was pretty well over the back part of the house. It was in the elevator, in the basement and in the third floor, and it was breaking out through the windows in the third floor when I saw it.

Q. Had the fire-alarm been given then?

A. I hadn't heard it.

Q. Was anybody crying fire then?

A. Yes, sir; some in the street.

Q. Was there much alarm, much outcry?

A. When I first saw the fire there was not. There was, a few minutes after.

Q. Did you hear the fire-alarm at all that evening?

A. No, sir, I did not hear it at all.

Q. From the time you saw the fire, how long was it before any hose-carriage came?

A. I didn't look at my watch. I should judge it was in the neighborhood of twenty minutes or half an hour. That is the nearest I could tell.

Q. How soon did an engine come?

A. That I could not tell anything about. I didn't see one, not at that time; not until after I went out of the house.

Q. What were you doing then?

A. I was in the house.

Q. After you saw the fire, did you go to the fire?

A. I remained in the house to help around the house. We passed water on to the roof for I should think two hours. The house was fired once or twice on the roof.

Q. Did you notice whether that hose carriage came fast or slow?

A. No, sir.

Q. Did you hear the fire roaring in the elevator?
A. Yes, sir.
Q. How was that elevator lined?
A. That I don't know; I never was in it.

SAMUEL F. PRESCOTT, *sworn.*

Q. (By Mr. RUSSELL.) At the time of the fire, where were you when it broke out?
A. At twenty-five minutes past seven, I locked our store, which is on Winthrop square.
Q. How soon did you notice the fire?
A. In the course of perhaps two minutes after that.
Q. Had any alarm been given?
A. I am not aware that there was an alarm given.
Q. Where was the fire? in what part of the building?
A. The fire, when I saw it, was in the south-east corner of the store of Tebbetts, Baldwin & Davis. I saw it by looking through the window, or perhaps the door which looks directly in front of their office; and the fire was then burning through the partition which separated the elevator space from the main store.
Q. In what story?
A. The first story.
Q. Was there any fire in the basement, or could not you see?
A. I saw none.
Q. Did you hear the fire-alarm after that?
A. No, sir.
Q. How long after you saw the fire did any apparatus arrive?
A. As near as I can recollect, I should think it was some fifteen minutes.
Q. What came then?
A. A steamer hauled by hand through Winthrop square.
Q. Was it going fast or slow?
A. The men were walking. They were walking when they passed Winthrop square. They were walking, coming through Winthrop square into Otis street.
Q. Do you know how soon they threw water on to the fire after they came?
A. I will not be positive. My impression is it was some twenty minutes from the time I saw the fire in the building before I knew of any water being put into the building.
Q. Was that put on by this steamer or by hose?
A. I am not aware. I did not stay at the place. I wish to say, immediately on seeing this engine, I went out from our store and took hold of the rope. By some exertion we succeeded in getting up a trot, and so passed through Otis street to the corner of Summer and Kingston streets.
Q. You helped draw the engine?
A. I did, yes, sir.
Q. And woke them up from a walk to a trot?

A. Yes, sir; all of us together. An effort was made, and we succeeded in getting up the speed a little.

Q. Did you notice anything else about the fire you wish to call our attention to?

A. Nothing, to my knowledge. I would like to state how I came to notice the fire. Our store was the Beebe store — Houghton, Perkins, Wood & Company. Our custom was, to go out of door No. 1, and lock that door last. The porter and myself were in the store, and no one else. I was detained a little, and didn't go away so early as perhaps I would at some other times. I went out of this door, and left the porter to lock it. I stopped at door No. 2, — there are two doors in front of Winthrop square,— and the thought occurred to me I would go round the block into Devonshire street, and let our porter pass this way and examine the doors on this side of the block, and our elevator door there. When I got into Devonshire street, I saw what appeared to be a cloud, a thin, vapory cloud, passing towards the east quite rapidly; and my first thought was "That cloud is running very fast;" and I also thought, perhaps the moon is in that direction. A second thought showed to me the moon was not there. I then went along two-thirds of the way into Summer street, from this point, and I heard some halloing. By the way, the second look I gave to this, I saw little sparks, little fine fibres, that were going up with this smoke. My first impression was, it was from some other building further south than the rear of the Summer-street block. I hastened my pace, and came round into Summer street, and as I came round there I saw no fire on the front of the building, and I went to the rear, the south-west corner of the building on Kingston street.

Q. You went round through Church Green?

A. No, sir; into Devonshire street, directly in front of the Summer-street block; and I came along to this corner, and, as I came along, I looked into the front of the store. I saw no fire whatever. I came round the corner of the block, and went to the rear, and there I saw the fire shining out of the rear of that block across Kingston street. There is a passage-way there. I looked into the store, and went up the steps (there is a door-way there which opens into their office, if I recollect rightly, with one window on Kingston street; the office running quite across the floor, across that room). I went up those steps and looked into the window of the door (the curtain was left up), and saw the fire coming through this partition, burning into the store from the elevator; and as far as I could see, the elevator space was completely on fire.

Q. You could not see it from the Summer-street side?

A. I did not see it from the Summer-street side in any portion of the building. I would add: Then I left that point and came back to meet our porter in Summer street, and I instructed him to go for our own Engineer. He had a small bundle he was carrying home from the store. I told him we had better go into the store and light the gas, and leave his bundle there. We did so, and went into our store at one of the Otis-street entrances. He immediately started for our Engineer, and got back to the store, perhaps I might say, in twenty minutes. I also sent for Mr. Houghton; pretty soon he came. The Engineer came and got up steam in our own boilers. During the time that the porter had gone for the Engineer, I went out and found Chief Engineer Damrell. I asked him for a line of hose that would reach up our elevator on to our building, and came with him to the elevator door in the rear corner of the block. He said he would have a line of hose there. I said I would have the elevator to take the hose on to the building as soon as the hose was ready.

Q. Did he furnish it?

A. He did, yes, sir; and I should judge as soon as his hose was ready, our elevator was ready to start. I started the elevator myself, and brought it up to the first floor, and the hose was attached, and the elevator carried it up into our attic. I did not go up into our attic; but, as I learned afterwards, they went up into our attic, and from our rear window threw water on to the building which is twelve feet from the rear of the block; a building owned by Faxon Bros., I think, fronting on Summer street.

Q. Could they throw on to the roof of that building?

A. Very easily.

Q. And did so?

A. I think they did, without any doubt.

Q. Was that a flat roof — that part of it?

A. Our roof, or Faxon's?

Q. Faxon's.

A. The top was flat, but it had this Mansard roof. It extended around three sides at least.

Q. Could not the water which they then had have passed over the Mansard front on the Summer-street side?

A. No, sir; it is too low for that.

Q. What became of it?

A. It must have rested against the side and on the flat roof of the building. It is possible that it may have been thrown on to Summer street, but I don't think it was.

Q. Where would it naturally run off, like rain-water?

A. From the roof of the building on the Otis-street side; also into this twelve-foot space in the rear of their store and ours.

Q. Was there any way to get hose on to the top of the Faxon building?

A. There might have been hose carried from the front of the Faxon building, but I think nothing from the side. There was a flight of stairs leading from Otis street up one flight on to the second floor in Faxon's building. Then you had to pass through the hall towards the front of the building, and then you would get on to the stairs that led from Summer street to the upper portion of the building.

Q. Was the hose saved afterwards? Was it taken down?

A. The hose came down. I think I heard it come down; but I am not positive in regard to that.

Q. From that position, could they protect the building on the corner of Otis and Summer streets on the other side of Otis street at all? On the west side of Otis, corner of Summer?

A. From our attic this building could have been protected, in a measure; but then — as I understood one of our men who was attached to the hose belonging, I think, to the fire brigade — the hose was placed out of the rear window; and in that case, but little water could have passed across Otis street to protect this building.

Q. Were there any windows in your attic on Otis street?

A. Yes, sir.

Q. If they had directed it out of there, could they not have protected the corner building on Otis and Summer?

A. No, sir. It is too far. I think Faxon's building must have been 110 feet long; perhaps, 120; then there was this 12 feet, and then our building, which is 164 feet. After placing this line of hose up our elevator, I went again for Chief Engineer Damrell, and I brought him to the store a second time through this rear passage of ours to the elevator, to the second elevator, which is in the further corner, the south-east corner of our store, towards Devonshire street. The Chief told me he was unable to give me a line of hose, not having enough to cover the territory, so much fire was raging, but as soon as he could give me a line of hose, he would do so.

Q. Did you see any hose playing on the building on the corner of Summer and Otis streets from any roof opposite the spot where the fire took place?

A. No, sir, I could not say I did. You should not place too much weight upon my testimony in regard to that, because I was interested in our own store so much. I was in and out of our store as occasion called.

Q. It might have been played there and you not noticed it?

A. Yes, sir; but I can say it was very hot indeed. I passed from our store through into Summer street. I perhaps passed there half-a-dozen times during an hour; perhaps less, three-quarters of an hour. Time of course flew very rapidly. There was a great deal to be done, and the last time I was through there, I think it was hardly possible for a man to stand there and direct a hose.

Q. How did the Chief appear?

A. He appeared very calm indeed.

Q. Self-possessed?

A. Very much so. The second elevator-door that I speak of was controlled by A. T. Stewart & Co. They used it for the hoisting of goods in and out of their lofts.

Q. That opened on Devonshire street?

A. The second elevator opens on the passage-way which leads from Devonshire street. We had no key to that door. I found a fireman who had an axe, and I asked him to remain there until I could see the Chief Engineer and get this hose, as I wished to have him ready when the Engineer gave his consent to break in the door and run in the hose. After the fire-brigade came and took possession of our store there was a line of hose brought in intending to carry it up the stairway to the top of our building, but the water came before we got it across the store, and they turned the stream into one of the offices in the rear of the building and directed it through the window on to this burning building in the rear, — Faxon's building, — the one east, fronting on Summer street.

Q. How far up did they get that hose?

A. Only the first floor. There was a large body of water. If I recollect right there was no nozzle to the hose. It was a hose that the water came through, I think, perhaps a three-inch hose.

Q. Did the Fire Department appear to be doing everything that could be done?

A. So far as I saw, the firemen were doing everything that could possibly be done. I think I heard the crash of the first building; that is, the building occupied by Tebbetts, Baldwin & Davis. I am very sure I heard the crash of that building, in about as near as I can judge thirty minutes after the time I saw the fire in the building. The last time I went in or came out of our building was perhaps twenty-five minutes past nine. At that time, I am very sure it was not safe for any person to go in. I was the last person, I think, to go in.

Q. Did you feel any serious alarm the first ten minutes after you saw the fire?

A. Yes, sir, I felt very much alarmed in regard to our own building, in consequence of there not being any water put on to the fire.

Q. From what you saw, do you think the fire might have been confined to the basement, if there had been no elevator there?

A. If there had been no aperture through the floor, and no hatch-way, and the fire had been discovered, I have no doubt it could have been confined to the lower, or second floor.

Q. Is it usual in buildings of that class, such as you and your neighbors occupied, to have those elevator passages open without any hatches?

A. Yes, sir. I am very positive that Mr. Beebe had hatches made for his building, but I am very positive we didn't use any ourselves; that those hatches were taken away before we occupied his store, and stored in the loft.

Q. Why were they taken away?

A. I should judge, from the inconvenience of opening them and shutting them morning and night.

Q. They were on hinges?

A. I think they were.

Q. You have never heard of self-opening hatches?

A. I have heard of them since the fire. I have never seen any.

Q. Have you ever heard of any being used in Boston?

A. One of the firm of Wellington Brothers & Co. informed me, the other morning, that they had those hatches at their store, and gave me an invitation to come in and see them; but I have been so busy since that time I have not had an opportunity to do so.

MARY F. COOK, *sworn.*

Q. (By Mr. Russell.) Where did you live at the time of the fire?

A. No. 27 Kingston street; I live there now.

Q. What time did you see the fire?

A. I should think it was about quarter past seven — from there to twenty minutes. I could not be certain.

Q. What called your attention to it?

A. Halloing and screaming.

Q. Was there any fire-alarm given then?

A. No, sir.

Q. Where was the fire then? in what part of the building?

A. When I saw it, I saw it first at the bottom, and I looked up and the blaze was from the bottom to the top.

Q. Do you know where the elevator was there?

A. No, sir; I don't. I ran into the house and reported, and my husband came out.

Q. Did you hear the fire-alarm that night?

A. Yes, sir.

Q. How soon after you saw the fire?

A. I should think it was five minutes, fully, before there was an alarm given.

Q. How soon after the fire did you see any engines or hose come to the fire?

A. It was fifteen minutes; and the first thing I saw then was a hose carriage.

Q. After the fire-alarm?

A. Yes, sir.

Q. Did you look at any watch or clock?

A. No, sir; I didn't, but it is what I should judge.

Q. Did you see any engine after that?

A. Yes, sir.

Q. How soon after the hose carriage?

A. I should think about from three to five minutes after I saw the hose carriage.

Q. Was there anything else about the fire that you want to bring to our notice?

A. We have a girl in the house that I think knows as much about it as anybody. She came from Charlestown with a bundle of clothes — some that she had got to wash — and she says when she passed by the building it was perfectly dark. She says all she did was to go up stairs, two flights, and take her clothes up; and she went out on the street again and saw the blaze; and she said that is all she was detained — just long enough to carry up her clothes.

Q. What is her name?

A. Althene Parker.

ALFRED D. NASON, *sworn*.

Q. (By Mr. RUSSELL.) Where were you on the night of the fire?

A. I was in New York; having been connected with the house of A. K. Young & Co. between three or four years — nearly four years.

Q. Were you a partner?

A. No, sir. I have been since three years ago the head confidential man, and manufacturing manager of the concern. Last year I had an interest in the business, but not as a general partner. This year I was on a salary.

Q. What was their condition, financially, at the time of the fire?

A. Their business at the time of the fire was more prosperous, in a financial point of view, than it has ever been before since I have been connected with them, and I think since they went into business, some ten years ago.

Q. Were they in such a condition as to be great losers by the fire?
A. Yes, sir; they are very great losers.
Q. Do you know what the stock was worth?
A. The amount of their insurance, I believe, was $17,600.
Q. What was their business worth in a year, — net profits?
A. I had an interest last year and their profits were upward of $30,000; and this year I will guarantee that our profits from Jan'y 1st to the time of the fire were over $40,000 net, above the losses we had met with.

ASINETTE COOK, *sworn.*

Q. (By Mr. Russell.) You live at 27 Kingston street?
A. Yes, sir.
Q. What time did you see the fire?
A. I should judge it was from fifteen to twenty minutes past seven.
Q. Where was it? in what part of the building?
A. The flame was bursting out from the third, fourth and fifth storis. I think it was five stories high.
Q. Could you see the basement?
A. I could see the basement, and it seemed to be light from the basement up.
Q. How soon did you hear the fire-alarm after you saw the fire?
A. It seems to me as though it was ten or fifteen minutes, but at such a time as that, the time seemed very long.
Q. How soon after you heard the fire-alarm, did you see the first hose carriage come?
A. I guess it was fifteen minutes before they were there.
Q. After you heard the alarm?
A. After the fire-alarm was given, I should think it was full fifteen minutes.
Q. How soon after that did any engine come?
A. They were there immediately after.
Q. You did not use a watch or clock in fixing any of these times?
A. No, sir.

MARY A. WARDWELL, *sworn.*

Q. (By Mr. Russell.) Where were you at the time of the fire?
A. At Mrs. Cook's, 27 Kingston street.
Q. What time did you first hear of the fire?
A. As soon as the cry was given.
Q. What time was that?
A. About quarter past seven, I think.
Q. How soon after that did you hear the alarm?
A. I should think about five minntes.
Q. How soon after that did you see the first hose carriage?
A. I could not tell. I should think it was about twenty minutes before the engine got ready to play on the fire.
Q. After the fire-alarm?
A. After I first heard the cry of fire.

Q. The engine began to play in twenty minutes after you first heard the cry?

A. Yes, sir, we furnished them with wood, to get up steam.

Q. You furnished them with wood.

A. Mr. Cook did.

Q. Is Mr. Cook here?

A. Yes, sir.

Q. Where was the fire?

A. It was in the three first stories. The three first stories were burning, and the window in the third story the flames seemed to burst out of the most. I stayed three or four minutes on the sidewalk and looked at it.

Q. Did you see any fire in the basement?

A. No, sir, it seemed to be up in the upper stories. There seemed to be the most fire there; the smoke and blaze were pouring out very rapidly.

WM. W. COOK, *sworn.*

Q. (By Mr. Russell.) You were at 27 Kingston street?

A. Yes, sir.

Q. When did you first hear of the fire?

A. I could not exactly state the time. I was sitting in the lower entry. We have a great many boarders at our house, and every Saturday night I sit in the entry to take the money, and while there I heard the boys in the street crying fire, and as soon as I could put my books and papers away, I jumped up and ran out.

Q. What did you see?

A. I ran up Kingston street and looked up the alley-way, and the place where I saw it was going up from the cellar to the garret. There was not much flame coming from the lower part, but I could see from the bright light that there was a fire there. It was going up through the elevator, and the place when I saw it was ten or fifteen feet in length, in the upper part of the elevator, coming out from the elevator windows, streaming across the alley. I should judge it was about three minutes after I heard the cry of fire.

Q. What time did you say it was?

A. I could not exactly state. I should judge it was somewheres from fifteen to twenty minutes past seven. I did not notice the clock; in fact, I was so excited at the time I ran out that I didn't take notice of the clock.

Q. Did you hear the fire-alarm?

A. I heard an alarm given. I should judge it was from four to five minutes, at least, after I heard the first cry of fire; four or five minutes, I should think it was. It might have been five minutes; I could not exactly state, because I didn't note the time.

Q. Did you see any fire apparatus,— hose-carriage or engine?

A. The first thing I saw in the way of fire apparatus was a hose-carriage drawn by men, coming up Kingston street from Beach; coming this way.

Q. Was it coming fast, or slow?

A. Very fast; as fast as the men could run.

Q. How long was that after you heard the fire-alarm?
A. I should judge it was very near ten minutes.
Q. How soon after that did you see an engine?
A. I should judge the first engine I saw stop at the fire was about fifteen minutes, I should think.
Q. After you heard the alarm?
A. Yes, sir.
Q. Not fifteen minutes after the first cry of fire? You said they were some ways apart?
A. The alarm was five minutes after I heard the first cry of fire. I heard the alarm in five minutes; in ten minutes after the alarm, the hose-carriage, and about five minutes after that the engine stopped there. They got out of coal while they were there, and they came into the house and got kindlings.
Q. Was that before they got up steam?
A. No, sir; that was as much as twenty minutes after they got up steam, and were playing.
Q. Do you know what engine that was?
A. No, sir.
Q. You say they got out of coal twenty minutes after they got going?
A. Yes, sir.
Q. Do you know they were out of coal?
A. The fireman came to the door and asked me if I had any kindling, or anything in the house he could burn. I told him yes, and he came in and got a basket and box full and carried them out and brought the basket and box back.
Q. Did you see any supply of coal come to them,— any coal cart?
A. No, sir; I did not see it when it came, but they had it there shortly afterwards, because I went out and asked them if they wanted any more, and they said their supply had come.
Q. Did their playing cease?
A. No, sir; the stream kept up right steady all the time. They had borrowed from other parties, they told me.
Q. How many engines were there when they borrowed?
A. I only saw this one. I was in the house and there might have been a dozen others in other directions.
Q. Which way did that engine come into the street?
A. I think she came from Beach street, up.
Q. Where did she locate to play?
A. At the hydrant just below my house.
Q. Corner of Bedford and Kingston?
A. Yes, sir.

GEO. W. ARMSTRONG, *sworn.*

Q. (By Mr. Russell.) Tell us all you know about the fire.
A. I saw the fire from my house at about a quarter past seven, and went direct to where the fire was. I went up on to the steps of a building just this side of where the fire was, with my wife, and stayed there from ten to twenty minutes before there was any water put on to the fire, and then the streams did not reach the third story.
Q. On what corner?

A. Right in that doorway there.

Q. Did you hear any fire-alarm?

A. No, sir; because, probably, my mind was on the fire; there was so much yelling in the streets.

Q. Was it on Kingston street?

A. The building where I stood was about No. 25 Kingston street.

Q. How long were you there before you saw water put on to the fire?

A. From ten to twenty minutes.

Q. You had no watch to see which?

A. I didn't look at my watch. I was surprised that there was no water put on to it; and when it was put on, it did not reach the third story.

Q. When you first got there what was the condition of the fire?

A. The whole Mansard roof — all but the corner — was in a blaze, coming up through the roof. It didn't come down and take the next story, but skipped down a story and came out of the third story.

Q. When the engines and hose carriage came, did they come fast or slow?

A. They didn't come fast. There was a steam engine drawn by men who seemed to be completely exhausted when they came up, and stopped right at the corner of Kingston and Bedford streets.

Q. Which way did they come?

A. From the south, — right up Albany street.

Q. That was the first one you saw?

A. Yes, sir. It stopped at the corner of Kingston and Bedford streets.

Q. Did you see any other engine or hose carriage arrive?

A. Shortly after that, a hook and ladder came. They came as slow as the engine did.

Q. Which way did they come?

A. From the south.

Q. Up Albany street.

A. Yes, sir.

Q. Did you see anything else that is worthy of notice?

A. Not at that corner.

Q. Did you anywhere?

A. Yes, sir. It surprised me to see no coal and wood where the engines were working. It seemed very strange to me. They were burning boxes.

Q. Where was that?

A. On Summer street, at the head of Lincoln.

Q. What time?

A. I am ashamed to say I can't remember. It might have been eleven o'clock.

Q. A good deal later than this?

A. Yes, sir.

Q. Did the steamer stop for want of fuel?

A. They stopped a good deal; whether it was for want of fuel, I don't know; they didn't work with the regularity they usually do. There seemed to be a great deal of stopping.

Q. Do you know whether it was from want of water?

A. No, sir; I don't.

Q. Did they call for water?

A. I supposed that was for coal. There was lots of calling all the time, toot, toot toot; two or three whistles, I could not say which.

Q. Did you see any other engines burning boxes or wood?

A. No, sir, I did not.

Q. Was there anything else that you noticed?

A. No, I think not. I live close by there, and my mind was on my own family.

Q. Where was your house?

A. 73 Beach, at the foot of Edinboro' street.

Q. When they were burning wood, was the steam up?

A. They were not playing at the time I saw them throw the wood into the fire-box. It might have been they stopped from some other cause. There was a number of engines stood in the square, two or three, and they were all burning boxes.

Q. In Church Green square?

A. Yes, sir.

Q. Did you see any lack of fuel when the first engine came on the corner of Bedford street?

A. No, sir, I did not.

Q. Did they get to work rapidly after they arrived?

A. No, sir; there seemed to be an omission of some kind. The people were so thick the firemen could not get in. The street was thronged before the engines were there. I was there with my wife, and some one said, I had better get the lady out of there as soon as possible, and I did.

Q. You say the firemen were troubled to get through the crowd?

A. At first they were, but they drove them back in a short time and kept them back.

Q. Do I understand that you got on to those steps as early as quarter past seven?

A. It might have been a few minutes later. I went there because there was nobody there to speak of. In ten minutes it was full.

Q. Do you mean to say you were there at fifteen minutes past seven?

A. It might have been a little later.

Q. You saw the fire from your house?

A. Yes, sir; and supposed it was Garcelon's stable, on the corner of Bedford and Kingston streets.

Q. What time was it when you got to the steps with your wife?

A. It could not have been more than five minutes.

Q. That would make it 7.20?

A. Yes, sir.

Q. You did not hear the fire-alarm?

A. No, sir; I could not say it was struck at all. My mind was on the fire after I saw it, and I didn't notice any alarm.

Q. The time when the steam engine arrived you didn't notice?

A. No, sir, only that it was a long time. I spoke to my wife and said, "Why don't the engine come?"

Q. Did you notice about the fire in the other part of the building?

A. The position I occupied was such I could not see the back. I didn't go any nearer the fire than the steps; all I saw was the roof and side towards Kingston street.

Adjourned to Friday, at three P. M.

SIXTH DAY.

FRIDAY, Dec. 7, 1872.

JOSEPH W. KINSLEY, *sworn*.

Q. (By Mr. RUSSELL.) What is your occupation?

A. Secretary of Faneuil Hall Insurance Company.

Q. When did you see or hear of the fire of Nov. 9th ?

A. I happened to be in the engine house of No. 4 when the alarm struck.

Q. Did you notice the time?

A. I should say it was twenty minutes past seven, or thereabouts. I can't say exactly.

Q. What was done?

A. When the alarm struck, Mr. Deering, the Engineer, threw the doors open of the engine house; the hose carriage was standing in front of the engine, nearest the door. While the gong was striking, he unreeled the rope (the rope rolls up on a little reel under the handle) and the men in the house and others swung it out. I stepped up to the dial and followed the box down with my finger, and when I saw it was fifty-two, I told them where it was, and we started with the apparatus.

Q. Started at once?

A. Started the moment I said "Bedford and Lincoln."

Q. How many had hold of the rope?

A. I should say at the time the carriage started, there were at least a dozen.

Q. Were you reinforced as you went on?

A. Every step we took, almost; they came out of the City Hotel and out of the Quincy House, quite a number. We went out of Brattle square into Brattle street, and down through Dock square and through Exchange street, and were reinforced all the way. Being somewhat familiar with the location, knowing that it was rather a bad locality, I took the head of the rope, and held it as long as I could. I kept on until they crossed Milk street on Devonshire street, right there by the new Post Office. I then stepped on to the sidewalk, and when I got on to the sidewalk, I could see the light of the fire. After the carriage got out of sound, so that I could hear, I heard the bell strike the last round of the fifty-two.

Q. How long were you in going to the fire?

A. I shouldn't think we could have been more than five minutes getting to that fire. I didn't go to the fire then; when I saw the light, knowing what the rules were, owing to the horse disease, I knew that it was a fire that would require the steamers, and the moment I saw the light, I turned back and ran to the engine house, hoping to get the steamer started before the second alarm could even be sounded, being but a short distance. When I got back, it seemed that somebody else had seen the light of the fire, or the second alarm had been struck while I was getting back, for the rope was all arranged, and they were just starting the engine out of the house when I got back.

Q. How much of a gang had hold of the engine?

A. I should say at least thirty were on the engine. There is always a crowd comes down to the engine house from Hanover street, Brattle square, Brattle street, and Tremont Row, when an alarm strikes. I have been there frequently when the alarm struck. I then went with the engine, and the engine went straight to the hydrant on the corner of Kingston and Summer streets. The fire was lighted before starting, and when the steamer got to the corner of Summer and Kingston streets, the hose company had a hose line on, and were playing with a hydrant stream.

Q. How long did it take the engine to get there?

A. They went up about as fast as I could run. I should say it was not over fifteen minutes from the time the alarm first struck before the engine was there. I allow for running up and back there a third time. I base my running time up there on my walking time that I have allowed myself to go to the depot. I know I can walk from the Albany depot, which is beyond that considerably, in less than ten minutes, and I know I can run faster than I can walk.

Q. (By Mr. PHILBRICK.) Can you walk from Brattle Square to the Albany depot in less than ten minutes?

A. No, sir. My office was on Congress street, and I calculated that the engine-house was about as far from my office on this side as the depot was from the fire on the other side, so that the distance would be practically the same. When we got there with the engine, the fire appeared to be coming out of the whole four stories on Kingston street. The fire hadn't got down but two stories on the Summer street entrance. The way I account for that, I am one of the committee of underwriters who have in charge the Protective Department, and I very frequently go into buildings, if I don't happen to see Engineer Green round, and assist in covering up goods, which is our special province in that department. I went in with three other men, thinking they would stop the fire on the Kingston street side, and it wouldn't come down to the second floor. I went in with a view to seeing if we could spread some covers there to advantage, but when I opened the door on the second floor, I saw in the rear, which would be along on the Kingston-street side, that the fire was then in the second story. There was also fire at the head of the second flight of stairs going to the third floor. Capt. Regan and Capt. Jacobs (Regan I know, and Jacobs I think was there) were there with a stream trying to get up that flight. We didnt't take any cloths into the building because we have had a good many cloths burned up, and we dislike to take them into a room if the room is absolutely on fire. I waited there a few minutes to see whether there was a probability they would stop the fire on that floor, to see whether it would be best to spread them on the floor below, and while there the order came to come out of the building. I came down the stairs, and when I got within two or three steps of the bottom, I heard the coving fall.

Q. Was it the corner coving?

A. I should judge it was, I can't tell exactly. The door was right next to the wall of the building. I think that Capt. Regan and myself were the last two out of that building. I know we stood there and saw it fall, and I thought that all we had got to do was to swing out by the wall, and we would be safe. We swung out and got on to the side and ran down.

Q. (By Mr. RUSSELL.) You speak of cloths — do these come in a wagon?

A. Yes, sir.

Q. Was the wagon there?

A. Yes, sir we had our wagon there. The man was there when I got to the fire; that came only from South street.

Q. (By Mr. FIRTH.) How is that wagon drawn?

A. We have two horses.

Q. You call that the Insurance Company's wagon?

A. We call it the Protective Department.

Q. (By Mr. PHILBRICK.) Was the wagon drawn that night by horses?

A. Yes, sir. I think we used our horses through the whole epidemic.

Q. (By Mr. RUSSELL.) How soon did the engine begin to throw water on the fire?

A. Well, they had a hydrant stream on the fire when the engine got there; they immediately disconnected the hose from the hydrant and attached the engine.

Q. Was it ready to throw water? was steam up?

A. They never wait for steam.

Q. They throw the water through the engine?

A. Yes, sir. That is where a good many people are deceived by seeing an engine throw water from a hydrant. They don't wait for steam; they let the water run through the engine; they get more force when they have steam, but they can get the same force through the engine as they can directly from the hydrant.

Q. How soon did they get up steam?

A. I can't tell you.

Q. (By Mr. PHILBRICK.) Was the fire kindled when you started from the house?

A. I didn't notice when it was kindled. I was at the head of the rope. I looked back several times, and could see that the smoke was coming out of the chimney. It might have been kindled before they started from the house.

Q. You saw it on the way?

A. Yes, sir. I think I saw it first on Exchange street. I didn't think of it at first; my first thought was to go back to the house and get the engine started. When we were in Exchange street, then I thought to be sure to have the fire lighted, and when I looked back, I saw the smoke coming out of the stack.

Q. (By Mr. RUSSELL.) How long did you remain at the fire that night?

A. I stayed until Sunday afternoon.

Q. How long have you been connected with the insurance business?

A. Since 1866.

Q. Have you been accustomed to attend fires?

A. Yes, sir, I have had an opportunity for the last four years of attending almost all the fires this side of Beach street, taking in what we consider the business portion of the city.

Q. How long have you been on that committee of the underwriters?

A. I think it is since 1869; 1868 or '9.

Q. You saw the fire cross to Otis street, I suppose?

A. It crossed to Summer and Kingston streets first.

Q. Yes; but were you there when it crossed to Otis street?

A. Yes, sir.

Q. I want to know if anything was left undone that could have been done to prevent that?

A. No, sir, I don't know of anything that could have been done. There were as many streams in Otis street as they could get there, and also on the building which was in the rear of the Winthrop-square building, and also on the Summer-street front.

Q. Do you think it was possible for the Boston Fire Department, with the means in their possession, to have prevented the fire from crossing to Otis street?

A. No, sir. I would state that just as it was catching the French roof on the corner of Otis street, I started for Cambridge. I made up my mind that it was going to be a large fire. I am personally acquainted with the department there, and I started to get the Cambridge Department over.

Q. Did you see any effort to stay the fire at the corner of Otis and Summer street?

A. Yes, sir.

Q. Do you remember what it was?

A. There were steamers 9 and 11, hose 3, and I think hose 8 or 5, I am not sure which, right in this corner, as we call it, trying to keep the fire out of Winthrop square. I can't tell what force was on the other side of Summer street. I kept backing with the fire. I know that engine 4 was on the opposite corner, because I could see them, and their stream was on that side somewhere, I can't tell where, and No. 7 was below on Summer street.

Q. (By Mr. Russell.) Did you get the Cambridge engines?

A. Yes, sir, the Cambridge Department came in when the fire was burning the A. T. Stewart half, if I may describe it so, of Beebe's block; before it got through that block, they got there.

Q. (By Mr. Firth.) Did you carry the message to them?

A. I ran up to the Cambridge car office, intending to go to Cambridge myself, but I saw a young man whom I knew just going over, and I told him to go to East Cambridge and give the alarm, and tell them I sent for them. I had done that before, and also when I lived in Cambridge I have come to this side, and given the alarm for the Boston Department to go to Cambridge.

Q. Was it your message which brought the Cambridge engines?

A. Yes, sir.

Q. (By Mr. Russell.) They all came in, first and last?

A. Yes, sir, they all got here. I think that the engines which answer the first alarm from the East Cambridge box came first. I sent over word that it was steamers we wanted more than anything else, feeling the necessity of force to throw the water high.

Q. How did the firemen behave that night generally?

A. I never saw them show more bravery or skill, as I thought.

Q. Does that apply to the whole time throughout the fire?

A. Yes, sir, from the time the alarm struck, until I left there, Sunday afternoon, I didn't see anything that looked like a disposition to shirk their duty, or anything of that kind.

Q. Now, looking back on the fire, do you think anything was left undone that ought to have been done?

A. I think there were some things done that ought not to have been done.

Q. What were they?

A. The use of gunpowder. The reason I speak of that particularly is, that I saw cases, where, in my judgment, buildings would not have been burned had it not been for the gunpowder, alluding particularly to my own office.

Q. (By Mr. Firth.) Do you think it was gunpowder, or the unwise use of it?

A I think it was the unwise use of it.

Q. (By Mr. Russell.) What number in Congress street was your office?

A. Number 32.

Q. What did you see there?

A. I saw, at the corner of Congress and Water streets, what I call a very fair job, so to speak.

Q. (By Mr. Firth.) That is, it was well done, comparatively?

A. Yes, sir, and I think if they hadn't attempted to blow up on the opposite corner, the fire might have been stopped. If the firemen could have stayed there, with the sort of square there was there, I think the fire might have been checked; but as soon as that building was down, or, very soon after, they put the powder into this building, which of course drove the firemen back, and it came up on that side without any interruption.

Q. (By Mr. Philbrick.) Did they fire these two buildings, one after another?

A. No, sir; the building on the corner was down before the other was blown up. After the first one was down, the fire came back of this building and they went to work blowing that up; then they put powder into the second or third building from the corner, and for some reason or other, the powder didn't explode until the building burned down into the cellar where the powder was. In the mean time, the firemen were kept back under orders from Gen. Benham, Mr. Carpenter, and others there, and the fire went across the street into Farwell's printing office in Simmons' block. The reason that it got in there was because the powder didn't explode until the fire got down into the cellar, and they wouldn't allow the firemen to go beyond it.

Q. How long did they have to wait for the fire to burn down to the powder?

A. I think they may have waited half an hour; then, when that powder did go off in that building, they put powder into the building on the corner of Lindall street, which was then on fire on three floors, and when that explosion took place (I don't know how long it was in there), it took every square of glass out of our building and filled the bank building full of burning embers. I claim that if they hadn't blown up that building, our building, being a low building, with a fire-proof roof, they could have stopped it there. Engineers Farrar and Smith were in our building, and I took them on top, and showed them that it was fire-proof, and that they could stay there and fight the fire, and that if a hot brick fell on the roof, they would be safe. I think there were five lines at one time ready to go into the building, but the explosions kept coming, and after awhile they filled our building full of fire; of course, it couldn't help but burn.

Q. (By Mr. Philbrick.) Supposing the buildings on the opposite corners of Congress and Water streets had been both exploded at once, wouldn't the result have been better?

A. I think it would, as there was an alley-way between this building on the corner and the next one, so that it need not necessarily explode the building next to it. If the two buildings had been blown up together, I think there would have been no trouble stopping the fire in that direction.

Q. Would it not have been much better to have exploded the powder before the fire reached the point, than to wait until that time?

A. That is what I asked them to do in one case, on the corner of Lindall street, so that the building might be a mass of ruins, and thereby save our building; but the powder being in that building, and not exploding until the fire got down to the cellar, the firemen didn't dare to go into our building.

Q. The fuse didn't burn?

A. Somebody said they didn't take any fuse with them. I think the failure to make a successful explosion there cost us that side of Congress street. Why I say that is, because it was getting pretty near home with me.

Q. Did you see the Chief during that night?

A. I saw Mr. Damrell as often as once an hour all night.

Q. How did he appear?

A. He appeared perfectly calm. I met him down on Purchase street, and he called my attention to a light that we could see through some narrow buildings, and asked me to go down and ascertain what that was, telling me where he was going, so that I could overtake him. I went down and ascertained that the fire was on a coal wharf, and went back and told him that the water-boat had come up, and was taking care of that. He said, "It is all right; I sent for the boat some time ago, and I am glad to know they are on hand." He asked me if I saw Mr. Scott, the man who had charge of the boat, and I told him I did. He seemed to be satisfied with that; it was in compliance with his orders. It seemed to be working according to his orders. I inferred from the fact that he had ordered the boat there, that he was fearful of South Boston, and when I told him that the fire was in some coal, and the boat was there, he seemed to feel relieved about it. That was before the fire had got to the north side of Franklin street. When the fire had got so far that the firemen had to back down Franklin street into Devonshire, I went to him, and he told me to find Capt. Regan, who works for James Boyd & Son, the manufacturers of hose, and tell him to go to the store and take every foot of hose there was there and bring it into Devonshire street, to ascertain when it was there, and report as soon as possible.

There was another young man with me, and I told him, "You hear what Capt. Damrell says; now we will go in different directions, and see if we can find Mr. Regan." I didn't succeed in finding him myself, but in my travels I met this young man, and he told me that he saw him.

Q. (By Mr. Russell.) Was there any trouble from lack of water that night?

A. Yes, sir; that was the great trouble.

Q. Where?

A. Well, from the start, that is to say, after there had been half a dozen streams attached to the hydrants. The second and third alarms would bring in several hose companies, who run without steamers; they are always anxious to get a stream of water on, and they would attach to the steamers, and undertake to get two streams, and they couldn't get sufficient water. When they had shut off one stream, then they would get one very good stream. I have noticed the same scarcity of water in that section before except where they could get at a reservoir such as there was at the foot of Franklin, on Federal. They have always made what use they could of that reservoir in case of a fire in that direction, on account of the hydrants being light. At the time of the great wool fire in that vicinity, they had three streams from that reservoir, because they could get so much better supply of water from that than from the hydrants.

Q. (By Mr. Philbrick.) When you arrived, were you surprised at the extent of the fire?

A. Yes, sir; I couldn't account for it. Ordinarily, I shouldn't have expected to see any more fire, if I had waited for the second or third alarm. It looked about such a fire as we generally see when they strike the second or third alarm, and that was the reason why I ran back for the steamer, because I could see from the light that it was such a fire as would call for a second alarm, and I wanted this company to be ready. I thought if I could save a little time, it was important at that time.

Q. Have you, as an underwriter, or your associates, ever had anything to say in regard to the construction of the elevator hatches?

A. Yes, sir. I don't know that we have gone so far as to attempt to oblige anybody to have self-closing hatches, but we have always preferred to have them. There are very few stores, however, that have them, but we always make that a point in favor of the risk, when we go to examine a building, if it has them.

Q. Have you ever heard any valid objections to these self-closing hatches?

A. Not the slightest; I never heard any objections raised. On the other hand, I have heard a good deal said in their praise, both as a protection from fire, and dust and dirt, and also as a protection against people backing down into them. I don't know what objection there can be to them. I think they are a great improvement.

Q. Did you ever know any to be removed after they were once put in?

A. No, sir.

Q. (By Mr. Russell.) Was there any scarcity of fuel that night?

A. I didn't notice any. I heard them telling in some of the back streets, where they got into a narrow alley-way, or something of that kind, about using boxes, or wood, or something of that sort, in one or two instances.

Q. (By Mr. Cobb.) When you first reached the fire, was the fire attacked with the energy and vigor that fires usually are by the department?

A. Yes, sir; and I can confirm my belief in that condition of affairs by stating that I went one floor above the fire, feeling perfectly confident that they would stop it at that height. I went one floor above where I actually saw the fire, to spread our covers. I thought there might be an elevator there or something of that kind, and I know they have been very successful in getting inside of elevators and stopping the fire.

Q. (By Mr. Russell.) Will you, as an expert, give the cause of the fire becoming so uncontrollable?

A. The French roofs.

Q. Was it the form of the roofs or the amount of timber in them?

A. It was both.

Q. Do you think that form of roof, made of any possible material, objectionable?

A. I don't know what material could stand the heat that was got up there. I don't think iron would have done it, unless it was very heavy iron, as they had not only roofs, but there were those large skylights.

Q. Suppose the skylights hadn't been made of wood, and the Lutheran windows hadn't been made of wood?

A. If the window casings and skylights had been made of iron, that would have been different, but not only the roofs were made of wood, but the skylights also. I know I went up into the third story of the second building that caught, on the corner of Otis and Summer streets, when the fire didn't look as if it had got beyond their control in front, yet the skylight was on fire, and the stairs were burned down one flight. That was before it showed a great deal on the outside. I went into that building. The first five thousand dollars the company lost were lost in that building.

Q. (By Mr. Philbrick.) What I wanted to ask was whether, in the old-fashioned, simple style of roof, if the building had been so constructed, and finished with wood cornices and Lutheran windows, in the style that most of those buildings were, it would not have been just as likely to take fire as if it had a Mansard roof?

A. Not quite so much so, because there wouldn't have been so large a space to cover with a stream. If a stream can cover a space four or six feet square, like the ordinary Lutheran window, it would have more effect than it would if it had to cover the whole side of the building, as was the case with the building at the corner of Winthrop square and Otis street.

Q. Suppose the windows were the same?

A. Then there was the wooden cornice.

Q. Then the trouble doesn't arise from the form of roof; the Mercantile building had a very heavy wooden cornice.

A. There wasn't so much wood to it.

Q. (By Mr. Firth.) As I understand, the French roof is a question entirely independent of its material; those were wood?

A. That is the point; it is the large amount of wood, so high up, out of all reach. It was not so much the form, as it was the material. The difficulty was from having so much wood up there, and so high.

Q. That is, it is the *wooden* French roof that is objectionable?

A. Yes, sir.

Q. (By Mr. RUSSELL.) Wasn't another cause of the fire becoming so uncontrollable, the time that elapsed before the alarm was given?

A. The fire had got great headway before it was detected.

Q. Did you ever see any fire that had got such headway before?

A. No, sir. I never attended a first alarm in Boston when a fire had got such headway, unless there was some difficulty, as was the case in the State-street block, when they went to one box and waited some time, and had to go to a second box; but when they have got an alarm from the first box, I don't recollect of attending a fire where it had got such headway upon the first alarm.

HENRY W. WELLINGTON, *sworn.*

Q. (By Mr. RUSSELL.) Where is your place of business?

A. No. 66 Chauncy street, corner of Bedford.

Q. How many stories high?

A. It is pretty difficult to tell; it is the old church. There are about four floors in it.

Q. What sort of hatches do you use to your elevator?

A. They denominate them the "Automatic Hatches," I think. I don't know any other particular name they give them.

Q. How do they work?

A. Very well, sir.

Q. How long have you had them?

A. Four and a half years, in my store.

Q. Have you had any trouble with them?

A. Never.

Q. What are the advantages of them?

A. They are always closed, except when a load is passing through. Mr. Kimball's life would have been saved, and Mr. Frothingham's son, and a great many other people's lives, the last few years, if they had had them.

Q. (By Mr. PHILBRICK.) What is the expense of those hatches, the size of yours?

A. I can't tell; not much more than the common hatches that are used.

Q. (By Mr. FIRTH.) Where are they made? There is a patent on them, I suppose?

A. I don't know that there is a patent on them.

Q. (By Mr. PHILBRICK.) How did you get them?

A. I happened to be in one of the mills at Fall River, and stood beside the elevator when a load came up. I noticed it, and as I was about fixing up my store, I put them in.

Q. Do you know of any others in Boston?

A. I don't think there are any others. I will say, that I put them in our mill in Newtonville afterwards, and our rope broke at one time, and the hatches worked so well, that although the load came down as quick as it could come, every one of them opened and shut with the exception of the last, which threw it over. If there had been a little pine block, we could have stopped it.

Q. It didn't stop the elevator?

A. No, sir; nothing would stop that. I didn't pay anything for the patent right. I contracted with a party to put in the elevator at Newtonville. I think they asked me a hundred dollars for the patent right to put it in there. I sent the man there who put in my elevator, Mr. McLaughlin, on North street, and I think he got some deduction on the patent right, I don't know. I paid him a certain price, and he was to pay for the patent, and put it in. It has worked admirably at my store, and mill, and at the Fall River mills. I have inquired frequently about them there.

MRS. SARAH E. YOUNG, *sworn.*

Q. (By Mr. Russell.) You came out from Mr. Young's building on the Saturday night of the fire?

A. I did, sir.

Q. At what hour?

A. At twenty minutes before six.

Q. Did you come out with Mr. Young?

A. I came out with my husband and three others. There were four of us altogether.

Q. Everything was quiet then? no fire?

A. Everything as usual.

JOSEPH R. GROSSE, *sworn.*

Q. (By Mr. Russell.) Where is your place of business?

A. 109 Court street.

Q. Will you tell us what you know about this fire?

A. I hardly know where to commence.

Q. Begin where you first heard of it.

A. Well, I crossed over the extension of Broadway on to Albany street with Alderman Powers, and I guess we had gone about the length of this Court-house, full as far as that, and perhaps a little more, and we were looking ahead of us, looking at the street lights, and all at once the heavens seemed to light right up.

Q. What time was it?

A. I should think it was from quarter to twenty minutes past seven; something like that.

Q. How soon did you reach the fire?

A. We didn't go directly to the fire; we went down Albany street to Essex street, through Essex street to Mrs. Montgomery's saloon, where the Alderman's two children were, and from there to the Boston Theatre. We saw a hose-carriage, I should think it was, on Harrison avenue, but there was no alarm struck from the time we saw it until the time we entered the Boston Theatre; at least, I didn't hear it, and suppose it wasn't struck.

Q. Was your attention called to the fact at the time?

A. Yes, sir, by, I should suppose, fifty or a hundred making the remark on the street, "Why don't the bells ring?"

Q. (By Mr. FIRTH.) No alarm had been given when you entered the theatre?

A. No, sir.

Q. Should you have heard it if there had been? Wasn't there too much noise in the street?

A. There couldn't have been much noise in the street at that time; there was a bell on the Boylston-street market, right near us, and I think if it had rung, we should have heard it, but still there is a bare possibility that we might not have heard it.

Q. (By Mr. PHILBRICK.) Did you hear any alarm after you got into the theatre?

A. No, sir.

Q. (By Mr. RUSSELL.) How long did you stay at the theatre?

A. It was after ten o'clock.

Q. Do you know anything about the fire?

A. Only I was with Aldermen Powers and Cutter, and remained all night, until about ten o'clock Sunday morning.

Q. Did you notice anything special?

A. Not particularly, as I know of; only general opinion; that is all.

Q. Have you ever been connected with the Fire Department?

A. I was in the department some twelve years as a member and volunteer.

Q. How long since you have been in the department?

A. I have not been in the department since steam came in.

Q. (By Mr. FIRTH.) About when was that?

A. I guess it was about eleven years ago. I think I left the department in 1858. There might have been steamers then, but our company did not have one. Yes, there were some steamers at that time. I recollect the "Miles Greenwood."

Q. How was this fire managed?

A. Well, so far as I could see. The only deficiency, I should say, was in the amount of hose. I can't think of anything else. They seemed to be standing round with no hose; they all complained that they hadn' those enough. I know it was so particularly on Summer street, because I went to one of the Engineers and told him he must get some hose for No. 10, I think it was. I took that responsibility.

Q. Hose 10, of Boston?

A Yes, sir. That is located in Washington Village, where I live, and I know the most of the company, so I took that responsibility.

Q. Was there any other hose company that had the same trouble, that you know of?

A. I should think there were half a dozen that could get only just so far. They didn't seem to have hose enough. They would want ten, twenty, or thirty feet more; there seemed to be a deficiency. There seemed to be enough of it round, but it was all bursted.

Q. Whether or not those were Boston engines?

A. Not all of them. I should think I saw four Boston engines, and wo or three of the out-of-town engines, more particularly where I stood at the head of Milk street, near Washington, in Liberty square, and down on Chauncy street.

Q. (By Mr. Cobb.) Was there plenty of water?

A. In some places I shouldn't think there was; sometimes, they would get two or three streams on a hydrant, and it seemed they couldn't reach any particular spot; but take away one stream, and the other seemed to do a good deal of good. There seemed to be a good deal of effect to it; but it scattered all round; the stream seemed to be light. I will say (I don't know that it is material), that I was with the Chief on top of the City Hall. I was in the Mayor's office at the time when word came in that the Chief was crazy, and the Mayor spoke of putting Capt. Quinn at the head, and I rather objected to that. I thought it was not his duty, and just at that time the Chief came in. I think it was the Chief of Police who suggested it, and the Mayor sent for Mr. Damrell.

Q. (By Mr. Firth.) What was the word that came?

A. That the Chief was crazy, and they had sent him home in a carriage. I think the Chief of Police brought that word into the Mayor's office, and soon after that the Chief came in.

Q. Was he crazy?

A. If he was, I am. I think that is the best answer I can give. No, sir; he was as calm and cool as ever I saw a man in my life. I was very much surprised, under the circumstances.

Q. Did you go to the top of the City Hall with him?

A. I did. I should think we were up there ten or fifteen minutes, making suggestions. The only thing I thought of was, that he would have to look out for the district where the Post Office was.

Q. (By Mr. Cobb.) What did he say?

A. He said himself, that that was the only weak point; that he had engines enough at other places; but he was afraid that before he could get them round and get them to bear, the fire would get ahead of him at the head of Water street, and down that way. The engines were all massed about Summer street and Washington street, and it is a long distance to go round and come down through; that seemed to be his only fear, as far as I could judge; he seemed to be pretty sanguine that he had the best of the fire, so far as this side of the street was concerned. He didn't seem to be at all alarmed about the Washington-street side.

Q. (By Mr. Firth.) About what time was it when you were on top of City Hall?

A. I should say it was about three o'clock Sunday morning.

Q. Were there any others there with you?

A. Oh, yes, sir. I think Alderman Cutter told me I had better go up with him, as I knew the Chief better than he did, and having been a member of the department, I might suggest something, and we went up together; but there were eight or ten, perhaps a dozen, on the top of the building at that time.

GEORGE W. CARNES, *sworn.*

Q. (By Mr. Russell.) Where was your place of business?

A. 43 and 45 Summer street.

Q. How soon did you hear of the fire?

A. I learned that there was a fire as early as eight o'clock in the evening, and took the nine o'clock Brookline train into the city. I reached my store about half-past nine o'clock. At that stage, the fire was in the block below Chauncy street, and had extended across to the opposite block, near the corner of Arch street. I felt uneasy with reference to my store, and therefore took my money, a number of account-books and insurance papers from my safe. Those I sent by my eldest boy, who accompanied me, to the depot. I then desired to get a clearer knowledge of the probability of the fire reaching my store, and went, soon after, on the top of the building, where I had an extended view of the fire. At that period, there seemed to be no preparation with reference to meeting the contingency of the fire at my corner — the corner of Chauncy street and Summer street. My own store was located next to that.

Q. Was your store a part of the Post-Office building — Capen's Post Office?

A. No, sir; it was the next above it.

Q. Next to Hovey's?

A. No, sir; there was one brick store between Hovey's and mine, occupied by Mr. Walko, a fur-dealer, and by other parties in the chambers. The want of preparation made me feel uneasy, as regarded the safety of my store. I knew that unless a stream was brought through on to either the adjoining building, the Post-Office building, or my own, it was only a question of time as to the destruction of the building. Being anxious with reference to my stock, and fearing that parties might pass it out through the door, I went below and conferred with two other occupants of our building, as to the prudence of removing the stock. At this stage I was hopeful as to the preservation of the building. It seemed to me, as the fire was working very slowly against the wind, up Summer street, that ordinary precautions as to this corner would avert the destruction of that part of the block. I looked upon this corner as the key to a block of immense value, including, as it did, the stores of Hovey & Co., Mudge & Sawyer, Lawrence & Co., Jordan & Marsh; and it seemed to me a natural course, that special attention would be given to this locality by the Fire Department. At a later hour, — I think it was not far from twelve o'clock, — four hours, or more, after the fire had taken at the corner of Kingston street, — the fire then had crossed Arch street, and was working its way in the rear of Mercantile Building, and working up Franklin street — I could see the buildings occasionally fall down in Franklin street, between Arch street and Hawley, and my chief anxiety arose from the very tall building which had recently had heavy additions made to the roof, on Chauncy street, opposite the old Post-Office building. At about this time, not far from twelve o'clock, I was greatly relieved by a hose, manned by a strong force, brought up through the Post-Office building, on to the tin or metal roof of that building; our own was a gravelled and tarred, flat roof. My brother-in-law remarked: "George, your building is now safe," and I felt considerably relieved. It seemed to me the fire could be repelled with that aid alone, unless, owing to the great height of this building by the side of the Post-Office building, the flames should stretch across the street; but I was hoping that as the block was being consumed gradually, the wall might fall, and that would afford relief in the direction of Kingston street. I cannot state in detail; I cannot seem to recall the precise occurrences, but I passed below stairs, being anxious with reference to the stock. I should remark, that while on the roof, one of the firemen remarked to me that a passage-way should be opened through the building, which I occupied, that they might pass in. or out, as occasion called.

Q. (By Mr. PHILBRICK.) As a place of retreat?

A. Yes, sir; a place of retreat from the roof. In the vicinity of fifteen or twenty minutes, being at the foot of the stairs, I met quite a number of the firemen, I infer an entire company, who passed down leisurely, remarking as they went out: "It is too hot to remain there." I looked upon it with some surprise, because the position they had taken on the corner building could have been changed to my own building, where they could have been amply screened, either behind the chimneys, or the tall projection on the front, and also by the skylight, through which they passed down.

Q. (By Mr. PHILBRICK.) Do you know what company that was?

A. No, sir, I am not able to say.

Q. (By Mr. COBB.) Do you know what Engineer was there?

A. I did not see any Engineer in the building. The firemen remarked that by orders of the Engineer they had the privilege of passing through our store. I told them they were free to use it. At a later hour, wishing to see what the prospect was as regarded the corner building, fearing that the trimmings might be ignited, I stepped into the middle of the street. There was a hose company in the middle of the street at that time. They were playing on the front corner of the Post-Office building. They appeared to me to be doing very little good, although some of the window trimmings were burning; they might have allayed the fire in that respect, but it had very little bearing upon the preservation of the building. At that stage, looking up to the top of my building, I saw a little fire, perhaps the breadth of a foot or two in extent, at the uppermost parts of this tower-like structure that was built up. A gentleman from Brookline was standing by my side, connected with the Eire Department of Brookline. I remarked to him, "It does seem too bad that that building should be destroyed with that small beginning." "Well," said he, "I will try to find an Engineer." As he left me, one thought suggested itself. This fire had not yet attracted the attention of the firemen, and I impulsively stepped forward to the men who had the pipe playing upon the corner building, and proposed giving them five hundred dollars if they would put a stream on my building, or carry a hose up through the building. In regard to carrying the hose up, one or two responded that it would be as much as their life was worth to go up there. Knowing well the construction of the building, and the easy approaches to that point, and the ease with which one could escape from that position, either in front or at the back, — and I may say here, that the construction of the building favored its protection more, perhaps, than any other build ing that was consumed that night; there was a passage-way in the rear, and by a short ladder, — I think even by climbing — they could have got on to the lower part of Hovey's building, making the centre of their main hall, — I felt disturbed by the response that it would be hazardous to go up there, and replied that if they would follow me, I would lead the way; upon which it was said, " We cannot go without the authority of an Engineer."

The proposal to change the stream from the corner, which I felt justified, under the circumstances, in making, because the stream, in my judgment, was doing no good, whereas apparently it might have done much towards the preservation of the building which I occupied,— that proposal wrought like magic upon them. There might have been some six or ten men in the cluster. No. 3 was on the caps of some of them. I do not know whether it was a Boston company, or what it was.

Q. (By Mr. Cobb.) What time was this?

A. This was, I should say, about one, possibly nearly half-past one. The proposal to pay them five hundred dollars excited them considerably, and they made the remark, one to another, " There is a prize offered," and in their impetuosity to get their stream to bear, they either fell to the ground, those who held the pipe, or the hose burst; I am unable to say which; but in the meantime, wishing to calculate as to the chances of the early destruction of the building, knowing that from that beginning it would work its way into our work-room, that was in the upper story of the building, I went up the stairway, and went into the room, and approached to the front windows. At that time, in the corner of the room, near this fire on the outside, there were little jets of light to be seen through the cracks in the plaster, and while I was standing there, a small piece of the plaster fell, perhaps two feet in length, and that began to sprinkle fire among the cotton goods, linings and such like, which we had been using in the manufacture of our boys' garments. I then passed down, feeling certain that without a hose the building would be destroyed.

In the mean time, my friend, Mr. Kenrick, of Brookline, an Engineer I think of the Fire Department, returned, and said he was unable to find an Engineer, but if I saw a man with a white fire-cap on, speak to him. Almost immediately after, I saw one, and accosted him. Said I: " I would really like to save that building. I think if a hose is carried up inside, that fire can be put out." He was looking in that direction. Said he: " We have no hose;" and I knew then that the building was doomed. In a little while after, the smoke began to issue from the upper windows, and shortly after, flame, and by degrees it burned to the next story, and passed down from story to story in that way, covering the space of an hour or more.

These are the facts. It might be superfluous for me to express my view of the inefficiency of the branch of the Fire Department in that locality. I have no other knowledge of the Fire Department, except what I saw in connection with that building, and on the street.

There is one thing I would like, with your permission, to suggest. I was surprised at the inappropriateness of the tools, or instruments, made use of to reach points where the fire was burning on other buildings. The building directly opposite mine, the Mercantile Building, with heavy eaves, projecting over the front, and a building, I think only two stories and a half high, might be accounted a very low building, as compared with ordinary warehouses. Not far from the time my building began to burn, the eaves adjoining the White building opposite Chauncy street, had taken fire, — a small stretch of the eaves, just adjoining the White building. It attracted the attention of a fireman having a pipe, and he directed the stream towards it, but could not reach it. Shortly after, there were two streams playing. The fire was not spreading with any rapidity along the eaves, but seemed to be burning just on that corner, and I saw, after the space of from three to five minutes, two streams directed to that point, with great efforts on the part of the firemen to reach it with the water. They would toss the pipe so as to jerk the water and reach it, but it appeared to me that hardly a sprinkle of the water reached that point.

I omitted to mention, that after I had come down from the work-room and passed again into the street, they had adjusted their pipe, and were successful in reaching the eaves of the house, playing higher than they had on the opposite side of the street; but they could only sprinkle a little of the water on the roof, which was doing no good, and the building was destroyed from that small beginning. I feel sure from this, that could I have anticipated this contingency, an ordinary hose attached to a faucet in the building would have put out the fire. One single hose from any engine, steam or hand, would have put out the fire in my building.

Q. (By Mr. Russell.) You say there would have been no trouble in carrying a hose up there?

A. No, sir; it would have been a pleasure rather than a rash performance to have done it myself. There is a mystery to me about the hose carried to the top of the corner building. The firemen came down through our building, and passed out. Whether this hose was withdrawn or destroyed, I am not able to say.

Q. (By Mr. Philbrick.) You did not see them take the hose out?

A. No, sir; I did not see them withdraw the hose.

Q. Was this hose carried up through the corner building?

A. I did not see the entrance; I only saw it as it emerged from the sky-light; but our porter says that this hose was carried up through the front door of the buildinga djoining our store. That same hose, had it been withdrawn and located up in our building, it is a question whether the corner building could have been saved; it needed, I think, water from without on the trimmings; but I feel sure that it would have saved our building, and the fur store between Hovey's and ours, next to ours.

Q. (By Mr. Russell.) You cannot tell who the Engineer was that you spoke to?

A. No, sir; he was a stranger.

Q. (By Mr. Cobb.) Did you say anything to the Chief that evening?

A. No, sir; I did not.

Q. (By Mr. Russell.) Do you know what those steamers were that were playing ineffectually on the Mercantile Building?

A. No, sir; I do not think I looked to see. I only looked at the stream and hose as they were being used. I feel aggrieved, as a citizen, at the inadequacy of the preparations made with reference to the protection of that corner. The fire was hours in approaching. It was apparently almost the natural boundary of the fire in that direction, and but very little effort was needed to prevent the fire from working into that block; and had there been any directing hand, it seems as though it would have been only the exercise of common sense to have made some provision with reference to persistent efforts in saving that corner. The efforts appeared to me irregular, fitful, left almost to the choice of the men; and the Fire Department in that section appeared to me more like a mob than anything else.

There were incidents connected with the fire, on the street, that annoyed me very much. Our porter was perhaps a more particular witness of them, but I saw firemen ranging the street, not far from the front of Mercantile Building, with articles of merchandise in their hands, congratulating each other as to what they had got. One of them had a paste-board box, that appeared to me to contain a muff, or some article of fur for ladies' wear, and he was telling one of his comrades what he had got. There were many of the firemen who were perfectly listless as regarded the igniting of buildings. This was at a time when there was very great danger of the Mercantile Building being destroyed, as the fire was then working its way into the rear, and particularly into the India-rubber store adjoining Holbrook's.

Q. (By Mr. Firth.) You cannot tell whether those were Boston firemen or not, can you?

A. No, sir.

Q. (By Mr. Russell.) Do you know more than that they had firemen's hats on?

A. They had firemen's garments on.

Q. Anything but hats?

A. Yes, sir.

Q. (By Mr. Cobb.) They were in uniform?

A. The ordinary uniform worn by firemen. I do not know that I could specify as to the entire rig. It was that form of dress which I have been accustomed to see firemen wear at fires; fire caps in particular.

Q. (By Mr. Russell.) I would like to have you recollect, if you can, whether they wore anything but the fire caps?

A. Nothing that attracted my attention.

Q. (By Mr. Cobb.) Anything like a uniform?

A. No, sir.

Q. (By Mr. Firth.) Were the men who had the muff, or something like a muff, the same who had been up in your building?

A. I could not have recognized one of the men who were in the building, and the countenance of this man was not impressed upon me. It was at a later hour, — it might have been an hour later, — and the firemen were mingling with each other in the street. There were a good many men in firemen's dress, who seemed to have no particular duty to perform, other than to enter some of those stores, and to move through the streets with these articles. This was between my store and Trinity Church, almost in front of the Mercantile Building.

Q. (By Mr. Russell.) What is your porter's name?

A. James Quirk.

Q. Where is he to be found now?

A. He is at my store.

Q. Was your building of such form of roof as to allow you to go on the top of the highest part?

A. The whole roof was flat. The tower was slated and came up to a point.

Q. Where was the fire?

A. It was upon that slated part.

Q. Was it between the upper and lower corners of the Mansard?

A. Yes, sir; I infer that this ridge was of wood. It began to burn near the top, and worked its way into the lathing.

Q. Were you the owner of the store?

A. No, sir; it was owned by A. C. Hersey, of Hingham.

Q. (By Mr. PHILBRICK.) Was there any point from which you could have hung carpets, or clothes, over that tower?

A. Had I anticipated this, I think I could have thrown them over that.

Q. Had you any means of wetting yourself?

A. I could have poured water on. I admit that I had not the presence of mind to do it. Soon after the fire commenced, a fireman came in and said he was very thirsty, and went down into the cellar; I let the water on, and he quenched his thirst. The difficulty appeared to me that the pipes threw too large streams; that the calibre of the pipes was too great. I wondered that they did not use smaller pipes.

Q. (By Mr. PHILBRICK.) Did you see anything of the way the fire was fought on Hovey's building, while you were on your building?

A. While I was standing on the roof, they were covering the upper wood-work, the framing of their windows above the eaves, — the eaves were of stone, — with blankets, and appeared to be throwing water on (I did not see any hose), as they stood near the eaves. They had a standing place where the windows set back from the eaves.

Q. Were those firemen?

A. They appeared to be men connected with the store.

Q. What time was that?

A. That I should say was not far from twelve o'clock.

Q. (By Mr. PHILBRICK.) Were they doing that before the fire got on to your building?

A. Yes, sir; long before that.

WILLIAM B. WHITING, *sworn.*

Q. (By Mr. RUSSELL.) Where is your place of business?

A. 67 Devonshire street.

Q. What can you tell us of these self-opening and closing hatches.

A. I have been somewhat conversant with them ever since they were introduced.

Q. How long is that?

A. I should think about eight years. When they are in good order, we regard them as a very good safeguard against fire passing from room to room.

Q. How many have you seen in operation?

A. I cannot tell, as I inspect about five hundred different cotton mills, and most of them have one in; I cannot tell the exact number; hundreds, I think, very probably.

Q. You consider them in fixing the rate of a cotton mill?

A. Yes, sir; the hatch, or the want of it.

Q. How much does it affect the rate?

A. I do not know as it would affect the rate very seriously. It might have the affect of determining whether we took the risk or not. There is no great variation in our mutual rates, only say from eighty one-hundredths to one and one-eighth per cent.; and the want of these hatches may deter us from taking the risk at all.

Q. (By Mr. PHILBRICK.) Is there any particular objection, that you know of, to introducing them into elevators?

A. None whatever, except that the elevator might be situated so that it might not be convenient to do it. At the same time, there is no general difficulty in introducing them anywhere.

Q. Merely in matters of detail, to provide for them at some particular point?

A. That is all. They are applicable to almost any elevator.

Q. (By Mr. COBB.) Of what company are you Secretary?

A. The Boston Manufacturers' Mutual.

Q. (By Mr. FIRTH.) By what name do you call this particular form of hatch?

A. I generally term it the "Thompson Automatic Hatch." William H. Thompson, President of the Manchester Print Works and the Kearsage Mills was the man who first brought it into notice. It was patented by a young man in his employ, and first introduced by him.

Q. (By Mr. RUSSELL.) Do you know what it costs?

A. I think, for cotton mills, it is one or two cents per spindle.

Q. (By Mr. FIRTH.) Are they used to any extent, except in factories, to your knowledge?

A. Not very much.

Q. (By Mr. PHILBRICK.) Is there any good reason why they should not be?

A. None at all, that I know of. There is only one thing to be looked out for, in case the hatches are put in, that is, that they work. They are pushed apart by a wedge-like projection from the top of the car, and if they are not well oiled, they will sometimes stick.

THOMAS MINNS, *sworn.*

Q. (By Mr. RUSSELL.) This statement of yours in the "Boston Journal," of Nov. 13th, is a correct statement of what you saw and did on the night of the fire?

A. Yes, sir.

I was unable to go to the fire till about half-past ten, and after seeing its extent in the neighborhood of Summer street decided that a line of buildings around it must be blown up by gunpowder. I sought to find Chief Engineer Damrell, to urge that course upon him, and followed him down Bedford street, towards Broad street, and there learned he had gone to Pearl street. I then turned and went to the City Hall, where I found Mayor Gaston and Alderman Jenks and urged that immediate preparations should be made to blow up a cordon of buildings. Finding that by law the Chief Engineer has supreme authority at a fire, the Mayor, Alderman Jenks and myself sought Mr. Damrell in the direction of Pearl street. We found him in Federal street, between Milk and Franklin streets.

He said he had sent to Chelsea and another place, I think the powder-boats, for powder, and would blow up the buildings on the east side of Federal street. He added, "Now I want you to understand one thing. an explosion will produce a great mass of light debris that will burn fiercely, and I must have a large quantity of water at once, I am afraid I shall not have water enough."

I then went. at Mr. Damrell's request, to learn how the fire was at Mercantile Building, and on my return found the Mayor and Chief Engineer had been summoned to City Hall, where I went. A few gentlemen were in the Mayor's office, and others soon entered. General W. L. Burt, Charles H. Allen, and others, and Mr. Damrell, soon entered, saying, "Gentlemen, here I am, what do you want?"

Mr. Burt said, "We want the Common opened to receive goods, and gentleman appointed to organize gangs of a hundred men to remove goods, and Mr. Mayor, I think you should send to the Navy Yard for powder to blow up buildings, and the Marine Corps to preserve order, and have the Militia called out."

Volunteers were then called for to take charge of parties of men and blow up buildings, and Mr. Damrell gave them written authority to that effect, and said they were authorized to take possession of any team for that purpose.

The Chief of Police was summoned to detail police for special service.

As soon as I received my commission, I proceeded to the corner of Milk and Federal streets. Six kegs of powder had been placed in a building on the east side of Federal street, half-way from Milk to Franklin street by the Engineer, but the fuses had not ignited it, and the firemen were unwilling to approach the building.

The powder was in kegs of twenty-five pounds, and canisters of ten pounds, and when six kegs were put in a building it was very difficult for inexperienced persons to make one explosion of the whole. although we used fuses of the same length in each. At first we used fuses of too great length, and time was lost.

Afterward, a few kegs of one hundred and twenty pounds each were obtained, and with them great effects were produced.

I have no doubt that if we had had powder plenty in large packages of one hundred and twenty pounds or more, the fire would have been stopped at Milk street.

I continued all night in the neighborhood of Milk, Kilby and Congress streets. At about six o'clock in the morning I had got a line of hose through the building on Kilby street next the Shoe and Leather Bank, playing on the rear of those buildings and on the Merchants' Exchange.

I broke through the iron shutter of the Sub-Treasury room, and explored the room about the dome and in the upper story, which was filled with a dense smoke. Finding the fire in the rear of the dome could be reached in this way, a line of hose was carried up the entry over the dome.

The Chief Engineer soon appeared here and said, "I want to get into the upper story of this building," and I went up with him. He soon had two more lines of hose in the upper stories, and finally six or seven lines altogether playing in this building.

I cannot doubt that the great exertions made by Mr. Damrell to save this great building, and the fire-proof character of the building itself, stopped the spread of the fire in this direction.

THOMAS MINNS.

JAMES POWERS, Alderman, *sworn.*

Q. (By Mr. Russell.) You were coming from South Boston by the Broadway extension on the night of the fire?

A. I was, sir.

Q. Where were you when you saw the light?

A. I think I must have been near the Catholic church on Albany street, between the Catholic Church and the bridge that crosses the Albany Railroad, on Albany street.

Q. Did you hear any alarm?

A. No, sir; I did not.

Q. Where did you go?

A. Well, I was walking along about that spot, looking, of course, directly ahead, and as sudden as a flash of lightning, it appeared to me, the sky was illuminated, and immediately there was a hurrah in the street from children, boys and girls. They sang out, "Fire," and all, of course, ran in that direction. I was walking along with a person who had been a fireman.

Q. (By Mr. Cobb.) What was his name?

A. His name was Grose, and he remarked to me, "I wonder there is no alarm." I made the same remark to him. We walked along a little faster; and occasionally we would both say, "It is strange there is no alarm." We walked on until we got to Essex street. When we got to Essex street, we could not see the light, or it was not so brilliant or apparent to us as it was when we first saw it. We stood there awhile, hesitating whether we should go to the fire or not. We were going to the Boston Theatre. In the mean time, we remarked again that it was strange that there was no alarm, and we concluded, as we could not see the light so brilliantly as we could at the start, the fire must have been "a flash in the pan," or something, and it had gone out; and so, instead of going to it, we switched off to the left, and went through Essex street to the Boston Theatre. Still there was no alarm. We mentioned it as we went along. When we got about up to the Globe Theatre, an engine or hose-carriage, — I cannot specify which, — came around the corner, but still we had heard no alarm. Everybody was halloing "Fire," and running. We went to the Boston Theatre, and up to the time we got there, we heard no alarm.

Q. (By Mr. RUSSELL.) Was it a subject of remark at the time, that there was no alarm given?

A. We had no conversation with anybody except ourselves. We remarked to each other a dozen times, I should think, at least, that it was strange we heard no alarm.

Q. Then your attention was called to it. If there had been an alarm given, could you have failed to hear it?

A. I do not see how we could have failed to hear it. Still, that is negative testimony. If I heard a man swear that he did hear an alarm, I should not of course want to dispute him, but neither of us heard any alarm.

Q. (By Mr. FIRTH.) Although you were listening?

A. We were listening and watching. Every one was running to the fire, but we heard no alarm at all, until we got to the Boston Theatre, and went in. I judge it must have been fifteen minutes from the time we first saw the fire break out; it came like a flash of lightning from the sky.

Q. (By Mr. RUSSELL.) Did you go to the fire when you came out?

A. Yes, sir.

Q. How long did you remain?

A. Perhaps an hour, or thereabouts, when we went at that time. Then we went to our houses. We saw that the fire was stretching along so rapidly towards South Boston, that we were of the opinion that eventually it must go over there, and we thought our people must be alarmed at home, and we both went over. One reason for our going home was, that I had two of my children with me, — two young children. That was the principal reason why I went home.

Q. Did you go to the City Hall?

A. Yes, sir; after I came back from home, I came to the fire, and then went to the City Hall. I think it might have been nearly midnight when I got to the City Hall.

Q. Did you see the Chief there at any time?

A. I did, sir.

Q. What time was that?

A. I cannot say, with any degree of certainty, whether I saw him after three hours, or four hours. He was in and out there. I should think I saw him two or three times. I stayed at the City Hall with the Mayor, and saw Mr. Norcross and other noted gentlemen about there.

I think I remember him (Mr. Norcross) more distinctly than anybody. He seemed to be busy with the Mayor, — in consultation with him.

Q. How did Mr. Damrell appear? Was he self-possessed, or otherwise?

A. He did not appear to me at all unusual. I have seen him many times at fires, and I always considered him a man likely to get excited under such circumstances. He did not appear to me under any unusual degree of excitement, when I saw him.

Q. Did you go on top of the City Hall with him?

A. I did, sir.

Q. Did he state his plans there for extinguishing the fire?

A. I cannot remember that he did state any plans. I saw Alderman Cutter when I got there, and we went, with Mr. Grose, the gentleman who came over with me, out to Milk street, and found Alderman Jenks there. He said he was looking after things there. We found men there carrying off india-rubber goods and other things. There appeared to be a ribbon store, or something of the kind there, and we saw engine men carrying off different things that they were getting out of stores. They had a disposition to break into other stores, and Alderman Cutter and myself immediately interfered with their carrying off those goods. We did not care so much about the goods, but it seemed to us that they were neglecting their posts somewhere, and we interfered. They said the goods were given to them by the people who owned the stores. We remonstrated with them, and told them that was not what they were there for; that they were expected to do duty, and they were neglecting their duty; it was not a matter of the loss of the goods at all. He spoke to a policeman then, and he stopped them from breaking open other stores.

Q. Were they members of the Boston Fire Department?

A. I cannot say that. They almost all had white hats on, the shape of an Engineer's hat; those leather hats, painted white.

Q. Is there any company of firemen in Boston who wear those?

A. Not that I know of. I think our Boston firemen, as a general thing, do not wear those, except the Engineers. Those hats looked like our Engineer's hats, and most of those men who were in that place seemed to have those white hats on.

Q. (By Mr. Cobb.) Was there any want of water that night?

A. Well, I saw a want of force to the water. I saw, of course, a great want of engines, also. When I came to the City Hall and consulted with the Mayor, Aldermen Cutter and myself went the circuit of the fire twice, all around it, that is as far as any one could get until we met it where it had burned down through on to Broad street, and then we went the other way. I stayed there all night, went home in the morning, and came back again and stayed all the next night. Of course, I saw buildings burning up where there was no water and no engines at all to play on them. All the engines, I supposed, were at work in other places.

Q. (By Mr. Cobb.) There were not enough to go round?

A. No, sir.

Q. (By Mr. Firth.) Can you fix the time when you saw the firemen taking those goods?

A. That must have been somewhere about one or two o'clock Sunday morning. Well, all the way along from one o'clock to three. I saw them also in Summer street, carrying off india-rubber goods, but where I saw the most of it was out here in Milk street. I saw engine men with a number of coats on their backs; some of them appeared to have half a dozen. When I was in Summer street, I saw some going towards Washington street with them, and other firemen coming towards them, and they would say, "Give us a coat," and the others would reply, "Go and get them yourselves." They would pass on with all they had. It appeared to me that they were going to put them in some safe place.

THOMAS L. JENKS, Alderman, *sworn.*

Q. (By Mr. Russell.) You are an Alderman of the city?

A. Yes, sir.

Q. How soon did you reach the fire?

A. I went immediately after the third alarm.

Q. Please tell us in your own way all you saw that is worthy of notice; anything you think we ought to know.

A. Soon after I got there, I met the Chief and suggested the practicability of blowing up those high buildings, in the immediate vicinity, for the purpose of stopping the fire.

Q. What time was that?

A. I should think in the vicinity of nine o'clock.

Q. What did the Chief say?

A. He said he didn't see any line where he could make a break of that kind.

Q. Was there any further conversation on that subject?

A. He said that he had sent to Salem, Lowell, and Lawrence for aid, and requested me to go to the telegraph office and see if the despatches had gone right. I went, and found I could get no response from Lowell, and in addition to that, I telegraphed to Providence and to Worcester, and reported the fact back to him. I then went to City Hall and found the Mayor there.

Q. What time was that?

A. I have no idea of time after that during the night. I suggested to him to turn the city carts out, to carry away goods; and he said, "Certainly." And we despatched three or four messengers to look for the Superintendent. I then went with the Mayor to the fire, and found the Chief there, and told him we would sustain him in doing anything he felt justified in doing to stop the fire. A consultation was held with the Engineers, and it was decided to blow up some buildings.

Q. Where was the consultation?

A. My impression is, that it was on Federal street.

Q. What was done in pursuance of that, if anything?

A. I think they sent for powder. I went back to the City Hall with the Mayor; we went into the fire-alarm telegraph operator's room, where we could get a good survey of the territory. After doing that, we came down into the Mayor's room, and different parties there were assigned different positions at the fire.

Q. Did you have, in the consultation with the Engineers, any definite line of defence with gunpowder?

A. It was decided to blow through to the next street a block of tall buildings that were there, that were immediately followed by some low buildings; they thought they could control the fire at that point.

Q. The next street in what direction?

A. Westerly, on Devonshire, I think. The parties when they left City Hall were assigned different positions; for instance, I had Milk street, from Devonshire to Washington, and I remained there until seven o'clock in the morning.

Q. Did you see any explosions?

A. One.

Q. Where was that?

A. Corner of Washington and Milk.

Q. What was the result?

A. The result was, to take a large amount of combustible material from the top of the "Transcript" building, and thereby, I think, save the steeple of the Old South.

Q. From the top of the building?

A. Yes, sir.

Q. Was there any powder put in the "Transcript" building?

A. No, in the building adjoining.

Q. Currier & Trott's building?

A. Yes, sir.

Q. Was the "Transcript" building nearly burned then?

A. There was a large wooden structure upon the top of it that was in flames; the building was in flames from the top to the bottom, and the jar of this explosion shook that down — the whole of it. The buildings upon the opposite side took fire several times during the night, and were put out. The fire did not cross Milk street on my district — not to do any serious damage.

Q. How did the firemen in your district work?

A. Not well, sir.

Q. What was the trouble?

A. I think it was a Charlestown company that was there. There seemed to be promiscuous plundering.

Q. Did they neglect their duty to plunder?

A. There did not seem to be a large amount of duty done by them on the street. The Chief came along one time in the night after I was there, — the roof of the building on the northerly side was on fire; I had been unable to induce anybody to go up there, and he sent some parties up there, and they put the Lutherans out that were on fire.

Q. What building was that?

A. I think it was the second building from Devonshire street.

Q. Did you notice any company that were engaged in plundering besides this Charlestown company?

A. Almost everybody that I saw had material.

Q. Almost every fireman?

A. Almost everybody that was about the fire there. There seemed to be promiscuous plundering.

Q. Was it given to them?

A. One of those buildings that was not burnt on the opposite side of the street was broken into by some parties, and goods taken out.

Q. What was the material? What were the goods?

A. My impression is, it was india-rubber. I saw any quantity of india-rubber coats and boots.

Q. To what extent did the firemen engage in this?

A. Almost every one I saw either had a coat or boots. Some of them sat down and changed their boots.

Q. Firemen?

A. Yes, sir; they had firemen's hats on; that is the only way I knew.

Q. Do you know what companies were in your district besides this Charlestown company?

A. A company came in the morning from Portsmouth, N. H.

Q. Was that before or after this plundering?

A. After.

Q. I mean, at the time the plundering was going on, was there any other besides the Charlestown company?

A. I think not.

Q. You don't know what number that was, or what name?

A. No, sir, I don't.

Q. On what building was that engine playing?

A. They played upon Ives' store, and one or two buildings this side of that.

Q. Were they firemen from that company who went up on the building you spoke of to put out the fire?

A. I am not positive. Mr. Damrell called somebody that he knew and sent them up there, and they put out the fire.

Q. You saw the Chief at different times, — when you saw him, was he self-possessed or otherwise?

A. I saw him once or twice when he was excited, perhaps, as anybody would be under an emergency.

Q. Did he seem to know what he was about? What he wanted to do, or otherwise?

A. I hardly know how to answer that. I saw him no time in the night when he did not give orders as he was passing from place to place.

Q. Could you give any judgment as to the period between the time you advised the use of gunpowder and the time when that consultation was held in Federal street?

A. It must have been about an hour and a half, — it might have been two hours.

Q. Who superintended that explosion of Currier & Trott's building that was so effective?

A. One of the Assistant Engineers, I think.

Q. You don't know which one?

A. I do not.

Q. Did you notice any want of water for the engines?

A. I did, in different places. Where there were two or three streams playing, apparently from the same point, there was not a sufficient quantity of water.

Q. Did you notice any case where fuel was wanting?

A. I think I saw them breaking some boxes in one place.

Q. Did the engine stop?
A. No, sir, it was going.
Q. What time did you reach the fire?
A. I left my place immediately after the third alarm.
Q. Where was the fire when you got there?
A. I think it was on the four corners.
Q. Did you notice any particular endeavor to stop the fire on the corner of Otis street from extending over in that neighborhood? Was there any water poured upon that building, or any ladders put up?
A. I don't think I did.
Q. Would you have been likely to have noticed it?
A. I should, if it had been done.
Q. Were you in Winthrop square soon after?
A. I think I went down through Winthrop square to the telegraph office. Winthrop square was not on fire, — not what you might term Winthrop square — I think the corner was on fire, but Winthrop square had not been destroyed. I had an impression if these high buildings were knocked down, we might control the *débris* and keep it from getting beyond that point.
Q. Had the fire worked some way down Otis street on your arrival?
A. No, sir, I don't think it had.
Q. Was there any apparatus at work on Otis street, fighting it?
A. I would not be positive.
Q. Was it too hot then for apparatus to work at the corner of Kingston and Summer?
A. I was there close to the corner of Kingston and Summer, and stayed there some time. The heat when I arrived there was not anything to what it was afterwards.
Q. Where were the engines playing when you arrived? Where were they stationed?
A. There were three or four, I think, on Summer street; one of them, I think, by the church.
Q. What church?
A. Trinity.
Q. Did you see any down Kingston?
A. I did not notice.
Q. Did you think the firemen did everything that could be done at that time, while you were there?
A. Perhaps I am hardly a judge.
Q. You have never been connected with the Fire Department?
A. No, sir. I was very strongly impressed with the idea of using powder when I first got there.
Q. When you first arrived?
A. Yes, sir.

GEORGE GARDNER, *sworn*.

Q. What can you tell us about the fire? If you will tell your story, probably that will be the shortest way.
A. I saw a good deal of the fire, and was very much interested in it. I had been dining at six o'clock.

I suppose it was somewhere from half-past seven to eight, when I went to Summer street, and to the neighborhood of the fire. It was then in the building that it took in at the lower corner of Kingston street; it may have reached on to the other, but not sufficiently that I decided that it had; but this building was entirely in flames from top to bottom. I stayed in that neighborhood for a time. The wind was bearing away from the other side of Summer street — perhaps towards the south-west, I should say. I saw on the other side of Otis street, the eaves of a building were beginning to smoke; then there was some water thrown up, or some water attempted to be thrown up, but it seemed to reach it rather in spray, — and then suddenly that all burst into flames. At that time, I hadn't any alarm in regard to the fire, because I thought there was a fair possibility of its being arrested in that neighborhood, although I saw the heat was so intense in the first building that it prevented any one getting very near for an efficient purpose. I then remained in that neighborhood for a time until it had worked this way one or two stores — I should think about two, or it might possibly have been three stores; and I afterwards went home (I live at the corner of Beacon and Charles), and reported the state of things, and got something to eat and some refreshment. Then I went down again to the fire. I then felt that it was very dangerous for Hovey's store and the upper part of Summer street. I felt that if it got to Chauncy street, the chances were it would get above that. When I got back I found it had worked this way. I should hardly think it was more than half way between Kingston street and Chauncy street, and on the other side. It had moved about half way between Otis street to Arch street. I didn't go down to the fire that time. I went immediately to Hovey's store. I went into Hovey's store and looked round there and went up on to the roof, and I told them to wet blankets and put them on and nail them up around the wood-work, etc. When I went in, I found they had made the usual preparations. They had filled their buckets with water, although at that time I had strong hopes it would not come to us. They had filled what buckets they had, and they had a pretty good supply, and distributed them about the building. I went into the basement to see how they got water. The water usually runs up in the store, but they were drawing too much that night; it was very feeble. There was but one faucet that run water, and that but slowly. It seemed to me it took an age to fill a bucket.

Q. How high up was this?

A. This was in the basement. All the water had to be carried up by hand. They will occasionally, on a Saturday, once in a few months, perhaps, put out their fire and let the boiler cool down so the fireman can go into it on Sunday and clean it out; and it so chanced on that afternoon the fireman had drawn off his boiler, and let his fire cool down, so we could not use the elevator, and everything had to be carried up by hand; and from the feeble stream of water that was running there he had to fill his boilers and get up his fire with cold water before he could get his steam. It was quite a long time before that was accomplished.

In the mean time, the water was carried up by hand in these buckets and the blankets were wet. After taking these precautions, the fire was still distant; it had not crossed Chauncy street, but still, as I remarked to some one, it was worth fifty per cent. to insure the building then. I thought there was a chance of its not reaching us; that it might be stopped. There was nothing to be done but to wait for the fire to come up to us, and that time was occupied in protecting the goods and keeping out people that wanted to come in. Then the fire began to come, and there was a great call for water to be carried up by hand, because the heat was drying the blankets. Then after a time, before the fire got dangerously upon us, the elevator was at work. That was a very great relief, because they had filled the iron ash barrels down there. The water ran so slowly that when you sent down your buckets from the attic it would seem as if they never would get back again, and we lost all the time the water was not running by not having anything to draw it into. They filled what things they could find which could not be carried up before, and they were put into the elevator and carried up into the attic. That gave an immediate supply for wetting those blankets, as the heat, although it was at a considerable distance then, required that they should be constantly attended to, — particularly those on the roof. The difficulties to contend with were the want of water and the difficulty of getting water throughout a part of it, and we had to economize our water in every respect. In fact, a little water is as good as a great deal. Then the fire came. Among other things they took down all the little sun-curtains; pulled them down, because they would catch, and it would take a tumbler of water to put them out, and water was too precious. These sort of things I speak of more in detail, because they were successful, and it does not always occur to a person what to do; what has been done suggests to another what to do, Speaking of the scarcity of water, knowing that scarcity, when I got all the wood-work covered with wet blankets, it happened to occur to me, there is the gutter; our water is too precious to have it running to waste, and we plugged up the conductors, which turned out fortunately; they held all the water which otherwise would have been wasted, and they afterwards dipped some of their blankets in it, and there was a necessity, at that time, of the utmost economy of water. Then we went on for a time. I passed from one part of the building to another to see what was going on. We had covered all the side windows. They pulled down the upper part of the windows and put out the blankets, wetting them. At that time those blankets remained without being disturbed, because the store next to us, and next but one, had not taken fire; but it was very hot on the roof, and the store on the opposite side below the Mercantile building was on fire, rolling up flames, and it was coming to us over the roofs, and the heat was increasing excessively. One of the men came in and said, "We can't stand it; the heat is too great." However, he rushed out again. I remained in the attic for a time, and he rushed in and said again, "We are all on fire." When he said that, he saw there was a bucket of water there, and he seized it and dashed out again and went at it.

I saw nothing more of these men, except they would come to the window and cry "Water," and we were hurrying all the water we could to this place. There was a Lutheran window at the end; opposite was the great heat from the building on fire above the Mercantile Library's Building. That end Lutheran window has been burned all the way along the side and charred by the fire. Water was passed out there, —

all we could spare — from the next story and everywhere, and from where the forces had been distributed, they were all brought up there. The heat was intense. Those fellows stood it and got burned, and fought it like heroes. The next roof was lower; but the one beyond was pretty high; and they had to take that fire behind with the heat from the other side. Those fellows stood it all. I was not out on the roof, although I was first inside, and I can't conceive how they did stand it; they did, however, and they held to it until those roofs fell in, and the fire was carried down and turned the corner. I can't tell precisely how many men were there. It was an exciting time. I took no note of time, nor any special observation, further than to say, I made the round of the building, up and down, to see what we wanted; and among other things, it occurred to me the fire might suck into the conductors and the cold-air boxes, and we might get fire on the floor without knowing why; and I directed them to shut the windows, which let the draught in, to prevent the sparks from coming in through. There might have been small sparks drawn in under the floor before you expected it. I felt then that we had passed the most dangerous time, but not that we were secure; and I made the remark at the time, "This building is worth ninety per cent. to insure, but I think ten per cent. is worth fighting for." I said this to keep them in good spirits. I went down into the next story, and then passed down into a lower floor, having my mind relieved in regard to those points, and was passing by the sky-light. (The building is recessed about seven feet — seven feet by some thirty on that side. In the recess there are three windows in each story for the purpose of light. Those windows were all blanketed. On the first story there is no recess, it being covered by a sky-light.) I was about in the centre of the store, when crash came the wall of the next building, and with it came a lot of cinders through the sky-light, breaking it all in. I chanced to be close to it; the first floor was all entire (that was the width of the building, and light was procured by having a recess above, and that is covered by glass). I chanced to be there, and it gave me rather a feeling of satisfaction. There was quite a rush when this came down. I exclaimed: "No harm is done; it is all right." I knew the fire was there, and they had all to go down, and the sooner the better; and I immediately stationed some men there with buckets of water, and what fire was brought in at first was put out. There was a great deal of calling still, at the upper part of the building, for water. There was only a piece of the wall came down at that time, leaving some height above, and it brought in a good many cinders. A tumbler of water would put out a few cinders, and an injunction was given to the men, to use no more than was wanted to put it out, and they acted on that.

We took a bucket and put in about a charge, in order not to waste the water, and if any cinders came in the men would take it and give them a dose — just enough to put them out; and we kept those cinders down very easily. It was arranged that some of the men were to remain there. I went up into the fourth story; the fire was fully upon us in this recess, only seven feet off. The next building was all on fire; the men there were defending the windows. They pulled down the top of the window a little way, taking wet rags and squeezing the water round on the upper part of the wood-work and letting it run down the sides. They couldn't hold their hands out long, it was so hot. Then I discovered, what had been overlooked, that there were little slots of windows on the side to let light into the building, and also into the elevator. Those were in the end of the recess. A fellow got round there and discovered it before I got up there. In fact he told me, "We have forgotten those windows on the side." He got round there. The flames did not come in through, but a shower of cinders and smoke rolled up into this recess. He got a blanket out there, and he would squeeze the water round the window and then shove it up again as quick as he could. It was impracticable to put a blanket there, because there were the cinders coming up. The smoke and cinders were pouring up and it was extremely hot there, and the glass was cracked into hundreds of squares, but did not fall out. I expected every minute to see the wood on fire there. There was a man stationed there with a bucket of water, with directions not to put any water on, because, if he had thrown on water, he might have broken a hole in the glass and made it fall out; he was not to put on any water unless the wood took fire. In that case, he was to put on just enough to put it out. You cannot make wood burn if you keep it a little damp. We had no water to spare. At that point, it seemed to me very critical. Then there came a dash of water from a hose, which struck the upper part of the window and ran down, and I think it was the most refreshing sensation I ever had in my life when that dash of water came. It struck just over the window and swept down over it. The firemen may have seen this point. The stream was followed then by others, and the water struck directly on the windows. It was all cracked into little pieces at that time, and I expected every moment to see it come through, and if it came through, then there would be a draught of cinders. There was a parcel of woollen shawls at hand, and orders were given not to put any water on, but if the glass was broken to clap a shawl up there, wet it, and keep it wet. After a time a piece more of wall fell, and then the fire was below us somewhat. At the same time, the heat was very intense, although it was lowered. In the mean time, we had got to that stage of the business that we had got a hose in. It must have come two hundred feet or more from Avon place; then it was up perhaps forty or fifty feet, and we had got a window open — the fire was below us, and the firemen put the nozzle of the hose out and pointed upon it. I don't know how far off the engine was to which it was attached. The heat was so great, I feared we could not stand it. The firemen cried out, "Play away, No. 2!" and we got more and more anxious, but the hose did not fill. Then it passed my mind, I don't know that we can stand this five minutes longer; certainly not ten, and as I looked down to the hose I saw the water coming in, and it began to swell and there went a good stream out of it, and I felt we were safe. We weathered it. I would not have given ten per cent. then to insure the store. I went down stairs and found another piece of the wall had fallen and brought in some quantity of cinders, and we dashed on the water in the buckets until we put it out. We put it out pretty quick, and rigged up a staging, so a fellow could stand on it and reach round the edges of this skylight, which kept taking fire, and put it out. He dashed on a few buckets and got it pretty well wet there. The cinders kept pouring in, and there was a man passing water up from down in the basement, and it was passed up from the counter to this place that was raised up on the little staging, and after dashing on a few buckets he got it pretty well wet around the floor. Another precaution to save water was this. Three or four cinders would come in, and the order was given, "Don't put any water on,"—because it had got very wet round the floor. I should think four out of five went out of themselves, so we could use our water for the fifth. When one began to blaze around it, we gave it a dash of water and it was all over.

Q You were not there Sunday night?

A. Yes, sir. I went home by daylight both mornings.

Q. Can you tell us whether there was any water thrown from the department on to your roof before the next building took fire?

A. I don't think there was any water thrown or any firemen in there, but I will say this: of course I should have liked to have had it myself, but I felt we were not to depend on outside help, and my experience of that night is, I believe you can save a building from the inside, economizing your force and using it with discretion, a great deal better than by dashing water on the outside. I looked out from up there in the roof, and I saw this great fire coming on. I don't know whether the Fire Department did their duty or did not, but people have made these remarks to me: "They ought to have done this, that and the other." I say there is one thing I agree would have been better, if such a thing could be practicable; it is important on certain occasions to be able to raise your water. You cannot throw it from the street to be of any effect. It becomes mere spray before it gets up. There ought to be some mode of carrying the hose up as it was into my fourth story. There we got as much force as we wanted. Then I want to say one word about the buildings, as the result of my observation of the fire. There is a good deal of talk about the Mansard roofs. I think there is too much wood put upon them. I have been astonished that the city would allow such buildings, as some of them are, to be erected. There is one at the corner of Water street and Devonshire, which is thirty to forty feet high of wood-work,—simply wood-work, trimmed with wood. If that gets on fire, it will be a great bonfire in the air. That always struck me as a dangerous building. My observation was a little curious that night. Perhaps you may have seen a little card I put in the paper. I felt grateful to those fellows that fought for me. That, and the roof of the Mercantile Building, saved my building.

Q. What was that covered with?

A. It is a composition roof,—a gravel and tar roof; something of that sort.

Q. You got your men pretty well disciplined in the latter part of the fire?

A. They behaved like heroes in the beginning. There were a good many of them, and they were ready men. If they had any idea that was practicable, they took hold of it readily. I want to say, also, that I regard woollen blankets, wet as these were, as one of the best means of protecting a building; I regard woollen as a non-conductor, and wood also, if green or kept wet. I believe that the fire could have been stopped by sheathing the buildings with wood and keeping it wet. It will not burn as long as it is kept damp.

WILLIAM ENDICOTT, Jr., *sworn.*

Q. (By Mr. Russell.) On Sunday night, what time did you get to the fire?

A. I was there all Sunday night. We had about twenty of our clerks remaining there, in case anything should turn up, and I stayed in charge.

Q. At what time was the alarm?

A. I should say about one o'clock.

Q. What was the first you heard?

A. I had been on the roof several times, looking about. About eleven o'clock, I went up for my wife. I thought she would never have a better opportunity of seeing a fire than there. She came down and went up with me, and then I went home with her, and got back about twelve o'clock, and heard those explosions. I supposed they were blowing up buildings. Suddenly, it exploded next door to us, and then, in a few minutes, on the opposite side of Summer street. Then I should think there were half-a-dozen explosions on that side of the street, between that point and Lovejoy's store. That was a very heavy explosion; it threw out the front wall. The front and side wall were standing, and this explosion threw the front wall out into the street. I ran to the front window to see what the matter was, and got there in a moment or two, just in time to see that young woman jump out of the window of the store opposite. There was a line of flame running across Summer street to the opposite side of the street — a straight line almost across the street. The building she was in was all in flames, which were bursting out apparently in several stories. She jumped from the second-story window, and I heard at the same time several voices in the building, saying, "Save us! save us, for God sake!" and the firemen brought a ladder and put it up; but they were, apparently, unable to reach where they wanted to go. I had to look out for our building, and went back. I asked a soldier on guard if they got them out, and he said, "No, they went up on the roof. If they had stayed at the windows they could have reached them, but they went up on the roof, where they could not reach them." So I suppose there were two persons burned in this building; one was the mother of this young woman, and there must have been another, because they used the plural. Then I went back; but a moment before I came back the building next to it flamed up. I suppose the gas spread over those two buildings, and they flamed up instantly, and there was no time at all to escape from them. I thought we might have the same thing in our own store, and it was not safe to stay there, and I went up and told the men to come out. We took them all out of the building, and we cleared the inside safe. Then three of us went down cellar and shut off the gas. We have four large meters. There was a pretty strong smell of gas in the basement. I think the concussion in the neighborhood had shaken our pipes and they were leaking. We had three boiler fires, and I was afraid if we went off and left it our store would blow up. I made up my mind that we would leave it secure, and got all the men together, turned off the gas, and quit.

Q. Did you take a light with you when you went to shut off the gas?

A. Yes, sir; we had to have a light to see to do anything. It took a hammer and a wrench. I went up to the gas-office and told them they ought to shut the gas off from the whole city; that it was exploding in all sections of the city. That was about one o'clock. At that time, those two buildings were all in flames,— the two I spoke of. They said they had just sent some man out to do that very thing. I went up to the house and reported that I was not killed, and then went back. Shreve's store was pretty well on fire. I noticed the gas-lights were all out on West street and Bedford, so I supposed they had shut the gas off, and I went into the store and stayed there.

Q. Did you fight the fire much from your building?

A. Yes, sir; the flame was very hot. The wind kept shifting; one moment it would blow on to our building, and the next moment the other way. I suppose it was a current of air made by the fire.

Q. Did you fight it with wet blankets?

A. Yes, sir. John Hall, of the Quincy Fire Department, was very efficient. He was there both nights.

Q. He is one of your regular clerks?

A. Yes, sir. We prepared all the windows just as they had been the night before, and also the roof, and got water up into the store all ready for it.

Q. It was the other side of the store?

A. Yes, sir. We put a couple of men on the roof of the Avon street building, and sent three buckets of water there. I find a little water at the right moment is as efficacious as a good deal a little later. When we had the fire at the theatre, it burned out six of our windows, and the only way we kept it out was by being on hand. We had men with buckets of water and tumblers, and when the sash took fire, they put on water with a tumbler. I think the Fire Department did good service Monday morning. They worked well between our store and the corner.

Q. Did you see efforts made like yours by any of your neighbors?

A. No, sir. I remarked that night that the buildings between us and the fire seemed to be deserted; there was nobody on the roof. They were on Jordan's, but the other buildings seemed to be deserted.

Q. You had your gas burning up to the time of the explosion?

A. No, sir; we had a lot of lanterns.

Q. What led you to use lanterns; on the ground of safety?

A. Yes, sir; we thought it might not be safe to have gas there.

Q. You didn't shut off your main?

A. No, sir. I suppose the explosion of the gas was in the sewers. That night I supposed it was in the pipes, but I know it must have atmospheric air mixed with it, and I suppose it was in the sewers. The bricks were thrown up in two places in our cellar on the drain, showing that the explosion was in the drain, and I supposed from that explosion the gas worked along in the sewers, and in running across the street, I suppose it must have been the connection with the main sewers from those buildings on each side. I suppose the flame went across in those drains. The explosions were apparently simultaneous. I went to the window immediately, as soon as I could, and when I got there, the building on the opposite side was all in flames. There was no perceptible difference in time, apparently.

LEWIS L. SOLOMON, *sworn.*

Q. (By Mr. Russell.) Where were you when you saw the fire?

A. Corner of Winter and Washington streets.

Q. What time was that?

A. About from ten to fifteen minutes past seven.

Q. Did you look at a watch?

A. I left at five minutes past seven, and it would not take me more than that time to walk up.

Q. Did you go to the fire immediately?

A. I walked right down to the building.

Q. Did you hear the fire-alarm?

A. It had not been given when I got there; nor for some time afterward.

Q. How long after you got there?

A. About five minutes.

Q. In what condition was the fire when you got there?

A. The roof was all smoking.

Q. Was the fire in any of the stories?

A. The building was high, and I was on the opposite corner. I could not see any fire, if there was any, up above. After I had been there a few moments, a gentleman directed my attention to the basement, and looking at it, I saw the fire in there.

Q. How soon after the fire-alarm did any engines come, or hose?

A. The hose came first and the hook-and-ladder next.

Q. How soon did the hose come?

A. I should say fifteen minutes after the alarm, — from fifteen to twenty.

Q. Did you time it by a watch?

A. I didn't think it was necessary. I thought it was that time. I didn't think it of any importance to take note of it. The building adjoining seemed to be at the same time all lit up. That might have been from the hatchway burning. I didn't go down to it.

Adjourned.

SEVENTH DAY.

SATURDAY, Dec. 7.

WILLIAM BLANEY, *sworn.*

Q. (By Mr. RUSSELL.) Were you Engineer of the building that burned first at the great fire?

A. Yes, sir.

Q. How long had you been such?

A. A little over two years in that building — two years last August.

Q. What time did you leave the building on the night in question?

A. About twenty or twenty-five minutes past five.

Q. In what condition did you leave the boiler?

A. With the fire down low and the doors shut top and bottom, — that is, the top doors were probably open an inch. I always burn the fire down very low. The bottom doors were shut close.

Q. How much steam on?

A. Ten or fifteen pounds.

Q. What is the full ordinary amount?

A. I carry fifty-five. It is insured for sixty-five, but I never carried it higher than fifty-five.

Q. Was there any way in which the fire could communicate from that boiler?

A. No, sir, not any way at all.

Q. Have you any theory as to how the fire took?

A. I have not.

Q. Who employed you?

A. Mr. Klous.

Q. How often did you draw your fire?

A. It was every Monday morning. I never hauled fire Saturday night.

Q. Of course, you did not haul it this night?

A. No, sir.

Q. When was the last time you hauled it?

A. The week before the fire, Monday morning. I let the fire I have in remain until Monday morning, and then I haul it out.

Q. Do you generally find much there Monday morning?

A. Oh, no, sir; the fire is all out entirely.

Q. What is the power of your engine?

A. It is about twelve horse power.

Q. About what amount of coal did you consume per day?

A. Well, I burned about seven or eight hundred pounds a day.

Q. What were your hours of running?

A. I used to get there in cold weather about six o'clock in the morning. In the summer season, I didn't get there till eight o'clock in the morning.

Q. How late did you run?

A. I used o get through sometimes at five, and sometimes at half-past five, and sometimes at six, according as their business was in the store.

Q. Did you have more than one boiler?

A. That was all.

Q. Did that heat the whole building?

A. Yes, sir. We heated by direct steam.

Q. What experience did you have before you went there?

A. I had been in that business for about twelve or thirteen years.

Q. Who did you run for last before you went to this place?

A. Down in Connecticut.

Q. Where before that?

A. No particular place, only I was over in the Navy Yard. I had charge of all the steam-piping there. It was in 1861–'62, and 1863.

Q. Who was in charge of the Navy Yard?

A. Admiral Stringham was there and Commodore Hudson, when I was there.

Q. Do you know how this elevator was lined?

A. It was sheathed up with spruce, I am sure of that.

Q. That was inside?

A. Yes, sir.

Q. Was there any brick partition between the fire-room and the engine?

A. Yes, sir.

Q. Were there any openings in it?

A. Yes, sir, there was a window in it exactly opposite the engine and boiler. The engine stood between the boiler and the elevator.

Q. (By Mr. Firth.) Had you ever had any doubts about the safety as regards fire?

A. No, sir, I never did. I used to leave everything all straight.

Q. Had any painters been at work in that neighborhood?

A. No, sir, not to my knowledge.

Q. Did you hear anybody express any doubts about the safety of the elevator as regards fire?

A. No, sir, I never did.

Q. In going for fuel, did you pass through the room where they kept the dry-goods boxes?

A. No, sir, my coal bunker was out under the street. I wheeled my coal through the engine-room into the fire-room. It is just an open space.

Q. Then you passed by the elevator with your wheelbarrow?

A. Yes, sir, right through the little entry.

Q. What did you kindle your fires with?

A. Broken cases that I picked up in the building.

Q. Where were those kept?

A. All they made down stairs they used to give me. Tebbetts, Baldwin & Company's folks, and Young's folks, kept theirs up in the upper loft of all.

Q. When did you do your breaking up of boxes?

A. Any time when they fetched them to me. They were old broken boxes. I used to keep them on hand till I wanted them. I would keep the broken pieces in between the boiler and the basement partition. There was a passage-way around the boiler, — between the boiler and the partition that partitioned off the basement floor from the boiler-room. It was a wooden partition, nothing but common sheathing for a space about two and a half feet wide.

Q. Was there kindling there at that time?

A. I had just about enough to kindle my fire Monday morning.

Q. Was it usual for you to leave that kindling there?

A. I always had left it there.

Q. The fire was no more than usual.

A. There was very little fire. I presume they will find the same in the boiler now when they dig down to it. There was very little fire in the furnace.

Q. Is it a horizontal boiler?

A. Yes, sir.

Q. Do you know who the private watchman was?

A. No, sir, I do not. The private watchman was outside the building. There was no watchman *in* the building at all, only *outside*.

Q. Who hired that watchman beside the occupants of this building?

A. As I understand it, the different firms of the several buildings. He had a beat all around that neighborhood.

JAMES QUIRK, *sworn.*

Q. (By Mr. RUSSELL.) What is your occupation?

A. I am the porter of George W. Carnes & Co., Nos. 43 & 45 Summer street.

Q. Did you see any proofs of the firemen's not doing their duty?

A. It may be bad judgment on my part in thinking so, and it may not. I will tell you what I saw. I was on the roof of our building with Mr. Carnes, in company with a gentleman named Mr. Gookin, and for an hour or so they run up a line of hose on the roof which formed the Post Office building. There were quite a number that came up there that didn't appear to have anything to do, and they went down through our store. I started down after them, because I thought they looked as though they were looking for what they might find lying around. Finally, they got to going up and down there, and they didn't take any more interest in the fire than if they didn't belong to the department.

Q. Do you know whether they did belong to it?

A. No more than that they had fire hats on and appeared to be firemen. I don't know whether they were Boston men or not.

Q. Of course you don't know what company they belonged to?

A. No, sir.

Q. Did you see them doing anything besides that?

A. No, sir. There was a man who said he was sent there by one of the Engineers to see that nobody but firemen went up and down there. There was quite a number that went down there. After they had been into Clapp, Evans & Co's store, they brought in some rubber goods and laid them down by the side of our door, and asked this man to look out for them, and then they went back and got some more, I thought.

Q. (By Mr. FIRTH.) Were they firemen that brought in the rubber goods?

A. Yes, sir. It was from Clapp, Evans & Co's.

Q. Was that store burning at the time?

A. Yes, sir. It was just catching in the rear. I could see the light of it from our door-way. I was standing in our door-way and looking over.

Q. Was there anything else that you noticed?

A. No, sir, nothing in particular.

Adjourned to Monday afternoon, Dec. 9th.

EIGHTH DAY.

MONDAY, Dec. 9, 1872.

GEORGE P. BALDWIN, *recalled.*

Q. (By Mr. RUSSELL.) What was the amount of insurance on your stock?

A. The sum total of insurance amounted to $172,000, $47,000 of which was upon the package-stock (stock in the loft), and $125,000 upon our open stock.

Q. (By Mr. PHILBRICK.) On what floor was the open stock?

A. It was upon the first floor and in the basement.

Q. (By Mr. RUSSELL.) What was the value of the stock?

A. The net value of the stock in the package-room, that is, the upper floor, according to our books, was $36,000; and upon the lower floor and basement, between $131,000 and $132,000, according to the showing on our books. That is what our merchandise account calls for, making it up on a cash basis.

Q. How long a lease had you?

A. Our lease expired on the first day of January, 1873.

Q. Did you intend to continue in that same place?

A. No, sir. I think the store was rented the very day of the fire to the firm of Burr Brothers.

Q. (By Mr. PHILBRICK.) Was the boiler covered with an iron shell, or was it covered with brick?

A. The boiler was cased in brick.

Q. You couldn't see any part of the boiler except the brick-work?

A. That was all.

Q. Could you pass round it here [referring to the plan]?

A. Yes, sir; there was a space between that partition and the boiler; also, on the end.

Q. That side is against the party-wall, isn't it?

A. Yes, sir; the probability is that there was no means of passage there; but here there was a passage across the ends, and on the side.

Q. That was a wooden partition, was it?

A. Yes, sir.

Q. Leaving a passage for fuel to come in there?

A. Yes, sir.

Q. Do you recollect what kind of a floor there was in that passage?

A. I think it was a wooden floor outside. I think that below was a brick floor; you step down here into the engine-room.

Q. Was that passage-way all open to the engine-room?

A. There was no partition, except as shown on the plan.

FREDERICK S. WRIGHT, *sworn.*

Q. (By Mr. RUSSELL.) Where do you live?
A. South Boston.
Q. When did you first see the fire?
A. I saw the fire before the alarm struck.
Q. Where were you?
A. I was in my store, corner of East and Federal streets.
Q. What time was it?
A. I should say it was somewhere in the neighborhood of half-past seven; I can't say exactly.
Q. Where did you see the fire?
A. My boys halloed "Fire," and I went out, and could see the light of it from the corner of East and Federal streets.
Q. How long after that did you hear the fire-alarm?
A. I went up to the engine-house and took hold of the hose-carriage, and helped them up there, and we were at the corner of Essex and Lincoln-streets — say three minutes — when I heard the alarm. When we got there, some of them left, and went and got the engine.
Q. Where is that engine-house?
A. In East street.
Q. You didn't look at any watch or clock, I suppose?
A. No, sir; I didn't have any time.
Q. (By Mr. COBB.) You say you got there in about three minutes?
A. In about three minutes.
Q. (By Mr. FIRTH.) You didn't notice the time when you saw the fire?
A. No, sir.
Q. (By Mr. PHILBRICK.) It shone very brightly, did it?
A. It did. I thought it was some wooden building in Essex street. I have belonged to the department some twenty-two years, and felt interested to get up there.
Q. (By Mr. FIRTH.) Are you a member now?
A. Yes, sir; foreman of Engine 1.
Q. Did the hose-carriage go to work as soon as you got there?
A. Yes, sir; I took the pipe and put a stream on the fire.
Q. About what time was it you got the first water on?
A. Within two minutes after the bell struck first.
Q. Where did you play the water first?
A. Into the basement. The basement was full of fire, and it was going up a large elevator.
Q. (By Mr. FIRTH.) Was there any fire above the basement?
A. Yes, sir, all the way up into the roof.
Q. It was so when you arrived?
A. Yes, sir, it was coming out of every window clear into the roof.
Q. (By Mr. COBB.) How long after you got there did the engine arr ve?
A. I should say about five minutes.
Q. What engine was it?

A. No. 7. Part of the men dropped off when we got to the corner of Essex and Lincoln streets, and went for the engine.
Q. Where did that engine go to work?
A. She went to the corner of Lincoln and Bedford streets.
Q. (By Mr. PHILBRICK.) Was there any delay in getting steam up?
A. No, sir.
Q. (By Mr. COBB.) Did you see the Chief?
A. Yes, sir.
Q. About what time did he get there?
A. I don't know what time he got there, but as soon as I was relieved by the regular hose-men who belonged to that company, I went in front of the building, and saw the Chief there. I asked him if I should go to South Boston and get my engine. I should say it was some fifteen or twenty minutes. He told me to go and tell all I saw to come right along. I didn't see him again till about one o'clock.
Q. How did the Chief appear?
A. As he always does.
Q. Level-headed?
A. Yes, sir, just as much as we are.
Q. Did you see the fire when it crossed Summer street?
A. No, sir, I was at work in the rear.

JOSEPH A. LAFORME, *sworn*.

Q. (By Mr. RUSSELL.) Will you tell us what you know about the fire?
A. Well, I was at the Union Institution for Savings that evening on a committee matter, and at a quarter past seven, or very near that time, at least, because I remember looking at my watch just before the alarm was given, and I should say it was about quarter-past seven that we heard the cry of "Fire" outside. Mr. Wm. O'Brien, of Jordan, Marsh, & Co's, was with me, and we went out and found the fire was at the corner of Kingston street, and was burning quite fiercely. When we got there, we found there was quite a crowd on Kingston street, already, so we didn't attempt to go that way; we went round through Bedford street, and walked along slowly, watching the fire as we went, and went round by Church Green corner into Summer street. When we got up nearly to Kingston street, we saw a ladder going up against the burning building. At that time, there was no fire on the front; the fire was all in the rear. The ladder was just going up on the front of the building on Summer street, as we passed there,—a long ladder as high as the building,—and we hadn't got more than across Otis street, when the flames burst out from the two upper stories in front. I should say that it was then about half-past seven. I calculated that it took us about fifteen minutes, the way we were walking, and stopping to look at the fire, to get round there. Then it was burning very fiercely from the two upper stories, and very soon the whole building was in flames. What became of the ladder I don't know.
Q. What time should you say the fire-alarm was struck?
A. That I can't say. I couldn't have heard it if I had paid attention

to it, because there was considerable noise there, and I shouldn't have noticed it. I went out on the cry of fire. We had a committee meeting at eight o'clock. We looked at our watches, and saw it was quarter-past seven, when we heard the cry of "Fire."

Q. Was there anything else?

A. Then in a very few moments the fire broke out of the front of the building on Summer street. It burned very fiercely, the flames extended way up into the air, and the heat was very intense. The flame seemed to sweep across Summer street, and very soon the building on the corner of Otis street was on fire up in the Mansard roof. It didn't burn very fast in the beginning, but it caught fire, and I remarked then to the friend who was with me, that I didn't see why no attempt was made to put out the fire on the corner of Otis street; that there was great danger of its extending down the block, with all those Mansard roofs. I was there until probably five minutes of eight. I should think that the building on the corner of Otis street commenced to burn probably about twenty minutes of eight. I looked at my watch at a quarter of eight; as I was going to the meeting, I wanted to be on time. I looked at my watch at about quarter of eight, so far as my recollection serves me now, and the Mansard roof was already burning then, slightly.

Q. Was any attempt made at that time to stop the fire?

A. Not the slightest that I could see on Otis street. I think the engines were playing on the rear of the building in Kingston street. I saw one engine come while I was there; that came along just about the time I saw this ladder going up, I should say about half-past seven. That engine came down Summer street, drawn by hand-power, and was the only engine I saw, although I understand there were other engines in the rear of the fire, but I didn't see them, as they came from the other direction. The only one I saw came down Summer street about half-past seven, drawn by hand-power, and that was stationed at the corner of Arch street, and while I was looking at the fire, about quarter of eight, I remember I got a ducking from the engine.

Q. Where did that play?

A. It played on the fire in the main building, on the corner of Kingston street. I saw no attempt made whatever to put out the fire on the corner of Otis street while I was there, and I was there until five minutes of eight; then I left and went to the supper, and went back about nine o'clock.

Q. (By Mr. Cobb.) Did you see the Chief Engineer?

A. No, sir. I shouldn't have known him, if I had seen him. I don't know him by sight.

Q. Did you see any Engineer who seemed to have charge?

A. No, sir. I was looking at the fire, rather than for Engineers. They might have been there, and I not have noticed them. It struck me at the time as strange that no attempt was made to put out that fire in the French roof on the corner of Otis street, and it was remarked by several people around me that it was very strange that the firemen made no attempt to put that out. That was really, to my mind, the cause of the extension of the fire, — the fact of the fire getting into that corner.

Q. (By Mr. Philbrick.) Did you look down Otis street to see if there were any engines there?

A. I looked down, but saw none. I looked down as I went along.

Q. And Winthrop square?

A. I saw none there; they might have been there, but I didn't see them. The fact is, from the time I passed the building, when that ladder was going up, until I left, at five minutes of eight, I stood between Otis street and Arch street. There might have been engines all around without my seeing them.

Q. (By Mr. COBB.) You saw no water thrown on that building?

A. No, sir.

Q. No ladder put up?

A. No ladder put up. I saw no attempt made. It seemed apparent that no attempt was being made to put it out, and that struck me as rather strange; in fact, so far as I could judge, the engines seemed to be trying to prevent the extension of the fire in the rear of the building where it caught.

Q. (By Mr. PHILBRICK.) Did you see it spread down Summer street?

A. I saw it spread after nine o'clock.

Q. I mean, before you left?

A. No, not before I left. I only saw this building on the corner of Otis street burning, without any attempt to put it out.

Q. (By Mr. COBB.) How far was it under way when you left?

A. The French roof was burning very hard, but not so hard but that I should think it might have been put out very easily if they had had the water there, when I left.

Q. (By Mr. PHILBRICK.) Could anybody operate in front of that building, in that heat?

A. I should say not, because then the other building on the corner of Kingston street was burning very fiercely.

Q. (By Mr. FIRTH.) Had that fallen in?

A. It hadn't when the other building caught fire. The building on the corner of Otis street caught fire before the Kingston-street building fell in. It fell in before I left.

Q. (By Mr. COBB.) What would have been your idea of attacking the fire when it was so hot there?

A. It seemed to me that the moment they found the opposite building was in danger, they should have got the hose up through the building.

CHARLES E. POWERS, *sworn.*

Q. (By Mr. RUSSELL.) What do you know about this fire?

A. Well, I was not aware that I knew enough about it to give anything to this commission, but, for the first time in my life, I was at a fire pretty early.

Q. How early?

A. I should say about twenty-five minutes past seven.

Q. Where were you when you saw the fire?

A. I think the first fire-alarm had been given; I don't know as they had got entirely through with the first alarm; I am inclined to think not; at all events, I had procured tickets for the Globe Theatre that evening, and was intending to be there at half-past seven, at the time the performance was advertised to commence. The fire was right in the immediate neighborhood of the Globe Theatre, and I approached it from Essex street and Kingston, and I think I took a position first, right at the corner of Bedford and Kingston streets. The large building was on fire on the right-hand side of Kingston street, in the direction in which I was looking, and one engine, I think, had arrived when I got there, — perhaps it was a little before me, — and they were getting up steam, and I am inclined to think were able soon to throw a stream of water. I noticed particularly, that there was no coal in the neighborhood, and as soon as they got steam sufficient to blow the whistle, that was done most vigorously; still, no coal arrived, and one after another engine came up.

Q. (By Mr. PHILBRICK.) Where did that first engine locate?

A. Just about upon the corner of Bedford and Kingston streets; a little in Kingston street, I think.

Q. (By Mr. RUSSELL.) What did they burn?

A. I think it was, at first, nothing more than the kindling that they carried with the engine; perhaps there might have been a very little coal, but I didn't see any at all. The second engine arrived soon after, drawn by men. I saw no horses at all, until about the time I left, which I think was about nine o'clock. The second engine, after they got up steam, immediately commenced blowing the whistle.

Q. (By Mr. PHILBRICK.) Where did they locate?

A. Somewhere to the right of the first engine, and about, I should think, across Bedford street.

Q. On the same corner?

A. Yes, sir; a little in the rear of the first one.

Q. (By Mr. RUSSELL.) Did you see what they were burning?

A. They had kindlings, I think, at first. I saw no coal at all. The first I saw of any appearance of coal was some little time after, and then the first load of coal, I think, came, drawn by four or five men, in a light express-wagon. The coal was at once unloaded in the street, and it was immediately put in the furnace of the engine, and was almost immediately consumed. At once they commenced blowing the whistle for more coal.

Q. (By Mr. PHILBRICK.) What time did that coal arrive?

A. It is impossible for me to say. I was very much surprised to find it was nine o'clock when I looked at my watch. I had no idea of it. I didn't suppose we had been standing there more than half an hour. It would be utterly impossible for me to form any idea of time. I was very intently engaged in watching the flames, for there were four or five dwelling-houses immediately opposite, or nearly so, and when I saw the flames, I had some little solicitude to know what would be the effect upon those buildings. I saw the people in them. While I stood there, the large stone warehouse or building caught fire, and was nearly consumed while I was there, and one of the dwelling-houses this side caught fire. There was a third engine arrived that was drawn by men, and there might have been a fourth, drawn in the same way; and in the mean time, some two or three hook-and-ladder companies had arrived. They were drawn by quite a large number of men, but I didn't see that they were of any use at all. I don't know that it was necessary that they should be used.

Q. (By Mr. COBB.) Did you see any hose-carriage when you first got on the ground?

A. Yes, sir, I think there were one or two hose-carriages there, at least. I was informed while there, that the engines had suspended playing, but that I don't say of my own knowledge. I have that from hearsay. I know they were very clamorous for coal; but at the time I left, they were doing very good service indeed. They had succeeded in extinguishing the fire in the dwelling-houses, I think wholly, before I left, and were making pretty rapid progress towards extinguishing the fire in this large stone building, which was a new warehouse, I should say. I don't think it was occupied or ever had been. That was the only direction in which I saw the fire, and I naturally inferred from the fact that it was being suppressed there, that it was being suppressed on all sides. I left and went to the theatre, about nine o'clock, or quarter past nine, and had every hope and expectation that the fire would be entirely put out, and was very much amazed when I emerged from the theatre to find the whole of Boston in flames, or that part of it, certainly. My household furniture was stored in a building on High street. I thought of that at the time, but receiving the impression that the fire was being subdued everywhere, I had no anxiety in reference to that. That was all destroyed.

Q. (By Mr. RUSSELL.) You don't know what engines those were which you saw first?

A. I can't describe them.

Q. Were you near enough to see, had they had any coal?

A. I was, I should say, within fifty feet of the first one; and as the crowd commenced to increase, I didn't care to get wedged in at all, and moved back all the while, until finally I was back some five or six hundred feet from Bedford street. I didn't see any coal, and I looked, I know, for coal, because I was wondering what they were whistling for; it was something new to me, and I inquired what it meant, and was told by parties in the crowd that they were out of coal. I looked very sharply for coal, and didn't see any.

Q. (By Mr. FIRTH.) Did the engines stop while you were watching them for want of coal?

A. I was told that they were stopped, but the stream of water was at such a distance from me that it would be impossible for me to tell whether the water was forced from the engine there or not; a considerable portion of the time I saw no stream at all; part of the time I did.

Q. Was the machinery going all the time?

A. At one time the engines were going, and were doubtless throwing water; and then again, when they commenced to whistle for coal, no coal appearing, the engine seemed to cease that vigorous movement that is always observable by a stranger; but the machinery was moving slowly.

Q. (By Mr. COBB.) Then they did not actually stop at any time?

A. I don't think the machinery stopped, but I certainly don't think it was going fast enough to throw any water at the time; that is all that I know about it.

Q. (By Mr. PHILBRICK.) Was that whistling for coal commenced immediately after they began to work?

A. Almost immediately. I know I was considerably surprised that apparently there was no provision made for coaling these steamers, and I very naturally expected — I know it came across my mind at the time — that the firemen, or somebody connected with the engines, would try to procure coal from some locality or other. It occurred to me that they might get it from the houses, or some of the stores in the neighborhood; but I saw no movement of that kind; all I heard was the whistle; and after some time, some number of minutes, the first load of coal arrived, in a light express wagon. I shouldn't suppose there was more than a ton of coal in the wagon at that time, perhaps not so much. That wagon was drawn by five or six men; the second load, which came afterwards, was considerable of a load.

Q. (By Mr. PHILBRICK.) How much delay should you judge there was in waiting for coal? How many minutes did the engines cease their vigorous action?

A. Well, I should say twenty-five minutes; of course, that must be taken with some considerable allowance.

Q. (By Mr. FIRTH.) Not by your watch?

A. No, I didn't look at my watch until just before I left, and I was very much surprised to see that it was very nearly nine o'clock. Certainly, time passed there very rapidly indeed.

Q. (By Mr. PHILBRICK.) Did you notice that after that period of waiting, say twenty-five minutes, they acted more vigorously?

A. Yes, sir.

Q. (By Mr. COBB.) There was a perceptible difference?

A. Yes, sir. Well, the fire was increasing very rapidly; the building on the opposite side of the street had taken fire, and this four or five-story building was completely on fire; and fire had broken out in the first dwelling-house next to this large building, so that the blinds were on fire, and I should think the frame-work of the windows was on fire, and part of the roof, and the fire seemed to be increasing until after the second load of coal arrived; then the firemen, I think, suppressed it entirely; that is, the fire on Kingston street.

Q. (By Mr. FIRTH.) When you first came in sight of the building where the fire originated, in what part did the fire show itself?

A. The top of the building was on fire, and the flames were bursting out of the two upper story windows.

Q. Where you stood, could you see the basement?

A. Yes, sir. There was no fire in the basement that I could see at all. The greater body of the flame was coming out of the upper story windows.

Q. Do you remember observing about the basement?

A. Well, my attention wasn't called particularly to it, certainly; I saw no fire there at all. My impression is, that I saw men at work at the basement. After I came out of the theatre, I went almost immediately to the same locality where I before stood, for the purpose of seeing whether the fire had gone any further in that direction, and it had not; it had made no advance whatever from the time I left.

Q. (By Mr. PHILBRICK.) Did you go round towards High street?

A. Afterwards I walked round in that direction, but I found I couldn't get to the place where my furniture was stored. I made up my mind then that it was gone, which proved to be the case. I went down to the United States Hotel, and went up that street, I think it was Lincoln street, as far as I could go.

JOSEPH FRYE, *sworn.*

Q. (By Mr. Russell.) What time did you see this fire of Nov. 9th?
A. I saw it soon after it broke out. I was at a distance from it, where I was.
Q. Where were you?
A. I was in Washington Village, South Boston.
Q. Will you tell us what time it was, as nearly as you can?
A. I should suppose it was somewhere in the vicinity of seven or seven and a half o'clock when the first alarm sprung in. I saw it then, when the alarm was given.
Q. (By Mr. Firth.) You did not see it before the fire-alarm was given?
A. No, sir.
Q. (By Mr. Russell.) Did you come in?
A. Yes, sir.
Q. Were you ever connected with the Fire Department?
A. Yes, sir. I am an old settler in the Fire Department.
Q. How long were you a member of the Fire Department?
A. Something like thirty years.
Q. How long since you have been connected with it?
A. One year this January.
Q. Where did you come when you came in to the fire?
A. I put myself in the vicinity where I had some valuable property, in Federal street, — the carriage bazaar.
Q. Did you stay there until that was burnt?
A. I stayed there until the wall fell in and covered the whole machine.
Q. How was that fire managed and fought, as far as you saw?
A. Well, sir, I don't know that I could say that I would be competent to pass an opinion; it was one of the first times in my life that I was ever a spectator at a fire. I have always been a workman, and when I was at my business I never saw what was going on outside of me. I made the remark once or twice during that fire, that that was the first time for many years, — since I was a boy, — that I was a spectator. I may not be so well able to judge. In fact, I was not in the working district of the Fire Department. They were in Summer street at that time. There was no protection at that time in Federal street or in Congress street, when I was there.
Q. You mean, nothing was done?
A. There was no apparatus in that section. The fire was making its own headway, without hindrance.
Q. In what streets?
A. In Federal street, until it crossed into Congress street, and from

there into Pearl street. I was there when it crossed over the three streets.

Q. The fire had its own way?

A. Yes, sir; it was beyond the power of any man to have said what should be done.

Q. (By Mr. PHILBRICK.) Did it sweep through that district very rapidly?

A. Yes, sir; it went like a tornado.

Q. (By Mr. FIRTH.) Did you notice the wind?

A. Yes, sir; it created a wind.

Q. (By Mr. RUSSELL.) Whether it was going with the wind?

A. Yes, sir, it was going with the wind, but there was a phenomenon that was rather peculiar about the wind. When we got down to Broad street, we took the wind to be blowing strongly from the eastward; so much so, that it took my hat off. As we looked up above, we saw that the current was exactly as we supposed it was, from the westward; the rarification of the air was such that it created an easterly wind on Broad street, so that it took my hat off.

Q. The upper current was north-west?

A. Yes, sir, north-west; coming towards the harbor.

Q. Is there any particular in which you would criticise the action of the Fire Department that night?

A. No, sir. I don't think I would be justified in doing that at all; only the general uproariousness and demoralization of almost everybody. I did express myself at one time that I thought everybody appeared to be perfectly demoralized. I don't know as I was a sufficient judge to say so.

Q. What should you say now about that?

A. Well, I told you in the first place that I had not been a spectator at a fire for a great many years, but it did appear to me that the multitude was demoralized. I believe the leave which was given to a great many people to take goods was very demoralizing. I think that had a demoralizing effect.

Q. (By Mr. FIRTH.) Did you see anything of that?

A. Yes, sir; I was in Otis place, and had to lean back against a stone building to let a current of people go by me with goods which I supposed they were saving for somebody, but come to find out afterwards, they were saving them for themselves.

Q. (By Mr. RUSSELL.) What sort of goods?

A. They appeared to be dry goods. Bundles of blankets, silks, broadcloths, etc.

Q. (By Mr. FIRTH.) Do you know where they came from?

A. They came from Winthrop square; from the direction of Mr. Beebe's store, and opposite there.

Q. (By Mr. COBB.) What class of persons had these goods?

A. All classes.

Q. Firemen?

A. I would not say that I recognized any firemen. No, sir; I should think not, at that time.

Q. Did you at any time?

A. Sunday morning, I thought the firemen were pretty busy round among the ruins.

Q. Did you see them take anything away?

A. No, sir; I didn't see them take anything away, particularly.

Q. Were they Boston firemen to whom you allude?

A. Yes, sir.

Q. (By Mr. RUSSELL.) What were they doing about the ruins?

A. They appeared to be doing anything but attending to any fire duty; so much so, that they excited my curiosity, and I asked some of them where they were stationed; and the reply was, they were not stationed anywhere; that their hose was burned, or they had lent it, and they had nothing to work with.

Q. Where was this conversation?

A. This conversation occurred in a building which I give myself some little credit for saving; I think it was No. 32 Devonshire street. I went up on the roof, through the hall; the offices appeared to be all locked; I had my veteran badge on, which gave me a permit through the lines. I went to the roof, and found a little place on the roof on fire. I came out and met the Chief Engineer on the street, and told him if I could have a single line of hose up through that building, I could save it. He told me to take anything I could get, and use my own judgment; and I got a line of hose up there, and did good execution, and that building was saved.

Q. How did the Chief appear when you saw him?

A. He appeared to be pretty well fagged out.

Q. (By Mr. COBB.) What time was that?

A. That was about eight o'clock, Sunday morning.

Q. (By Mr. RUSSELL.) Did he appear to be self-possessed, rational?

A. Oh, yes, sir.

Q. (By Mr. FIRTH.) He at once acquiesced in your suggestion, it seems?

A. Yes, sir; he appeared to be very glad to have all the outside aid he could have, and I believe he always reposed a good deal of confidence in me in matters of fire business, and he gave me leave to order any line of hose that I could get and put it up into the building; and I did so.

Q. (By Mr. RUSSELL.) It was in that building that you had this conversation?

A. Yes, sir.

Q. Was it before you went up with the hose?

A. No, sir; after I went up with the hose. I found afterwards some stragglers came up on the roof.

Q. Was this talk on the roof?

A. Yes, sir; the talk was on the roof.

Q. Did you know from their badges to what engines they belonged?

A. No, sir; I didn't take cognizance enough of that; they were pretty smutty and dirty.

Q. Do you know they were Boston firemen?

A. Yes, sir.

Q. Do you know they were attached to an engine?

A. They were not, then; they were doing nothing.

Q. Do you know whether they were firemen, or whether they were parties with firemen's hats on?

A. They had their fire-hats and fire-coats on.

Q. (By Mr. Cobb.) How do you know they were Boston firemen?

A. I recognized them; I used to be very familiar with almost all of them.

Q. Cannot you call any of them by name?

A. I do recollect one, particularly. I recollect the foreman of Hose 6, of East Boston; he was on the roof.

Q. (By Mr. Russell.) He was one of the parties with whom you had this conversation?

A. Yes, sir.

Q. Was his hose burned?

A. He said his hose was lent or burned, or something to that purpose, and he was out of duty.

Q. (By Mr. Firth.) Why should they have gone on that roof?

A. Well, curiosity, perhaps; seeing a line of hose through the building, they thought they would go up and see what was being done. There was quite an accumulation of loafers there after awhile, after everything was all over.

Q. (By Mr. Russell.) Is there anything else you noticed in the conduct of the firemen?

A. No, sir; I don't know that I noticed anything. I was down in the vicinity of Liberty square and all around the fire that morning, and they appeared to be doing diligently all they could do.

Q. (By Mr. Cobb.) Was there plenty of water?

A. There appeared to be. Everything appeared to be going well enough for water. I guess, if there had not been anything but water there, some of them would have done a little better.

Q. (By Mr. Russell.) Were any of them drunk?

A. I saw a considerable number of men drunk. I do not mean to say they were firemen, but I thought liquor was rather plenty. There was one little circumstance that attracted my attention particularly. I was trying to assist a man in Liberty square to turn a stream on a building,—I think it was an out-of-town company,—and a man came along, knocked the head of a champagne bottle off and handed it to the foreman. He took it and dashed it on the sidewalk, and said, "Don't you give my men any of that damned stuff." I spoke of it quite in commendation. I said I wished all of our firemen were just such men.

Q. Do you know who offered it to him?

A. No, sir, I didn't notice, particularly. I noticed some one come up — he thought he was doing an act of kindness, I suppose, to refresh them, but the foreman took it otherwise. He dashed the bottle on the sidewalk, and said, "Don't you give my men any of that damned stuff." That rather met my approbation at the time.

Q. (By Mr. Cobb.) Did you say you saw any Boston firemen intoxicated?

A. I can't say, in particular, Boston firemen, but I think there was a general demoralizing effect there for a day or two among the multitude. I was a little astonished, I know, by the transactions. I thought when the city ordered all the rum shops to be shut up, they did an act they might have done a great many years ago.

Q. There was a good deal of intoxication about?

A. Yes, sir.

Q. Was that order carried into effect?

A. Yes, sir, it was carried into effect effectually this time. I know the police stepped into the bar-rooms and said, "You must shut up your shop or go with me," and it was done. I know in my neighborhood every place was shut up on the Monday night immediately following the fire. I organized a special police for our district, of good and responsible citizens. I enrolled about forty men, and they complimented us in City Hall by giving us certificates, I believe, that we were police force without pay. But we found no rum-hole open in our place those three or four nights, although we watched diligently. It had an effect, sir, when the officer told them, "You must shut up or go with me; those are my orders."

CHARLES ANDREW BODGE, *sworn.*

Q. (By Mr. Russell.) When did you first see the fire of Nov. 9?

A. As near as I can calculate, it was about eighteen minutes past seven.

Q. Where were you?

A. In Winthrop square, in front of Houghton & Perkins', and Anderson & Heath's stores.

Q. Where did you see the light?

A. I heard the cry of fire before the alarm was given; I heard a dozen voices, I should judge, I can't tell the exact number, but a good many voices, and I listened. Mr. Crane, a city officer, was with me. We didn't understand, at first, that it was a cry of fire, but when we discovered that it was fire, we ran directly from where we stood to where the fire was. It would not take more than one minute to go from where we stood to the fire.

Q. Then what was the condition of the building?

A. The fire then was down on a level with the ground floor.

Q. Was it in front or back?

A. In the rear, sir.

Q. Was there any fire above that?

A. There was fire above, I think, in two or three stories, but I think I saw no fire below in the elevator. I was somewhat confused, of course, being private watchman for the parties. I watched for Baldwin & Tebbetts, and a good many others, outside, on the street.

Q. How far does your beat extend, as a private watchman?

A. From Devonshire, on Summer, to Washington street and down Franklin to Devonshire. Nothing below Devonshire on Franklin, and nothing beyond Baldwin & Tebbetts on Kingston. That was the extent of my route, — through the cross streets, Arch and Otis streets.

Q. You were employed by a considerable number of parties?

A. Yes, sir.

Q. All on that route?

A. Most of them; I had a large number of stores.

Q. How long had you been employed?

A. It will be three years the 21st day of March, since I commenced.

Q. How soon after you saw the fire, or heard the cry of fire, was the fire-alarm given?

A. Well, I think soon after I arrived at the fire; perhaps it might have been five minutes, possibly more; I was somewhat confused and excited, being one of my stores. I should judge it was five minutes, I don't think it was longer than that.

Q. (By Mr. PHILBRICK.) Did you do anything about giving the alarm yourself?

A. No, sir.

Q. Was not that part of your duty?

A. Yes, sir; but some one said that Mr. Page, one of the city officers, had gone to give the alarm.

Q. How many minutes do you think it was from the time you first heard the cry of fire, until you heard the fire-alarm?

A. It might have been six or seven minutes; it took me about a minute to run across, it might have been a few seconds more, but I don't think it took me more than a minute to run across; I ran very quick.

Q. Did the fire go up the elevator after you got there?

A. Yes, sir.

Q. How fast?

A. Very fast indeed; so fast that I was surprised to see it.

Q. (By Mr. PHILBRICK.) I understood you to say, that when you first saw it, it was not only on the ground floor, but two or three stories above.

A. It was, but the chairman asked me how quick it went; it travelled very quick.

Q. (By Mr. RUSSELL.) Travelled up the elevator?

A. Yes, sir, travelled very quick.

Q. Was it in the second and third stories without being in the lower story at all?

A. No, sir; when I got there, the fire was below the second floor.

Q. You mean, that it was all below the second floor?

A. No, sir, not all; it was down on the second floor and above; it hadn't burst out of the roof; it was confined inside of the building.

Q. (By Mr. PHILBRICK.) Did you go down past the building in Kingston street?

A. I came straight across Summer street and went into Kingston street; I went into the rear.

Q. (By Mr. COBB.) How near the fire did you go?

A. I went round the corner of Kingston street, and into a passage-way in the rear; just stepped in, and saw the condition of the fire; then I waited perhaps five minutes, and then I started for the parties who occupied the stores. I started for Mr. Tebbetts, and met him on the Common. I was running across the Common, and saw Mr. Tebbetts, and stopped and told him the condition of affairs.

Q. (By Mr. FIRTH.) Did you look into the basement windows?

A. No, sir; I did not notice below the ground floor.

Q. (By Mr. PHILBRICK.) In what part of the ground floor did you see the fire?
A. I saw it in the elevator, through the windows in the rear of the building.
Q. Through the elevator windows?
A. Yes, sir.
Q. Could you get into the passage-way then?
A. Yes, sir, I could have got in, but I knew it was impossible to stop it, you know, and I went at once to notify the parties, which is part of my duty.
Q. I want to find out the exact appearance of the fire when you got there.
A. I can't say it was in the basement, but it was in the second floor.
Q. There was none above the second floor?
A. Yes, sir, there was fire above.
Q. But it was below, on the ground floor?
A. I can't say it was away down as far as the elevator, but I could see the light from below on the second floor; it was burning briskly above.
Q. (By Mr. PHILBRICK.) You saw it travel upward?
A. I stayed but a short time; I went immediately to notify my parties.
Q. (By Mr. COBB.) Was there any fire apparatus there before you left?
A. I think there was a hose company there.
Q. Do you remember what hose it was?
A. No, sir, I don't.
Q. (By Mr. PHILBRICK.) As you approached the fire from Summer street, could you see the light through the front windows?
A. No, sir, I didn't notice any through the front windows; the curtains were down.
Q. Where did you see the light of the fire?
A. I could see the reflection on Hatch's building, on the opposite side of the passage.
Q. Could you see it from the Kingston-street windows?
A. I didn't notice it there.
Q. Was the fire spouting out of the lower windows?
A. No, sir; it was not coming out of the windows themselves.
Q. Only the light?
A. Only the light.
Q. (By Mr. RUSSELL.) How many keys are there to that alarm box?
A. Really, I cannot tell.
Q. How many are there that you know of?
A. Mr. Farwell and Mr. Page have keys, and there are two other men who have them.
Q. Did you have a key?
A. Yes, sir, I have a key; I presume one key fits all the boxes.
Q. Are there not a number of stores about there where they have keys?
A. I do not know; that is the only store that I have on this side, except I have Mr. Glazier's, on this corner.
Q. (By Mr. PHILBRICK.) Is there any other fire-box on your beat?

A. That is the nearest; there is another one on Channing street, and the next is at the Old South; the next is in Winter street, near the Music Hall.

Q. No. 52 was the nearest?

A. Yes, sir, until I came to Bedford street again on the corner of Bedford street and Washington; there is no box near me on Summer or Franklin streets, until you come to Milk street; one at the Old South, one near the corner of Chauncy street, and one on Bedford street.

Q. When did you first ask if an alarm had been given?

A. I heard it.

Q. You say it was five or six minutes after you heard the cry of fire, before you heard the alarm?

A. Yes, sir; some one told me that Mr. Page had gone to give the alarm, and spoke of its being a good while before they got an answer from City Hall. I heard that remark made.

Q. When did you have that conversation?

A. I did not have it myself; I overheard it.

Q. How long after you arrived on the spot?

A. It may have been three or four minutes, possibly; I can't tell exactly; I was excited, as I say, in regard to it.

Q. When you first arrived on the spot, didn't it occur to you that it was your duty to go to the alarm box?

A. Yes, sir; it was my duty as well as the other officers who were with me. There were three city officers there at that time.

Q. But you say you waited four or five minutes before you heard anything said about the alarm?

A. I can't tell how long it was before I heard this remark; I can't tell the exact time, but somewhere in the neighborhood of five minutes. I can't tell exactly.

Q. (By Mr. Cobb.) You heard some one say that he had been gone a long time?

A. Yes, sir; that he had been gone long enough for the alarm to be given.

Q. You knew he had but a short distance to go; why didn't you start then?

A. I don't know why I didn't. I suppose, if he had gone, I knew he was in advance of me, and of course he would give the alarm before I got there.

Q. (By Mr. Firth.) Did you ask the question of anybody whether an alarm had been given on your arrival?

A. No, sir, I didn't, not to my knowledge; I don't remember asking.

Q. (By Mr. Philbrick.) Why didn't you go to the box?

A. Because some one said that Mr. Page had gone, the officer on that route. Of course, if he had gone, there would be no necessity for my going.

Q. But you said you waited two or three minutes before you heard that remark made; those two or three minutes were very valuable minutes at that time.

A. Yes, sir, I know, but if he had gone in advance of me——

Q. But before you found out that he had gone, you say it was two or three minutes?

Mr. RUSSELL. He says he was excited.

WITNESS. Yes, sir, I was excited.

Q. (By Mr. FIRTH.) Looking back upon it now, don't you think you ought to have started quicker for that box?

A. If I had been cooler, I presume I should; but if I had, I probably should not have had the alarm rung any quicker, because there were other officers there. There were three officers went over with me. If I had been alone, it might have made a difference, but there were no less than five officers, — Mr. Farwell, Mr. Page, Mr. Crane, Mr. Dodd and Mr. Matthew, — who all went directly to the fire, sir.

JULIUS F. GAGE, *sworn.*

Q. (By Mr. RUSSELL.) What time did you see the fire?

A. Well, about fourteen minutes past seven.

Q. Where were you?

A. In Chauncy street, about a rod beyond Bedford.

Q. Did you go immediately to the fire?

A. No, sir, not immediately; I went down to the corner of Essex street.

Q. How soon after you saw the fire did you hear the fire-alarm?

A. I should think it was not far from seven to nine minutes.

Q. You give the time when you first saw the fire exactly fourteen minutes past seven, P. M.; did you look at your watch?

A. Well, I fix that time from the fact that I went from Bedford street to Essex street, got off the car, and helped the ladies off, and said, "We will go back," and they said they had not time. I then looked at my watch, and it was fifteen minutes past seven. My watch said twenty minutes past, but my watch was exactly five minutes fast.

Q. How extensive was the fire at that time? Did you actually see the fire?

A. I did not in the first place, sir.

Q. What did you see?

A. I saw a little reflection on the corner building,— I think it is Forbes, Richardson & Co.'s.

Q. Where is that?

A. That building stood on the corner of Summer and Chauncy streets.

Q. (By Mr. PHILBRICK.) Did you go to the fire?

A. I went into Rowe place, from Essex street, immediately, and saw the fire from there. I went to the fire, as you might say, by going into Rowe place, as soon as I got off the car. That was the reason I had occasion to look at my watch.

Q. Did you go to the fire before the alarm was sounded?

A. I went into Rowe place, where I could see the fire right straight across, distinctly.

Q. (By Mr. COBB.) What did you see there, distinctly?

A. I saw the fire was burning on the corner of the building, at the top, and I stood there until the alarm struck, and then immediately went round to the fire.

Q. At that time you could see a light in the upper front of the building, when you got into Rowe place?

A. Certainly; that was where the reflection came from, when I first saw it. I saw it then when it burst out from the upper windows, and so on. I made the remark that I never saw a fire in my life when the alarm was so long in being given; and just as I said that, they struck the alarm.

W. F. JENKINS, *sworn.*

Q. (By Mr. RUSSELL.) When did you see the fire?

A. I should say it was from fifteen to twenty minutes past seven o'clock. I was writing at the time at a desk in J. A. Hatch & Co.'s, Nos. 14 and 16 Kingston street. Our office was in the front of the store, the side nearest the alley. I heard a sound like the clinking of glass, as if the whole window had been broken in. I listened a moment and heard the roar of flames, and saw that the room was full of light. I looked up the alley (I forget whether there were two or three basement windows between the elevator and Summer street) and at the first window nearest the elevator the flames were coming out, and they were coming out of the first two windows in the elevator. There were no flames above the second story. In this window in the basement, it seemed all on fire, and it was going up very rapidly from one story to another. There were then a dozen people looking on, on the other side of the street. I asked if any one had given the alarm. They said, "Yes, a man had just run to give it." I ran back to the safe and took out the books and papers and carried them down to the corner of Bedford street, and carried out what silks and shawls I could, and a few of my own things (I roomed in the store and worked there), until the flame came in, and it was getting pretty warm, and I stopped from going any more. The passage up stairs was No. 18. There were three policemen that I saw there at once. I unlocked the stairway door and asked the policeman to station some one there to see that no roughs went up. When I came in the last time, he told me not to go in again, as they expected the roof was coming in. Then I went across the street into Mr. Pratt's, and stayed there for an hour. I got the books out the back way. I carried the goods up to Jordan & Marsh's. I should think from the time that I saw the flames until the time that there was any water put on was fifteen minutes, or it may be twenty minutes, as I should judge now, although it may not have been so long.

Q. How long was it before the alarm was given?

A. I was rushing around so that I didn't hear the alarm, and I can't tell who sounded it. When I came home from supper, it was about half an hour before the fire broke out. I saw a man in the alley-way just before the fire broke out.

Q. Did you hear any report before you heard the noise of the fire?

A. No, sir; I did not. Where I was sitting was but fifteen or twenty feet from where the fire broke out. I didn't hear anything unusual before I heard the noise of the fire. I should have heard it if there had been anything unusual, because I was so near. Rag-pickers go into that alley frequently, and people after old wood, and I always hear them or any other unusual noise.

Q. What was the first fire apparatus that came that you saw?

A. That I could not tell. I remember the hose being carried up stairs, and I think the first thing was an engine at the corner of Bedford street, but I could not say definitely. The hose was carried up the stairway of Nos. 14 and 16 to No. 18, up stairs. There was no hose carried in at our door down stairs. I noticed firemen up stairs when I last went out. It seemed a great while before there was any of the Fire Department on the grounds.

Q. Does the building you are in have any windows on the passage-way?

A. Yes, sir. We had, fifteen feet from the ground, windows not more than eight feet wide. Along on the other side were gratings, except on the highest flight. Our basement was full of heavy goods. On the floor where the office was were samples. On the floor above that were samples. On the floor above that were fancy goods, and a good deal of straw. They were in large cases, and in the packing of them there was a good deal of straw used. In the attic were manufactured suits.

As I looked up, the whole flame was coming against those windows, and it got in there. There were half-sized windows in the alley, but I could not look down from them. I noticed the reflection of the light of the fire on our wall when I first looked out. There was not anything in that to excite my alarm, but after hearing the glass rattle, in a moment I heard the roaring of the flames. I did not see anything but a light shining on our ceiling, as if it were shining from a lower point.

Q. When you went out, did you look at the basement?

A. Yes, sir. There was where I saw the fire first. Perhaps there were two or three windows between the elevator and Summer street, as it looks to me now. It was in the window this way on the alley-way, and it was in the two first windows from the elevator, and also below those in the basement. There was no fire in the attic as I looked up. I feared for our upper stories and roof, and therefore I looked up immediately.

Q. Was there anything to excite your suspicions about the man you saw in the alley-way?

A. No, sir. I should say now that he was a rag-picker, or that he went in there to make water. There was nothing suspicious about him. Before going into the office, I went through our store, as I always do, and saw to all the locks and bolts. Everything was straight in our store, — J. A. Hatch & Co.'s.

Q. When you first looked up the alley, after going out, were the basement windows burst?

A. One was, that I am certain of. As I think now, it was the one nearest the elevator, because the flame was sweeping out of that and out of the two windows in the elevator, — out of the ground floor and the second floor.

ALBERT BOWKER, *sworn.*

Q. (By Mr. Russell.) Please tell us anything you know about this fire.

A. I feel a great deal more than I know.

Q. State anything that you think ought to be brought to the attention of the Commission.

A. I am so appalled by this measureless calamity that I hardly know whether I am on my feet or not. I am in the habit of attending all great fires, and for twenty years I have attended all small ones also. I have always made it a rule to have my horse saddled as soon as the bell is rung.

Q. How long have you been connected with Insurance Companies?

A. Nearly a quarter of a century. Within the last two or three years, I have not been so frequently at the small fires as formerly. I used always to make it a point to go to all fires within any reasonable distance of the city.

Q. How soon did you reach this fire?

A. I did not reach it until it had made considerable progress, for the reason that I had purposely constructed on the top of my house an excellent lookout, so that I could witness fires, and note their progress. Since we have had an Underwriters' Brigade, I have not felt it necessary to be on hand to save property as I used to. This fire had made considerable progress before I got there, and I had to take the statements of others as to what occurred.

Q. Did you notice anything after you got there that is worthy of remark?

A. Yes, sir.

Q. What time did you get there?

A. I should not dare to speak as to the time. I was there during all the night and all day Sunday; I can't tell you the hours; for four or five of us connected with the Insurance Companies went around the fires constantly, and we would go right back to our offices and make up our minds how much we had lost. We would do it by means of a "Plan" on which we have everything located. But I don't pretend to have been on the ground at the time the fire first burst out, or anywhere near it; and I didn't note the time.

Q. Can you tell anywhere near the time when you left home?

A. No, sir; but I should say that it was within fifteen minutes of the breaking out of the fire. I went right into my cupola. (I am on the highest land and overlook the whole city.) In about fifteen minutes I started for the fire. I could get there in twenty minutes easily. I went past my office and looked in, expecting to find some of my clerks there.

Q. What did you notice?

A. I noticed that the fire had made considerable progress, and had extended to several buildings; and I immediately went (I am not sure now whether it was the first or the second time) into C. F. Hovey & Co's store, where we had risks. I went on to the top of his building and gave more or less directions in regard to shingling the windows with blankets and carpets. It was a copper roof. I assisted a little in removing goods. After that I went immediately around the fire again, as near as I could get around it.

Q. When you first went there, was Otis street on fire?

A. No, sir; not to my recollection. It would not answer for me to swear positively to particular buildings or particular streets, because it was so alarming that I have not the facts definitely in my mind.

Q. Did you see the fire cross Otis and Summer streets?

A. No, sir. I think it was the second time that I went around it before the roof of the Freeman's Bank (in which I am a Director) was burned. That was on Church-Green street.

Q. State anything that you noticed as to the management of that fire.

A. There was no management about it when I was there. All the water they put on promoted combustion, it seemed to me. It was not easy to get near where they were pouring on water.

Q. Did you notice any want of water?

A. My impressions are of a general nature entirely in regard to that fire, with the exception of in regard to particular places — such a place, for instance, as Hovey's building, where I went on to the roof.

Q. Did you see any misconduct on the part of the firemen?

A. No, sir. I have no doubt that the firemen, as individuals, showed great intrepidity, and made heroic efforts. I occasionally spoke to an Engineer; but they seemed to be powerless when I saw them. Indeed, I was very seldom able to get near the Engineers, but only met them occasionally.

Q. Did you happen to see the Chief that night?

A. No, sir, I didn't see him at all.

Q. (By Mr. Cobb.) What is your opinion about covering windows with blankets? If other people had done so, would not more buildings have been saved?

A. I have no doubt of it. But Hovey's was a copper roof. It was so hot you could hardly stand on it. The men were about to leave, but I begged them not to. It was frightfully hot up there. There was a small army of men moving goods.

Q. Was there a large flat roof where they could walk about?

A. Yes, sir.

Q. Towards Summer street there was a steeper pitch, with dormer windows?

A. Yes, sir. Those windows were the ones that they were about to give up covering. I told them they would save that building if they kept on. They went right out from the attic on to the eaves. We had some improvised steps to get up with. We stood right on the level roof. There was great excitement. Mr. Lawrence was there. I was so appalled that I even asked him his name, and yet I knew him well.

Q. (By Mr. Philbrick.) Did it ever occur to you that we were in danger of such a large fire in Boston, from the character of the architecture here?

A. I think there is a printed speech of mine in New York, in which I said that I thought we were the worst-built city in the Union — especially the new part of our city — except Cincinnati. (In Cincinnati, they build as high as they can, and then put a wooden roof on top of all.) I have been in every city in the United States east of the Mississippi, except two that had the yellow fever — New Orleans and Mobile.

Q. Are you still of the same opinion in regard to the architecture of Boston?

A. I don't know of any city where they put so much kindling-wood on top of stone-work.

Q. Do you conceive that it was in the power of the Fire Department to put out that fire after it got a half-hour's start?

A. No, sir; not after that time. It must either exhaust itself for want of materials, or else the buildings must be blown up.

Q. Did you see any blowing up?

A. No, sir. I saw the effect of it, and I was as near as it is prudent to be; but I didn't see the process.

Q. What was your judgment as to the effects of blowing up buildings?

A. So far as I understand, they were perfectly laughable. There was no practical blowing up that was really useful. The buildings were not lifted up bodily and tumbled in a mass of fragments into the cellars, as they were in Chicago.

Q. Were those that you saw in Chicago that had been blown up, full of merchandise?

A. No, sir. Almost all that I saw were brick dwelling-houses. They used very large amounts of powder there.

Q. Did you see the building on the corner of Water and Congress streets after it was blown up?

A. No, sir, — not to observe it particularly. But I have been over the district and observed other buildings particularly. I noticed Currier & Trott's building, and some in Summer street. Really, I am not posted on the matter of blowing up, here.

Q. Do you think, then, that if the powder had been used in a proper manner, it might have been very useful here?

A. Certainly. There might have been a space made around that fire. There is no doubt about that at all.

Q. How early, when you went around the fire, were you impressed with that fact?

A. I was so impressed that I went back the first time and said, "We have not lost over $100,000, and the fire is under control. They will subdue it before it has passed much farther." The next time I came around I found that we had lost $200,000 or $300,000, and the next, all had gone.

Q. Did it appear to you before the fire that some other organization was necessary?

A. I am glad you asked that question, because, when I came back from Chicago, at either the regular meeting of the Board of Underwriters (composed of the Boston Presidents of Insurance Companies) or of the Underwriters' Union (of which I am also President), I stated (I think it was before the latter) that I had deliberately and thoroughly investigated Boston's preparations against fire, and that what we wanted here was a corps of men who knew how to blow up buildings, and how to do it quickly without waiting for red tape, or sending to the Navy Yard and getting a permit from the Commodore. That recommendation of mine was received with shouts of laughter, — a regular "guffaw" — derisively.

Q. You did not publish those remarks?

A. No, sir. They were received with derision.

Q. Did you bring those views before the public in any other way, or before the City Government, or the Fire Committee, or the Fire Department?

A. No, sir. I talked privately with Capt. Damrell, in Chicago. I thought that he came away "a changed man," as we say in religious meetings, — converted — "to powder."

Q. Did Capt. Damrell confess to you that an immense fire was possible in Boston?

A. No, sir. But I think his views were modified.

Q. Did you observe anything in respect to the force of the current of air created by the fire?

A. When I was in High street, the wind came as if there were a blowpipe. It was blowing right through from High street down towards Federal. It was blowing towards the fire. It was the induced current.

Col. E. O. SHEPARD, *sworn.*

Q. (By Mr. Russell.) At what time did you see the fire first?

A. It was about 8 1-2 o'clock. I did not go to the fire at first.

Q. At what time did you go to the City Hall?

A. It was between one and two o'clock.

Q. Before you went there, did you see anything worthy of notice?

A. No, sir. Nothing more than what a great multitude would testify to.

Q. Did you go there to consult?

A. Yes, sir. I went to see what was going to be done. It looked as if the city was all going, and I went up to the Mayor's room.

Q. Who was there?

A. There were fifteen or twenty people there, I think. I remember that Chief Engineer Damrell was in there when I went in, seated at the Mayor's desk, — also Mr. George O. Carpenter and others. At the time I got there, Mr. Damrell was writing the orders to give to people for them to blow up buildings.

Q. Did you receive an order?

A. Yes, sir.

Q. Have you one here?

A. Yes, sir. Here it is. [Reads.]

"Col. Shepard will blow up buildings or remove goods, as his judgment directs.
"(Signed), J. S. DAMRELL, *Chief Engineer.*"

Q. About how many others were given out?

A. I think they were given, one each, to Aldermen Jenks, George O. Carpenter, General Burt, Mr. Bicknell, Mr. Page, and Mr. Loring of the Council.

Q. Did you hear the Chief make any remarks at that time?

A. Yes, sir. Somebody said something about powder, and he said, "I have already taken measures about that; the powder-boat is already coming to the wharf with powder, and men are already engaged about that. I have also sent to Charlestown for powder, which is probably on its way here by this time." That is all that I remember that the Chief said.

When these orders were written, we were standing about the table in the centre of the room, and various persons were talking about what should be done, and how it should be done; and Mayor Gaston inquired if he should call out the military. Gen. Burt replied, "That is a good idea. They should be called out."

Q. Whom did the Mayor inquire of?

A. He seemed to inquire of those who were there. He named their names and said, "Had not the military better be called out at once?" I think General Burt replied, "Yes, as quick as they can."

Q. Was there anything farther from the Mayor?

A. I don't remember of anything farther.

Q. Did the Chief Engineer seem to be self-possessed, or otherwise?

A. Well, he appeared self-possessed, I think. He was laboring under some excitement.

Q. How was the Mayor?

A. The Mayor was about the coolest of the party assembled there. He seemed to be in full possession of his faculties, — very cool, and yet not phlegmatic. The most excited man that I saw there, I think, was General Burt.

After these orders had been given out, some one suggested that Gen'l Burt be chosen the Commander, and that was adopted; and then we all started right off without any organization, or without knowing where we were to go, or what we were to do, and I suggested to Alderman Jenks that we seemed to be going off like a mob. Mr. Jenks then turned to the party and suggested that we be marked off in localities, — directed to go to special localities, — and upon that we were designated. I was stationed at the corner of Summer and Washington streets. We went down into the office of the Chief of Police, and each had a policeman assigned to him, and I went away with my policeman to the corner of Summer and Washington streets. I don't know the name or the number of the policeman. I felt that it was a fearful responsibility for me.

Q. What did you do in pursuance of that authority?

A. We went to the corner of Summer and Washington streets. The fire then, I think, was just reaching Trinity church. It had not got down Washington street as far as Macullar, Williams & Parker's store. It was burning up there. The firemen were at work in Summer street throwing water upon the opposite buildings; and they were in Washington street, nearly opposite the "Transcript" building, playing upon the opposite buildings there. The wind was blowing down Winter street pretty strong. My judgment was that the firemen would save that without any explosions being made.

I saw Alderman Woolley there, and he was of the opinion that the firemen would save it. I impressed a team and took my policeman, and we went down Dock square to Mr. Reed's store to get powder. We didn't get it, but got five hundred feet of fuse. Then we went up to a store on Cornhill, and found the store broken open, and that somebody had been there. Then we went back to the fire, and shortly after I got there (perhaps we were gone three-quarters of an hour), some powder arrived. Mr. Page came there with powder, and various citizens were about there. They were very anxious that the building should be blown up, when they found out we had authority, and they were very anxious to have Mudge's store blown up. Finally between Mr. Page, myself, and some others, there seemed to be a general opinion that it must be blown up, and somebody took some powder into the building. The engine at the corner was moved away and the firemen all deserted Summer street and Washington street, and the powder was touched off. It blew out the glass, but it didn't make a great noise. They put some more powder in and ran. That powder didn't go off at all. Well, some time passed, and then Washington street and Summer street were cleared, and it was cleared for some distance up Winter street, everybody expecting momentarily that this building would blow up. But after waiting about ten minutes, I saw that the buildings on the other side of Washington street were getting very hot, and I saw the necessity of having water thrown upon those buildings. The wind was pretty strong then. The fire then had got down to this Mudge's building, and the store beyond was in flames. This building was alone. It seemed certain then that the fire would not cross Washington street if water was thrown upon the buildings opposite, and that it would not cross Summer street. There seemed to be a necessity for having water thrown upon the buildings. I was trying to rally the firemen back to their places, but they were very much afraid of this powder and refused to go. Finally, I found a white-hatted Captain of a hose company who seemed to realize it. I told him that I knew who put the powder in there and how much there had been, and that there was no danger whatever. I told him that I would be the first man at the nozzle of the hose, if he would come down Washington street. He said he would go where I would. He got a hose and came down into Washington street and played on the building opposite, and shortly afterwards two or three other hose came in there and played on to the burning buildings and on to this Mudge's building, and then they got a hose down into Summer street, and the building didn't blow up or burn down either.

Q. How many minutes were lost in that place by using powder?

A. Well, sir, I should think more than half an hour, and, perhaps, three-quarters of an hour. It is very difficult to judge of the time.

The sentiment of those people about there seemed to be that it was a wise thing to do; and I thought that if it was not blown down, and the fire *should* cross Washington street, it would be said that it was in consequence of its not being blown down. It was very difficult to decide what was best. It seemed then that it had got to burn if it was not blown up.

Q. Were there any Fire Engineers on that spot?

A. I saw no Engineer.

Q. To your knowledge, no Engineer gave an opinion for or against it?

A. No, sir. Alderman Woolley was the only one that I saw who seemed to have authority when we tried to rally the firemen. They called for an Engineer. I inquired where he was. They said they didn't know. I pulled out this paper and said that I was an Engineer for the time being, and that I would take the responsibility of directing them. I tried to impress them with the fearful authority of that paper.

Q. Do you know what became of that second dose of powder?

A. No, sir. So far as I know, it is there now.

Q. You say "they" advised doing it and you thought you had better not. Whom do you mean by "they"?

A. They were men that I didn't know. I remember ——— Taylor and Mr. John Brown of Temple street. He was very anxious that the building should be blown up. He was the only man that I know. Councilman Page was there, and he thought it should be blown up, and he brought the powder, with a couple of firemen.

Q. Who appointed General Burt as Commander?

A. Somebody suggested it. I don't know who it was. He suggested that General Burt should be put in command of this force; others said "Yes." There was no formal vote. General Burt started off the moment that he received that authority, and we were about following him, like a mob. He assigned me to Summer street. When we came back, at the suggestion of somebody that we had better be organized, the Mayor's Clerk sat down at a table and wrote off the names and the places. I think they were asked to volunteer, and one said, "I will go here," and another said, "I will go there," and they rather chose their places. I was quiet and didn't hanker after responsibility, and I took what was left.

Q. Did General Burt accept the command?

A. Yes, sir. He did in fact; I don't know that he did in words.

Q. Did he issue any orders whatever?

A. No, sir. I think as soon as they appointed him Commander in this way, he says, "Come, let us go!" and we were starting off without knowing where we were going or what we were going to do.

Q. Was any section assigned to General Burt?

A. Yes, sir. I think he said he would go down in Federal street, or somewhere in that vicinity.

Q. Did you blow up any other buildings besides Mudge's?

A. No, sir. I didn't blow that up. I didn't see who went and put the powder in.

Q. Where was Mr. Page's district?

A. It was not there. It was a usurpation. He was invading my dominion.

Q. That was the only explosion you witnessed?

A. Yes, sir. I stayed there until about six o'clock, when I saw that the fire was under complete control in that section, and then I went back to the Mayor's office and reported to him that it was all safe there.

Q. Did you see your Commander at any later time?

A. No, sir.

Q. Were no reports made to the Commander?

A. No, sir. I reported to the Mayor, and I think Mr. Cobb was there when I returned. Then I went home and went to bed and remained there until half-past nine o'clock.

Q. (By Mr. Firth.) How was it in regard to the conduct of the fire as it came under your eye?

A. It was excellent, with the exception of those men who declined to go into Washington street, because they were afraid of the explosion of that building. I don't think they were to be blamed much for that. I think it was an out-of-town company. I told them that there was not a formidable quantity of the powder. But they were inclined to think that that was a fib.

The second charge was put into the farther extreme corner, so that it was rather a dangerous thing to attempt to go in to get it out. There didn't seem to be anybody very desirous of doing it.

Adjourned to Tuesday afternoon, Dec. 10th.

NINTH DAY.

TUESDAY, Dec. 10.

WILLIAM W. GREENOUGH, *sworn.*

Q. (By Mr. RUSSELL.) You are the treasurer of the Boston Gas Light Co.?

A. Yes, sir.

Q. What means do you have of shutting off gas from a burning district?

A. Perhaps I had better make a statement, so that you may understand the whole thing more clearly.

In 1835, at the time when our corporation was reorganized, there were placed outside of the meters, a cock, and outside of the house, at each service pipe, a cock, by which the gas could be stopped in case of a conflagration. When I took the management of the works, in 1852, some few of the outside cocks still remained, a great number having been previously discontinued as useless in case of emergency, for the simple reason that, having remained in the ground for a series of years, they became rusty, and wouldn't turn when occasion required. Shortly after I became manager, my attention was drawn to the importance of having some provision for the streets, whereby the gas could be shut off from districts, and I began and continued a system of water valves, the only known valve then in use, and deemed suitable for the purpose, whereby gas could be shut off in the main before reaching buildings. Some three years since, a slide valve was invented, which, after careful investigation, I made up my mind to trust in the streets, and began slowly to introduce them. At the time of the fire in November, we had in use in the streets of the city eight hundred and thirty-four valves on the street mains, of which six hundred and fifteen were water valves, and two hundred and twenty-nine slide valves. By a slide valve, I mean an iron gate. I believe that is a larger number than is in use in any other city with which I am conversant. In most American cities, they have no provision in case of fire except the cock on the service pipe outside the house, so that I supposed, previously to the fire, that we had all the provision which it was possible to have for the protection of the city and ourselves. When the fire came, all these preventives proved worthless; the water valves in the districts which were on fire were inaccessible, and the fall of the heavy granite buildings broke our mains from ten inches in diameter down to the smallest sizes.

I should explain, that the distribution in the streets consists mainly of 3, 4, 6, 8 and 10-inch mains, with large arterial mains, conducting gas from the works to the reservoirs. During the time of the fire, it was not possible to get hand-carts enough, nor men enough, to convey water in barrels to the water valves; but at six o'clock on Sunday morning, our street foreman and his assistants began, with their gangs of men, to shut off as fast as they could, their first work being to fill the 18-inch water valve at the head of Summer street.

Q. What is the name of your street foreman?

A. William H. Durell. He can tell you very much more than I can of his own movements, as I know nothing of what he did except by hearsay.

Q. He only did what he was told to do, I suppose?

A. He wasn't told to do anything. It was his duty to do it, without waiting to get any command from me. It was his duty to cut off all the gas from the district, in all cases of fire. I can say this, that he went on with his work, and continued steadily at it, Monday, Tuesday and Wednesday, until all connection with the burned district was cut off. On Sunday night an explosion occurred, breaking our great arterial main connecting the works with the two Federal street gas-holders. *Directly* connecting, I should say, because we had an outlet connection with the works, but the means of supply was through this 18-inch main; and the gas was shut off at the works immediately subsequent to that.

I think I have now given all the substantial facts.

Q. The gas that continued to burn in some places was what remained in the pipes after this shutting off?

A. Yes, sir.

Q. You could see gas burning dimly in some of the streets?

A. Yes, sir; the gas continued to burn in places about town, on the high ground, and so on, very dimly. The specific gravity of the gas being lighter than the atmosphere, of course it went to the high portions of the city. I think in some houses, on Mt. Vernon street, for instance, it did not go out at all.

Q. How did these water valves work?

A. The water valve is a seal of water. It usually is in the form of a circular box, of greater or less depth, according to the size of the main which it is to stop; through the centre of it, at the top, comes an iron partition, which extends within a few inches of the bottom If there is nothing in the valve, the gas passes under the partition, and through it; when the water is filled in, so that it is up to the level of the bottom of the pipe, then the gas cannot pass from the street main on one side to the street main on the other side, without going down through the water.

Q. (By Mr. PHILBRICK.) Exactly like a trap in a sewer?

A. Yes, sir; exactly like a trap in a sewer.

Q. When you want to use them, you fill them with water?

A. Yes, sir; for instance, that eighteen-inch main water-valve (which is the largest we have in use) takes three or four barrels of water; on that eighteen-inch main, however, we have substituted two slide valves, in places where there were water valves before. The great difficulty has been to get valves which work after having been in the ground for a long while. About three years ago, there was invented a valve of a V shape, which fitted into the bottom of the valves in this way, the old valve having been square, and squarely entering the cavity at the bottom of the valves; when that form became rusty no human power could pull it out sometimes, although it worked with a screw. But we found that the new slide valves that we used worked very well, and we are now largely continuing their use. When the explosion occurred on Sunday night, it blew the water out of the water valves in the immediate vicinity, so that we were left as if nothing had been done.

Q. (By Mr. FIRTH.) Was that something new in your experience?

A. Entirely. We have never had any considerable explosion of gas in any case of fire, so that when Monday morning came, we had nothing to do except to cut our mains bodily around the district, which was accomplished by Tuesday night.

Q. (By Mr. RUSSELL.) How many men did you employ?

A. I can't tell you. Mr. Durell can tell you.

Q. (By Mr. PHILBRICK.) How do you account for the explosions of gas that occurred?

A. My theory of the matter has been this: that among the breakages of the mains, there came a break in the vicinity of a sewer, by which the gas was let into the sewer, and from that went into the cellars of some of the stores that were on fire. There was no force previous to the explosions to have broken that eighteen-inch main, which we found broken in three places, when we çame to strip it, as we did as soon as we could get access to it, the whole length of Summer street, with the exception of the places where there had been no granite stores to fall upon the mains. We found the mains broken only in the vicinity of the explosions, where the ground was upheaved, in front of the store where I suppose the main explosion took place, from the account which was given to me by Mr. Greenleaf, of the firm of Hovey & Co., who gave me the only definite account which I have had of the successive explosions. But my theory, as I have before stated, has been, that the gas got into the drain, and from there into the cellars. And what confirms me the more in that opinion is that on Monday afternoon, the gas being on for a little while, I was standing at the head of Summer street, and an explosion came through the drain, blowing off the covers of the drain, I should think, two or three times while I was standing there. The gas was shut off Monday morning, but it was let on again a little while Monday afternoon, to see if everything was tight.

Q. How do you explain satisfactorily the occurrence of the explosions in the gas mains by the leakage of gas into the sewers? As I understand it, gas doesn't explode without air.

A. No, sir.

Q. Could any air get into your mains?

A. No, sir. There were four explosions, as I understand; the first below Chauncy street, on Summer, on the right-hand side going down; the second nearly opposite Hovey's; the third was in the store between Trinity church and Mudge's, and the fourth explosion was in the cellar of another store, I forget the name of the occupant. That explosion broke this main, upheaved it from below. Whether the main was broken before or not, I have no means of saying, but when the explosion took place, it blew to pieces the water-box of the eighteen-inch valve at the head of the street. Of course, we can do nothing now except form a theory about the matter. We found our gas was pouring into the district, notwithstanding all the valves we could command were shut; there was no means of getting access to all of them. I don't know the exact position of the sewer, but it was very near to our main.

Q. The explosion in the sewer created a shock that broke your main?

A. Yes, sir; it broke our 18-inch main at that time, and that let the air into it; but that would not blow out the 18-inch main. The syphons that were blown out were blown out of the other mains, which had but very little connection with the 18-inch main. This was an arterial main; it had but two connections with Summer street, one 6-inch, near the corner of Kingston street, and another 3-inch, near the corner of Hawley street, which were entirely insufficient to produce such results on the water valves. What other explosions occurred through the district, I have no means of knowing, but we found our seals were gone.

Q. Did you examine them to see if the water was gone?

A. I can't tell you what examination Mr. Durell made. It is his business to look after the valves. I came into town between six and seven o'clock on Monday morning, and the moment I understood the situation of things, I ordered the mains to be cut. I felt that it wasn't safe to trust the valves any longer.

Q. (By Mr. Cobb.) Have you any means of ascertaining what the wastage of gas was?

A. Only approximately. The consumption on that night was about three and one quarter millions cubic feet. On Sunday morning, at six o'clock, there was no gas left in the holders. I think the consumption on the night before (Friday) had been about two and a half millions.

Q. (By Mr. Philbrick.) That is, in the normal state of things?

A. Yes, sir, the normal condition of things on Friday night. That would leave a balance of 750,000 feet to be accounted for. The town was lighted as for a festival that night; everything was burning on Saturday night. Our rules have been, in case of fire, to let our gas go, for the reason that property must be saved. If we had shut our gas off that night, it would probably have added to the loss by the fire millions upon millions. Suppose here is a store in a street, and the fire approaching it. The people are getting out their stock; they light their gas, and when they are done with it, go away and leave it burning. I have not yet heard of an individual who went to a meter and shut off his gas. A number of merchants have said to me since, "If you had shut off our gas, we couldn't have saved our property."

Q. (By Mr. Firth.) Did the propriety of shutting off the gas occur to any one that night, so far as you know?

A. No, sir.

Q. (By Mr. Russell.) The propriety of *not* shutting off had occurred to you before?

A. Yes, sir. I shouldn't shut it off unless there was an absolute necessity for it. That is, we prefer to suffer the loss of our gas, in case of fire, rather than that people should lose their property in consequence of being deprived of it. Think what it would have cost if we had shut off our gas that night on Franklin street!

Q. How long does it take to shut these slide valves?

A. It depends upon the size; they work with screws. To shut an 18-inch valve would take about three minutes. I shouldn't think it would take more than a minute to shut a 3-inch valve.

Q. How many valves were there in this district?

A. I can't tell you. The important fact at this time was not the number of valves in the district, but in the territory surrounding the district.

I think there were in this district something like twenty-five or thirty valves, and a great many more in the surroundings.

Q. (By Mr. PHILBRICK.) Were there a sufficient number of slide valves in the immediate neighborhood of the district to isolate it?

A. No, sir.

Q. You were depending upon the old water valves?

A. Yes, sir; we depended upon the water valves, which we had never learned to distrust before.

Q. Do you know any loss of pressure on the gas to allow of the introduction of air in the mains?

A. Not unless those mains had been broken previously to our knowledge. In one of the mains just above Hovey's, there was a piece blown out three feet long, I should say, by, perhaps, twelve inches wide at the widest part; an oval-shaped piece, that looked as though it had been blown from the inside outward. If that took place, of course that was sufficient to account for any explosion in the main.

Q. If there was an explosion in the main, I can see how the water came to be blown out of the valves, but I don't see how air could get into the mains as long as there was gas there.

A. Of course we were not aware of all the damage that was done to the mains until subsequently to the fire. I had no suspicion. I didn't suspect, for a moment, that the mains were broken so extensively as they were by the fall of buildings. We had occasion to take up our Milk-street main for the purpose of restoring gas in the Old South block and the Devonshire-street buildings, immediately after the fire, and we found that pipe broken in seven places between Washington street and Devonshire street. Those breakages were sufficient to let plenty of air into that pipe.

Q. Could the air get into your pipes while they were under the pressure of gas?

A. No; but there was no supply of gas at that time; it was all out on Sunday morning. The gas was all gone, and no pressure existed in the pipes.

Q. The reservoirs were exhausted?

A. Yes, sir.

Q. (By Mr. COBB.) I understand you as saying that these water-valves proved a failure?

A. Yes, sir, I think so now.

Q. In view of that, what would be your recommendation for the future?

A. Slide valves; such as we are putting in.

Q. How frequently?

A. I have been going on with the work, with the view of gradually displacing the water valves by slide valves. For instance, since the fire, we have had an opportunity to put in twenty-three valves. During the present year, we have taken out twenty-two valve boxes and substituted for them gates. This we have been doing wherever we had an opportunity, but feeling perfectly safe all the time with our water valves. I am not aware that any other city in the world has these slide valves in use.

Q. (By Mr. PHILBRICK.) If you had had these slide valves supplied in the place of the water valves, would there have been enough of them to have isolated that fire district during Sunday?

A. That I can't tell you, without looking at the map of our distribution and seeing the position. Perhaps it would enable you to understand this matter more fully, if you would go to my office and see the great map we have of the position of all the valves. I have no doubt that district could have been isolated by going out far enough on its circumference, and shutting the gas off from the neighboring districts besides.

Q. Well, if there had been a sufficient number of these slide valves, there would have been no trouble in shutting them, as to time, during Sunday?

A. No.

Q. (By Mr. Russell.) Is it your intention to go on and displace all the water valves?

A. Yes, sir, in time.

Q. In what time, probably?

A. Well, that I can hardly say, because there are certain positions in which the water valves will answer pretty well for the present. In districts that have granite buildings, I shouldn't want to trust them. I should want this year to replace all my water valves in those districts where there are heavy stores; but where there are houses, where the fall wouldn't break our mains, the water valves will answer.

Q. In all places where there are heavy stores, you mean to put in slide valves at once?

A. Yes, sir, during the coming year. The fall of a brick building will not break the main, unless it is an enormous building, like the old Gerrish Market. When that fell, it broke our small main, running through Sudbury street; it did not break our eighteen-inch main, directly under it. The rule is, to lay the top of our pipe three feet from the surface of the ground. Speaking of Gerrish Market, recalls to my mind a fact in relation to that which is noteworthy, in connection with the safety stops outside. When that building was in process of construction, I said to myself, it is merely a question of time when it will burn, and I will put a water valve on the large supply pipe which goes into the building. It was done, but when the fire came, we couldn't get within three hundred feet of it. Our people were ready to rush in, but the Fire Department wouldn't let them.

Q. Do you remember the explosion on Hanover street and Blackstone street? We have heard something of that. Was it caused in the same way?

A. No, that wasn't from fire; a break had occurred in the main from frost.

Q. There was no fire before the explosion?

A. No, sir.

Q. (By Mr. Firth.) Some of the firemen have reported here that when that explosion took place they were on duty at a fire?

A. There was no alarm of fire occurred, to the best of my recollection. The explosion occurred about eleven o'clock, and I first heard of it from my assistant foreman, who came to my house, and I went down there, I should think about eleven o'clock that evening. The main had broken, according to the best of my recollection now, near the corner of Hanover and Blackstone streets, and leaked into a cesspool, and through that into the drains fed by some of the houses in Salem street, and the explosion occurred in consequence of the explosive mixture reaching a stove in one of the rooms of a house in Salem street.

Q. (By Mr. PHILBRICK.) Did it ever occur to you, that it might be worth while to put your pipes deeper than three feet, to escape the danger of breakage from falling buildings, and by the frost?

A. They have been kept at three feet because the water people elected the four-foot level. When we first laid the mains, we took the three-feet level, which was deeper than the level at which pipes were laid in Europe. The first European Engineers who came here were in the habit of laying the pipes as they laid them in London, two and a half feet deep. I can't tell you at what time our company began to lay their pipes three feet deep. It was before I had any knowledge of their affairs. When I came to their office, they were laying their mains three feet deep, and when I made the inquiry why that custom was adopted, I received the same answer that I give you, that the water people had elected to lay their pipes four feet deep. If we took a five-feet level, it would make it very expensive to get to the main, in laying service pipe, etc. If we took too high a level, it of course brought us under the action of frost. In St. Petersburg, I think their mains are laid five feet deep, to be below their frosts; but frost in Boston seldom goes below three feet, at least in original soil.

Q. (By Mr. FIRTH.) On this question of depth, the danger from falling walls was never thought of?

A. No, sir; I had no apprehension of falling walls.

Q. (By Mr. RUSSELL.) When your intended plan of putting in slide valves is completed, will you be able to isolate such a district as this?

A. Yes, sir.

Q. How long will it take?

A. That I can't say, of course, without having the number of valves which it would require to isolate it.

Q. I don't expect an exact answer, but approximately.

A. The valves in such a district would be six, four, and three-inch, and with gangs of men who understood where they were going,—of course the location of the valves could not be carried in the memory, and they are very frequently covered up with dirt so that they cannot be seen in the streets; there can be but a few people who know exactly where they are, and know which ones to shut; that is a business for which the Superintendent of street work and his assistants must be immediately responsible. We require everything to be put in black and white that we have in our underground work, so that in case of the absence or death of the individual in whose memory the fact is stored, it is to be found on this map, which is a very large map, and made to scale, and we have a descriptive book which shows the position of every valve, and everything in the surrounding houses.

Q (By Mr. RUSSELL.) How many assistants has your foreman for this work?

A. He has precisely the number of men which his work requires; for instance, when we were laying this eighteen-inch main, he had a very large number of men, all the men he could work; but his ordinary gang consists of about twenty-five men. These men are employed in the service of the company the year round; during the summer, in laying mains, and looking after the syphons, and the general care of the machine, and in the winter they are occupied in looking after leaks.

Q. (By Mr. Cobb.) When your proposed plan is completed, how small a district in the business portion of Boston will you be able to isolate?

A. I have not yet made up my mind on that subject; it is a question of expediency. Suppose a fire occurs, I will say, on a long street, and is confined to one side of the street without a break in it, of course, the natural thought would be to govern that side of the street by a valve at each end of it; but there might be reasons why I shouldn't dare to shut it off, or which would render it bad policy to shut the gas off of that district. Of course, I should wish to have the means in my control, but it might be utterly inexpedient to do so until the fire got directly upon us, and forced us to shut off the gas.

Q. Don't you think it would be necessary to have the means to do it?

A. I think so, and that is what I have been attempting to do, but which has proved utterly useless.

Q. (By Mr. Philbrick.) Was part of your plan to have your valves at every street corner?

A. No, sir. Our plan was to take it in districts. The theory of thorough distribution is thorough circulation.

[The witness, by a diagram, illustrated the system which he proposed to adopt.]

Q. (By Mr. Cobb.) By doing that, wouldn't you render the district dark, and do greater damage in that way?

A. Yes, sir; I might do that.

Q. Are these valves expensive?

A. Yes, sir; slide valves are. For instance, here is the cost of the ninety-three slide valves we had in 1872,—$2,301. The 12-inch valves cost $75; the 3-inch, about $15, which is the smallest. An 18-inch valve, of course, costs very much more. These two 18-inch valves, which I inserted in the 18-inch main in place of the water valves, were made by the Boston Machine Shop. The men worked night and day until they were ready. There were none in the country that we could procure.

Q. (By Mr. Firth.) How recent is this invention?

A. I should think it is about three years since I saw the first valve I dared to trust in the street.

Q. (By Mr. Russell.) You spoke about one explosion on Summer street, on the left-hand side below Washington — who told you about that?

A. Mr. Greenleaf. He was describing to me on Monday morning what had occurred.

Q. (By Mr. Philbrick.) There is nothing to prevent isolating any district, however small, except the limited number of valves, and the expense of applying them?

A. No, sir. We should not consider the question of expense at all, in connection with the public safety.

Q. What I want to get at is, whether the presence of so many valves would be an incumbrance upon the system, in increasing leakage?

A. No, sir; I don't think they would add anything to the leakage.

Q. (By Mr. FIRTH.) You would consider that such a number would add a good deal to your care?

A. Of course; we would have to open them and keep them in order, and see that they would work when required to work.

Q. (By Mr. PHILBRICK.) Is it an iron surface that slides?

A. Yes, sir. It is subject to rust, of course; but it has been generally considered that the cock inside, at the meter, was an all-sufficient protection.

Q. In the house?

A. In the house, if people would attend to it themselves, and shut it off in case of danger from fire. Applications have been made since the fire, for cocks outside of the houses, on the supply-pipes.

Q. How do they get at those?

A. With a key, through the sidewalk, down under the ground on the supply. As I said before, we have found them utterly inoperative. When we wanted to turn them, we couldn't do it; they were utterly useless; yet there are large cities in the United States whose sole reliance is upon these cocks now.

Q. Does that stem pass out through the top?

A. It is the shape of a T, with a square at the end of it, turning the cock below. The head of the cock would turn off.

Q. How would you get at that cock?

A. There would be a pipe leading down to it from the surface of the ground.

Q. (By Mr. FIRTH.) From the information you have, what should you say in regard to the turning off of the gas that night? Did anybody turn the gas off?

A. I don't know of anybody, except that Judge Russell has mentioned that Mr. Endicott, of the firm of Hovey & Co., turned off their gas Sunday night.

Q. (By Mr. PHILBRICK.) Supposing every service-pipe had been turned off, don't it appear to you probable that there were leaks in the main from the shocks, which would have made considerable leakage?

A. Yes, sir; explosions would naturally occur where mains were extensively broken by falling buildings at the time of a fire, and the gas had opportunity enough to mix with air and form an explosive mixture.

Q. So that slide valves are the only reliance?

A. Yes, sir. That was the first practical conclusion I came to after the fire, and I so stated to the editor of the Gas-Light Journal, who immediately published it in his paper, that the fire in Boston had shown the utter worthlessness of every valve except the slide valve.

You asked me a question, with regard to the consumption of gas on Saturday night, which I did not fully answer. I began by stating, that our consumption then was three and one quarter millions feet, and our average, two millions and a half, leaving 750,000 feet to be accounted for; then I went on to say, that the whole town was lighted as for a festival. Of course, it would be only guess-work; but my estimate was, that we had only lost about ten per cent. by the fire, which seemed to be a very moderate sum — 325,000 feet on three and a quarter millions. On Sunday morning, at half-past one, I went into several shops, and said to the people, "I pray you, don't burn your gas in this way; at any moment it may go out; I can't tell when. There is plenty for ordinary consumption, but not for any consumption like this." So that, considering that, probably only ten per cent. had been consumed by the fire, the idea didn't occur to me that any such loss could take place as did occur on Sunday.

[See Appendix.]

MALCOLM S. GREENOUGH, Chemist of Boston Gas Light Company, *sworn.*

Q. What is your position?

A. I am assistant-engineer of the Boston Gas Company.

Q. (By Mr. Russell.) Will you state the reason why you didn't shut off the gas on Sunday morning?

A. I left the office of the company about five o'clock Sunday morning. Having been there nearly all night, to see if we could do anything, and finding it impossible from the office, I went to the works and found that there was not a foot of gas in the entire city; the holders were absolutely empty, for the first time in the history of the company. I supposed that it all came from the consumption in the city, which, as my father has said, was enormous, everything being lighted; so I set the works going to their fullest extent making gas. Mr. Durell had gone for his men, and I knew that at six o'clock, he and his foreman would start round the district to shut all the valves, not expecting they would have anything like the difficulty they did. So we began to make gas as fast as we possibly could. I went down there again in the evening, and got the reports from the different men who had gone to the gas-holders to see what the supply was; and then I found that the gas had been running into the ruins all day Sunday. Even if we had not been requested by the Chief of Police not to make any more gas, we should not have continued to do so, after we had found that out.

WILLIAM H. O'BRIEN, *sworn.*

Q. (By Mr. Russell.) You were with Mr. Laforme on the night of the fire, at the Union Savings Bank?

A. Yes, sir.

Q. When did you hear an alarm of fire, or a cry of fire?

A. I did not hear any alarm of fire. I heard a racket on the street.

Q. How long did it take you to get there?

A. We rushed down Bedford street to the foot of Kingston street.

Q. What was the condition of the fire then?

A. I looked up Kingston street, and the roof of the building at the corner of Kingston and Summer was in flames; perhaps a portion of the rear part was not entirely, but most of it was in flames.

Q. Did you hear any alarm then, or at any time?

A. No, sir. We went down Bedford street, turning around Church Green, and up Summer street. At that time, the upper story, the fourth story, and the third story of the building, were in a blaze, and the flames were so hot that I had to hold my hands up to my face to pass through. The first thing I noticed was their putting up a ladder, at that time, on the building directly east of the one that was on fire, and I made the remark (I had never seen the process before), how nicely it was done. We passed further up Summer street, crossing the head of Otis, and stopped half way between Otis and Arch streets. A hose was laid there, and they were playing on to the fire. We made no delay at any of these points particularly.

Q. Was there any steamer there?

A. I think there was a steamer at the corner of Arch and Summer streets. I am very sure there was, but I would not swear positively that there was at that moment, but there was very soon after.

Q. Did you see the fire cross Summer street to Otis street?

A. Yes, sir; when it first crossed.

Q. What was done to stop it?

A. I saw nothing done, and I remarked to the gentleman with me, that it was strange they did not do anything. I do not say they did not, but I saw nothing.

Q. Where did it take in the Otis-street building?

A. It took on the mouldings, the frame-work of the windows, in the Mansard roof; the sill, that is probably what you call it.

Q. That being of wood, I suppose?

A. Yes, sir. There was an immense volume of flame coming out of the building in which the fire originated, and it made two or three attempts, and finally caught this woodwork, very slightly at first.

Q. At that time, could the firemen stand in Summer street and play on this front?

A. Well, that is a pretty difficult point. There was an immense volume of flame from the fourth story and roof of the building which first took fire, crossing Summer street; I do not know what the heat was, because it was some ten minutes after I had passed up, but I don't think it was any longer than that. As a matter of opinion, I should say they could, but I do not know that.

Q. Do you know whether there were any streams carried up inside of the building, and thrown upon those roofs?

A. No, sir; I will tell you, that seeing this fire taking on the north side of Summer street, I said to the gentleman with me, "It is very strange they do not carry a hose through that store, and put that out;" and from the time it took, I watched it for fifteen minutes, and it never decreased; it was increasing all the time; that I am ready to testify to, for I took particular pains to observe it, and remarked that it was strange they did not do something to stop that. I considered, as a matter of opinion, that that was the vital point of the whole thing.

Q. Do you know how many engines were on the spot at that time?

A. No, sir; I do not.

Q. What time did you say it was when the fire crossed Summer street?

A. Well, sir, I should say it was not later than fifteen minutes of eight.

Q. Did you consult your watch at all?

A. I did not then, but I had an appointment at eight o'clock, and I consulted my watch at other times.

JOHN W. REGAN, *sworn.*

Q. (By Mr. Russell.) Where were you when the fire broke out?

A. 5 Columbia street — my home.

Q. How long have you been connected with the Fire Department?

A. About nineteen years.

Q. At what time did you know there was a fire?

A. At eleven minutes past seven.

Q. Did you look at a clock, or a watch?

A. Looked at a clock.

Q. Was your clock right?

A. It generally is, sir. I have a fire-alarm telegraph in the room.

Q. How did you know there was a fire?

A. Heard somebody hallo fire in the street.

Q. What did you do?

A. I immediately went to Kingston street.

Q. What was the condition of the fire then?

A. The fire was then in the three upper stories of the building, and down in the lower story in the rear, on the passage-way.

Q. In the rear, were all the stories on fire?

A. They were all on fire. The three upper stories were on fire, and a part of the three lower stories; that is, it seemed to go down in the elevator to the three lower stories.

Q. What did you do?

A. There was a building in the rear of it. I knocked at the door, and a young man answered my call, and I asked him if he had a key to the door leading to the stairs, and he said he had; and I asked him to open the door, and he did so. I then went to the front on Summer, to see if any of the department had arrived. I found there, in a very few minutes, the Insurance wagon. I asked the driver of the Insurance wagon to bring an axe, as I wanted to break open the door on Summer street. We tried it, and seeing that it would take too long to break it open, we gave it up, and went to the rear. I took No. 4's stream to the upper story of the rear building, and remained there until the other building fell on to it.

Q. Did you notice when the fire-alarm was given?

A. No, sir, I did not. I could not hear it there, but before taking No. 4's line up in the building, I met an officer, and told him to go to the box, and give three more alarms. That was before any of the department had arrived on the ground.

Q. What came first?

A. My impression is Engine 7, although I cannot say. She came in at Bedford and Lincoln streets. Hose 2 was the first apparatus I saw.

Q. Can you tell me when she came?

A. I cannot tell.

Q. Do you know whether she had steam up, or not?

A. I suppose she had; I do not know. She is under my charge, and she always has steam up.

Q. What did you do next?

A. I next came out of the building into Kingston street. The falling of that building cut our line in two. The engine remained on Summer street, and I sent a hoseman round to report to the Chief. I then took Hose 2, who was in the same building with us when the building fell, on to us, and put him on the dwelling-houses directly opposite, on the roof. No. 13 came and reported, in the mean time, and I went back again into the building I had come out of, but thought it was not safe to remain there any longer, as it was on fire up and down, and we had to come out; and I got No. 13's stream to work in the street. After I came down from the roof where I put Hose 2's stream, I called Capt. Smith and Capt. Colligan into Summer street. I told them we had a terrible fire, and we must separate and attack it at different points. Capt. Smith said he would go to Chauncy street; Capt. Colligan and myself remained in Kingston street, and Capt. Munroe went to the corner of Columbia and Bedford streets. A short time after that, the Chief Engineer sent for me to go and get all the hose I could, and I did.

Q. To Mr. Boyd's?

A. Yes, sir.

Q. Was that the first time you saw the Chief?

A. I did not see the Chief this time. He sent the message to me.

Q. Had you seen him before?

A. Yes, sir. I think I saw him half an hour after the fire had crossed Summer street. I saw him in front of Mr. Beebe's store.

Q. What was he doing?

A. He was ordering the building to be cleared of its goods,

Q. Was he self-possessed, or otherwise?

A. He was self-possessed.

Q. After you got the hose, what did you do?

A. I immediately returned to Chauncy street, and there found that Capt. Smith had gone, for the Chief Engineer had sent for him to go to the north of the fire, and meet him. I asked if the Chief had sent for him, and they said, "Yes." I said, "It is strange that Captain Smith should leave this point." They said the orders were positive from the Chief for him to go. I then stayed in Chauncy street some time, and went to work on the store of Lewis Coleman and Co., and there stopped the fire.

Q. What did you have to work with there?

A. My impression is that No. 13 was one of them; No. 18 was one, and I think a Newton engine. I think we had three engines at work there.

Q. After you stopped the fire there, where did you go?

A. I immediately went to the corner of Bedford and Columbia street, to prevent the fire getting into the Columbia building. It had then taken on the other side of Bedford street, in those dwelling-houses.

Q. Where did you go next?

A. I next went on Lincoln street, and cut it off there.

Q. (By Mr. PHILBRICK.) Can you tell us about what time you left Chauncy street?

A. I think it must have been nearly twelve o'clock.

Q. At that time, the old Post Office building (Capen's) was all burned up?

A. Yes, sir; that was all gone, and the new building where they had put it out had taken fire again.

Q. Can you tell me why that building of Coleman and Co. did not take fire on the roof, as well as the others?

A. I do not know, because I was not there at the starting of it.

Q. It does not seem to have taken fire at all?

A. No, sir; I never ascertained why. I never understood the construction of the old Post Office building.

Q. (By Mr. RUSSELL.) You did not play on Mr. George W. Carnes' building, did you?

A. No, not that night.

Q. (By Mr. PHILBRICK.) Did you take any hose at any time on top of the old Post Office building?

A. No, sir; that was done before I got there.

Q. Where did you go next?

A. On South street. I cut off the fire on South street, the first dwelling-house on the left; then I went down to Federal street, but I had very little to do. I found the fire cut off. I came back again on to South street. I left three engines in charge of the foreman of Engine 1. I was then the only Engineer south of the fire. I then went to Washington street, and made up three engines, and carried them to the north of the fire, — No. 7 among others. It had then got to be seven, or half-past seven o'clock. I put No. 7 at work on the corner of Chatham street and Merchant's row. I then seized a horse and wagon south of the fire, and carried hose to the north until eleven o'clock in the forenoon.

Q. What did you do then?

A. I then put some lines to work at the corner of Milk and Batterymarch streets, and some on Kilby street, and worked all over the ruins about the rest of the day, — on the Post Office, and various other places in Congress street and Congress square.

Q. Was there any want of water that night?

A. Yes, sir; there was a scarcity of water. At our first start with No. 4 we did not get water enough to protect us in the business.

Q. What was the trouble?

A. That I never ascertained. We did not get enough water.

Q. That was when you had the hose up in the brick building?

A. Yes, sir.

Q. Was there any want of steam?

A. That I do not know. I have never made the inquiry, on account of this investigation.

Q. (By Mr. RUSSELL.) Was there any other want of water that night?

A. Yes; there was a want of water at the corner of Columbia and Bedford streets. Engine No. 12 stood there. We could not get but one decent stream from that engine, where we ought to have had two.

Q. Did you know what the trouble was there?

A. My impression was that the trouble was in the small water pipes; we have had trouble in that district for years.

Q. No. 12 had steam enough?

A. Yes, sir; she was in good working order.

Q. (By Mr. PHILBRICK.) Did you have a reservoir in Chauncy street?

A. Yes, sir; we had a reservoir and a hydrant, both.

Q. Sometimes did you run the reservoir down?
A. Sometimes we did, and sometimes we didn't.
Q. (By Mr. RUSSELL.) Was there any other place where there was a want of water?
A. Yes; there was a want of water on the corner of Bedford and Kingston street; Engine 3 stood there.
Q. The same trouble there?
A. Yes, sir; we could not get but one stream.
Q. Plenty of steam there?
A. Yes, sir; plenty.
Q. (By Mr. PHILBRICK.) Did you see that engine when it first arrived?
A. No, sir; I did not. I was in the building at the time she arrived.
Q. Was there any want of fuel that night, that you saw?
A. Yes, sir; there was a want of fuel; that is, there was a want of coal, but we had plenty of fuel without.
Q. What steamer wanted coal?
A. Number 3 wanted coal at that time.
Q. What time?
A. I think it was between ten and eleven o'clock.
Q. What did she have instead?
A. She had boxes, and various other things in the shape of wood.
Q. Did you suffer for the want of fuel?
A. No, sir.
Q. Did you lose steam for want of fuel?
A. No, sir.
Q. Any other place where coal was wanted?
A. I didn't see any.
Q. (By Mr. PHILBRICK.) Did you see any lack of steam for want of fuel any time in the night?
A. No, sir, I did not.
Q. Did you see Number 3, or Number 4, when it first came?
A. I took Number 4's stream into the building. I did not see either one of them when they came on the ground.
Q. How long could Number 4 have been there, before you took the stream?
A. It could not have been there two minutes.
Q. (By Mr. COBB.) You were in the building when it came?
A. No, sir; I was in the street when Number 4 run off, because I had nothing to go up into the building with. I took Number 4's stream up into the building myself.
Q. Was No. 4 supplied with coal when she arrived?
A. Yes, sir.
Q. Did you see No. 3 when she came on the ground?
A. No, sir; I didn't see her until she had run her hose off, and got to work.
Q. (By Mr. PHILBRICK.) What amount of coal did they carry?
A. Some engines will use more than others; some engineers will use more than others, in the same time. They generally carry coal enough for an hour.

Q. Was there any scarcity of coal in the engine houses in consequence the horse disease, that you know of?

A. I never heard of any.

Q. (By Mr. Russell.) How did the hose work that night?

A. Very well, sir.

Q. Was there any more than the usual bursting?

A. There was not so much, that I saw.

Q. How did the men behave?

A. The men behaved remarkably well.

Q. Was there any trouble with any of the men of the Boston Fire Department?

A. There was trouble with one man that night. A citizen came, and reported to me that Badge ——, — I have forgotten the number now; but he said that the man was drunk, and was very quarrelsome with officers and citizens, and I went to the place, but the man was gone. He has since been discharged from the department.

Q. Do you know to what engine he belonged?

A. I think it was No. 13.

Q. Do you know of any other case of drunkenness?

A. I do not. I did not see any other.

Q. Did you see any firemen helping themselves to goods?

A. I did.

Q. Where was that?

A. It was on Devonshire street, upon my return from Boyd & Sons.

Q. What time?

A. About twelve o'clock. I can't tell exactly the time now.

Q. What kind of goods?

A. My impression is they were rubber goods.

Q. Were they Boston firemen?

A. Some of them were.

Q. What did they do with them?

A. I told them they must take them off immediately, and leave them on the sidewalk. They said the store was burned down. I said: "You must take them off, and lay them on the sidewalk. You must not handle those goods."

Q. Did they obey you?

A. They did.

Q. Did they go to work immediately?

A. They went to work immediately. I organized a company, and saved a large quantity of hose that was left in Devonshire street. I got them to draw it to the other side of Milk street. There was about one thousand feet of it. I asked whose hose it was, and was told that the most of it was from out of town.

Q. Did you see any other instance of firemen helping themselves?

A. I did not see any other instance; but on Monday morning, one of the firm of Jordan, Marsh & Co. brought out a case of blankets, and commenced giving them to the Fire Department. As soon as I saw it, I said: "This must be stopped." He said: "These are my goods." I said: "No, they are not; they belong to the Insurance Company, and you have no right to give them away." I said: "You are making thieves of the Boston Fire Department." He said he was not. I said:

"Yes, you are. These men are wearing these blankets in the streets, and in the estimation of the public, they are thieves." He said: "Well, if you say stop, I shall do so."

Q. (By Mr. COBB.) Was there any unusual delay in getting the apparatus to the fire?

A. No, sir; on the contrary, when I came out of this building, after it was crushed, I met the Roxbury Board of Engineers in the street, and I asked them how they got there so quick. I thought they got there quicker than usual.

Q. Did they bring their apparatus with them?

A. Yes, sir.

Q. How was it about the city engines and hose-carriages?

A. I think, under the circumstances, they got there as quick, if not quicker, than they would with horses.

Q. That is qualified; this is what I want to get at; whether they were any later than usual, in your judgment?

A. No, sir; not after the bell struck, they were not.

Q. You didn't hear the bell strike?

A. No, sir; I know nothing about that, except from the report I got at the telegraph office.

Q. (By Mr. RUSSELL.) You did not see any explosions that night?

A. No, sir; I had nothing to do with that.

Q. (By Mr. COBB.) Did you notice that that fire had made unusual progress when you got there?

A. I did, and I ordered three alarms to be struck, which would bring the engines from Mattapan and Neponset, having no horses. That was about five minutes before the Chief got there. The Chief and Captain Green were my seniors, and they lived within five minutes of the fire; but I did not wait for either of them. I took that responsibility, that I suppose no man ever did before, and gave the order to have three alarms rung. I understood that an alarm had been given. When the officer went to the box, he came back and reported to me that he found an officer there, who was waiting for the first alarm to get through.

Q. Whom did you send?

A. I think it was officer Crane, of station two.

CHARLES A. R. DIMON, *sworn.*

Q. (By Mr. RUSSELL.) What time did you go to the fire?

A. I was at my house at the time of the fire.

Q. Do you belong to the Fire Brigade?

A. I am attached to it as one of the Secretaries of Boston. I am not directly attached to it, except that the Secretaries are detailed to have the general superintendence at all fires.

Q. (By Mr. FIRTH.) What is the exact title of the Association?

A. The "Boston Protective Fire Department Association."

Q. What time did you reach the fire?

A. I cannot say; I should judge it was quarter to eight, or somewhere near there.

Q. What was the condition of the fire when you got there?

A. The building at the corner of Kingston and Summer streets was in flames entirely, and the cornice of the store at the corner of Otis and Summer streets had then taken fire. I then met Captain Damrell, and reported to him.

Q. What was he doing?

A. He was superintending the placing of a ladder on the side of the building on Otis street, occupied by Maflyn, Mullen & Elms. It was impossible to put a ladder on the side towards Summer street, owing to the heat of the other building.

Q. How far from the corner of Summer street was the ladder put?

A. I should think fifteen feet.

Q. (By Mr. RUSSELL.) Was the ladder put up?

A. The ladder was put up on the building.

Q. What was done then?

A. I cannot say; I did not stop there. I spoke to Captain Damrell in regard to covering up the goods of Maflyn, Mullen & Elms.

Q. What was your conversation with Mr. Damrell?

A. I spoke to him of the necessity of covering up those goods on the first floor, and asked him whereabouts Capt. Green and the wagon were.

Q. What did he say?

A. He said he thought there was no necessity for it; that the building could not be saved. He spoke to me about the shortness of his ladders, and also of the difficulty of getting a stream up on that high roof. This was in the course of a conversation which was very hurried, as I left immediately to go down in search of the Brigade Wagon.

Q. (By Mr. PHILBRICK.) Did you notice whether or not the ladder reached the roof?

A. It did not.

Q. (By Mr. COBB.) Was it a spliced ladder?

A. I think it was; I won't be certain. I think it reached to about the third story.

Q. Do you know whether anything more was done to save that building on the corner of Otis street?

A. No, sir.

Q. I understand you to say, that it was impossible to stand in Summer street, in front of the building on the corner of Otis and Summer?

A. You could not get at the building on Summer street, between Maflyn's building and the building that was burning.

Q. Now, in Federal street, what did you see?

A. I noticed that the windows in the attic lofts of Howland & Luce's wool warehouse (No. 114, I think it is) were all open, and the wool was stored right up against the windows. I tried to get in, shook the door, and a clerk came along, and said he belonged there. I told him I must get in and shut those windows, and he finally consented to have the door broken in; and we broke in the door, and went into the upper lofts. The stairway was in the rear of the building, and the upper loft was packed from that stairway to the front, so that to get from the rear to the front, where the windows were, we had to crawl in some cases. There was hardly room enough to get under the rafters. When we got through, we found we could only shut two of the windows, as the wool was piled up against them; and the sparks at that time were coming in at the windows from Winthrop square. The middle one we could not close, as the wool was piled up against it, and the bales were too heavy for us to move.

Q. Did you see anything further worthy of note during the fire?

A. No, sir.

Q. (By Mr. COBB.) Referring again to the building at the corner of Otis and Summer streets, in your judgment, was everything done after you got there that could be done to save the building by the Fire Department?

A. I should judge that the proper steps had been taken by Capt. Damrell, so far as it was in his power to take them, to stop the flames. There seemed to be very few men there working on Otis street.

Q. In general, how did the firemen behave that night?

A. I think in some cases very foolhardy, that is, reckless.

Q. Did they expose themselves unnecessarily?

A. Yes, sir.

Q. (By Mr. GREENE.) You mean, in incurring danger?

A. Yes, sir; there was one case in particular, on Summer street. A building was burning there, which I knew contained fireworks, for I inspected it; and I immediately notified one of the Engineers, — I do not know which one it was, — that there were fireworks in it. He notified his men, but they seemed determined to get water up the stairway, when there was immediate danger of those fireworks exploding.

Q. (By Mr. RUSSELL.) In general, did they behave well or badly?

A. So far as I could judge, they behaved very well. I saw them in several cases that night, and that morning, during the explosions. I saw Capt. Damrell again on Washington street, at the time Currier & Trott's store was blown up. He was giving directions then, and they seemed to be very obedient and very active.

Q. How did Capt. Damrell behave? How did he appear?

A. To me, he seemed very cool, sir.

EDWARD H. SAVAGE, *sworn.*

Q. (By Mr. RUSSELL.) What position do you hold in the City Government?

A. I am Chief of Police.

Q. How long have you been connected with the police?

A. About twenty-one years.

Q. At what time did you first hear of the fire?

A. I had been out on Thursday and Friday nights all night, both nights, without any sleep, night or day. Saturday night, I went home and went to bed a little before seven o'clock, with my pants on. The first that I knew, my bell was ringing. The fire had got somewhat under way. I don't know what time it was. I jumped out and put on my clothes. I went directly to Station No. 2. There was no one in the hall. I shifted the telegraph on to the hall. We have a telegraphic communication from the Central Office into each of the police stations, and help was called by means of the telegraph that night.

Q. What do we understand by your shifting the telegraph?

A. In the evening, when we close, (we close at six o'clock,) we throw the switch so as to telegraph to that station, it being the nearest. The officers throw it into Station No. 2, instead of communicating to the Central Office, in the night time. Station No. 2 is but a few feet from the corner of City Hall.

Q. Did you remain there through the whole night?

A. Yes, sir; I didn't leave there until the next Monday night, at half-past seven o'clock.

Q. Did you sleep during that time?

A. No, sir; not at all. I slept a little on Saturday night. Besides that little, I did not sleep at all Thursday, Friday, Saturday, or Sunday nights.

Q. When did you see the Chief Engineer that night?

A. The first time that I recollect seeing him was in the Mayor's office.

Q. About what time was it?

A. Really, there was so much excitement, and I had so many calling me, and so much to do, that I have little recollection of the time. I think, however, it must have been half-past twelve o'clock. It was at the time that he was giving orders for blowing up.

Q. What orders did he give, and what did he do?

A. I was called for the purpose of furnishing police officers to go with those who were to blow up buildings, and was requested to give my police badges to the gentlemen who had the commission. The papers that I saw were given to different parties giving them permission to blow up buildings. When they came down to my office, I gave badges to those who showed me those papers signed by Mr. Damrell.

Q. How many did you assign to each?

A. Some had four and some two. When they first came, they wanted four each, but I could not give them that number, and the last ones who called for them had two, I think.

Q. When did you first see the Mayor that night?

A. I should think that I saw him within perhaps an hour or two. I should judge that it might have been eleven o'clock. It might have been later. It was in his office.

Q. Do you know whether he had been there before?

A. I don't know what time he came. I can't be positive whether it was eleven o'clock or not. As near as I can fix the time, I suppose it may have been somewhere about that.

Q. Did you have any conversation with him about the orders for the police? Did he give you any orders in regard to the police?

A. I don't recollect that he did. I think that the arrangement for the policemen had begun to be made before I got there. As the fire spread, the officers had to fall back, and we had to call for more men to extend the lines.

Q. How many officers are there?

A. I have five hundred and twenty-two to-day. There were four hundred on the lines that night.

Q. What orders did you give in regard to the fire besides detailing policemen, and what steps did you take?

A. When I first came, I sent for more men. Lieutenant Childs, and Sergeants Foster and Bates were in charge of the men on the lines. Lieutenant Childs was in charge on the Washington-street side, on the upper end, and Sergeant Foster was on the side next to Broad street, and Federal street. Sergeant Bates was on this side most of the time. Childs had the general supervision at the first start. The Deputy was there.

Q. Were any orders of any consequence given during the night?

A. Yes, sir; they were given at all times. I took one officer and selected out twenty-seven men for special service; and the officers were detailed here and there, and everywhere. I suppose that there was not ten minutes at any time during Saturday night and Sunday but what there were some orders given for police. We were called everywhere and anywhere.

Q. How many arrests were made that night for larceny?

A. Our folks began to take in everybody that they found taking off goods. They soon found that there were a great many people carrying off goods who had a right to carry them off — owners, etc. They took in a great many clerks who proved to be clerks. They took off some three hundred persons, but it was found that the people who owned the goods had told these people to take them up and carry them off; that it was as well for them to carry them off as for the goods to be burned. In the majority of cases that was found to be the fact; at least, we could not make cases in court. Capt. Vinal, of Station No. 2, had a dozen cases in one day, as he told me. Judge Parmenter said that under such circumstances, where there was a probability that the goods had been delivered to persons of good character, we could make no case. On Monday morning, the Captains were all present, and there were some questions as to what they should do with parties whom they had got locked up. I gave instructions to make a case against every party that they could. Those that they could not make cases against, of course they had to let slide.

Q. Were there any convictions?

A. About seventy odd they reported to me. The Police Court took jurisdiction.

Q. What was the punishment?

A. I don't know. They were charged with stealing from a building on fire. I asked how many cases were made, and they gave it to me in detail.

Q. Can you furnish us with the record of all the sentences?

A. I suppose I can get them at the court. Each Captain keeps his own; but they do not always get them until afterwards.

Q. Were not the sentences generally light?

A. I think they were. We thought there ought to be more cases made, but we could not make them.

Q. Were there many cases of drunkenness that night?

A. There were very few. There were not many arrests for drunkenness. There was very little drunkenness during the next ten days. They shut the shops up.

Q. Tell us how thorough the closing was. What was the order?

A. On Monday morning, you recollect very well what the circumstances were. There was a very large number of people here, and a large number of military out, and a large number of firemen, and all the people were under a state of more or less excitement. I thought it was justifiable to remove, if possible, any exciting cause of disturbance. Monday morning, I gave my captains this order, — "Captain ——, stop the retail liquor trade, including beer, during this crisis,"— and signed it with my name.

Q. You did it on the ground of an exigency, not on the ground of law?

A. It was but for a short time. I sent out Mr. Ham with the men that were on secret service, with the same order; and in a few hours a good many gentlemen came in and wanted to know what authority I had to shut off the beer, and under what law I was acting. I said: "We are not endeavoring to enforce any law. We are endeavoring to remove a great exciting cause, which may create riot and bloodshed in our city." Then they said, "Why do you shut off beer?" I said, "Because so many people get drunk on beer." The places were closed up remarkably well. Gentlemen who were in the beer trade came in and gave me their word that they would not sell any beer; and I have good reason to think that a majority of them did not.

Q. (By Mr. Firth.) Did you find much objection?

A. When I issued the order, I told my officers to go out and give them my compliments, and ask them, from me, to close up. I gave it to all the retail dealers. There were very few reported that did not shut up. They did not say they would not. I gave the order that afternoon that if any man would not shut up, to bring him in to me. There were only a half dozen brought in.

Q. Did all comply after that?

A. I presume there was a little sold after that, and but a very little. In the month of November, 1871, there were 986 persons complained of for drunkenness, which amounts to between 32 and 33 per day. For the ten days that the crisis lasted, there was not half that number, with all the excitement that prevailed. During those ten days, I believe it was about 16.

Q. Do you know anything about the gunpowder, except what you have stated?

A. I know that my officers were sent for it.

Q. Where were they sent?

A. The first man that went out of City Hall for powder was Capt. Quinn. He went down to Reed's. Then I sent to Charlestown and Chelsea, and I sent down for the boat and the powder from that I got. The first lot was ordered to be carried to the new Post Office. But after the fire got up in that vicinity, we were ordered to carry it to Liberty. square. I believe the heft of the powder, however, was left down at the end of Central wharf. My officers were detailed to get fuel for the engines a great many times. I sent two of them to shut off the gas Sunday night, — the most reckless thing that I had done.

Q. Where did you send them?

A. Down to the gas-house. It was at the time that these explosions occurred.

Q. Did they get there before it was done?

A. Yes. At first, I supposed that somebody was blowing up more buildings. I did not see why they should. The next thing was, that a Sergeant came in and said that the paving-stones kept flying in Washington street so that he could not keep his position. I told him to fall back out of harm's way, and yet keep up as near as he could. Two or three other gentlemen came in as the explosions kept coming. Finally, one of the officers came in and said that they were blowing the covers off of the sewers twenty feet high; and it occurred to me that the pipes had been all burnt off. There was a big 18-inch pipe in Summer street. It looked rather pokerish. I sent Lieut. Goodwin as hard as he could run to the gas-house. Somebody went to West street. I told him to tell Old Jimmy at the gas house to turn off the gas, or we should all be blown to the devil. That was at the North End — the gas-house, the only place where it could be turned off. Then I started the telegraph machine to Station One. Then I started a horseman. They got old Jimmy O'Neal out, and he shut it off. Lieut. Goodwin told him that it was the order from the Chief of Police, and that it must be obeyed or we should all be blown to atoms.

The next day Mr. Greenough came in and told me that it was right, and saved some trouble. I believe on Monday night they turned it on a little again and had some little explosions. It was shut off Tuesday night, I think. It was shut off two nights.

Q. How often did you detail officers to supply fuel?

A. I guess I sent a dozen or fifteen, or it may be twenty.

Q. How late in the night was that?

A. I think I sent some officers for fuel for steamers down to the north side before I went into the Mayor's room. I should judge that it was before twelve o'clock. Their orders were to take the first team that they could get.

Q. How did you hear that the fuel was wanting?

A. It was reports from citizens and from firemen themselves. At that time there was an explosion, and just then a gentleman came in and said that there were two Connecticut and Rhode Island steamers in Washington street (he gave their names), that were in a nice position to play on the fire, and had not a pound of coal. Sergeant Spear of Station One came in just at that time, and I sent him up to Tremont street, to take the first team he could get down to Charles street to get some cannel coal.

Q. Were there any other special orders that you gave?

A. I don't remember now what they were, but I was giving them all the time. I was in the office, and they were bringing in goods, and, people were running after this thing, and that thing, and the other thing, so that I could hardly remember what orders I did give, without some one's calling them to my mind.

Q. You remained, for the most part, at your office?

A. I stayed there pretty much all the time; and I had pretty much all I could jump to while there.

Q. Have you known any other cases at other fires, where goods were given away by the owners?

A. I don't know that I recollect any. I never saw a fire like this, where there was so much excitement.

Q. What was your view of the action of the military during the time they were on duty?

A. I think they did nobly, sir. There was a little fear expressed that they and our folks (the police) would not fraternize. But they were our old friends and neighbors, and we were engaged in the same cause.

Q. Don't you think it would be a good idea to have some call or alarm for the military?

A. I don't know, sir. On Sunday morning, we had 400 men on the line.

Q. Do you know at what time they were summoned, — the 400, — and what time they were there?

A. They were there I think by twelve o'clock. We kept calling them. When I first came the Deputy called some, and Mr. Childs. He found out where the fire was and sprang to the station house. They telegraphed for men, and the Deputy got there before I did. When I got there I threw it off from the Central Office, and inquired how many men they had got on the lines from each office and how many had been sent. I guess they got there about eleven o'clock; possibly it was half-past eleven when the last squad came. Station 1 had forty men; Station 2 had seventy (all that they had in the station house except four); Station 3 had forty-two; Station 4, sixty; Station 5, forty; Station 6, forty; Station 7 (East Boston) ten; Station 8 (Harbor Police) fifteen; Station 9, thirty-two; Station 10, thirty-three; Station 11 had nineteen; making about four hundred in all. I kept calling as the fire progressed and made my calculations from appearances and from what I learned.

Since then, our officers have been under instructions, when there was a general alarm given, for all the men that could to go to the station house; and that night the men went to the station house — both the men who had been on duty during the day and those on duty all night. The day-men went on duty at eight o'clock Saturday morning, and some of them remained until five o'clock Sunday morning. They had been on duty from fifteen to twenty-four hours; and in the morning we had nobody to relieve them with, and I said to the Mayor that we should have to have some help from some quarter; that it would take four hundred men to relieve our own. I don't know but he did call before that. After the call came, the military responded very quick.

Q. At what time did you speak to the Mayor about it?

A. It must have been after daylight. I can't tell what time. It was daylight Sunday morning. Our men had had a very hard night's work, and it was necessary for them to leave. There were no men to relieve them. I don't know of any means that the Mayor had of calling out the military before morning; yet I don't know but he did have such means.

Q. Did he call them through you?

A. No, sir. I presume it was through General Cunningham. I think he sent for that general.

Q. Did I understand you that that request from Capt. Damrell was not to ring the second alarm unless the fire was higher than the second story?

A. I guess you have the order here. My recollection is that there was to be only one alarm given if the fire was not above the second story.

When the military came, I detailed them along the lines to take the places of and relieve our men.

We kept two lines Sunday and Monday. On Tuesday, I took my men off the lines, except at certain points, and detailed them inside upon the burnt district, and then formed a line upon the outside, through South Market, Cornhill, Tremont, Boylston and Essex streets. That became necessary in order to get travel along, and also to cut off any rogues that we might catch.

Q. Do you know at what time the marines appeared?

A. No, sir; I didn't see them that night. I understood, however, that they were on the lines before morning.

Q. What time was it when the first company appeared?

A. I think it was about nine o'clock. It might have been a little earlier.

Q. How about the roughs coming here from New York? Did you have any evidence of the presence of a large number of unruly men here?

A. No, sir. We received a dispatch about half-past eight o'clock Sunday night from an employé of the telegraph, saying that there were fourteen car-loads of roughs that had left Springfield for Boston, by special train that evening. Shortly afterwards, I was called into the Mayor's room, and he had a similar dispatch.

Q. Was there a name attached to it?

A. Yes, sir. It was "Atwood." I think I have the one that was sent me, and also the one that was sent the Mayor. It came from Springfield.

I immediately ran down State street, around on the line where my men were with the military, and I got thirty men, pulled off their uniforms, and got them into hod-carriers' clothes as quick as I could; and then I took twenty men with uniforms, off the other side, and got Capt. Smith with twenty-five horsemen, and went to meet the cars. I telegraphed to Worcester and Groton Junction, and two or three places, but I never had any communication from them, and don't know whether it reached them. I sent some officers to the Know-Nothing Station. The cars came in at half-past eleven o'clock. There was about that number of cars, and a good many empty seats. We took in six men. I found that they were sporting men, probably. I asked, "Where are the rest?" They said, "Got sea-sick, and went home." I have no question but what there was a large number of them that came as far as Worcester; but they didn't come here. If they had, we should have had some fun with them.

Q. Were there any cases of incendiarism during the week?

A. Captain Adams thought there was one out at Roxbury. It was a case where some boys undertook to put some matches into a stable. I don't know of any other case where the fire was supposed to be incendiary.

We have some local thieves here, but I don't think we had anybody from outside of Boston. There was no house-breaking or anything of the kind. I had a great deal of anxiety about it, and expected that the roughs would come; and so I carefully covered every point that was to be reached.

Q. During the ten days after the fire was crime more abundant than usual, or less so?

A. After the crisis was over, drunkenness began to increase. In regard to crime, we had but very little for the ten days.

Q. Was there less than usual?

A. There was no more than at ordinary times, — I think less. I have not looked it over to see just how it would compare, with the exception of drunkenness.

Q. What did you say you thought about the plan of having an organization of military to be ready at short notice?

A. I hardly see how they could have an organization that would spring to their work any quicker than these men did at this fire. I don't know but it might be well. We have not policemen enough for such an emergency as that. If we had had a thousand men, we could perhaps have handled it without the military; but we could not have handled it with any less than that.

Q. Is there any good reason why you should not avail yourself of the military organization which you happened to have?

A. No, sir.

Q. (By Mr. FIRTH.) Have you had complaints of the loss of time in announcing fires either on that night or before?

A. No, sir. We have had no general complaint, — none reported to me.

Q. What would you say about the origin of the fire?

A. I had considerable anxiety about the matter of giving the alarm. I think it will appear to you that there were four of our officers that got there pretty early. There were certainly two, and I think three men who got there thus early. Our man got there before the man who had the key and lived right opposite to the fire. I don't know but you have had him before you. The man who had the key told me that our folks were ringing the second alarm before he got there.

All the officers carry a key to the alarm-box. I don't know who else has keys. The officers on the beat would know. There is on every box a note telling where the key is to be found.

Q. From the best information you have been able to obtain, are you entirely satisfied that your officers responded as quickly as they do under any ordinary circumstances?

A. I don't know why they did not. Officer Page was on Lincoln street chasing some boys. You have heard his testimony. Officer Moulton, who lives near, ran to the box without his hat. There were three officers there very early. The officers in going out at night have a great many papers, letters, etc., to carry; and some if not all of these officers had been about distributing these letters and messages from City Hall and all the departments.

Q. Are the officers specially impressed with the duty of giving an early alarm of fire?

A. Yes, sir, they have it in their rules. There is nothing that is more strenuously impressed upon them. There was a special talk about it at the time of the horse disease.

Q. Do you know what portion of the alarms are given by citizens?

A. Mr. Cunard, the Superintendent of Fire Alarms, could tell you. I think he keeps a minute of it. We make reports to him every morning. The Captain reports who gives it and what time. Our men report who sounds the alarm, if they give it. If they learn who else gives it, they mention that. I think, if you summon any officers who were on their beats that night, you will find they were there very early. I have no reason to think that they did not get there as quickly as usual.

At first, I was afraid that they were deficient. I called thirteen of them to my office and took their statements. If they did not lie to me abominably, they did their duty pretty well.

When a building is shut up, as this one was, a fire would burn a good while before it becomes conspicuous, if the fire took in the bottom. It was back in that alley-way, so that there were but very few except those that lived right opposite that would have an opportunity to see it.

WILLIAM H. DURELL, *sworn.*

Q. (By Mr. Russell.) What is your connection with the Gas Co.?

A. I am Superintendent of street work.

Q. How long have you held that place?

A. Seventeen years.

Q. When a fire takes place, what is your duty in regard to shutting off gas?

A. We have no regular instructions in regard to it, because it is not very often that we have anything dangerous enough to require the gas to be shut off; but in case we do, I go to work as quick as I can and cut the pipes off and plug them up, in case we have no other way. I do it on my own responsibility. I don't have special instructions. If it is anything very important and I can get at Mr. Greenough, I should consult him first. If not, I should do it on my own responsibility.

Q. How many men do you have to work with you on that?

A. I have from twenty-five, upwards, according to the nature of the work and the time I am engaged in it.

Q. How many can you summon to your help if you should need a large force?

A. In a short time I could summon forty odd men.

Q. How often have you done that at fires?

A. I can't think that I have ever done it more than perhaps three times.

Q. What did you do at this fire?

A. Saturday night I was not able to do anything. I did not know of the extent of the fire until after eleven o'clock, not being out until that time. In the night, it is almost impossible for us to do much of anything on that kind of work, and with a crowd around, we could not get at what we would like to.

Q. When did you begin?

A. I began Sunday morning, early.

Q. How early?

A. Well, I started at six o'clock myself; and my foreman that I have on went to the North End. We started about six o'clock in the morning to get our men together. I went up to the South End and got them up as quick as I could. About seven and a half o'clock, I think I had about twenty-five men. Then I went immediately to filling a valve box that we have at the corner of Summer and Washington streets, and then I filled some at the foot of Summer and Broad streets — filled them with water.

Q. What others?

A. Then there were a few scattering ones — small ones — around, one at Federal street, one on Devonshire street, and then some down on Broad street, that I filled that day.

Q. Did you keep at work through the day?

A. Yes, sir. After I had filled what boxes I could, — after I got particularly the large boxes filled, — I put part of the gang to digging down and cutting off pipes where I could get at them. There were not many places Sunday that I could get into. The police kept us out. I had no way of getting into half the places that I wanted to get into. I told them what my purposes were. I could get through the day police without trouble, but the night police did not know me, and I could not get through them.

Q. Didn't you have tools with you?

A. Yes, sir. But they would not admit us. They said that they had had strict orders not to let anybody in but firemen. Then I worked farther off upon the outskirts of it.

Q. What course did you pursue? Did you cut pipes and plug them?

A. Yes, sir.

Q. Did you do anything Sunday night?

A. Not after dark, no, sir.

Q. When did you go to work Monday morning?

A. It was about seven o'clock.

Q. Then how long did you keep at work?

A. All day Monday and all day Tuesday.

Q. By that time was the work done?

A. Yes, sir. I thought I had it nearly all cut off Monday. We tried the gas and found we had not got it cut off. We shut it off. Then I went through it more thoroughly Tuesday afternoon. We tried it again and found it right. We thought we had it all shut off, but Mr. Greenough didn't think it prudent that night, but thought we had better take it early in the morning, when we had more time to get around.

Q. Do you see any difficulty in using these slide valves so that you could cut off any portion of the city from the rest?

A. I have not, so far as my experience has gone. We have not been able to get anything to use until within three years. All we had tried to use previous to that would either get rusty and stick, or the gas would make them stick so as to cause them to leak. So far as we have had a chance to try them I liked them, very well and have had no trouble with them.

Q. When you get completely provided with those, you will be able to isolate any district so far as you please?

A. Yes, sir.

Q. Is there any trouble about it except the expense of providing them?

A. The only trouble would be arising from their leaking. They have what we call a stuffing box that the vertical shaft goes through. That is packed with yarn and tallow. It is apt to get dry and get to leaking, which has been one argument against their use.

Q. How often ought they to be tried?

A. What I have had in I have tried about twice a year. I never have had to repack any stuffing box.

Twice a year was as often as I needed to go to them. I have had them three years. There has not been much trouble in regard to leakage. On reflection I would say that I did have to repack two last summer. I don't think they could have been packed as they ought to have been when we took them. They had been in about eight months, I think. Otherwise than that I have not had to touch one of them.

Q. Did you have to dig them out of the ground in order to repack them?

A. Yes, sir, because our pipes are not deep enough so that we can carry a box down far enough for a man to get into it. We have to dig them up to repack them.

Q. You think, in the case of those two last summer, that if they had been in proper condition when put down, you would have had no trouble?

A. No, sir, I don't think we should have had any trouble.

Q. (By Mr. Philbrick.) Do you think that many breakages of the mains occurred from the falling of buildings?

A. I have not had a chance to see except in two places. In those two they were pretty badly broken. One was in Summer street, right opposite Thorndike Hall and the church. They had a 3-inch main there, besides our 18-inch one. That main was all broken up and there were pieces not more than one foot long.

Q. Have you known cases before of breakage from falling buildings?

A. I have only had one case. That was at the time that the Gerrish Market, on Sudbury street, was burned. The main then was broken in five or six places, so that we shut off the gas and left it shut off all winter. At the late fire we overhauled the pipe in Milk street from Washington to Devonshire and I found that the 6-inch main was broken in six places. I also found at the corner of Kilby and Central streets, where I stopped a pipe, that the pipe was badly broken there. Those are the only two cases that I have seen, except the 18-inch main on Summer street.

Q. Have you ever had them broken from frost?

A. Yes, sir.

Q. Does it often occur?

A. Yes, sir, we average from three to four per day all winter. Last winter I think I averaged four per day all winter.

Q. Does not that incur considerable risk from leakage?

A. Yes, sir. You can't have gas come into a place without some risk. We try to be as cautious as we can, and work on them as soon as we hear of them.

Q. Did you ever know so severe a season as last winter?

A. No, sir. I think it was the most severe season for gas or water works that I have ever known in the course of seventeen years' experience.

Q. If you were to begin over again would you not advise that the mains be put deeper?

A. In some respects, I should. In other respects, I should not be particular.

Q. I mean on account of breakage from frost, when there must be a kind of upheaval?

A. I have noticed that most of our breakages occur in a particular way, where they have dug a drain out of a house and we have dug right across underneath it. In the winter time it generally freezes harder in that trench than it does on each side of it, and the consequence is, in accordance with the theory that I have taken, that it operates the same as a lever, and will break our pipe off even with the side of that drain. I have had notices of hundreds of cases like that where they dig a trench for service pipe for water or any drain. We have more troub from that than from any other source. We have pipes that don't lie over eighteen or twenty inches below the top of the ground, and there never has been a leak in them, to my knowledge, since I have been on the works.

In some cases it is about as well to be frozen solid all round as to be below the frost. Here in the city it is almost impossible to get any rule that you can go by. Last winter we found frost four or four and a half feet deep in the city, and even five feet deep.

Q. If they were put six inches deeper would you not avoid a certain amount of frost?

A. Yes, sir, we might. The frost would not be so hard either. Take it on the Back Bay the frost goes a good deal deeper than anywhere else in the city. That sand seems to hold the frost.

Q. Would not putting the pipes deeper get them out of the way of shocks of falling buildings?

A. I don't know but what it would be better on that account. Our pipe is a little different from the water pipes, being put together with cement. It is perfectly solid. There is no give to it. Whenever any jar or shock comes the joint will not give at all like a lead joint.

Their water pipes not being broken is owing to their being laid a little deeper and having lead joints. Our joints are all perfectly rigid, and the pipes are stronger at the joint than anywhere else.

Q. Would not the fact that the water pipes are deeper, account for it in part?

A. Yes, sir. But as regards the frost I have my doubts about it, whether there would be anything gained.

Q. Is there not a good deal less frost at four feet than three?

A. Yes, sir. But I think the weight of the pile of dirt on top has a tendency to press it down. Most of our soil here in the city is not solid. Not much more than one-third of the city can be calculated upon as solid ground. I mean the foundation of it.

Q. Is it not softer at four feet deep than at three?

A. Yes, sir, I think it is. The top of the ground is trod harder. I notice that the first foot that we dig digs harder than any other.

Q. Do you want any better bottom than good gravel or sand?

A. No, sir. I might take it for such work as was done upon Commonwealth avenue. With our deepest pipes, I have had more trouble than with those that lie shallow. In Chauncy street, I have never had to look at it for seventeen years. There is no knowing but it is as perfect as ever it was.

Q. Is there any practical use in these outside cocks that people have?

A. No, sir, they will not work, and it would be dangerous for a man who just began to play on a fire to shut them off. All the good it would do is the shutting off of the gas from that building. Practically, they would rust very soon and be of no service.

PATRICK H. RAYMOND, *sworn.*

Q. (By Mr. RUSSELL.) When did you first see the great fire?

A. [Examines his memorandum book.] On the evening of November 9th, we had an alarm in Cambridge from Box 27 at 7.35 o'clock. That was the first intimation that I had of the fire.

Q. What is your connection with the Cambridge City Government?

A. I hold the position of Chief Engineer of the Cambridge Fire Department.

Q. What did you do on receiving that alarm?

A. Upon receiving that alarm I responded to the box, as is the custom, and there learned that there was a serious fire raging in Boston, and that assistance was sent for. I despatched at once two steamers and their companies, and one hose-carriage with the full complement of hose. Subsequently to that alarm, we had a double alarm from Box 13. I responded to that box, and on arriving there I had another message that more help was needed. I then despatched another steamer with a hose-carriage tender having about 500 feet of hose. Still later, at 9.30, another alarm came in from Box 6. I then despatched the hook-and-ladder company. That is the amount of help that I rendered on that evening.

Q. At what time did you come in?

A. I came in the next morning to the fire, about half-past eight o'clock.

Q. Where did you go?

A. I went directly to the Merchants' Exchange building, where one of my steamers was at work; and upon entering the building, Engineer Green, of the Boston Department, requested me to take command of the streams in that building, he being then very much fatigued. There were some four or five streams of water. I remained in that position until three o'clock Sunday afternoon, and succeeded in preventing the fire from passing north of the sub-treasury rooms, where the greater part of the water was directed.

Q. You had charge of that building, and of the fire at that particular point?

A. Yes, sir, at the instance of Captain Green. I think I could give you the names of the companies that were located at that position: No. 3 steamer, of Boston; No. 21, of Boston; No. 2, of Cambridge, and the Arsenal steamer, from the United States Arsenal. I think that was all that were inside of the Merchants' Exchange Building, over which I then had control.

Q. How did the firemen behave on these four engines?

A. They behaved most admirably. When the dome of the sub-treasury came in, those men were inside of the room with myself, and they displayed a good deal of bravery. They did not forsake their posts, I can assure you. They fell back in a very orderly manner.

The fire being checked about three o'clock, it was deemed advisable to dispense with the services of some of the out-of-town companies; and upon consulting the Chief Engineer of Boston, I made up — as we term it — the Cambridge companies, and returned home with them. That is all that I can speak of for that day; but subsequently, on Monday morning, I sent in steamer No. 3, and it remained here until Tuesday morning about three o'clock.

Tuesday morning, about twelve o'clock, I sent in steamer No. 1 with the company, and they remained until Wednesday afternoon at three o'clock. I was in the mean time with those companies, and during all that time there were relays of men detailed from the different companies in the department, to come over and render relief to the Boston firemen; that is, to take charge of certain streams, and tender their services. They kept that up until Thursday night in that way.

Q. Did you see anything of our Chief, Sunday morning?

A. I ran away from the Merchants' Exchange building, and took a course down into Liberty square, where the Cambridge engine was stationed, to look after their welfare. I found the Chief there. He recognized me, and shook hands with me right on the ground.

Q. How did he appear?

A. Considering that he had been through so much, I thought that he was the most collected man I ever saw in my life. It was John Damrell that I saw on Sunday, and nobody else. I have known him from boyhood, and went to school with him, and know his characteristics.

Q. What time on Sunday morning was it when you went down there?

A. I should judge that it was between quarter and half-past nine. I went to look after my engine company located in that direction.

Q. Can you give an opinion as to how the fire was managed?

A. I can only say directly what I saw at the time I was here.

Q. What do you think of that?

A. That everything that could be devised to extinguish the fire was being put into very effective use.

Q. Do you think at the time you were here it was advisable to use gunpowder, during any portion of that period?

A. No, sir, I did not; and I omitted to state, Mr. Chairman, that while battling with the flames in the Merchant's Exchange building, that building was mined with gunpowder, and the firemen knew nothing about it. I wish to protest against that, and to name it as one of the most reprehensible acts that was committed during that whole night. There was no notice given to the firemen about its being mined.

Q. Do you know that it was mined?

A. I don't know, of my own personal knowledge. It was so reported to me. Also, that the sub-treasury building was. It may have been immediately under that building and not under the granite building of the Merchant's Exchange. It was reported to me that a whole section, in which a portion of the Post Office was located, was mined. I did see five kegs of powder taken out of the cellar of the building joining Bond's chronometer store, on Congress street, by some hook-and-ladder men. The heads of the casks were ripped out after they were taken out into the street, and the powder was poured into the gutter. I saw that myself. That building had been seriously injured by fire, and the fire had been extinguished by the firemen entering the building and fighting it from the inside. It was a low structure. Those men stated there, within the hearing of my men who were inside of the fire lines, that it was a gross piece of carelessness. Captain Zenas W. Smith, one of the Engineers, told me that he had been in that building and knew nothing of the existence of that powder on the premises.

Q. Did you see anything else of gunpowder?

A. No, sir; that was all.

Q. Did you see any of the effects of it in buildings that were blown up?

A. I saw the effects of the explosion at the corner of Hawes and Kilby streets. I made up my mind when I saw that, that that square building in Liberty square would not have been burned if it had not been for the explosion of that large building, for by that means the heat and flames were opened right upon the square building, and it was ignited. It was at that point that I met Captain Damrell Sunday morning.

Q. Was anything said to you by Captain Damrell in relation to the powder?

A. No, sir. The only officials that I spoke to about the powder were Captain Smith and Captain Green.

Q. Is it your opinion that gunpowder can be used with advantage in the stopping of conflagrations?

A. Well, now you have asked me rather a posing question. At this recent conflagration in Boston, I don't think, as near as I could see, that the gunpowder was of the least use in staying the progress of the flames.

Q. Have you any suggestions to make as to how gunpowder should be used, or as to what should be used instead of gunpowder?

A. I don't know that I would care to give an unscientific opinion upon a matter of that kind.

WILLIAM E. DELANO, *sworn.*

Q. (By Mr. Russell.) Where do you reside?

A. In Charlestown. I am Chief Engineer there.

Q. How long have you been connected with the Fire Department?

A. Some twenty years. It is my first year as Chief.

Q. What was the first you knew of the Boston fire?

A. I reported to Chief Damrell, I think, at about five minutes of eight, on Otis street. I got the alarm over in Charlestown, and came over and reported to him, and asked if he wanted assistance. He said that he wished that I would send him all the assistance that I could, immediately.

Q. What was the condition of the fire then?

A. I did not go over into Summer street. But as near as I could judge, it was on all four corners of Otis, Summer, and Kingston, and in the front of Beebe's block, on Summer street.

Q. How did the Chief appear at that time?

A. He was very cool and collected.

Q. What did you do?

A. I went right back to our city and struck Box 21 in the Square, and sent over a steamer and three hose companies, and stationed my engine at the corner of Franklin and Devonshire streets, and reported with our streams at Beebe's block; and the Chief told me to stop the fire from crossing Devonshire street, if I could. That is on the left-hand side of Beebe's block. We worked there as long as we could, and then shifted on to the other side of the Square. We were there in Winthrop square from half to three-quarters of an hour, before we were driven out by the heat.

Q. Was there any falling of granite there?

A. Yes, sir, Beebe's block; and before we left that position I had a stream up in the upper story on the left-hand side of Franklin street, and worked there some fifteen minutes in the upper story, and seemed to be doing a good deal of execution; but the fire worked in underneath them so that we had to take the men out very lively.

Q. Did you have plenty of water?

A. Yes, sir, we had a reservoir there.

Q. Could you reach the top of Beebe's block?

A. We could on the side fronting the Square, but there was such a draft of wind that it was almost impossible to get a stream up on the narrow streets. There was a wide space in front there. There were three or four streams with us.

Q. Did you see the fire cross Franklin street?

A. No, sir. I mean on the left-hand side of Franklin, coming towards Washington. One of our men was hurt in that building coming down. I attended to him. In the mean time, our engine was moved to the Old South. We stayed there until they blew up Currier & Trott's building. Then we moved to Court Square. We stayed there until everything was all safe. We worked on top of the "Transcript" building for an hour, or very near it.

Q. Were you on top of the "Transcript" building?

A. Yes, sir. We had hose carried up right through the building. There was only one of our streams there. There was some other out-of town stream there. I don't know what stream it was.

Q. Where did you next go?

A. From there we got notice that they were going to blow up Currier & Trott's building. We went into Williams' Court first, and attempted to attach to a hydrant. It was of a small pattern, and we could not make the connections. It was in the centre of the court. We then went up into Court Square and took a station at the reservoir back of the Court House. Then we ran our stream down to the "Daily Post" building.

Q. Where next?

A. We next went from there to the corner of Broad and Custom-House streets, I think, and ran a stream through to the corner of Milk and Oliver streets, and were stationed in where the fire was stopped that afternoon at three and a half or quarter to four o'clock.

Q. Did you have sufficient water there at the fire?

A. When at the Old South church, we were bothered some in getting water. There were three engines stationed at the reservoir, and I should judge that the supply pipe was not full, but finally we had plenty of water.

Q. Was there any want of fuel that night?

A. We did want fuel when we were in Winthrop Square. We burned boxes, counters, and shutters.

Q. Did you at any time stop for want of fuel?

A. No, sir, the fuel that I obtained sufficed to keep up steam. We worked right straight along.

Q. How did the men of the Fire Department behave that night, all told?

A. I never saw them behave any better, or work any better.

Q. Was there any flinching from the fire?

A. Not to my knowledge.

Q. Any intoxication?

A. I did not see any among the firemen.

Q. Was there any stealing from the stores?

A. Not by the firemen, to my knowledge. I saw a good deal done by outsiders. Our stream was stationed immediately opposite Weeks & Potter's. When the wall fell and caught those men there and the two firemen, our men went in to save them. It was my idea that the two Boston firemen were in there, but in conversation with the company they seemed to think that they were somewhere else, and I supposed that they knew more about it than I did. I had the impression that all the firemen that went in to save those outsiders did not come out, and so it proved.

Q. In your opinion, was that fire managed well or badly?

A. The general management, in my opinion, was admirable. I saw the Chief several times. We were there, and reported somewhere from eight, to ten or fifteen minutes past eight. He was with us in the different positions I have stated, and seemed cool and collected, and gave his orders in that way.

Q. Can you now think of anything that could have been done to have prevented the fire from becoming so large?

A. No, sir; I cannot.

Q. Should you know how to manage that fire better than it was managed then?

A. No, sir.

Q. What were the principal causes of the fire becoming so uncontrollable?

A. The narrow streets and high buildings, and, as I said before, in the positions where we were in Winthrop square, the draft was so strong that we could hardly get a stream anywhere. We could hardly hold our hats on, and we could hardly live there; but the men held out. On Washington street we were more fortunate.

Q. (By Mr. Cobb.) When you first reached the fire-ground, you say that there was fire on all four corners of those streets. Did you see any effort made to attack the fire at the corner of Otis and Summer streets?

A. No, sir. I went to Chief Damrell directly, and I did not notice. At the time I got back, the fire had got out all over Beebe's block. It was coming out at all parts of the block.

Q. (By Mr. Firth.) For how long was there a force here from Charlestown?

A. We left at about half-past three or quarter to four, Sunday afternoon. We were there from about eight o'clock with four hose companies. We reported Monday with steamers, Tuesday with two companies, and Wednesday with one.

Adjourned to Wednesday afternoon, Dec. 11th.

TENTH DAY.

WEDNESDAY, Dec. 11.

BENJAMIN CALLENDER, *sworn.*

Q. (By Mr. RUSSELL.) What time did you go to the great fire?

A. The first time, I should think it was twenty-five minutes past eight o'clock.

Q. What buildings were on fire then?

A. The building at the corner of Summer and Otis streets, I think.

Q. Will you tell us anything you observed that you think is worthy of notice?

A. I was in the upper part of Summer street. It seemed to me that only one of the streams that were being thrown on the building went to the top, and that one didn't do any good.

Q. Why didn't that do any good?

A. That didn't seem to be able to put the fire out at all.

Q. Could you tell why the other streams didn't go to the top? Could you tell whether it was owing to the want of water, or steam, or what it was?

A. I couldn't, sir.

Q. Did you see any steamers that had no fuel?

A. I didn't, sir; not that were pretending to be at work.

Q. Did you see any insubordination among the firemen? any breaking into stores, or anything of that kind?

A. I didn't.

Q. Did you see any neglect of duty by the firemen?

A. I did not.

Q. Any intoxication?

A. No, sir.

Q. Was there anything else you observed, at any time, which you think we ought to know?

A. I have my own theory about the matter. I don't know as you want to hear that. I went from Summer street to the corner of Bedford and Kingston streets; I saw an engine drawn at rather a moderate gait by men —

Q. Do you know what engine it was?

A. No, sir. There was such a crowd, I was glad to get out of the way, and didn't stop to see the number. It came down Bedford street.

Q. What time was that?

A. I should think it might have been then quarter to nine o'clock.

Q. Was there a crowd on Bedford street?

A. Yes, sir, so large a crowd that I couldn't get through to the United States Hotel, where I lived, and turned round and went back again.

Q. (By Mr. GREENE.) Was not the reason why the engine moved so slowly because of the crowd in the street?

A. I didn't think so at the time.

Q. (By Mr. RUSSELL.) Did you see anything else there?

A. That is all that I saw there.

Q. Anywhere else?

A. I then went to the house and stayed there until about half-past nine, I should think, when some one remarked that Anderson, Heath & Co's store was on fire. I then thought it was time for me to go to my own store, which I did by going round through Broad street to Congress street, down Congress to Channing, to my store, which was at the corner of Channing and Federal streets.

Q. What did you observe there?

A. I think nothing that had any bearing upon the fire at all.

Q. Did you see anything further that night that you think ought to be reported to the commission?

A. No, sir, I think not.

Q. (By Mr. PHILBRICK.) You spoke of seeing an engine which threw a stream to the top of the building on Summer street, when you first arrived, — can you tell where that pipe was playing that went up to the top?

A. No, sir, I can't.

Q. Was the other stream, that fell short, in the immediate vicinity of it?

A. Yes, sir; the streams were going up side by side. One of them, for aught I know, may have been from a hydrant, may not have been from an engine. There was such a crowd there, that I didn't care to go through it.

Q. (By Mr. COBB.) Mr. Callender, do you think of anything that might have been done to stop the spread of that fire, that was not done?

A. Yes, sir, I do.

Q. What, for instance?

A. I think, if horses had been provided to draw the engines to the fire, no such fire need to have occurred. I think that previous and subsequent fires substantiate that statement. I think that there was no reason why there shouldn't have been horses.

Q. (By Mr. PHILBRICK.) You were not there before eight o'clock, were you?

A. I was not.

Q. (By Mr. GREENE.) You saw engines at work then?

A. Yes, sir, I saw engines at work then. I saw, as I have stated, two streams going up at that time.

Q. (By Mr. RUSSELL.) Do you think that the use of horses, after you arrived there, would have helped matters much?

A. I think if there had been a suitable number of engines in the city proper, that fire could have been stopped.

Q. What do you consider a suitable number?

A. I think, if I was on the committee of the City Government, I should insist upon their having at least twelve engines in the city proper.

Q. That is aside from the question of the use of horses. Do you think horses would have helped the matter after you arrived there?

A. Yes, sir, I think they might, because they would have got a larger body of engines there, and I think if they could have had a larger body of engines and massed them in those two streets, the fire would have been stopped there. I have very seldom been to a fire, but when I have been, I have noticed that the most effect has been produced by throwing water across, not throwing it up. I mean, if the building opposite us, for instance, was on fire, the most effectual way of extinguishing it would be to get a hose into this building and carry it to the top, and throw the water across, instead of throwing it up from the street.

Q. Did you see any chance of accomplishing that, after you arrived?

A. I rather thought, when I was looking from Bedford street, that if there had been engines enough on Otis street and Devonshire street, the fire might have been stopped in the building that lies between those two streets, in the manner I spoke of.

Q. (By Mr. RUSSELL.) You mean Beebe's building?

A. Yes, sir.

Q. (By Mr. PHILBRICK.) Wasn't that on fire when you first arrived on Summer street?

A. No, sir. I think when I first got into Summer street, but one building there was on fire, possibly there might have been two, but I think it was the building on the corner of Summer and Otis streets.

Q. Did it look to you, after arriving there and seeing how little the engines accomplished, as if any number of additional engines would have accomplished much more?

A. I don't think it occurred to me at the time, because I went home supposing this fire would be put out, like most others, and as a citizen, not connected with the Fire Department, I was only in the way.

Q. Did it occur to you when you saw this stream playing short, that there was not water enough?

A. My idea at the time was that there was a want of power in the engines; but as I said before, I don't know whether the stream that fell short was from an engine or from a hydrant.

Q. Did you see more than one stream playing short?

A. No, sir. I saw but two streams; one seemed to reach the top of the building, the other didn't.

Q. What building were they playing on?

A. They were playing, or trying to play, on the building on the north side of Summer street, near the corner of Otis and Summer. I don't think I saw any stream playing on to the other buildings. I don't recollect that I did, now. I didn't stay there, probably, more than ten minutes, at the outside, but I believe if the engines had got to the fire with the alacrity they got to the fire at Rand & Avery's, that fire would never have spread as it did.

Q. You mean, if they had arrived on the ground soon after the outbreak of the fire?

A. Yes, sir.

Q. Have you any means of knowing how soon they got there? That is what we want to know.

A. Not of my own knowledge, only what I have heard from different people. I didn't get there, probably, until half an hour after the fire broke out.

J. H. CHADWICK, *sworn.*

Q. (By Mr. RUSSELL.) What time did you go to the fire?

A. About ten o'clock.

Q. Your building, Nos. 22, 24 and 26 Oliver street, is occupied by the Boston Lead Works?

A. Yes, sir.

Q. Won't you state what took place after the fire got into Oliver street?

A. The fire that got into Oliver street came from the rear, in Pearl street, through the block of stores exactly opposite.

Q. What did you do?

A. We had in the room above some parties who were just experimenting in making half a dozen portable organs. I let them have a small part of the second story, and didn't charge them any rent. They had their tools and stuff there up at the windows; the frame-work and everything of that kind for the organs was there. About seven o'clock Sunday morning, we moved all that stuff back, and wet the windows, and wet the floor with water, and got everything out of the room, — the room was perhaps twenty feet across, — so as to leave no chance for the cinders to come through the windows and set anything on fire there. We moved everything out of the windows below, at the same time, and wet all those windows. It was exactly ten minutes past eight when the fire broke out in the block opposite. I looked at the clock when it first broke out, and made a minute of it. We then filled our buckets with water, and carried them up on top of the building, and kept the windows wet, and wet the roof, and stamped down the fire, I think, for half an hour, until it fairly broke out of the roof of the building opposite.

Q. What is the top of your building covered with?

A. Gravel and tar. It was very nicely covered; it had a great deal of gravel, and we could keep the fire down very nicely. Some very large brands came from the building opposite; if we had let them burn there five or ten minutes, they would have burned through to the roof.

Q. Would that coal-tar furnish a blaze of itself?

A. Yes, sir, it would blaze.

Q. Through the gravel?

A. Yes, sir. I never saw a building on which the tar wouldn't come out through the gravel, more or less, in the summer season; keep it warm enough, and it will blaze in time. We had two or three men up there, and they stamped the fire out. We kept doing that all the time until the other building was burned flat.

Q. How long was that?

A. We were at it two hours, I should think. I came down myself, and saw that we had got to go. I saw that all the windows were on fire, but I went through the ceremony of wetting down again, and went out and found a hoseman, who turned out to be a member of No. 2 of Lynn, and I met Engineer Kimball of Lynn at the same time, and told him if he would give us a line of hose, we would save that block, and I would pay him liberally. He gave us a line of hose from the rear. I opened all the scuttles on the front side of the building way up to the roof, and we put a stream across from the second story on to the fire on the other side; as soon as we deadened it there, we pulled in the butt, and played up through the scuttles, and that wet the whole outside of our front, except the cornice, and that we wet with buckets. We kept doing that until the block opposite was flat, then we carried our hose on top, and played on the other buildings beyond. One thing that aided us in doing it, was the fact that the coving was stone; if we had had a wooden coving, we should have had a hard fight of it.

Q. (By Mr. RUSSELL.) Do you think you could have saved it if the cornice had been of wood?

A. Yes, sir, I think we could have saved it if it had been of wood. We were bound to save it. I didn't move a thing in the store. I told my partners that the store wouldn't burn; still, it might. Then I went and found Capt. Munroe, and got him to send down Steamer 12, from the Highlands, and stationed her at the corner of the street, and the hose was carried right down in front. I then got Capt. Munroe to go down in the rear, and I went down with him part way. I asked him to go in behind the store of Brooks, Robinson & Co., and see if he couldn't do anything to save it. He said he had been there, but I asked him to go again, to accommodate me. I said, "We have saved this block, and we shall depend upon you to save that store." I left him there, and I think he was there from ten o'clock until twelve; it may have been half-past nine or ten. Mr. Damrell came there about nine o'clock, I think. He came into the rear of the store. I met him just he came in, as I was going up stairs. I asked him how he did. He said, "I am used up." "Well," said I, "it is a pretty hard time." Said he, "Can I go up on the roof of this building?" Said I, "Yes," and I went up ahead of him, and we went on to the roof, and went along on to the next store in the same block, which was occupied by May & Co. The scuttle was down, and he said, "I want to pull that scuttle up. I want to go down that way." Said I, "There is no need of your going down there, you can go down through my store." He said, "I want to go through there;" so I called two or three men, and they pulled up the scuttle. He went down that way, and I didn't see anything more of him.

Q. When you saw him, how did he appear?

A. He appeared used up.

Q. How did the firemen work?

A. The firemen worked very well; they were encouraged, you know.

Q. Did you see any disposition to loaf at any time?

A. No, sir. This was a Lynn company we had. The Chief Engineer of Lynn was a very pleasant man, but he appeared to be a little demoralized; didn't seem to be quite equal to the occasion; still, he did very well. I have no fault to find with him.

Q. Did any of you get scorched at all?

A. No, sir. I found the men wouldn't go unless some one would go ahead, and I went ahead myself and stood in advance of the pipe all the time. I said to the men, "I will stay here as long as you do." Engine No. 12 was stationed right on the corner of the street, and I said to Capt. Southwick, "I want you to stick by." He said, "I will stick by as long as you do." I told him, "If there is any danger, you have a chance to get out, but I have not." I am satisfied we should have lost our store, if I hadn't been there; that is my feeling about it. You can ask my partners; they went out of the back door, and said they were not coming back.

There was not an engine playing on the fire in High street, except the first part of it. There was an engine in there at first, but they had to run up with the engine; but they were right in the middle of the street. They didn't go into the block on the other side and play on the buildings on the other side, as we did in our store; if they had done so, every stream of water would have gone across the street with the effect it did in our case. If you were in the third story of a building, you could reach out of a window and play on to the cornice of the building opposite.

Q. (By Mr. FIRTH.) Did you see where the engine was that furnished you with water?

A. I think the engine that furnished us with water was in the rear, on the corner of Batterymarch and Broad. I should say that we were troubled about water. It seemed as though it was six months, but it probably wasn't more than two or three minutes. It was only a very short time, long enough, probably, to fill the pipes after the water had all been drawn out.

Q. The engine wasn't out of steam?

A. I don't think it was. I didn't go down to the engine; they sung out, "We are short of water," and then we had to wait two or three minutes.

Q. (By Mr. PHILBRICK.) Did the fire go through High street from end to end?

A. Yes, sir, it went right along on the covings. It started on the lower end of High street, and went right through the street.

Q. Do you recollect how long it took the fire to go through High street?

A. I should say that it didn't take more than an hour and a half; it may have been two hours.

WILLIAM F. BROOKS, *sworn.*

Q. (By Mr. RUSSELL.) You are a member of the City Council?

A. Yes, sir.

Q. What time did you go to the fire?

A. As nearly as I can judge, I should say it might have been from half-past ten to eleven o'clock when I arrived there.

Q. (By Mr. COBB.) Where was the fire when you got there; how far had it extended?

A. It was then in Franklin Square.

Q. (By Mr. RUSSELL.) Did you see it cross from one side to the other; or was it on both sides?

A. It was on both sides of the street when I arrived there.

Q. What did you see that you think we ought to know?

A. I only went from place to place, to see where I might do anything that might be useful; to see if anything was not properly managed by the Fire Department. I saw nothing that would warrant me in saying that the department did not do the best they could, under the circumstances. I thought at the time, and made the remark, I think, to some members of the City Government and some gentlemen who were with me, that the attempt to blow up buildings was a mistake; I consider that a perfect failure. It seemed to me that the Fire Department lacked power; that is, there did not seem to be department enough to cope with such a fire as that. For instance, on Federal street, when the fire first struck the long block there, I took out my watch and timed it, and it was only fifteen minutes before the walls began to fall. It didn't seem to me that any firemen's life was safe who attempted to play upon those buildings; the streets were so narrow and the buildings so high. It was a large block of granite stores. I do not know how many stores there were in the block.

Q. (By Mr. Cobb.) How many stores should you think there were in that block?

A. I think there were five stores. I consider that the firemen did all that mortal men could do, under the circumstances, and I so remarked the next day.

Q. Did you see the Chief that night?

A. Yes, sir, several times.

Q. How did he appear?

A. Perfectly calm and cool, as I have met him on many occasions at large fires; for instance, the large fire at East Boston.

ROBERT C. NICHOLS, *sworn.*

Q. (By Mr. Russell.) What time did you go to the fire on the night of Nov. 9?

A. I left my house at the Highlands about half-past nine o'clock.

Q. What time did you go to the City Hall?

A. I went to the City Hall between twelve and one o'clock. In going to the City Hall the first time, I met Mr. Burt, the postmaster, and he asked me if I would accompany him. I did so. We went to the station house, and asked for the Mayor. They knew nothing of the thereabouts of the Mayor. We then inquired who had charge of the City Hall, and we went into the basement of the building accompanied by a lieutenant of the second station, met the officer having charge of the building, and Mr. Burt inquired for the Mayor. The officer said: "The Mayor left here a few minutes ago; about fifteen minutes since." Mr. Burt said: "The city is being burned, and the City Hall is all in darkness; we want to find the Mayor. We want the Board of Aldermen; we want them up stairs. We want the Chief of the Fire Department here in the building; he should make this his head-quarters. Now, I want you to go up stairs, and light up the Aldermen's room, the Mayor's room, and the whole building; light it all up."

Q. (By Mr. Cobb.) Did you know who that officer was?

A. No, sir; the officer turned round and said to me: "Who is this man who gives these orders?" Said I: "This is Mr. Burt, postmaster of Boston." Mr. Burt asked me to accompany him to the fire in search of the Mayor, and perhaps some Aldermen. We went down School street, but could not get near the Old South, so we went down Spring lane, and through Devonshire street on to Milk street, near the new

Post Office building; and continued our walk down through High to Purchase street and through Pearl, talking with some of the policemen occasionally, and making the same inquiry; if they had seen the Mayor or any of the Board of Aldermen. When we got back to the City Hall, we found the building lighted up. We found ex-Mayor Shurtleff going up to the Mayor's room, and spoke with him on the stairs. Our conversation at the station house, by me especially, was if there was any way to telegraph an alarm to bring out the militia. The officers informed us that there was no such alarm; that there was no way to get out the militia. I saw the necessity of having the militia out as soon as possible, and I suppose General Burt did. When we went into the Mayor's room, we found the Mayor there, and Gen. Burt said: "Mr. Mayor, what is going to be done? The city is all burning up, and there is nothing being done. There is no head governing this fire, or having charge of it." The Mayor said he was willing to do anything it was in his power to do. The Chief of the Fire Department, Mr. Damrell, sat at a desk, and Mr. Burt addressed his conversation to him then, more particularly. He said to him: "Why are not the gates of the Common opened, to allow people to cart their goods there; that is a good place to deposit them, and the station houses are all full." The Chief of the Fire Department said: "I will authorize any one to go and open the gates of the Common." Said he: "How do I know where to get the keys; how can I open them?" Said he: "If you cannot get the keys, I authorize the gates to be broken down."

Q. (By Mr. PHILBRICK.) Who said that?

A. Mr. Damrell.

Q. To whom was it addressed?

A. Mr. Burt. Then Mr. Burt said there was only one way to stop the fire, and that was by blowing up buildings; there should be powder obtained and buildings should be blown up; and I understood Mr. Damrell to say that he had attended to that, or that he was going to attend to it. I will not swear distinctly which, whether he had attended to it, or was going to. I thought we could obtain the marines by sending to the Navy Yard, and suggested to Mayor Gaston going over for the marines. He said yes, he wished I would do so. I asked him for a written order, and he said that was not necessary; just carry his respects to the Commodore, and say he would like the marine corps, just as many as he could spare, to come over and go on duty. I then said to Mr. Burt, as I left the room: "I am going to Charlestown for the marine corps." I took a carriage at the Parker House, and went to the Commodore's private residence, rang the bell, and he came to the door. I told him my errand, and he said he would do anything in his power to aid the authorities of Boston; that he had already sent over two steam fire-engines, all he had in the yard, and I understood him to say that parties had been there for powder, or that he had sent some. He asked me in regard to blowing up the buildings, and I told him I understood it was in charge of a naval officer. He wanted to know the name of the officer, and I told him I did not understand the name of the officer. Mr. Damrell, or some one in the Mayor's room, told me that the powder was to be in charge of a naval officer, and I so stated to Commodore Parrott. Commodore Parrott called his officers, and directed them to get the guard ready, and I returned to the City Hall, and notified Mayor Gaston that the marines would be over. They were to report at City Hall. I obtained a policeman's badge, by order of the Mayor, and remained on duty doing police work until some time after the troops arrived. I carried quite a number of men into the station house, and unloaded them of large quantities of boots and shoes. I found I was about the only one attending to that business, and soon got sick of it, and left; it was too much.

Q. What time did you start for Charlestown?

A. It must have been nearly two o'clock.

Q. Did you impress a carriage?

A. I did. There were four gentlemen in a carriage just turning away from the Parker House. I told the agent of the carriage that I had an order from the Mayor of the city to go to the Charlestown Navy Yard for a marine corps, and I wanted that carriage, and must have it. He ordered the men out and I got in.

Q. (By Mr. Cobb.) Do you know anything about the use of gunpowder that night?

A. No, sir; only I heard explosions and saw a carriage driving round the streets near the fire, said to contain packages of gunpowder.

There was one matter in regard to Mr. Burt that I did not mention. When Mr. Burt and myself went into the Mayor's room, the Mayor said: "I am willing to do anything in my power that can be done." He then asked what could be done. Mr. Burt said: "We can get citizens enough to volunteer, and organize them into companies, and put squads into the different streets under the charge of different citizens;" and he volunteered to take charge of one of the squads, who were to be placed in each street, with supreme authority coming from the Chief Engineer.

Q. (By Mr. Cobb.) Supreme power to do what?

A. To have control of the streets, and the people in the streets. His idea was to have a squad in each street.

Q. (By Mr. Philbrick.) To do police duty?

A. To do police duty. I think Doctor Ainsworth was present, with others, and they said they were willing to do anything of the kind. My object in going to the City Hall was to tender my services as police in case they were needed. This remark was made by Mr. Burt, and the Chief Engineer sat down and wrote an order, which he gave to Mr. Burt. The nature of that order I do not know.

ELEAZER W. THATCHER, *sworn.*

Q. (By Mr. Russell.) Where were you on the night of the State-street fire?

A. Near Atlantic avenue.

Q. Did you observe the fire?

A. Yes, sir.

Q. What did you see?

A. I saw smoke coming from the top of the building.

Q. Did you try to give the regular alarm?

A. I tried to find a policeman, and cried fire.

Q. (By Mr. PHILBRICK.) Do you know what time that was?

A. It was twenty minutes of ten when I discovered the fire.

Q. (By Mr. RUSSELL.) Did you find an officer?

A. I saw a man who wanted to know what the trouble was, and I told him there was a large fire in State-street block. He said: "All right," and started on a run. I supposed he was a policeman.

Q. Didn't you give the alarm?

A. No, sir.

Q. Do you know what time the alarm was given that night?

A. It was given at eight minutes past ten.

Q. (By Mr. COBB.) How long after you had given the alarm by crying fire?

A. Twenty-eight minutes. I took particular notice of the time. It was eight minutes after I saw the man before the alarm was given. That was twenty-eight minutes after I first saw the fire.

Q. You didn't know anything about any trouble with the fire-alarm boxes that night?

A. Afterwards, I asked the man how it happened that he was so long giving the alarm, and he said one of the boxes — either sixteen or seventeen, I don't remember which — was out of order, and he had to go to another box.

Q. Do you know who the man was?

A. No, sir; I don't.

GEORGE B. UPTON, *sworn.*

Q. (By Mr. RUSSELL.) You were at the head of the Fire Department of Nantucket in what year?

A. For a number of years, down to 1845.

Q. You were an advocate of the use of gunpowder and carried it through the town meeting, that it might be used in case of fire?

A. Yes, sir. Nantucket was then a compact, wooden city of about 10,000 inhabitants.

Q. Was that vote passed before the great fire in Nantucket?

A. It was before either of the great fires. The fire that destroyed the most property was the first fire, in 1842 or 1843. Then they had one in 1846 which destroyed many dwelling-houses.

Q. You were head of the Fire Department at that time?

A. I was, up to 1845.

Q. In what year did you begin?

A. It was some years prior to 1842.

Q. Did you try any experiments with gunpowder before the fire took place?

A. Yes, sir.

Q. Go on and state all about the matter.

A. It was a wooden town. The supply of water was moderate, by cisterns; and it always seemed to me that if they had a severe fire, we should have to resort to powder. I had some correspondence about the use of powder. I think, upon writing to Hartford, I was informed that powder would not blow down a wooden building. A man had a mill which he wanted destroyed, and I got him to let me try the experiment upon it. I tried it, and was entirely successful and blew it down.

Q. What was the size of the building?

A. It was a building of considerable size. One of those old-fashioned, oak-framed wind-mills. Whereupon, the town voted to give the Fire Department liberty to prepare to use powder, and I prepared it.

Q. What preparation did you make?

A. I prepared it, according to the best information that I had, in stout, iron-bound casks of about forty gallons capacity each — fifty or sixty pounds of powder in each. It was put in loose. That is the secret in regard to the use of powder.

I will state here, for your information, that to get the full effect from powder you must give it surface. I have seen the experiment tried, of taking the head out of a cask of powder and dropping a coal into it. The effect was that three-quarters of the powder blew away, and didn't explode.

Q. You don't get surface in a cartridge in a gun?

A. That is a very small amount. If you will try the experiment of putting in an ordinary charge of powder without any shot, and firing it at a piece of paper, you will find that you can go and pick out the kernels of powder out of the piece of paper, showing that you want a gradual combustion of powder, and that you want to follow up the ball after it starts, clear up to the muzzle of the gun. In blowing buildings, you want the powder all to explode at once. You will find that if the powder is in a compact form in a cask, that it will not all explode, but that a considerable portion of it will blow away.

Q. What was this powder that you used for blowing down buildings?

A. We had to use ordinary cask powder. The kind of powder required would be that with a very large grain. I think that no city or town should have an organized Fire Department, without having connected with that department a powder department, entirely under control of the Fire Department. I have given the matter more or less consideration, and I should say what was needed was an iron cylinder with a handle at each end, and a hundred pounds of powder in it. It need not be made very heavy. The cylinder should weigh from 100 to 150 pounds. Two men could easily take that by the handles and carry it where it would blow down almost any building in town. A cylinder of that kind would give the powder a chance to lie loose. You would want a cylinder of just such dimensions that two men could carry it. Such a cylinder could be made to hold from 50 to 60 gallons.

Q. You think it ought not to be full of powder?

A. Oh, no, nothing approximating to that.

Q. What was the result with you?

A. The first house that I applied it to was a large double house, with two front rooms and an old-fashioned entry running through the house. I took the powder into the cellar and exploded it, and the building came flat down.

Q. How did you get the powder into the house?

A. One man and myself went in with it.

Q. What sort of a fuse did you use?

A. We had no fuse. I had seen the men blow rocks, and the only idea I had about it was to knock the bung out of the cask and put some tow into it and set fire to the tow. Every building I fired came down flat. I think I fired seven. They not only fell flat, but there was very little fire about them, and no fire was communicated from the explosion. One engine, if I remember, took care of them after that. We stopped the fire entirely by that means.

Q. Did you ever have occasion to use it again?

A. No, sir.

Q. What kind of buildings were these?

A. Five of these were large dwelling-houses, one was a large boat-builder's shop, and I forget what the other was used for.

Q. Were all of the buildings of wood?

A. Yes, sir.

Q. Do you know whether they kept up this same system afterwards?

A. They undertook partially to do it.

The truth in regard to the use of powder is this: it is of no use if the persons who are to use it have any fear of it. After I left Nantucket, they had a severe fire in the town, and undertook to use powder. (I can only tell it from second-hand.) We had a number of old-fashioned firewards at Nantucket when I was at the head of the Fire Department. I proposed to some of them to go in with me to carry in these casks, which were too heavy for one man to carry, and it was necessary to carry in a lantern at the same time. One Quaker spoke up and said, "I'll go with thee, George;" and the Quaker and I did the business. Afterwards, when I left, they undertook to go in with the powder, but did not fire it. Some one told me that they carried it in, and the buildings took fire, and that they did not succeed in blowing down the building, for the reason that the persons who had charge of the powder were afraid of it.

It is a dangerous thing for people to use, unless they have confidence in it and confidence in themselves. The man is just as important as the powder. It ought to be in charge of the Fire Department. In regard to selecting the buildings that are to be blown down, I would say select those that are not too strongly built — those that you know the powder will demolish. On the night of the fire here, they put powder under the building where the Webster Bank was. In my judgment, it would not have blown that building down.

Q. Was it not put in there for storage?

A. No, sir. I understood that notice was given that the building was to be blown down. It was a very strongly built building, and for that reason was not to be tampered with unless people knew what they were about.

Q. Has it not iron floors?

A. No, sir, but a portion of it is iron.

Q. It is iron and brick, is it?

A. Yes, sir — a very strong building. I think as a rule that powder ought to go into the very lowest part of the building.

Q. Did you confine this that you used in any way except with the casks?

A. No, sir. There were some strong casks with double heads that I made. That was the only form then. I set the casks right down and turned them on the bung so that the powder would come out of the bunghole. The tow was on the floor.

Q. Was anybody hurt?

A. No, sir. We came pretty near it though, from not having sufficient tools. It so happened that we got into one blind cellar, and in lighting the tow my friend blew the light out, and I did not know the way out of the cellar and could not find it. It was one of the early preparations that we made. It was soon after I had the powder-house built. In that case, I put my foot on the tow and extinguished it pretty quick and we commenced operations again.

Powder is a very dangerous element, and is to be used only by persons who have perfect command of themselves and know what they are about.

Q. Should they not be drilled in its use for this sort of purpose?

A. It is not a thing to be played with in any form. You may pick out men in the Fire Department who have perfect confidence in themselves, and have nerve enough to be trusted with it.

Q. Should you not think it more prudent to have a military man at the head of the powder brigade?

A. I think not. I think that it ought to be under the control of the Fire Department and included in that organization, so as to make the organization complete. I have a different opinion from many in regard to the organization of a Fire Department. I don't mean to say anything against the Chief Engineer of this city or the Assistant Engineers. But I think such officers ought to be men who know something more than the mere matters of coupling hose and such details. It requires an amount of judgment and wisdom greater than almost any other position in cities where there is liable to be a great destruction of property from fire.

Q. Would you not also say that they should have special training in that direction?

A. I should, certainly. If you had to call out the powder brigade under the command of the Chief Engineer, I should want them trained so as to know what to do, — to understand who was to have charge of the powder, and to have perfectly cool men, who felt themselves entirely competent for the business, and knew the proper method of proceeding, and had perfect command of themselves, — not men who are undertaking to fire powder for the first time in their lives.

Q. You have no special knowledge in regard to this Boston fire, I suppose?

A. No, sir, except that I was at the fire early. The bells struck in an unusual manner and I went out, and was there while that first building was on fire.

I think there was a want in our Fire Department at that fire in this way: There was a want of carrying up hose. The engines were playing too much on the lower parts of the buildings when the upper parts were on fire. I saw that the fire was getting the entire control of the department the moment that it got into these narrow streets with high buildings. There was no arrangement for carrying up hose. They were not prompt enough. It is of no use to play on the third and fourth stories of buildings when the fire is in the fifth and sixth, and is coming down. It does not do anything; the fire just spreads from one building to another. I watched the whole fire until the next morning at ten o'clock.

Q. Where did you observe this style of playing that you speak of?

A. On the very first building that burned and on the others generally. I spoke of it at that time. Four or five engines would be playing on the lower part of a building when it was the upper part only that was on fire.

Q. Had the fire crossed Summer street when you arrived?

A. No, sir. I think that it would not vary but very little from half-past seven o'clock when I arrived. The first building was only fairly on fire. It was a question then about the fire's crossing Summer street. I said then that I wondered that they did not get up their ladders and get the hose upon the other side. As a general thing, without going into details, the water did not get at the fire.

Q. In regard to the first building, was that practicable when you arrived?

A. Yes, sir. They could have taken up the hose on the opposite side and played into the building. There were but one or two engines there when I arrived. There was no reason that I know of, why with such an alarm as that there should not have been a number of engines there. To me the alarm sounded in a very unusual manner. I started and went right down when the bells first struck. As a rule, I never go to fires, but this alarm sounded in so unusual a manner that I went right out. I live just below the corner of Charles and Beacon street. I went across the Common and right straight to Lincoln street. When I arrived, I think I found but one engine there. I did not see but one stream, at any rate, and there was no water reaching the fire at all. They were playing at it and not reaching it efficiently.

Q. Where was the engine stationed that you saw?

A. It was on the street where the fire was. It was on Kingston street, right opposite the burning building.

Q. Whereabouts in the building was the fire when you arrived?

A. It was in the upper part of the building.

Q. Do you remember looking below to ascertain whether it was not below also?

A. I think it was not below. I did not notice it there. I noticed one single engine playing, and in some conversation that I had there, I asked where in heaven's name the other engines were, and they said that they were bringing them up by hand. My own impression would be that there was a want of hooks and ladders, especially ladders, to aid in getting up the hose.

Q. Did you come down Summer street from Washington?

A. No, sir, I went through Bedford street to Kingston street, when I went to the fire.

Q. Was there no engine at the corner of Bedford and Kingston streets?

A. No, sir, I did not pass any. I did not undertake to fix the location of any engine. I directed my attention to the fire, to see what was the effect of it.

Q. Was it too hot to pass through Kingston street to the fire?

A. No, sir, I did not undertake to do that. I went within four or five blocks of it.

Q. Did you turn up Kingston street?

A. I think I did, after going down Bedford. That is my impression. I was not a great ways from the fire. I went up far enough to see the basement of the building and its whole length. While I stayed there, the fire got in the upper stories on Summer street. Then I went round into Summer street to see what would happen next. I said, " Is it possible that they are going to let that fire get into Summer street? "

Q. Did you go through Church Green or Chauncy street?

A. I went through Chauncy street. After it got into Summer street, I stayed there some time, and then I went into Franklin street and saw that the fire came down there, and then I spoke up and said, " They ought not to allow that fire to go the other side of Franklin street. They ought to have used powder there."

Q. Did you ever see powder used in that class of buildings filled with merchandise?

A. No, sir; I never did.

Q. Did you see anything of its use that night or the next morning?

A. No, sir; nothing from which I could form an opinion. I was not near enough.

Q. Was there gas let into those houses at Nantucket for lighting purposes?

A. No, sir. That is to be considered. It is a great danger, of course. There is no doubt about that.

AUGUSTUS LUCE, *sworn.*

Q. (By Mr. Russell.) Where do you reside?

A. At 15 Linden street, East Boston.

Q. How early were you at the fire?

A. I was there I should say within five minutes after the first bell struck.

Q. Where were you when the alarm struck?

A. On the corner of Broad and Summer streets.

Q. Did you see anything of the fire before the alarm?

A. Yes, sir.

Q. How long had you seen it before the alarm?

A. Not more than a minute.

Q. When you got there, what was the condition of things?

A. When I got there, the end of the building nearest to Bedford street was on fire, and the flames were showing themselves.

Q. Was there any fire apparatus there at that time?

A. Steamer 7 was on the corner of Lincoln and Bedford streets.

Q. How soon did that steamer begin to play?

A. I kept right around the fire on Bedford and Kingston streets, and then went on to Summer street. I there met Deputy Chief Regan. He gave orders to some men who were with him to cut through the front door on Summer street; and, as they were cutting through, the remark he made was like this: " Where in the devil is Steamer No. 7? " and I replied, "She stands on the corner of Bedford and Lincoln streets." He says, "What is she doing there?" I said, "The other end of this building is all in flames." He instantly took his men away from that door and went down Kingston street, and I followed him. There was one stream, if not two, going on to the fire then.

Q. How many minutes after you heard the alarm did you see the stream going on to the fire?

A. I should think it was not over ten minutes.

Q. Do you belong to the Fire Department?

A. No, sir. I belong to Station No. 2. I am a policeman.

Q. You don't know about the giving of the alarm?

A. No, sir.

Q. Did you see any other steamers while you were there?

A. No, sir; not right away at that time.

Q. Did you see any hose carriage?

A. Yes, sir; right in the street. The crowd gathered in there very thick. I don't remember what hose carriage it was. In a very few minutes I was on Summer street again, and a hook and ladder company had come then. I saw no other steamer directly at that time.

Q. Did ,you save some women from Kingston street?

A. Yes sir.

Q. What time was that?

A. It was very soon after I went down Kingston street with Officer Regan. These women got scared, and could not get out through the crowd. I went into the house and took them down through the crowd. It was right opposite the fire on Kingston street, I think the first house next to the new store that they are building, — Mr. Rogers' house.

JOHN M. PAGE, *re-called.*

Q. (By Mr. Russell.) What is your occupation?

A. I am a policeman at Station No. 4.

Q. The outlines of your beat are Kingston, Essex, South, East, Federal and Summer streets?

A. Yes, sir.

Q. What time did you pass the corner of Kingston and Summer streets?

A. As near as I can judge, it might be five or ten minutes before seven o'clock.

Q. You noticed nothing then, of course?

A. No, sir.

Q. You went down Kingston?

A. I went down Kingston, towards Essex.

Q. You met a woman there, did you?

A. Yes, sir. I left the corner and was coming down Essex street when I met a woman. She had some complaints to make about parties, and about her husband; and detained me there five or ten minutes, perhaps.

Q. Then where did you go?

A. I went to the corner of Lincoln and Essex.

Q. What took place at Lincoln?

A. I was standing on the corner a few minutes, and there was a party of rough boys half way up Summer street, making some disturbance and noise, and I started to go up and drive them off. They saw me coming, and they ran towards Summer street, and I followed along after them. When we got up to Summer street, they began to hallo fire. I supposed they were doing it to plague me. I ran pretty fast after them up to the corner. I didn't know but what I would touch them with my cane a little. I got up to the corner, and sure enough, there was plenty of fire on the corner of Lincoln and Bedford streets. It appeared to be coming out of the top of the buildings. I could not see the building that was on fire. There was a high building between that and me, that ran farther back.

Q. How many minutes was that from the time you passed that corner of Kingston and Summer streets?

A. It might have been twenty minutes or more.

Q. How near you was box 52?

A. I was right at it. It was right on the corner where I stood. I took the key out and gave the alarm as soon as possible.

Q. How soon did you give the second alarm?

A. I could not hear the bell, there was so much noise. I waited what I thought would be time enough to strike the bell, and then I gave the second alarm.

Q. How many minutes were there between the first alarm and the second?

A. I should judge it was five minutes or so.

Q. Why did you give the second alarm?

A. There was word came from an Engineer to give the second alarm, although I had made up my mind to give it without having any orders. I gave a third alarm. That I had orders from an Engineer to give. But it was an order throughout the whole department, in case the fire was above the second story, to give a second alarm immediately, without having any orders. I gave the third alarm as soon as I thought the second had done striking. I gave the first and the second within five minutes of each other, and the third as soon as the second had got through. I could not hear the second strike. I did not hear any answer that night.

Q. Did you get any response from the box?

A. Yes, sir; I could hear it ticking in the box.

Q. As soon as you gave the first alarm did you hear it ticking?

A. Yes, sir.

Q. Had any one spoken to you about the alarm before you gave the first one?

A. No, sir; there was nobody there.

Q. How many seconds was it from the time you heard the cry of "Fire" until you gave the first alarm?

A. It was as quick as I could put my hand in my pocket and take out my key — taking up five or six seconds. The box was located on the corner of Lincoln and Bedford streets. I was right at the box. When I got around the corner far enough to see, I gave the alarm. I was right there at the box when I saw the fire.

Q. While you were giving the first alarm, what officers came up?

A. There were a number. I think the first officer I saw was Mr.

Moulton, right close there. He came there without any hat or coat, and with his key in his hand.

Q. What other officers?

A. Mr. Farwell, Mr. Hoffman, Mr. Crane, and quite a number of others.

Q. Did you hear any other alarm except from those boys?

A. No, sir. That was my first intimation of the fire. I had been standing at the corner of Essex street for four or five minutes. If there had been any outcry in Summer street, I must have heard it.

These boys shouted as soon as they got there, and I was then after them. I was going up Lincoln street towards Bedford and Summer.

Q. Can you tell what fire apparatus you saw come, and when you saw it come?

A. I saw one steamer come up Lincoln street with some men on it, and I thought they had light teams to haul the engine with, and I appealed to the crowd to take hold and help haul it along, and there were a number that took hold.

Q. What time did they reach the fire?

A. I was waiting at the box to give an alarm. I think it was the second alarm. It must have been that.

Q. What steamer was it?

A. I suppose it was No. 7. I did not notice. It came up Lincoln street.

Q. Where did it locate?

A. It stopped right at the hydrant at the corner of Lincoln and Bedford streets. It came within five minutes after the first alarm.

Q. How soon did it begin to play?

A. I don't recollect about that. I think before it had got to playing I had left the box.

Q. Where did you go?

A. I went up Bedford street. The boys had got up into a yard, on to a shed, and I went there to drive them out and stayed there for some time.

Q. Did you see any other steamers come before you went up Bedford street?

A. No, sir; I don't think I did. I was there half an hour or more.

FREDERICK HOFFMAN, *sworn.*

Q. (By Mr. Russell.) What is your occupation?

A. I am a policeman, connected with Station No. 4.

Q. On the night of the fire, where were you when the alarm was given?

A. When the alarm was given I was at the fire.

Q. When did you see the fire first?

A. I saw the fire from the corner of Bedford and Lincoln streets. My beat runs from the corner of Essex and Lincoln down Lincoln to Beach, along Beach to Federal, up Federal to East, through East to South, up South to Essex, and then through Essex to Lincoln.

Q. What time was this that you saw the fire?

A. I should say, to the best of my knowledge, that it was between fifteen and twenty minutes past seven. The fire was in the rear of the building.

Q. Was there any fire in front?

A. No, sir.

Q. How far up was it?

A. I should say that it was the second or third story.

Q. Did you notice any fire below?

A. Yes, sir, I did. From the front part of the building, I could see the light of the fire through the basement windows from the Summer-street side.

Q. How long after you saw the fire did you hear the alarm?

A. I could not hear any alarm at all, there was so much noise around the fire. I ran up to the head of the street and met officer Page at the box. I went around by the front of the Freeman's Bank to Summer street, and Engineer Regan was there and the driver of the Insurance wagon. They tried to cut into the front door and make an opening through so as to unbolt it, but it was a centre bolt and they could not unbolt it. Engineer Regan told me to go round and give a second and third alarm. I told him the second was rung. He said ring the third right after it. I went round to the box and told officer Page. Our orders were then if the fire was above the third story to give the second alarm. Officer Page gave the second alarm while I was at the box. He had given the first alarm and had just closed the box when I got there.

Q. How soon after the second alarm was the third given?

A. I could not say exactly. I got back I should say in about two or three minutes. As soon as I ran around to where the Freeman's Bank is, then I came right back again and told officer Page.

Q. Did you see any fire apparatus there?

A. Yes, sir, I saw Steamer No. 7, and there was a hose from Hudson street. I saw the hose there, but could not see the carriage. I had seen Steamer 4's hose carriage come round through Otis street right into Kingston.

Q. How soon did Steamer 7 get there after the first alarm?

A. Steamer 7, I should say, was there within about five minutes from the time that I got to the box,—less than that. I could not tell anything about the alarm, because I did not hear it. What I judge by is that officer Page closed the box. Some one went down and gave notice to the steamer, that was located right in East street.

Q. Where did it stop to get water?

A. It stopped in Bedford street, right at the rear. I could not see exactly where it did stop. They got the hose over the shed right in the rear of the building.

Q. How soon did they get water on to the building after they got there?

A. I should say it was ten or fifteen minutes; I could not say exactly.

Q. How soon did the hose get there from Hudson street?

A. I saw the hose there in fact sooner than I saw Steamer 7's water.

Q. How soon after the first alarm was given?

A. I could not say exactly. It might be six or seven minutes. I know they were a very short time ahead of Steamer No. 7.

Q. How soon did Hose 4 get there?

A. It was some time before Hose 4 got there. The fire had got up through the roof at that time. The fire had got out on the Kingston-street side, through the windows, at that time.

Q. How many minutes, to the best of your knowledge or opinion?

A. I should say about eighteen or twenty minutes.

Q. (By Mr. Firth.) As I understand, you were at the corner of Bedford and Lincoln streets when you saw the fire?

A. Yes, sir.

Q. Then you went from there to the fire?

A. Yes, sir.

Q. Why didn't you sound the alarm?

A. When I came there, officer Page was at the box.

Q. Was officer Page there when you were there?

A. When I came there, officer Page was there. I was standing at the corner of Essex and Lincoln streets, when my attention was attracted to it by the noise and the cry of fire. I ran up for the box. When I got there, officer Page had given the alarm and was just closing the box. That was before I had been to the fire. I had seen officer Page on the corner opposite to me a short time before that. I thought he went out of Essex towards Kingston, but instead of that he had gone up Lincoln and was there before me.

BENJAMIN F. FARWELL, *sworn.*

Q. (By Mr. Russell.) What is your occupation?

A. I am a police officer connected with Station No. 4.

Q. Where were you when you first saw the fire?

A. I was in Lincoln street, on my beat.

Q. What part of Lincoln street?

A. I was near the building called Lincoln building, or Crystal Palace.

Q. What did you see?

A. The first that I saw was that a lot of young men and boys came running up the street, from the lower end of the Palace. They were in the middle of the street. I had not discovered any fire at that time. I went in the middle of the street and looked up, and saw a light there, and went up to the box at the corner of Lincoln and Bedford streets, as quick as I could.

Q. Whom did you find there?

A. I found officer Page at the box.

Q. Did he tell you what he had done?

A. I heard just as I got there the click. I could hear the lever, and I stopped there a moment and I heard the tick.

Q. Did he give a second alarm while you were there?

A. No, sir. I don't know. I left then. I heard the click and then I went through Bedford street. There is a Mrs. Foster who lives there, and a lot of young men had run through her yard and were going over her sheds. I went in and drove them out of her yard, and then I went around up Kingston street to the fire.

Q. In what part of the building was the fire when you got there?

A. It was in the top part, beyond the elevator, in the rear end.

Q. How soon did you see any fire apparatus come?

A. I went into the building next adjoining that, — I went to the door of Tebbetts, Baldwin & Davis first. That was bolted and I could not get in. Then I went up into the building next to it, clear to the top. There was a fireman that went in with me at that time, up to the top of that building. I think he was an Engineer. I stopped there until there was a hose run up the three flights.

Q. Do you know what hose that was?

A. I don't know. I suppose, however, that it was Steamer No. 7's. This hose was carried through the building on the right, — I. H. Hatch & Co's, just across the alley-way to the right.

Q. How many minutes after you left the box before you met this Engineer?

A. It might have been four or five minutes. I should not think it was over that, to the best of my judgment. It might have been five minutes.

Q. What time was it when you reached the building which was on fire?

A. I don't know.

Q. What should you judge?

A. Twenty minutes past seven o'clock, I should say, or in that neighborhood, as near as I can judge. It might have been later than that, and it might have been not quite so late.

Q. How soon after did you see any engine?

A. I was in that building, and could not see.

Q. (By Mr. Firth.) Were there any words between yourself and officer Page at the box, about what he had done?

A. All that was said by him was, "Do you hear the bells?" I said, "I hear the tick," and then I could hear the clicking in the box. He says, "Go out there to Mrs. Foster's;" and I started. That was all that was said.

FRANK R. CRANE, *sworn.*

Q. (By Mr. Russell.) What is your occupation?

A. I am a policeman connected with Station No. 2. My beat is Washington, Summer, Devonshire and Franklin streets.

Q. When were you first out on the night of the fire?

A. It was at six o'clock.

Q. At what time did you hear the cry or alarm?

A. Well, it was just a few minutes before the bell struck — probably not more than two or three minutes.

Q. Where were you then?

A. I was just at the corner of Franklin and Devonshire streets.

Q. Who was with you?

A. Mr. Dodd and Mr. Mather.

Q. What sort of a cry did you hear?

A. When I heard it, I did not think it sounded any more like fire than anything else. I did not recognize it as being an alarm of fire. I thought it was parties passing up Summer street. It is a very common thing there to hear such noises.

Q. Then you say that two or three minutes after that cry you heard the alarm. What did you do then?

A. I thought then that this halloing might be "Fire." I started and ran right through to Summer street. When I got through there I could see the reflection of the fire in Kingston street. I went right around, and came up from Devonshire into Kingston street as soon as I could, and went in the rear of the building.

Q. Was anybody there at that time?

A. I don't think there was when I went there, but when I came out of the passage-way I met Mr. Regan, one of the Engineers. He told me to go and give the second and third alarms.

Q. What did you do?

A. I went to the box and found officer Page there, and told him what Capt. Regan had told me.

Q. Did he give another alarm then?

A. Yes, sir. He said he would give it as soon as the bell had done striking the first alarm.

Q. Then you had come all the way from Franklin street before the first alarm got through?

A. From the time the first bell struck, — before the three rounds of the bell had struck.

Q. How many minutes would it take you to do that?

A. Well, three or four minutes.

Q. After that, what did you do?

A. I was about there all night, in Summer, Franklin, Washington and Devonshire streets, making myself as useful as I could, under the command of Sergeant Foster.

Q. What fire apparatus did you see first?

A. I could not say what it was. I saw that which I supposed to be Steamer 7's hose carriage.

Q. How soon did you see that after the first alarm?

A. That was before the bell had done striking. It was on Kingston street, right opposite to the building that was burning.

Q. Was it before the first alarm had done striking?

A. Yes, sir.

Q. When did you see the next apparatus?

A. I could not tell, but it was right away. It was but a very few minutes before I saw Steamer No. 7, there in Summer street.

Q. To the best of your knowledge, how many minutes after the alarm was first struck?

A. I should not think it was more than fifteen or twenty minutes. It might not have been so much as that.

Q. What time did you reach the fire?

A. I could not tell — not to a minute. But it was somewhere between quarter past seven and half past.

JOSEPH DODD, *sworn.*

Q. (By Mr. Russell.) What is your occupation?

A. I am a policeman, and am connected with Station No. 2.

Q. On the night of the fire, where were you on duty?

A. I was on duty, watching stores at the corner of Franklin and Devonshire streets.

Q. Did you hear any noise there?

A. I heard some one halloing and a noise.

Q. What did you do?

A. I started and ran in that direction, towards Summer street.

Q. Did you hear anything of the alarm?

A. No, sir, I did not hear the fire-alarm on my way.

Q. Did you hear the cry of "Fire"?

A. Yes, sir.

Q. What did you see when you got there?

A. I went across Summer and Devonshire streets to an alley-way back of the building which was on fire, and I heard glass breaking, and I looked up and saw the fire just coming out of the window. I thought then that it was in the third story.

Q. Did you hear the alarm at any time?

A. I heard the bells ring, but I did not count the strokes to know what the number was.

Q. How soon after you started and ran did you hear the bells ring?

A. I could not tell. It was after I got to the fire.

Q. About how many minutes would that take?

A. It would not take more than two minutes to go from where I was, if it did as long.

Q. What did you do then?

A. I went and helped Lt. Childs get a rope off the hook and ladder truck.

Q. When did that truck arrive?

A. It was pretty soon after I got there. I don't know how many minutes. I don't believe it was more than a minute or two after I got there. The hose got there about the same time I did. I turned around and saw them coming. I thought it was quite a spell before a steamer came. I could not tell exactly how many minutes it was after the bell struck.

Q. Give it, to the best of your judgment.

A. I thought at that time that it was about five minutes, but it might not have been so long.

CALEB T. MATHER, *sworn.*

Q. (By Mr. Russell.) What is your occupation?

A. I am a policeman connected with Station No. 2.

Q. Where were you on the night of the fire?

A. I was on my beat, corner of Devonshire and Franklin streets. I was there about ten minutes previous to the fire's starting.

Q. When did you hear anything unusual that attracted your attention?

A. I was talking with Mr. Crane, and simultaneously we heard some one hallo; and there was another officer that came along about that time and said he guessed there was a disturbance up the street, and we started towards Winthrop square, up Devonshire street; and then we distinguished the cry of fire and proceeded in that direction. I went by the way of Devonshire street, that being on the line of my route. I got about opposite Beebe's building and I heard the fire-alarm. At the time I got to Summer street, I distinguished the number.

Q. How long after the alarm was it before you saw any fire apparatus?

A. After I got to the corner of Summer and Devonshire streets, on my way up, I saw the smoke and got the direction of the fire, and I went immediately there and rushed to the door of the store on the Kingston-street side, and the fire appeared to be in the rear — from an alley-way in the rear of the counting-room, and Mr. Crane rushed by me up into the alley-way, and came up and started back, and met Mr. Regan, who told him to go and give the alarm — the second and third alarms. I remained there. It was not many minutes before the first and second lines of hose came into the street. I could not tell exactly how many minutes had elapsed. Time seems much longer under such circumstances. It seemed to me rather slow.

Q. How many minutes was it, to the best of your judgment, between the alarm and the arrival of the first apparatus?

A. I might have stood there from seven to ten minutes. It might not have been as long, but it seemed to me so. Then I saw two lines of hose running up the street. They started up the stairway of the building beyond the alley. I don't know whether they got a stream on the fire or not. They soon ran back.

Q. Did you see the hose arrive?

A. I saw these two lines of hose run into the street. I did not see the carriage.

Q. Did you see the steamer come?

A. No, sir.

Q. You were at work on the fire all night with Sergeant Bates?

A. Yes, sir. I stayed there as long as I could. I stayed there until the heat drove me away, and then I went down Kingston and Bedford streets, and around in the rear, and saw steamers enough there. On my way around, I went from there to the Freeman's Bank entrance, and remained there until the fire crossed Summer street, and the Deputy Chief came to the door where I was and said, if I had any families living on the route, I had better proceed in that direction; and I did so. I remained on the route as long as I could be of any service. Then I reported on Summer street, and was with Sergeant Bates the rest of the night.

SERGT. JOSEPH H. BATES, *sworn.*

Q. (By Mr. Russell.) You are an officer of the police force?

A. Yes, sir.

Q. Where were you when the alarm was given of this fire?

A. I was going down Hanover street. I listened to the first alarm, and the second alarm was turned in so quick that I returned to the station-house and put on my uniform, and went immediately to the fire.

Q. How many minutes did it take you to get there after you heard the second alarm?

A. It was probably ten minutes, as near as I can judge.

Q. In what condition was the building?

A. The building at that time was all of a light flame.

Q. Was there any fire apparatus there?

A. Yes, sir. Steamer No. 4 was all the engine I saw. She was attached to a hydrant, and the stream was on the fire.

Q. Did you see any other steamer come?

A. No, sir. I had a line across the head of Summer street, at that time. On the other lines were Sergeants Foster and Childs. They were below me on the other side.

Q. How long were you on duty?

A. I was on duty until the next morning at nine o'clock, and all through the day afterward, in fact.

Q. Did the officers come promptly from your station, or otherwise?

A. After I had been at the fire some time, I judged it would be quite a fire, and went to the station-house and reported that I must have more men, I had hard work to hold the line with what I had. He sent me three or four, and the men from other stations came within an hour. Station No. 8 reported to me, and Station No. 5, and then I had some of Station No. 4's men, and, in fact, the officers from other stations reported up to ten o'clock and past that hour.

Q. You say you had hard work to hold the lines. What was the trouble?

A. It was on account of the crowd. There were so many people crowding down. That was the great difficulty all that night. It was a trouble to the firemen as well as to the police. We were obliged to let the firemen through. We always gave them all the privileges necessary.

Q. Was the crowd troublesome to the firemen?

A. No, sir, I should judge not. There was a line of hose run up Summer street. We would always say to the firemen, "Pass through the centre. Your line of hose is open ready for you." We used every means in our power to give them a chance. When the apparatus arrived, we dropped our lines and let them pass through. A crowd will usually let the engines pass through without any hindrance. They take care to keep clear of the horses, and give an engine plenty of room.

Q. Did the crowd give way when the engine was drawn by men, as in former times?

A. It was about the same — nothing different.

Q. How did the police officers behave?

A. They behaved well. We had not a particle of trouble with a single man. We had some fifty during the night.

Q. Did you see any of the firemen disorderly?

A. No, sir.

SOLOMON S. FOSTER, *sworn.*

Q. (By Mr. Russell.) Are you a member of the police force?

A. Yes, sir. I am attached to Station No. 2.

Q. Were you out at the time of the fire-alarm?

A. Yes, sir. I was in Merchants' Row when the first alarm struck. I went right over to the fire as quick as I could go.

Q. When you got there, what was going on?

A. The fire was burning pretty rapidly on the top of that building on Kingston street. The flames were coming out of the upper windows.

Q. How many minutes did it take you to get there? From the time the alarm struck until you got there, how long was it?

A. I ran all the way through State and Devonshire streets, right to Otis, and right through to Summer street.

Q. Did you see any fire apparatus when you got there?

A. The 7's had got there. The hose-carriage came about the time that I did, I think.

Q. What hose was it?

A. I think it is No. 2, or else it is No. 3. They were in Kingston street, near Bedford.

Q. What did you do?

A. Then I went right to work getting the crowd away, in order to give the firemen a chance to work.

Q. Did you have officers from different stations?

A. Yes, sir. I sent word to Lieutenant Burleigh to telegraph, and he sent all the officers he could get, and as quick as he could get them there. We formed our lines on Franklin and Devonshire streets, and fell back, as the fire came through to Milk street, from point to point, as the fire drove us.

Q. Were you employed in driving crowds from buildings that were to be blown up?

A. We were, at the corner of Milk and Devonshire streets.

Q. How long did you hold those lines?

A. It was all night.

Q. How did the police officers behave that night?

A. They behaved well.

Q. Was there any trouble with any of them?

A. None that I know of.

Q. Did you see any firemen drunk or disorderly?

A. No, sir.

Q. Did you see firemen robbing stores, or helping themselves to goods?

A. Yes, sir. That was at Peck's fur store on Devonshire street.

Q. Were they Boston firemen?

A. I could not tell, there was such a crowd. They said that Mr. Peck told them to take what they could, and also told other citizens the same. I took care of what stuff I could, and cleared the place out, and put some officers in there.

I can't tell what firemen it was that took these things, or where they belonged. It was pretty late. The fire had got past Franklin street towards Milk. It had not got to Peck's store, by two or three stores. Mr. Peck's was on the left-hand side, as you go through to Milk street.

Q. What is your opinion of the practice of giving away goods?

A. I think it demoralized the people and the firemen, by telling them to go in and help themselves. The crowd would rush and we could not keep a line. It was hard enough to keep a line with 500 people behind it, even if nobody said anything. As soon as one of these men spoke, we would not have much show. The crowd broke the lines a number of times across Milk and Devonshire streets. We could not hold the lines when these men would sing out for the people to come through. We were powerless the moment that these store-keepers would say that thing. It would demoralize everything.

Q. Did you ever know that thing to be said before?

A. No, sir.

Q. Did you see it at any other place besides Mr. Peck's?

A. I saw the same thing up in Washington street. I went in there and drove them out of two stores on the corner of Franklin street. There was a collar store there — Bradford & Anthony's.

Q. A little to the left of Franklin?

A. Yes, sir; as you go up.

Q. Did you make any arrests that night for larceny?

A. I brought one man in, I believe. I took away a good many goods from people in those stores, and I put the people out.

Q. How could you tell a thief from a man who had had a present?

A. I made them leave it all. I told them I did not think they had any right to give things away, and I got them out as quick as I could.

Q. How many years have you been an officer?

A. I went into the department in 1849. I have been in the department ever since it was organized with the watch.

JOHN H. WESTON, *sworn.*

Q. (By Mr. Russell.) Where do you live?

A. In East Boston.

Q. Where were you at the time of the fire?

A. In East Boston.

Q. How soon did you come over here, after the first alarm?

A. We don't come to Boston unless by special order. At the striking of the fourth alarm, we are ordered to report at the Ferry. We so reported, and were ordered back by Captain Barnes, to the house. On his so doing, I went to my place of business. A member of Engine Co. No. 5 came and told me that we were ordered to go to Boston at once. I started to go to the Ferry. Just at that time an alarm came in from box 154. We went to the fire there, and then immediatly came back. I am attached to the Fire Department — to hose company No. 6.

Q. What was the condition of the fire when you got there?

A. We were ordered to report on Devonshire street. At that time, the fire had hardly got into Franklin street. Mr. Dunbar ordered me into the clothing store on the corner of Franklin and Devonshire. I went on to the roof of the building to see what kind of a chance there was. I went up and found the building then ignited. I told him that we could not get up there and remain there more than three or four minutes. He then told us we had better take our line out and go into Franklin street, which we did. We were driven back from Franklin street into Devonshire, and remained there some time. After that he went away, and I thought I saw a good chance to make a stand on a block of buildings consisting of four or five stores on Devonshire street. I took my stream up on to the roof of the building, and Engine No. 8 took their stream on to the building. 2 of Cambridge and the Lynn company were in the lower part of the building. We were doing excellent execution. I have no hesitation in saying that had we not been called out of it, we would have made a pretty good show. We had made things look black on both sides of us. The buildings on both sides of us being low we could pour water right into them. There was some little space next to us and we had an excellent opportunity to fight the fire. I was congratulating myself and saying that we were doing nobly, when we received an order to come down instantly. I said, "For what purpose?" I asked whether it was an Engineer that gave the order. The man said, "No." I said, "Go down and ask what I am to come down for." He came back and said they had put gunpowder in the building on the opposite corner and were to blow it up. I made some kind of a remark about the use of gunpowder under such circumstances, which I do not care to repeat. We came down and went into State street and remained there (I glanced at the clock), in connection with seven or eight streams, an hour and a quarter, waiting for the explosion. As I understood, the powder was put in and the fuse was lighted, but it went out. We had to wait until the fire had got to the gunpowder before we could go back and fight the fire again.

While waiting for the machine to get to work again, we went into the new Post Office and waited until the explosion. I was a little curious to see how gunpowder would work in such a case and I watched it pretty thoroughly. Some ten minutes after the explosion the wall fell in. Then we went into the street and around the new Post Office and had a pretty severe fight. Then we went into the building on the opposite corner and extinguished the fire, and proceeded up Milk street, and stopped the fire as we went. After we got the fire put out there, we went down into the "Post" building and stopped the fire there. After that, we were sent around to a number of different places.

Q. What is your opinion now as to the effect of using gunpowder?

A. I could not see the benefit there. I think it was a detriment to us instead. The building, I think, was right on the corner of Milk and Devonshire streets, opposite the new Post Office, on the upper corner.

Q. Do you think you would have extinguished and stopped the fire there if you had not been called off?

A. I am inclined to think that we would. I don't think it would have come into the building where we were, at least, for I think we had it, sure.

The powder was put in without our knowledge, and we were warned out. I could not tell who the man was that sent for me. I did not see him. It was not put into the same building that we were playing in. It was put into the building on the opposite corner.

Q. You have no way of helping us to find out who put that powder there?

A. No, sir.

Q. Did you see the man who had sent the order to you when you came down?

A. I says to the man, "Is that the gentleman who ordered you to go and tell us to come down?" He had on a city badge. I did not have time to notice him particularly. I think it was an Alderman. I think the Aldermen have badges. This man had a gold badge.

Q. Was it from that circumstance that you thought he was an Alderman?

A. Yes, sir.

Q. Do you know what time of the day or night this was?

A. I could not say anything about the time. It was towards morning; pretty late, at that. I should judge that it was between three and four o'clock. I could not say exactly.

Q. Was that new Post-Office building a barrier to the flames on account of the way in which it was built?

A. It was somewhat. There was considerable fire in and around it, and we had pretty sharp work to extinguish the fire in and around it.

Q. What was there in it to burn?

A. There were stagings, scaffoldings, and other things in and around it. There was a good deal of lumber in and around it and on top of it.

Q. So far as it was fire-proof it was a barrier, was it not?

A. Yes, sir.

Q. With almost any other building there, do you think the fire would have stopped there?

A. I should not want to say that it would under existing circumstances, with the gunpowder as it was used at that corner. I think that the gunpowder would have been likely to have thrown the matter around so much that it would have scattered the fire everywhere, and cracked the glass the whole length of the street. The building was actually on fire when the explosion took place. The fire burned down to the powder, but the fuse didn't light it.

Adjourned to Thursday afternoon.

ELEVENTH DAY.

THURSDAY, Dec. 12.

C. W. ELLIOT, PRESIDENT OF HARVARD COLLEGE, *sworn.*

Q. (By Mr. RUSSELL.) At what time did you go to the great fire of Nov. 9th?

A. I don't know exactly; I was in Brimmer street, and heard the alarm strike, and immediately looked out of the window, and there was a great blaze in the sky at the time the alarm struck. I went as quick as I could to the place, and might have been ten minutes in crossing the Common and going down West street.

Q. When you reached the spot, what was the condition of the fire?

A. The whole building seemed to me to be in a blaze from top to bottom. I should say there were at least three engines playing on it when I reached there.

Q. Did you see it cross to Otis street?

A. Yes, sir, I saw it cross to the cornice and roof.

Q. How long was that after you reached the spot?

A. I can't tell how long it was. I don't know; I did not look at my watch during the night, that I know of.

Q. Did you see any effort made to prevent that crossing?

A. No, sir; I could see none. I was standing below the fire in Summer street. I distinctly remember thinking how extraordinary it was that no effort was made.

Q. (By Mr. PHILBRICK.) Were you in a position so that you could see down Otis street, to know whether there were any ladders there or not?

A. I was below the fire on Summer street, looking up.

Q. You couldn't see into Otis street, then?

A. Oh, no; I saw the fire on Summer street, so to speak.

Q. (By Mr. RUSSELL.) You couldn't see into Otis street, nor see whether anything was going on there?

A. No, sir, I couldn't see into Otis street.

Q. (By Mr. PHILBRICK.) Do you think it was practicable, at that moment, when the fire got across the street, for any man to have operated directly on the Summer-street front of this building or to have scaled the front of this building on the north side of Summer street?

A. I think it would have been a dangerous and altogether injudicious operation to have attacked that fire in front on Summer street, at that time. It was the wrong place altogether to work.

Q. (By Mr. COBB.) For what reason?

A. Because the hose would then have been carried up to the place where it would have been most exposed to heat, and of course the firemen might have been obliged to retreat at any moment.

Q. (By Mr. Philbrick.) Where do you think the firemen should have attacked it?

A. From Otis street and Devonshire street.

Q. (By Mr. Russell.) State anything you noticed that night which you think should be brought to the attention of the Commission.

A. The thing I noticed most that night, up to twelve o'clock, was that water was not put on the fire.

Q. Where was it put?

A. The great bulk of the water was thrown on to the vertical walls of those granite and brick buildings. The water didn't go more than three stories high, as a rule; sometimes it went a little higher, but seldom more than three stories high. It then fell down in front of the building, across the sidewalk, and went into the street. The hosemen didn't break the windows, as a rule, and the water therefore didn't penetrate the buildings at all. I over and over again saw powerful streams of water used in that way, where the upper stories and roofs of the buildings on which they were playing were in a light blaze. I saw it repeatedly during that night, and as late as eight o'clock on Sunday morning.

Q. On what streets did you see that?

A. I don't know that I shall be able to answer that with precision. The places where I remember it most distinctly were Otis street, Devonshire street (on the water side of Beebe's block), on Milk street, a little above Batterymarch street, I think, and another place that I have not been able to identify since, where I stood nearly fifteen minutes. It was in the vicinity of High and Purchase streets, but the ground is entirely burnt over; the buildings they were attempting to save were burned, and I have not been able to identify the place, although I went there for that purpose.

Q. (By Mr. Philbrick.) Did you occasionally see streams that played higher than three stories?

A. Yes, sir, I occasionally saw a stream where they were using a smaller nozzle than usual, which would go a little higher than usual, but the streams were very ineffectual then, they were so much divided before they got to it. I don't think I saw a single stream used in that way from the street which reached the top of the building that was burning. I will say I didn't see the effort to prevent the fire from crossing Washington street, opposite the Marlboro' Hotel. I understood they did get the water to the top of that building. That was the most astonishing thing during that whole night, to see Americans using superb resources in that way. I would not have believed it; nothing would have induced me to believe it. During the night I several times asked hosemen, and persons whom I supposed to be Engineers, — but I generally found they were not Boston Engineers, but country firemen, — why they didn't go on to the roofs, instead of staying in the street. Of course, that was a very disagreeable question, and I generally got pretty short answers, but I got at three different reasons in the course of the night. One was, that it was much hotter on the roofs than in the streets; another was, that it was too dangerous; and another, that they couldn't carry their hose up without bursting them. Some of them said, because the pres sure of the water would burst the hose at such a height; and others said that there was no way of getting the hose through a building without making a good many turns, and that the turns increased very much the danger of bursting. Those were the only reasons that I got at during the night, but of course it was a bad time to give reasons. But, as I dare say the gentlemen of the Commission have heard, those difficulties were all overcome later in the fire. They did carry hose to the top of buildings on Sunday morning, as high as the buildings which were burned Saturday night.

Q. (By Mr. FIRTH.) Did you think that what they alleged in regard to the excessive heat on the top of the buildings was true at that time?

A. I did not.

Q. (By Mr. PHILBRICK.) Were you around the fire during Sunday forenoon?

A. I was; that is, I was there from half-past eight until eleven; after eleven, I had other work. I should say that the next thing that struck me during the night was a lack of foresight from hour to hour in the operations of the Fire Department. They would work on a building which was inevitably to be burned, until it was too late to take any efficient measures to save the next building.

Q. (By Mr. RUSSELL.) Where did you notice that, if you remember any place?

A. I noticed that repeatedly. The place where I first noticed it was in Winthrop square, when Beebe's block was on fire. The block on the lower side of Devonshire street was lost because they played on the three lower stories until it was too late to do anything on the roofs. I noticed the same thing on Federal street. I passed through Federal street several times before the fire swept it, and saw no measures whatever taken to preserve the lower side of that street. Still later in the fire, Federal street went with a rush, but at that time, so far as I saw, that part of the field was abandoned. I saw no firemen there.

Q. What would you have suggested in regard to that block near Beebe's?

A. I did suggest that three powerful streams which were playing on the sidewalk should be carried up through those buildings, but it was not done. Of course, nobody had any right to make any suggestions.

Q. Did you suggest that to any Engineer?

A. I did. I suggested it to Mr. Damrell. I ought to qualify that by saying that I didn't know Mr. Damrell, but this person was pointed out to me by two police officers, and by a man whom I afterwards ascertained to be a Charlestown Engineer, as Mr. Damrell, and I have no doubt it was Mr. Damrell.

Q. What did he say?

A. He looked up at the place, and said something to this effect: "Do you think the men could stay up there?" It wasn't put in the way of a negative answer, it was put in the way of an inquiry; at least, I so understood it; but I ought to add that it was too late to begin operations to save that block. The roof was not in a blaze, but it was smoking, and very hot. These streams, however, had been playing upon the stone walls of the building as much as fifteen minutes from the street, and they were three superb streams of water.

Q. (By Mr. PHILBRICK.) When you saw the fire checked during Sunday forenoon, did you think the check was due to the different tactics, or to the different style of architecture of the buildings?

A. To both. I thought it was emphatically due to the change in tactics, and I also thought that a building like the Merchants' Exchange was a more favorable building to meet the fire in.

Q. Was there not a larger concentration of force there Sunday forenoon than could have been possible on any large scale Saturday night?

A. Yes, sir, I have no doubt that there was; but that wasn't the true way to fight that fire, to concentrate on single blocks at the outset. That is, at the outset, a still greater concentration was possible than was ever possible afterwards, until it was extinguished; that is, from eight to nine o'clock on Saturday night, when the Fire Department had arrived.

Q. Do you think there was sufficient apparatus on the ground between eight and nine o'clock to have successfully fought the fire under the circumstances?

A. I don't feel competent to answer that, because I don't know how many engines there were. There seemed to me to be a good many magnificent streams of water between eight and nine o'clock, but I don't know how many there were. I noticed another thing at that time, that nobody seemed to know where Mr. Damrell was, and nobody had any definite orders to do anything. That was quite as true of the police officers as it was of the hosemen. I was close to a group of half-a-dozen police officers in Winthrop square. They were debating among themselves to whom they should report. I heard three of them say simultaneously that they had no orders, and they did nothing. There was another thing that I noticed during the night, and that was, that the crowds that were rushing about the streets were very much in the way of the Fire Department, and interfered with them constantly at every turn. They were particularly in the way when the firemen wished to change the direction of their hose. It seemed to me that there were two defects of organization that were pretty conspicuous. One was, that the Chief Engineer had apparently no means of commanding the whole field, and he had no means of sending orders. I saw this person who was pointed out to me as Mr. Damrell run two or three times across Winthrop square in the course of fifteen minutes, carrying his own orders, and of course fatiguing himself very much. He didn't seem to have any means of getting intelligence from the different parts of the field. In short, the Fire Department seemed to me to lack the methods of an army altogether, about receiving intelligence and conveying orders. Then I couldn't but sympathize with the reluctance of the firemen to go on such high roofs. One reason was, that there were not firemen enough to handle the hose up those high buildings, and to station men all along the line, at short intervals, to a place of safety. I think hosemen who are to go on roofs are entitled to that protection. They are entitled to feel that there are experienced men all along the line of hose on the line of retreat, who will warn them of danger and secure their retreat. It seemed to me there were not men enough attached to the hose and hose-carriages to do that.

Q. (By Mr. Russell.) You say three of the police said they had no orders, — did you hear any firemen say that?

A. Oh, yes. I asked quite a number, perhaps half-a-dozen or a dozen persons, in the course of the night, in different places, if they had any orders to do what I saw them doing. It struck me so many times as extraordinary and preposterous, that I couldn't help asking that question, and they always said they had no orders.

Q. You asked them in each case if they had orders to do what they were then doing?

A. Yes, sir.

Q. (By Mr. Philbrick.) What did the police officers appear to be doing, besides keeping the crowd back?

A. The police officers to whom I refer were not keeping the crowd back; they were not doing anything at the time; they seemed to be at a loss what to do. The crowd had free admission to Winthrop square at that time. I entered the square with Mayor Norcross, Dr. George Ellis, and Mr. Phillips Brooks, and we went right up close to the place where the firemen were working. There were hundreds, I don't know but thousands of persons in the square at the same time, that being, at that moment, the critical point of the fire.

Then there was another thing I noticed. I don't know exactly what use is to be made of this conversation, and this is rather a hard thing to say, perhaps; I don't know the causes of it in the least; but the firemen all the first part of the night, up to midnight, didn't seem to me to work with what I call desperation. I didn't see a man work as the crew of a ship do, for instance, when they are in danger. There was a sort of nonchalance about them, an easy-going way of working, which was not coolness; it was more than coolness, more than indifference to danger. They seemed to me to be thoroughly impregnated with the idea that it was impossible to do anything with a combustible roof, on top of a five or six-story building. They seemed to me to have that idea thoroughly ingrained, that it was not to be expected; that they couldn't do anything.

Q. (By Mr. Philbrick.) Did you see any marked difference the next morning?

A. I did, very great.

Q. Among buildings with a similar style of roof to those on Winthrop square and Franklin street, with granite walls?

A. Yes, sir, I should say I did. I watched for some time the fate of the buildings on Water street below the building of the "Boston Post." The fire was stopped at the building of the "Post" newspaper. I should say the firemen there worked with much greater energy and desperation. They went up into the building next to the "Post" building, and a powerful stream of water was directed upon the fire after it had penetrated the "Post" building; in fact, the fire was there put out after it had well started in the "Post" building.

Q. Did you see many chips of granite fall from the building?

A. No, I didn't see anything of that. It seemed to me that the firemen had one great excuse for not working in the last part of the night with vigor. They were not fed all night. To the best of my knowledge and belief, no food was given to the firemen during the night. They began work at half-past seven, and it seemed to me they were left without food until the next morning at seven or eight o'clock.

Q. When you saw the engines playing in the street up against the sides of those buildings, was it more or less hot there than it would have been on the roofs of the buildings against which they were playing?

A. The circumstances were various. As a rule, I should say it was cooler down in the streets than on the roofs, but I saw men expose themselves very much indeed several times in the street where the buildings were on fire on both sides, when it was exceedingly hot in the street; so hot that I couldn't penetrate where these men were working. I saw many times men behave with great gallantry. The heat before Hovey's store was pretty intense. According to Mr. Gardner, there were only two men on the roof.

Q. (By Mr. Russell.) Was there anything else that you noticed?

A. Yes. *Apropos* to this sort of indifference of the firemen, I noticed a great deal of what I should call straggling. I saw firemen at a distance from the real work walking about the street. They seemed to me to be, and I have no doubt they were, firemen who had come in from the country.

Q. (By Mr. Firth.) Did you see any stragglers whom you recognized as Boston firemen?

A. No, I couldn't recognize them, they were all dressed so much alike. I simply saw, over and over again, firemen a long way from the fire, and not doing anything.

Q. Did you notice any plundering by firemen?

A. I did not. I heard a conversation among firemen about plundering. It was to the effect that they had been interfered with by the police for helping themselves; and they thought it was rather hard that the police interfered with them rather than with civilians who were plundering.

Q. (By Mr. Philbrick.) What do you think of the practice of giving away goods on such occasions?

A. I think it is a most pernicious and vicious one. I saw a great deal of plundering, which I was entirely powerless to prevent; and not only plundering boots and shoes out of stores, but I saw carts being driven away from the fire containing goods taken out of stores, followed by men and boys, and the goods taken out from the rear of the carts, in spite of the driver and the man accompanying him. Those were goods on the way to a place of safety, which was a little worse than taking goods which might be burned up.

Q. (By Mr. Russell.) Can you tell who those firemen were who complained that they had been interfered with by the police?

A. I am sorry to say, they were from Cambridge.

Q. (By Mr. Philbrick.) Did you see any lack of force to the streams for want of fuel?

A. Oh, yes; over and over again.

Q. How early?

A. As early as half-past nine. I saw them burning boxes which they had brought out of the stores in Franklin street, and broken up, as early as half-past nine, I supposed for lack of steam. The engine was doing nothing.

Q. Had it been playing before?

A. It had been playing, and was in a position to play; that is, was attached to a hydrant; but the engine was doing nothing, and the men were breaking up boxes at the side of the engine, and were putting the wood into the fire.

Q. (By Mr. COBB.) Do you remember what engine that was?

A. I didn't notice. I afterwards saw other engines, over and over again, out of coal. They seemed to me to whistle for coal. I repeatedly heard them whistle, and not get any, apparently. Of course, I only saw it in passing by. I didn't stand by the engine; I passed by, and saw that condition of things.

Q. (By Mr. FIRTH.) In the cases you now refer to, were the engines throwing water while whistling?

A. I should say not, all of them; some of them were. I saw engines repeatedly which were stopped, whistling for coal; if that was what the whistling meant.

Q. (By Mr. RUSSELL.) To the best of your opinion, how many did you see not working, but whistling?

A. I should say four or five before midnight. I only remember seeing them breaking up boxes for fuel once.

Q. (By Mr. PHILBRICK.) Did you see anything that appeared like a lack of water supply for the engines?

A. No, sir; I saw nothing of that. The supply of water seemed to me to be superb all night along.

Q. Didn't it occur to you that the lack of height in the streams might be due to the fact that the engines expended their power in drawing water from a small hydrant, where it did not flow to them?

A. It did not occur to me. The lack of height in the streams, I supposed to be due to the fact that they were using, as a rule, a very large nozzle, and also to the fact that they did not force the engine to do its utmost; I suppose, because they were afraid of bursting the hose; however, that is mere supposition on my part. I saw, Sunday morning, splendid streams of water played over the top of the building called the City Exchange, on Devonshire street.

Q. Were those streams played from the street?

A. Oh, no, sir. The hose was carried up on the inside, and then a very powerful stream delivered on the roof. I never saw a stream of water thrown over a building on the street, that I know of, during the night; I don't remember seeing any such.

Q. (By Mr. RUSSELL.) Do you think of anything else?

A. No, I don't think of anything else.

Q (By Mr. PHILBRICK.) Did you see any of the results by the explosion of powder?

A. No, I can't say that I did. I saw attempts made to blow up buildings, that were unsuccessful. I cannot say that I saw a successful explosion, one which produced a result in the way of stopping the fire.

Q. Where were the unsuccessful ones that you noticed?

A. There was one at the corner of Milk and Washington streets — the Currier & Trott building. There was another in Kilby street, perhaps half way between State street and Liberty square, on the upper side as you go from Lindall street; that building, I think, was afterwards blown down.

Q. What was the condition of that building?

A. It was well down. It was not on fire when I saw it.

Q. Well shaken down?

A. Well shaken down, yes, sir.

Q. Do you think the fire was checked by the use of powder, so far as you saw it, in any case?

A. I saw so little of the blowing up that I should not feel competent to say anything about that.

Q. (By Mr. FIRTH.) Did you notice the withdrawal of the engines from the neighborhood of Currier & Trott's building, while the preparations for blowing up were being made?

A. No, I did not.

Q. (By Mr. RUSSELL.) Did you see any drunkenness on the part of the firemen?

A. I did, Sunday morning.

Q. Where was that?

A. On Water street and Broad street.

Q. To what extent?

A. Perhaps I saw two or three men, not more, and it struck me as very excusable.

Q. In the case of men who could not get food, and could get liquor?

A. Exactly. I did not blame them at all, as it seemed to me the neglect was on the part of those who did not feed them.

Q. (By Mr. PHILBRICK.) When you first arrived at the fire, did it occur to you that there was a probability of having a great fire?

A. I intended to go home, so little did it seem to me possible that the fire should extend beyond that place; but it occurred to me that I would walk around the water side of the fire, and go up Summer street, and it was then I saw the fire cross Summer street, and it struck me as so extraordinary that I stayed.

(By Mr. FIRTH.) Was not the rapidity with which the fire spread very noticeable to you from the beginning?

A. It was, on that building at the corner of Kingston street, on Church Green; but that it should cross Summer street without resistance, that, I should say, struck me as most astonishing at the time; and the rapid course of the fire along both sides of Otis street was astounding.

Q. (By Mr. PHILBRICK.) Were there many cases of fire passing from one building to another, except from one roof to another?

A. Not in the early part of the fire. I should say, not before half-past nine; but later in the night, on Federal street and Pearl street, I saw buildings burst into flame throughout, apparently, at once. The roof took a little at first, but the buildings were all in a blaze nearly simultaneously.

Q. That was owing to the previous roasting, was it not?

A. That was in consequence of the great roasting. The conducting power of granite is very considerable.

CYRUS A. PAGE, *sworn.*

Q. (By Mr. RUSSELL.) You are a member of the City Council?

A. Yes, sir.

Q. What time did you go to the fire?

A. I should judge it was about half-past eight, as near as I can remember.

Q. What time did you go to the City Hall, if you did go there?

A. I think I went to the City Hall between one and two o'clock, if I remember right.

Q. Who did you see there?

A. I saw the Mayor, Alderman Jenks, General Burt, and Chief Engineer Damrell.

Q. Did you receive any written document from Mr. Damrell?

A. I did.

Q. Have you that here?

A. I have not got it about me.

Q. What was it?

A. It was a permit to blow up buildings and remove goods.

Q. Did you have any talk with the Mayor?

A. Yes, sir; general conversation.

Q, What was the conversation with the Mayor about? The fire?

A. Well, I don't know; general conversation. I don't remember anything in particular. He requested me to send any members of the government I might find around the fire to the City Hall.

Q. How did the Mayor appear? Did he seem self-possessed, or otherwise?

A. Well, quite calm, I should think; a little nervous, of course, but not particularly excited.

Q. How did Mr. Damrell appear?

A. He was considerably excited, I should say.

Q. Did you receive charge of any section of the city?

A. My permit did not designate any.

Q. Did you have any verbal instructions?

A. Yes. They sort of districted us off a little.

Q. What was your district?

A. Mine was Franklin street and Washington street, if I remember right.

Q. You do not mean the whole of Washington street?

A. Oh, no; Franklin, near Washington.

Q. Did anybody tell you to take that district, or did you say you would take it?

A. I guess they asked me. I do not remember whether they asked for a person to take charge there, or requested me to go there. I cannot say about that.

Q. Did you see any explosions in that portion of the city?

A. I should prefer not to answer any questions in regard to explosions.

Q. (By Mr. Cobb.) How far had the fire progressed when you reached the fire ground?

A. I went down Washington, through Bedford to Kingston; and when I got there, it had not crossed Summer street, if I remember right. I did not go to the Summer-street side of the fire until afterwards. I went up into Kingston street, and not having my badge with me, I could not get by. I went down Bedford street into Summer, and then went down Summer on to Broad street, through Pearl, and all round through there.

Q. Did you see the fire cross Summer street at all, right in front of the first building that took fire?

A. I do not know that I saw it cross; but I saw the fire after it crossed.

Q. Did you see anything done to extinguish the fire at that point?

A. I saw steamers there.

Q. Did you see any streams?

A. I did not see any streams of water on the fire there, at all.

Q. Did you see any ladder?

A. I do not remember that I did.

Q. Could you see the side of the building on Otis street from where you stood?

A. No, sir; because I was down Summer street, near Church Green, and I could only see what was done in front.

Q. So that they might have been at work in the rear, and you not noticed it?

A. Oh, yes, sir.

Q. (By Mr. PHILBRICK.) In view of your experience that night in the use of powder, would you, in any similar case, advise the blowing up of buildings?

A. I do not consider myself an expert on that matter, exactly.

Q. Whether, in your judgment, anything was gained, on the whole, by the use of gunpowder that night?

A. I should rather prefer to leave that an open question.

THOMAS HILLS, *sworn.*

Q. (By Mr. RUSSELL.) What is your present position?

A. I am chairman of the Board of Assessors.

Q. Have you prepared any figures in reference to the loss by the fire?

A. I made some on the day of the fire, on Sunday, the tenth of November, which I gave to the editor of the "Boston Journal," for publication on Monday morning, the substantial accuracy of which I have since seen no reason to doubt. I placed the loss then at eighty-five millions of dollars, claiming throughout that it was an over-estimate; and really believing, when I made the figures, that seventy-five millions was nearer the total loss than eighty-five millions.

Q. (By Mr. COBB.) What does that loss consist in?

A. In buildings and in personal property. Perhaps I ought to say, that in making the estimates in the manner I did, I was obliged to take gross amounts. There was no time for details at that time, and I threw everything that was in doubt in my own mind in favor of loss, in order that no person should be able, when they got at the details, to prove that I had underrated it, because I felt that my natural tendency would be, perhaps, to underestimate, or understate. The reasoning I gave is all in print, and is at your service. I would only like to say on this point, that I have since had an opportunity to verify my estimate of the loss in the Fifth Ward, that is, everything south of Milk street, — which I claimed was twelve and a half millions, — by our books, and I find that the exact amount was, $11,991,300. I have had that taken from the books by the clerk of that ward, who is thoroughly conversant with the books, and it is about as much of an over-estimate as I expected.

Q. Have you the number of buildings destroyed?

A. Yes, sir. The same paper will give you, with a very few errors incident to the haste with which the work had to be done, the buildings destroyed, the names of the owners, and the names of the occupants. It was drawn off on Sunday, while the fire was still raging, in the office, and I myself called off some of the figures, and some of the clerks the rest. I have since revised it, and I find an omission of only two buildings, at the northerly end of the fire, where I suppose they were in some doubt whether the buildings had burned or not, when the paper went to press.

Q. (By Mr. RUSSELL.) Does your office specify the value of the buildings, and the value of the land?

A. Yes, sir; the value of the land, as will be seen by the statement I have made, was, as nearly as may be, two-thirds of the whole estates. The value of the buildings, fine as they were, was only one-third. These estimates were made because at that time the figures were getting to be enormous; people talked about them as though they did not know what figures meant. The loss was stated as high as one hundred and fifty millions, and even two hundred millions. I thought such figures as these might have a tendency to stop that exaggeration; and although I made no mention of that element, it was one of the reasons which induced me to say that when I put it at eighty-five millions, I considered that estimate as something which could not be gone beyond.

Q. (By Mr. COBB.) What should you state to-day, as the probable loss?

A. Seventy-five millions.

Q (By Mr. RUSSELL.) You have allowed for salvage?

A. Yes, sir; two millions.

Q. (By Mr. COBB.) Have you thought sufficiently on the subject to be able to state what would be the difference in the value of the land to-day, as compared with the value it had before the fire?

A. Not materially changed, I should say. The sales made since the fire are of such a character that it leads me to say that our valuation of it was a good one, and has been sustained. Take, for instance, the sale in Pearl street, where the land with the old material on the ground, which was thrown in, was sold for thirteen dollars a foot. Our valuation was twelve dollars a foot. There has been a sale of land in Devonshire street since, which we valued at sixteen dollars a foot; Mr. Gardner Brewer pays a little over nineteen dollars a foot. A piece of land has been sold in Summer street, within a day or two, for which the parties realized seventeen dollars a foot; our valuation was eleven dollars.

Q. Whereabouts was that?

A. That was opposite Church Green.

Q. (By Mr. RUSSELL.) Have you the valuation of the real estate — the land?

A. No, sir; I have not got that here, but it is just double the value of the buildings. I tested that in two or three ways, and found the value of the buildings was one third of the value of the estate. Taking these very figures, twelve and a half millions in Ward 5, and one million, six hundred thousand dollars in Ward 4, — that is, north of Milk street, — double that amount, and you will get as nearly as may be the value of the land. Of course the higher the price of the land, the larger proportion the land would bear to the buildings. It costs almost as much to put up good buildings on land worth eight dollars a foot as it does in places where land is worth twenty dollars a foot. If you take twelve dollars a foot as an average price for the whole territory, I should not think you would go far out of the way. The cost of the buildings, of course, varies; still I should say, that would not be very far out of the way for the cost of the buildings at the time they were erected. They could not be erected now for that, or anything like it. The amount insured is a pretty fair test. An article was published in the "Daily Advertiser," of Nov. 21st, giving a statement of the amount of insurance on the property. I roughly cast up the amount, and found it to be fifty-two millions; and consequently I was not at all surprised when I found in the "Herald," of December 8, that they placed the entire loss by the Insurance Companies at $52,076,600; and it seems to me, in the proportion at which property is usually insured, that is another very strong indication that seventy-five millions is as nearly as may be the amount of loss. There is one other item, — the item of wool. Mr. George William Bond has made a very careful estimate, and I got this document from him within a day or two. He puts the loss of wool at four and a half millions; but if we had credited the accounts that were given of the immense loss in that line a few days after the fire, two or three firms would have lost more money on wool than the total loss as there represented. I make the number of buildings destroyed 547; that might be varied as people would count, but not much. One man might call two estates what another would call one, and then, where the fire ended, one man would call a partially burnt building a destroyed estate, and another would say, "No, that was not destroyed."

Q. (By Mr. Philbrick.) In the case of a block of buildings built and owned by one party, how do you estimate it?

A. I take them as separate estates.

Q. Each number?

A. Not each number, because, you know, some of those mercantile firms will have two or three numbers to one estate, perhaps not more than twenty feet wide, but where there are party-walls, we call each one a separate estate. Of those five hundred and forty-seven buildings burned, there were two churches, sixty-eight dwelling and lodging-houses, and four hundred and seventy places devoted solely to business.

Q. (By Mr. Firth.) Did you know how many persons were in those dwelling-houses?

A. That could have been obtained, but we didn't go into that. They were pretty thick for the number of dwelling-houses. The dwelling-houses were in South, Summer, Bedford, Kingston, and Purchase streets, and a few scattered around in the places on Fort Hill, where the occupants were very numerous. I think twenty-eight out of the sixty-eight were on Purchase street.

Q. How was the south side of Oliver street; were there any dwelling, houses left there?

A. They had all been taken away. Fortunately, Fort Hill had been taken down, and that saved property enough to cover all the expense of its removal. I make out by our books that about nine hundred and eighty-five business firms, that we assessed, were dispossessed of their localities. A young gentleman, who was formerly connected with our office, went over the books, as a matter of curiosity, and he made nine hundred and ninety-nine.

Q. (By Mr. PHILBRICK.) That is about double the number of stores?

A. Yes, sir; but many places had four or five tenants. That number would not include very many other persons who did business there; for instance, the agents of corporations, express offices, and out-of-town people who paid taxes elsewhere, and not here. It includes only those that we assessed. Very many of the shoe and leather people have nothing but samples, and yet do a very large business, but they are not assessed by us. On the question of loss, Mr. E. H. Derby prepared an article, which was published in the "Advertiser." I had some conversation with him about it, and found that he arrived at the same figures which I believe in, by a different method. His method was, to take the taxes of the United States upon sales, which last year shows sales to the amount of nine hundred millions. He estimates that it is a thousand millions to-day, and from that he estimates the amount of stock on hand for three months, and then the proportion in the burnt district, and he comes to the same conclusion.

Q. (By Mr. FIRTH.) Did he come to that conclusion before these data had been published?

A. I think he did, because I made my figures in rough, on Sunday, before I left the office, and took them home, and that night put them in shape, in pencil, and the next morning took my pencil draft from the desk and wrote it in ink for the paper. I had just finished when Mr. Derby came in, and asked me what I thought of the loss. He expressed his views, which I heard with some interest, and then handed him my paper, and I remember that he stood for ten minutes trying to get me to take off that ten millions, so that he and I would come together. But my purpose was to make an over-estimate, and claim it as an over-estimate, for I did not want to be ciphered down by anybody.

The following note was received and read from the City Surveyor: —

BOSTON, Dec. 12, 1872.

HON. THOMAS RUSSELL, *Chairman of Fire Commission:*—

SIR. — By approximate estimate, the Burnt District (by fire of Nov. 9th and 10th, 1872) contains sixty-five acres. This includes the *whole area* within the fire limits.

Very respectfully,

THOMAS W. DAVIS, *City Surveyor.*

WILLIAM L. BURT, *sworn.*

Q. (By Mr. Russell.) You are the Postmaster of Boston?
A. Yes, sir.
Q. At what time did you go to the fire?
A. As soon as the alarm was struck. I was then at the South end, and went directly, as quick as a car would carry me, down to the fire, and arrived there before it had got beyond the two adjoining buildings.
Q. Did you see it cross Summer street to Otis?
A. Yes, sir; I saw it just as it was crossing the other side from the corner of Kingston street.
Q. How did it cross Summer street to Otis? Where did it take on the Otis-street side?
A. It caught in the window of the building on the corner of Otis towards Washington, on the ornamentation of the frieze of the high window. I found the street crowded, and went round and came down on the Summer-street side, in order to see. The wind was driving the smoke and fire the other way. I went down on the High-street side, and then came round up the other side, so I did not see at that precise point how it crossed. I saw it where it had taken, where it was burning.
Q. Did you notice what means were taken to prevent its crossing?
A. I did not. The department were gathered in stronger force, though, to the leeward of the fire, than on the other side, at that time. It was very obvious that they were stronger on the leeward side than they were on the Summer-street side. At first, all the engines as they came, — the lighter engines of the regular service here, — were put in that direction. The reserve, the old engines, — there were four of them, I think, — were soon on the ground, within an hour and a half, and they were placed in very strong force in the direction in which the fire was working. My impression is, that as the wind was carrying the fire, they did in the first instance what any one would do: put the strength of the department in that direction.
Q. Which way was it carried; straight down Summer street?
A. No, sir; the wind was carrying it at an angle. As it took in the corner, the wind carried it almost in an angle from the old Church Green block, right across Bedford street, and towards Lincoln street. The wind was very positive, and the effect was obvious. Until I got around to the corner of Devonshire street, I did not feel very much concerned in regard to the spread of the fire in that direction, as I did the other way. The fire beat up to the windward faster in the course of an hour, than at any fire I ever saw.
Q. Did you notice anything that you think the Commission ought to hear, until the gunpowder period of the fire?
A. Yes, sir. Knowing exactly where the lookout is on the City Hall, and where the fire was, it seems to me a miracle that it was not seen from the lookout before the alarm was given from the box. If you go to the top of City Hall, you can look down on the corner where that building stood; there is nothing intervening.

After the fire crossed Summer street, it spread in every direction, crossing Otis street and attacking the Beebe block in the upper stories. All those buildings were on fire very quick, so that the firemen were driven back; then the impression on my mind was this, that there were no means of reaching those buildings to operate with the Fire Department satisfactorily. That the fire was beyond our control was just as evident at ten o'clock that night as it was the next morning. You would see buildings take fire above, and the upper stories would be all consumed before any fire was apparent in the lower story. For instance, Beebe's block (that is as good an illustration as you could have) was burned out above, the roof had fallen in, and one could look directly through to the sky, when the lower stories were entirely untouched, down to the ground; and in many cases, the *débris* falling from the roofs to the sidewalk kindled a second fire before the stores had burned down through from above.

One suggestion in regard to means of reaching these high buildings. The firemen will not go into such places. Take the Beebe block, bounded by Otis and Devonshire streets. It was very soon evident that any men who should go on to those roofs would be driven back from roof to roof, and finally, at the end of the block, there would be no escape for them. Our ladders were not long enough to reach the roofs; the fires got under the Mansards, and they would burn first. It was evident there would be no means of escape. That was the terrible peril to which firemen would be exposed who should go on to such buildings without any preparation made for their rescue finally, if they should be driven back over the block, as they would be in every case. There was no stand made against the fire in this direction. There were points where the firemen attempted to control it, but there was no concerted stand made in two or three streets at once, so that the firemen in one street would feel that they would be assisted by those in the adjoining streets. The fire would soon flank them, and they were driven back hour by hour all night. There was no systematic attempt made to reinforce the men who were fighting the fire on Summer street by those in Franklin street. There was a great depth of buildings between Summer and Franklin, and there were places where it was possible, it seemed to me, to control it; in the rear of the Mercantile Building, for instance. But I saw no where any any such co-operation as would give the firemen the confidence needed at such a time.

Another thing I noticed. The engines which came in from out-of-town located themselves without much direction or pre-arrangement. The reinforcements which came in to take part in the battle (for it really was a battle with fire) should have been located with precise reference to what it was proposed to do, with reference to some plan. The fire was then getting so large that it required a systematic defence, a systematic resistance, and no such defence appeared to be made. These things impressed themselves upon my mind strongly, when I saw how the fire was working this way. It told its whole lesson in an hour. It was as obvious what we ought to do in one hour from the time the fire started, as it was towards morning.

Q. At what time did you go to the City Hall?

A. The first time, before twelve o'clock.

Q. What took place there?

A. I went there four or five times. The first time I went to the City Hall, I went in at the rear entrance and went up stairs. I went there with this view, to have the Mayor and city authorities, as many as could be found, meet at the City Hall. I supposed as soon as people saw the condition of things, they would all look for some head-quarters, because there must be some place where everybody who was doing anything that night could report for instructions, orders and co-operation. I supposed that very early they would begin to gather there. I could find no one who could give me any account of anybody, except that I was told that Capt. Damrell had been there only a little while before, and had gone back to the fire. The clerk of the Chief of Police was at the telegraph in Police Station No. 2, adjoining the City Hall. I asked the man in charge of the City Hall, at the lower door, to light it up. He said he would like to do so, if he had authority to do it. I told him I would be very glad to take the responsibility; that they did not know the danger the city was in, and asked him to light up the Aldermen's room and the Mayor's room, particularly, and if any question was asked, whatever the result was, I would be personally responsible, so far as any citizen could be. He hesitated, and finally asked me to go into the 2d Police Station and see the clerk of the Chief of Police, as I understood him. I went there and found some of the officers of the station. I found they were bringing in men with little packages of goods, whom they appeared to be arresting for stealing. That was before twelve o'clock. I urged them to stop that at once, and organize a system to take care of the goods; that the amount that would be stolen in that way would be trifling; that nine men out of ten would not steal at such a time, but all could be relied upon, if organized, to assist in getting the goods out of the stores and taking them to a place of safety. I went to the fire and returned to the City Hall three or four times, in great anxiety. I don't think I ever suffered more in two hours, mentally, than I did that night from before twelve o'clock until half-past one. I urged them again and again to light the City Hall, and they promised that it should be done, but it was not done, and there was no light in the building, whatever else may have been done to call the people in, until nearly two o'clock.

Q. What took place then?

A. I came again to the City Hall, and seeing lights above, I hurried to the door. As I came to the door, this same watchman came to me and said, "The Mayor is up stairs now; he has just come in, and Capt. Damrell has gone in with him." I hurried up stairs and found ten or twelve people there, among whom was Capt. Damrell and four five of the Aldermen, whose countenances I recollected. The impression was made on my mind that we had men there who would be recognized wherever they were seen as men in authority in the city.

Q. What conversation did you have with the Mayor and Chief?

A. This conversation occurred. The Mayor said: "We are here; what do you want?" I told them that I had urged sending for them, because it seemed to me that the fire was destined to sweep the whole city, unless there was some organized resistance, and it seemed to me that the time had come when we should accomplish nothing, unless we blew up buildings; that the firemen were falling back before the fire, they were losing confidence, and that some energetic action was required. The Mayor said: "I have no authority in the matter; that is in the control of Capt. Damrell by law." I replied, "Mr. Mayor, before to-morrow morning, if you look out of that window (if the City Hall is saved, which I doubt, unless there is something done), you will see the shipping in the harbor."

Said he, "Would you take the responsibility of blowing up buildings?" I said if I had the authority, as he had it, I certainly would. He said I was mistaken; he had not the authority; that by law it was vested in the Chief Engineer and the Assistant Engineers of the Fire Department. I told him it was an exigency that required immediate action; the people would not hold us blameless (using that expression), if we allowed this city to burn. I then told him that I had already commenced packing my mails at the Post Office; that the fire would shortly come to State street; that if we could not stop it in a broad street like Franklin, we could not hope to stop it in narrow streets like Water and Lindall, and that it seemed to me the peril was imminent for the Post Office, the Sub-Treasury, and all the banks. On that, Capt. Damrell said, "I have determined to use powder, although it is against my judgment. I think the experience of Chicago is against it." The Mayor said, in connection with that, "Yes, sir, and as we are situated, the risk to lives will be very great." I replied to Capt. Damrell, that it was absolutely necessary, in my judgment, to use powder, and in answer to the suggestion of the Mayor, I said, "To-morrow morning will see ten men killed in fighting this fire with water, to one killed in fighting it with powder." This conversation was all very hurried, and what they said to me was not in the way of fault-finding, but of suggestions as to what was their duty as men in responsible positions. I then said to them, that we had all the United States Government property in our custody, as well as that of the city and citizens, and if no one else was to take the responsibility, certainly we must do something; it would be disgraceful to have this city burn down, as it had been burning for the past four hours, or since nine o'clock. Then the Mayor turned and asked if I was willing to take the responsibility of using powder, if I had the authority. I told him I was. He said, "I will give you the authority, so far as I have it." I told him I did not care where it came from; I wanted it in proper form, and I should certainly take the responsibility. He said, "Capt. Damrell alone can give that authority. I said, "I want it in writing, and when I have it, I will advise with him how it ought to be used." The Mayor then asked Capt. Damrell to come to his desk, and the Captain sat down and wrote such authority as would protect me in doing what I proposed to do. After he had done this I asked for eight or ten citizens to take charge of each of the streets around the fire. I said, "Let each of these men go to each street, with two policemen." Then Capt. Damrell said, "Who will volunteer?" I turned to two gentlemen whom I saw there, whom I knew, and called upon them to aid us. One was the chairman of the Water Board, and we made out six or seven in all, and each man went with two policemen, and every street and place was designated. Capt. Damrell said he would take care personally of the district from Franklin street around towards the south part of the city.

Q. (By Mr. Philbrick.) Did Capt. Damrell allot the other districts to the several men?

A. No, sir; I allotted them. There was little said but what I said at this meeting. I requested that an order should be given to the police to open the gates of the Common, to form lines to the burning district, and pass the goods from the western section of the fire to the Common, and from the easterly section to the open ground on Fort Hill. There was no place where goods could be saved except on the Common on the one side, and Fort Hill on the other. They asked if I thought the fire would spread in the direction of Fort Hill. I told them that it was already burning on the Fort Hill district, and the people were piling up goods in the streets in that direction, which would obstruct the firemen, and the goods would inevitably be destroyed. I said, "You can make nine out of ten of the men in the crowds of service in helping to remove goods to those places and watching them, and we will have them all organized into a system in half an hour." The gentlemen to have charge of each street were named, and the places where they were to go designated. I remained in the hall until I saw four or five of them go out, each with two policemen, and these instructions. We were told there was powder sufficient for all purposes; that the powder-boat had come round to the end of Central wharf, or City wharf, and the powder would be delivered to us in the streets as soon as we got there, and that fuse had been provided. The suggestion was made, if we got short of powder we should go down to Reed's gun-shop and get powder there. I told them it would not do. It seemed to increase the danger, in the disordered state of the city, for mere citizens to break into a store, distant from the fire, to procure powder; but that the police should go to the store, find out what powder there was there, and have it taken out properly, if we had to resort to that.

I went down to my district with two policemen. I told them that I would take charge on Devonshire street and Federal street; that I would not be further off than the old Post-Office or new Post-Office building. I took a paper and marked out the line that we must try to save on Washington street; put the engines in there, take the line of the Old South, the new Post-Office building, and the old Post Office, and fight the fire on that line, and not fall back, no matter what it cost; not to blow up any buildings west of Washington street until we had met together in City Hall, and to report there, if there was any emergency or special disaster, and let each other know what they were doing. I think, decidedly, that the position which was then taken helped us to hold that line. The first difficulty we encountered was, that the powder furnished us was used up immediately. There was but little of it.

Q. What amount of powder did you have first?

A. We had less than four hundred pounds, all told, in the kegs that were brought; twenty-five pound kegs and some small canisters. We used that up at once. Before leaving the Mayor's room at City Hall, I said to the Mayor and Capt. Damrell, "I shall go down to Winthrop square, or as near as I can get to it, and blow up the entire block between Federal and Devonshire, running back to the new Post Office. If we can do that, I think we can keep the fire under control in that direction." The first plan was to blow up the buildings on the south side of Franklin street, below Devonshire, to prevent the fire from crossing Franklin street.

Q. (By Mr. PHILBRICK.) Had not the fire crossed from Devonshire to Federal street at midnight?

A. No, sir; it had not at Franklin street, at twelve o'clock. What I said was, if we had got to work an hour earlier, the fire could have been held from crossing Franklin street. It crossed over and came on to the Gardner Brewer estate, the old theatre estate on the opposite corner, and from there to the other side of Franklin square, going across Devonshire street into the Revere-Bank building.

Q. What was the first use you saw made of powder?

A. In the blocks of stores between Devonshire and Federal streets. We used it between Franklin and Milk streets, lightly, at first, but we used it quite severely afterwards. I will say here, that I cannot give you localities; I will give them to you generally, and in the confusion it would be impossible for me to locate particular stores and numbers on the streets. I will say this, that there was no building blown up that night for which I would have given an ordinary straw hat, at the time we did it, no matter how much the building might have cost. There was some very severe blowing up in the buildings below Morton place, and there were strong hopes that we were going to keep the fire back there. All that prevented it from crossing Milk street and attacking the Old South church estates was blowing up the buildings in the rear, east of Morton place. It was held back until the buildings were sufficiently burned out, so that when the walls fell, the flames did not cross the street.

Q. Where did that powder come from?

A. That night, before I left the hall, I asked the Mayor to have the militia called out; to send to Gen. Cunningham's house, in Lynde street, and have him order the militia out instantly, get them out before morning, and to send to the Navy Yard for powder, in which I would join him, and also for Marines, which we should have to protect the government property. I knew we could get them at once. All these things were suggested at City Hall before we left, and the first powder that we used that was of any service came from the Navy Yard. The first I knew of its arrival, a man with a red cap on came up to me on Devonshire street, and said, "We have the powder here."—"Where is it?"—"Back here in Devonshire street." I went with him to the place, and found a one-horse load of powder, covered with blankets. I said, "Where is your driver?" At that time, engines were working on Devonshire street, and throwing their burning cinders in every direction. I told him the powder was wanted up in front. He said his driver had run off and left it. I told him to get on the wagon and take his flag, and I took his horse and led him by the engines. The blankets were covered with sparks, but we got the wagon up to the front, and then we went behind the wagon, shook the sparks off of the blankets, and took first a one hnudred pound keg and carried it into a building; that was the first hundred-pound package that was used. A number of men came up as soon as the first flurry was over, to assist, and we had some seven or eight men who were exceedingly efficient, taking every risk that men could on such an occasion. We emptied that load and used it south of Milk street. In fact, I satisfied myself that we should be able to stop the fire on the line laid down, as far as the new Post-Office building, and save that building. We were then between Milk and Franklin streets, towards the head of Milk.

Q. (By Mr. Russell.) Did this powder-man want a receipt?

A. Yes, sir; when these other men came up, which they did immediately, he turned round to me, and, touching his hat in military style, said, "General, now I shall want my receipt for this." That man went twice to Charlestown and brought us two loads. I then sent the wagon that goes with the fire brigade to Chelsea for a load from there. I kept a little run of what we used, and my impression is that we burnt between three and four tons that night, and I had five tons in the street, when we stopped the next morning. I had two tons in North Market street, a ton and a half in Dock square, and a ton on State street. In the doorways on the north side of State street, kegs of powder had been placed ready for use if the emergency required.

Q. (By Mr. PHILBRICK.) Where did the bulk of the powder come from?

A. I think Commodore Parrott arranged, after we sent to the Navy Yard for the first load, to have it from Chelsea. Some came from the powder-boat, and also some from the forts.

Q. Did you get it as fast as you wanted it?

A. Yes, sir; but not till about four o'clock. I think we did wrong in stopping the use of it when we did; we could have prevented the fire from going to Liberty square. It must not be forgotten that the buildings between Milk, Water and Lindall streets, south of Congress, were all old-fashioned, plain granite buildings, with ordinary small windows, and with partitions carried through to the roofs. These burned one by one, none of them catching by the roofs, as in the case of the Mansards, and for three hours the fire burned through these streets, finally reaching and crossing Liberty square. I think we could have saved two hours of that burning with powder. I would have gone in and blown out some of the stores in these blocks.

Q. (By Mr. COBB.) Why did you not do it?

A. The controversy with Alderman Woolley caused a revocation of the order and we were stopped.

What we did was this: When it became evident that we were first getting the fire under some control, we had blown up a number of buildings, one of which was near the new Post Office, on the easterly side. It was the merest chance in the world that the fire crossed into Simmons's block, on the north side of Water street. Five minutes would have enabled us to save that, and it was the merest chance that the "Post" building was saved. It burned around the corner, and into the window, and had got fairly started, but by going into the new Post-Office building, and working from the inside of the "Post" building itself, it was saved. This is the only wooden Mansard that was thoroughly on fire and yet was saved, in the city; and it could not have been done but for the protection of the fire-proof building, the new Post Office, in its front. The charge of powder that was put in the building below the new Post Office was not heavy enough; the building was slight in its construction, and the explosion raised it and pitched it forward into a pile; the firemen came up and had three streams there instantly; in fact, the firemen stood just round the corner as the fuse was burning; they did not fall back, and had it not been for the gas that came up and set the whole pile on fire, and drove the firemen back, we should have stopped it there, and it would not have crossed to Simmons's block. The gas was the greatest danger and trouble we had that night.

Q. (By Mr. PHILBRICK.) Did you shut off the gas supply?

A. No, sir, we could not find the gas company's men. We sent to the gas office on West street, and I went once myself, but no officer could be found connected with the gas company that night, from the time the fire broke out until it was broad daylight. I could not find a man who knew anything about the street pipes or knew where any one could be found who did know. The office in West street is usually kept open all night. Mr. Greenough is a very efficient man, and how it happened that no one who had control of the pipes in the street could be found that night, I cannot understand. There was never such a combination of misfortunes anywhere as there was during that night and until nearly ten o'clock the next morning.

Q. Won't you describe how the gas worked?

A. We blew up one building so that the firemen could come up and control it. The roof fell in, and the whole came down, so that we were in shape to control it. The firemen got to work, and there came a second explosion that raised the whole of the *débris;* fire shot out through it in every direction, and in five minutes from that time it was one mass of flame; and the building burned up with a stream of gas as large as my arm, pouring out close to the sidewalk into the ruins, until a space twice the length of this room was filled with the glare of gas. No man could do anything under such circumstances. This experience was repeated half-a-dozen times. If we could have got at the mains and shut off the gas, that difficulty would have been avoided, but this was the situation. Very few of the stores along the street there were opened by the men who occupied them; the doors were broken in, in most cases, nobody belonging to the stores being there. The occupants were not there in one case out of ten, and when we did find a man who belonged to the store, he had no more idea where the gas or water pipes were than the man in the moon. Some of them occupied the upper part of the building, and some the lower, and where they occupied the whole warehouse, they could not tell where the gas could be shut off. Take one instance, that of Wright & Potter's large printing establishment. The question was asked on the ground, where we could cut off the gas supply, and whether it all came into the same meter; and the answer was, that they had two or three meters, and they did not know where it could be cut off. In hardly any instance did we succeed in getting the gas cut off. Another difficulty in cutting off the gas was, that people were relying upon it to a certain extent, and that was continued until four o'clock in the morning. It finally got so, through the loss of gas by the open pipes in the ruins, that the supply was exhausted. I found in one instance where we blew a building down to the basement on Lindall street, the explosion had this effect upon the meter; it evidently drove the meter in forcing a wave of gas through the main pipe, and every gas burner went out down State street and in all the buildings; it had got sufficiently weak for that. It got so finally in the Post Office, that when we were about to blow up a building, the clerks prepared matches to relight. We lighted up the Post Office several times after the gas had been extinguished by these explosions.

Q. (By Mr. Russell.) Is not that a serious drawback to the use of gunpowder?

A. Yes, sir. It is not the destruction of the building, or the danger of fire getting into it; it is just exactly that. It is obvious that the city needs some way of cutting off the gas at the sidewalk, and we must be able to shut off a whole district. There were secondary explosions all over the burnt district that night, and the heat of the gas was intense;

there was enough oxygen combined with it to make it terribly hot. I saw, in the most intense part of the fire, huge bodies of gas, you might say twenty-five feet in diameter — dark, opaque masses, combined with the gases from the piles of burning merchandise — rise two hundred feet in the air and explode, shooting out large lines of flame, fifty or sixty feet in every direction, with an explosion that was as marked as the explosion of a bomb. That occurred half-a-dozen times. Where a building had been blown up, so that it fell in ruins, these streams of gas would go up to an immense height and explode, so that you could see the flame, I presume, fifty or sixty miles.

I knew that we had mails due that night, one at ten o'clock, from the north, and another about half-past eleven o'clock, from New York and the west; and about eleven o'clock I sent word to the Boston and Albany depot to have their mail held at the depot, and for the mail wagons to come to the Post Office and assist in moving the mails. The man who came on the wagon told me that the Engineer on the train on the Boston and Albany railroad said, that when they crossed the summit at Charlton, he saw the light distinctly, and soon began to see the reflection on the sky. That must be sixty or seventy miles from the city. He told me that this Engineer said, when they came under the railroad bridge at Albany street, it seemed as though they were running directly into the flames. They were so high and so immense, that it looked almost like running the train into the fire; and many passengers jumped from the cars and left the train before it reached the station.

Q. (By Mr. Russell.) What was the effect of the new Post-Office building in stopping the flames?

A. The greatest effect was this — it was perfectly reliable as a standpoint; it was like a fortification; the engines could fall back there, knowing that they could stay there and would not have to move. Everything about the building was reliable, and there was a crowd on top of the building all night. I directed the Engineers to permit no water to be thrown upon it, and the water was kept off of it; and, although the stagings finally burned, they did not communicate fire even to the lumber inside. Everybody looked upon that as a sort of place of refuge. The line of defence marked out proved just as reliable in fact as it did in theory when we left City Hall.

(By Mr. Philbrick.) What was the best way of placing that powder, in order to do the greatest execution, in the hurried way you were obliged to use it?

A. It was not so hurried a thing, with the fire burning a whole day. The question is, what amount of work can men do in twelve hours? There was no danger of the powder exploding prematurely; not a spoonful burned any quicker than we intended it should. There was not half the danger that people supposed attending it. Take your powder, as many kegs as you need, and put them together; open one of them — one is all you want — and put in your fuse; and if you have anything to confine it, use it. In every instance, we told the men to put on plank, or timber, if they could get them. In one instance, in Lindall street, we had two joists, set upright over the kegs in such a way as to hold them firmly. When that powder went off, it blew a granite column, which was three and a half feet square, clear across the street, and made a clean sweep of the building. In one instance, the powder was placed under an arch, in the wall where the flue came down. In that instance, it carried the wall up, raising it four stories, to the roof. Get anything you can to brace it down, in order to get the full effect of the first explosion; that is what you want; the kegs will take care of themselves.

Q. Will it communicate without loss of time from one keg to another?

A. Instantly; there is no question about that; every keg opened is a loss of power. The powder will take care of itself a great deal better than you can take care of it. There is no such thing as hearing two kegs explode separately inside of a building; when the explosion comes it is instantaneous for all of them. All that is required for the use of powder, and using it efficiently, is that it shall be put in the right place. There is where a mistake was made opposite the Old South Church. Persons came to me three times and desired to blow up the Old South Church. I told them, "There is no necessity for it; we can stop the fire there." Finally, they did get some small packages in the building opposite the Old South on Milk street. This was a mistake. They put that powder on the back side, towards the rear wall; it should have been placed in front, and any bearing they got should have been on the front, not the rear wall. That would have thrown the building out into the street. Some of the men understood that very well. If the explosion at the head of Milk street had been managed in that way, it would not have blown out the windows merely, but when the explosion took place, it would have blown down the walls if they had been two feet thick. As it was, nearly all the effect of the explosion was upon the partition wall of the adjoining building. I told the men repeatedly not to use less than four or five hundred pounds. It was said by some that one hundred and fifty pounds was enough. After the experience we had that night, I should now say, put in six hundred pounds of powder, shore it up, and raise the building from cellar to roof. The firemen should be ready and right upon the ground to co-operate. The fuses used were in many cases altogether too long; some of them would burn eight or ten minutes. Thirty seconds was sometimes long enough, and we used some that only burned that time. If the firemen stood by and saw the effect of the powder, they soon discovered that the danger was very small indeed, and that the explosion opened the way for them to do their work. There was not an instance where there was anything thrown out of a building by the explosion to injure any one. The explosion of powder lying on the ground is ten times as dangerous as in one of those buildings. They put two or three hundred pounds into a building not far from the Post Office, and put in a ten-minute fuse. They were moving one of the steam engines, and wanted to get it out of the way. I went round into the Post Office, went up into my room, within three hundred feet of where the explosion was to take place, and said to my clerks, "We must get out of the way, for when the explosion comes, it will throw us all down." I thought we had about seven minutes to work, but the explosion came before we got down stairs, and it blew some of the men several feet, and laid us all flat. It blew all the windows out, the heavy doors on that side were shut, the large window inside was blown out, and up in the room where we had just stood, there was not a piece of glass left in the windows as big as my three fingers.

It is a sort of cushion of air, that carries everything along with it, and if there is anything near where the powder is exploded that can be moved, it will be carried with great force; but an explosion in an open room above will not carry anything. There was powder used in the Sub-Treasury building. There was a building all on fire, with an iron roof; it was a perfect oven of flame; the girders were two feet in diameter, of wrought iron trusses, and the pressure of the roof was crowding the walls out, and it was evident that there must be some relief. The only thing that saved the Sub-Treasury was a charge of powder, the explosion of which doubled the roof up. Some of those large iron girders that twenty men could not have carried out, as they struck the floor curled up, making two turns as they came down. The powder was put close under the eaves, and took the entire corner out. The roof over the Sub-Treasury was of iron and all girded together; the powder was used to blow the wall over, so that the roof would begin to fall; it fell over the corner and came down into the building; the other portion of the roof stands to-day.

Q. (By Mr. Firth.) Did you see the fire engines cease to play at any time?

A. Yes, sir; for two hours we were short of water. We could not get water enough to play above the second story. Our whole system of pipes is radically wrong. I don't know who is to blame. There was not sufficient supply of water in Milk, Federal and Congress streets, and all that region, for two hours. We tried the engines singly, and for two hours' time we could not get more than fifteen minutes' play before the water was gone. I don't know anything more about it now than I did that night, but such was the result. Some engines stopped to give others water; if it became a matter of necessity to get a stream to any height, we could not get it.

Q. Did you see any of them stop for want of fuel?

A. We got out of fuel very early. I don't think any of them actually stopped. By the way, those old reserve engines that night did just as much service, and I think more, as the light engines. If we had had another grade of heavier engines, they would have been what was needed; but the reserve engines worked splendidly; none of them failed. I had supposed they were out of repair, and expected every minute they would fail us, where we were relying upon them, but they did not. Some of them worked three or four hours without stopping. An old rotary engine, which would have failed if anything did, was working three hours continuously.

Q. (By Mr. Russell.) How many are there of those reserve engines?

A. Five or six in all, I think. But we were out of water along our streets, the hydrants were not large enough, and when so many engines came to draw from them, it exhausted the water. When they had two pipes, one would be cut off, and then the water would fail utterly and the engine stop playing. There were two hours when the fire was driving us five or six hundred feet an hour. It was terrible.

Another thing I noticed which caused much trouble was this: the moment we took the hose up to any height, it would burst; there is no hose in this city that would stand being carried to the top of a building one hundred feet high, with the steam engines that we have; you may rely upon that. The experiment was tried, and I think it is so. I would have run hose to the top of the new Post-Office building, if I had not been perfectly satisfied that the water could not be carried there. One of the best engines around the new Post Office was the Watertown Arsenal engine; that was worked by regularly enlisted men. They did just as my men did. When I told them to go, they went; when I told them to stay, they stayed; they relied on somebody else to take care of the risk and the danger; they would do what they were ordered to do, and felt that their chances were better in that way than in any other. This engine followed on the line of the fire, falling back when they were compelled to do so. The men went into every building they were asked to go into, and took their hose with them, but it burst once or twice. They went into the Simmons's block to see if they could not do something to control the fire opposite, but their hose burst, so that a length had to be taken out, and they came out of the building just before the upper part of the wall fell in.

Q. (By Mr. Cobb.) If there had been an abundant supply of water, what difference would it have made, in your judgment, in fighting that fire?

A If the supply of water had been ample, it would have obviated one great difficulty; but whether the fire could have been controlled at that time, even with the water, is doubtful. The want of water demoralized the firemen.

Q. (By Mr. Philbrick.) When did you first observe a want of water?

A. I observed a want of water before twelve o'clock, and from one to three it was very marked, and I do not know but still later.

Q. (By Mr. Russell.) Did you observe it earlier in Summer street?

A. No, sir.

Q. (By Mr. Cobb.) You didn't answer my question whether there were not some causes operating which were beyond control, even if there had been plenty of water.

A. I confess I don't see how we could have got that fire under any control, unless we could have placed the firemen on the roofs, and have them in a shape to fight the fire from above, and do it by combination. Here were four blocks on fire, with the streets behind them, all burning — neither you nor I would ask the firemen to form a line of defence in the middle of one burning block. You have got to do it with all the blocks and in all the streets. At one time, I seriously thought of going into the attics of the line of buildings, from the Revere Bank, back, and blowing the Mansards off. It seemed the best thing to do, and if we had had the powder, it would have been tried. We could not have been sure, however, that the water would not fail us, for it so happened that very soon after, we could not get the water into the second-story windows. If we could not get the water so that the men could reach the upper stories of the buildings, it would have been impossible to keep the fire from crossing the street.

It is said that the fire spreads and extends by the blowing out of windows. That is an utter fallacy. There was no communication of fire by any such process. It would seem, at first, that there would be that danger; but the more buildings we blew up, the better they could be reached.

Q. Was not the fire communicated nine times out of ten from roof to roof?

A. Yes, sir, and under the roofs. I would to-day rather take my chances of stopping a fire after blowing off the Mansards, than with those roofs on. I think if we had blown off the entire roof of the Revere-Bank building, just as we were there, we could have done more in stopping the fire and holding it, than we did do. The gas did not trouble us at all in any building where we blew it up in the second story. Blowing off the roofs would have given us a very good place to operate.

Q. (By Mr. Cobb.) Did I understand you to say, that it would have been a very good thing if there had been some means of escape from the roofs?

A. Every block in this city should have, from the second story, a fire-escape running to the roof, so placed as not to obstruct air or light. In such a fire as that, the only way you can get the firemen to take the risk of going on the roofs of large buildings, one hundred and fifty feet or so in depth, some of them more and some less, and of varying heights, as they are, is by providing some means of retreat. I would have gone up myself with the men, if I had known that there was means of escape. We require communication with a base. You must not ask men to go where you cannot control them with an order or relieve them in an emergency. Take the Cathedral block, — when the fire was crossing Devonshire street, I would not have dared to put men on the roof of that block, unless there were means of escape. It would have been perfectly foolhardy to have done it.

Q. (By Mr. Russell.) Do you blame the firemen for not going there?

A. They gave us, in the order from the City Hall, the control of the firemen where we were, and they did not refuse in a single instance to obey. I did not ask them to go on any such buildings, because it would have cost them their lives. I would not put men where I would not put myself, and I would not go myself unless I had some place where I could work and fight the fire, as we did at the new Post Office, where we had a means of escape. There should be an upper iron ladder so placed that the ordinary ladders can reach it. The proprietors of the "London Times" sent me their articles on the fire in the flour mills there, and I noticed that that fire began the same time as ours, and burned three days constantly with the whole Fire Department at work. The Fire Department of London consists of three hundred and eighty men, and no more. There are about one hundred men who go with the fire-escape in detail; there are fifty divisions in London having fire-escapes, with a detail of two men to each of those divisions. They are so organized that every hour in the twenty-four there is a man ready in each of the fifty divisions to take charge of the fire-escapes; that is, to save lives. They have no such means as we have of quickly reaching fires; they do not need them; their buildings are so constructed that they burn slowly; and they do not lack the means of escape from the roofs and upper stories. The whole vitality of our Fire Department consists in the rapidity with which we can reach a fire and control it, at the start; if we do not do that, it is perfectly clear that we have no adequate means of stopping it subsequently. The city of New York is just as much at the mercy of a fire that gets beyond control as we were.

Q. (By Mr. Cobb.) You said that towards morning you noticed that the men seemed to work as if they lacked confidence — did they work with alacrity when you got there?

A. After they got to the fire in Summer street, the firemen went to work gallantly. The engines came in slowly; it is very seldom that we ever get so late a delivery of engines at a fire. The hook-and-ladder companies were there in advance, and they were ready for the engines when they came. The engines got up their fires slowly. At a later stage of the fire, the men took dry-goods boxes and broke them up, and I sent down to the wharf for Cannel coal, and dumped loads down in the streets. I sent one of the mail wagons, as soon as it got there, for fuel, but we could not keep wagons at work to supply the engines with fuel of any kind, regularly, no matter what supply we had, for we had to fall back to save ourselves in time from the fire. In State street and Liberty square, we could have dumped down coal, but in a narrow street like Devonshire street, it would have been an obstruction; it would have been in the way; we wanted to go in and out. Dry-goods boxes and everything that could be burned were taken out and used for fuel. At one time, I counted around me some thirty-two steam fire engines, actually running. No previous forethought could have supplied so many with coal or fuel. They would come up and take the first available hydrant; nobody could know when they would get there and have the coal on the spot. We were short of fuel, but it must be borne in mind, that instead of twelve or fifteen engines, comprising our department, we had thrown upon us seventy engines, distributed all over the territory, for which a supply must be improvised in some way.

Q. (By Mr. Philbrick.) Was there any lack of fuel in firing up?

A. I don't know about that. They did not get their engines started as they ought to have been. I don't know when the first one was started. I saw five or six fire up myself that night.

Q. They worked slowly?

A. They started slowly; some of them, I think, did not have their fires up when they got upon the ground. I think the first engine coming from this direction did not get its fire up until the second engine got there.

Q. (By Mr. Cobb.) Did I understand you to say that those men worked with alacrity early in the night?

A. They did. I think the disheartening time to the firemen, and when things looked the bluest (and from that time for two hours there was not much faith in anything), was after the fire had come through and burned the Cathedral block, caught on the Revere-Bank building, and was running up Franklin street, and crossing to the other side. I think I never saw men who were evidently more discouraged than the firemen at that time, and it was a disheartening task.

Q. (By Mr. Firth.) Did you see any giving away of property?

A. Oh, yes, sir, a great deal of it.

Q. What was the effect of that, so far as it came under your eye?

A. It had very little effect where I was, on Federal and Devonshire streets. I thought the effect was good. It took the rabble out of the way. It did not demoralize anybody who would have done us any good but got a good many out of the way. If a man stole five dollars' worth and ran off, it was a perfect godsend in our direction.

Q. (By Mr. Russell.) You did not see the firemen demoralized by it?

A. I don't think there was anything of the kind in our region. There were human supplies wanting; they wanted something to eat and drink. There were firemen who worked all night without a mouthful to eat or drink. I don't believe Capt. Green or his men had anything to eat or drink that night, until they almost fainted away. The same was true of whole fire companies. For myself, I will say, that I was finally so exhausted that I could hardly stand up when it came twelve o'clock the next day. I stayed by until after twelve o'clock the next day, without eating, drinking or resting, of course, not aware of the strain that was on me. The firemen could not work under such circumstances. If it had been a cold night, I do not know what we should have done. The Watertown company worked up to the last moment, without leaving their position; every man known to be there.

Q. What was the result?

A. At twelve o'clock the next day those men were drenched through, and a team was sent to Watertown to bring them some dry clothing. They had had nothing to eat, and were not supplied until Sunday afternoon. They came away without any money; it was Sunday morning; the restaurants were not open; it was the worst possible time for the men to get anything. Three hours of the work of a fireman, getting hose into buildings and tending the pipe, will exhaust the strongest man. One of those streams as now thrown by a steam engine, will knock three men down. It took five of us to move the hose out of the way of an explosion, to prevent being thrown down in the street. A man cannot work on that strain, wet through as those men were, and not have it tell on him.

Q. (By Mr. Cobb.) What in your judgment, in view of your experience that night, was the effect of the use of gunpowder?

A. The fire would have gone into State street, and burned the Sub-Treasury, as certainly as I sit here, even with the appliances we had, if it had not been for the powder; nothing in the world saved us but that. Take such a street as Lindall street, with buildings five stories high, and the street only thirty feet wide. The fire burned across two streets and came into the upper windows into the third story of our Post Office. The only way in the world to stop it was to level those buildings. I do not make the least question that every building that was blown up would have been destroyed by the fire if gunpowder had not been used, with the exception of the building at the corner of Milk and Washington streets, and an old wooden building on Broad street. Those buildings might not otherwise have been destroyed, but there was hardly anything else that would not have been destroyed, and the powder saved millions of property. That is my best judgment, after carefully looking it over.

Q. Did you see any powder put into buildings that did not explode?

A. Yes, sir, I did, and we were obliged to keep out of those buildings. In regard to that, I will say, that there was not a place where powder was used where it extended the fire a single foot however.

Q. (By Mr. Cobb.) Was there any loose powder put into the Webster-Bank building, at the corner of Congress street?

A. No, I think not. We had made a regular set-to with the fire, when we had the trouble with Capt. Woolley. The buildings were all blown out on those corners, and I told them we would blow up every building on Kilby street, from foundation to roof, to keep the fire from State street. In fact, if it had caught there or got into the "Traveller" building, I don't see where we could have stopped it. There was the Sub-Treasury, opposite were the Safety-Deposit Vaults, and many of the principal banks. Of course, there is not a place in Boston, or in the world, that I know of, that it would be a greater peril to have a fire reach, or a greater disgrace. I had no doubt that we could make a clean sweep of Kilby street, but at the same time, I said to the men, "We won't use this powder; we have got force enough here; we have blown out the corners, and I think we can control it, and use our judgment in regard to blowing up any buildings here." Just then Capt. Woolley came up, and went in back of the Hide and Leather Bank building, the high freestone building on Kilby street. It is useless to blow up such a building as that; you must blow up the surroundings and let that stand as a bulwark in itself. I asked them to be ready to blow up the other side, out to State-street corner. We had put our powder into the buildings beyond, and all the men understood it. Capt. Woolley came up and said it must be taken out. I heard what was said, and went down to the men with the hose and told them that the use of the powder was in our control; to pay no attention to him, but stay where they were. Very soon, I heard a loud voice saying that the firemen would fall back unless that powder was taken out, and as I looked back, I saw Gen. Benham and ex-Alderman Carpenter and Alderman Woolley at the building, having a controversy. Alderman Carpenter appealed to me. I said we had put the powder in the buildings; that I would stay with the hosemen down in front; that no powder should be fired until we were ready for it; but that we must make our stand there. The men with the hose, hearing the controversy, fell back, I should think, a hundred and fifty feet. I took hold of one of the pipes myself, and helped drag it down street, and went fifteen or twenty feet nearer the fire than we were before, where it was almost impossible to stand. The men stayed there and others came up with their hose, as they always will; they are ashamed to do a cowardly thing before others, and we made a stand near the Revere Copper Company's building, and held it. I understood that somebody had started for the City Hall, and very soon afterwards, perhaps ten minutes, I was told that all authority to blow up buildings had ceased, and all power was in the hands of Capt. Damrell and his subordinates.

Q. (By Mr. Firth.) How did that word come to you?

A. A person from the City Hall brought it directly to me.

Q. (By Mr. Philbrick.) Did you want to blow up the buildings there?

A. Not at that time. We should have stopped there, if we stayed the fire where we were at work; but if we could not hold it at that point, there was no other place where we could stop it on Kilby street. We did hold it there. The powder was taken out of Capt. Woolley's building; but it was not taken out of the Post-Office building, or any other, until the next morning.

Q. When you speak of the Post-Office building as one of the buildings from which the powder was not removed, you mean the building fronting on Kilby street used as part of the Post Office?

A. Yes, sir. As to the second fire, Sunday night, I was not at all surprised at what occurred in Shreve, Stanwood & Co's store. The same thing might have happened on the top of Beacon Hill, or in the State House, as well as where it did happen. The gas of this city is a more serious danger to life and property than any convenient thing we have. In my judgment, we could have stayed the fire long before we did but for the gas. It is perfectly evident that we should have legislation immediately, compelling every gas company in this Commonwealth to put in cut-offs to the mains in the street, and to the service-pipes in every building, so that the gas can be controlled. It is not enough to put the control on the inside; you cannot get into the basements and under the sidewalks, where the cut-offs are. If it is found that these cut-offs wear out once in three years, renew them once in three years. It is nothing but a plug of iron, that can be easily changed; it is not like a water-pipe, which you have to protect from frost; it can certainly be reasonably controlled.

Q. (By Mr. Philbrick.) Would it not often get so hot when a building was on fire, that when you wanted to shut it off, you could not get at it?

A. No; when a building caught fire, it should be shut off instantly. You should not allow a building to burn, with the gas pipes reaching through it — to the attic.

Q. (By Mr. Cobb.) Supposing that one of those tall buildings was on fire in the upper stories, the parties in the lower stories might want to use the gas in order to save their books and goods?

A. I would go in and shut it all off, nevertheless. You must have the control of the gas; it will not do to run the risk of having the fire communicated to the surrounding buildings, without some means of cutting it off.

Q. (By Mr. Philbrick.) With the rapidity with which the fire spread through Federal, High, Purchase and Pearl streets that night, could any gang of men have accomplished that thing?

A. Yes, sir. If I could have got hold of the men, we could have dug up the mains in every one of those streets, and shut off all the gas. The fire did not burn rapidly; it caught along from building to building; but the fire did not go as rapidly as fires do when driven over a city by a gale. It was from seven o'clock on Saturday night until one o'clock, Sunday afternoon, in covering this territory, beginning where it did. In that time, with an average gang of men, you could have dug up all the pipes, if you had known where they were, and plugged up the pipes. I intended to try it, whether it could have been done or not; and I think I could have accomplished it, if I could have found the men who knew where the pipes were.

Q. (By Mr. Russell.) You say you were not surprised at what took place on Sunday night. Did you anticipate that explosion of gas?

A. I did. It was a constant element of danger. I was not surprised at the spread of the fire in spite of the firemen. We could have done better with gunpowder, if it had not been for the gas. The gas troubled us more than the lack of water.

Q. (By Mr. Firth.) Did you observe any trouble from the wind?

A. Our streets are narrow, and the buildings high; and in almost every street it was like the tremendous draught of air that you observe at a brick-kiln, or at the foot of any high chimney. I had to hold my hat on, and my coat would be drawn towards the fire as I turned to go back; and in every street it swept the dirt and dust into this immense current that was rising so rapidly. The rarefied air went so rapidly up, that the outside air came in with a rush, and the draft along near the ground was tremendous, but the wind after the first hour caused no trouble.

Q. (By Mr. Cobb.) Do you think the Fire Department, as a whole, did all they could do under the circumstances, from the time you were there?

A. That I must answer in this way: The Fire Department of this city, in its engines, is entirely inadequate to our wants. We ought to have to-day two steam fire engines, of not less than ten tons, requiring from four to six horses, capable of throwing a three or four-inch stream, through a wire-bound hose, two hundred feet in height. The Fire Department of this city to-day is just as incompetent to cope with the fires we are liable to have, as it was fifteen years ago, when we outgrew the hand engines.

Q. In what respects?

A. The buildings are so high, that unless we have additional power to throw our streams, and additional strength to our hose, we can do nothing on such high, deep buildings. These smaller engines will reach a fire quickly, they are managed easily, and moved rapidly, but they do not meet the emergency of a great conflagration, such as a city like this is liable to have. We have just as much outgrown our steam fire engines as we had outgrown the hand engines.

Q. What hose would you recommend?

A. I am not an expert. I know the hose we now use is inadequate.

Q. Did you notice whether it was the rubber or leather hose that burst?

A. Some of the leather hose was old. I found they had coupled new and old together. There was hardly a line of hose by morning that wasn't all mixed up. I think many of the couplings did not fit. I noticed that the out-of-town engines were supplying the water when I got back on State street. We had no trouble about water at that time. More engines were massed in State street, filling the entire street, before I got my stuff finally out of the Post Office. While all this was going on, I had the office running, and was getting out my material.

Q. Did you see much of the Chief?

A. I saw him at the Hall. I think we went out together about the last ones that went out. I heard from him once about daybreak, up in Milk street. When I saw him next was when our own building, the Merchants' Exchange, was on fire. He came up to the Congress-street entrance. You understand that all the doors of our building I kept barricaded that night. No one was permitted to come in who was not recognized, and I continued the same strictness after the building was on fire and while it was burning, on account of the exposure of the government property in the Sub-Treasury. Had the watchman of the Sub-Treasury and our own watchman there. Mr. Damrell came to the Congress-street entrance; the door was fastened with a Post-Office lock, and could not be opened. I broke open a window, reached through and put my arms under his, and lifted him in. Then I went with him through the building and showed him the condition of things there, and he helped us in our building for the next three-quarters of an hour. That is my only recollection of seeing him after meeting him at the City Hall.

Q. Did he appear to be self-possessed when you saw him?

A. I don't know Capt. Damrell sufficiently well to judge. He was earnest. A man judges another by his own feelings. I was impressed with the tremendous danger with which we were threatened, and he seemed to be, too. He took hold efficiently to do what was to be done. He certainly did his duty there. My impression at the City Hall was this,—that he felt that the appliances we had could not control the Mansard roofs, that powder was a hopeless resort, and that it was a terrible alternative. I know I went out of the City Hall feeling that I had not a single man going with me, or approving what we were then undertaking; that I was really running counter to his judgment, and that is a great oppression to a man situated as I then was, but since the men who went out with me have said it met their entire approval, and hundreds have told me the roar of the explosions was the first sign of hope, and sent a thrill of joy through the whole city.

Q. (By Mr. Russell.) You have told us that the means of battling with the fire were utterly insufficient—how did the firemen use the poor means which they had?

A. They certainly did not go back from a building until they were compelled to, anywhere; they stayed until the last moment, and whenever they were asked to make an extraordinary effort at a given point, they did it in every instance. I was in every street leading to the old Post Office and the new one, almost as fast as a man could go, back and forth, and I saw nothing in our own firemen which was discreditable. My attention was called to two firemen from out of town who were drunk, and I started to arrest one of them and put him in the lock-up; but the Captain told me that he was not a regular fireman, but came in with the Company as a volunteer. I know the Boston firemen by their badges, and I do not think I saw a man where I should criticise what he was doing or the way he was doing it.

Q. (By Mr. Russell.) Have you looked into the law in regard to the use of powder?

A. No, sir. I was very careful not to. I was afraid I might know something about it. That opens this question. I made up my mind that what little authority I could get, whether it was good enough to stand me in hand or not, I would use. On such an occasion as that, I think no man should stop to study the law. It was evidently a necessity which made a law for itself. I would have blown up those buildings any way. I had come to that conclusion. I wanted something to stand behind me; I wanted some organization that would set men to work with co-operation, and I wanted some apparent authority for bringing the powder in here; but it was absolutely necessary to do it, to save ourselves that night. I felt so then, and I have not changed my mind.

I am perfectly certain I would not have let the Post Office and Sub-Treasury burn without blowing up the buildings on Lindall and Kilby streets. I should have done it, as the saying is, "On my own hook."

I think the Mayor's statement that he had not the legal authority to blow up buildings, but that it resided in the Chief Engineer and Board of Engineers, was probably correct, but precisely how it resides in them, I don't know. Such an emergency is just as likely to occur again as it was before this fire, and it should be determined where this power does reside, and in what way it can be exercised.

Q. (By Mr. FIRTH.) Don't you think that needs legislation as much as anything?

A. We must have the means of doing whatever is necessary to stop the spread of such a conflagration in a crowded city. For instance, suppose the fire in the building at the foot of Cornhill (it so happened that I got there before the alarm was given) had crossed Brattle street in one direction and Washington street in the other, it might have required the blowing up of Cornhill in less than an hour. If it becomes necessary again, powder will be used; if there is no law for it, there should be.

I have understood that other parties had authority given them to blow up buildings. When our authority was given, I requested Mr. Bradley, who is connected with the "Herald," to take down the names, which he did, to make a record of where they were to be sent, and the Mayor and Chief Engineer were to approve it. They were to do nothing except in their own localities; they had no power outside. Mr. Allen, President of the Cochituate Water Board, was to go down to Broad street, and blow up buildings to prevent the fire from going round Broad street, and getting into the Fort-Hill District. I understood and felt that night, that if he had gone to Bedford street, and commenced blowing up buildings, he would have interfered with the plans of Capt. Damrell to such an extent that he would have been liable personally for it. I had no idea that this thing was to be done in any loose, chance way. I felt that every man should have his place and go there; that if there was any additional authority needed, he should get it from Capt. Damrell.

It was distinctly stated, that nothing should be done above or west of Washington street, and if the fire finally crossed that street, the course to be pursued should be considered at City Hall. If it had crossed that street, what we should have done I don't know; it is terrible to contemplate; but nothing was to be considered as trusted to any man in advance. Down this way it was different. I had my theoretical idea that I would keep the fire from State street, and the valuable property around there. I directed that four or five buildings should not be blown up. The Old South Church was one, and the building below the Old South Church on Milk street. The question came up in regard to the "Traveller" building. I said no, the emergency hadn't come; we would not do that. The fire was coming through, if it came through at all, in the building where the Sub-Treasury was.

There is one other thing which it seems to me we must always have in view, and that is, the construction of buildings. It was very obvious, during that fire, that iron beams were less safe than wooden ones. As soon as they were heated to a red heat, they curled up and came out, story after story, while the wooden beams would stand until they burned off. If there is any process by which wooden beams can be made less combustible, I am satisfied that a hard-pine beam, or an oak beam, is safer for such buildings than iron. As the buildings with these iron beams fell in, the pressure crowded the walls out, and in almost every instance, let the next story down, and when rooms, filled with merchandise, as many were, burned, the fire heated the iron beams red-hot. It was like putting them over a blast furnace.

Q. (By Mr. Cobb.) Did you notice that when the iron posts sustaining those massive fronts got heated, they would come down, and the whole front fall with them? Do you think that is the proper way to construct a building?

A. That did not happen in any case until the building was burned clear down below. Very likely a good many people were a little disappointed, in looking over the ruins the next day, to find that so few of the walls of those immense warehouses, the most solid of any in the city, were left standing. The fact is, that the effect of the explosions was to take them down. We cleared the ground behind us all the way through; nobody had any occasion to use powder the next day to blow down walls along the line on which we operated.

Q. (By Mr. Firth.) About how many effective explosions should you think there were?

A. We must have had not less than twenty, and my opinion is, over thirty, in our region. Not less than seventeen or twenty that were tolerably effective. But the difficulty was, we did not use powder enough. We ought to have used a hundred and fifty or two hundred pounds more than we did. If we had put in two hundred pounds more at the corner of the street below the new Post-Office building, the fire would never have crossed into Simmons's block. If we had spent just that much more on powder in that building, we should have saved half a million dollars on the other side of the street. The front went down flat, but the heat was intense; it lay shingling back, piled up; the rear part of it was up to its full height, and the front down almost to the sidewalk, and presented a great surface of flame. What we ought to have done was to let that building down into the cellar; and it would have gone into the cellar, if we had put in two hundred pounds more.

As to another means of protection of large buildings from fire, we ought to have iron pipes in these large buildings, connected with the hydrants on the streets, so that the hydrant can be put on it, or an engine attached to it, and water thrown on that roof, or into the building. A few hundred dollars spent in each warehouse would furnish means of carrying water over the building, and to use upon each roof upon the adjoining buildings, and then we should have no trouble from bursting hose. We have, as I said before, outgrown our fire apparatus; we have not outgrown the men. Those men will be equal to any firemen in the world, if you will give them the appliances; give them the hose and engines, and fire-escapes they ought to have.

Mr. Mullett, the supervising architect, when we commenced preparing plans for the new Post Office, was very decided that it should be a thoroughly fire-proof building. His opinion was not coincided with by any man that I know of, who had anything officially to do with the matter in Boston, except myself. So far from it, Mr. Alpheus Hardy, who was a member of the commission for the purchase of the site, desired to put up a building similar to Macullar, Williams & Parker's building. He insisted upon it so strenuously that he made a proposition to the Treasury Department, offering to put up a building in that style, and fixing the price; and that single thing gave Mr. Mullett and myself more trouble than any other one matter; for he represented a large estate; he said that a building of that character was perfectly safe; that he had money enough to build with; and yet was erecting such buildings under the direction of architects who could not be mistaken. Finally, when a committee of investigation was appointed, Hon. Ginery Twitchell telegraphed me, and I went to Washington, and the whole question came up in regard to the construction of our City Hall, to which reference was made, and whether we should have a fire-proof building, or such a building as Mr. Hardy proposed to build for eight hundred thousand dollars, and which he had urged the Secretary to accept. Now, had we built such a building, we should undoubtedly have occupied it, and we should have lost everything in the Treasury and Post Office.

Instead of stopping the fire, it would have carried it through to State street. In other words, you cannot impress too strongly upon people in cities of the size of Boston, the absolute value, in dollars and cents, of fire-proof buildings, thoroughly reliable. That building was reliable; the outside walls might crumble, but if it had contained a hundred millions of property, every farthing would have been saved. I speak of that as showing what this experience demonstrates in regard to the value of fire-proof buildings. Mr. Hardy represents a class of men who, by this fire, are taught that there is still another thing to be learned in this great city. We have got to go one step beyond Macullar, Williams & Parker's. Every man who has a Mansard roof on his warehouse should be compelled to line it up and fill it in solid. I should think every man would do that at once.

Q. (By Mr. Philbrick.) Do you think we have the frames to bear it?

A. I am afraid not. In that case there is no other way but to take them off. Mr. Mullett is entitled to all praise. A young man, he carried his plan through on his own judgment, and I felt on the night of the fire, when I drew that line at City Hall, and said, "There is the line on which we will fight this fire," that our Post-Office building was worth all it had cost, by this confidence it gave us; that, possessing such a structure, we could save State street; and so it proved. It saved ten times what it cost, yet it was against the judgment of Boston, and of Boston architects, that the building was constructed in that manner. Those consulted, disapproved the plan.

Q. (By Mr. Firth.) Did they disapprove of the fire-proof character of it?

A. They said that it was unnecessary; that the expenditure on such a building to render it fire-proof to the extent proposed, was unnecessary; that there was no exposure that warranted such an expenditure.

Q. Would it have been fire-proof, if finished?

A. Absolutely; just as much as it is now, and a little more so. We have carried up a frame-work of wood, and have platforms for the steam engine that is used for hoisting, etc. All the fear I had was that the fire might reach this wood-work and heat the iron beams, and press the walls out. I had that in my mind; but if we could keep the fire out of the inside, I felt we were perfectly safe; and we did. In other words, the exposure when the building is finished, will not be one-half what it was that night, while the fire was burning.

Q. (By Mr. RUSSELL.) Is there anything further you desire to say?

A. Speaking of what is needed in Boston as a further protection against fire, the danger from the height of buildings is also guarded against by the width of streets. It seems to me we should have, here in Boston, with the opening and opportunity that the burnt district gives us, a new and distinct plan for protection against fires made to conform to the wants of the city for business purposes. We need it for health, we need it for convenience in our business. The plan that has been so far adopted in reference to streets by the Street Commissioners, extending Washington street and Devonshire street in a straight line to Haymarket square, would seem to make it desirable to extend in the same line through Federal street to the foot of Summer street, and make the street at least eighty feet wide, as a sort of fire barrier. This street would run from the Boston, Hartford & Erie depot, through by the new Post Office building, across State street, through Haymarket square to Charlestown bridge, in an air line, making a continuous street, and the larger portion of it can be made of sufficient width to be a protection against fire, and a reliable one. If we had had such a street as wide as the area in the central part of Franklin street was, there would have been no possibility of the fire crossing from one side to the other. Not only would it be a direct protection against an extension of fire, but you would have a street where you would be safe in locating your steam fire engines, making a permanent position for fighting a fire. It would be invaluable in this respect. Then coming from the new Post Office (which can be relied upon as an absolutely fire-proof building, as much so as the Custom House), in the direction of the City Hall through School street, take out the buildings in Water street, between the new Post Office and Washington street, which would give us an eighty or ninety feet width there. Then by simply cutting off the old buildings, as far up as City Hall, we strike the church above, which can be turned around and placed in the burying-ground, which belongs to the city, and thus, at a very small expense, make an open avenue which becomes a cross barrier in a westerly direction, the only place where we can get it.

There is not in the whole line of streets in Boston, any place except Beacon street, which will justify any such amount of widening from east to west as is required for a fire barrier, except School street. The City Hall, being located where it is, with sufficient room in front to be appropriated to sidewalks, a street and area can be opened there at a very reasonable expense. The question of expense is always an important item, and the difference between widening fifty, sixty, or eighty feet, would be saved actually in the insurance-money, the actual risk of the insurance. I do not mean by this the mere premiums charged for insuring; I mean there will be enough saved in the actual fire risk of the city in a few years to pay the entire additional expense. It seems to me that, as we are now situated, we should at once fix upon these two short lines from the new Post Office to the Boston, Hartford & Erie depot, and the line in this direction from the new Post Office through

School and Beacon streets to the Common. If necessary, instead of assessing all the betterments for such improvement upon the mere locality, let the whole city pay for it. This will divide the city up in such a way, that hereafter it would be almost an absolute protection from fire beyond the local district.

No one who looks at the city can fail to see that there is no reason why, if a fire should break out on the west side of Washington street, say in the Music Hall, or in the rear of the Adams House, or in the rear of the Parker House, it should not sweep from Washington street to the Common, and spread north. I believe that the opportunities for the spread of such a fire are greater in that region than in the section where our great fire took place.

Then looking at it in another view: Take the neighborhood of Dock square. We are in the same difficulty there, and the exposure is the same. Moreover, making one part of the city safe as against another is a great protection to personal property, for, if it cannot be moved to a place of comparative safety, without hauling long distances, then it is substantially lost the moment a large conflagration occurs. We can save in the actual increase in the value of property, personal and perishable, as well as in the improvements upon real estate, in a short time, by taking advantage of the condition in which we are now to open these wide avenues, more than they will cost. I wanted to make a special point of that, because it is rather my weakness to look in that way.

I would say another thing, that there are advantages to be derived from these wide avenues in other respects. For instance, in winter, our narrow streets accumulate large amounts of snow when there is a heavy snow-fall, and we have to cart it off on to the Common or some other place, and a fire is entirely unapproachable by the engines. How much better it would be to have these avenues, that would be of sufficient width to allow of fire-engines being located there, and worked advantageously and without obstruction, than to have that portion of the city built up with streets forty, fifty, or sixty feet wide. Give us something wide enough so that a body of snow shall be no obstruction to business, or to the engines in case of fire, or other emergency, and also furnish, at other seasons of the year, the means of doing the business of the city.

Q. (By Mr. Firth.) Have you mentioned this plan to the Street Commissioners?

A. Yes, sir. I have urged it there, and I am urging it everywhere.

ADJT. GEN. JOHN A. CUNNINGHAM, *sworn.*

Q. (By Mr. Russell.) At what time were you called upon to order out the military on the night of November ninth, or morning of the tenth?

A. At two o'clock precisely. The clock was striking when the Alderman was speaking to me at my house.

Q. What Alderman called?

A. Alderman Cutter.

Q. Where is your house?

A. 36 Lynde street.

Q. What did you do to get the military out?

A. As soon as I presented myself to the Mayor, he said he wanted troops. My reply was, it was for him to order, and for the State to obey. He desired that I should order such troops as I pleased, — he knew nothing about the organization of the troops in Boston. I asked him if he thought a regiment of four hundred or five hundred men would be sufficient. He thought so for that time, and I ordered out the First Regiment.

Q. How did you give notice?

A. I went myself to East Boston to the commanding officer, Col. Proctor. I did not find him in, and left an order with his wife for the Colonel to report with his command, as soon as possible, to His Honor the Mayor. Not feeling quite satisfied with that, and feeling that Col. Proctor might not return to his home, in the morning I went myself to South Boston and ordered out Col. Finan with his regiment.

Q. The ninth?

A. The ninth.

Q. What followed in the way of getting them out?

A. I had nothing to do with it. Other troops were ordered out during the day.

Q. What other troops?

A. The First Battalion of Cavalry, the First Battalion of Artillery, the First Battalion of Infantry, and the Second Battalion of Infantry.

Q. Did you have occasion to observe how the men behaved, — those that were on duty?

A. I thought very finely. I made grand rounds myself through the night.

Q. (By Mr. Firth.) How much force was there out in all?

A. On Wednesday there were twenty-one hundred men on duty.

Q. How many had you out on Saturday in answer to your call? How fully represented were the regiments?

A. At four o'clock, Sunday afternoon, we must have had twelve hundred men.

Q. (By Mr. Russell.) Do you know what company came first, and at what time they came?

A. Major Gaul reported first with one company. Next came Capt. Colligan of the 9th Regiment.

Q. When did Major Gaul come?

A. He reported to me at City Hall at half-past five that he had them in his armory ready for service.

Q. When did Capt. Colligan come?

A. Half-past seven.

Q. Have you thought of the question, whether it would be well to have some signal for calling out the military?

A. I have thought it was very desirable, although I must say I think our troops responded very promptly.

Q. Can you suggest any signal?

A. Only some signal from the fire-alarm, so that when the men connected with the military should hear that signal they should assemble at their armories and be ready for orders.

Q. (By Mr. PHILBRICK.) Should you think it worth while to have them assemble at every fire-alarm?

A. No, sir, only that on an alarm signal that had so many strokes the military should assemble.

Q. A preconcerted signal for the purpose?

A. Yes, sir; like the signal for dismissing the schools, for instance.

Q. (By Mr. FIRTH.) Unlike anything that is now used?

A. Yes, sir.

Q. What would you say of having a military organization drilled for the purpose of sapping and mining; that is, using powder when necessary?

A. I can't say. I cannot give any opinion upon that.

Q. (By Mr. PHILBRICK.) If it is ever to be used, don't you think it ought to be done by expert hands?

A. Yes, sir.

Q. (By Mr. FIRTH.) Can you get them except by having persons trained to it?

A. I should think not.

Q. (By Mr. PHILBRICK.) Are you in doubt as to whether it ought ever to be used?

A. I can't give any opinion about it; I know so little about fires or stopping fires.

JOHN S. JACOBS, *sworn.*

Q. (By Mr. RUSSELL.) You are an Engineer?

A. Assistant Engineer.

Q. Of the Boston Fire Department?

A. Yes, sir.

Q. How soon did you go to the fire?

A. As soon as the bell told me where it was.

Q. The first alarm?

A. Yes, sir, the first alarm, although I am not called to the first as a fireman.

Q. About how long did it take you to get there?

A. Five or six minutes, probably; not far from six minutes.

Q. What was the condition of things when you got there?

A. The upper part of the building was well on fire. That is, I could see it from the street.

Q. Any fire apparatus there when you arrived?

A. Yes, sir, there were two lines of hose in the street

Q. What did you do?

A. I went into the building that was on fire and took a line of hose in with me.

Q. How far up did you carry it?

A. I carried it on to the second floor; that is, so as to play into the second floor.

Q. (By Mr. COBB.) Which side did you go in?

A. Summer street.

Q. (By Mr. RUSSELL.) How long did you stay there?

A. Time is a peculiar thing at a fire. I suppose I might have stayed there five to eight minutes.

Q. Then were you driven out?

A. Well, I was up the stairs with a hose, and there was an order came from outside for the hose to be taken out of the building. I said, "Who ordered the hose out?" and the reply was, "An Engineer." The hose was taken out, and when I got down to the front door I saw how bad the state of the building at that time was. In fact, I did not hardly dare to go out of the building, but hesitated whether to go out of the door or not, but I said to myself, "If I don't get out here, I can't get out anywhere," and I took my life in my hand and went out.

Q. Was the stone falling then?

A. Yes, sir, from the coving.

Q. (By Mr. Russell.) What did you do next?

A. I opened the first door below; the adjoining building, on Summer street, and ordered a line of hose into it; that is, it was opened by my orders. Then I received orders from the Chief to go to the building opposite, — on the opposite side of Summer street. I took one line of hose into that building, and ordered one into the adjoining building. The windows were then taking fire, and the coving or the wood work round the top of the building, and I sent for extinguishers and used the hose to the best advantage.

Q. (By Mr. Cobb.) How far up did you go in that building?

A. Out through on to the roof.

Q. (By Mr. Russell.) With hose?

A. Yes, sir.

Q. (By Mr. Cobb.) Was that the building on the corner of Otis street?

A. No, sir, the adjoining, — that would be the second building.

Q. (By Mr. Russell.) Where did you throw the water?

A. Inside and out, on the roof, and on the inside of the building and round the front, round where the Lutheran windows go.

Q. (By Mr. Philbrick.) Could you cover the corner building from where the hose was?

A. Not after the fire burst up there; the heat was so great.

Q. After the fire burst through the first building, you mean?

A. The one on the corner of Otis and Summer. The stream would not go a great ways. It didn't seem to penetrate very powerfully.

Q. Had the fire got through the roof when you got the hose up there?

A. No, sir, not when I first came up; there was not a great deal of fire coming out of that roof on the corner of Otis and Summer.

Q. What prevented you from quenching that?

A. I was in one building that was on fire and the fire was in the adjoining building.

Q. Wasn't it all on the roof?

A. No, sir, not all of it.

Q. Was there fire inside also?

A. Yes, sir; the most of the fire on the north side at that time was on the corner of Otis and Summer streets. I was in the adjoining building, saving that, and doing what I could to save the other building — the corner one.

Q. (By Mr. RUSSELL.) Was anything done to the corner building, except what you did?

A. I could not see, there was so much fire and smoke; and that fronted on another street. I stayed on that roof until the flames made a complete arch over me.

Q. (By Mr. FIRTH.) Did you throw water on the corner building?

A. Yes, sir, and played on to the windows in the rear?

Q. If you had been there ten or fifteen minutes earlier with your hose could you not have saved that corner in your judgment?

A. No, I don't think I could.

Q. Was it too hot for one stream?

A. Yes, sir; I had two streams up there.

Q. Was it too hot for them?

A. Yes, sir; I had one on the building I went up through, and one in the third building, but both came on to the second building.

Q. (By Mr. PHILBRICK.) What I want to get at is, if your hose had been up there before the fire began to burn this building on the corner, whether you could have stayed there; whether the fire on the opposite side of the street would have driven you away?

A. The fire on the opposite side did not drive me off; it was the fire in the adjoining building on the corner of Otis.

Q. If you had got there before the fire had such a start on the corner of Otis, could you not have held it in check?

A. I don't know as I could have done any better than the engineers and firemen did in that building; we could not put water wholly on to one building.

Q. Would it not have been possible, if the apparatus had been there fifteen minutes earlier, to have held that building?

A. I should not want to answer that.

Q. (By Mr. RUSSELL.) Do you mean you cannot?

A. No, sir; I could not answer that.

Q. (By Mr. PHILBRICK.) Couldn't you form an opinion?

A. I should not want to, sir; I think the chances were against us.

Q. Did the water come freely when you called for it through this hose?

A. Yes, sir; we had good streams.

Q. (By Mr. RUSSELL.) Was it possible to stand in front of that building on the corner of Otis street, and play on to it from the street?

A. I wouldn't have done it; I should not have dared to.

Q. Where did you go next after you were driven away from there?

A. I went into Devonshire street, from four to six buildings from Summer street. I thought I would get a hose in there and be prepared for the fire when it got to me. I broke open a store and went up into the second story and found the building on fire.

Q. (By Mr. COBB.) Inside?

A. Yes, sir. There was no fire then on Devonshire street. I went to the water faucets and tried to get some water to throw on to it, but could not get a drop. I then went on to the street and ordered some fire annihilators or water into the store to put the fire out that was kindled there.

Q. (By Mr. PHILBRICK.) How do you suppose the fire got into that store?

A. My judgment is it was set.
Q. A separate fire?
A. Yes, sir.
Q. (By Mr. Russell.) How far was it from the fire?
A. The fire then was along on Otis street, but it had not come through into Devonshire.
Q. (By Mr. Philbrick.) Which side of Devonshire street was this building you went into?
A. On the east side; on the water side.
Q. (By Mr. Russell.) In what part of the building was the fire?
A. The second story.
Q. Were the windows broken?
A. I could not say whether they were or not.
Q. Did you notice whether they were open?
A. I have forgotten whether they were open or not?
Q. What was the building used for; what goods were in it?
A. There were boxes or bales. I don't think the building was on fire; I should think the fire was on the goods, — the bales or boxes.
Q. Did you put that out?
A. No, sir, I didn't get back again into the building. I ordered the annihilators in there.
Q. (By Mr. Firth.) Were they carried in?
A. I could not say.
Q. (By Mr. Russell.) Did you think, at the time, the fire was set?
A. I thought it very strange that it should be there.
Q. (By Mr. Cobb.) I wish you could remember about the windows, — whether they were open or closed?
A. I do not remember.
Q. (By Mr. Firth.) I suppose the fire was dropping about you in the street, — the sparks?
A. Before I left the roof of the building I came off from, the fire seemed to go a hundred feet, and likely to annihilate us at any moment.
Q. Was there not plenty of fire dropping in Devonshire street down to this building you went into?
A. There was any quantity dropping down.
Q. So if the windows were open, the fire might have got into the goods?
A. Yes, sir, it might possibly.
Q. (By Mr. Russell.) To what point did you go next?
A. I went into a narrow street or passage-way still lower down Summer street. I went where the Chief gave me orders.
Q. When you went to this place in Devonshire street, did you go by order of the Chief?
A. I think not.
Q. Do you think you consulted with any one about going there?
A. I don't think I did, sir. Sometimes we have to act to the best of our judgment.
Q. What did you do there in this narrow street?
A. The buildings had got on fire in the rear on the roofs, and I got some lines of hose in there. I got two lines, I think.
Q. How long before you were driven from there?

A. I was not driven from there, but was ordered by the Chief to make a stand on the corner of Summer and High, I think. That is, to the best of my recollection. The thing was done very quick.

Q. You say you got two lines of hose; did you get them on to the roof? Did you carry them on to the roof?

A. I think I did not get them on to the roof.

Q. Did the men go up on to the roof?

A. The fire was on the inside as well as on the roof. I don't think the men went on to the roof. The fire was travelling so fast that we had to work to keep ahead of the fire. That is why the stands we made were so short, on account of the fire going so fast.

Q. What did you do at the corner of Summer and High?

A. I took a line of hose up into the second building on High street.

Q. On which side?

A. On the water side. I thought the men never would get out of the front door where we carried them in, and I must get them out some other way. I came down and went on to Summer street, and took a line of hose up into the building, and ordered a roof ladder up on to the roof and to drop down to the scuttle where these men were, provided they could not hold the building and get them out. The ladder could not be got up. We got the ladder half way up and got it blocked; the ladder was too long. The men went up on to the roof, climbed up and crawled along on the roof, and halloed down the scuttle to them to go out of the front door as they could not get off of the roof, and they came out through the fire.

Q. What did you do next?

A. Then, with Engineer Straw, I concluded we would make a line from South street to Federal street in the rear and try to stop it there, and fought it successfully.

Q. There you stopped it?

A. Yes, sir.

Q. What did you do after that? Where did you go?

A. Then I went up to Washington street round the fire to Pearl, I think.

Q. What did you do there?

A. Got all the engines to work that I possibly could at every available point.

Q. (By Mr. Cobb.) In Pearl street, did you go to work?

A. I set the engines to work; some engines that came in from out of town at that time, or about that time, or had been shifted from some other quarter, at every reservoir and hydrant.

Q. Where were the hydrants and reservoirs where the engines were stationed?

A. Liberty square, and Batterymarch street.

Q. Was the water carried to Pearl street and thrown on to buildings there?

A. I will not be certain whether there was any carried from Liberty square to Pearl, but I put them to work there on each side of Pearl street.

Q. Was the water thrown on the water side and the other?

A. The north-west side when I was there.

Q. (By Mr. Cobb.) Thrown from the street or from the rear?
A. From ladders from the street. I sent men into the buildings.
Q. Did the men get on to the roofs of any of those buildings?
A. No, sir, I don't think they did.
Q. (By Mr. Russell.) Could they have got on to the roofs?
A. If I had thought it would have been of any avail I should have ordered them there.
Q. How many streams were thrown on the buildings in Pearl street?
A. Really I could not say.
Q. More than three?
A. Yes, sir, I should think there was.
Q. How long was water thrown in Pearl street?
A. I could not say, for I left that point.
Q. Who was in charge when you left there?
A. There was an Engineer from out of town, I think a Salem Engineer. He seemed to be a pretty good kind of a man and worked in pretty readily.
Q. Do you know his name?
A. I do not.
Q. Where did you go from that point?
A. To Milk street, to the best of my recollection.
Q. What did you do there?
A. I fought the fire down to Batterymarch street on the northerly, and to Oliver street on the southerly side.
Q. Were you there when it was stopped in that direction?
A. Yes, sir, I was there.
Q. What time was that?
A. I should think along in the afternoon; four or five o'clock, to the best of my recollection, Sunday afternoon.
Q. (By Mr. Cobb.) You were there in that neighborhood all day Sunday?
A. Yes, sir.
Q. How did the firemen behave?
A. As well as men could behave.
Q. Any exception to that, to your knowledge?
A. No, sir.
Q. How was the supply of water; did you have plenty?
A. At the first of the fire we seemed to have plenty of water, but the streams were not so good at the end.
Q. Was there any time when any of the steamers failed to throw water on account of a short supply?
A. Yes, sir, at the Batterymarch street reservoir I shut down three engines. There were four engines at work on the reservoir, and I ordered three of them shut off, because one of the engines was playing in a very important place, and I wanted her water. I had to shut them down for a few minutes.
Q. People complain that a great deal of water was thrown on the second and third stories when the fire was up above on the roof; can you account for that? In the first place, was that so?
A. Yes, sir.
Q. Why was that?

A. Some of the engines were playing through very long lines of hose, and I suppose, also, owing to the scarcity of water.

Q. Did you see any engines playing on stone fronts instead of playing through the windows or on the wood work?

A. No, sir, not when their streams would reach the windows.

Q. If that happened, you mean it was because it would not reach, so the water would fall on the stone fronts?

A. Yes, sir.

Q. Was there any want of fuel where you were that night?

A. No, because we used dry-goods boxes. There was no lack of fuel. I never heard of any complaint on that score. There was one man reported to me they were out of coal, and I told him to take dry-goods boxes for his fire.

Q. Did that engine stop playing?

A. Not to my knowledge.

Q. How did the hose work that night; was there much trouble from the bursting of hose?

A. Well, there was some, but nothing more, I think, than usual. There were a great many teams driving through the streets, and that is liable to cut hose.

Q. Were you troubled by the crowd of spectators?

A. Well, a portion of the time we were.

Q. Were the police able to hold the lines?

A. No, I don't think they were after the fire spread. That is a matter of judgment.

Q. Did they hold them, I mean?

A. They didn't trouble me much.

Q. The crowd didn't trouble you?

A. No, sir, they opened right and left.

Q. Did you see gunpowder used?

A. Yes, sir.

Q. Where?

A. I saw it on Milk street. On the left going down from Washington; the corner of Milk and Congress, I think it was.

Q. What was the effect there?

A. It took the building down pretty well.

Q. Was the effect to give you a chance to play on the ruins?

A. I think the building would have burned up full as quick.

Q. (By Mr. PHILBRICK.) Didn't it make the fire more manageable and less likely to spread to the next building?

A. No; in my judgment it made about as much fire.

Q. (By Mr. RUSSELL.) Did you see any other explosions?

A. I piled up some powder in one building on Water street, by order of the Chief, — about eight or nine barrels or casks.

Q. Was that exploded?

A. I kicked the heads out and put the fuse in.

Q. Did you light the fuse?

A. No, sir.

Q. Did anybody?

A. I think the Chief did.

Q. What was the effect there?

A. I didn't see the explosion. It was a very dangerous operation. The fire was coming into the building when I kicked the heads out.

Q. How long have you been connected with the department?

A. About twenty-five years.

Q. Suppose you had just that same fire to go through again; is there anything you could suggest that would prevent it becoming uncontrollable?

A. If I had to fight that fire over again, I don't know where I could make any better points than I was ordered to by the Chief.

Q. Do you think of any way in which the fire could be better managed than it was?

A. No, sir.

Q. (By Mr. Philbrick.) In looking back, can you see any reason why the fire got such an early start, or got control of you? You were there among the earliest; why was it that that fire spread in spite of all your efforts, from the first, as compared with other fires that you have often checked?

A. The alarm, in my judgment, was given late. We have had fires before, in my judgment, that would have burned as much as that if there had been fuel for them to burn.

Q. That is, if they met as combustible material on the way?

A. Yes, sir; there were the Commercial street and Fort Hill fires. I told a Councilman that night the fire was in Commercial street, if the buildings extended to Long Island they would go.

Q. The bakery, do you mean?

A. No, sir, since the bakery; the fire that took in Matthews' block.

Q. How long ago; was it since we have had a steam department?

A. It was at the time the Merrimac had the fight in Hampton Roads. I was sitting on a bale of goods playing on the fire when the news came.

Q. If a fire should break out in any of these high buildings that are left, of a similar nature, should you expect the same experience?

A. We have not got a chance in Boston to have another such fire as that was.

Q. Perhaps not so many buildings of that class, but there are a good many of them left.

A. I would answer that question as I answered a good many people after the Chicago fire, when they asked if it was possible for us to have such a fire as they had there. I told them yes.

Q. (By Mr. Cobb.) What were your reasons for saying we might have such a fire?

A. I knew if it got away from the building we were in, we could not stop it.

Q. Because the buildings were so high?

A. So high, and the streets narrow, and so much wood-work on the top of the buildings.

Q. Was there sufficient apparatus at the fire early?

A. I had all the hose that I asked for; I did not have to hunt for any. When I wanted a line of hose, all I had to do was to ask for it.

Q. Did it seem to you at any time during the continuance of the fire that there was enough apparatus on the ground?

A. No, sir.

Q. (By Mr. PHILBRICK.) Did it occur to you that the fire had got an extraordinary start when you got there?

A. Yes, sir.

Q. Did any apparatus come with you, or near you, from Salem street?

A. I went in with Hook-and-Ladder 1. I generally come with them. We generally come together in Dock square, and I went in with them that night.

Q. (By Mr. FIRTH.) How did they travel as to speed?

A. I usually meet them in Dock square. I come down Marshall street; they come through New Friend, and we usually meet.

Q. In regard to speed, did you come quick that night?

A. Yes, sir.

Q. As quick as if you had horses?

A. Yes, sir; I don't think that there was much difference. We went as fast as I could run.

Q. Can you generally keep up with the horses?

A. For a short run, I can.

Q. For the distance that you did run?

A. Yes, sir; sometimes, perhaps, I might not, and then again I would. A man cannot always run alike.

Q. (By Mr. PHILBRICK.) How soon after you got there did you apprehend a very serious fire?

A. When I saw I was getting outflanked on Otis street.

Q. How long was that after you got on to the spot, should you think?

A. Fifteen or twenty minutes. The reason that I went into the first building, I thought I could go right up into the building and take the life of the fire out. That is why I went into the first building; to stop it right where it was. A light fire will not go across a street; the heat will not set the buildings on fire across a street unless there is a large body of it. My idea was to put the stream up into the building and take the life out of it where it began.

Q. (By Mr. COBB.) You think the best fight was made with that fire in the beginning that could have been made?

A. I will stake my reputation as a fireman on that.

Q. (By Mr. PHILBRICK.) You mean after you got there?

A. Yes, sir.

Q. You might have done a good deal if you had been there a quarter of an hour before?

A. Yes, sir; if the alarm had been given earlier. I have done more than twenty-five years' fire duty, but it seems as though it was all condensed into twenty-four hours; and I have had some hard duty.

Q. You saw as much that night as all your life before?

A. It seems as though the whole of it was condensed into that. There has been considerable said in regard to our not working well, and the like of that. I never have seen a man belonging to the Boston Fire Department that has flinched one iota. I took a man by the collar in that building opposite where the fire took, and pulled him out of the scuttle, and carried him to the next building and threw him up on to the roof. He was there like a bull-dog, and would not leave until he was driven out.

Q. (By Mr. FIRTH.) Was the spirit of the men as good at the beginning as the next morning, or at any time later in the fire?

A. Their pluck was good, but the men did not have that strength later, to work. There was one point that I forgot to mention, where I worked in a building and had Engine 5 in with me, and the men worked nobly. That was on Summer street; I am not sure whether it was on the corner of Devonshire or that narrow street — it was one or the other. The men stayed in that building, and I had to tell them more than once to come out, to save their lives, because the fire was in the stairways underneath.

Q. Would there not have been a good deal more confidence in scaling roofs if you had always been sure of a safe retreat? Would you not have felt inclined to order them up oftener? I mean, if there had been any means provided more than there were. Suppose there had been permanent outside ladders that you knew you could get down from, on every block, would you not have had more confidence in going up there?

A. We should not take men down so quick sometimes. We must see our men out of buildings when we order them in.

Q. Is not that the most effective way of fighting a fire, — to go on to the roof?

A. No, sir; the best way to fight a fire, in my judgment, is to go into the building.

Q. After the fire gets started, and it gets too hot in the building?

A. Then you must keep it from spreading on the outside: from the roofs and windows of the adjoining buildings. You cannot wet the windows in front of the building you are in.

Q. When the fire spread, say when it was crossing Summer street, you went on to the roof because it was your best chance?

A. Yes, sir.

Q. Could you cover the front of that building by an engine playing from the street? Could you play high enough?

A. Yes, sir; until it was extended down the street so the men could not go up in front.

Q. It was too hot in the street?

A. Too hot and dangerous.

Q. (By Mr. RUSSELL.) Did the men have anything to eat that night, or the next morning?

A. I don't know; I didn't.

Q. When did you eat, yourself?

A. I got a cup of coffee somewhere during the day.

Q. Sunday?

A. Yes, sir.

Q. Did the men suffer from the want of food that night or early the next morning?

A. I don't think they did; they could not have suffered a great deal.

Q. Some people think, being overworked, they ought to have been supplied with food; I want to know whether the men thought of it. Was there any complaint?

A. I didn't hear any complaint.

Q. Do you think the men were worn out for want of food or refreshment?

A. No, sir ; I don't think they were.

Q. Didn't you feel the need of food?

A. No, sir. The excitement was so great. The first thing I did when I got through, I was very near blind, and I held my eyes open and went to the Eye and Ear Infirmary.

Q. Couldn't you see without holding them open?

A. No, sir.

Q. From the fire and dust?

A. Yes, sir.

Q. Do you think the men would have worked much better if they had had coffee provided?

A. A cup of coffee will enliven a man, I have no doubt.

NATHAN L. HAYDEN, *sworn*.

Q. (By Mr. RUSSELL.) How early did you see this fire?

A. About five minutes past seven.

Q. Where were you?

A. Hudson street. I was opposite about No. 66, when I first discovered the fire.

Q. What did you do?

A. I halloed "Fire," and went into the house and got my fire-hat, and ran across the street to Hose Two's house and helped haul it into the street.

Q. How soon did you get to the fire?

A. Inside of four minutes.

Q. What o'clock was it when you got there?

A. I could not tell you what o'clock it was.

Q. As near as you can. You mean from the hose house you got there inside of four minutes?

A. Yes, sir ; for when the alarm struck we were at Harvard street, and there was quite a number took hold there, and we went down very fast, quicker than any horses could go the road we went.

Q. (By Mr. PHILBRICK.) You got to Harvard street before the alarm struck?

A. Yes, sir.

Q. (By Mr. RUSSELL.) When you got to the fire what was the con dition of the fire?

A. It was all over the building, the basement and all the way up on the back side. We went into the back side of Kingston street and took the hydrant on the corner and went right in there.

Q. How soon did you get a steamer on after you got there?

A. I should think it was not over three minutes after we got there. We ran right off, and connected with the hydrant just as fast as we could.

Q. You say you saw the fire five minutes after seven ; did you look at a timepiece?

A. No, sir ; I came right out of the house. It was about seven as I came out of the house, and when I got on to the street somebody spoke and said, "See the fire!" I looked at it and could see it plain.

Q. When had you seen a timepiece or heard a clock strike last?

A. I heard the clock strike seven.

Q. Do you know whether your clock is right?

A. I could not swear to that.

Q. (By Mr. PHILBRICK.) Did you have anything to do with holding that hose when it was played?

A. Yes, sir; I held the pipe.

Q. At what point did that play?

A. Into the basement.

Q. Through one of the windows in the alley?

A. Yes, sir.

Q. Did that look like the hottest place?

A. Yes, sir.

Q. (By Mr. FIRTH.) Had it begun to run up when you got there?

A. It was through the roof when I got there. That is where I discovered it, coming through the roof.

Q. Had any other apparatus arrived when you got there?

A. Steamer 7 was there, but they had not got any water on. They were in the alley.

Q. How soon after did they get water on?

A. Just about the same time. There was not more than a minute's difference. We sung out about the same time, but our water came before theirs did.

Q. Where did their stream play?

A. They played in the basement with us, but we didn't play more than a minute before it got so hot it drove us away. It was very narrow, and the glass and stuff began to fall so quick, we had to get out.

Q. From the time the first alarm was given until you got a stream of water on, how many minutes was it?

A. About five minutes.

Q. It was about six minutes before Steamer 7 got hers on?

A. I should think it was.

Q. How long did it take you to get your hose out, and as far as the corner of Harvard street?

A. Not more than a minute and a half. We were very quick. The driver said, "Stop and get the box." I said, "There is no need of getting the box, the fire is very near." "How do you know?" said he. "Look up and you can see it," I said.

Q. How many minutes from the time you saw the fire until you were on Harvard street?

A. About two minutes; long enough for me to get my hat and go down to Harvard street.

Q. Do you remember what apparatus came next?

A. No, sir, I do not. I was busy at work, and there was a good deal of excitement. One thing that delayed us was, there was such a crowd we could not seem to get to work. After I came out, after it drove us out of the alley-way, I gave the stream up to their Company and went to see about my own Company, and when we came in we took the same stream and had to fight almost to get to work. All the way we could get to work was to take billets of wood out of the engine and strike right and left. They delayed us as much as six or seven minutes.

Q. Engine 3?

A. Yes, sir.

Q. Where was she stationed?

A. Corner of Kingston and Bedford streets.

Q. There is a reservoir there?

A. No, sir; we took the same hydrant that Hose 2 had.

Q. Had she steam up when she came?

A. Yes, sir.

Q. Any fuel?

A. Yes, sir.

Q. How long did the fuel carry her?

A. We kept getting it. We went into the neighbors' houses and got wood.

Q. You didn't lose any steam?

A. No, sir. We kept steady at work. We got out of coal, and a gentleman there said he had plenty of wood in Kingston street, and we could have it, and we went into his house and brought out wood. Then the coal came.

Q. Do you know who that was?

A. No, sir. I could not tell the house. We were growling because we had no fuel, and he told the fireman, "I have got plenty of wood, and you can have it all." Then we got boxes from a grocery store.

ALBERT S. JENNESS, *sworn.*

Q. (By Mr. RUSSELL.) You were formerly the Engineer at this building where the fire began?

A. Yes, sir.

Q. When?

A. Something over two years ago. It was two years ago last September when I left there.

Q. How long had you been Engineer there?

A. Nearly a year.

Q. What was the condition of the furnaces and boiler when you left?

A. The boiler was in good condition, with the exception that the front smoke-arch was burned out a little in the casing; I had asked to have it fixed quite a number of times.

Q. It hadn't been done?

A. No, sir.

Q. Did you regard it as safe when you left?

A. I regarded it as safe until such time as the iron had burned down to the boiler.

Q. (By Mr. FIRTH.) Was there anything about the arrangement then that seemed dangerous?

A. Nothing, if properly taken care of. The partition round the boiler was merely matched boards. It was something like eighteen inches from the brick-work of the boiler.

Q. (By Mr. PHILBRICK.) How did the fire-flue get out of the building from the boiler?

A. The fire passed under the boiler, back through the tubes and through the chimney.

Q. How did the fire-gas go from the smoke-arch to the chimney? What kind of a flue was it?

A. Sheet-iron; very short from the boiler to the chimney. The boiler was against the party-wall. Everything in that regard was safe enough.

Q. You spoke of the smoke arch being burnt out?

A. On the under side, where the smoke arch goes on to the lap of the boiler, where it is riveted on to the boiler, it began to burn off towards the front side, towards the apron. The iron had burned away on the front, and left exposed the sheet, and that had burned a hole perhaps as big as my three fingers; nothing so but I could lay a piece of brick on to it, and the dust would settle on it and cover it up.

Q. Suppose that had been neglected, would that present a dangerous place for communicating fire outside?

A. No, sir, it would cause a leak in the boiler, and the water would run into the fire-box and put the fire out.

Q. The damage would have been to the boiler?

A. Yes, sir; it would have made it leak, and would have extinguished the fire.

Q. Where did you keep kindlings when you were there?

A. Between the brick-work and this partition wall; but the brick was never so hot but what I could put my hand upon it, or lean up against it. We used to keep kindlings there, but we always considered it safe.

Q. There was no way of communicating between the fire and the kindlings?

A. No, sir. The only way I can suppose the fire could communicate with that wood or with the partition would be by leaving the fire unbanked, and having a piece of coal drop out and roll against the partition. There used to be a platform about three feet wide, and one step, that went down on to the brick-work, and the ash-pit door used to swing against this partition. It was, perhaps, twenty inches in length. I used to be careful when I left my fire at night in the winter to take a hoe and crowd my fire back one-half of the grate, leaving one-half of the grate exposed, and bank what fire I had left, so that in case coal should start from the fire it would roll on the grate and remain there; it could not roll out of the furnace; but if the fire was left so that a coal might drop out and roll against this step, or against this partition, it would communicate with the partition.

Q. Could that occur without leaving the ash-pit doors open?

A. The ash-pit doors are kept shut at night to stop the draft. In leaving the fire at night, I used to crowd the fire back. Some Engineers bank a fire right on a level, and put on wet ashes against the front of the door and swing the door around within an inch or two inches. There is a great difference in men in that.

Q. If you shut the door it would burn out?

A. It would burn out at night. It is policy in the winter to keep a little heat all the time. Men are different; some work one way and some another.

Q. Did you ever know coal to drop down in the way you speak of?

A. Yes, sir; not out of that boiler, as I know of, but others I have.

Q. Were you ever troubled with the idea that the coal might roll out and burn the building at night?

A. I used to think of it, but I used to be careful that such a thing did not happen. Every man that handles a steam boiler or engine has a reputation to look out after; if he is careless in one place, it is hard work to get employed in another.

Q. How far is the wooden step from the partition?

A. It used to run on a line with the partition opposite the boiler.

Q. Was the space between the boiler and that partition floored over on a level with the boiler, or up to the step?

A. Nearly as high as the step. I can't say whether it was the brick work that ran a little higher, or whether there was a platform there. I think the main floor of the basement ran to the brick work, and then this partition was built up.

Q. There must have been a step there?

A. Yes, sir.

Q. Which side were the hinges and which side the latch of the fire door as you face the door?

A. There were two fire-box doors opening in the centre, right and left.

PATRICK H. POWERS, *sworn.*

Q. (By Mr. Russell.) Where are you in business?

A. Lawrence & Co., 13 Chauncy street.

Q. How many years have you been with that firm?

A. Over twenty-nine years.

Q. How early were you there on the night of the fire?

A. At the store or the fire?

Q. At the fire?

A. I got down a little after ten o'clock.

Q. Tell us anything you noticed that is of importance for the Commission to know. We understood you were there at the outset.

A. I didn't get there until about ten. I suppose the only thing I know about the fire that is of interest to the Commission is the fact that during the time our store was in danger,— say from a little before two o'clock until half past three, or between that and four, an hour a half or two hours, — there was no Engineer in the vicinity to be found, as far as I could ascertain.

Q. Did you look for one?

A. Yes, sir; after I had been in the store perhaps half or three quarters of an hour, and had been up stairs and down on the roof (I was up in all the stories, probably six or eight times during the night, watching the course of the fire and the lay of the surrounding houses, calculating the chances of it coming to our store), when I made up my mind that it was crossing over, and our store was to be in danger. I went on to the street and tried to get some streams up there. That was after the old Post-Office building on the corner was on fire, — the store adjoining ours. within about six feet of us. That was in a blaze, burning up through the roof. I could not get a stream up there. The firemen said they had no right to come without being commanded by an Engineer. I asked them where I could find one. They said they did not know, but they described the dress and uniform of an Engineer, and I went to look for one. I went through Chauncy as far as Bedford, and up Avon street,

It was rather difficult getting through the lines and through the crowd. I did not see any Engineer there, and feeling very much interested in the store, I went back again. I went up stairs and found the fire still nearer, and went down again and tried to get a stream up, and after half an hour of teasing, and using every exertion and every means to induce them to go up there, I got one foreman to go up stairs with me, all through the building, and showed him the place, and he was satisfied, as I was, that that was the place to stop the fire, and we got a stream up there, and finally another and another. The last stream came in just in time to stop the fire from coming up our elevator. We got it stopped there, and then an Engineer made his appearance. He was not a Boston Engineer, and when I asked him to send more streams up there, he said he was not a Boston fireman and had no authority. I infer from the fact of a Newton company being there, and it being near our store then or a little time afterwards, that he belonged to Newton. Newton No. 1 was the company, I think, that was in our store, and did service for a couple of hours.

Q. Do you know who the firemen were that declined to go up because they had no orders?

A. I cannot tell you what company it was. I recollect that Hose 4 was there from Boston, and my impression is, a No. 2 was there, and a No. 20, if there is such a one. It seems to me that there was a No. 20 there.

Q. No. 20 steamer?

A. That I could not tell you, whether they were steamers or hose companies. I know No. 4 was there, because several men had their badges on, and one man I knew connected with it, who, I think, was a newspaper reporter.

I omitted to tell you one thing. The first Engineer that made his appearance was this out-of-town Engineer. He said he had no authority whatever, and no right whatever to order any of the Fire Department, so I failed to get anything through him. Later, perhaps half an hour later — it must have been an hour and a half, or two hours from the time we first got a stream, — a Boston Engineer made his appearance. He was a low-sized man, and wore whiskers. After going up there with me and looking through the building, he seemed to be satisfied with the way the thing was being managed by the firemen, and went away, leaving us in the store to keep a look-out up stairs and around, to see that the fire did not take in any other part of the building. I don't know but he may have come back. There was a building directly opposite us, a new building that had never been occupied, and that I thought was, from its situation and character, a grand place, as well as our building, to stop the fire, and it did stop it for a good while. They stopped it until the building on the south-east corner of Chauncy street was all burned, and there was no danger from that, but some sparks had caught up on the roof; and in one of my excursions up to the roof of our building, I saw this spot on the top of the roof of the new building on fire, —perhaps covering a space of six feet square, — you could only see it from the top of our building, — and I went down stairs, and I met this Engineer and took him up high enough to show it to him, and told him a stream put up there for five minutes would save that building, but if it was left alone for fifteen minutes, it would be destroyed. He went away saying he would put a stream on there, but there was not any put on until it had worked down, and the first thing I knew it burst out of the windows. Somebody told me there was a stream got into the lower part of the building, and the firemen were afterwards ordered out.

Q. Was there anything further that you observed?

A. No, sir.

Q. Was not the building occupied by Lewis Coleman & Co. between you and the old Post Office?

A. No, sir; they were under us. We were in chambers above them, in the same building.

Q. Did your attic window finish take fire?

A. No, sir.

Q. Why?

A. In my opinion, the real cause of the escape of our building was in the fact that it was a great deal higher than the buildings on fire immediately around it; that is, than the old Post-Office building. These buildings were very close together. The passage-way between our building and the old Post Office was about six feet wide. The windows running up and down in some places in that building were opposite to ours, and without shutters, so that the flames burst out right opposite to ours; but on the roof, I question if any part of our building was even singed. I was up there a great deal, and there was no time I could not stand on the edge of the roof nearest to the burning building. I attribute its safety to the fact that it was twenty odd feet higher than the others, and that the wind blew away from our building. The danger to our building was at the windows, and the windows of the elevator.

Q. What was your roof covered with?

A. It is a gravel roof; what the material under it is I cannot say. Mr. Mudge, who was at the fire all the evening, spoke of his building as being unusually well put up. I know that all those things that are generally exposed are stone or iron, and I understand the roof is similarly protected. I know the roof is not injured. There are dormer windows in the attic on the roof; they are painted, I don't know whether on iron or wood.

Q. They were not severely heated, you say?

A. No, sir, I could not tell what the frame-work is. I could not say whether wood or iron. I know there was at no time heat enough to set any part of them on fire.

Q. The fire was so much below you?

A. Yes, sir. There was a time when I was down in the lower story somebody said, "They say outside that the roof is on fire." I expressed a disbelief of it, but wanted to be sure, and I went up stairs. I went up to the attic windows, which brought me above the gutters, and looked out, but could see no signs of it, and went out on the roof. On the corner of the building there is a portion of the roof surrounded by an iron railing, where I could go to the edge, but I could see no signs of any fire.

Q. You had no occasion to carry water up there?

A. No, sir.

Q. How were the firemen engaged to whom you went, and asked to go on to your roof?

A. They were playing and working very hard with three or four streams on the front of the buildings in Chauncy street. The buildings were on fire at the back and all around, and they were playing on the front of the buildings. What struck me as a great deficiency was that while those men were working bravely where they were doing little good, and working hard, there did not seem to be anybody looking round to see where the fire was spreading, and get at the points where it could be conquered. The top of our building was a splendid place to observe and find out all the points where to attack the fire successfully; but during the whole night, I question if there was a person in authority in the department up on top of that roof; during this time the store was in danger, only one Boston Engineer made his appearance there, and he for a short time, and the out-of-town Engineer that I have mentioned.

Q. How did they stop it on the other side of Chauncy street?

A. I think the new building stopped it from running up on the opposite side of the street. It was a new building with thick walls. The partitions had not been built. The timbers were large and solid, and there was nothing else combustible in the building; the roof of it, I think, had walls that went up like battlement walls. The wall went up higher than its own roof, and above the roof next to it.

Q. Did that get on fire once?

A. It got on fire from the top.

Q. That is the one that caught fire in the upper stories?

A. Yes, sir.

Q. Did they extinguish that?

A. Yes, sir, after it had burned out the two upper stories.

Q. How did they apply water to that?

A. They got one stream out of our windows across the street. I notified some of the firemen in the rear part of our building that the flames had burst out there, — the Engineer was not there, — and they brought a stream round and played out of one of our front windows on to it, and then they got on to a building south of that. Next to this high building there is one that is low; and below that another, that is quite as high as this new one; and they got a stream or two up on this building, and played across on to the one that was on fire. Then they might have had streams on it from the rear, that I could not see on Chauncy street.

Q. At what time did you think you were safe?

A. Not until — it must have been half-past four.

Q. In the building?

A. Yes, sir, I judge it was that; although, in the excitement, I took precious little notice of time. I recollect when the younger member of our firm, Mr. Amory Lawrence, came back, being a young-looking man, they would not allow him to pass through. I got through, but they would not allow him to pass through, and when he got back the danger was nearly over; and that was nearly five o'clock. I should say by half-past four the danger was nearly over; our danger really came from half-past two to four.

Q. How long did they have that hose up through your building?

A. Playing on the opposite side?

Q. Yes, sir.

A. Not very long; they got that under very soon. What I was afraid of was, the street was very narrow, and the flames came out at first with great force. I felt myself quite secure from the fire in the old Post-Office building, and we were all congratulating ourselves that we were safe, when this fire broke out suddenly. I should think the flames came out twenty feet right across. I was afraid it would catch our store and we should have to leave it; but they got it under very soon. There was one stream in our building during the early part of the fire, playing from our front windows on a building opposite.

Q. Playing on to this new building?

A. On the corner building, which was on fire and had been for some time, and I think I went to the men who had charge of that and asked them to take it round and play on to the burning building adjoining us, but they did not do it. I think the reason was they didn't have orders. I am not certain whether it was I or some one else who asked them, but I know they were asked.

Adjourned to Friday, at 3 P. M.

TWELFTH DAY.

FRIDAY, Dec. 13.

ARTHUR REED, *sworn.*

Q. (By Mr. RUSSELL.) Where is your place of business?

A. 66 State street.

Q. What time did you go to the fire?

A. I started from my house at the foot of Bowdoin street, immediately after the second alarm.

Q. (By Mr. COBB.) How far had the fire progressed when you got there?

A. When I first got there, it seemed to me it was only in the two upper stories. I stood there in the street and about that spot perhaps twenty minutes, and by that time the roofs of the opposite buildings on Summer street had begun to take fire. Then I went round through Hawley street, and into Winthrop square, and was in that neighborhood for an hour.

Q. (By Mr. PHILBRICK.) Did you see any efforts made to stop the fire from crossing Summer street?

A. I saw streams playing on the first two or three stories of the building where the French roof was burning, if that can be called an effort.

Q. Playing on to the fronts?

A. Yes, sir.

Q. Did you see any stream playing from the roof of the adjoining building?

A. I did not, sir.

Q. (By Mr. COBB.) From where you stood, could you look up Otis street so as to see what was being done there?

A. Not from Hawley street; but when I went through Hawley street into Otis street, I found an engine there, and the hose was clear along towards Summer street. Where it was playing, I can't tell.

Q. What were the most noteworthy incidents in regard to the spread of the fire in this half-hour?

A. It was the taking of the building on the opposite side of Summer street first, and going down through that street, and along the block which fronted on Winthrop square. I watched it go from one store to another as far as I could in Winthrop square, and stood there until the westerly side of Beebe's block was all on fire; then I made up my mind it was going to the water, and went round into High street to look after matters there.

Q. What matters?

A. Matters of my friends, who had stores there.

Q. Did you stay in High street until the buildings caught fire?

A. I did, except going over to my place in State street, carrying divers bundles, bags of books, etc. I made two or three journeys to

State street. I was in High street when that large block of Mr. Webster's, in the centre of High street, finally took fire.

Q. Did you see any of the Fire Department on High street?

A. I saw firemen. I have no recollection of seeing an engine there.

Q. (By Mr. COBB.) Were any streams of water thrown on the building?

A. I think not, sir.

Q. (By Mr. PHILBRICK.) Do you recollect between what hours High street was burned?

A. I can't say positively. My recollection is, it was about eleven o'clock when that building burned.

Q. Were the occupants of the stores pretty generally about there saving their property?

A. They were not when I first got there, and there were not a great many at any time.

Q. (By Mr. FIRTH.) Were those who were there employed in removing their own books, papers, etc?

A. Yes, sir, they were, so far as I saw. I remember the first journey I made from High street to State street with bags of books, I met scarcely anybody, and we were looked upon as very strange people, carrying things away from High street. One or two whom we met wondered what we were doing.

Q. (By Mr. PHILBRICK.) Were there any fires in High street at that time?

A. No, sir.

Q. (By Mr. FIRTH.) In regard to the spread of the fire, what did you think of it at the time, from all you observed?

A. When I saw Beebe's block and Winthrop square so entirely out of control of the firemen, as I said, I made up my mind that there was nothing to prevent its going to the water, as what little wind there was was in that direction.

Q. Was the spread of the fire very rapid and beyond anything you had before seen?

A. Very far beyond anything I had ever seen.

Q. (By Mr. PHILBRICK.) Was it mostly on the roofs?

A. That is where it took in every instance, so far as I saw, and worked down through the buildings. It held in the Beebe block, I should think, twenty minutes. I knew there was a very firm partition wall between that block and the store on the other side, and I remarked to the gentleman who was with me that that would save it, if anything would; but as we watched it, we saw it go over the roof and go down on the other side. When I saw that, I left.

Q. (By Mr. FIRTH.) After the fire reached High street, how rapid was its progress? What time should you have had then to have taken away your goods?

A. Scarcely any time at all.

Q. Did you notice anything about the wind at that point?

A. Yes, sir. I noticed a tremendous wind drawing right up High street towards the fire. I went out into the street once or twice when the brands were flying, and the wind was drawing them almost horizontally. They didn't seem to strike on the sidewalk, but were drawn right up the street.

Q. (By Mr. PHILBRICK.) How was the wind above the houses?

A. The wind above the houses seemed to be towards the east.

JOHN B. BROWN was called and sworn, but could give no information except upon points already covered.

EDWARD ATKINSON, *sworn.*

Q. (By Mr. RUSSELL.) At what time did you go to the City Hall on the night of the fire?

A. It would be impossible for me to say positively on that. It was, I should say, in the neighborhood of two o'clock.

Q. What took place there?

A. My first visit was to find out what the arrangements for the use of powder were, and to see if the attention of the parties at City Hall, or whoever had charge of the use of powder, could not be drawn to the line of Water street as a line of defence; that is, above the new Post Office, between Spring Lane and Water street, to make a gap where the fire had not reached, and below the Post Office, on the south side, where there were low buildings, of small value, the fire then being distant therefrom, but working that way.

Q. Whom did you see there?

A. I saw the Mayor, and, I think, Mr. Norcross.

Q. Did you have any talk with the Mayor?

A. I had a talk with the Mayor, and he at first said that Mr. Damrell had authority, and then he said that he had also granted authority to sundry persons, naming Gen. Burt. I didn't ask any authority for myself, because I didn't feel competent to use powder. I didn't know how.

Q. Did you meet Gen. Benham?

A. I did not, at that time. I went back to State street, and, the use of powder still appearing rather desultory, and too near the line of fire, as it appeared to me, I was speaking with Mr. Wise, of the firm of Wise & Russell, and making a remark upon it, when he said, "If we had Gen. Benham, or some other officer, it would be a good thing." At that moment, I looked out on the street, and there stood Gen. Benham. I went to him and asked him to go to City Hall. He consented; and I went with him to the Mayor. Gen. Benham then said that he should need men, if he was to have any authority, and I volunteered to go down to the Fort and get some regulars, taking an order from the Mayor for a tug.

I obtained twelve regulars, two sergeants, and a lieutenant, and I caused them to report at the City Hall, hoping they would be assigned to Gen. Benham for that use. They were not, but were put on guard somewhere.

Q. You did not blow up any buildings yourself?

A. No, sir. I do not know what responsibility I would not have taken, but I did not feel competent to do that; and I was very much mortified to see my name put in the newspaper in that connection by a reporter.

The most I did was to act as powder-monkey, to get the powder to one or two points where persons, who had authority, thought they needed it, and there to leave it under their control.

Q. Did you see any explosions?

A. I saw an explosion on the corner of Lindall and Kilby streets.

Q. What was the effect?

A. I thought the intention had not been carried out, of destroying the building. I knew that attention had been drawn to that corner long before, but at the time of the explosion, it was too near the fire, and the first effect seemed to be an immediate flash of flame, which, for the moment, looked as though the powder had done more harm than good; but I watched it through, to see the end, and it seemed to me that it brought the whole burning material low down, and made it easier to put the fire out, and to put it out in the next building to which it spread from that. I thought there was a good effect of the powder then, although I think the delay in getting off the charge had brought the explosion altogether too near to the line of fire.

Q. Did you see any other explosion?

A. I did not, near enough to have any judgment about it. I saw several, but not sufficiently near to have any judgment which I should be willing to give in evidence.

Q. Is there anything which you think the Commission ought to know, that you noticed?

A. As I walked up State street, after dawn, with the twelve regulars, the Engineer in charge of the engines stepped out to the lieutenant, and asked him to get his men detailed to protect his hose. He said that wagons and carriages were continually running across his hose and he could not protect it. That was the hose on which the safety of State street depended. There was an absence of any bridge or apparatus for the protection of the hose, which seemed to me to show negligence somewhere.

Q. Do you know what Engineer that was?

A. I do not. It was whoever had the apparent control of the engines at the head of State street, as we passed. I spoke of this afterwards to a hoseman, and he said that a model of a hose bridge had been presented by Mr. Damrell long before, and was lying in the City Hall, and had not been adopted; and he made a rather savage remark, which I will not repeat.

I noticed two points in regard to construction, which I understand you are going into a little. I happened to know the iron roof over the rotunda of Merchants' Exchange building, and I felt very anxious about that building, when I saw the fire getting from the rear into the upper stories, because I knew that those upper rooms — formerly intended for hotel purposes — were stored with furniture, and very inflammable; and I went to the top of the Columbia Bank, with young Mr. Coolidge and others, and watched the fire there, or rather should say watched the smoke, for we could see no fire, until the floors had been burned through, and the whole of the material had fallen into the rotunda. The reason why we could see nothing, and the reason of the safety of the building, was that there was a good, substantial flat iron roof through which the flames only appeared at the extreme corner from us, and there I think they only appeared through a window, not through the roof. There, I thought I saw evidence of good construction.

Q. (By Mr. PHILBRICK.) How did the fire get in under the roof?

A. It got in through the windows that were on the corner towards Congress street — the rear corner, towards Lindall and Congress streets. Another thing, of absolutely bad construction, not Mansard, I think ought to be noted — Monks' Building, one end of which was on Congress street, and which ran through, making the back of Congress square and joining City Exchange, where Charles Head's office is. That building had a flat roof, with a wooden coving projecting about two feet, and it was burned, catching fire entirely from that wooden projection. That wooden projection burned, in my judgment, at least half an hour before any injury was done to the main building. I pointed it out to two or three people when it caught, and saw it gradually spread until the building burned, and then the whole thing came down. It was one of the grave dangers on that part of State street.

Q. I would like to ask if you saw any evidence of organization or unity of action in the process of blowing up buildings?

A. No, sir; and could not find any. That was what I tried, in my humble way, to establish. It had seemed to me, from observation, at some distance to be sure, that the blowing up was desultory and altogether too near to the line of fire. I should not have presumed to meddle with it, except that I thought I could see a line on which an effective defence could be made.

There was a man, — a very brave fellow, I cannot give his name or identify him, — who, I think, touched off a good many charges in different places. He did not seem to have any hesitation in going in and touching them off. I do not know who he was. When I was escorting those policemen with the powder in charge, to the point where it was supposed it would be wanted, this man said: "I don't want that d——d sort; that is sporting powder. I want mortar powder; that brings them down."

Q. (By Mr. FIRTH.) What were your observations with regard to the conduct of the firemen during that night?

A. My only observation about them was on Sunday morning, after I came up from the Fort, and then it seemed to me that wherever there was a chance to concentrate a stream of water upon a low building, and make a fight, they did it. They did it wonderfully well, and, in my judgment, their use of water in the upper stories of the Merchants' Exchange building was very judicious.

Q. (By Mr. PHILBRICK.) Did you think their tactics were good?

A. So far as I could observe at that time. All the early part of the night, I was engaged in saving the goods of J. C. Howe and others; miscellaneous work.

HON. AVERY PLUMER, *sworn.*

Q. (By Mr. RUSSELL.) While you were an Alderman of the city, did Mr. Damrell call your attention to the want of water, in what has now become the burnt district?

A. Not particularly to the want of water, that I recollect. He repeatedly called my attention to the want of fire apparatus in the burnt district and vicinity, but I do not recollect of his mentioning that there was any deficiency of water.

Q. Did you go there with him?

A. I do not recollect as to that particular locality, but I went all over the city with him.

Q. Were you on the committee that had charge of that matter?

A. I was Chairman of the Committee on Fire Department for four or five years. The particular point with reference to this district was at the time the engine-house was located here in Bulfinch street, when the city bought the Smith estate. I was opposed to it, and Alderman Jenkins was also opposed to it. We felt that this immediate part of the city had as much protection as was necessary, while this large extent of territory, where so many warehouses were, was not protected. And the city had a tract of land on Batterymarch street that was lying idle, and the house could have been built there at no cost for land. But we were overruled, and this house was put up on Bulfinch street.

Q. (By Mr. FIRTH.) Was it proposed at that time by anybody to put an engine-house down on Batterymarch street?

A. Yes, sir; by gentlemen on both committees, I think, the Building Committee and the Fire Department Committee. I do not know whether there was any one else with me on the Committee on Fire Department who was in favor of it, but I was decidedly in favor of it. I thought that was the proper place to put it.

Q. (By Mr. FIRTH.) Did it present itself rather as a question between two places? As between the two, you would go there?

A. Yes, sir; I would go to Batterymarch street, rather than to Bulfinch street. In the first place, because I thought (and I believe the Chief Engineer thought so too) that that part of the city needed more protection; and, in the next place, on the ground of economy.

Q. Did it impress upon you that that was a point, by itself, requiring an engine house?

A. Yes, sir. There is no engine house, if I recollect right, along the water front, from East street, until you come round to the North end, below Union Wharf, I think.

NATHANIEL J. BRADLEE, *sworn.*

Q. (By Mr. RUSSELL.) How long have you been an architect in Boston?

A. Twenty-one years, for myself.

Q. Is there any difficulty in building Mansard roofs which shall be non-combustible?

A. No, sir.

Q. How should they be built?

A. They should be built with iron rafters and beams, and covered either with copper or iron; I should prefer copper, being lighter.

Q. Is there any less expensive material than copper which you consider safe in such a place?

A. Yes, sir; composition roofing (gravel and tar) is next to copper.

Q. Is that better than tin?

A. Yes, sir; you can heat through tin much quicker than through composition or copper.

Q. (By Mr. RUSSELL.) What do you think about the danger of a composition roof burning?

A. I have tried it on several occasions, making considerable fire, and never could set it on fire.

Q. Was that when the roof was new?

A. New and old both. I have tried it in all stages.

Q. (By Mr. FIRTH.) So far as your observation went, what should you conclude from the experience on the night of the fire with regard to the comparative safety of different kinds of roofs?

A. I think the slated roof did more harm than any other. The slate cracked from the heat and exposed the wood at once. The roofs covered with composition took fire last, and then they did not take from the top, they took from underneath.

Q. (By Mr. PHILBRICK.) Do you think a wooden cornice, if covered with sheet-iron, the proper finish for a wall sixty feet high?

A. No, I do not; I think if covered with galvanized iron, leaving an air space between it and the brick wall, it would be safe; but I wouldn't attach it to wood.

Q. You wouldn't attach the galvanized iron to the ends of the rafters?

A. By no means.

Q. How should they be attached?

A. By iron stays, let into the brick wall, carrying the brick right up.

Q. Iron furrings?

A. Yes, sir.

Q. (By Mr. COBB.) I would like to ask you if you saw any of the results of the use of gunpowder on the night of the fire?

A. In two buildings that I have had charge of, powder was used,—Mudge's store at the corner of Summer street, and the Merchants' Exchange building.

Q. What was the result?

A. The only damage done to Mudge's was by powder, which in my opinion was uselessly used. There was some fire in the Merchants' Exchange building, but the damage was increased by the use of powder, blowing off the iron roof. To illustrate that: The Sub-Treasury had an iron roof, and wrought-iron girders, trestle girders, and over the L part the same. The roof over the Exchange room was blown off, blown all to pieces, and down on the Sub-Treasury floor, carrying everything with it. The roof over the L wasn't blown off, and remains perfect to this day, although the building had wooden floors there, which were all burned out.

Q. What damage was done to Mudge's building?

A. The easterly wall and part of the northerly wall were sprung about half an inch, and the lower door-way and stair-case were blown into Summer street, and about $2,000 worth of plate glass broken.

Q. How much damage in dollars and cents was done to the Merchants' Exchange by the use of powder, in your judgment?

A. I should think the loss by the use of powder was at least $30,000, which might have been saved if powder had not been put there.

Q. Don't you think the fire would have done much more damage there, if powder had not been used?

A. No, sir, the fire was pretty accessible.

Mr. PHILBRICK. The advocates of the use of powder claim that they rendered the fire accessible by blowing that roof off.

WITNESS. I would like to have you examine the premises and see for yourselves how that was. You will find that the windows in Merchants' Exchange room are whole, and but very little burned. The fire came in, apparently, through an iron door-way in the L part, which was burned at first, and could have been easily managed without touching that roof.

Q. Didn't it get into the lofts where the furniture was stored?

A. It got into the rooms in the further end; the rooms at this end are still intact. It got in quicker after the roof was off than it would have done if the roof had been allowed to remain, and they could have stopped it without blowing off the roof.

Q. (By Mr. FIRTH.) Have you seen the elevator in use at Mr. Wellington's store on Chauncy street?

A. No, I have not.

Q. Have you seen any of the automatic elevators, where the hatches close after a load passes up or down?

A. No, sir.

Q. (By Mr. PHILBRICK.) Shouldn't you consider that a desirable appendage to the elevator trunks in the city?

A. I should. I should consider it a very decided improvement.

Q. (By Mr. COBB.) Both as a protection to life and against fire?

A. Yes, sir; and not an expensive one either.

Q. What is your opinion of the feasibility of introducing permanent water trunks into the large warehouses, which has been suggested by some of the correspondents in our papers, in order to avoid taking hose into the upper parts of the buildings?

A. It struck me very favorably. We have put one now into Jordan & Marsh's, and they also have a connection with the Cochituate main, so that they can turn it on themselves.

Q. (By Mr. COBB.) How recently has that been done?

A. Since the fire; the connection with the main pipe was to be made to-day.

Q. (By Mr. PHILBRICK.) I suppose, in case of fire, the Cochituate head wouldn't rise to the top of that building without a pump?

A. I think it might. If they had turned on the high service at Roxbury, and used the two engines, they might have increased the force somewhat.

Q. (By Mr. RUSSELL.) Didn't they do that?

A. No, sir.

Q. Is the high service in a condition to be immediately connected with the lower part of the city?

A. Yes, sir, by just opening the gate at Beacon Hill, the water would be let down this way.

Q. (By Mr. FIRTH.) How high are those pipes carried in Jordan & Marsh's store?

A. To the upper story.

Q. (By Mr. COBB.) How large is the pipe?

A. The pipe is three inches in diameter.

Q. (By Mr. RUSSELL.) How high is the upper story?

A. The upper story of the building is about sixty feet.

Q. (By Mr. FIRTH.) Can they tap it in any story?

A. Yes, sir, in each story; the head of the Cochituate is about twenty feet above the top of their roof, but of course, when they tapped the pipes in a great many directions, the head would be reduced at once.

Q. If the fire broke out in that building, they would have the full head?

A. Yes, sir; when the fire broke out, they would have the full head.

Q. (By Mr. PHILBRICK.) Have you any knowledge that the connection was not made with the high service on the night of the fire?

A. I know it was not.

Q. (By Mr. FIRTH.) Who is the person who has charge of the high-service pipes?

A. The east division of the Water Works is under the charge of Mr. Jones. I suppose he had as much as he could do that night to keep the supply round in this direction.

Q. (By Mr. PHILBRICK.) Are those stationary pumps so arranged that they can both be worked at once?

A. Yes, sir. We keep them for alternate service, so as to keep them in order, but they can be worked together.

Q. (By Mr. FIRTH.) Have both of them ever been used on any special occasion?

A. They have not. We have never had any fire in the district with which the high service is now connected since they were introduced.

Q. (By Mr. PHILBRICK.) Do you think, if the high service had been connected on the night of the 9th of November, that the supply of water would have been ample in this district?

A. I can't say that. I don't know as it would have increased the supply; it would have increased the head.

Q. Wouldn't that have furnished a great deal more water in a given time?

A. Yes, sir; that is, the head would have been increased; the pressure would have been greater on the pipes.

Q. Are the pipes in that part of the city adequate to sustain that pressure?

A. They have never been tested by that pressure, but there is no reason why they shouldn't bear it. The original pressure by which they were tested was more than that would have given them.

Q. While you were on the Water Board, was the subject ever prominently brought before you of introducing the Lowry hydrant?

A. That hydrant was introduced in some instances.

Q. (By Mr. RUSSELL.) Who brought it up?

A. The first Lowry hydrant was placed in Winthrop square some ten years ago, I think; when we extended the pipes into Roxbury, we put the Lowry hydrant throughout that section, and we have also used it in the Dorchester district.

Q. Was there ever any request or demand that it should be placed in Boston proper?

A. No; the objection to having it here then was that the firemen were not acquainted with it; they would have been obliged always to carry one of the heads; and to have one part of the city one way and part the other would be bad. Then there was another objection: The Lowry hydrant, to be efficient, must be placed over the centre of the pipe, and they were an obstruction in the streets; whereas, the hydrants which we use in the city proper are on the sidewalk. Then, again, in case of snow and ice, it became a question whether they would be so desirable in our narrow streets, where, in winter, there are sometimes two or three feet of snow, and you couldn't get at them; but the sidewalks are always cleared. Those in the Roxbury and Dorchester districts are all over the pipes; that is one of the advantages claimed for them, that they are right over the main. Mr. Cobb knows what an inconvenience the caps are in the streets.

Q. (By Mr. Firth.) After your experience, to what conclusion have you come in regard to the Lowry hydrants?

A. I don't see that they are any advantage over the other hydrants, although the firemen claim that they are.

Q. Are they not capable of furnishing more water?

A. I think not. They reduce the head at once; you may get more water to run seventy or eighty feet high, but the more taps you put into any pipe, the more you reduce the head.

Q. That would depend upon the size of your main, would it not?

A. The mains are all calculated for the natural supply, not for a large conflagration.

Q. (By Mr. Cobb.) Ought they not to be provided to meet that necessity?

A. Under the circumstances, I don't think they should be. I think, if you should lay pipes to meet such a contingency as we have just had, they would cost more than the whole water supply. The pipes in Kingston street, for instance, are now six inches in diameter, and they are ample for the ordinary wants. If you were to put in pipes twelve inches in diameter, they would cost at least ten times as much.

Q. (By Mr. Philbrick.) It is not a continuous outlay, it is a plant of capital. It would not increase the current expenses, would it?

A. Well, you take the cost of the distributing pipes in the city proper, which, if my memory serves, was some $6,000,000, if the streets were to be piped the size necessary for such a conflagration as that, it would cost at least seventeen or eighteen millions of dollars. The city wouldn't be justified in making such an expenditure.

Q. (By Mr. Firth.) If the question was a new one, what would be your judgment?

A. I shouldn't make any change in the pipes. I think everything depends, in case of fire, on its management at its starting-point.

Adjourned to Monday, at half-past seven.

THIRTEENTH DAY.

MONDAY EVENING, Dec. 16th.

WILLIAM COPELAND, *sworn.*

Q. (By Mr. RUSSELL.) What is your connection with the Police force?

A. I am attached to Station No. 5.

Q. Were you present when the cellar and boiler of the building first on fire were uncovered?

A. Yes, sir. I found one of the doors of the furnace open about an inch, and the other open about four inches. It was a double door.

Q. What was the condition of the boiler?

A. The boiler to all appearances was good — all that I could see.

Q. You have not been able to see the top yet, have you?

A. No, sir.

Q. What was the condition of the coal?

A. I should judge that there was from one-eighth to one-quarter of a ton of coal in the fire-box, on the grates, under the boiler pushed back. It was partially burned coal; but I took out one piece and found that it was fresh and not burned at all. That was just off of the grate. The body of it was pushed back.

Q. Was there any in front of the fire-box, on the floor?

A. There was, I should think, one-eighth of a ton of fresh, new coal there.

Q. (By Mr. PHILBRICK.) Was that on the brick hearth?

A. Yes, sir, — about twelve inches below the floor of the cellar.

Q. Was there a step there?

A. Yes, sir.

Q. What was it made of?

A. That was brick.

Q. Was any part of the wooden floor of the cellar remaining?

A. There was a small piece left there; perhaps the whole of it would not amount to the size of your table there. It was enough to show the level.

Q. Would it show where the floor came against the boiler?

A. It was about twenty inches from the boiler-wall.

Q. Was there an unburned edge to show where the edge of the floor stopped formerly — before the fire?

A. Yes, sir. It stopped at the edge of the sunken place in front of the boiler. I found a straight, clean edge there.

The hearth was about eight feet square, I should judge. The edge of the wooden floor came to within three or four feet of the boiler door. There was no wooden floor nearer than four feet. All the fire in the grate had been pushed back.

Q. How near was the nearest of it to the door?

A. I should think ten or twelve inches — perhaps twelve inches.

Q. Did you find the remains of the shovels?

A. The shovels were taken out of there with the handles burned off; I was not there at the time, but I saw them afterwards.

Q. When was this that you dug down to it?

A. It was last Saturday forenoon.

Q. Was the fire banked with ashes, or in any other manner?

A. I could not see any ashes there. I could see nothing but coal.

Q. (By Mr. FIRTH.) The appearance inside did not indicate that it was affected by the outside great fire itself?

A. No, sir.

Q. Did it look as if there had been no outside fire? Did the coal inside of the grate look as it would have looked if there had been no outside fire?

A. Oh, yes, sir.

Q. Under the ordinary course of things, if the fire had been left in that way, would not the coal have burned up probably?

A. Probably in back it had burned. But the grates were about twelve inches from the front of the doors, and this piece of coal lay on the flat part of the iron — not on the grate.

Q. Would it not burn down to less than one-eighth of a ton before going out?

A. I should think that it would. I should have thought that it would have all burned up.

Q. What prevented it from burning up?

A. I cannot tell, unless the draft was shut off in the chimney. The front ash-doors were shut tight.

Q. (By Mr. RUSSELL.) Was there any kindling wood about there?

A. Nothing that I could see. Furthermore, I waited there until they shovelled everything out, and there was nothing in the shop but old coal, cinders and the like, in the space that was bricked. I was very particular about that.

Q. No old rubbish?

A. There was some calico, prints, or something of that sort that was taken out. But probably that fell there. It was buried up in the rubbish, partially burned.

Q. Did you see anything that looked like kindling-wood?

A. No, sir. There was some charcoal. But that probably was from the ruins.

Q. What seemed to have prevented this piece of floor from burning?

A. I cannot tell, unless it was the stuff falling on to it, and the water playing in. That was all of the floor that I saw.

Q. This was twelve inches down from the floor to the brick work?

A. Yes, sir.

Q. Was it all one step?

A. Yes, sir; there was no appearance of the step being divided.

Q. (By Mr. FIRTH.) Was there any appearance of fire having been communicated from that?

A. I should think not. The walls of the boiler appeared to be perfect, with the exception of something falling against it in one case, — I mean the brick casing.

Q. Did you see the skin of the boiler at all?

A. No, sir; only the ends, — what is called the bonnet. I believe you could see the tubes — all of them.

Q. Did you see the communication with the chimney?

A. Partly. The flue was gone. It went from the front up to the right-hand corner. There were some bricks in the wall gone. The flue in the wall was gone. I could not see where it went up, but I should think it went up along flat, horizontally, for eight or ten feet. There was flagging-stone set in there for some reason, and we concluded that that was the flue that was the draft of the engine-room. The engine-room was between there and the elevator; but there appeared to be a brick wall between the boiler and the engine.

Q. Did that flue pass as far as that brick wall?

A. Yes, sir; I should think that it passed by it.

Q. What prevents you from seeing where the flue went up?

A. The wall has fallen; it has fallen about even with the top of the setting of the boiler. There is one place where there is the appearance of a flue; but if it was a flue, there has something fallen out from it. That is some ten or twelve feet from the boiler; it might be a little more than that.

Q. (By Mr. Cobb.) From all you saw, is there anything that led you to believe that that fire originated in or about that furnace?

A. I could not see the first thing.

Q. You were looking for that particular appearance?

A. Yes, sir; I have been a fireman myself for seven or eight years, and am an old hand in the department.

WILLIAM M. FLANDERS, *sworn.*

Q. (By Mr. Russell.) Have you been on the Fire Department Committee?

A. Yes, sir; for the five years ending this year.

Q. Has Chief Engineer Damrell ever called your attention to the want of facilities for extinguishing fire on what is now the burned district?

A. Yes, sir; a great many times.

Q. What has he said?

A. I think as long ago as 1869 he took me down through Franklin street. We went down together. (I could not fix the time exactly, it may be longer ago than 1869.) He called my attention to it, and had a little map drawn out. He told me the extent of the hydrants, and how they were located, — in particular a Lowry hydrant, which is located nearly opposite Donahoe's printing establishment, I should think, and which he was very anxious to have remain.

As he had it dotted out on the map, he said, "Now I have not got a hydrant here in Devonshire street, until I get away over to this part of Devonshire street; and in case of any conflagration here, I don't think that our service-pipe is large enough to give us a sufficient quantity of water to put out the fire."

Q. (By Mr. Philbrick.) By "service-pipe" you mean the street-main?

A. Yes, sir; it is perhaps more properly the street-main. We took some action in our Fire Department Committee at that time to call the attention of the Water Board to the fact. I remember urging it very strongly that as long as our department paid for $60,000 or $70,000 worth of water, we should control the hydrants; that they did really belong to us, — I mean our Board, or the Committee on the Fire Department.

The Water Board would go to work and discontinue hydrants, without ever notifying our Board. In taking up the streets, as they are constantly doing for re-paving, sewerage and the like, I don't think in a single instance did the Water Board notify the Fire Department that they had disturbed a hydrant. At the same time, we paid this awful sum of $60,000.

The Chief Engineer took the ground that if the Fire Department had the control of the hydrants (it coming out of our appropriation, we paying twelve or fifteen dollars for every hydrant put down, and for the Lowry hydrants twelve or fifteen dollars more, we have always urged that we should have the Lowry hydrants) that in winter and cold weather we could see to the management of them better than the Water Board had heretofore done, by the proper packing and trying of them and everything of that nature, and that we should have control of everything that pertained to the hydrants.

I will now come down to another period, viz.: that when the House of Correction took fire. Mr. Cobb was on the Board at that time. I was called to go there, but was not a member. That was a year ago last April, I think.

The Chief was very anxious that I should see the first Engineer that got there and talk to him about the supply of water there. I found that they had not any water of consequence there. You could get it through a squirt-gun as well as through that hydrant. They were compelled to go to the ocean for water, and also out to the Glass Works, where there was a large mud-pond. We had to run our hose out there. If it had not been for that, we should never have stopped that fire where we did. It was all owing to the small pipes that they had, and to their not being properly packed. Capt. Regan found an old reservoir there and succeeded in getting what water we wanted.

Then, to come down a little farther, I think it is about a year ago this month that Steamer 7's house caught fire, in this way (if I am properly told by the Engineer that has the charge of the engine of that house): the water, it seems, had been turned off by the Water Board, and the Fire Department Committee, the Chief Engineer and the other Engineers had not been notified; they thought the water was frozen up, and they went to work to thaw it out, when there was no water there, and in that way they set the building on fire. When the engines got down there, there was no water to play upon it. Whether there was any blame to be attached to any one for that, I don't know.

Then to come down to the time just after the conflagration at Chicago: the committee and I were very anxious that the Chief should visit Chicago and learn all he could in regard to the use of gunpowder, and how the fire was managed. He came home, and we went down through our district — took his horse and buggy and rode around. He said,

"I dread a fire here at a time when we have a great drought." We were going through part of the district lately burned. He said, "If a fire should get in here and we should have a short supply of water, I don't think that any agency, human or divine, could stop it." I said, "We must keep up our apparatus, have new hose, and, if there is a necessity for more engines, we must have them." We took pains to keep the apparatus in good order, and I think at the time of the fire the department never was in better condition in respect to the supply of hose, and everything except in regard to the condition of the horses.

Q. Did Capt. Damrell call your attention to the supply of water in this vicinity?

A. Before going into that I might speak of this fact: In the location of engines, we have always had a great deal of trouble to get one located. If we wanted one in a certain place, some committee would want it in another. Take the matter of the location of Steamer No. 4, which you are well acquainted with. In the first place, a member of the Council introduced an order asking for authority to locate it under the Court House. Mayor Gaston said he would see the Judges, but he thought they would object to its being located there. They did object. Our friend, the editor of the "Commercial Bulletin," came out with a red-hot article against me, saying that I was trying to put up a job. We advertised. Some wanted to put it down in Bowker street. The Chief said he never would consent. He wanted it nearer this way. We advertised for proposals for Steamer No. 4. They came in — from $75,000 to $150,000. I went to see Mr. J. B. Smith, and he told me that he had been assured that he could get $60,000 for his site. I told him that we never could advocate that amount. Here was a large amount of valuable property left uncovered if we took it away. Then I went and saw Mr. Clapp, the editor of the "Journal," and told him that I would like to have him see Mr. Smith and see if he could not get his price down. We got his price down to $55,000. We carried it through and got the steamer located there.

The Chief has always been for bringing apparatus nearer the centre, instead of locating it on the outskirts of the city.

That night of the fire I had just left my house; and before I heard the alarm, living in Edinboro' street, very near where the fire was, I heard people halloing fire, and running towards Kingston street. When I got to Kingston street (I think before the alarm was sounded), the flames seemed to be right out on the roof, coming through the windows. I heard Steamer 7's gong strike as she came out of her house. They must have seen the fire. It was very clear, and you could hear the gong a good ways. I could not swear that it was No. 7, but no other steamer being in that direction, I took it for granted that it must be Steamer 7. I had no idea but what the Chief would be able to stop the fire, because we always had stopped fires.

Within three or four months, I called the attention of our committee (which consists of Alderman Woolley, Alderman Clark and Alderman Cutter) to the fact that I thought it very important that we should have control of the hydrants. It was not three months ago. You will find it on the record, before we thought of any conflagration. I have urged it very strongly in the committee that we should have control of the hydrants so long as we paid for them. It was brought before the Water Board, but no written report was made in regard to what action they took in the matter.

Q. (By Mr. Cobb.) Has there been any record made in the committee about the Chief's asking for greater facilities, — both as regards apparatus and water?

A. He never has called for any apparatus, to my knowledge, but what he has had it.

Q. You said you had taken some action in the committee regarding water and the putting in of Lowry hydrants?

A. I presume there has been a record made of that, because it was entrusted to Alderman Cutter. It was about three months ago.

It has been talked in general committee, and I have talked outside that we ought to have it. I have always said that we ought to have control of the engine-houses, which we do not.

Q. You have felt the necessity of having a large supply of water there?

A. Yes, sir; I have, from the very fact that the Chief has always called my attention to it, and I have been in favor of it.

Q. Why have you not introduced it into the City Council?

A. We never could get any full vote of the committee to do it. Alderman Cutter, being on the Water Board for three or four months, called their attention to that fact.

Q. Can you get that record?

A. I presume so. While we are on the subject of the Lowry hydrant, I would say that our department has always been considered a very expensive department, and the Water Board thought that these other hydrants were just as good as the Lowry hydrants.

Q. You didn't think so?

A. I only knew from what the Engineers told me.

Q. You think the pipes had lost their pressure often, with this small hydrant?

A. It struck me so. There didn't seem to be any pressure that night. That was early, — when they first got a-going.

Q. Did you see the Chief?

A. He was rushing right around among them all. I hailed him, but he said he could not stop.

Q. Did he seem to have a definite plan?

A. Yes, sir.

Q. I understand that your impression is that the difficulty was in the Water Board?

A. I merely tell you what our efforts have been to get control of the hydrants. If we had had control, we would have had in the Lowry hydrants.

Q. Is the location of hydrants determined by the Water Board?

A. Yes, sir. They put them in where they are a mind to. Never to my knowledge have they consulted with the Chief Engineer. And in putting in these fire-alarm signals, they put them in where the fire-alarm committee say. That is a special committee — the Committee on Bells and Clocks.

C. W. FREELAND, *sworn.*

Q. (By Mr. Russell.) At what time did you reach the fire?

A. It was a little before nine o'clock; I should say about quarter before nine.

Q. Where was your place of business?

A. 14 Devonshire street is my office. I did not get to the fire at that time. The President of the Hamilton Bank (of which I am a Director) and the Cashier of the Massachusetts Bank were there, and we were in conversation about the prospect of the fire coming there.

At eleven and a half o'clock, we hired a large truck-wagon and brought it to the front door, and kept it there until we wanted it. I was in the building there from ten to fifteen minutes, so as to notice the fire. It worked along to Milk street. The Post Office made a barrier there; and we were there until seven o'clock in the morning before we removed the valuables out around in the rear.

I told several gentlemen at the Hide and Leather Bank (I don't know that they were firemen), that I thought it was very strange that they did not get on top of the buildings more.

The "Post" building got on fire, and the buildings below that were on fire and burning down. Much surprise was expressed that there were not more firemen on the tops of the buildings. It would be easy for them to get off, because they could run from one building to another.

After the Hide and Leather Bank building was burned, I went down to the brick building below the cross street on the right of Water street. That building was on fire. It is only a two or three story building. It was on the right side. I think drugs and paints are sold there. It was apparently about falling in when I was there. I thought that it was so far away from the Shawmut Bank that that building was perfectly safe and would not take fire.

I came back to the banks and reported to the President and Directors that I did not think that there was one chance in twenty that the fire would get there. It was not long after that that the Shawmut Bank took fire from some source, and the fire kept going to the north of the Hide and Leather Bank building.

Our valuables were taken to a place of safety. One was in Hamilton square, and the other was opposite the Athenæum. I went up there, and the fire had just begun to drift north, where the Hide and Leather Bank was.

My coachman brought me up in a carriage. I told him to go into this square and remain there. When I came up past here I could not see him.

I was not gone from the building half an hour before I was back there, and then everything had burned up to the rear of the Exchange, including Monks' building and another. They were almost totally destroyed. They were all flat. [Illustrates with a diagram.]

Here is a solid wall. I leased this building of Mr. Howe for twenty-five years, and filled it up. When I did so, I put a brick wall there a foot thick. These two buildings were built together. I intended to put up a battlement-wall, but didn't think of it in time.

These roofs were together. There was no entrance except through the entry-way here.

Those were the only two vital points in this building. When I returned I went down to the end of the building to see the condition of things, and found that everything was flat. There is a road-way that runs along by this building. Out of the fourth story of my building was going a stream of water on to the wooden cornice of *that* building. There were two or three streams of water playing on to this building that was on fire. I told the firemen that I wanted a stream of water upon the top of this building immediately. They told me that it was useless — that the building was so high, that it was impossible to do anything towards saving it. I found it impossible to get any of them to play upon it. I spoke to all the men there who appeared to be in command.

I immediately came back here into Devonshire street and saw at the "Post" building several white hats. I went there as quick as I could, because I was afraid of this roof. The first man that I spoke to proved to be Capt. Damrell. I didn't then know him from any of the rest of them. He listened to me and immediately sent to State street and placed two streams of water under my command. I had told him of the importance of the thing.

I told the men that I wanted a stream as quick as it could be brought there. We started and came *here*, and I myself assisted in taking the hose up to the top of the building. We got it up in a reasonable length of time.

I told the men to take axes and cut away the roof from the back side of this brick wall, anywhere. There was some one up there who also gave them instructions to tear off the wooden roof, which they did. I told them that they must not in any event allow the fire to cross that wall.

I then went down and got the other line of hose and took it up into another building (which was fire-proof — of stone and marble) and fought the fire. There was not much fire in the first story. The men went up stairs, and it seemed to be very difficult to get at the fire. My great anxiety was for fear the hose might burst in being taken up those stairs. I had very little time to observe what was being done elsewhere. After I got back, about half-past twelve o'clock, I confined myself to this place. The work was done very well. My ideas were carried out. They seemed to be short of hose in carrying it up. There was no lack of hose on the top of the building.

Q. Do you think that in the absence of your giving them this information as to this line of defence, it was sufficiently apparent to any of the Fire Department for them to have seen it?

A. No, sir, it was not. There was no one else there probably that knew the vital points. I knew them, because I built the wall myself and occupied the building, and, in an instant, as soon as I saw the fire in the rear of my office, I thought of these things. There was one building on fire there that was higher than the other. There were two low buildings where Bond's chronometer watch establishment is. At the end is Congress square. There was a solid brick wall between the high and the low buildings, and I knew that when that had burned out the other buildings were perfectly safe, because the fire had been stopped on the opposite side of the street. I knew that those buildings were perfectly safe, and I had nothing to fear upon that ground. I presume the firemen, if they had known the points of defence, would have taken care of it, and done it in time; but there was not a chance in fifty of its being done, because they did not know the construction of the building. It was the key to the whole situation, as you see by the diagram.

Nobody would know anything about this unless they were familiar with the premises. If I had not been there it would have burned. Capt. Damrell was quite ready to listen to me in an instant. He didn't see it; but I told him what it was and what I wanted.

Q. Did he seem to see it from your statement of the case?

A. He listened to me at once, and he went and gave me the relief I asked for at once, so that I inferred that he took in the whole situation.

Q. What do you think of wooden cornices in case of fire, — from what you saw of them that night?

A. My building there had a stone cornice on both sides. When I rebuilt it I put on a stone cornice in front. I should not put any wooden cornice on any building. I put on my own dwelling-house not only a stone cornice, but a stone dormer window.

Brick is the best building material there is. There is no question about that. Mr. Brewer and many people have been to see me about building material, knowing that I have built considerable, and I have invariably said that I would only use brick or iron, and my preference was brick. If I was going to erect a handsome building in Devonshire street, I would have it of heavy iron in the first story, because you want to get in a good deal of light, and in that respect there is no substitute for iron. Above, I would have it of brick, with some light stone trimmings, and I would paint the brick of some suitable contrasting color, and have handsome plate-glass windows. I believe the General Government are going to give us plate-glass cheap for a time.

Q. Did you notice anything about the way in which the granite stood the fire?

A. There were no walls fell while I was there at the place before spoken of. While I was in the banks during the night, from what I learned, it seemed to me that they didn't fight the fire enough from the tops of buildings. Standing in the street, they had little effect. The danger was from the tops of buildings rather than from the bottoms — from those wooden dormer windows and wooden cornices. If the heat was sufficient to set the stores on fire on the north side of Franklin street, just from the heat on the south side, it would seem hard to tell where you could use water. It would be pretty rough on top if it was hot enough to set buildings on fire on the north side of Franklin street. The fire looked very bad when I first saw it.

Q. Did you ever see a fire spread like that?

A. Never anything to approach it.

Q. (By Mr. PHILBRICK.) Do you consider the present style of elevators running from cellar to attic, prudent?

A. The elevators at our factories have sliding doors at every floor, and they open and shut of themselves. If any of you, gentlemen, have been in mills, you know how they are constructed. I can show you. It is a very desirable thing to apply to all Boston elevators. It is desirable on more accounts than one. You avoid the danger of falling down the hatchway. They are thus constructed in all modern mills, so that when the elevator passes up it crowds the doors open, and then when it comes the other way it shuts right down again. In my opinion, it should be rendered compulsory. The cost is moderate. Nobody now builds a first-class mill without one of those.

Q. Do you know what the cost is?

A. I can't tell you to-night, but I can send it immediately, because we are putting in several.

Q. Is there a patent on it?

A. I think that there is a patent on it still. I think that W. H. Thompson, treasurer of the Manchester Print Works, has the patent. I think it was invented at Biddeford. He has a patent on it, or an interest in it.

Q. Send whatever papers about it that you have to us.

A. I can inform you, because we have several of those elevators going in at Chicopee Mills. They are made at Holyoke of the same pattern. It is my impression that the cost is $1,200 or $1,500 dollars. On my return from Chicopee I will send you an exact statement. I don't know what the cost of these is. The patent right is a very small tax upon it. The only difference between this and the ordinary elevator is in this opening and shutting of the doors. Then you have the expense of the doors and of the attachment. There is a royalty, I think, of $300 on an elevator. One elevator answers for quite a large warehouse. I suppose from the experience of this fire it is shown that gravel roofs are much safer than tin or slate. I think gravel preferable to tin, and I suppose tin and copper are not very different, except that copper is thicker. Other than that, there is not much difference, because the danger arises from its being heated through on to the wood underneath. Both are soon heated through.

Mr. Powell, the mason, was telling me to-day about the Mercantile Building on Summer street, that there were quantities of fire and of inflammable materials, and of materials on fire that fell on to that building and went out, and that this building didn't take fire as quickly as Trinity church, which was covered with slates.

Q. How extensively have you built in Boston?

A. My experience has been more in dwelling-houses than anything else. I have built a million dollars' worth or more of dwelling-houses, and I built over the Exchange, which was substantially the same as erecting a new building.

It must be an understood thing that when a fire breaks out, a certain number of firemen or hosemen must run up and go upon the top of the building.

Q. (By Mr. PHILBRICK.) Is it not very difficult to keep the hose from bursting when it is carried up in that way?

A. That fire went up six stories high, and the water was carried 75 feet after they got on top of the buildings.

Then you may have iron stand-pipes. It is no matter about having them on the outside of the building, only to have a connection outside. That is what we have for factories. We have iron stand-pipes on the outside of mills, with a fire-escape right alongside of them that can be run out of the building for the people to go down the steps; we have a stand-pipe about every 100 feet.

Q. Would not the value of the upper stories pay for having the two upper stories indestructible?

A. That tends to enchance the cost. I don't expect they would erect buildings more than five stories high, but the lower the building the greater the cost. All about Franklin street and Devonshire street, these upper stories were as full as hives, and they all paid well. They would not pay in State street, because you could not get a class of tenants that would pay. Beebe had rented to outside parties, Skinner & Co., and Leland, Allen & Bates, one or two stories for storage. It was a convenient place, near by, and they were kept rented all the time.

Take the actual addition to the cost from putting on six stories rather than five, and in the percentage there is no expense except the actual expense of the walls, the iron, and the putting on of another floor. The percentage received from that additional expense is just as good as the percentage that would be received from the whole building. With steam-elevators, the fifth or sixth stories are just as good for storage as the second.

GEORGE SNELL, *sworn*

Q. (By Mr. Russell.) For how many years have you been an architect, in this country?

A. I came to this country in the latter part of 1849. I have been here since 1850.

Q. Do you know any difficulty about building Mansard roofs of incombustible materials?

A. No, sir, I know no difficulty at all about it.

Q. Of what materials would you build them?

A. There is a variety of fire-proof materials that I would use. The dressings, architraves, cornices, or whatever it might be about the dome or windows, I would have of incombustible materials, it may be of brick, stone or iron. The mouldings, if any, down the steep front, and the flat at the top, or the less steep inclination, I would have of iron, or at least covered with copper or tin.

Q. If they are so made, are Mansard roofs objectionable in regard to fire, or more exposed to fire than other roofs?

A. I think I can show you that the very best form of roof is what would be called here a "Mansard roof" *i. e.* any steep roof.

Q. How would you cover the steep portion?

A. I don't suppose that slate is absolutely combustible, but one could do much better than that. If it was very steep, it could be iron, or covered with copper. I saw the other day a material made of Neufchatel stone, for roofing, which they told me they could make slabs of, to cover the upright surface.

Q. You have not tried that?

A. I saw the experiment of it on a flat roof. I was there after the fire had been burning some time and when it was nearly out, and I could not see any effect that it would have on the roof. I went underneath and put my hand on the inch-board — the one thickness of board that is underneath it, — and it was scarcely warm.

Q. What was the thickness of the preparation of stone?

A. I should think it was about half an inch.

Q. (By Mr. FIRTH.) Where is that prepared?

A. They are going to prepare it in Boston, if they can get a business. They are preparing it now in New York. The probable cost would be fourteen dollars per square, and it is quite reasonable.

Q. Is it a new composition?

A. I am told not. They used it as long ago as before the fire in Hamburg. It has been used in London and England. It has been tested, as they told me, by the military authorities in England, where they had had two roofs that they had built covered with this material. They built a fire upon one roof and kept it on there a long time, and it had no effect upon it. They put another roof up, and put a fire underneath it, and after a while, the wood under it was burned and the roof fell down and put the fire out. When that which supported it was burned, the fire was put out. This composition is prepared in the form of paste and spread upon the roof in a connected mass.

Q. Do you consider slate on a wooden boarding a proper and efficient protection against the steep inclination of these roofs, when they are heated by an adjoining building?

A. I would rather have copper. But I would much rather have slate on one of these roofs than on one of the old-fashioned roofs.

At the fire, I didn't see roofs take fire through the slate; but I noticed particularly the effect of fire upon one building in which the value of parapets properly constructed, and of party-walls projecting in front of steep roofs, was strikingly illustrated. I saw a remarkable instance of that, — an instance in which the fire was entirely stopped, although the moulding that was down the steep part and the flat at the top were of wood, and the dressings on the dormer windows were of wood, and one dormer window was, I think, about three feet only from the parapet-wall. It was one of the Hunnewell blocks. The exposure to the heat in this particular one was lengthwise in the block. The other had caught fire in front and in the rear. But this one at the last, after I was obliged to leave the scene, was no doubt set on fire by the building just opposite to it, viz.: the Cathedral block.

The building I was in caught fire from the buildings adjoining. That Cathedral block was only distant from it about ten feet, and the windows of it were opposite the windows of the other. There was an opportunity of testing precisely whether a fire would spread from one building fiercely on fire, with a properly constructed parapet-wall, or parapet running down a steep roof in front, the cornice being of stone, — whether that would communicate fire to the other. It did not do so in this instance. There was not a single stream of water played upon the building, because the firemen were engaged entirely in putting out the fire upon the building opposite, — in order to save Wright & Sons' building, and stop the fire there if possible.

Q. Do you consider the common method of constructing elevators in our warehouses a prudent thing?

A. No, sir. I think it very imprudent indeed to have an opening from the cellar right up to the top — a sort of ventilation-shaft, as it were.

Q. Have you seen any building constructed with self-closing hatches in the elevator?

A. There was a model brought to my office, a few days after the fire, in which there was a very ingenious contrivance for shutting the hatches as you came up. The platform as it rose impinged against some cams that turned around and opened the scuttle above, so that as it approached it, it opened in the way which I now illustrate, and as it left it, it shut it again. The scuttle was a hinged scuttle.

Q. There is one in operation in Mr. Wellington's store, which operates automatically?

A. I have not seen that. But of course there must be a great many different ways of closing hatches.

Q. If the closing of hatches were left to the care of attendants, do you think it would be done efficiently?

A. I am quite certain that it would not be done efficiently.

Adjourned to Tuesday afternoon, December 17th.

FOURTEENTH DAY.

TUESDAY, December 17.

THORNTON K. LOTHROP, *sworn.*

Q. (By Mr. RUSSELL.) At what time did you go to the great fire?

A. I left my house about half-past seven o'clock in the evening.

Q. What was the condition of the fire when you arrived on the ground?

A. I suppose I got down there about quarter before eight; it is difficult to tell precisely. I stopped on my way, waiting for a gentleman who was on his door-steps to go down with me, and we went down first to the head of Summer street, and then round through Franklin street, into Winthrop square, and in that vicinity.

Q. Had the fire got into Winthrop square when you reached there?

A. No, sir.

Q. Where was it?

A. Klous's building, which was the first building which took fire, was pretty well in flames, but nothing had fallen. The wood-work of the building on Carney's old estate, on the opposite corner, had caught more or less. I can't answer as to the front of the building opposite Klous's, on Summer street, — that is, where John C. Gray used to live, but the wood work on the side, the windows, cornices and so on, had very slightly caught. I suppose the front may have been well in flames; I didn't see it at that time. There was a ladder up on the building two or three doors further down Summer street. The firemen were playing water on that Klous building (I can't tell about Carney's), and on the side of the building on Otis street opposite.

Q. You say there was a ladder further up on Summer street?

A. Yes, sir, a little further up, but even nearer the fire than Minot & Pierce's store was, for I remember wondering whether that would catch or not. The fire was substantially, it seemed to me at that time, confined to that building, the others having caught a little. At the same time, the opposite corner of Summer street may have been all on fire in front; I can't tell about that. I stood in Winthrop square, I should think, between half and three-quarters of an hour, and I didn't feel at all apprehensive, while I was in the square at that time, that the fire was going to spread any further. I didn't go out into Summer street at that time. When I left there, the side of the building on Otis street had caught a good deal more, and it looked to me as though that building would probably go; at the same time, I didn't think the fire would then jump that gap from there to Weld and Beebe's building. There was no one on top of the building, or anywhere about it. I left there and went round through the back alleys and into Milton place and High street, and so up into Summer street, and came up nearly to Church Green. I was some considerable time in getting round there, and when

I got round there, the fire in Summer street showed signs of stretching down towards Church Green, — not much, but still a little.

The ladder I spoke of had been moved further along, and I saw firemen going up the ladder outside, but there was no hose going up that I could see. They were still washing down the granite outside, without reaching the fire. I stayed there, I suppose, some twenty minutes; perhaps I might say I was gone from Winthrop square twenty minutes; while I was standing there, there was a sudden rush of flame and great masses of burning wood. I say "masses;" I mean that pieces six inches long came over directly where I was standing, so that the people about there turned up their coat-collars first, and then, as another shower came over, started and moved back a little. I moved back a little. I then went back into Winthrop square, and when I got there the policemen were just drawing a line across the square. The steamers had moved back to those blocks on Devonshire and Franklin streets; perhaps not so far back as that, but still well back of Winthrop-square block. In two minutes after I got there, the Winthrop-square block seemed to be lighted from bottom to top with a flash of flame; the whole thing was evidently on fire. I stayed there five or ten minutes. I can give you the judgment which I expressed at the time,— not an after judgment at all. I turned to the gentleman next to me and said what I should say now, "This fire will go to the Custom House, unless it is stopped by blowing, or something else; it is entirely beyond the power of the firemen now." I didn't think it was going to stretch up towards Washington street, from the way it had been going (I had observed the way the flames were tending), but it seemed to me it would go square down in front of the Custom House, unless something was done to stop it.

Q. Did you notice any facts in regard to the conduct of the firemen?

A. The individual firemen whom I saw worked extremely well. The water at that time in the evening didn't touch the fire at all; an occasional spurt of water would strike the cornice or heavy projections of a building, but it was a very occasional stream of water; that was the best a man could do if he was standing on the sidewalk, and spurting at a fire which was very high up. It was impossible to hit it except by accident.

Q. When you first arrived at Winthrop square, did you see any ladder up, or men on the roofs of the buildings on Otis street?

A. I think the ladder was up when I first got there; it might have been put up afterwards, but I am quite sure there was a ladder up there, and some men appeared on the top of the buildings on the side where Mr. Gray's building was, on my left as I was standing. There was no ladder while I was there, I am very sure, on the southerly side; but there was no hose playing on the top; whatever water was played, was played from the bottom. When I came round on the other side of Winthrop square, there was a hose carried up, if I recollect rightly, through a low building between the Winthrop-square block and the building at the corner of Summer street; there was a passage down there, and a small brick building, and a hose was carried up to the top of that building, and across the roof; how far it went I can't say; it wasn't light enough to see; but I saw a hose carried up there, and carried over the roof of that building, so that it could reach the fire from that side. They were playing with some success on this side of the building in that back passage-way, but where the granite fronts were, there was nothing that hit the fire at all.

Q. (By Mr. Russell.) Was there anything further that you noticed?

A. No; I came away. I looked round to see if I could see the Chief Engineer, proposing to ask him if he had sent for the Lynn steamers, and if he had not, to suggest if I couldn't do something for him by going to the station. I didn't succeed in finding him. I then went home, intending to return, but when I got home, I found that every man, woman, and child had deserted that part of the town, and as my wife was not well, I was obliged to stay there. I understand that there was no request made for the engines on the line of the Eastern road until twelve o'clock. The manager of the road, Mr. C. F. Hatch, told me that he was called from his bed about twelve o'clock, and asked to send down and get the steamers on the road; he can tell you what he did about that. I was just as confident, when I went home, at nine o'clock, that the fire was beyond control, as I was at three o'clock in the morning, when I went to bed. Everybody observed the state of the atmosphere. I saw the flame from almost the first; the fire bells hadn't sounded three minutes before I saw the flame; that was what called my attention to it. It went up straight as could be. I think the bulk of the engines were working on the other side of the fire, towards Bedford street.

There was no hose played off the ground, except in this back place to which I have referred, so far as I could see; whether they could or couldn't, I can't tell. I observed (what everybody observed) that the firemen were standing there washing granite walls; they were doing that in various places on Summer street and Otis street.

Q. (By Mr. Cobb.) Apparently, they couldn't reach any higher with the streams?

A. They couldn't reach; given that the men had got to stand on the sidewalk, they were doing the best they could with their hose. Of course it is patent to anybody, if you stand on the sidewalk, in front of a building, and the fire is way up in the roof five or six stories above you, you can't reach it.

Q. Do you think the engines did their best as well as the men?

A. The engines at that time were doing their best. There were not a great many engines there; all the Boston engines hadn't got there then. The engines came along one after another. I know at nine o'clock, when I was in Franklin street, there was a Boston engine came, drawn by men. In my opinion, the fire so early got beyond control, that is to say, in an hour and a quarter, that no one except a very big man, who was willing to take extraordinary measures, to withdraw himself from the immediate supervision of any engine, and take in the fire as a whole, could have successfully contended against it; and I don't know that anybody could have done it.

GREELY S. CURTIS, *sworn.*

Q. (By Mr. Russell.) Will you tell us what time you went to the fire?

A. At the third alarm.

Q. Directly to the spot, I suppose?

A. To Summer street.

Q. What was the condition of the fire when you arrived?

A. It is impossible for me to say; it was burning fiercely.

Q. Had it crossed Summer street?

A. It had crossed Summer street, to the best of my belief.

Q. How long did you remain at the fire, in various places?

A. Until twelve o'clock Sunday noon.

Q. Will you tell us any facts you noticed which you think ought to be brought before the Commission?

A. At half-past eight in the evening, I found the fire was beating the firemen at that particular point where I was. I went round the fire to see what luck they were meeting with on other sides, and they seemed to be meeting with equally bad luck. When I got back to Summer street, I went round it again, to see where the firemen would probably stop the fire. On my return again, I went round to see where the fire would stop itself.

Q. Did you notice any facts about the conduct of the firemen, or their manner of contending with the fire?

A. I thought I saw at first one stream thrown from an upper story window, to an equal height opposite upon the roof, and one only.

Q. Was that over the building next to the corner of Otis and Summer streets?

A. It was the building at the corner of Kingston street that the stream was going on; not the corner, for I think that was already burned down, but the building that was down from the corner towards South street. That building is still standing. Later in the evening, there may have been more, although I didn't notice them, because it was obvious to my mind that water was of no good; but up to half-past ten, that was the only stream that I saw thrown from roof to roof.

Q. Was there any other fact which you noticed?

A. I noticed that the first time I went to the fire, there was one, if not two engines which were out of fuel and whistling for fuel, and at times were breaking up packing-boxes to keep their fires up.

Q. Were their fires slack?

A. I can't say whether their fires were slack, but they were breaking up boxes to keep their fires going. I can't say whether they were slack or otherwise.

Q. (By Mr. RUSSELL.) How late was that?

A. That was early, not later than half-past nine.

Q. (By Mr. COBB.) Were the machines at work?

A. I think that particular machine was stopped at the time.

Q. (By Mr. RUSSELL.) Where was that?

A. That was near the corner of Church Green.

Q. You can't give us the number of the machine?

A. No, sir, I can't.

Q. Did you see that at any other time?

A. I heard the whistling of engines for fuel at other times, but I did not see any means taken to supply them.

Q. Is there any other fact which you think ought to be brought to the attention of the committee?

A. There is hardly anything which I should think of any importance. I noticed, in going round to find where the fire would stop, — or at least where I tried to imagine it would stop, — that the coals were falling on the Hartford & Erie Company's station, and the wooden buildings in that vicinity, and there was nothing there to protect them; that was the first time I went round. The second time I went down there, I found that the coals had done their work, and set those buildings on fire; that the fire had made a jump, skipping the buildings on High street. There is one thing I should like to say which may have a bearing, and that is, that the buildings in the early part of the fire which I saw, caught in the roofs, and no one of the streams that I saw reached the roofs. When the fire attacked the block, or the end store of the block on Devonshire street, where it joins Summer street, I saw a very light flame, and asked one of the firemen if it wasn't possible for them to get a stream up there; it could have been easily put out if they could have got a stream up by a hose through the building.

Q. What did he say?

A. He said he had too much to do.

Q. (By Mr. PHILBRICK.) Was that an Engineer?

A. I don't know whether it was an Engineer or not; it was a fellow who seemed to be looking around there after fuel.

Q. Did he have a white hat on?

A. I didn't notice his hat.

Q. (By Mr. COBB.) Did you see the Chief?

A. I didn't, unless you call the Mayor the Chief.

Q. (By Mr. RUSSELL.) Do you know Mr. Damrell?

A. I don't know him by sight; all I know of him is merely through hearsay. One other thing which I noticed, and which I suppose everybody else did, was that they were spurting on the outside of the houses, instead of reaching the roofs. That is one thing we were all talking about. I was with Charles Elliot, Pres. of Harvard College, the second time I went round, and we noticed that almost universally.

I afterwards went to the Mayor's office. Having in mind that they would begin to use powder at about eleven o'clock, between eleven and twelve o'clock, I went down to a friend's office on Kilby street, near State street (I having set State street mentally as the limit of the fire), to help him move out, or get hold of his clerks, if they were there, he being out of town, which shows that at that time I thought the fire was beyond water; and after waiting several hours, I went up to the Mayor's office, to see if I couldn't induce him to take the same view of it.

Q. (By Mr. RUSSELL.) Did you see him?

A. I did.

Q. Did you have any conversation with him?

A. There were three of us in the party, and he stated that he had given Gen. Burt full authority. That was previous to any explosion. We went down to see if there was anything being done in the way of powder, and after waiting some time, we went back and saw the Mayor the second time, and he again repeated that Gen. Burt had received full authority to act. We pointed out to him that Gen. Burt was doing nothing, apparently. He said that he couldn't do anything more than he had done; that we must find Gen. Burt, and that he was at the new Post

Office. I went down to the new Post Office and searched round for him, but couldn't find him. I don't know whether I went back the third time to the Mayor's office or not; if I did, it was merely to hear the same thing, — that we must find Gen. Burt.

Q. Who was with you on these visits?

A. On the first visit, there were Col. Lee and Mr. Henry L. Higginson, I think, but I would not be positive.

Q. The first time you saw the Mayor, did he say that he had given Gen. Burt authority, or that Gen. Burt had authority?

A. I didn't pay any attention to that shade of his meaning. I thought at the time, from what he said, that he thought he had the authority, but I would not be willing to say that he used any particular form of words, such as you suggest, either one or the other.

Q. (By Mr. COBB.) He may have used either?

A. He may have used either.

Q. (By Mr. PHILBRICK.) Did you see anything of the results of the explosions?

A. I saw the result of one explosion, which was the blowing out of a lower story, and the hanging, apparently, of the upper part — three or four stories.

Q. Where was that?

A. I think that was at the corner of Water and Congress streets. At five o'clock Sunday morning, I saw that Summer street, near where the fire broke out, was a lake. I wish to throw that in, because I understood there was some doubt as regards the supply of water. I know it was there at five or six o'clock, for I was paddling around in it myself, surprised to see so much water in the street.

Q. Did you see anything like thieving or stealing on the part of anybody?

A. It could hardly be called thieving. I saw things taken out into the streets and men helping themselves; but I didn't look upon them as thieves.

Q. Do you know whether the goods were given away?

A. I don't. I saw in Pearl street, I think it was, a building very much on fire, and some fellow was throwing cases of goods into the street, and then the men outside smashed them in, and they received a sort of free distribution.

Q. Were they firemen?

A. Oh, no; I should think they were outsiders.

Q. Did you see any intoxication among the firemen?

A. None whatever. I thought the firemen worked splendidly. I never saw a braver set of men, or men who were working with less of head. They were standing up to it like good fellows. It seemed to me there was no management at the top of the ladder.

Q. (By Mr. GREENE.) When you visited the Mayor's office, was it in consequence of your opinion that gunpowder should be used?

A. Yes, sir. I had been convinced of that for at least two hours, at that time, and had been hoping to hear some explosion; feeling confident, all the time, that however late that conviction might come, it must come finally.

Q. You were unable to find any one who had authority to use powder, after visiting the Mayor?

A. I only searched for Gen. Burt, understanding from the Mayor that he was the one who was placed in command.

Q. You supposed that he had general authority?

A. I thought he had general authority.

Q. And you were unable to find him?

A. I was unable to find him.

Q. Where did you seek for him?

A. I looked for him at the new Post Office; there is where I understood the Mayor to say he was.

Q. You saw no other party using gunpowder that night?

A. No. I saw powder going through the streets in charge of policemen. I saw one or two explosions, but I didn't see the head man.

Q. You saw no one who gave the authority?

A. I saw no one to whom I could speak. The policemen were keeping the streets clear for the explosions.

Q. (By Mr. Philbrick.) How did it appear to you that the police duty was done during the night, in keeping the crowd away from the firemen?

A. I thought that where they had their orders to keep the crowd away, they did very well.

Q. They have general orders to that effect, haven't they?

A. I thought they were rather good-natured. They let us come in quite close to the firemen.

Q. Did they have ropes to keep the crowd back?

A. They did later in the evening; not when I first went there. I was prevented by no policemen from going anywhere I chose; the heat of the fire was the only limit. Afterward, there were policemen, soldiers and sailors. It seemed to me, at half-past ten, that the quicker powder was used the greater the safety, and the less blowing there would have to be done; and that if a belt were blown at that time from Washington street, if necessary, or from Hawley street, down to Fort Hill, that it would be a good plan. I thought that would be a good plan at half-past ten. I don't know what time I went up to the Mayor's office; it could not have been before one o'clock, and I don't think it was so early.

J. M. CRAFTS, *sworn*.

Q. (By Mr. Philbrick.) Will you state what you know about the origin and spread of this fire, that you think of importance?

A. The points that I noticed particularly were, that in very few cases the water was carried up to the roofs of the buildings.

Q. How early did you arrive?

A. At about quarter before eight o'clock, and remained there on and off. I happened to be going to the theatre with some ladies, but instead of going in, I went to the fire; and during the performance I was there perhaps one-third of the time. I afterwards went back about twelve o'clock, and stayed until four. In Summer street, during the early part of the fire, I noticed very often that streams of water were playing against the fronts of buildings without at all reaching the parts of the buildings which were on fire, and in very few instances was the stream directed downwards on the fire, or on a level with the fire. After being in Summer street during the time, after going back and forwards through Summer street, the remainder of the night I passed at the north end of the fire, near Pearl street — I didn't see the part near Washington street — and there the same thing was apparent. I noticed that on some buildings near Pearl street the water would sometimes be squirted partially on the roofs, but in very few instances did it go over and fall on the flames. In a great many cases they were playing quite uselessly on the fronts.

Q. Was that from lack of power in the stream to reach the roofs, or lack of direction?

A. Lack of power in the stream; it couldn't be carried high enough. The men apparently received orders to play on a certain building, and played upon it from the ground, but the fire was above the point that the water reached.

Q. Wasn't most of the fire communicated from roof to roof?

A. Yes, sir; almost entirely. The fire didn't spread in the direction of the sparks. It caught almost entirely from the radiant heat, the heat on one side of the street being intense enough to ignite the wood on the other side of the street, or from building to building in that way. As to the management of the fire, I saw two instances in which the engines were out of coal. In one instance, the engine was burning boxes which were taken out of a store; and in the other case, it was not burning anything at all. The Engineers told me in both cases that they were out of coal, and coal was brought from a store. They wanted cannel coal, and they got it through private individuals.

Q. Did they have to stop playing for want of fuel?

A. One of the engines stopped for a time, and then began to burn boxes; they were not apparently throwing any stream.

Q. How early was that?

A. That was about two o'clock. It was on Pearl street. One of them was stationed directly on Milk street, just around the corner from Pearl street. The other one was in Pearl street, I should think, about one hundred yards from Milk. It was suggested to one of the Engineers that they had better get some coal from the stores. They said they wanted cannel coal, and didn't know where it could be found. They said the Engineer's cart hadn't got round that should supply them, and accordingly gangs of men went round, and after inquiring at two or three stores, they found some cannel coal, and the people gave it very freely. I wanted to carry some coal to one of the engines, but the men told me they were going to move from where they were, immediately. I asked them where their next station would be, and at first they couldn't tell me, but afterwards they told me where they were going, and I got a load of coal and went to the place, but didn't find the engine, and dumped it in the street. There appeared to be a want of anything like a staff appointment to carry orders to the different engines as to their stations. Then there were two instances, one at the corner of Milk and Broad streets, and the other in South street, where the suction-pipe of the engine didn't fit. They were delayed in consequence of it; at least, that is the reason the Engineer gave. He said they were going somewhere (I don't know where) to get the necessary screw connections.

Q. When you say they appeared to be employed uselessly, how did it occur to you they should be employed?

A. That is a point which is scarcely within my province. It occurred to me at that time that the only way was to employ some other means than engines; that is, attempt to blow down a line of buildings and make a gap across which the fire might be prevented from passing.

Q. Did it appear to you then that it was beyond the control of any Fire Department?

A. At this point, the engines which were stationed there were doing absolutely nothing.

Q. Did you see any use of powder afterwards?

A. Yes, sir. I saw the use of powder in Kilby street. The first building where I saw powder used was a low building. The explosion blew out a portion of the side and tore down the flooring. I think it came down in a jagged way. It didn't throw down the building. The next time they attempted to blow up, the powder was brought, and the fuse didn't explode, and of course there was considerable delay before they ventured to put in another barrel, and that exploded. That was a large building owned by the heirs of the Sturgis estate, in Kilby street, I think, at the corner of Lindall. The first attempt at exploding wasn't successful, and the next attempt only blew out the windows, and apparently a small portion of the building. The building didn't come down, and at the time that was made, the building had caught in the upper part. The powder was carried in rather a dangerous way, I thought.

The only other point which I noticed which would be interesting, was the want of any attempt to organize means of saving goods from the fire. There were a number of men with badges, I don't know whether they were special policemen or not, standing about, but I didn't see that they did much work. They were usually lookers on. I didn't see any single attempt to organize the bystanders into gangs of men to carry goods out of the buildings. Back of Pearl street a large amount of goods could have been saved, if the owners of the property could have trusted the persons about there. In one case in particular, a crowd went into a building that was already burning, at very considerable danger to themselves, and removed the goods. After attempting in vain to find some one who had authority there, it was done by private individuals.

Q. What did you think of the conduct of the police during the night?

A. As I told you, I was in that part near Pearl street. I don't remember seeing a policeman. Of course, one might have escaped my notice, but at one time, in reference to the building I speak of, I looked for a policeman for some few minutes and didn't see one. After that the subject occurred to my mind, and I didn't see any down there. Of course, I can't say what number were there. Those firemen who were not employed at their engines were not assuming the office of police in any way at that part of the fire; that is, they were not attempting to save goods from the buildings nor attempting to keep the crowd out of danger, but simply looking at the fire.

Q. (By Mr. COBB.) When you reached the scene of the fire, at quarter before eight, did you observe any fire apparatus at work?

A. Yes, sir.

Q. How many engines were there?

A. I didn't count the engines. I went through Kingston street, and went down the first street behind the building which was on fire, and got a view of it there. There was an engine on the corner of that street when I got there already working very well. There was another at the corner of Kingston and Summer streets, and there were one or two in Summer street at that time.

Q. Did you see any hose carriages?

A. I didn't take notice.

Q. Did you see any ladders?

A. I didn't see any, but they might have been there without my seeing them, because I wasn't taking any particular note of them. I thought in the early part of the fire the crowd seemed to impede the movements of the firemen. It was a little boisterous; the boys would get up a cry that an engine was coming, make a rush, and the people were in danger of being trampled upon. I didn't see that elsewhere. The crowd in other parts of the fire were very orderly. I didn't see any cases of stealing except where the building was evidently on the point of burning; then the people would go in and take the goods.

Q. Did you see any firemen take any goods from the stores?

A. No, sir. I saw the firemen carrying off boots and shoes. I didn't see them take them from the inside of any store; they might have taken them when they were thrown out. In regard to the police, I saw the police arresting men near City Hall, who were carrying off boots, as I was going home, but there was no attempt to stop plundering on the spot.

WILLIAM G. RUSSELL, *sworn.*

Q. (By Mr. RUSSELL.) At what time did you reach the fire?

A. I reached it, I should say, about half an hour after the second alarm was given; that is, I went as far as the front of Trinity Church. That was the nearest I went to it.

Q. Did you notice whether the fire had crossed Summer street at that time?

A. It had crossed Summer, and had crossed Kingston street.

Q. How long did you remain watching the fire in different places?

A. I stood about there, for perhaps an hour, and then went down on the northerly side of the fire into Winthrop square.

Q. Will you state any facts you saw worthy of notice?

A. I don't think there is anything that I saw that will be of use to the Commission. Possibly, from my position when I first saw the fire, I was not a good judge whether or not more effort could have been made to check it upon the westerly side of Kingston street, but the judgment I formed was, that that was neglected; that is, there appeared to be no effort to put out the fire when it first caught, or when it was but slightly developed, on the western side of Kingston street.

Q. (By Mr. COBB.) How was it on the opposite corner, — the corner of Otis street?

A. That I didn't see, so much. I stood on the northerly side of Summer street most of the time, so that I could see diagonally across. I noticed at one time two streams thrown from the house on the westerly side of Kingston street, next to the corner store, into the building where the fire originated, which, it appeared to me, might have been much better directed to the westerly side of Kingston street, where the fire was catching and spreading; but there may have been good reason why it could not be.

Q. (By Mr. PHILBRICK.) The fire did not spread up Kingston street, did it?

A. It crossed Kingston street and came up Summer. I meant the store at the corner of Kingston and Summer streets.

Q. The unfinished store?

A. Yes, sir.

Q. Did it seem to you at first that the fire was likely to get beyond the control of the firemen?

A. I saw no reason why it should, at first.

Q. How soon did it look so?

A. As soon as it crossed to Otis street and spread down towards Winthrop square, I thought it was to be a very serious fire, and went home with my daughter, whom I had with me, because I thought I would come back alone and stay longer than she would like to.

LAWRENCE CURTIS, *sworn.*

Q. (By Mr. RUSSELL.) At what time did you reach the fire?

A. Not later than twenty minutes of eight. I left Charles street about half-past seven. The fire had not crossed Summer street when I first noticed that there was going to be a very serious fire. It was then confined to the corner building, and every now and then, as parts of the building fell in, large sheets of flame flew out and across the street. Then I began to notice that the flag-staff that stuck up from the front of Mr. Gray's building opposite — the first one that caught on the other side — began to burn with the heat of the fire, although no flames reached it. That must have been twenty minutes after I got there, I should think. Then the wooden cornices on the roof began slowly to catch fire. At one part I should say the flames spread more than two yards in length. It burned very slowly, apparently attracting little notice from the department, who were pumping vigorously into the solid flames, that nothing could control. No attention was paid to this building. I don't say they could have reached it, because it was so high up. I doubt if any water could have been brought to bear on this point, on account of its height.

Q. You speak of the building at the corner of Otis?

A. I am not familiar with the streets, but it was the building directly opposite the corner which first took fire.

Q. The John C. Gray estate?

A. I think so. I think it was the same estate where Wm. Gray's office was before the fire; the same building where Wheelwright, Anderson & Co's office was. Then I was in the crowd, and came across Mr. Higginson, of Lee, Higginson & Co. I remember his noticing that the firemen did not seem to be doing much. I said, if I was a fireman I should not know what to do; because it seemed as if nothing could possibly be done. Then we decided to take a turn round the fire and see how far it would go. We walked through Arch or Hawley street, and got into Winthrop square. There Mr. Higginson remarked to me, he thought that whole building was doomed, and the fire would burn through to Beebe's office, and A. T. Stewart & Co's, on the front of Winthrop square. We then walked through, round the other side, and got behind the fire, back through Summer street, and back to, I think, Bedford street. There the fire was apparently marching along towards a lot of low tenement-houses, of not more than two stories. Before it got to them, there was one very high building which did burn, and the fire seemed to stop there. I went there this afternoon with a view to look at the ground again, and I think what saved those buildings was the lowness of them, and the tall building; the tall brick wall that is now standing apparently acted as a screen to those buildings. If one of them had caught, I don't see why it would not have burned to the Old Colony depot. The street is very narrow, and the houses are not high. I think two or three stories are the average.

Then I went through Chauncy street again to where I first was, and there the fire was already under no control whatever.

Q. In Chauncy street?

A. In Summer street. There was nothing to be done.

Q. You think nothing could be done at that point?

A. I should say not. There, as early as eleven o'clock that night, people began to say freely, they ought to resort to blowing up buildings.

Q. Do you know anything about the blowing up of buildings?

A. Nothing whatever. I was down on State street.

Q. Did you go to the Mayor's?

A. I did not go to the Mayor's.

Q. Was there anything further that you noticed?

A. I was on duty at the Union Safe Deposit Vaults until about two o'clock on Sunday, so I did not have many opportunities. As soon as State street began to appear to be in danger, I went there, and did not leave, beyond going to the head of Devonshire street, to look down and see the extent of the fire as it came nearer and nearer.

Q. Are you employed there?

A. Yes, sir, I am a clerk in the office.

Q. What was there to be done there Sunday?

A. Nothing but to stand at the door and persuade depositors, who were afraid of their securities being burned up, that everything was safe, and the vault could stand anything that might occur to it.

Q. There were some loud demands?

A. Pretty loud; but I said then, and have had occasion to say since, that I was very much surprised at the moderation that was generally shown. There were a few rabid cases; but generally, moderation was shown, and great firmness.

Q. There was firmness inside?

A. Yes, sir, there was. Some of the men said, they had seen the fire, and had driven in ten or twelve miles, and would feel better if their boxes were in their pockets. All I could say was, there was nothing to be done, and the vaults would not be opened. Many of them, as soon as they heard that, were satisfied.

Q. (By Mr. Firth.) I was told that it entered into your plans, as a last resort, to have water in the vaults. Was that part of your plans?

A. That I am not familiar with.

Q. When you reached the place where the fire was, did you notice anything about the fire apparatus; how much there was there?

A. No, sir; I did not.

Q. Did you notice some?

A. I noticed some, certainly; and I noticed at a comparatively early part of the evening, I should say, four or five streams playing into the building then on fire, but I didn't notice then any attempt to cut off the fire by heading it off. They always seemed to be behindhand; one building behind.

Q. What part of the building seemed on fire when you first arrived?

A. At first the building seemed to be burning in the middle, upon the roof, and then later on, the whole thing fell in, and all the flame came out and shot right across the street. Huge volumes of flame would fly out as soon as anything fell inside.

Q. Was it practicable for any one to stand between that building and the one on the other side of Summer street?

A. Yes, sir; all the firemen were at work there, directly opposite.

Q. How soon were you there after the alarm was given?

A. I don't think I was more than ten minutes after the alarm was given. I was in Charles street, near where the engine is, and I started when I saw the engine start, and walked leisurely to the corner of Charles street, and, as soon as I saw the magnitude of the fire, ran all the rest of the way.

Q. While you were there did it become too hot to remain?

A. No, sir, it didn't.

Q. You think the fire took on the opposite side of Summer street higher than an engine could reach from the street?

A. I should say so, most decidedly. I think one instance that showed how valuable it is for streams to be played from neighboring houses, instead of from the street, was the fire at Rand & Avery's. I was inside the lines and gave particular attention to it. They had a stream played from this side, — from the Dock-square side, — and they had five streams or eight streams playing from the different windows of the hotel just in the rear of the building. They did great execution. All the water was brought to bear directly on the fire and into the fire. It ought to be the object as soon as a fire is discovered to get some stream of water to play on to it and not up to it.

Q. Was there any point in Summer street from which a hose could play out of a high window on to the front of that building, opposite where the fire originated?

A. Well, at first they could have done so from this same building that took fire first on the other side of Summer street.

Q. I mean to the front of that?

A. No, sir, I should say not.

Q. What other points could it have been watered from?

A. I don't think it could have been watered at all. Of course there are certain positions where such things would fail.

Q. You see no way where the department could have done better at that juncture?

A. No, sir, I don't say that the department is to blame in any way.

Q. Was not that a very critical point — the crossing of Summer street?

A. I think that was decidedly the critical point.

Q. Could any amount of apparatus, if the apparatus had been there sooner, have prevented that?

A. I don't think I am competent to answer that.

Q. Did the water that was poured into the building when you first arrived there, appear to have any effect? I mean into the building where the fire originated?

A. Not the slightest; any more than if it had been oil they were pouring in.

Q. How many streams were pouring in when you first arrived?

A. I should say four or five, or shortly after I arrived. I can't say when I first arrived, because I do not remember; but within a short time, I should say there were four or five in Summer street.

Q. Did you see any ladders placed against any of the buildings?

A. I do not remember any ladders being used.

GEORGE SNELL, *recalled.*

Q. (By Mr. Russell.) Have you examined the elevator at Mr. Wellington's?

A. Yes, sir.

Q. What do you think of the working of it?

A. I like it very much indeed, sir.

Q. Is there any trouble about the working of it?

A. None at all that I can see. It is very simple. I like it better than that I saw the model of. It is simple.

Q. Is it adapted to general use?

A. I should say it was, decidedly. It might be made more fire-proof than it is. That is to say, it might be made to fill up the surface more completely than it does there. It was not intended for that purpose, but it can be made so.

Q. That is a matter of detail?

A. Yes, sir.

Q. It was designed chiefly for security of life and limb?

A. Yes, sir; so no man or any goods should fall more than one story at a time.

Q. You consider it a perfect protection against accident?

A. Yes, sir.

Q. And it would retard a fire?

A. It could be made so as to almost entirely retard a fire at a very slight expense, — the one they have there now. It is simply to go straight against the ropes and up within about four inches from the wall. It may be very easily cut round the rope and made to touch the wall. It is perfectly simple; they could do it themselves very easily.

Q. It might be made of sheet iron?

A. It might be made of sheet-iron or covered with tin as it is, and that portion that was added to it to make it fit might be joined to the other by something elastic, — india-rubber, for instance, — so that there would be no draft through it at all, if that were necessary.

Mr. Wm. E. Perkins, member of the Common Council, appeared in obedience to a summons from the committee, but stated that he had no testimony to give which would be instructive to the Commission, and was not examined.

S. B. Schlesinger, called in response to summons from the Commission, and stating that he had no testimony to offer, was not sworn. He, however, made the following statement: —

I do not feel that the fire was managed properly. I do not think that the fire was under any kind of control or system. There was no system about it. I did see a good many windows washed. I was about the fire all night, and thought there was a good deal of want of management, not to say mismanagement. I gave one of my teams to the Fire Department to help haul coal. A good many of the steamers did not have coal. Mr. Walko told me his building could certainly have been saved if they had had coal. He also said he could not get to his place in Summer street to get at his stock, because there was a crowd of spectators, and those who had business were not admitted. There were teams enough about on that night, and if there had been a proper system they would have had the military seize them and compel them to carry coal to save the buildings. So far as it strikes me, there was any amount of mismanagement.

EDWARD S. PHILBRICK, *sworn.*

I have been a Civil Engineer for twenty-five years; for the last two years have been Consulting Engineer for the Governor and Council, on the Hoosac Tunnel. I am familiar with the experience on the tunnel work from the beginning, where all sorts of explosives have been applied with various success. The use of explosives is generally classified into two leading divisions, first, their use on projectiles from fire-arms; and second, for blasting rock or tearing things in pieces. The nature of these processes is essentially different. For projecting missiles from fire-arms, an explosive is wanted which will not expend its whole power instantaneously, but will burn with a sustained force while the projectile is in the barrel, and follow it the whole length of the barrel. If the whole force of an explosive is exerted instantaneously in a fire-arm, it necessarily destroys the arm — bursts it. For blasting rock, and for blowing up walls or other structures, we do not want to project missiles; it is rather to be avoided. We should rather have an explosive which has an instantaneous effect, and the greatest destructive force possible.

All explosives known in commerce except fulminates, are composed of carbon in different forms treated with nitric acid, this acid being the cheapest form of applying oxygen to promote the rapid combustion of carbon without air. There is no form of gunpowder which is sufficiently instantaneous in its action to be so well adapted to blowing up walls and structures as other forms of explosives. Various other forms have been tried, such as gun-cotton, and nitro-glycerine. The great drawback upon their use has been the liability to premature explosion. Nitro-glycerine, properly manufactured, has thus far been the best and safest material for that particular use. It is used very largely, and has been for years in the Hoosac Tunnel and various other mines, in the liquid form. Where used continually from day to day and week to week, there is no valid objection to using it in a liquid form; but where kept on store for occasional use, the liquid is subject to deterioration and leakage, and of course great risk would be incurred from leakage. In order to avoid this objection, various substances have been experimented upon as a vehicle or sponge for carrying the glycerine in the form of powder. Those have been known under the names of dualin, dynamite, and litho-fracteur, — the French name for a similar substance. A like compound has been used in the California mines for years, under the name of giant powder. Perhaps that is the safest known form for using glycerine for general purposes. It is a form of dynamite, or litho-fracteur, and made in or near New York. It has been recently introduced into the New York market by eastern manufacturers. It is now used in the Hoosac Tunnel quite largely, under the name of giant powder. It is essentially the same thing as dynamite; it consists of infusorial earth, with a certain amount of glycerine held in it as in a sponge.

Infusorial earth is an inert, neutral powder, incombustible, a sort of marl, serviceable only as a sponge for carrying glycerine. Under this form, or as a liquid, the explosive can be freely burned, if *in the open air*, without any explosion. Within a few days, twenty-five pounds of this powder in cartridges were lying in a box in the Hoosac Tunnel, from which a blaster was to take some cartridges for charging his holes. He had a miner's lamp on his head, and as he stooped down a drop of burning oil dropped from the lamp on his cap on to those cartridges, and the mass flamed up like a mass of pitch, but there was no explosion. It burned about five minutes with a great flame. The explosive power of this substance is claimed to be about ten times that of an equal weight of gunpowder. It will not explode by being dropped or thrown or jammed, overthrown in a wagon, or in a collision of a train of cars. I think it by far a safer material than gunpowder, and much better as an exploder for destructive action; but, like any other exploder, it should never be used except by trained hands. The best way of exploding it is by primers prepared for the purpose by the manufacturers, composed of caps like percussion caps, in which is inserted fulminating powder similar to that used in percussion caps, but in greater quantity. The sharp shock of the explosion of the fulminate in the cap explodes all the oil that is in the cartridge in an instant; and not only in that cartridge, but in all neighboring cartridges, which may have no connection, except proximity. It is difficult to explode it without a certain amount of confinement. To blow down a wall, the cartridge should be put in a piece of gas tube, or something of the kind, to confine it. It could be carried about and kept in that form with one end open. The primer could be inserted in a fuse in the end of the tube, and a cap could be screwed on in a minute and be ready for use. Without that confinement, the gases are evolved as from a mass of pitch or turpentine without explosion, but with the confinement, the incipient combustion causes a great pressure of the gases within the confining vessel. That pressure, with the heat combined, produces an instantaneous explosion of the whole mass. The cap used as a primer is easily fired by a fuse made for the purpose, similar to the common blasting fuse. For general use, it is much the readiest way of firing them, but for use in the tunnel, they are generally fired by electricity, the wires being a permanent attachment to the side of the tunnel, and a battery being located at a fixed point. That is the most convenient and safest method of firing them in such places, but for portable use, the burning fuse would be much more proper. The cost of this article — the market price — is now about one dollar a pound, and as a pound of it is supposed to exert, and apparently does exert, the force of ten pounds of gunpowder, it is of course much more portable, and a more compact material for storage and conveyance. As it will never explode from any of the cartridges falling or being set on fire, till confined, it is infinitely safer than gunpowder. The inventors claim it does not deteriorate if it is kept where the oil will not soak out of the powder. If it is kept in water, the water displaces the oil, the oil floats out of the powder, and the water take its place. Glycerine is an oily substance; it is the best article in the market that I know of for blowing up buildings.

Q. How would you apply it to the blowing up of a building?

A. It ought to be kept in these cartridges ready for the purpose, and perhaps enclosed in gas pipe, for the sake of confinement; and to save time in applying it in an emergency, of course the gas pipes could always be kept on it, open at one end, till primed.

Q. Where would you put the gas pipe?

A. I should put the cartridge right against the side of the wall you mean to blow out; scarcely any confinement is necessary beyond that of the gas tube. I have seen five pounds of it exploded in a case on the surface of a boulder about the size of this table, shattering it into small blocks, without any drilling; simply exploding it on the surface. At the same time, if you touched a match to it, without the confinement of the case, it would burn up harmlessly.

Q. How long has it been known?

A. It has been used in California in the mines for some years. They have been improving upon it.

Q. Was the use of glycerine in this form discovered there?

A. No; nitro-glycerine and this dynamite were first invented in Germany. Noble invented the glycerine, and these various forms have been experimented upon in Germany. It was introduced in the form of dynamite in the early part of the Franco-Prussian war with great effect in destroying bridges and other structures by a military corps.

Q. By the Prussians only?

A. I don't know about the French. They had it in the Prussian army as their chief exploder for that purpose. It is good for nothing for fire-arms; it destroys the arms. It is very similar to dualin, but dualin is made by soaking glycerine in sawdust, with a little of other ingredients perhaps, and is not such a permanent compound as a neutral sponge like this infusorial earth. The sawdust with the oil combined is apt to cause fermentation, and either evaporates the oil in time by fermentation or explodes it. There is a risk of exploding it. It was dualin that caused the trouble at the Worcester Junction. Dualin as an explosive, aside from the risk of keeping it and handling it, is essentially the same thing as this dynamite.

Q. Can it be used for purposes that this powder cannot be used for?

A. No; I think it has no superior merits, and has not the advantage of being kept without danger for a long time. It is subject to fermentation and spontaneous explosion, — subject to that risk where the dynamite is not. The only precaution in keeping dynamite is to keep it in vessels where the oil will not soak out of it. It is put up by the manufacturers in paper cartridges which can be cut in two with a knife. They are made of various sizes, adapted to the different sized holes for blasting. They are from six inches to a foot long, and are put up in boxes.

Q. In preparing it for use against an emergency, your suggestion would be to have it in gas pipes?

A. That seems to me the cheapest form of confining it ready for use; but I should keep one end open till primed.

Q. How large a pipe?

A. So that a cartridge would fill it compactly. It ought to be stowed compactly in the pipe, one end closed with a screw-cap, and the other end with a cap fitted to screw on with a little hole for the fuse to come through. I should on no account have the fuse kept in it, because the fulminate is a very unstable compound, and liable to explosion.

Q. How long a pipe would you have?

A. I should have different sizes, according to the different charges it is found advisable to use. I have never had any experience in blowing down walls. The officers who are to use such an explosive ought to have some previous experience before attempting to use it on occupied buildings. The present ruins would form a capital place to experiment with it without harm.

Q. Is it generally known?

A. It is known among contractors and among blasting men pretty generally, now, I think, and ever since the French war it has been known to all scientific and military men, and it has been used more or less in California for two or three years in the mines. It has grown rapidly there in use, from its merits. That degree of safety has been attained by careful experiment, I suppose, during the California use; at any rate, it is the result of experiment.

Q. If I understand you, you say this substance spread over the surface of a rock will blast it?

A. Not in a loose form. It is difficult to produce the explosive action when it is loose. It must be compacted in a tight case or tube to make it explode readily.

Q. What do you do with the tube? You do not insert it in the rock?

A. Lay it on top of the rock and it will explode it; but it will take perhaps ten times as much to break a rock in that way as if inserted *in the rock* with a drilled hole. The economical way to blast a rock would be to drill a small hole, and put in the charge. I simply mentioned that to show what power it has when exploded on the surface, but in case of blowing down buildings, we cannot stop to drill the walls. It must be put on the surface, and you must use it at a waste, therefore.

Q. How do you say it compares with gunpowder?

A. Ten pounds would be equal to one hundred pounds of gunpowder.

Q. The application of it seems to be very much simpler than powder. How would you use powder for throwing down a building?

A. I have no experience at all. The testimony that we have received here has informed me more than I had before learned, but it has been very various and conflicting. Sifting it down from my own reasoning and sense, I think the most rapid burning powder should be used.

Q. And that should be confined?

A. Yes, sir.

Q. What do you think of the statement, that having but one head open, where you have half-a-dozen or more kegs, is just as good as more?

A. I have known a powder magazine to blow up where one hundred kegs have exploded, and no particle of a keg ever found again. That was done in Vermont. I do not think there is any waste of time in the explosion passing from one keg to another where a whole keg explodes. I think it is instantaneous, but I think the powder rarely burns all up when it explodes in that way. The first keg you fire smashes the other kegs, and the explosion runs from one to the other almost instantaneously, but there is a great deal of powder blown off into the air and wasted. Glycerine never blows itself away. When you explode it, it all flashes into gas at once; it is all consumed.

Q. Of all the preparations, you say that this which is popularly known as giant powder is the best for this purpose?

A. Yes, sir. There are two qualities made, Nos. 1 and 2, possessing different force; No. 1 is one dollar a pound; No. 2, fifty cents a pound. Although the No. 2 claims to have three-quarters of the force of the No. 1, I think you want concentrated action, the greatest possible power, for this purpose, and there would be no economy in using No. 2 quality. In blasting rocks, it is often found more economical to use the cheaper material, because the rock is easily drilled, and a little additional drilling will enable you to use the cheap powder.

Q. Have you ever had anything to do with torpedoes?

A. No, only in exploding the glycerine charges. They always use a little torpedo to explode glycerine, as you do in exploding this powder. Glycerine will burn slowly. I can pour a pint of it on this table, and light it with a match, and it will burn like tar or turpentine, without any explosion; but if I drop some of it on the hearth, and happen to drop the end of a poker or shovel on it, it will explode the whole mass and blow me out of the room. A mechanical shock of heat and pressure combined is necessary to explode it in any form.

Q. You say if you use a match to it on this table there would be no explosion, but if you struck it, it would cause an explosion?

A. The liquid form of glycerine is liable to that risk; the powder form is not; that is, if it is an inert mineral powder like the dynamite, composed of an earth. Dualin is not an inert powder; it is a carbon sponge, — sawdust — and is more liable to explosion from a fall or shock. But on burning this dynamite, the powder is left. You burn it over an open plate or dish, and it leaves a mass of ashes equal to the whole of the powder. There is nothing burned but the oil. If I take a handful of the powder and put it on an anvil and strike it with a hammer, it will explode a small quantity of it directly around the contact of the hammer and the anvil. The rest will not explode, but will burn. If I pour liquid glycerine on the anvil, — a spoonful of it, — and strike the wet spot with a hammer, the whole will explode, and perhaps blow the hammer out of my hand.

Q. Where is this made?

A. It is made in New Jersey and in California. I have the address of the manufacturer's agents in New York.

Q. In what form do you usually buy it?

A. In these cartridges, done up in brown paper ready for use.

Q. How about transportation?

A. The cartridges are packed in boxes, and the railroad companies and other carriers take it at first-class rates.

Q. Passing under its proper name?

A. Yes, sir, it is known. They did not take it until it was satisfactorily proved to them that it was a safe material, and that if these cartridges were set fire to there was no harm that would come except as combustible material. The cartridges are made for an inch hole, a three-quarter inch hole, or a two-inch hole.

Q. What quantity does a box contain?

A. They are about as big as a candle-box; I don't know how many pounds.

Q. Is it very heavy?

A. No, it is not so heavy as sand, but it is heavier than flour. It is a little heavier than the same bulk of gunpowder.

Adjourned to Wednesday, Dec. 18.

FIFTEENTH DAY.

WEDNESDAY, Dec. 18th.

DANIEL H. JOHNSON, *sworn.*

Q. (By Mr. RUSSELL.) What is your official position?

A. I am Superintendent of the Water Works of Salem and Beverly.

Q. Were you at the Boston fire?

A. Yes, sir.

Q. What time did you come in?

A. I came right at the corner of Milk and Congress streets, say at fifteen minutes past one o'clock.

Q. Can you tell us anything you saw that night worthy of notice, or any fact that you observed?

A. I hardly know just what points to speak of.

Q. Anything in regard to the management of the fire, the working of the engines, the working of the hydrants, or the connection of the hose with the hydrants.

A. Although Superintendent of the Water Works, I am foreman of a steamer in Salem, that is held in reserve, in case the Water Works give out; and that engine I brought to Boston that night. I came to the corner of Milk and Congress streets with the engine. I was in business in Boston four years at the corner of Bath and Milk streets; and, knowing no one to report to, I went myself to the hydrant in Bath street, with the engine, and ran her hose some seven hundred feet up Pearl street, say to the corner of Sturgis place and Pearl street. But all that we could do was merely to delay the flames moving down Pearl street. There was no water, of course, in the rear in Congress street, and it was perfectly plain to me that it was only a matter of time when it would burn down that side of Pearl street, and we kept taking off sections of hose until we got down to the corner of Pearl street, and the fire then had reached the corner of Congress and Water streets, and it appeared as if we should be cut off from getting out of Bath street that way; and I knew myself that the nearest hydrant was in Lindall street, and I moved the engine to that point, and then ran her hose out to the corner of Congress and Water streets, and there we did very good execution.

We afterwards moved from this hydrant to the cistern at the corner of Broad and State streets, and ran our hose up Lindall street.

Q. How long did you remain?

A. We remained until two o'clock Sunday afternoon.

Q. While you were there, what did you think of the conduct of the firemen?

A. The firemen are usually very noisy and boisterous; but they got that all out of them. They settled right down into work; and if the delay by blowing up the buildings, which required us to move from Lindall street, had not prevented us, and we had not been obliged to move from

Lindall street, I would be willing to give an opinion that the fire could never have got by the Mercantile Agency, which is on the corner of Congress and Water streets.

I want to say in relation to the blowing up of buildings, that in my business as Superintendent of Water Works, we have had a great deal to do with blasting; and a number of times when all the other companies were ordered out of that street, I was satisfied with having three or four, or eight or ten, brick walls between me and the explosion,— I was satisfied that I need not leave that street, and I never left it.

I saw that the effect of blowing up all the buildings that were blown up there was very disastrous indeed. When the fine new building where the Shawmut Bank was, opposite the Mercantile Agency, was blown up, every pane of glass in that freestone building on the opposite corner, in every window of every story, was broken out, and also in every story of every building about there. I consider that if the glass could have remained, it would have been a great preventive against the fire spreading as it did.

I can only say that the manner in which they blew up buildings about there certainly was a failure.

Q. In what respect?

A. In this respect: — that in no case did they level a building, so that we could put in water upon it to extinguish the fire.

Q. How many did you see blown up?

A. I saw five buildings blown up.

Q. Did you see others after they were blown up, besides those five?

A. No, sir; I never left that neighborhood, and only know about the blowing up of buildings in that neighborhood.

Q. In your opinion did that blowing up do any good?

A. It was one of the chief causes of the fire's spreading in that locality. I went up into these buildings to see if there were any points that we could make by playing in other localities there, and I found that every pane of glass in every window from the bottom to the top of those buildings was blown out.

Q. Aside from the blowing up, what is your opinion of the general management of the fire?

A. The trouble about my telling about the general management of the fire was this, that I did not know personally any Boston Engineer in the whole time that I was there, not being personally acquainted with them. They were about there; but seeing what we were doing, and the manner in which we were trying to put out the fire, they never gave us any orders to change our hose.

Capt. Damrell came around once when we were in Pearl street, and once at the corner of Congress and Water streets, and once in Lindall street, and paid some compliment to us,—that we were doing well. I don't know any of your Boston Engineers.

Q. (By Mr. Cobb.) You didn't see any of them to know them?

A. No, sir.

Q. You received no orders from them?

A. No, sir. I received no orders that I know of from any Boston Engineer.

Q. Then you went on to the fire-ground on your own hook?

A. Yes, sir,—because I knew where that hydrant was. I have no doubt that they were about there; but when they saw that our hose was connected with that hydrant, they didn't give any orders. We received orders once from the Chief on Lindall street. He asked us to change our position, and if we could not go through a store and play in a certain direction, and we said, "Certainly," and followed his directions.

Q. How did you get fuel?

A. I was satisfied that it wanted a little energy to do the thing, and I went myself personally to State street. I found the policeman who had charge of that matter and told him that we were getting out of fuel, and he said they would send us a cart-load of coal.

There was a great scarcity of hydrant keys, and when we could not steal one, we would get some one to go and shut our hydrant off.

Q. Would you go to some fireman whom you happened to meet?

A. Yes, sir. I was acquainted with one or two firemen here in Boston, and they were very kind to come and shut our hydrant off when we wanted it.

You will see, that in our position, located in Bath street, playing up Pearl street, the fire working down and we delaying it, it was all plain work with us, and then in moving to the next hydrant, of course I moved on my own responsibility, for I knew where it was. I think the Boston Engineers about there were satisfied that we were doing well.

Q. Did your hose fit the hydrant?

A. Yes, sir. I would say that, in my position as Superintendent of Water Works, I am a little more familiar with your hydrants here than most people are; and I went back to the house and got two couplings to fit your hydrants, and brought them with me. If I had not brought those up here, I don't know that I could have been of any service. I did not know of any place where our couplings would fit. I don't know what cisterns there are about there that we could play from.

Q. (By Mr. Russell.) What is the difference between the Boston hydrants and the Salem hydrants?

A. Many of the Boston hydrants have a two-inch thread, while ours have a two-and-one-half inch thread. As Superintendent of the Salem Water Works, I followed the Boston thread on our works. I made a point of that, because I thought that if ever the Boston apparatus came to Salem, I thought I would like to get them to screw their hose into our hydrants. So we followed Boston upon the Salem Water Works.

Q. Do you use the same hydrant in Salem that is used in Boston?

A. No, sir; we use the Lowry hydrant, such as they use in the Highlands. We have 320 Lowry hydrants in Salem. The town of Beverly has such hydrants as yours, except that theirs are a post hydrant, and yours are what are called the flush hydrant.

Q. What are the comparative merits of the Lowry hydrant and the one that we use, — the difference in the amount of water they can deliver in a certain time?

A. I would say that all our hydrants are right on the main pipe, and we can play from any hydrant, or we can take four or five hydrants right in the same locality, and we can play six streams from every hydrant and play them from 80 to 100 feet. In the most thickly-settled parts of Salem, — say around the City Hall, — we have played forty-two streams of water just by putting on our pipes. We had an exhibition of that kind, and Capt. Damrell was down. We played forty-two streams right over any building that we have there.

Q. What is the size of your mains?

A. Our main pipe is 20-inch. Then in every one of our principal streets we have either an 8, 10 or 12-inch pipe.

Q. There is nothing smaller than an 8-inch?

A. Nothing smaller than an 8-inch pipe in the principal streets.

Q. Do you have the Lowry hydrants upon an 8-inch pipe?

A. Yes, sir; they give plenty of water. In speaking of these, I would say, that when we put a Lowry hydrant on a 6-inch pipe, we have it fed in two ways, so that it is really fed by an 8-inch pipe.

Q. How is that done?

A. Your hydrants lead by a 4-inch pipe from the main to the sidewalk. By putting a hydrant in immediately upon the street, it is fed down the street and up the street at the same time, being situated on the main pipe itself.

Q. (By Mr. Cobb.) Is there any objection to placing the Lowry hydrant in the street on account of the projection it makes in the street. Do you find any such objection in your paved streets?

A. Not in the least, sir. There is not a complaint in Salem about it, not even now in the winter time. The Water Works take care of these Lowry hydrants. We make a large dish-hole about them. We don't dig a hole which would be just large enough for a horse to step into, but we make a large hole, and grade it off carefully all around the hydrant, so that it is just like these cradle-holes which you have here in the streets in Boston where there are no hydrants in the street; and you can never break a sleigh-runner or a carriage-wheel by passing over those holes. We have had no trouble from either runners or wheels. We have narrow streets, and a good deal of travel, both heavy and light, over the main streets.

Q. Did your men go upon the roofs where you were at work and play from the roofs?

A. No, sir. There were no ladders used this side of Sturgis place to State street, where we were playing — no ladders used at all.

Q. Was there any opportunity to go upon the roof and play from the roof?

A. The trouble with me was that I belonged to the Fire Department, and went there to put the fire out; and really, outside of my own engine, I could not say. I inquired about the others.

Q. Did your men in any instance take hose upon the roof?

A. No, sir. We went into the third stories of buildings. We have a very powerful Manchester engine, and could play upon almost any roof there is about there. We run our steam up a good deal higher than you do here in Boston, so that we could command the roofs even of the Mercantile Agency building, and cover the roof entirely.

Q. Was there any occasion for your men to go upon the roofs?

A. No, sir. Because in Pearl street it was a foregone conclusion that there was no use to go up on a roof to fight the fire. It was sure to go down that street, and we were to make a stand at the foot of Pearl and Milk streets.

Q. I will call your attention to the interview with Capt. Damrell — when was that?

A. It was of peculiar importance to me, so that I made a minute of it at the time. It was Sept. 23d, 1870. Capt. Damrell was invited to Salem on a parade of the Salem Fire Department, and after the review of the department, he made some inquiry about our Water Works, and finding that we had such large mains in all our streets, I think he was surprised that we should go to such expense in running such a large pipe. He said he would like to have a trial of our hydrants. The Chief Engineer wanted to know if I would take some of the Water-Works men and go and show Capt. Damrell the operation of our hydrants, and I at once put this hydrant to work and showed him how quickly we could put the water on and play six streams of water from eighty to one hundred feet. There were some very poor nozzles among them. We did not have any selection of nozzles. We played from eighty to one hundred feet right over the building. This is the remark Capt. Damrell made. He says, "Capt. Johnson, there is in Boston a locality bounded by Bedford, Broad, State and Washington streets, that has simply a twelve-inch pipe running round that territory, with a sixteen-inch pipe running down Milk and up Pearl, and the rest of these streets have nothing but six and four-inch pipes." Says he, " They were laid twenty years ago." And he said I must certainly know something about the matter of the rusting up of pipes. He said, " Probably those pipes are reduced by rust to one-third of their diameter, and right in the heart of the city, where all our business is done, we have these small pipes, and of course a great scarcity of water, and in case of a large conflagration, I don't know what would become of us." I asked him if he had called the attention of the authorities to it, and he said that he had repeatedly.

Q. What is your opinion about the reduction of the diameter of pipes by rust?

A. We have another aqueduct in Salem and use iron pipes there, and I am familiar with it. We have pipes in Salem that have been laid twenty years that are nearly wholly obstructed by rust; but our water in Salem has had a peculiarity which affects iron very badly indeed, more so than your water, because in the same ratio it would hardly seem as if any water could pass through them.

Q. How large pipes are stopped up in that way?

A. We have three and four-inch pipes. I would also say that I was very particular to observe our engine and water pressure at these different points. Being Superintendent of the Water Works it interested me. We never got at Bath or Lindall street more than eight or ten pounds water pressure.

Q. (By Mr. Cobb.) What should you expect?

A. I should think it should be somewhere from forty to fifty there, where we got from eight to ten. There was a time when we did not have water enough to run our engine; we had to run her very slowly indeed.

DANIEL B. LORD, *sworn.*

Q. (By Mr. Russell.) What is your position in the Fire Department of Salem?

A. Chief Engineer.

Q. Did you come to the great fire in Boston?

A. No, sir; I did not. I received a telegraphic despatch from the Chief Engineer of Boston.

Q. At what time did you receive it?

A. I received it, I think, somewhere about twenty minutes to eleven o'clock.

Q. You sent an Assistant Engineer, did you?

A. I think at first, when the despatch came, it was not dated. I got it from the Eastern Railroad, *i. e.*, they sent it to the Police Station, and the marshal sent two policemen to my house. I was then just getting into bed, as some one rang the bell, and I spoke up rather loud (it was rather late, you know), and he says: "I have a despatch from Boston. There is a big fire, and your assistance is wanted." My wife was up, and I told her to open the door and let them in. I said, "You open the despatch and read, and I will tell you what to do while I am dressing." They read the despatch, as follows: —

"Send all the engines you can possibly spare, immediately.
(Signed) CHIEF ENGINEER DAMRELL."

I said to one of them, "You start for the Eastern Depot to notify Mr. Glover that I want a train ready. The other one go to the Second Baptist Church, and ring the bell;" and they started as quick as a wink, and I took my coat and hat and started for the steamer. The bell was ringing by the time I got out of the house. When I got the steamers out, I found a number of the department there. The Engineer was there, and asked who was going. I said, "I detail you, Mr. Osborne, and you, Mr. Woodbury, of Steamers No. 1 and 2."

Before the horses got out, they took the drag-ropes, and away they went for the depot. That brought out the whole department to the depot, and all the hose-carriages, — six in number.

Mr. Glover made his appearance, and wanted to know what was going, and I told him. Then he had to start his other cars upon the north side and get an engine and cars that had just come in. We got what we could put upon those cars, and then I said, "We had better put on an extra one." As quick as he got those cars loaded, we had another one ready. They proceeded, but were detained in Lynn — because they had an engine there which they wished to send — three-quarters of an hour to help load that engine. Mr. Glover telegraphed to Boston, the telegraph going through Lynn, that we were making preparations to go to Boston. I telegraphed to the Chief Engineer that I had sent two steamers, three hose-carriages and three Assistant Engineers.

Q. Give us the names of the Assistant Engineers.

A. J. H. Bell, Josiah B. Osborne, and Ezra Woodbury. I telegraphed to the Chief Engineer what I had sent, and then waited at the depot, and got a telegram that they had arrived safely in Boston, and that all was right.

Q. Did you use your horses that night?

A. I did not use them that night, because there was such a large crowd there.

Q. I mean in Salem. Didn't you use them in Salem?

A. We used them in drawing, on Sunday, after they came back. We did not take them out. They were all harnessed.

Q. You could not stop for them, could you?

A. We were so anxious, that I never made any arrangement about horses. The horses were sick some time. I always found that there was one pair ready in case we needed them; but that night they were harnessed, and were all ready, and came out of the door all ready to hitch on. But the men thought they could go it just as well without them, and it didn't make any difference. It was but a little distance, and was down hill.

EZEKIEL R. JONES, *sworn.*

Q. (By Mr. Russell.) You are superintendent of a division of the Water Works?

A. Of the eastern division, yes, sir.

Q. What are your general duties?

A. To take the care and management of the practical part of the work, extensions, etc.

Q. And of repairs?

A. Yes, sir.

Q. Were you out during the great fire?

A. I was out from half-past nine until four that night. I was very weak that day and ought not to have gone, but the necessity of the case took me down there, and I stayed longer than I ought to. I was not out on Sunday.

Q. Can you tell us about the relative merits of the Boston hydrants and the Lowry hydrants?

A. I think I can. That is, I have an opinion in regard to them. The Lowry hydrants are a much larger hydrant, being nine-inch capacity, — the barrel of them.

Q. Nine-inch section?

A. In diameter. The Boston hydrants are only three. The Lowry gives four outlets, sufficient for any four engines; the Boston hydrant only for one engine. The Boston hydrants are placed on the sidewalk, and a branch taken from the main with a small-sized pipe to the hydrant; the Lowry hydrants are set in the mains, so it makes two or more, up to four, supplies to a hydrant. If we put one on a pipe, it is supplied from each end. If we put them at the intersection of two pipes, it has four supplies, where a Boston hydrant, or even a Lowry hydrant on the sidewalk, only has one supply.

Q. The Boston hydrants are all at the end of a branch?

A. Yes, sir.

Q. What is the size of that branch?

A. Four inches, formerly; now we put in six, and have for two years.

Q. What is the size of those in the burned district?

A. Four; generally about four.

Q. Within two years you have been putting in six-inch?

A. Yes, sir; but for the Lowry hydrants (they adopted them, and after first putting them in in Roxbury, they put them in in the sidewalk), we take a nine and twelve-inch branch.

Q. In Roxbury are they put in the sidewalk?

A. A portion of them were put in in the street as originally intended, in the first place, but there was some objection on the part of the Water Board to having them in the street, so they put them afterwards on the sidewalk. The few I put on the Fort-Hill district, I put in the street,— about five of them, I think. That is since the fire. I have laid some new pipes down there. I showed the Water Board what I considered the advantages and the disadvantages; that is, the advantages of them in the street, and the disadvantages in the street.

Q. What are your ideas on that point?

A. There are four essential advantages in having them in the street to two disadvantages. In the first place, they are much cheaper. It is much more economical to have them in the street. They do not cost much more than half as much in the street as in the sidewalk. Then, in the next place, they give a much larger supply of water.

Q. Because they are applied directly to the main?

A. Because they are applied directly to the main. It does not have to turn to go off on to the sidewalk.

Q. And you draw from two directions?

A. From two to four. The third essential advantage is, they never freeze. That is, where the pipe is, there is a continuous flow of water. It flows by the valve, and keeps the hydrant from freezing. Then the fourth is, by having them in the street, you can group your engines better than to have them on the sidewalk. You can get three engines around and give them plenty of water. I was going to state, the first Lowry hydrant we had was put in as an experiment, previous to the introduction of water into Charlestown, for the benefit of the Charlestown Water Commissioners. It was put in on the burned district, in front of Beebe's building, in Winthrop square. That was put at the intersection of one pipe with another,—six-inch pipes,—and our Fire Department volunteered to test the hydrant. There were four engines put there, and I am quite positive there were two streams from each engine, in the presence of the Water Commissioners of Charlestown, the Fire Department Engineers of Boston, and such guests as were invited, and they could not exhaust the water from that one hydrant.

Q. At the intersection of two pipes?

A. I don't know whether you call it an intersection; we call it a T. There was a supply from three ways to it, and with a twelve-inch pipe there would be four supplies to one point. That supplied four engines, and, I am quite confident, with two streams each.

Q. You said there were two disadvantages?

A. One is a heavy snow in the winter. That I think can be easily overcome by a little labor. We have but few large storms.

Q. The difficulty is in digging them out?

A. The difficulty can be overcome by carting away the snow, but you would have to take it away some distance. If we cart it away from twenty to thirty feet each side, and make a gentle slope down to it, there is no difficulty. If the snow was merely removed from the top, the trouble would be that it would cave in and cover up the hydrant. Another difficulty is, the cover comes up an inch above the street.

Q. Worse than a sewer cover?

A. I don't think it is so bad. Either of them are bad enough, but not a serious matter.

Q. In your judgment, if you were to re-pipe and furnish hydrants for that district, what pipe would you recommend; what size?

A. In regard to that, it would be only an opinion, if I should give it. That territory is better piped than any other portion of the city, but I should think the piping might be enlarged advantageously in some instances.

Q. Such as what place?

A. Federal street. There might be a 12-inch pipe put through Federal street.

Q. Where else?

A. I don't think of any other place.

Q. You would put the Lowry hydrants over those pipes?

Q. By all means.

Q. The pipes there, in your judgment, would furnish water enough?

A. Yes, sir; the pipes that are there now. For instance, where the fire commenced on Summer street, on the corner of Summer and Kingston. This pipe on Summer street,— anybody would naturally think, it being a 6-inch pipe, it would not give much water, but it has six supplies. It is supplied from Washington street, from Church Green, making two, and then the other streets branch into it. The supplies coming from these sources make a good supply at the commencement of a fire, but when you come to a large conflagration, it does not amount to so much.

Q. Those pipes were put down in 1848, have they not filled up with rust?

A. Yes, sir; they have become reduced somewhat in size.

Q. How much should you think?

A. I should think perhaps nearly an inch. I should not think they would average more than 5-inch pipe.

Q. If these Lowry hydrants are so vastly superior to the others, why have they not been adopted?

A. I cannot tell. I can only say I have recommended them. I can't say anything further.

Q. Do you think you would get the full efficiency of Lowry hydrants on 6-inch mains?

A. They have been adopted in Roxbury and Dorchester, on all our new piping there. We have laid but little in Boston. In Dorchester, on the new territory, they have been adopted. In East Boston, they were put in. There was a territory laid out to be piped with new pipes, and they have been put in with Lowry hydrants.

Q. What time was that?

A. It was commenced last year and finished during this year.

Q. Has East Boston the Lowry then?

A. Yes, sir.

Q. And no other?

A. On that portion that was newly piped.

Q. Was that where the large fire occurred?

A. Yes, sir; in that vicinity.

Q. Whether you think you can get the full efficiency of the Lowry hydrants from a 6-inch main?

A. I think you do, for this reason. Even putting it on a 6-inch main without any intersection, there are two 6-inch supplies to it; and where we have a branch, what we call a T branch, there are three sources of supply; then it is made with a large capacity at the bottom; it goes into a large pot down below. The hydrant has a large base to it, where the water enters and then comes up, and it has a capacity of twice 6-inches to supply a 9-inch valve.

Q. Did you visit the territory the day after the fire?

A. No, sir; I was laid up ever since.

Q. Some of the hydrants were left open?

A. I got the information in regard to that from my foreman. At the time of the fire, everything was all excitement at our head-quarters. I stayed there all the night, and the engines as they came in and could not get to the reservoirs came to us for tools. We let our tools go as far as we dared to, saving some for ourselves for opening the reservoirs, and then, instead of lending the tools, I sent the men out, and a man took charge of a certain number of reservoirs. Those they shut off, but there were from sixteen to eighteen in use during Sunday, and we found nine of them running on Monday. They were running the full head. These things in a large conflagration are serious matters, because you take a 4-inch outlet from a 6-inch pipe, under ground, and let it run continually, you take the head almost entirely down. Not only that, the falling of the buildings broke our mains in three places.

Q. Was there not a large waste from the broken service-pipes in the buildings?

A. Yes, sir.

Q. What steps were taken to stop that waste?

A. We shut off the district as soon as we could. We could not immediately afterwards. I sent men round to shut them off. We could not dig in the streets, but wherever we could send them into the buildings to shut it off, we did so, but the falling of the buildings cut off our shut-offs in the street.

Q. Have you ever had the mains broken before by the falling of buildings?

A. Not to my recollection. To show how much a 4-inch pipe will take off of a 6-inch pipe, I will state a circumstance that happened in 1860. We laid a new 40-inch main, and on the Milldam we put a blow-off, — a 16-inch outlet. That blew off one night. The three mains were then connected. The 36-inch, the 30-inch, and the 40-inch were all connected. In opening that hole of sixteen inches in the 40-inch main, it took all the water the 40-inch would supply from Brookline, and emptied the water from Beacon Hill, and all over the city took it down so low you could hardly draw it in the basements.

Q. That was pretty near tide-water?

A. Yes, sir. There is one serious matter in these reservoirs. There is an outlet to each of these reservoirs, down about six feet, about eight inches in diameter, and when the water comes to that point it runs to waste in the sewer. If it came to the top, the firemen could see it and shut it off; but if it don't come to the top, they think there is no occasion to shut it off, and it runs continually.

Q. That is unnecessarily low?

A. It cannot be stopped very well unless the inlets are stopped. You see, the original supply of water to the reservoirs came from the eaves of the houses and came in drains to the reservoir. Then there was an overflow so that after it filled to that point it would run away. If the overflow is stopped so it will not take the water away, it backs into the stores, and gets into the cellars, and does damage.

Q. Cannot they be stopped up?

A. Yes, sir.

Q. Is there any object in keeping them so?

A. No, sir.

Q. Could they not be readily stopped from the inside?

A. I made a report to this effect; I made this statement; but it would not do to stop up the overflow unless you turned the course of the inlets on account of the damage it might do to the stores. All the stores have valuable property in the basement, and it would not do to have this water get into them.

Q. You would have these inlets diverted to the sewers?

A. Yes, sir.

Q. Did the firemen of the country engines come to you when they could not couple, or send to your office?

A. When they could not open the reservoirs.

Q. Not in regard to the coupling of their hose?

A. No, sir.

Q. How much below the street are these overflows generally?

A. About six feet, I judge.

Q. Should you think there would be any objection to having them fixed at three feet or four?

A. Yes sir, I would not have any of them. If it came over the top, let it come. There is nothing to fill the reservoirs, or ought not to be, but the Cochituate, and when the gate is open so as to let the Cochituate in, if it overflows let it flow into the street. That would be a warning that it was full. You see an eight-inch outlet in a reservoir will take a great deal of water away.

Q. Have there been any reservoirs built since the introduction of Cochituate water?

A. Not to my knowledge; I think not.

Q. Were there any hydrants left running?

A. We found one only. That was where a building tumbled and the firemen were probably obliged to get away as soon as possible. Each engine and each hose carriage carries a wrench with them so they can shut off a hydrant, which they have to do before they can take their hose off. It is not so with a reservoir. The Fire Department have only a wrench to open the reservoir with, that goes with each hook-and-ladder company. That is why they had but a few tools to open them with.

Q. If they could have had the tools convenient, they would shut them with the same tool?

A. Not during the excitement; they are not so apt as they would be with a hydrant, because they have to shut them off before they can take their hose off the hydrant.

Q. They could use the same tool if they had it on hand?

A. Yes, sir, but there was not enough made for every reservoir that was open. We and the Fire Department together hadn't tools enough to have one to each reservoir.

Q. Has any information been brought to your knowledge from the Chief Engineer of the Fire Department that the pipes were not sufficiently large in that district to provide against fire?

A. I have not heard anything from that district particularly. Quite frequently, when there is a large fire, he will say that the pipes are not big enough.

Q. What is your opinion?

A. I don't think they are large enough for a conflagration of that kind, but they are large enough to prevent it.

Q. With the present hydrants, do you think?

A. It has always been so. I don't know when it has not, except this last time. I can only say, if I was going to pipe the district anew, I should put in Lowry hydrants.

Q. Is there any reason, except the expense, why the Lowry should not be put into the present pipes?

A. I don't know of any.

Q. After the experience of the fire, what would be your own judgment on that point, — about putting in the Lowry hydrants?

A. I should put them in by all means. I don't think I should ever put in the Boston hydrants; even before the fire, I should not.

Q. How about making the change; whether it is worth while to make the change now?

A. I think I should myself, yes, sir.

Q. What is the cost of the Lowry hydrant?

A. Eighty-five dollars is the first cost.

Q. What is the cost of the Boston hydrant?

A. Thirty-five dollars.

Q. About fifty dollars each difference?

A. Yes, sir.

Q. Where do you get the Lowry?

A. They are manufactured here.

Q. If I understand it, the Lowry hydrants are used generally in the suburbs?

A. Yes, sir.

Q. But here in the city we use the Boston?

A. Yes, sir.

Q. And when these out-of-town people come in from the Lowry hydrants, they cannot work with the Boston hydrants, on account of the coupling?

A. No, sir, it is not the coupling; it is the wrench that opens them. The couplings of the Boston and the Lowry hydrants are the same. For the Lowry hydrants, they carry a chuck.

Q. It requires a different instrument to open them?

A. Yes, sir, but that they all have, because they all have Boston hydrants somewhere in their locality.

Q. Do you know anything about the cause of the difficulty of coupling the country engines?

A. They had a different thread on the hose.

Q. You had nothing officially to do with that?

A. No, sir. In Chelsea, for instance, their couplings are the same, but the thread is different. There should be a uniform thread, not only here but in New York — the same as there is a gas thread all over the State.

Q. It should be national?

A. Yes, sir, national; of course we should not expect to get any engines from over the water.

Q. It should be a congressional law instead of a legislative law?

A. Yes, sir. Speaking about piping the territory again, I should adopt the plan they have now. All the new pipes we put in are coated pipes. They make a smooth flow for the water, and we do not know of any corrosion.

Q. What do you coat them with?

A. A composition of bitumen and linseed oil.

Q. From what quarter has come the opposition to the Lowry hydrant?

A. There is no opposition that I know of.

Q. Why hasn't it been put in?

A. We have put it in. They were put in in Roxbury as an experiment; when Dorchester was annexed it was continued there, and the little we have laid in Boston, we have continued in the Boston style. I have no authority to take out the hydrants now in.

Q. My question is why hasn't it been done?

A. I don't know.

Q. Who would have decided that question; to whom does it go?

A. I presume it would come upon the Water Board. They would have to get a larger appropriation for them, because they are more expensive.

Q. Was the Lowry hydrant applied in Roxbury and Dorchester after annexation?

A. Yes, sir.

ATWOOD D. DREW, *sworn.*

Q. (By Mr. Russell.) What department are you connected with?

A. I am Chief Engineer of the Fire Department at Watertown.

Q. You were in here on the night of the fire?

A. Yes, sir, I was.

Q. How many engines were in from Watertown?

A. Only one. We have only one steam engine.

Q. What time did you arrive?

A. I arrived here about half-past four with the engine.

Q. In the morning?

A. Yes, sir. I came in myself about half-past twelve.

Q. Where were you stationed?

A. On the corner of School and Tremont streets.

Q. Were you there most of the day?

A. I was there until about ten o'clock, when we were ordered to the foot of State and Broad streets.

Q. Who gave you those orders, — the Chief or one of the Assistant Engineers?
A. A policeman, I think.
Q. Not a member of the department?
A. No, sir, I think not.
Q. Where did you go from there?
A. Corner of Broad and State streets.
Q. Did you work the engine on the corner of Tremont and School?
A. Yes, sir, we worked what time we were there, playing on to the "Transcript" building and down Milk street.
Q. Your hose led the whole length of School?
A. Yes, sir. I brought in 800 feet of hose with me, and borrowed some in here to make out the line.
Q. Did you connect on the corner of State and Broad?
A. No, sir, we hadn't any connection.
Q. What was the difficulty?
A. The difficulty was the two-inch hydrants. We had a two-and-a-half-inch connection.
Q. How did you play on Tremont street?
A. We were in a reservoir.
Q. Were there other out-of-town engines about you?
A. Up at Tremont street?
Q. Yes, sir.
A. There was one, — I think it was from Charlestown.
Q. Did you see the Chief Engineer during the fire?
A. I did.
Q. Did you receive any orders from him?
A. Not especially; not anything further than to fight the fire.
Q. Where did you first see him?
A. I saw him shortly after I arrived, on the corner of Milk street and Washington street. He came there and spoke about blowing up the building. I asked him if he intended to blow the building up, and he said that was the orders. I said to him I thought it could be stopped without resorting to that extreme measure. I told him I thought we could stop it by fighting, and he then said, "Give it a desperate fight," and left. Shortly after, he came back and said he was going to blow the building up.
Q. What building was that?
A. Just below the corner of Milk and Washington, next to Currier & Trott's. I asked him, when he returned, if he intended to blow the building up, and he said that was the order and it must be obeyed. That is what he told me.
Q. When you first came in town, you say you went to the corner of Tremont and School. How did you happen to go there?
A. I met a man and asked him where there was a hydrant or reservoir. He seemed to be a man having charge of the reservoirs and hydrants.
Q. An Engineer was he?
A. No, sir, not that I know of. He had no badge that I could distinguish him by. He said, "Your location is here," and he went and took up the reservoir cap. He seemed to have authority, and he said, "I will

let the water on in a few minutes." He seemed to be some person that understood where the reservoir was, and how it was situated.

Q. Then you went to work without any further orders?

A. Yes, sir.

Q. When you left, did you shut the water off from the reservoir?

A. No, sir, I did not. There was some person there that did.

Q. When you connected with the reservoir and run your hose down School street, did you do it on your own hook?

A. On my own responsibility.

Q. And fought the fire where you thought you could do the most good?

A. Yes, sir.

Q. Without any orders from anybody?

A. Without any orders, yes, sir.

Q. What do you think of the management of the fire generally; have you formed an opinion?

A. My opinion of the management of the fire was like this: I thought it was managed, under the circumstances, as well as it could be managed after it reached the magnitude it had when I arrived there.

Q. So far as you observed, the Fire Department did their duty to the utmost of their capacity?

A. I think so.

Q. Did you have plenty of fuel?

A. Yes, sir, I did.

Q. Plenty of water?

A. Plenty of water from this reservoir.

Q. How did you get your fuel?

A. I brought enough with me, probably, to last about twenty minutes, or fifteen minutes, and after I got my hose laid, my 800 feet of hose came just to the corner of Washington and School streets. I saw there was a line of hose lying there not used. I don't recollect what line of hose it was, but I went to the hoseman and told him they were doing no good as they were, and I would like their hose. My company, — the engine company, — were all in here. They left at the first alarm and came in, and I went out and got the engine and brought it in without my men, running my risk of finding them when I got here. I found that line of hose not doing any service. I got the hosemen to disconnect their line and make a connection with my engine, and by that means I got a stream on the fire. One of the firemen came down and said, "We have no fuel," and somebody passed the remark that the orders were to take boxes or anything I could find. I saw a team taking out goods from the store next to the corner store. I went to the teamster and told him I wanted his horse. He refused, but I told him I could not take any refusal, and I sent and got one of my men and put him in the wagon, and said, "You go and get some coal, and see that it is delivered to the engine. I don't want any noes, ifs or ands about it;" and by that means I got the coal.

Q. How did you draw your engine in from Watertown?

A. With horses.

Q. Were they the regular team that belongs to the engine?

A. No, sir.

Q. Where did you get them?

A. From an expressman.

Q. Had you provided beforehand for spare horses while yours were sick?

A. Ours were not so sick but what they could be used at all times in the village, although I had made preparations and had ordered the driver to go to a place perhaps within 200 or 300 feet of the engine house, and take a pair of horses at any time in case of an alarm of fire; and Saturday night, on the evening of the 9th, I told my driver to make preparations to take that pair of horses, should there be an alarm. The night of the fire our horses were not in a condition to come so far. The Newton Engineers sent me down word that they had gone to Boston, and requested me, in case of a fire in their town, to go to their assistance. The 11 o'clock train came out and brought news that there was a large fire in Boston. Our Engineer had been in during the evening and said there was a large fire and we ought to go to their assistance. I said I thought if the fire was such that Mr. Damrell needed assistance, he knew where we were and could send a dispatch for us. I waited until the 11 o'clock train got out, and then I thought I would come in and see. So I walked into Boston to see the fire, and when I arrived I saw the necessity of help; that it needed every and all help that could be got. I met an Engineer on Summer street, and he said, by all means use every exertion to get our engine here as soon as possible. I then went out and procured those two pairs of horses and came right back.

Q. Did you walk out again?

A. No, sir, I rode out.

Q. How many miles is it from your engine house to State street?

A. I should suppose about six miles.

Q. How long were you coming?

A. Fifty-five minutes coming in.

Q. With four horses?

A. Yes, sir. I was just an hour walking in. It was just one hour from the time I left home until I got to Summer street.

Q. Were those horses any worse for the trip?

A. No, sir, we didn't consider them so.

Q. Had they been sick?

A. Yes, sir.

Q. Convalescent?

A. Yes, sir.

Q. Did you have any change in your rules in consequence of the horse disease?

A. No, sir, not anything further than that all preparations were made in case they were worse, or anything of that kind, to get horses; that was all.

Q. Is there anything else you have to communicate in regard to the fire, or any suggestion?

A. I don't know of anything in particular. I think from what I saw at the fire that there was a lack of water.

Q. In what places?

A. I saw some engines that they said were without a sufficient supply of water. On the corner where I was located there were five streams, and there were only three of them that were doing any execution. I asked the question what was the trouble with those engines, that they didn't play a better stream, and I was answered that the hydrants did not supply them with water enough, that they were running away from the water.

Q. When you got to Broad street you had no coupling?

A. No, sir.

Q. And were unable to do anything at all?

A. Unable to do anything on account of that. I went to City Hall to get a reducer, but could not get any; and also went to Hunneman's place, but could not find one there.

Q. How long did you remain there?

A. In that neighborhood until about three o'clock in the afternoon. I went to one of the Engineers, who was then there where the fire stopped — I think Oliver street runs across there — and told him my situation, and he passed the remark, I had better go down on to the wharf and set my engine, and he or some other Engineer would come down in time and form a line of engines so as to supply us with fresh water, and we could use salt water from the docks. I went on to the wharf next to Long wharf. Engine 8, of Boston, was there, down below the Custom House. I waited there some time, and went up on to Broad street, but did not find anybody to assist me, or tell me where I could find the hydrants, or much about them. Finally, we went and borrowed a connection, just about the time of leaving, and we found a hydrant way down on India wharf, I think it is, but we hadn't hose enough to reach the fire and could not do any good, and as our town was left bare, I thought we had better go home.

Q. What sort of a coupling do you use with your engine when you attach it at home?

A. We use reservoirs altogether at our place.

Q. You have no hydrants at all?

A. No, sir. We have a hydrant connection with our engine; that will connect with a two-and-a-half-inch hydrant.

Q. What kind is that?

A. The same as the Boston hydrants; two and a half inches is the size. I understand that section of the city has two-inch hydrants; something smaller.

Q. Did you see anything of the use of gunpowder?

A. I did. I was present when the building was blown up on the corner of Milk street and Washington.

Q. Did you see anything of it in the lower part of the city?

A. No, sir.

Q. Were your men ordered back on account of the blowing?

A. Yes, sir.

Q. They were withdrawn?

A. Yes, sir.

Q. How much time did they lose?

A. I should not think they lost more than five minutes.

ALFRED KENDRICK, Jr., *sworn.*

Q. (By Mr. Russell.) You are the Brookline Engineer?
A. I am, sir.
Q. What time did you get in to the great fire?
A. About twenty minutes past nine. I came in on the nine-o'clock train from Brookline.
Q. Did you go out again to get the Brookline engine?
A. I sent out. I sent a messenger out.
Q. Is it a steam engine?
A. No, sir, a hand engine.
Q. How many came in?
A. The only one we have, sir.
Q. How was it brought in — by horse or by hand?
A. By hand. I sent out word for them to get horses if they could, but the messenger did not do his errand, or there was some misunderstanding, and it came by hand.
Q. What time did they arrive?
A. They told me (I did not see them when they arrived) that they arrived about half past ten.
Q. Do you know how long they were on the way?
A. About thirty-five minutes.
Q. What is the distance?
A. Four miles, I suppose it would be called.
Q. What did you do with them?
A. I didn't see them. The place I ordered them to report to me was all on fire, and I didn't see them for several hours. I lost track ot them entirely.
Q. What were they doing?
A. They were at work in the mean time under the direction of Boston Engineers, in different localities. When I found them, they were at work on Broad street.
Q. Where did you first find the fire?
A. I went up Lincoln street to the junction of Bedford and Summer.
Q. Where was the fire then?
A. The fire then had worked down to the corner building — the Freeman's Bank building — where the church used to stand, and on the other side it had got down nearly opposite.
Q. On both sides of the street?
A. Yes, sir, nearly through to Winthrop square.
Q. Were there many engines there?
A. There were two I think in the square, draughting water from the reservoir.
Q. How did you think they were operating?
A. I should think they were doing as well as they could under the circumstances. It was very hot there.
Q. What other part of the fire did you see?
A. I was next up on Chauncy street. After being driven away from the corner of Bedford and Summer streets, they seemed to check the fire there. I supposed from appearances they would, and they did

finally check it. I then went round and came down Summer from Washington. The fire was working up Summer street, and had got up to the corner, or nearly up to the corner of Hawley, on the north side, but not quite so far up on the other side.

Q. Did it then appear to you impossible to prevent its coming up Summer street?

A. I thought it could be stopped on the south side, but I did not see any way of stopping it on the north side until it burned to the church. I thought the church would stop it, perhaps.

Q. Did the department that you saw at work there appear to be doing all that could be done?

A. I think they did. There was not department enough for the fire.

Q. Was not apparatus enough?

A. No, sir.

Q. Did you see any lack of water there?

A. I thought there appeared to be a lack of water. I noticed that engines draughting from a reservoir were much more effectual than those taking water from hydrants.

Q. That you observed in different places?

A. Yes, sir; and as the fire increased, it grew, of course, worse.

Q. Did you see any attempts made to fight the fire from the roofs of the buildings?

A. Yes, sir; not from the roofs of the buildings in which the fire was, but from the opposite side of the street. That was done in Chauncy street, and along on Washington street.

Q. How late did you remain?

A. I left the fire somewhere about five o'clock in the morning, for two or three hours.

Q. Did you notice any scarcity of fuel?

A. No, sir; there seemed to be plenty of fuel, such as it was.

Q. Not always coal?

A. No, sir.

A. More boxes than anything?

A. Some boxes; in some cases I saw them used.

Q. Did you see any engines stop for want of fuel?

A. No, sir.

Q. They kept the machines moving?

A. Yes, sir; the wood seemed to make a pretty good, hot fire.

Q. Did you see any engines idle?

A. No, sir; I didn't.

Q. Did you see goods given away anywhere where you were?

A. No, sir; I can't say I did. I went into one store where they appeared to be helping themselves; whether it was by direction of the proprietor, or not, I could not say.

Q. Firemen?

A. Yes, sir; I think I saw firemen with rubber goods.

Q. Did you notice the company or the number?

A. No, sir; I did not. I think I saw policemen, too.

Q. Policemen helping themselves?

A. They appeared to be.

Q. What building was that?

A. On Summer street, just below Trinity Church, on the same side; a rubber store.

Q. Were those firemen city firemen, or couldn't you tell?

A. I could not say whether they were or not.

Q. Did you see much water wasted by throwing it on to places where it did no good?

A. Yes, sir; I saw water wasted, because it did not reach where it was required.

Q. Would not go high enough?

A. No, sir.

Q. Was this long continued?

A. I saw it used in that way a considerable length of time on Summer street, on the south side.

Q. To what did you impute that?

A. To there not being power enough in the hydrants to throw it high enough, and the high buildings.

Q. Were those hydrant streams?

A. The stream I allude to particularly was a hydrant stream.

Q. Did the engine streams play as high as they ought to?

A. Not so high as engines ought to play, if they had a full supply of water.

Q. Did you see how this water could be more wisely used?

A. No, sir; I did not. It was so intensely hot in those localities they could not go on to the buildings, and they had to get as near as they could, and direct the stream towards the fire.

Q. Your opinion was that the progress of the fire was owing to the inadequacy of the department to contend against it, rather than a want of skill in managing the force they had?

A. Yes, sir; that is the impression I had. When I got to the fire, I thought it was beyond all control, and immediately sent a messenger back to Brookline to send the whole department; that is, in addition to the engine, a hose-carriage and hook-and-ladder.

Q. Did you see anything of them?

A. I saw them all in the course of the night. I saw one or two Boston Engineers, and told them the department was coming, and they said if I did not find an Engineer, to set them at work where I could to the best advantage, and if they saw them, they would set them at work.

Q Did you see the Chief?

A. Only once during the night; at about quarter-past ten, I should think.

Q. Where?

A. In the square at the junction of Bedford and Summer streets.

Q. Did he give you any directions?

A. No, sir; he did not. He seemed to be in a great hurry. I told him my department was coming; he said, "All right," and I think he passed down Summer street.

Adjourned.

SIXTEENTH DAY.

THURSDAY, Dec. 19.

HON. EUGENE L. NORTON, *sworn.*

Q. (By Mr. RUSSELL.) You were interested, I believe, in this burned district?

A. Yes, sir.

Q. What time did you reach the fire?

A. I reached my store about ten minutes past ten.

Q. (By Mr. COBB.) Where was your store?

A. 81 High street.

Q. (By Mr. RUSSELL.) Are there any facts within your knowledge which you think ought to be known to the Commission?

A. When I arrived at my store, the fire was on the west side of Congress street; it had not reached the vicinity of my store by some five hundred feet. I noticed that the buildings all took in the roofs, and that the engines were not powerful enough to throw the streams, apparently, more than three stories high; no water reached the roofs of the buildings on High street while I was there. There was a single steamer in the street when I arrived, and I remained until the store I occupied was burned down, and the adjoining stores were well on fire. While there, a second steamer arrived, but the labors of the firemen were wholly ineffectual, from the want of power in the steamers, I think. The roofs, as far as I noticed, were not reached at all by the water.

Q. Can you tell what the want of power was owing to?

A. I cannot; there seemed to be no deficiency in the supply of water.

Q. Anything further?

A. Nothing further, except that — if opinions are admissible — I should say that the fire might have been arrested if the buildings had been blown up before it reached that quarter, and others that I noticed after.

Q. (By Mr. PHILBRICK.) Did you see the actual effect of the blowing up?

A. I did not.

Q. (By Mr. COBB.) That is on the theory that water could do no good?

A. Yes, sir.

Q. Did you see anything noticeable about the general management of the fire by the Chief or his Assistants?

A. No, sir; nothing came under my notice.

Hon. OTIS NORCROSS, *sworn.*

Q. (By Mr. Russell.) At what time did you reach the fire?

A. As near as my recollection serves, it was about eight o'clock.

Q. Did you see any fact on the spot that you think should be brought before the Commission?

A. I don't think I went near enough to say anything in regard to the management of the fire, or to express any opinion about it. When I saw that the fire was likely to go through into Otis street, I retreated and went round into Winthrop square. The fire went across to Mr. Weld's building, and from there to the other side of Devonshire street, and took those Mansard roofs, followed the tops of the buildings across all the way, and seemed to have its own way, pretty much. The water from the engines did little or no good; I didn't think it did any good; it didn't reach far enough. We stayed there until we were driven away by the police, who said that the building over our heads was on fire.

Q. (By Mr. Cobb.) Did you see any effort made to put out the fire upon the roofs while you were there?

A. There was nobody on Mr. Beebe's building or this other building, — nobody on the roofs, that I remember. I don't remember seeing any, and I think I should have noticed them if they had been there. There were one or two engines and some hose in this street, playing up in front of the building, but the stream did not reach the fire.

Q. (By Mr. Russell.) Did you go to City Hall?

A. I stayed in Franklin street for a while, and then went home to report myself, and laid down a few minutes. I should think it was three or four o'clock when I got to City Hall, but I can't say exactly what time it was.

Q. Before you went there, had you seen the Mayor or Chief Engineer?

A. No, sir; I started from home, thinking that the Mayor might want some friend to be with him, and I went to City Hall. The Mayor said he was glad I had come, and requested me to stay with him, which I did until morning.

Q. Did you have any consultation as to what measures should be taken to check the fire?

A. Not directly as to what measures should be taken to check the fire, but very many people came in, and as various questions came up, there was a great deal of conversation about the fire and so on, but no conversation directly as to taking the management of anything, other than that people came in and wanted to know about blowing up buildings.

Q. Were you there when General Burt came in?

A. I was not when he came in the first time. I saw him there oftentimes during the fire, but I understood from some communication that he was there before I went there.

Q. Were you at the City Hall when General Burt was there talking about blowing up buildings?

A. No, sir, I was not there.

Q. Then I will ask you generally whether anything took place there worthy of notice?

A. A great many people came in, wanting the Mayor to order such and such buildings blown up; and the Mayor, whenever anything was said about blowing up buildings, always coupled whatever he said, with the direction that the Chief Engineer must be consulted. I think there was no instance while I was there that he did not give that direction.

Q. Did he say that he had no authority?

A. I don't know that he said he had no authority, but he said repeatedly, "No action must be taken in this matter unless you confer in the first place with the Chief Engineer;" and I thought that was very good advice. It won't do to have too many heads.

Subsequently, Mr. Norcross was recalled, and made the following statement: —

I recollect Gen. Benham's asking authority, two or three times, for blowing up buildings. In no case was any authority given, except that he should confer with the Chief Engineer. There must be no action except in conference with the Chief Engineer. Mr. Atkinson came with Benham two or three times. They came to renew the request. Mr. Atkinson was desirous that Gen. Benham should have authority to act on his own discretion — not that he put the question in so many words — but I got the impression that he wanted that authority for Benham, and that Benham wanted it for himself. I felt the importance of not giving such authority to Gen. Benham. I thought there would be great danger to the firemen. The result of it was that Gen. Benham would give the benefit of his skill and experience to the Chief Engineer. The Mayor advised with me continually, that night. There ought to be one head in using powder, and this was kept in view. All Boston would have been blown up, if all requests had been granted, and if the material had been provided.

Many persons asked to be appointed as police officers to guard their property. The Mayor said he would do so when the Aldermen came, on proof of their fitness.

JAMES F. MARSTON, *sworn.*

Q. (By Mr. Russell.) You are a member of the City Council?

A. Yes, sir.

Q. At what time did you reach the fire?

A. I should judge from ten minutes to a quarter of an hour after the second alarm.

Q. What was the condition of the fire then?

A. At that time, it had got across Summer street; there were one or two stores that were on fire on the opposite side, when I got there.

Q. Will you state any fact that you noticed which you think the commission ought to know?

A. It has always seemed to me that the great trouble with the fire was that the alarm was not given soon enough; it seemed to have got too much headway before the alarm was given.

Q. What experience have you had in connection with the Fire Department?

A. I have had twenty years' experience, sir.

Q. (By Mr. PHILBRICK.) Have you any connection with the Fire Department now?

A. I am on the Committee of the Fire Department of the City Government.

Q. (By Mr. RUSSELL.) As an expert, how do you consider that that fire was managed?

A. It was managed as well as any living man could have managed it, in my judgment, from what I saw of it.

Q. How did the firemen behave?

A. Very well indeed, as far as I saw.

Q. Did you see any misconduct among them?

A. Not among our own firemen; there were some out-of-town firemen there who behaved very ungentlemanly indeed, it seemed to me; they would not obey anybody's orders.

Q. How many times did you see the Chief during the night?

A. I only saw him twice, from eight o'clock until three o'clock the next morning. As near as I can remember, I saw him about nine o'clock at the foot of Summer street.

Q. How did he appear?

A. Very calm indeed; that is, as calm as I could expect him to under existing circumstances.

Q. Looking back upon the fire now, can you think of anything that ought to have been done that was not done to stop it?

A. I don't know that there was anything. I can't see how anything different could be done if the same thing should occur again. There is a difference of opinion in relation to the use of powder. In my opinion, it is good if you can blow the building down; but if you only partially level it, it is more of an injury than benefit.

Q. The conduct of the firemen has been criticised because they did not go on the roofs more; can you give any reason why that was not done more than it was?

A. I haven't heard of any case where they refused to go upon a roof when they were told to go there.

Q. Were there any cases, so far as your observation extended, where they did not go when they might have gone?

A. No, sir; but I was on Broad street, among those low buildings. I fought the fire on that street, and was not in a situation to see how it was managed in other localities; I did not leave that position at all; I stayed there at the request of the Chief.

Q. When you first got there, did you see the firemen playing on the fronts of buildings, washing the fronts, as it is called, and using water in that way that could have been used to better advantage elsewhere?

A. I saw one stream on this side of Summer street which was played as high as it could, but it only reached to the third or fourth story.

Q. Was that doing any good?

A. No, sir, I don't think it was, so far as that stream was concerned.

Q. Were they wasting the water at that time?

A. I should think they were. It was only for a few minutes; the stream was changed into a building in the rear and carried up inside. They played two or three minutes when they first got there, and then they were ordered by some Engineer into the building in the rear, and went up inside.

Q. How did the hose work that night?

A. Very well indeed, as far as I saw.

Q. Has Mr. Damrell ever brought to the attention of your committee the want of water or apparatus in this part of Boston?

A. He has spoken a number of times in relation to the smallness of our water-pipes; I have heard him suggest that it would be a great deal better if the pipes were larger, and that the hydrants should be tapped from the main pipe.

Q. Has he talked about the Lowry hydrant?

A. Yes, sir.

Q. Has he urged the adoption of that?

A. He has, to a certain extent. I don't know how hard he has urged it, but I know he has been very strongly in favor of their being placed all over the city.

Q. Has he ever spoken of the fact that the most exposed part of Boston, or the most wealthy part of Boston, was destitute of steamers?

A. I think I have heard him say that there should be an engine at the foot of State street, or somewhere in that locality. I think I have heard him say that quite a number of times.

Q. (By Mr. COBB.) When Mr. Damrell has spoken of the water-pipes as being too small, has that been in committee?

A. Once, certainly, before the committee, and I think once or twice in his office, outside.

Q. Has any action ever been taken in your committee on that subject?

A. Nothing definite.

Q. Any vote ever been taken?

A. Not to my knowledge. I believe there was last year, before I was in the government.

Q. Not since you have been there?

A. No, sir, not since I have been in the government.

HON. GEORGE W. WARREN, *sworn.*

Q. (By Mr. RUSSELL.) At what time did you reach the fire?

A. About eight o'clock.

Q. How far had it got then?

A. I left Hotel Pelham with my wife, thinking there was a good chance to see something of a fire. I went down Winter street and stopped for an hour, and then took her back and put on an old coat and my glazed cap; got my Alderman's star, which I had in 1864, and went to the fire. Having been one of the young firemen in the days of the volunteers, I take some interest in the department. I went down, intending to assist Mr. George H. Rogers, a friend of mine, on Kingston street, whose house I heard was in danger. I got there a little before nine o'clock, I think. I found there was plenty of water and plenty of power, and that the fire was not likely to go in the direction of Hotel Pelham. I then went down Bedford street to get below the fire, and came up Summer street, going round the Church Green estate. I found that there were three or four engines there and the fire burning so fast that it frightened me. I remained there—it seemed hours, but it was perhaps fifteen or twenty minutes. I noticed that the fire was crossing Devonshire street, and called the attention of a fireman to the necessity of playing upon it to stop its crossing the street. He said, "I can't reach it." "Can't reach that," said I; "we used to reach it with our old tub engines. Aren't there any engines in the department that can play there?" He said, "I don't think there are any." Says I, "Then the fire has got to go as far as these high buildings last." "I don't see but what it has," said he. I stepped back perfectly overpowered with the thought. I never dreamed of such a thing. The idea of those buildings burning up was to me something beyond possibility until that moment. I stopped to see it cross, and I think the second building had taken fire when I asked where Chief Engineer Damrell was. They did not know. I started then to find him and as I turned around, I found the fire had crossed to the south block in the attic. Not a drop of water had been thrown on that side, and there was no engine that could play on the fire as it caught. I went round back to Chauncy street again, asking for Mr. Damrell all the way. I got the answer from a fireman that he had gone to the Insane Hospital. I don't know who the man was; I don't know that he knew who I was, because I don't generally appear in a glazed cap, except when I go down the harbor; it is one I bought for that purpose. I kept on up to the fire, in pursuit of Mr. Damrell, as near as I could get, but I couldn't find him. I found, however, that there were plenty of engines and plenty of water; it seemed to me that there were too many engines, more than were being used; some of them were not playing. I then went down Kingston street and round up Chauncy street, and worked through up Summer street, into Hawley street, inquiring for Mr. Damrell of every city man or prominent man and fireman I could.

I said to this fireman, "If you can't reach it with water, then you have got to use something else besides water." The same answer came, "I don't see but what we have;" and it was for the purpose of suggesting powder to Mr. Damrell that I was after him. I was working my way round to the corner of Franklin street, when I met Barney Hull. I thought then I had got a live man, whom I could interest. I said, "Mr. Hull, we have got to do something to stop this fire." "Oh," said he, "we are going to have forty engines; they have telegraphed everywhere for them, and they are coming in, and we shall stop it." I said, "You may have forty thousand engines, and if they can't do any more than the engines on the south side are doing, you can't stop the fire." Then I told him what I had seen. He said, "What will you do?" I said, "I would blow up all the south side of Franklin street before I would stand and see the fire burn as it is burning. And I would not only blow up Franklin street, but I would blow up Federal street down to Summer street if necessary." "Oh," said he, "You have lost your head." I remained at the corner of Franklin street, and near by there until the fire came through those buildings, and there was not an engine nor any water there; whereas, if they had had engines there and fought the fire as they did on Washington street through the stores, which could have been done with perfect safety, having an opportunity to retreat by the back way, they could have stopped the progress of the fire there. The hose could have been carried up through the buildings to the fourth story, and if they had had half the steamers on Franklin street that they had on Summer street and that neighborhood, they could have prevented the fire from spreading in that direction. I remained there until half-past twelve o'clock, and then I must say I despaired of the city. There was no other one point where you could have concentrated a force and worked to so much advantage as you could have done on Franklin street. Three engines in Franklin street, playing from the north side, or carrying their hose up through the stores and playing down upon the fire from the rear, could have extinguished it. That was the simplest and first thing that it seemed to me would suggest itself to any fireman.

I did not find Mr. Damrell, though I sought for him up to twelve o'clock at night, but while I stood in Franklin street I got again the answer from a fireman, that he had lost his head. Those two answers I had from different firemen. One said that he had gone to the Insane Hospital, and another that he had lost his head. Everybody else spoke respectfully of him when I inquired for him; that is to say, they used no slang expressions.

Q. Were these Boston firemen?

A. Boston firemen, at work on their engines. I felt then, and I feel to-day, more sorrow over the bad management of the fire, as it seems to me, — that is to say, the disgrace of it, — than over the loss. I think we can recover from the loss, but I am afraid it will be a long time before Boston will stand where she has, for after seeing that Norwich engine playing three streams of water up into the cupola of the building on the corner of Summer street, at the Sunday night fire (we had no such exhibition on Saturday night) — after seeing that, I made some inquiries, and was told by Engineers, that we have no first-class engines in the Boston Fire Department. I asked if we had any second-class, and the reply was, that we had third-class, but they could not say we had second-class. At any rate, that fireman told me they had no engines that could reach the fire, when it was in one of the buildings on the corner of Devonshire street, where it enters Summer.

Q. If you had been in command when you were in Franklin street, should you have used water or powder?

A. Both. I should have sent for powder. I said to Barney Hull, "Oh, for one hour of despotism!" I should have called in the military and had the powder.

Q. Didn't you think, at that time, that the fire could have been stopped with water?

A. I do think it could have been stopped in that direction. I have no hesitation in saying, that I think three steam engines could have stopped it, had they been stationed in Franklin street. Of course, on such a night, you cannot speak of time; but I should say it was near ten o'clock when I reached there, and I think the fire must have got into that street within thirty-five minutes after I got there, or somewhere about half-past ten; and yet it might have been twelve o'clock, for all I know. I went home at half-past twelve, and then came down to State street to remove my books.

Q. Did you see anything of the blowing up?

A. I went home at five o'clock, and slept until nine, and then went out again. I saw nothing of the blowing up.

Q. (By Mr. PHILBRICK.) You speak of a Norwich engine as better than the Boston engines. What was that engine called?

A. I think there was but one. That was called the Norwich engine. It arrived Sunday, and was at the fire at the corner of Summer and Washington streets, after the explosion.

Q. Have you been familiar with the playing of the Boston engines previous to this fire?

A. I have not been, except as an occasional spectator. I was three years on the hose, in the days of the volunteers, as a young fireman.

Q. I mean these same steamers?

A. I have had no experience with these steamers, except I have always supposed we had a power that could not be tired out and that was equal to any height or quantity of water.

Q. Who was it that spoke to you of the Boston engines as second or third class?

A. I asked a gentleman, who has been in the Fire Department, and who has been present before you and testified this afternoon (Mr. Marston) in regard to it, and I have asked the question of three or four others, firemen, until I became satisfied, from the various answers, that we had no first-class engines.

Q. (By Mr. COBB.) Did you notice any want of water during that night?

A. I heard that there was no water to be had at the corner of Franklin street. Sometime between eleven and twelve o'clock, the report came down, "No water;" but nowhere else did I hear it. There seemed to be an abundance of water on the Summer-street side, but it was wasted, generally, on the third stories.

Q. May there not have been a short supply even there, so that the engines could not work with their usual efficiency?

A. I never saw so great a quantity of water poured upon a fire as I saw in Summer street, from the various pipes; but they were playing, I think, generally, two or three streams instead of one. In fact, I put the question to some of the firemen, when the fire crossed to Church Green, if they could not, by using one stream, reach the fire, and they said no. The thought that struck me was, that we wanted high service rather than quantity; we wanted to reach the fire.

Q. Did you hear anything about there being a scarcity of fuel that night?

A. Yes, sir, I think they were waiting for fuel near the Old South Church.

Q. Had the engine stopped?

A. The engine was stopped.

Q. Was it a Boston engine?

A. I think it was a Boston engine, but I would not speak with any certainty. I know that at one time, and I think it was there, an engine was stopping for want of fuel.

Q. You spoke of seeing several engines stop during the night?

A. No; early in the evening, on the south side, there were a number not playing.

Q. What did they appear to be doing?

A. Standing and waiting for orders. They may have arrived from out of town. I was so anxious and so excited myself, and in pursuit of one object, that I did not pay the attention which I think I should a second time, as to the names of the engines and other matters. But the number of engines on the south side of the fire surprised me. I said to myself, or took it for granted, that they were help from outside, but I have no knowledge of their being such.

HENRY HUNTING, *sworn.*

Q. (By Mr. Russell.) At about what time did you reach the fire?

A. I should judge, as near as I can calculate, between four or five minutes after the alarm was struck.

Q. Are you connected with the department?

A. Not at present.

Q. How long were you connected with it?

A. About eight years, I think.

Q. What was the condition of the fire when you reached it?

A. The entire upper story of the building in which the fire took appeared to be in flames.

Q. How many engines were there, hose and apparatus?

A. I saw at that time but one.

Q. What was that?

A. That was the engine that I assisted to the fire — No. 4 — and their carriage.

Q. Did you go from the engine-house?

A. I did.

Q. How long did it take No. 4 to reach the fire?

A. I stated on Sunday morning, and I should adhere to it, not over four minutes.

Q. From the time of the alarm?

A. Yes, sir; I speak of the carriage. The engine was later.

Q. How long after the fire-alarm did the engine reach the fire?

A. I cannot state positively, but very soon. I know that before we had fully completed our connections from the carriage to the hydrant, the engine arrived.

Q. How soon did you get water on the fire?

A. The hose was run towards the fire immediately, but whether there was any water put on the fire I can't state. I superintended the hydrant myself, and turned on the water, but whether the men had got their pipe on the building, I am unable to testify.

Q. How soon was water thrown by the engine on the building?

A. Not very soon from this particular engine, from the fact that before they got connected, they were obliged to move, on acoount of the extreme heat, etc. They were directed to move by the Chief.

Q. (By Mr. Cobb.) Then you did no work until after the Chief got there and gave the order to move?

A. No, sir, the engine did not get to work.

Q. (By Mr. Russell.) How many minutes do you think it was after the fire-alarm before you got water on the fire from steamer No. 4?

A. I should judge it was ten or twelve minutes, perhaps.

Q. Do you know anything about the arrival of other steamers?

A. No, sir, I don't, only in the case of No. 18. I happened on this night to be in No. 4's house. It being a company which I formerly commanded, when it was No. 11, under the City Hall, many years ago, I have always felt an interest in it, and occasionally drop into the house, and I happened to be in there when this alarm came in. The carriage was put in front of the engine, the order from the Chief being for the carriage to run in case of fire, and the engine to follow. There were no horses in the house; they had been taken out and were in Grove street. The moment that the alarm struck, we sprung for the reel, opened the doors of the engine-house, and run off the rope. We were obliged to wait until we got the number of the station, inasmuch as the company does not run except to certain stations. As soon as I got the number — 52 — I took the head of the rope, passed down Brattle street into Exchange street, through Exchange into State, and then across to Devonshire. The light of the fire was quite plain as we entered Devonshire from State. We ran directly through, and took the hydrant at the corner of Kingston and Summer streets. It will occur to you that we must have been in very good season to have taken that hydrant, as it was the nearest hydrant to the fire, and there were other companies very much nearer to that station than No. 4's company. We attached to the hydrant, and the hose was led off towards the fire. I have heard that the pipe was taken into the building, but it would be of very little use to take a pipe in there with a hydrant stream.

Q. Do you think you were later than you would have been if you had had horses?

A. I think the engine could have made better time with horses.

Q. How much?

A. Not much.

Q. How many minutes?

A. I should think they could have got there a minute sooner. That is my idea, from what I have seen of their movements.

Q. Were they prepared to work when they got there? Was steam up?

A. The engine had steam, yes, sir.

Q. How long did you remain at the fire?

A. I stayed there until about a quarter-past eleven. I cannot say anything about the spread of the fire, as I did not attend to it at all. The place where the engine stood was a very warm place, and I concluded to stay there until we got out of it, and did stay there until the engine was hauled out. We then went to draft at the reservoir on Chauncy street, and until this time I saw no other engine except No. 10. She stood at the corner of Arch and Summer streets. That was the only engine I saw. Where the department was located, I don't know.

Q. Did you see the fire cross Summer street to Otis street?

A. I did.

Q. What was done to prevent it?

A. Streams were thrown from the street, — I saw some few, — and an attempt made to take hose into the building. I don't know that any was taken in, but I think there was. I think there was a long ladder put up on Otis street, on the building at the corner of Summer and Otis. I am pretty confident, although I can't say positively, that a line of hose was up.

Q. (By Mr. PHILBRICK.) Did the streams play from the street on to the roofs of the buildings?

A. No, sir, not effectively.

Q. (By Mr. RUSSELL.) Could not hose have been carried up in the buildings?

A. From Otis street, I think very likely it could, and, as I said, there were ladders put up there, but whether those streams were taken in there to any effect I can't say. I hardly moved from the position I first took until the engine was taken off; until the wall fell and broke the connection of the engines, so that we could get no water. Then we were obliged, as a matter of course, having no water, to fall back.

Q. (By Mr. PHILBRICK.) Do you think the engines played as well as usual when they first got to work?

A. I should say so, yes, sir. I know No. 4 was run with very little water, so as to make steam rapidly. I know that when a large piece of granite fell and cut our connections, the fires were pulled immediately, in order to save the engine, because she was running very low.

JOHN COLLAMORE, *sworn.*

Q. (By Mr. RUSSELL.) At what time did you reach the fire?

A. I think about half-past seven o'clock; as soon as I heard the first alarm.

Q. Will you state anything that you noticed at the fire that you think we ought to know?

A. Of course, it is not gracious to criticise any one, when he is doing all that it is possible to do, nor is it considered, I think, a very great thing to be a prophet after the event. But it does seem to me that the fire ought never to have crossed Hawley street. That is to say, if we could have got a supply of water and enough engines, Trinity Church ought never to have been allowed to burn. I think the firemen should have gone right into Trinity Church and fought the fire through the windows. There were no dormers there. There was the Mercantile Building, — not a high building; and there was a rear passage-way to Arch street, and there was a large space where the rear of the stores came, and anybody could have stood on George Winslow's roof, and played right down on the fire. There is no use in playing on the two lower stories of a stone building, when the upper stories are on fire. It don't amount to anything at all. There was an engine stationed in Hawley street, between Summer and Franklin streets, and I think the men might have gone up the passage-way leading to the rear of Macullar, Williams & Parker's, and fought the fire there, or gone into the passage-way on the other side, or gone into Mr. Donahoe's building, on the corner, and taken the carpets and hung them over the windows and kept them wet. I think if there had been one-half the energy displayed there that was manifested to save Hovey's, nothing would have been burned west of Hawley street. I do not say it was the fault of the Engineers. There might have been the same difficulty that there was at the head of Franklin street, when the reservoir gave out. There stood an engine, but there was no water.

The engine at the corner of Bromfield street at times got water, and sometimes it did not. There was great want of water. The store south of me was where George Warren formerly kept a carpet store, only a two-story building, and I could have stood at my back window and played directly on that, if I could only have got a stream of water. I did not see anybody who had any water to spare, although I tried three hours. My store never went down until half-past five o'clock Sunday morning. They stood and played on the carpet store, and after a while they knocked in the windows of my store, but I saw it was no use then. They ought to have gone in on the back side, and protected it in that way. If they could have gone directly into White, Brown & Davis', on the north-west corner of Franklin and Hawley streets, and played on the building on the opposite corner, they might have stopped the fire in that direction. On the east side of Hawley street, most of the buildings were common brick buildings, not more than thirty-five or forty feet high, and if they could have massed a force there (I do not say whether they could or not), they might have prevented the fire from spreading to the west side, for, as I view it, there were no high buildings there, such as would endanger the west side of Hawley street. Of course, the store of Burrage Brothers, and another on the opposite side (I forget the name of the occupant), were the two points that were dangerous for the west side of the street.

I think, sir, that after twelve o'clock, I saw no Boston engine there. I labored very hard with two out-of-town Engineers to get them to take a stream through this building, and Sheriff Clark labored in the same direction; but it was of no avail. They said, "Get one of the Boston Engineers; we are under their orders; we are out-of-town engines." After the fire got into the buildings on the west side of Hawley street, it worked up very fast.

I think the great want, — as I say, I watched it very quietly, although very anxiously, and I dare say I might have felt very anxious, knowing one of my stores had gone, and the other was going, — I think the great want was water; and my impression is, that our apparatus is not all that it should be. I was myself connected with the Fire Department, as an Engineer, with Col. Amory, and our hand-engines, in the olden time, had the ordinary four-inch and eight-inch pipe, and two-and-a-half-inch nozzle. Now, the steam engines have only four-inch pipes. They want more water. If they have got to go to a street where there is a large main, they may have to go through two streets to get their line where it will reach the fire, and they have not a sufficient supply. I think it is a very great protection to our city that we have the reservoirs we used in the olden time.

Q. (By Mr. Cobb.) Did you notice any want of fuel?

A. While in Winthrop square, a man said to me, "Have the engines burst?" "No," said I, "They are whistling for coal." In two minutes along came a man and asked, "Aren't there any boxes here?" "I don't know," I said; "break open the door, and if there are any there, throw them out and break them up; I will bear you out in it. Take the doors, or anything you can get for fuel." I think there should be a depot for coal somewhere near the centre of the city, and I think there should be two of our best first-class steam engines somewhere in the centre of the city; and also that Capt. Green, of the Fire Brigade, should have some tent or shanty in this vicinity, where he can make his head-quarters, instead of being away off in the outskirts. I think the city could not spend money to better advantage than to give us two engines somewhere down Summer street, or round Liberty square, in case they are wanted. My experience of some fifteen years as a fireman teaches me that the first fifteen minutes after a fire breaks out are the all-important minutes. There are occasions when you can supply almost everything but *time*, and you have none of that to spare. The Fire Brigade, as I think Mr. Cobb, who has been long connected with insurance companies, is aware, is a wonderful saving. The insurance offices support that brigade, and if they could have a place near the centre of the city, it would be, I think, most desirable; and if this Commission should deem it of sufficient importance to state to the city authorities not only the desirability, but absolute importance, of having one or two steam engines and a coal depot near the business centre of our city, I think it would have a good effect. I believe the Chief Engineer, as long ago as 1868, complained of the small supply of water. These small hydrants answered well enough for the hand-engines in the olden time; but things are changed. I know it is very easy to criticise, and very easy to find fault; and it did seem to me, as I saw some of those men the next day, after their twelve hours' hard work, as though they must be iron men, to be able to stand up and hold one of those pipes. A great many people, I think, love to grumble; but to say there were no mistakes made that night would not be proper. Of course there were mistakes made; the question is, whether anybody could have done any better.

BENJAMIN H. SAMPSON, *sworn.*

Q. (By Mr. Russell.) Were you at the fire on Saturday night, November 9th?

A. I was there on Sunday morning. It was past twelve when I arrived there.

Q. What is your position in the Medford Fire Department?

A. I am Chief Engineer.

Q. To what point did you first go when you came into town?

A. I think I went first into Franklin street.

Q. What part of the street?

A. Well, the fire was then raging; I can't tell you exactly how far down it was; it was some ways down the street.

Q. (By Mr. Cobb.) Did you come in with the steam engine?

A. Yes, sir, the steam fire engine and two hose carriages, that we have in Medford.

Q. On which side of the street was the fire when you arrived there?

A. On both sides.

Q. Where did you put your stream first?

A. In Congress street. Our steamer was located in State street; our stream was directed down Congress street.

Q. How long did you remain there?

A. We remained there until Sunday, about five o'clock in the afternoon.

Q. Did you see anything of the use of gunpowder that night?

A. Yes, sir.

Q. Where did you see it used?

A. I saw it used in Congress street, and in one building near the new Post Office — Water street, I believe it is. I believe I saw the first discharge that was made.

Q. What was the effect of that first discharge?

A. It merely blew out the windows.

Q. Did it do any good?

A. I did not see that it did.

Q. Did it do any harm?

A. I can't say that it did any harm or any good, so far as spreading the fire, or arresting its progress, is concerned. It merely blew the windows and doors out.

Q. Where was the second discharge?

A. That was in Congress street.

Q. Do you know what building it was?

A. I don't. I think it was on the corner of Lindall and Congress streets.

Q. What was the effect of that?

A. Well, the building was on fire before they had their arrangements fully completed, and they had to run and leave it, and the building burned down to the powder, and the powder exploded. That is all the effect I saw of that.

Q. Did that do any good or any harm?

A. I did not see as it did.

Q. (By Mr. Philbrick.) How much time did you waste there, when your streams were withdrawn?

A. I should say it was fifteen or twenty minutes before we dared to go near the fire with the hose. We had to wait for the fire to get at the powder. They did not get the powder in in season; the building was on fire while they were putting it in, and they got frightened and left.

Q. Did you see any other explosion?

A. After that exploded, they then put powder into the next building this side of that; I think it was on the corner of Congress and Lindall streets. That was put in the second story.

Q. How did that work?

A. That blew out the side of the building next the street completely, and tore off a portion of the roof, which fell in.

Q. Was the effect of that explosion beneficial?

A. I did not see that it affected the progress of the fire either one way or the other. The buildings below that were on fire, and it passed across to the street below that, and burned right through.

Q. Had it passed that point before the explosion took place?

A. The fire was down below, and passed Lindall street after this explosion. I don't think it had before. That was shortly after the explosion, because I know we took our hose up into the building opposite that, and undertook to play across: but we soon found that the fire was on the same side of the street where we were, near the Post Office.

Q. Did it catch on the roofs?

A. I can't say, for I was in the building the greater part of the time there; but as near as I can remember, it took the whole face of the building, all the wood-work, the window casings, etc., ignited, and it burned right through.

Q. What was the next building you saw blown up?

A. The next building was on the opposite side of Congress street, a small building, occupied as a restaurant.

Q. How did that work?

A. The building was completely demolished.

Q. Did that have a good effect in stopping the fire?

A. It did, for the time being; but the fire passed that place, and burned two or three buildings this side of it, finally. But it made an opening, whereby they could reach the fire beyond. If they had had sufficient water there, perhaps it might have had a beneficial effect, but as it was, it did not arrest the progress of the flames.

Q. (By Mr. PHILBRICK.) Water was lacking there?

A. Yes; they had not sufficient water to stop the fire.

Q. (By Mr. RUSSELL.) Didn't they have engines enough, or was there a want of water to supply the engines?

A. Where I was located, there was not a sufficient number of engines. I understand (I do not know this personally) that those which were connected directly with the water-pipes did not have sufficient water. Our engine played from a reservoir, and we had water enough all the time. The reason why we played from a reservoir was, that we found there were two sizes of couplings, and when we got ready to couple on to a hydrant, we found we could not do it, because there was a two-inch coupling on the hydrant, while ours were two-and-a-half-inch. Most of them are two-and-a-half-inch; but there appeared to be two sizes in Boston. That was a very serious matter. We spent some fifteen or twenty minutes in trying to find a reducing coupling. The next day I went and had a coupling made, so that, if we were called into Boston again, I should not have that difficulty.

Q. (By Mr. COBB.) How did the men behave, on the whole, that night?

A. As far as I saw, they behaved very well indeed.

Q. (By Mr. RUSSELL.) Were there any exceptions to that?

A. Well, I saw some who had plenty of whiskey, or something similar; but there were very few cases of that kind.

Q. (By Mr. COBB.) Were those Boston firemen?

A. No, sir; they were not.

Q. (By Mr. PHILBRICK.) Did you get anything to eat for your men during Sunday?

A. Yes, sir.

Q. (By Mr. RUSSELL.) Did you have any trouble for want of food?

A. No, sir.

Q. (By Mr. PHILBRICK.) Did you have any trouble for want of fuel?

A. No, sir, I believe not.

Q. (By Mr. COBB.) Did you see any people carrying away goods?

A. Yes, sir; when I first came in, I went down through Pearl street, and they were carrying off boots and shoes at a rapid rate.

Q. Firemen?

A. No, sir; those appeared to be citizens.

Q. (By Mr. PHILBRICK.) Did that distract the attention of your men?

A. No, sir; they were not there at that time. Our steamer did not come in until after I came in. I went out for her.

Q. What manufacture is your steamer?

A. The Amoskeag Co's.

Q. Do you know anything about the comparative merits of yours and the Boston steamers? Is yours any better?

A. We consider the Amoskeag engine as good as any there is made.

Q. Has Boston any of that kind?

A. Yes, sir.

Q. Did you see anything to lead you to suppose that the Boston engines were any better than yours, or not so good?

A. I could not discover any difference. I presume there are some that are better, and some not as good. Some of Mr. Hunneman's steam fire-engines are as good engines as there are made in this country.

Q. (By Mr. RUSSELL.) Were all the firemen from Medford directly under your charge all the time?

A. Yes, sir; I believe they were. After we got at work, I believe I did not leave until we got through, but once or twice, to get something to eat.

Q. (By Mr. COBB.) What time did you go home Sunday?

A. About five o'clock.

Q. (By Mr. RUSSELL.) Did you see anybody taking goods from Goodyear's rubber store, or any rubber store?

A. No, sir, I did not.

Q. (By Mr. PHILBRICK.) From whom did you get directions, when you first went to work?

A. I saw Mr. Damrell when I came in, and asked him where we should go, and he told me to work in the vicinity of State street and Washington street, and try to keep the fire from coming up at that point, which we did, and remained there. The last battle we had was in the Post-Office building.

Q. Were there any other engines drawing from that reservoir?

A. Yes, sir, there were three others.

Q. Did you draw it down so that the water gave out?

A. Not so but what we could get water. One of the other engines had to put in a piece of suction hose. We drew it down, but not dry; not so but what we had plenty of water all the time.

Adjourned to Friday, at three o'clock.

SEVENTEENTH DAY.

FRIDAY AFTERNOON, December 20.

WALTER H. STURTEVANT, *sworn.*

Q. (By Mr. RUSSELL.) What is your official position?
A. I am Engineer of Steamer No. 11, located at East Boston.
Q. At what time did you start for the great fire?
A. Somewhere about half-past seven o'clock.
Q. Have you any means of telling exactly?
A. No, sir. It was from that to twenty-five minutes to eight o'clock, I should think.
Q. What means have you of knowing what time it was when you arrived?
A. I went around and looked at the clock on the boiler of my engine. It was five minutes of eight.
Q. Is it your custom to look at it to get the time?
A. Yes, sir; it is for me. I generally look to see the time when I start for the fire, and when I come away from the fire.
Q. Do you make a record of it?
A. No, sir.
Q. What point did you reach?
A. I took the hydrant on the corner of Franklin and Devonshire streets.
Q. Which alarm did you follow?
A. I think it was the third alarm that we followed.
Q. Did you go with horses?
A. No, we did not.
Q. (By Mr. COBB.) How long does it take you, between the same points, when you come in with horses?
A. I should judge that, with the crew we had on that night, we could go no quicker with horses.
Q. Don't you know as a matter of fact?
A. No, sir.
Q. Did you go to the fire at the State-street block?
A. Yes, sir.
Q. How long did it take you to get there?
A. Twenty-five minutes. We had horses then.
Q. How long going to Rand & Avery's?
A. We were twenty minutes.
Q. You had horses at both times?
A. Yes, sir.

GEORGE W. BROWN, *sworn.*

Q. (By Mr. RUSSELL.) What is your connection with the Fire Department?

A. I am engine-man of Engine No. 9; i. e., I am Engineer. They term the Engineers "Engine-men."

Q. Where is the engine located?

A. At Perry street, East Boston.

Q. At what time did you start for the great fire?

A. At twenty-seven minutes past seven o'clock.

Q. How do you know the exact time?

A. I looked at the clock when I started.

Q. What alarm was that?

A. It was the second alarm.

Q. At what time did you arrive?

A. I could not tell you exactly; I had no way to get the exact time; but, as near as my judgment goes, I should say about thirteen minutes to eight, somewhere in that vicinity.

Q. (By Mr. FIRTH.) To what point did you go? Where did you stop?

A. We went to Church Green, and stopped at the reservoir.

Q. What would have been the difference of time, in your opinion, if you had had horses?

A. I don't think that it would have made any difference whatever.

Q. Did you go to the State-street fire?

A. Yes, sir; I did.

Q. How many minutes did that take?

A. It took about fourteen minutes.

Q. Did you go to Rand & Avery's fire?

A. Yes, sir.

Q. How long did it take for you to get to that fire?

A. That took eighteen minutes, for we did not catch the boats in East Boston. A great deal depends upon that. In the great fire we caught the boat and ran direct on to the boat. We didn't stop at all. We started right off. It was the same at the State-street fire. At the Rand & Avery fire there was a delay.

Q. When you came to the State-street fire, and to Rand & Avery's fire, did you come with horses?

A. Yes, sir. The night of the great fire we had no horses. We had them at both of the other fires.

JOSIAH S. BATTIS, *sworn.*

Q. (By Mr. RUSSELL.) What is your connection with the Fire Department?

A. I am Engineer of Steamer No. 5, of East Boston. It is located at Marion street.

Q. At what time did you start for the great fire?

A. Somewhere in the neighborhood of ten minutes of nine, as near as I could judge. I can't tell exactly.

Q. At what time did you arrive?

A. That I could not tell exactly, but we judged that we were from twenty to twenty-five minutes in going.

Q. Where did you come?

A. We came to the corner of South and Summer streets. We caught the boat. The boat was waiting for us. We came without horses.

Q. What would have been the difference in time if you had had horses?

A. I don't think there would have been any difference, with the horses in the state in which they had been. With the horses in the usual state, I don't think we could have done it much quicker. We had a large number of men.

Q. About how many men had you?

A. I asked the foreman the next day, and he thought there were one hundred and eighty on the rope.

Q. Did you come to the State-street fire?

A. Yes, sir. We came with horses. We judged that we were fifteen minutes in coming. We caught the boat at that time. It was waiting for us. We got right aboard.

It was about the same at the Rand & Avery fire.

Q. Did the same men come with you all the way from East Boston?

A. We picked up a good many more. We put an extra rope on the engine. We had on a good many men who came clear from the engine-house; it was after the third alarm struck. We did not start on the third alarm, but started when we got orders from Chief Engineer Damrell.

GEORGE O. TWIST, *sworn.*

Q. (By Mr. Russell.) What is your connection with the Fire Department?

A. I am attached to Engine No. 2 as Engineer. The engine is stationed on Fourth street, between K and L streets, South Boston.

Q. At what time did you start for the great fire?

A. About quarter to eight o'clock. I could not tell exactly.

Q. What time did you get there?

A. We were there, I think, about quarter past eight o'clock, as near as I can judge.

Q. How much quicker would you have come if you had had horses?

A. We did use horses. We got horses at the Broadway, South Boston, railroad station.

The draw of the Broadway bridge was what detained us. It detained us it may be ten minutes.

JOHN RAY, *sworn.*

Q. (By Mr. Russell.) What is your connection with the Fire Department?

A. I am engine-man of Engine No. 1 of South Boston. It is located on the corner of Fourth and Dorchester streets.

Q. What time did you come to the great fire?
A. I came at the fourth alarm. I could not give the time.
Q. Can you tell anywhere near the time that you got there?
A. I could not state the time when we arrived. I could state about the length of time that we were in coming.
Q. How long was it?
A. I should say from twelve to fifteen minutes.
Q. Was it by horses or men?
A. It was by horses.
Q. Where did you get the horses?
A. They belonged to the company, sir. They were our regular horses.
Q. On the way did you meet with any delay on account of bridges?
A. No, sir.

DAVID E GILMAN, *sworn.*

Q. (By Mr. Russell.) What is your connection with the Fire Department?
A. I am engineer of Steamer No. 15.
Q. Where is that located?
A. At South Boston, at the junction of Broadway and Dorchester avenue.
Q. What time did you start for the great fire?
A. It was at eight o'clock.
Q. Did you look at the clock?
A. I was looking at the clock to get the time.
Q. Did you come with horses?
A. We did not come with horses.
Q. What time did you arrive?
A. We arrived at five minutes past eight. We started at eight, and got there in five minutes.
Q. Where did you arrive?
A. It was on Kingston street, at the junction of Kingston and Bedford.
Q. How long would it have taken to have come with horses?
A. It would have taken a little longer, perhaps half a minute.
Q. How would you have lost half a minute?
A. On account of the bridge.
Q. Would you have had to walk across the bridge?
A. Yes, sir. It would not have been safe to have run across the bridge with horses as fast as the men came across. The track was not filled up outside of the rail.

LOUIS BRIGGS, *sworn.*

Q. (By Mr. Russell.) What is your connection with the Fire Department?
A. I am engineer of Engine No. 18.
Q. Where is that located?
A. At Mount Bowdoin, Dorchester.

Q. How far is that from the burnt district?
A. We call it about four miles and a half.
Q. What time did you start for the great fire?
A. I started immediately on the general alarm.
Q. Do you know what time that was?
A. No, sir, not exactly. I have forgotten.
Q. At what time did you arrive?
A. We were timed by a man named Rexford. It was fifty-five minutes. His place of business is up here in Bedford street. He is in the perfumery business.
Q. At what place did you arrive?
A. We arrived in Chauncy street.
Q. Did you come by horse-power or by man-power?
A. By man-power.
Q. How much faster would you have come if you had had horses?
A. Not a great deal.
Q. Did you ever come over pretty nearly the same route with horses?
A. Yes, sir; I did at the Rand & Avery fire, and also at the State-street fire.
Q. How long did it take you to reach the State-street block on the last occasion?
A. Forty minutes.
Q. How long did it take you to reach the Rand & Avery fire?
A. About the same period. At the State-street fire we had a better chance, because it was late at night and the streets were clear.
Q. How was it when you came to Rand & Avery's fire, in respect to the streets being clear?
A. The streets were fuller. It was earlier in the evening, and there were more horse-cars running directly down Washington street. We were from forty to forty-five minutes coming to the Rand & Avery fire. We then took the hydrant where Adams' Express Company used to be. We did not go so far at the Rand & Avery fire as we did at the State-street fire.
Q. Did you race with any engine on the way?
A. No, sir.
Q. You did not pass any horse-power engine, or have any horse-power engine come with you?
A. No, sir.

EZRA B. HIBBARD, *sworn.*

Q. (By Mr. Russell.) What is your connection with the Fire Department?
A. I am Engineer of Steamer No. 19.
Q. Where is that located?
A. At Mattapan, 16th Ward.
Q. How far do you call that from Church-Green street?
A. It is about six and a half miles.
Q. At what time did you start for the great fire?
A. At eight o'clock I came out of the house.
Q. Did you look at the clock?

A. Yes, sir. The clock on the school-house was just striking as we started.

Q At what time did you arrive?

A. We arrived at half-past nine o'clock on Purchase street.

Q. Did you come by hand-power?

A. Yes, sir; by hand-power all the way.

Q. How much quicker do you think you would have come if you had had horses?

A. About from fifteen to twenty minutes quicker.

Q. Did you come to the State-street fire?

A. Yes, sir.

Q. How many minutes did that take?

A. One hour and five minutes.

Q. How long to the Rand & Avery fire?

A. Fifty-five minutes. I had horses on at the two last-named fires.

Q. What made the difference between the State-street fire and the Rand & Avery fire?

A. We had a hired horse, which had never worked on the pole before. It was the first night he had run, on the night of the State-street fire, and he was a little awkward. It was one new horse and one of our old ones. At the Rand & Avery fire, we got a little more speed out of him, so that he came in a little quicker. It was one hour and five minutes at the State-street fire, and fifty-five minutes at the Rand & Avery fire.

EUGENE H. FREEMAN, *sworn.*

Q. (By Mr. Russell.) What is your connection with the Fire Department?

A. I am engine-man of Steamer No. 16.

Q. Where is that located?

A. At Lower Mills, Dorchester. They call it six miles from there to the head of State street.

Q. At what time did you start for the great fire?

A. We started on the repetition of the general alarm. I don't remember now just what time it was.

Q. How long did it take you to come in?

A. We were fifty-five minutes. I timed it by my watch.

Q. Was it horse or hand power?

A. It was horses.

Q. Did the team belong to your engine?

A. No, sir; they were livery-stable horses. If we had had our own horses, we should have come in a little quicker.

Q. Who hired the horses?

A. I sent to the stable after them.

Q. What was the condition of your own horses?

A. They were badly used up. They were the sickest that they had been at all at that time. They came down late with the complaint, and they had it the very worst just then.

Q. Can you give any opinion as to how long it would have taken to have come without horses?

A. I could not. We did not drag our engine entirely by hand.

Q. To what point did you come?

A. We came to Chauncy street. We were sent there to the reservoir between Summer and Bedford.

Q. (By Mr. Firth.) How long did it take you to come to the State-street fire?

A. We got to State-street block in forty-four minutes with our own horses.

Q. How long did it take you to come to the Rand & Avery fire?

A. We were forty-eight minutes. We came over the upper road that night, which made it a little farther.

Q. You had your own horses at both the State-street fire and the Rand & Avery fire?

A. Yes, sir, at both places.

FRANKLIN MURRAY, *sworn.*

Q. (By Mr. Russell.) What is your connection with the Fire Department?

A. I am Engineer and engine-man of Engine No. 20.

Q. Where is that located?

A. At Neponset, in Ward 16.

Q. How far from the head of State street?

A. I don't know that I can tell you exactly. I believe it is considered five miles from the depot in Neponset to the head of State street.

Q. At what time did you start for the great fire?

A. I started at twenty minutes past eight o'clock.

Q. What started you?

A. We started on the second alarm.

Q. What time did you arrive?

A. We arrived in Chauncy street at five minutes before nine.

Q. Did you come with horses?

A. Yes, sir.

Q. Were they your own horses?

A. No, sir.

Q. Were the horses hired for the occasion?

A. Yes, sir. We went out and got them. They were hired by the foreman.

Q. Did he have any orders from any one else about hiring them?

A. No, sir.

Q. What was the condition of your own horses?

A. They were very sick.

Q. Where did you arrive at eight fifty-five?

A. At Chauncy street.

Q. Did you go to work there?

A. Yes, sir.

Q. How long did it take you to come to the State-street fire?

A. Forty-five minutes with our own horses.

Q. How long did it take you to come to the Rand & Avery fire?

A. Thirty-five minutes with the same horses.

Q. What made the difference?

A. When we came to the State-street fire, it was the first time we had used them after they were taken sick, and we drove slow.

CHARLES C. LANE, *sworn.*

Q. (By Mr. Russell.) What is your connection with the Fire Department?

A. I am engine-man of Steamer No. 17.

Q. Were is it located?

A. At Meeting-House Hill.

Q. How many miles from State street?

A. I don't know the exact distance.

Q. What do you think the distance is?

A. I think they call it three miles.

Q. At what time did you start for the great fire?

A. Quarter to eight o'clock by my watch.

Q. What time did you arrive?

A. Quarter past eight.

Q. Where did you arrive at that time?

A. At Church-Green. That was by my watch also.

Q. Was it by horse-power or man-power?

A. It was by hand-power.

Q. How much quicker could you have come with horses?

A. I could not have come any quicker with horses.

Q. Did you pass any horse team or did any horse-team engine pass you?

A. No, sir.

Q. How long did it take you to get to the State-street fire?

A. Forty minutes, as near as I can judge. I did not take the time when I came in, but we ran the biggest part of the way coming in. The horses did not come any faster than we came by hand. They were the regular horses on the engine. They were sick.

Q. (By Mr. Firth.) How was it at the Rand & Avery fire, as near as you can judge?

A. We came in in thirty-five minutes.

Q. Did you take the time?

A. I took the time when we started — not when we came in. It was not the same horses. I came in with a hose-carriage horse at that fire. He is now dead. He did not live but three or four days after that fire.

JAMES T. COLE, *sworn.*

Q. (By Mr. Russell.) What engine are you attached to?

A. Engine No. 12, as engine-man.

Q. Where is it located?

A. At the corner of Warren and Dudley streets, in the Highland district.

Q. What alarm caused you to start for the great fire?

A. We started for the great fire on the fourth alarm.

Q. At what time did you arrive?

A. I could not give you the exact time. It was twenty minutes from the house to the hydrant, with all the connections made.

Q. Where did you arrive?

A. At the hydrant at the corner of Bedford and Columbia street.

Q. How far do you call it?

A. It is somewhat over eleven thousand feet. I forget the exact number. I did measure it on the map. It was a trifle over two miles.

Q. Did you come by horse or hand power?

A. By hand-power.

Q. How much quicker would you have come if you had had horses? I mean good horses.

A. I think we could have bettered it some five minutes, perhaps more.

Q. How many minutes did it take you to come to the State-street fire?

A. That I could not say, only to guess at it. I should say twenty to twenty-five minutes. We had the horses that belonged to the engine.

Q. Did you take the time at Rand & Avery's?

A. No, sir.

Q. How did you know that you came in twenty minutes?

A. There was a gentleman who came with us who timed it; we came on the run all the way. I can run considerable, and I had to get on and ride twice. Every now and then fresh men would run out and jump on to the ropes.

Q. Who was the gentleman who timed you?

A. His name is Henry Morse. He lives in the Highland district, on Warren street. I don't know the number.

THOMAS NANNERY, *sworn.*

Q. (By Mr. Russell.) What is you connection with the Fire Department?

A. I am attached to Engine No. 14, as engine-man.

Q. Where is that engine?

A. At Centre street, Boston Highlands.

Q. How far out on Centre street?

A. It is within two hundred feet of being three miles from State street.

Q. What time did you start for the great fire?

A. Well, sir, that is more than I can answer. I was on my vacation at the time of the great fire. I went to the great fire myself. I started off before the engine. I was eating my supper at the time I heard the alarm.

Q. Did you come in to the State-street fire with the engine?

A. Yes, sir. We came in in twenty minutes with our horses.

Q. How was it at the Rand & Avery fire?

A. It was just about the same time, twenty minutes.

Q. On both those occasions was steam up when you got there?

A. Yes, sir, the steam was all ready.

Q. (By Mr. Cobb.) Who did come in with your engine and take your place at the great fire?

A. Mr. Raymond. I have got the time from those who did come with the engine. It was twenty-five minutes.

Q. Where did they locate with the engine?
A. At the corner of Otis and Franklin streets.
Q. How was the engine drawn?
A. It was drawn by horses that night. It was our own team. They were not very well, and so the driver did not hurry them so much as he otherwise would have done.

GILMAN TYNG, *sworn.*

Q. (By Mr. RUSSELL.) What is your connection with the Fire Department?
A. I am on Engine No. 10.
Q. Where is it located?
A. At the corner of River and Mount Vernon streets. I am Engineer of the engine.
Q. At what time did you start for the great fire?
A. I could not say at what time we did start. We started when the first alarm was given, at about 7¼ o'clock. We started as soon as the first alarm was given.
Q. Do you know at what time you arrived?
A. No, sir, I don't know exactly.
Q. As near as you could tell, about how many minutes?
A. I should think that if we came in in ten or twelve minutes that we were doing very well. Some twenty-five or thirty men thought that would be the time that we came in on. I don't know exactly.
Q. How much quicker would you have come in with horses?
A. It might have made a minute's difference. I don't know that it would have made that much difference. I had, I guess, all of one hundred men.
Q. Where did you go?
A. We came right in by Boylston street, right down Essex street, and stopped at the corner of Arch and Summer streets.
Q. When you went to the State-street fire did you have horses?
A. Yes, sir.
Q. How many minutes were you in coming?
A. I calculated that we came in to the State-street fire in eight or nine minutes. We came in pretty lively. I thought we had had fires enough, and that I would come in fast this time. I don't think it was more than six minutes. We had a nice, clear road, and went along pretty lively.

THEODORE HUTCHINGS, *sworn.*

Q. (By Mr. RUSSELL.) What is your connection with the Fire Department?
A. I am Engineer of Eagle engine No. 3.
Q. Where is it located?
A. On Washington street, near the corner of Dover.
Q. At what time did you start for the great fire?
A. Somewhere about thirty-five or thirty-six minutes past seven. I can't tell exactly.
Q. Did you look at the clock?

A. No, sir.
Q. What alarm was it?
A. We had got out of the door before the third alarm struck, having seen the fire.
Q. Do you know at what time you arrived?
A. I could not tell. Probably it was some eight or ten minutes from the time we started.
Q. How much faster could you have come if you had had horses?
A. I should think one quarter faster, or in that vicinity somewhere.
Q. To what spot did you come?
A. We came to the corner of Kingston and Bedford streets, directly opposite the fire.
Q. How long did it take you to go to the State-street fire?
A. I should think somewhere about thirteen or fourteen minutes.
Q. Did you have horses?
A. Yes, sir.
Q. How long to Rand and Avery's fire?
A. About the same time as the State-street fire. It may be a minute less.
Q. You did not time either of these, did you?
A. No, sir.

DEXTER R. DEARING, *recalled.*

Q. (By Mr. RUSSELL.) You belong to No. 4, situated in Brattle square?
A. Yes, sir, it was formerly. It isn't now.
Q. What time did you start for the great fire?
A. It was inside of seven minutes after the first alarm sounded that we arrived at the fire.
Q. Did you time it by your watch?
A. No, sir. I had all I could do to get ready.
Q. How long did it take you to come to the State-street fire?
A. I should think that it took four minutes.
Q. Did you use horses?
A. Yes, sir.
Q. At the Rand & Avery fire you did not use horses?
A. We used horses, but we were there connecting when the bell struck. I started the engine myself, coming away in my plain coat.

CHARLES RILEY, *sworn.*

Q. (By Mr. RUSSELL.) What is your place in the Fire Department?
A. Engineer of Steamer No. 7.
Q. Where is it located?
A. At East-street place, which makes up on the corner of East street. The engine-house is about half way down.
Q. At what time did you start for the great fire?
A. I don't know what time it was.

Q. Was it before the alarm or after?
A. It was before the alarm. I was on the way before the bell struck.
Q. How long after you started did the bell strike?
A. It might have been four or five seconds, I should judge. I was out of the house.
Q. Where did you go?
A. To the corner of Lincoln and Bedford streets.
Q. How many minutes did it take you to get there?
A. I don't know exactly, of course. As near as I can tell, it took me about a minute and a half — not over that, to the best of my judgment.
Q. How far is it?
A. Really, I don't know, — it is but a short distance.
Q. How soon did you have a stream on the fire?
A. I should judge that we had a stream on in not far from four minutes. It was inside of five, I should say.
Q. Do you mean from the time you started?
A. Yes, sir.
Q. Did you have steam up fully?
A. No, sir; not a full head.
Q. Did you use the steam in four minutes?
A. I got the hydrant stream on in four minutes from the time I started, and steam on a minute later. I have hot water in my boiler nearly up to the boiling point all the time, and I had it at that time.
Q. Did you have plenty of fuel when you begun?
A. Yes, sir.
Q. Did you get out of coal at any time?
A. Yes, sir, I got out, but not to lose any steam, however.
Q. How soon did you get out of coal?
A. It was in perhaps an hour.
Q. Where did you go for fuel?
A. It was brought to me by a team and horses.
Q. Didn't you use any fuel besides coal?
A. Yes, sir.
Q. What did you use?
A. It was cases and boxes. Those were also brought to me.
Q. Who brought the boxes to you?
A. I could not tell you. They were brought by citizens.
Q. Was any wood brought to you?
A. No, sir.

BROWN S. FLANDERS, *sworn.*

Q. (By Mr. Russell.) What is your place in the Fire Department?
A. I am Engineer of Steamer No. 8, stationed at Salem street, between Parmenter and Prince.
Q. At what time did you start for the great fire?
A. At the second alarm.
Q. Did you notice the time?
A. It was about twenty minutes past seven o'clock — within a minute or two. I noticed it by the clock on the engine-house. It might vary.
Q. At what time did you arrive at the fire?

A. I have no means of knowing when we arrived at the fire. It is not customary to time us. To the best of my knowledge, it was eight and a half minutes.

Q. How much faster should you have gone if you had had horses?

A. I could not say.

Q. What point did you go to?

A. I went to the south-west corner of Winthrop square,—the corner of Beebe's building, at the opposite side of the street.

Q. Could you have gone any faster if you had had horses?

A. Yes, sir.

Q. Did you ever time the steamer going to a fire about the same distance?

A. We have been timed repeatedly by other parties. I never have timed it. I should judge it was from five to six minutes to a point about that distance off.

Q. When you said you went in eight and a half minutes, what time was that?

A. It was from the time when we started from the house.

Q. Now, from the time you started from the house to the time you got to the other fire was how much?

A. It was five and a half minutes with horses. I should judge about that.

JOHN C. TRAVER, *sworn.*

Q. (By Mr. Russell.) What is your place in the Fire Department?

A. I am Engineer of Steamer No. 6.

Q. Where is that located?

A. At Wall street.

Q. At what time did you start for the great fire?

A. I don't know what time it was. It was at the third alarm.

Q. How long did it take you to reach the fire?

A. It was about ten minutes.

Q. That was not by the watch, I suppose?

A. It was only estimated to the best of my judgment.

Q. Where did you go?

A. We were located at the corner of Devonshire and Summer streets.

Q. How long would it have taken you to go with horses?

A. I don't know exactly. Our time, I believe, is about eight minutes to that box with horses.

Q. That is something you have talked about before, is it?

A. We have been timed with horses at that box, and they allowed us eight minutes.

Q. It might vary two or three minutes?

A. Oh, certainly, three minutes. It depends upon whether the street is blocked up or not.

Q. Have you ever been timed with hand and horse power, at the same point, or to any point?

A. We have not, sir, to my knowledge.

Q. (By Mr. Cobb.) You went that night with hand-power?

A. Yes, sir.

Q. You don't know how many minutes you were going to the Congress-street fire?

A. No, sir; I do not know of anybody who timed us. Sometimes gentlemen outside will time us, and tell us.

Q. Were you timed when you went to the State-street block?

A. No, sir; we did not go; we were at work on the ruins. We had steam on all ready to make connections.

GEORGE W. BIRD, *sworn.*

Q. (By Mr. RUSSELL.) When were you Chief Engineer of the Fire Department?

A. I have been out about five years now, sir.

Q. (By Mr. FIRTH.) Can you state where the hand engines were placed when you were Chief Engineer? I mean those about the burned district?

A. Well, sir, we had one stationed on East street, and one on Purchase street, and one on Franklin street in that location, and a hook-and-ladder truck we had on High street.

Q. Did you have anything on School street?

A. No, sir; there was nothing on School street. There was one under the City Hall.

Q. (By Mr. PHILBRICK.) Were there no steamers?

A. When I was Chief Engineer, it was entirely changed from hand to steam. I changed it myself, and there was no hand engine when I left it.

Q. Were there steamers then at these points you have mentioned?

A. No, sir, — none at City Hall. There was one at Scollay's building — moved from there to the City Hall. I could not give the exact date when they were changed. The yearly report of the Chief Engineer will show that.

Q. Do you remember the year the change was made?

A. No, sir, I don't know that I do exactly. I am not very good on dates.

Q. (By Mr. FIRTH.) Were the steam fire engines in that vicinity any differently located when you left from what they are now?

A. Yes, sir.

Q. Where were they?

A No. 7, which is located now in East street, was then located in Purchase street. It was located at that place when Mr. Hatch was Chairman of the Committee on the Fire Department.

Q. Do you remember when the engine on Franklin street was moved?

A. There was one steamer on Franklin street. All the others were hand engines.

Q. The one in City Hall was also a hand engine?

A. Yes, sir.

JOSEPH BIRD, *sworn.*

Q. (By Mr. RUSSELL.) Where do you live?

A. I reside in Watertown. Mount Auburn is my Post-Office address.

Q. What connection have you had with the Fire Department at any time?

A. Simply since the great fire in Charlestown, in 1835, I have been watching to see how the department could be made better — seeing how we could have less fires.

Q. Did you come in at the great fire?

A. No, sir, I was sick.

Q. Had you foretold something of this kind?

A. Yes, sir.

Q. You were the author of an article in the "Advertiser"?

A. Yes, sir.

Q. There was a reprint of that on the Monday after the fire?

A. Yes, sir.

Q. That which you now produce is your statement?

A. Yes, sir. I ought to say, also, that that account is an account of what might happen in a gale of wind. The same month I wrote afterwards upon the subject of the Mansard roofs, and I wrote what would be the result if there was not a gale of wind. I can give you that also.

Q. We would like to see it.

A. I have it here. It is in the paper dated November 25, 1871. It is headed, "*Mansard Roofs.*" It is as follows: — [Reads.]

"In my paper upon 'Mansard Roof Buildings,' I only wrote of the danger to a city if a fire should occur in a gale of wind. I shall now show how much more likely a fire will be to take in them than in others when there is not a gale of wind. Examine one of the Montrose buildings running up to the heavens, and then go to State street and look at the fine stores not so high by two or three stories. What do you find? Every room in the common-sense buildings on State street will be found to be let to good, responsible tenants; while rooms without number away up in dangerous buildings are now and will be to let. While not occupied they become filled up with all sorts of merchandise — perfect tinder-boxes, to go off as the cigar or pipe-smoker throws his lighted match among them. But many of them will be owned by persons who have their money so invested that they must be let. What is then to be the result? Why, that tenants of no character, or of only doubtful business reputation, flock to them — occupations of the most dangerous kinds — such as the workmen on jute, so dangerous that it should be banished from all cities except in bales; nitro-glycerine, dualin, the making of torpedoes, or other kinds especially dangerous, will be carried on in them. And this is not all. Business falls away. Money is hard to procure, and creditors must have money to pay their debts.

"Go to the insurance office where your property is insured and ask the President whom you can address, what will most likely be the result of having such business tenants in the times that tries men's souls and the patience of insurance people. The officers of insurance companies know all about this. But let me tell them that they don't know yet the full danger to their insured property if these Mansard roof buildings once get on fire in a gale of wind.

"They may seem, to those whom they insure in such neighborhoods, to charge very high rates; but time will prove that if stern measures are not soon applied, merchants' banks and insurance companies will be involved in one common ruin.

"What happened at the Chicago fire? When it had burned a mile or two of the small houses, it came in the direct line of the gale to the great, beautiful and magnificent erections, most of which were covered with Mansard roofs. Now, indeed, it became a hell of fire. It went with redoubled speed on its fell work of destruction, with the wind.

"But that was not all, nor the worst of it. Those great structures made the heat so great that they set the neighboring buildings on fire against or behind the wind. The fire, when it came to them, spread not alone in the direction of the wind, but on each side and in spite of it, and near $200,000,000 were destroyed of the most valuable property of Chicago."

The point is that it showed here just exactly what must happen without a gale of wind: that the heat would throw this fire in every direction where Mansard roofs were near enough to it.

There is one thing that I would like to say, gentlemen, and that is, that there is a very large part of Boston that has Mansard roofs now, and needs protection. But the powers that be — as it was in the United States army when the war began — never move.

There is a power capable of stopping every one of these. There is a power, which should have been used, which has been pressed upon the city for four years, which would have made it perfectly safe at that fire.

Q. What is it?

A. It is simply a small portable engine carried on to the roof, — carried up to the Mansard roof. There is not to-day (for I have been over the city with my team), where there are not windows from which you may stand and reach out with a small hose from one of these engines and throw water back on to the Mansard roof so that you can strike all of these exposed places in less than ten feet, and every one of these small engines can play thirty feet [illustrating and exhibiting one of the small engines referred to]. Suppose that to be the fire up by that window. The man goes up on to that roof with his hand covered with wet woollen cloths. He puts his hand out and plays back upon that roof. The building is just as safe as if it were in the Atlantic Ocean.

Gardiner Brewer wrote an excellent article the other day, in which he said that he was going to have a Fire Department of his own. I went to his house and took this engine which I now hold in my hand. I have no pecuniary interest in any engine except one, in which I lost a thousand dollars several years ago.

Q. Where would you have got water to have used in a case like this of the great fire?

A. Hovey's place was saved without even an engine, and they got water with perfect ease.

Q. They would not have got it without their elevator. They got it with tremendous exertions.

A. It would have been a great deal better to have saved the first building with a great deal of exertion, than to have burnt up the whole district.

Q. At that time everybody was gone home and locked up.

A. I understand the objection, but let me say that 3,000 of these little engines, such as I have in my hand, playing a great deal more water than all the present engines of the city of Boston, will not cost half as much, and the expense of their working will not cost half as much as one steam fire engine. You must designate those of the police who are to use them. We will say that it is known that you are a good man for the purpose, and I am not. It is to be placed in your house, and if through your means it puts out the fire before it spreads, you shall have five dollars.

Suppose every hay place has them, every hotel stable has them, we will say, and is obliged to have them.

I can show you old laws of the city of New York, by which it is provided that every house-keeper shall have a leather bucket, and every baker three, and every brewer six.

I would have put up over every door directions how to use this engine. The people may just as easily be taught to fight fire as to be terrified by it. Now, if there is a fire, men, women and children become terrified and run away from it. People can be taught so as to act with presence of mind at the time of a fire, so that a woman or even a girl shall put it out. Dr. Hill, of Waltham, while President of Harvard College, taught his children what to do in case of a fire; and once his son while in college woke up and found the room badly on fire. He knew just what to do. The water was frozen up except one pump, and he had but one single pail. He put the water on in little dashes at a time, and then went back again and got more, and in this way put the fire out.

The simple truth is, that people may be taught to put out a fire just as they are now taught not to put it out, and thus save the first house that the fire struck upon. You would then see men carrying water up there with all their might in a minute. I can tell you of fire after fire that I have put out simply by acting promptly and judiciously, with very small quantities of water thrown by hand.

Q. I want to know what you think about these open elevators?

A. They are perfect curses.

Q. Supposing that they should be shut on every floor?

A. They should be shut on every floor always.

Q. Will you go down and look at the one at Wellington & Bros., on the corner of Chauncy and Bedford streets?

A. I will go there and see it before to-morrow night, and I should like to have you see Mr. Downer's method of putting out fires.

ARTHUR W. HOBART, *sworn.*

Q. (By Mr. Russell.) With what Insurance Company are you connected?

A. The Mutual Benefit Insurance Company.

Q. Were you at the great fire early?

A. Perhaps twenty minutes after the alarm sounded.

Q. Where did you go?

A. I went down to Summer street.

Q. What was the condition of the fire?

A. The whole building in which the fire originally commenced was well on fire.

Q. It had not crossed the street, had it?

A. No, sir, it did not until after I reached there.

Q. Will you state anything that you saw that you think the Commission ought to know?

A. I can merely say, that from being there for the next half an hour, the impression given me was that I never saw so little force gathered at the commencement of a fire, as at that; merely judging from the streams of water thrown upon it. Of course I could not see where the engines were stationed at all.

Q. Could you see those playing from Kingston and Bedford streets?

A. I could see those playing from Summer street and Kingston street, where I was standing.

Q. Do you mean that you could see no others?

A. I could not see any others. I was in the middle of Summer street.

Q. How many engines should you suppose there were there at the end of half an hour after you came?

A. I can't answer as to engines, but only as to streams.

Q. How many streams?

A. I did not see more than five streams of water.

Q. How far down Summer street were you?

A. I was down, I should say, where the Post Office was, on the corner of Chauncy street, between Chauncy street and Kingston street, in the middle of the street.

Q. Is there any other fact that you noticed?

A. Nothing more than the progress of the fire. I saw it cross the street.

Q. Did you see any effort made to prevent its catching the north side of Summer street?

A. I did not, sir.

Q. Was there anybody in those buildings at the corner of Otis street?

A. That I cannot say.

Q. Do you know whether there was any stream on?

A. I saw a stream on after the fire had caught.

Q. Was it playing from the street?

A. Yes, sir; that played from the street.

Q. Did it do any good?

A. No, sir, I should not say that it did.

Q. How high did it go?

A. It went up to the fourth-story window, perhaps.

Q. Did you see any stream from the windows of the adjoining building?

A. I did not.

Q. Do you know whether it was played?

A. No, sir.

Q. (By Mr. PHILBRICK.) Did it occur to you that something was not done that might have been done to prevent the fire from crossing the street?

A. It merely occurred to me that there was less apparatus with which to fight the fire and to prevent its crossing the street than there should have been.

Q. How was the heat?

A. The heat must have been intense, for this whole corner building seemed to be a mass of flame, for the two sides that I could see, on Summer street and Kingston street.

Q. (By Mr. FIRTH.) At that time, did it seem to you that an engine could have stood upon the street and worked so as to have played upon the fire?

A. Yes, sir. It need not necessarily have stood beside the fire to have reached it.

Q. Could you see whether there was another engine down Otis street?

A. No, sir; I could not see where I stood.

Q. Did you see any ladders down Otis street?

A. That I cannot answer, sir. I supposed there was another matter that I was summoned here to testify about. It is this. I had occasion to carry my securities from my office to my home, between twelve and one o'clock, because I felt that my office would take fire. My office was No. 29 State street. On my return, I passed down School street. It must have been between one and two o'clock, I should judge. I thought I heard a pounding, and Capt. Damrell's voice coming from the large front door of the City Hall. I of course supposed that I must be mistaken, and I stopped to listen again, and I heard a voice saying, "Let me in! Let me in!" I knew then that it was Captain Damrell's voice. I walked up to the steps and there was Captain Damrell standing on the steps with three or four persons around him. He was pounding on the door, calling, "Let me in!" It was the main large door right on School street. As I approached I heard him say to one of these parties that were standing with him, "Doctor, I am all used up. This whole fire is the result of the architects being allowed to pile up their Mansard roofs." I suppose it was the end of some conversation that he had been having with a man. That was all that I heard of it.

When I reached him near enough to speak, I said, "What is the matter?" He said, "I want to go in here."—"Well," said I, "the only way to get in is on the rear, Court square. That door is open to-night." Said he, "I am going in this way, sir." Said I, "Very well, sir, if that is the case, I will go around and see if I can get the door open for you." I accordingly went around to Court square and went in at the rear door, and up stairs, and I thought probably I might open the door. I went to the door and found that it was locked. The building was full of people. I turned around and saw an officer pretty near, and I asked him if he knew who had charge of that door. He looked around, and said, "Yes, sir; there is the officer who has the key." Said I, "Will you open this door?" Said he, "My orders are not to." Said I, "Yes; but Capt. Damrell is out there and wants to come in." Says he, "I suppose I must let him in." He went and unlocked the door and let him in. The Captain blew the man up for not having the door open. The man told him that those were his orders. (I cannot give the words that he used; it was merely in an impatient way, to think the door was closed.)

Q. At what time should you say that this was?

A. I should say, without knowing truly, that it was between one and two o'clock.

I followed the Captain up stairs, thinking that I had a right to know the cause of his visit at that time. He went to the Mayor's room, and took his hat off, and says, "Gentlemen, you have sent for me and I have come." Said the Mayor, "Well, we sent for you to consider in regard to blowing up buildings." "Well," said Capt. Damrell, "my opinion is, that it will do more harm than good; but I suppose that the public opinion will demand it, and I have been getting ready for the last few hours to blow up on Milton place." That was about the whole of the story. They then went on to consider the matter of blowing up buildings.

It was merely the point of Capt. Damrell's spending so much time in trying to get in at that door when he might have gone around.

Q. How much time was wasted there by him?

A. I should have said that it was ten minutes.

Q. Did you understand him to be quoting Metamora, when he said, "You have sent for me, and I have come"?

A. Those were the words. He said it with the tone of a man who was sorry that he had to come. Perhaps the thing made more impression on my mind than it should have done, because I had a great deal at stake in that fire, and every moment was an age to me. To see the Chief of the Fire Department spending so much time in trying to get in at one door when he might have got in at another door looked to me as if he had not quite got his head at that time, perhaps.

Q. How did he appear afterwards?
A That was all that I saw of him.
Q. After he got up stairs, did you see anything of his manner?
A. No, sir. All I noticed was that remark that he made when he went in. He said that he had been making preparations to blow up in Milton place..

BENJAMIN F. LEONARD, *sworn.*

Q. (By Mr. Russell.) What is your connection with the Fire Department?
A. I am driver of hook-and-ladder truck No. 5, situated in Fourth street, near Dorchester street, South Boston.
Q. At what time did you start for the great fire?
A. We started on the general alarm.
Q. You don't know what hour it was?
A. No, sir, I could not tell.
Q. Did you start immediately on the general alarm?
A. Yes, sir.
Q. What time did you reach the fire?
A. From the time of the general alarm until we were in Summer street, I should say it was not over eleven minutes. I only estimated it. We came with horses. We had our own team. We could not have come at that rate with hand-power.
Q. What is the distance?
A. It is hard on to two miles, or one mile and a half.
Q. How long would it take you to come by hand-power, to the best of your judgment?
A. It would take all of twenty minutes to get there by hand — that is, in the way that we should have to pick up a team on such an occasion as that.
Q. Have you ever run two miles with that company and that machine by hand?
A. No, sir, we never have.

JOSEPH E. THAYER, *sworn.*

Q. (By Mr. Russell.) What is your connection with the Fire Department?
A. I am driver of hook-and-ladder truck No. 2, of East Boston.
Q. At what time did you start for the great fire?
A. It was about half-past ten o'clock.
Q. Did you have horses, or did you go by hand-power?
A. It was hand-power.
Q. At what time did you arrive?
A. It was about eleven o'clock.
Q. Where was it that you arrived?
A. It was in Franklin street. That was the first place.
Q. Did you catch the boat?
A. No, sir, the boat had just started. I was detained fifteen minutes on account of the ferry.

Q. What started you at that late hour?

A. I am not authorized to leave the island without special orders. I am on the only ladder carriage there is in the second Ward, and they don't allow me to cross to this side, if they can possibly help it, on account of its taking so long to get back across the ferries. We started at half-past ten, and just at that time they halloed fire over there, and we had to stop and put out a fire on Summer street, East Boston.

Q. From Sumner street, how long were you coming to the great fire?

A. I was about twenty minutes; I don't think I was over that, that is, after I got started from the Summer-street fire. I was not fifteen minutes in running time. I allow fifteen minutes outside of the boat to get to the fire. It is only 1,500 feet that I have to come to reach the boat on East Boston side.

Q. Then, from the Boston side of the ferry to Franklin street, how many minutes did it take you that night?

A. It was not over ten minutes.

Q. How long would it have taken you if you had had horses?

A. I don't think I could have made the time any quicker with horses than I did make it. I had eighty feet of rope, and it was full of men. There was a very large company on the rope. I rode myself and managed the break to guard against any one's being run over. They got along very lively. The carriage is a very light one, and only weighs 5,500 pounds. It rolls very easy.

I started at ten o'clock, in the first place, to come to this fire, and as we were turning the Sugar House, they halloed fire over there in East Boston. It was just a short distance below Sumner street, and we were detained there about half an hour by that fire. We used the fire-extinguishers on a ladder-carriage until we got a hose-carriage.

This time is estimated; I have no time by the watch.

Q. Did you come to the State-street fire, and, if so, how long were you in getting there?

A. Yes, I came to the State-street fire, and I was about twenty minutes in getting there. I also attended the Rand & Avery fire. I don't think there was much difference in the times of getting to those two.

Q. Did you have horses?

A. Yes, I had horses both at the State-street fire and at the Rand & Avery fire.

Q. Did you start then with special orders?

A. No, sir, I went on the fourth alarm. Under the circumstances of this big fire (the men were at work and we were at home), we thought it was best to go on that account.

Q. Do you think with the horses at these two fires that you went no faster than you did at the great fire with your men?

A. No, sir, I don't think, actually, that it made difference enough to mention. I could not see the difference.

Q. How does your carriage compare with the steamer?

A. The steamers weigh about 8,500 lbs., and my carriage only weighs 5,500.

Q. You spoke about extinguishers. Have you extinguishers?

A. We keep one in the house. There is an extinguisher wagon in

East Boston. They came right down and we used them at the fire. Then there was a hose-carriage, and that came and we used that.

CHARLES BROOKS, *sworn.*

Q. (By Mr. Russell.) What is your connection with the Fire Department?
A. I am driver of hose-carriage No. 6, stationed at East Boston, Chelsea street, fourth section.
Q. What time did you start for the great fire?
A. At half-past ten. I was at another fire when they sent for me.
Q. Did you go with horse or with hand-power?
A. It was with horse-power.
Q. At what time did you arrive at the fire?
A. As near as I can judge, it was in about fifteen minutes.
Q. Was there any delay at the boat?
A. No, sir.
Q. How long would it have taken you to have come by hand-power?
A. It ought not to have taken me more than twenty minutes from the square where I left the other fire.

ALBERT L. PEARSON, *sworn.*

Q. (By Mr. Russell.) What is your connection with the Fire Department?
A. I am driver of hose-carriage No. 1.
Q. Where is that located?
A. At Salem street.
Q. At what time did you start for the great fire?
A. I was not on duty at the great fire at all.
Q. Did you go to the fire at the great wool warehouse in Congress street, two months ago?
A. Yes, sir. We went by horse-power that night.
Q. How many minutes did it take to get there?
A. I should judge that it would take about six and a half minutes, although I have never taken the time.
Q. How long would it take to go by hand-power?
A. I should judge that it would take eight or nine minutes.

JOSEPH R. GILBERT, *sworn.*

Q. (By Mr. Russell.) What is your place in the Fire Department?
A. I am Engineer of Steamer No. 21, stationed on Boston street, Dorchester district.
Q. What is the distance from State street?
A. From State street to Upham's corner is supposed to be three miles, and we are a short distance this side of Upham's corner.
Q. Did you come to the great fire?
A. Yes, sir.
Q. At what time did you start?

A. We started at twenty minutes before eight o'clock, and arrived at eight o'clock. It was by hand-power.

Q. How did you get the seven-forty?

A. I looked at my watch and made the remark that I would see what time it was.

Q. How long would it have taken you to come with horses?

A. Provided the horses had been well, we might have made the time perhaps some eight minutes different.

Q. At what alarm did you start?

A. Upon the fourth alarm. On the first blow on the tapper — before the alarm — we started. We were all ready, with rope, waiting for it, with the doors open.

THOMAS W. GOWEN, *sworn.*

Q. (By Mr. Russell.) What is your connection with the Fire Department?

A. I am driver of hose-carriage, No. 9.

Q. Where is it located?

A. It is stationed at B street, South Boston.

Q. At what time did you start for the great fire?

A. I didn't take the time. I don't know what hour it was. I started on the commencement of the general alarm. It was right away, before the stroke got through.

Q. Do you know at what time you arrived?

A. I didn't take the time; but I should judge not far from eight minutes.

Q. How did you come — by what power?

A. It was by hand-power.

Q. How long would it have taken you to come by horse-power?

A. I could have come quicker if the horses had been in their usual order.

Q. In how many minutes?

A. I could have done it in five minutes.

Q. Did you come to the State-street block fire?

A. Yes, sir.

Q. Where did you come to in the Summer-street fire?

A. I came to Church-Green street, and then ran a line from a steamer there.

Q. How long did it take you to come to the State-street block fire?

A. I could not tell the precise time, because I did not take it.

Q. Did you take the time at Rand & Avery's?

A. No, sir.

FRANK WALKER, *sworn.*

Q. (By Mr. Russell.) What is your place in the Fire Department?

A. I am driver of hose-carriage No. 2, situated in Hudson street.

Q. At what time did you start for the great fire?

A. At quarter-past seven. It was before the alarm. It was within a minute and one-half of seven and a quarter o'clock. It was probably half a minute before the alarm.

Q. How long did it take you to get there?
A. Three to three and a half minutes.
Q. Where did you arrive and where did you station your stream?
A. At the corner of Bedford and Kingston streets.
Q. How soon did you get a stream on after you got there?
A. It was a minute and a half.
Q. Did you see when the engine arrived?
A. No, sir, I did not.
Q. You don't know about that?
A. No, sir. All I have is a hose-carriage.
Q. (By Mr. COBB.) Did you go by hand?
A. Yes, sir.
Q. What difference would it have made if you had a horse?
A. It would make about a minute's difference.

THOMAS MERRITT, *sworn.*

Q. (By Mr. RUSSELL.) What is your place in the Fire Department?
A. I am driver *pro tem.* of an Extinguisher wagon.
Q. Where is that stationed?
A. At North Grove street.
Q. At about what time did you start for the great fire?
A. I could not exactly state the time. It was just as soon as the first alarm was struck. It was by hand-power.
Q. At about what time did you arrive?
A. From the time I left the house until I got to the fire was seven minutes.
Q. Do you know exactly?
A. Yes, sir, very near. I had 150 men on the wagon.
Q. Would you have come faster if you had had horses?
A. No, sir, not so fast.
Q. How heavy is the carriage?
A. About 2,000 lbs., I should judge. There are nine extinguishers on it. The wagon weighs about 1,000 or 1,200.
Q. Did you use the extinguishers?
A. I could not tell you the stores on which they were used. I lost five of the nine which I had.
Q. Do you generally lose them?
A. No, sir. I find them good things.
Q. Are they good in the beginning of a fire?
A. I once saw a fire put out with them down in Chandler's place. It saved many thousand dollars.
Q. How did it happen that the extinguishers were lost?
A. The men took them up into the building to put out the fire, and they were driven out and had to drop the extinguishers in order to save themselves. It was the third building from the corner on the opposite side. It was a building that the Chief and fifteen of us were in, trying to kill the fire. We were fighting it with these extinguishers; and if they had not driven us off from the roof, we would have done good service with them. The heat drove us off—the heat from the opposite side, and the heat of the building right alongside of it.

Q. Do you use them on the roof usually?

A. No, sir. We use them wherever we can get a good chance to get at a fire. They will play some fifteen minutes, by using good, careful judgment.

Q. How many men do you have?

A. Only two.

Q. What kind of extinguishers are these?

A. They are chemical fire-extinguishers. They are the Babcock extinguisher. They weigh eighty pounds.

Q. Was there anybody else there on the roof with a stream?

A. Yes, sir. Hose No. 3, and two or three more engines that I could not tell.

Q. Was there any other Engineer there besides the Chief?

A. Yes, sir; Capt. Jacobs was there, and two or three more.

Q. Which way were you playing? Was it up or down the street?

A. We were playing on to the building next to it — the one towards Washington street. It was right opposite the building that took fire. I arrived there before the fire crossed Summer street.

Q. Was that the first thing you did with the extinguishers?

A. We went on to the buildings around it to try to stop it. There was one building where the fire caught in the coving, and we put that out.

Q. How many wagons are there that carry extinguishers?

A. There are three at present in the department — one located at the South End, one at North Grove street, and one at East Boston. We always start at the very first alarm, anywhere in the city. Extinguisher No. 1 takes the North End, down to Kneeland street; No. 2, from there to Roxbury. Ours is No. 1. No. 1 takes everything this side of Beach street. Then Extinguisher No. 2 takes everything the other side to the Roxbury line. If there is a second alarm given, they go right to it, with all hands. They carry 400 feet of 2-inch hose, and 400 feet of 1½-inch hose. The 2-inch hose we use to make connections with, with the other hose, in case we want to shift a line of small hose, or to carry it up into the attic of some dwelling-house to put out a fire, or to connect it with some private faucet. The 2-inch hose is good for nothing on a steamer. We take and tap their line. We carry connection-pipe branches on purpose for that. Sometimes we have to make a fresh-water connection, where they pump salt water to street-engines on the wharves.

Q. No change was made in the rule with your wagon, by reason of the horse-disease?

A. No, sir. The wagon did not weigh much, and a hundred and fifty men could run away with it. We came almost the same distance with horse-power, and could not make the same time. It was at Rand & Avery's fire. We could not make as good time.

At the State-street fire, we could not do as well, because we had a good deal to contend with, and there were teams in the way.

WILLIAM BLAKE, *sworn.*

Q. (By Mr. RUSSELL.) With what machine are you connected?
A. With Hose No. 8, located in Church street.
Q. At what time did you start for the great fire?
A. It was somewhere in the neighborhood of seven and a quarter o'clock. It was immediately upon the first alarm. We calculated that we were eight minutes in getting to the fire, as near as we could estimate it. We went by hand-power. I don't think we could have gone any quicker with a horse.
Q. Suppose you had had a good horse?
A. They started out some two minutes or so before I could have done in that case, because I should have had to stop and harness.
Q. To what point did you go?
A. Right to the corner of Kingston street, right around on to Otis street, and took that hydrant on Otis street.
Q. Where was the hose carried?
A. Right up on to the first building that was on fire.
Q. How soon did you get a stream on after you arrived?
A. It was very quick.
Q. How many minutes?
A. I heard some of the men say to-night that they didn't think it was over two minutes. But then they had to back right out, they said. We coupled on to a hydrant.
Q. When you went to the State-street-block fire, did you have a horse?
A. Yes, sir.
Q. How many minutes did it take there?
A. I did not time it.
Q. You did not time it at Rand & Avery's?
A. No, sir.

HORATIO ELY, *sworn.*

Q. (By Mr. RUSSELL.) What is your place in the Fire Department?
A. I am driver of Hose-carriage No. 3.
Q. Where is that stationed?
A. In North Grove street.
Q. What time did you start for the great fire?
A. I did not start on the first alarm. I started somewhere between quarter-past and half-past seven o'clock. I started at the second alarm.
Q. How long did it take you to get there?
A. From the time the alarm struck until I got there, I should think was somewhere about fifteen minutes, as near as I could judge. I did not look at any time-piece. I went directly to Summer street. I took a steamer at the corner of Arch street. It was No. 10.
Q. You went by hand-power, I suppose?
A. Yes, sir.
Q. How long would it have taken you to go by horse-power?
A. I don't think it would have taken much less time to have gone with horse-power. It might make some little difference. It might make five minutes' difference.

Q. How much of a team did you have?

A. It was very light when we got the second alarm. Most of the men went on the extinguisher team; consequently, I had to take what I could pick up as I went along.

Q. What would be the difference between the time of your arriving, and the time of the wagon arriving with the extinguisher team?

A. They had a very large team to start with, and it might make some six or eight minutes' difference.

Q. Do you know what time it took you to go to the State-street-block fire?

A. I was sick at that time. Mr. Merritt, who was just in here, drove. I was also sick at the Rand & Avery fire.

Q. After you got to the fire, how soon did you get a stream on it?

A. I should not think it was more than some three or four minutes. We ran the hose directly into the building, and word was passed to play away. It was in the building on the left-hand side of Summer street. We took it (the hose) up the stairway to play out of the window, and went on to the roof until we were compelled to get off. I drive the carriage and don't have to go into the buildings except once in a while to light up the hose, in case of emergency.

Q. What drove you off of the roof?

A. It was the fire. I didn't go on the roof myself. I went back to the carriage after I got my hose in.

Q. What building was it that they took the hose into?

A. I don't know who occupied the building. It was directly opposite where the fire was in the first place. It was some three or four doors below Otis street.

G. W. STIMPSON, *sworn.*

Q. (By Mr. Russell.) What is your place in the Fire Department?

A. I am driver of Hose-carriage No. 7.

Q. Where is that located?

A. At 1044 Tremont street.

Q. At what time did you start for the great fire?

A. It was about half-past seven o'clock. It was at the general alarm.

Q. At what time did you arrive?

A. I arrived there at seven and three-quarters.

Q. Did you look at your watch?

A. No, sir. The estimate I have given is that of one of the hosemen.

Q. Did the hoseman speak from the watch?

A. Yes, sir.

Q. Did he speak from the watch as to the time of starting and arriving both?

A. Yes, sir.

Q. Where did you arrive?

A. It was in Bedford street.

Q. How soon did you get a stream on?

A. It was in about ten minutes.

Q. Was it from hydrant or engine?

A. It was from engine.
Q. From what engine?
A. It was from Steamer 12.
Q. Why did it take ten minutes?
A. We lent one hundred feet of hose and then went to work. I think it was to Engine 15 that we lent it.
Q. Where was the steam thrown?
A. It was thrown in front of Columbia street.
Q. How long would it have taken you to have gone with horse-power?
A. We could have gone there in about thirteen minutes, if not sooner.
Q. Did you use horse-power at the State-street fire?
A. Yes, sir.
Q. How long did it take you to get there?
A. It was twenty minutes.
Q. To what spot?
A. In front of the building that was burning — the State-street block.
Q. Did you use your own horses there?
A. We used a spare horse. We use only one horse.
Q. Was he well?
A. No, sir.
Q. At the Rand & Avery fire, how long did it take you to get there?
A. Twenty-five minutes.
Q. Did you use a sick horse then;
A. Yes, sir; not the same one that I used at the other fire. It was another sick horse.
Q. Suppose that both horses had been in good condition, what difference would it have made?
A. It would not have made more than three minutes either way. I might have saved three minutes if I had had a horse in good condition.

WILLISTON A. GALORD, *sworn*.

Q. (By Mr. Russell.) What is your connection with the Fire Department?
A. I am driver of Extinguisher Wagon No. 2, which is located on Harrison avenue, corner of Wareham street.
Q. At what time did you start for the great fire?
A. We started on the second alarm?
Q. What time did you arrive?
A. It took us about eight minutes to get down there.
Q. Was it by hand-power?
A. Yes, sir.
Q. Could you have come faster with a horse?
A. No, sir.
Q. How much does the carriage weigh?
A. We had our extinguishers and hose on the ladder truck all combined that night.
Q. Where did you stop when you got to the fire?
A. It was at the corner of Kingston and Bedford streets.
Q. What did you do?

A. Before we had fairly stopped, we were ordered with our Extinguishers into a building on Kingston street. I drove Extinguisher Wagon No. 2.

Q. Did you use them anywhere else?

A. Yes, sir. We used them in dwelling-houses on the left-hand side of Kingston street, towards Summer. We stopped the fire in those dwelling-houses.

Q. In how many houses did you stop the fire?

A. Two of those dwelling-houses we used them in, and saved them both. There were streams of water on the roof playing across, but nothing inside. It was where the fire caught in the window frames and in the windows, and burned through on to the plastering.

SILAS LOVELL, *sworn.*

Q. (By Mr. Russell.) What is your position in the Fire Department?

A. I am driver of Hose-carriage No. 5. It is stationed in Shawmut avenue, No. 398, between Canton and Brookline streets.

Q. At what time did you start for the great fire?

A. I started at 7.25. I looked at the clock. I arrived about twenty-five minutes to eight o'clock.

Q. Did you look at your watch then?

A. Yes, sir.

Q. Did you have hand-power?

A. Yes, sir.

Q. Could you have gone faster with a horse?

A. No, sir.

Q. No faster with a well horse?

A. No, sir; not with the horse I have at the present time.

Q. How is it with the horse you generally have?

A. The one I had previous to that is a very smart horse. This is rather an ordinary one.

Directly after arriving there, — not more than three or four minutes after — we attached to Engine No. 22. The stream was put on on Summer street, about opposite from the building that took fire first. It was towards Otis street.

Q. On what part of the building was it thrown?

A. It was on the coving. It was thrown from the street. It reached the coving.

Q. Why didn't you put it out?

A. It was a little too much for one man.

Q. Did you have to back out?

A. Yes, sir. We were ordered from the ground up into the fourth story of the building. We went up there and played across Summer street.

Q. Who gave that order?

A. Capt. Jacobs, I think. It was an Assistant Engineer. We then followed along from building to building as the fire drove us.

Q. Did you go upon the roof of any of them?

A. Yes, sir. We were driven up towards Federal street.

Q. On the roofs of how many buildings did you go?

A. We were on the roofs of two buildings and in the fourth story of a third one, I think.

Q. When you went to the State-street-block fire, did you have a horse?

A. Yes, sir. It took about seventeen minutes. To the Rand & Avery fire, it was about fifteen minutes.

Q. Was the horse well?

A. No, sir, not entirely.

Q. Do you suppose you could have got there as fast by hand?

A. Yes, sir, I think we could — quicker.

Q. Suppose you had had a well horse?

A. It would depend somewhat upon the ambition of the horse.

JAMES B. PRESCOTT, *sworn.*

Q. (By Mr. RUSSELL.) What is your position in the Fire Department?

A. I am driver of "Franklin" Hook-and-Ladder truck No. 3. It is stationed at No. 618 Harrison avenue, Boston.

Q. At what time did you start for the great fire?

A. I think it was twenty-five minutes past seven o'clock, as near as we could judge with our time. It was at the second alarm. We calculate that we were about eight minutes on the road — as near as watch could tell.

Q. Did you look at your watch when you arrived?

A. Yes, sir, I did.

Q. Did you come by hand-power?

A. Yes, sir.

Q. Where did you stop when you arrived?

A. We stopped on the corner of Bedford and Summer streets.

Q. Could you have come any faster if you had had horses?

A. No, sir, we could not.

Q. How long did it take you to get to the State-street-block fire?

A. I calculate that it took us about seventeen minutes. We had horses then.

Q. Were they well?

A. They were not entirely well; but then the order came to use them, and we did so.

Q. At the Rand & Avery fire how long?

A. It was fifteen minutes.

Q. Do you think you could have gone to the State-street-block fire as quicker by hand-power?

A. I should say that there would not have been any great difference, provided that we could have had the same number of men that we did at the great fire. We had a large team at the great fire — about one hundred and fifty men, as near as we could calculate it.

GEORGE W. THOMPSON, *sworn.*

Q. (By Mr. Russell.) What is your position in the Fire Department?

A. I am driver of Hook-and-Ladder truck No. 1, stationed at No. 148 Friend street.

Q. At what time did you start for the great fire?

A. At twenty-five minutes past seven.

Q. Did you look at your watch?

A. We went on the first alarm. Coming down street, we cannot hear the alarm, in consequence of the rattling of the ladders. We arrived in six minutes. We turned out of Otis street on to Summer street.

Q. Could you have come faster with horses?

A. I don't think we could.

Q. What does your team weigh?

A. It weighs about between 6,500 and 7,000.

Q. How much of a gang did you have?

A. We had two 75-foot ropes on, full of men.

Q. How long did it take you to go to the State-street-block fire?

A. In my judgment, it was about five minutes.

Q. Did you have a horse then?

A. Yes, sir.

Q. How long did it take you to go to the Rand & Avery fire?

A. Between three and four, I should judge.

Q. Did you have a horse?

A. Yes, sir.

JASON GORDON, *sworn.*

Q. (By Mr. Russell.) What is your place in the Fire Department?

A. I am driver of Hook-and-Ladder truck No. 7. It is stationed at Meeting-house hill, in the sixteenth ward.

Q. At what time did you start for the great fire?

A. On the fourth alarm, at quarter to eight. I didn't time it myself, but I took it from the firemen in the same house. I arrived at the fire at quarter-past eight o'clock.

Q. How did you get that time?

A. I got it from the Engineer of the steamer. He said that there was a man run in and took out his watch, and told them that they got in in thirty minutes. We went off right together with Steamer 17. We were right together. We went by hand-power.

Q. How long do you think it would have taken you with a horse?

A. I have some trouble in getting off, and I could not get in there so quick with a horse. I keep my horses in Steamer 17's house. My ladder house is about one thousand feet distant, across the hill. I have to go over, light a kerosene lamp, and put the pole in. We got in fully as quick by hand-power. If I had had horses well, and all harnessed, I could have come in in twenty minutes. Once in a while some of the company will come in and help me; at other times, I have to tie my horses, and go and run the carriage out, and put on the pole.

I went to the State-street-block fire, and also to the Rand & Avery fire, but did not take the time at either.

ALEXANDER P. HAWKINS, *sworn.*

Q. (By Mr. Russell.) What is your place in the Fire Department?
A. I am driver of Hose-carriage No. 10.
Q. Where is that stationed?
A. At Washington Village, Dorchester street, South Boston.
Q. At what time did you start for the great fire?
A. I started at half-past seven o'clock.
Q. What alarm was that?
A. That was the general alarm. I started as soon as it was given.
Q. Did you go by horse-power or by hand-power?
A. It was by hand-power.
Q. How long were you in coming in?
A. We were twelve minutes in coming in.
Q. Where did you come to — to what point?
A. We arrived at Devonshire street. That is where we took our water. We took water from Engine No. 8.
Q. Where was the stream thrown?
A. The stream was thrown into a building on Summer street.
Q. How soon after you got in was that water thrown on the fire?
A. Well, perhaps half a minute. I have not taken that matter into consideration. I should judge that it was half a minute.
Q. How long would it have taken you to come in by horse-power?
A. Ten minutes.
Q. How long did it take you to come in at the State-street fire?
A. It took me fourteen minutes to come in with a horse that was not well.
Q. How long did it take you to come in at the Rand & Avery fire?
A. It was fifteen minutes, with the same horse. He was not well.

BENJAMIN F. THAYER, *sworn.*

Q. (By Mr. Russell.) What is your positition in the Fire Department?
A. I am driver of Hose-carriage No. 4.
Q. Where is it located?
A. On Northhampton street.
Q. At what time did you start for the great fire?
A. I didn't take particular notice. I started on the general alarm.
Q. How long did it take you to get there?
A. I should think about twelve minutes.
Q. Where did you arrive?
A. It was at Otis street.
Q. Where did you get your water?
A. We were ordered to stand in reserve. Mine is a hose-carriage.
Q. How long would it have taken you to come by horse-power?
A. Well, in the condition in which the horse was that night —

Q. I mean with a well horse?

A. We could not have got there much quicker than we did.

Q. Suppose that you had used your sick horse, how long would it have taken you?

A. I don't think we could have got there with him.

Q. Did you go to the State-street-block fire?

A. Yes, sir.

Q. How many minutes did it take you?

A. I should think it was twenty minutes. It was with a sick horse at the Rand & Avery fire. I should say that it took eighteen minutes. I threw him three times going to the fire. The horse is living, but he is weak yet.

Adjourned to Monday.

EIGHTEENTH DAY.

MONDAY, December 23.

SANFORD H. BRIDGHAM, *sworn.*

Q. (By Mr. RUSSELL.) Did you time one of the Roxbury steamers on the night of the fire?
A. No, sir.
Q. Are you connected with the Fire Department?
A. Yes, sir.
Q. What are you?
A. Driver of Engine 21.
Q. Where is that located?
A. Upham's Corner, in the 16th Ward.
Q. What time did you start for the fire?
A. Well, sir, I am unable to tell.
Q. Did you use horse-power or hand-power?
A. Hand-power.
Q. How long were you coming in?
A. That I am unable to tell. I never looked to see what time it was when we started.
Q. Did you start at the time of the general alarm?
A. Yes, sir.
Q. As near as you can tell, how long did it take to come in?
A. I heard the Engineer say, after we got in there, that we were twenty minutes coming in.
Q. To what point?
A. To Church Green,—the reservoir on Church Green.
Q. How much quicker could you have come with horses?
A. I have been from our house to Haymarket Square in seventeen minutes.
Q. Did you come in to the State-street fire?
A. Yes, sir.
Q. How long did that take you?
A. That I am unable to say, but to the best of my opinion, I should say twenty minutes.
Q. Did you time the engine going to the Rand & Avery fire?
A. No, sir, I did not.

R. E. FLANDERS, *sworn.*

Q. (By Mr. RUSSELL.) You are a fireman?
A. Yes, sir.
Q. Connected with what?
A. Steamer 21.

Q. Do you know how long it took you to come in to the great fire?
A. No, sir, I don't.
Q. Have you any opinion?
A. No, sir.

GRIDLEY J. F. BRYANT, *sworn.*

Q. (By Mr. PHILBRICK.) Will you give us your opinion in regard to the style of Mansard roofs used in Boston, — whether they are conducive to conflagrations or not?

A. The Mansard roof, with wooden trimmings, is of course more dangerous than if the trimmings were galvanized iron.

Q. Is there anything in the form of the roof to make it dangerous, if the materials are proper?

A. Decidedly not.

Q. Is there anything in the shape of the roof which makes it difficult to use incombustible materials in its construction?

A. No, sir, it is really the simplest form of roof in outline.

Q. Have you ever had your attention called to elevators, as they are generally built in Boston, without any self-closing doors?

A. Yes, sir; it has been a subject of considerable thought among all the architects in active business, who are engaged in building large structures. Small buildings, of course, do not require them, but in large buildings, they are becoming a *sine qua non.* I do not speak of buildings requiring passenger elevators, only, but almost all buildings having power I think are using elevators open on all sides to each loft.

Q. What is your opinion of the self-closing hatches, as a means of preventing the spread of fire?

A. One or two different theories have been brought to my attention. It seems practicable to build them, and I think they may be made exceedingly useful.

Q. Have you ever seen them in practice?

A. No, sir, I have never paid any attention to them as actually built. I doubt whether there are many built in structures other than factories, but it seems to me, from the models that have been shown to me, they ought to be made useful, and can be exceedingly well arranged for cutting off fire.

Q. Have you any statements to make as to the part played by the new Post-Office building in preventing the spread of the fire on account of the character of the construction?

A. I believe the construction of the building, by its great massiveness, drove the fire certainly around it; and, had the building been left alone, so far as water is concerned, we should not have been in the condition we are to-day, in my judgment. While there was great heat, there would not have been the destruction of granite that there has been, but for the water.

Q. Was that caused by throwing water, in your opinion?

A. That seems to be the opinion, that a large part of the mischief was done by water.

Q. Did you see any water thrown on it?

A. No, sir; but I think you can have the evidence, as much of it as you want. I take that as report from our own people. Mr. Leighton, our Assistant Superintendent and Master Mason, was there. If you want him, he will cheerfully come at any time.

Q. Was the fire-proof character of that building considered in planning it?

A. Oh, yes, sir; what should be called the non-combustible character of it. I suppose we all agree that when a building is finished, having glass windows, that there should be as little inside finish of wood as possible. An iron door is not a practicable thing. It is continually jamming your fingers, and most non-combustible buildings have wooden doors. Originally, in fire-proof buildings, they tried iron doors, but it is not practicable to use them. The experience with those at the Custom House shows this. In the new Post Office, the architraves around the doors, the wainscotings, and everything but the doors themselves will be of iron. They are all contracted for. The doors themselves will be mainly of mahogany, but there will be, leading into the cash rooms, and the treasury in the second story, iron doors besides the mahogany doors, to cut off all communication with the corridors, but those are placed there more for safety from entrance than as a cut-off from fire, because we have fire-proof shutters to every window, and our floors are entirely of iron and brick, with tiling in the major part of the rooms. Nearly the whole area will be tiled. The roof will not have a piece of wood in it as big as your finger. It will be slated with very heavy slates upon wrought iron, without boarding, the rafters and purlins being of iron. The upper part, or flat deck of the Mansard, and the upright sides, will be covered with and composed of non-combustible materials, and that building will be, perhaps, as perfect in its construction as any in the country, for which the credit is entirely due to Mr. Mullett, who laid out the lines, and designed it.

Q. What is the top to be covered with?

A. Copper.

Q. Will the building be more fire-proof than it was the other night, when it is finished? Will it be more of an obstacle to a fire, or less?

A. It ought to be more, sir. If the glass had been in the other night it would have been ruined by the great heat.

Q. Was there not a good deal of wooden staging round the building which made a great deal of heat, which would have been avoided if the building had been completed?

A. The wooden staging created a great deal of heat that would not have been there if it was finished. The staging was only up against the rear wall, but it had a large quantity of lumber in it. Then the adjoining buildings in the rear, some of them, were as near as fifteen feet. The Peter Brigham estate, a very high building, some seven stories, was twenty or twenty-five feet off.

Q. I would like to ask your opinion of covering dormer window-finish on Mansard roofs with galvanized iron nailed on to wooden furring.

A. Nothing is a sufficient protection in case of a fire like that. You perhaps read in this morning's paper that in the Presbyterian church in Brooklyn, N. Y., the galvanized iron curled up like paper. My belief is, no material can be applied to the roof of a building that will be a sufficient protection in the case of a great fire; not necessarily so large a fire as this, but where there is great heat around the premises, — a square or two, or three or four buildings, — but of course we are all glad, and very glad, that iron has taken the position it has for the last few years; and it is unfortunate for our city that iron was not well received at an earlier date. It is unfortunate, also, that our original building act did not contain — as the New York building act did — a provision that no Lutheran window, no Mansard roof, should have other than iron trimmings on it. I think I am right in that statement. I would like to correct myself if I am not, and will do so. I have not looked at the New York building act for three or four years.

Q. I meant to ask if covering wood-work with galvanized iron was worth much? Whether to cover dormer window finish and cornices with galvanized iron was good for anything, if nailed on to wooden furring?

A. I should have less faith in it. I know what you allude to now. I know nine-tenths of the work is done in that way. I have far less faith in it than if it went home and met an iron frame. I am speaking as if it was slate or copper.

Q. Not for slating, but for trimming; for moulding, cornices, trimming and window finish; to take the place of wood, — as a covering for wood?

A. Heretofore, nine-tenths of our clients, if we talked of galvanized iron, or any kind of iron, would not listen to us. They would say it is a piece of extravagance, and would not listen to us. Galvanized iron, of course, is far preferable to wood in a location such as you name, and it is the material of all others to be used, unless you could afford, or had the foundation for putting on cast-iron, and even then it is a question, whether cast-iron would be as judicious as galvanized iron, taking into consideration the heat and water.

Q. I want to know whether you think it a proper thing to nail this galvanized iron on to wooden furring?

A. No, sir; I do not.

Q. The building act allows Mansard roofs to be built, if covered with non-combustible material, which would allow them to cover these wooden things with galvanized iron. I don't think it is a fit provision. Don't you think the wood would burn through in a few minutes?

A. There is a good deal in that.

Q. Have you seen tested the efficiency of mortar to go between the roof boarding and the slate for the steep surfaces?

A. I don't know that I have ever seen the results after a fire, but I have great faith in the use of an inch of mortar anywhere.

Q. Is there any practical difficulty in applying it on a Mansard roof between the boarding and the slating, or between the boarding and iron, if it is covered with iron?

A. No, sir; and my instructions from Washington are that the upper Mansard part of the Post Office is to be filled with mortar and with arches.

Q. There you have no boards?

A. No, sir.

Q. I mean for boarded roofs?

A. No, sir; there is no difficulty.

Q. It would require longer nails?

A. Yes, sir. All such things are excellent preventives.

Q. Were you here during the Saturday night of the fire as a witness?

A. No, sir; I was not. The Mansard is most useful as giving you an additional story without the increased height of masonry which would be necessary if you had any other form of roof. It can be made so it is a cool story as well as most useful, and can be finished inside — as many of our best houses are — so you do not know you are in the roof, inside, the rooms being square, with very little loss of room. Of course, I am saying nothing new, but I want to make my record that the Mansard roof is the most useful roof, and would be the hardest to dispense with.

Q. You mean properly constructed?

A. Yes, sir, of course.

Q. Do you consider the tar and gravel roof a good roof for flats in case of fire, as compared with tin?

A. I incline to answer that, that tar and gravel is safer than tin, and will endure longer. There are two or three different patents. I am not able to state in regard to the exact detail of the pigments used, and the parts of each pigment, but I am inclined to think it is safer. The examinations that have been made show that tar and gravel well put on, and applied in proper proportion of materials, made as fair an exhibit, after the fire, as most any other material.

Q. The tin is so thin, I suppose the heat penetrates it?

A. Yes, sir, and it curls up very quickly. Tar and gravel adheres.

Q. Do you think the provision in our building act, requiring four inches of brick between the ends of floor joist, is sufficient?

A. No, sir, I do not like that.

Q. Shouldn't it be more than four inches?

A. I should think one brick, — eight inches, — which of course is admissible on the theory that four inches entering a wall is all that a timber should enter. In warehouses, I believe in not entering the timbers, but resting them on projections, or entering them very slightly, and letting them lie on projections for a bearing; but eight inches would be my judgment as to what should be between the ends of the timbers in the two sides of a wall.

Q. I have seen a great many principal girders over iron columns made of rolled iron beams, on which the wooden floor joists rest. I have been unable to see what advantage that was. Can you tell me?

A. We have all practised it of late years, the theory being that it aided what is termed fire-proof construction, and that the wrought-iron girder left nothing but the floor-joists to burn out, and that the iron beams served materially to tie the front and rear of the building. We believed they would hold the walls of the building together, and that the floors would drop away from the iron without distorting it.

Q. From recent experience in this fire has that advantage been realized?

A. Not at all; the reverse of it. There is evidence all over the burned district of these beams curling up and falling from their positions.

Q. Judging from this experience, should you not think a good square, hard-pine beam superior in such places?

A. I will use the word safer. You can stand under it until it has about gone, and it will stay where it is. Iron will play the part of a snake and come out of its place very suddenly.

Q. Then, do they not sometimes expand and throw the walls out of place?

A. I have no doubt it is possible. They would not expand any but the front and rear walls, because we presume that kind of a structure goes from the street, or front end, back to the rear, and never the other way, unless a building is isolated. I have no knowledge of a wall being thrown out by the expansion, but we know the expansion is very great, and undoubtedly walls are thrown out of position.

Q. Would not a wooden girder act to sustain a building longer than an iron one, with merchandise burning under it?

A. It would on the average be as reliable. The wooden timber would, in my judgment, continue longer in place, under great heat, than the wrought-iron beams.

Q. That is what I meant to ask, whether it would not do its duty longer?

A. But the answering of the question in that way is not intended to say we will do nothing hereafter in iron; not intended to say, hereafter we shall not put in wrought-iron girders in similar positions; not intended to imply that we should not build non-combustible buildings, as far as possible, that the means at the disposal of our clients will permit.

Q. In your opinion, does the use of an iron girder supporting wooden floor joists add to the fire-proof qualities of a building?

A. Yes, sir. I ought to say I think it adds to the fire-proof nature of a building, but under a fierce heat, I should feel as safe inside of a building with a hard-pine girder twelve or fourteen inches square.

Q. How does the iron add to its being fire-proof?

A. There are very few contingencies that can come up to displace girders as they were displaced in that fire. In an ordinary fire, in the burning out of a single store, unless it was filled with something very combustible, it would not, in my judgment, throw iron out of place.

Q. Don't you think those iron girders were thrown out of place by the combustion of the materials in the individual stores in which they were placed, rather than the adjacent stores?

A. Not materials; perhaps you mean merchandise. I cannot conceive that the material of the floor —

Q. I do not mean the material of the building, but the material taken in connection with the merchandise. Was it not the contents and material of the individual buildings which displaced those iron beams, rather than the burning of the neighboring buildings?

A. Yes, sir; but there was such havoc made with all material, and a fire like that is of such rare occurrence, that it is difficult to define it strictly.

Q. Don't you think something could be gained by protecting iron work with mortar or plaster of Paris?

A. Yes, sir, we are going to try a bit of roof on the Simmons building in that way. The trustees of the Simmons estate are going to have removed, and have contracted to have removed, the wooden roof of the original Rialto building. There are a good many others in Boston who might follow suit, that will not, although it would be the best economy in the end. Mr. Philbrick puts the question as to the use of mortar as an increased safeguard to iron as well as wood, and I answer, unequivocally, that it is safer. Plaster of Paris is used very largely for that purpose. The Simmons trustees are going to take off the wooden roof of the Rialto and cover it with iron, backed with plaster of Paris. They are also going to take away the wooden towers and rebuild them of iron. We have received estimates for corrugated iron facings, and we have received estimates for stone. We have the foundation to put stone on. The dome which is to surmount the corner of the two streets is to be contracted for and put up of iron. That was to have been slated, but it is now changed to iron. The purlins between the rafters and the entire body of the dome is to be covered with corrugated iron, instead of slates, as originally designed.

Q. Whether or not, as a result of this fire, the architects of Boston will not recommend a change in the plans of their building?

A. We have asked very many times to be allowed to do these things. The trustees were very liberal to me. The will of Mr. Simmons required that the façade should be the same style as the one he built, and that being rather a pet investment, and having some pride in it, they allowed me to have a dome; and I said, "Don't talk of wood; let us have iron." It was intended to be covered with slate, but we have improved on that. All these things have come up since the fire. It has set us all to thinking.

EDMUND CALHOUN, *sworn.*

Q. Where do you live?

A. I am executive officer of the Navy Yard and captain in the navy.

Q. Will you tell us what time you were first summoned to take any part about the fire in Boston?

A. As near as I can tell, it was about half-past eight on the evening of the ninth. I took a walk in the upper part of the yard and looked at the fire (I had observed it at my house), and then went up to my house. I think it was that time, because at eight forty-five the first order was given for a steamer to leave the yard.

Q. What time did that first steamer leave?

A. Eight forty-five, sir. I reside at the lower end of the yard, and it is quite a distance from my house to my office. For that reason, the orders afterwards were issued immediately by the Commodore. I sent the first steamer out after having consulted with the Commodore, and afterwards sent the other steamer at eleven forty-five. I think there was an interval of three hours. It is the rule in the Navy Yard to keep one steamer in for emergencies.

Q. Do you know anything about the amount of powder used that night from the Charlestown Navy Yard?

A. I told you when the second steamer went, at a quarter of twelve. We have but two steam-engines. If I remember the time they summoned me about the powder, it was somewhere between twelve and one o'clock, I think. I sent an order immediately to the Ordnance Officer, Henry Truxton. I am Executive Officer, and I sent those orders to him, and afterwards it was not referred to me, because I told the officer who came to go and get the powder, and afterwards they went and got it, to what extent I don't know, but I think they got forty-five or fifty barrels.

Q. What was your order?

A. To let them have what they wanted. I think that afterwards when they came for powder they were referred immediately to the Commodore, because he is nearest. I live near the Chelsea bridge. They were referred immediately to the Commodore, and he gave them all they wanted. I sent all the available force I could. A master's mate went in charge of the engine, and then a boatswain who lives in South Boston, Mr. Choate, he volunteered, and made his appearance here about the powder. I didn't know he was engaged at all until he came about the powder.

Q. Would Henry Truxton know the exact amount?

A. Yes, sir; he is the Ordnance Officer and has charge of it. This first order was written on a small piece of paper in pencil, if I remember aright, and it was endorsed by the Commodore. I sent it with my endorsement to Mr. Truxton, and then they didn't refer to me at all afterwards about the powder. I was up all night, nearly, round about the yard, to see that we sent all of our available force that we had in the yard.

Q. How many marines did you send?

A. I don't know the number of marines exactly. The Commodore would know more about that, but we assisted not only on the 9th and 10th, but several days after that.

F. O. PRINCE, *sworn.*

Q. At the fire on Saturday night, I understand you overheard some conversation in regard to blasting and the length of fuse that was used?

A. Yes, sir, I heard some talk between Gen. Benham and somebody or other.

Q. Was the party who talked with Gen'l Benham, a party engaged in blowing up buildings?

A. I was in Lindall street about the time that Robinson's place was on fire. I had watched the fire with great interest from twelve o'clock, wondering why certain things were not done, and I met Gen'l Benham, a gentleman whom I know very well, and I asked him why they didn't blow up some more buildings, and he told me he was at that business there, and observed that they were about blowing up the building next to Robinson's, which surprised me. I said in my judgment, a more remote building should be blown up, and suggested that the building on the corner — the south-east corner of Lindall street — should be blown up. He said that he thought so too. "Then," said I, "why isn't it done?" And he said people would not obey his orders. I drew his attention, when he told me what he was blowing up, to the fact that to blow up buildings next to the fire would do more injury than good, judging from the Chicago experience; and he said people would not obey his orders. Just then, somebody came up, who seemed to be under his orders, blowing up buildings, and spoke about the fuses, and whether this stranger or the General made the observation, I don't know; but, at any rate, one or the other made the remark that the fuses were eighteen-minute fuses.

Q. Did the General make any objection to that?

A. Not at all.

Q. You say the fire was in the building next to the one he was blowing up?

A. Next to the one he told me he was blowing up.

Q. Do you know the other party?

A. No, sir; I do not. My impression is he had a quantity of fuses with him,—powder-works.

Q. Were his hands full of fuses?

A. Yes, sir; and a cart came down pretty soon, which they said contained powder and fuses, etc.

Q. Gen'l Benham stated to you that he was attending to that service?

A. Yes, sir; and complained that they would not obey his orders. I had one of my sons with me, who also heard it.

WILLIAM BIBRIM, *sworn.*

Q. Will you state what you did on the night of the 9th, in regard to the fire in Boston?

A. To the best of my knowledge, I think it was about nine o'clock when I learned that a steamer and carriage was over here from the Navy Yard. At that time I was on Milk street. I think I was full three-quarters of an hour before I found the steamer belonging to the Navy Yard, which was at that time stationed on the corner of South and Essex streets. I think an hour after I learned that another steamer had come over, and was stationed on Bromfield street, I was told. I came up, but could not find her. I went round the fire; I think I was absent an hour. Upon my return, I found the other steamer had gone to South street, found a reservoir and had gone to work. We worked there until, I should judge, in the neighborhood of four o'clock, when orders came to report on State street with two steamers. I went to State street, and after looking round some ten or fifteen minutes, found an engineer and reported to him. The orders were to take the steamers on to Milk street and report there. I gave orders for the steamers to go there and went down, and found they could find but one hydrant at that time that could be made serviceable. Another Engineer came up and asked me if I had any objection to one of my steamers going to Bromfield street. I said not, and sent an Assistant Engineer with that steamer, and that is the last I saw of her until I saw her in the Navy Yard again at eleven o'clock. I took a position at the corner of Batterymarch and Milk, and worked there until the building was exploded. I think it was the one on the corner of Water street and Liberty square. That frightened the men and drove the Engineer and men away from the steamer. All the other steamers had backed out before that, and I thought it was time for us to get out. After that we went down into Custom-House square, but could not get a chance to go to work with the engine, and went to work with the men helping Mr. Bickford get out his safe. Then we were ordered on to Oliver street.

Q. How long did you remain in Custom-House square?

A. I should judge two hours.

Q. Was there no place where you could work?

A. No, sir.

Q. What was the result of that explosion? What was the effect of it in checking the fire or otherwise?

A. That explosion was quite a distance from where I was stationed. My engine was on the corner of Batterymarch and Milk street, my hose leading up in the direction of Pearl street, and I had no opportunity to observe the effect of the explosion. One effect that it had was to drive my men away, because we were given to understand that we should be informed when an explosion was to take place. I asked, I think Engineer Jacobs, to be kind enough to let me know, and I guess in five minutes after he promised he would, the explosion took place without notice. After that, the men didn't care about going so near buildings. As soon as the explosion took place, the glass in the windows near where we stood, near where the engine was placed, was all blown out, and without any orders, they left the machine. I assured them there was no danger. There was an officer sent over to look after the safety of the apparatus, and he said he wouldn't take the responsibility. I said I would, but the men didn't care to go up street again and I ordered them back.

Q. You say you were in Milk street, and there was only one hydrant available?

A. Yes, sir.

Q. How long did the engine remain idle there?

A. One of the engines took that hydrant.

Q. Did the other one remain doing nothing, or go immediately to Bromfield street?

A. Went immediately to Bromfield street.

Q. Was there plenty of water?

A. Yes, sir.

Q. Did you have any trouble from want of fuel that night?

A. At times; but not for any great length of time, because we found boxes and used them until the coal arrived.

Q. Did you lose steam at any time on account of a want of fuel?

A. No, sir.

JOSEPH P. DAVIS, *sworn.*

Q. What office do you hold?

A. I am City Engineer, at present.

Q. Are you familiar with the Lowry hydrant?

A. I have seen it in operation. I have never used it myself. I know its general character and principles.

Q. Do you know any valid objection why it should not be generally used in Boston?

A. The only objection that I know of is against its being placed in the street, on account of snow.

Q. How much more efficient is it for the delivery of water than the common sidewalk hydrant in Boston?

A. That question cannot be answered as you put it. The sidewalk hydrants that are now used here are sufficient for a single hose. I think with the Lowry they have a chance for five hose; so the ratio would be five to one, provided you had a pipe large enough leading to it.

Q. Is it not less likely to freeze?

A. The Lowry? no, sir.

Q. Not on account of being near the main?

A. So far as I have known it has never been known to freeze.

Q. I say less likely?

A. Yes, sir, it is less likely.

Q. Are you familiar with the size of the street mains in the burned district?

A. Yes, sir; I know what they are on the map.

Q. Were you here during the fire?

A. Yes, sir.

Q. Did you see any indications of a want of water supply for the apparatus that was used?

A. I saw one place where I supposed the engines were short of water; that is, from the manner in which they were playing. Whether they were or not I cannot say positively. That was on the corner of Devonshire and Franklin streets, but then I could not say positively that that was the trouble.

Q. Under the present system of the construction of the reservoirs, is there not likely to be a good deal of water wasted in withdrawing the engines and leaving the reservoirs running into the sewers?

A. Yes, sir.

Q. Why should not these overflows be stopped entirely?

A. I can only explain that to you from statements I have heard. I don't know so much about it myself.

Q. Is there any good reason why they should not be stopped?

A. Not if all connection with the cellars was taken away from them.

Q. Could not the house-water be conducted directly into the sewers without inconvenience?

A. Yes, sir. I suppose it is done so now, since they do not build any more of those reservoirs.

Q. I suppose those reservoirs being of old date, and having their former supply from the house-pipes, retain that connection now, do they not?

A. So I understand.

Q. In case we stop the overflow, that house-water must be provided for by direct connection with the sewers?

A. Yes, sir.

Q. Are not the reservoirs a valuable auxiliary to the Fire Department in equalizing the flow of water?

A. I think the trouble at the corner of Franklin and Devonshire streets was from the fact of that reservoir being there. There is a 6-inch pipe leading down there, and a 4-inch nozzle leading into the reservoir. That is equal to the supply of a certain amount of water, but not to the number of engines they massed there.

Q. Do you think that a 4-inch supply to a reservoir is sufficient?

A. It depends upon how many engines you want to put in one spot.

If the idea is to have eight or ten in one spot, there should be facilities for it.

Q. Suppose there was a 6-inch supply; could not the stop-cock be gauged to supply one or two reservoirs without overflow?

A. Yes, sir; but perhaps a 6-inch pipe is not equal to that supply.

Q. It would be more than double a 4-inch, would it not?

A. Yes, sir. There is probably less than twenty feet of 4-inch pipe. It would not probably make much practical difference.

Q. The short spur, you mean, between the main and the reservoir?

A. Yes, sir; the branch leading from the main.

Q. If the Lowry hydrants were put in once in two hundred feet, would they acquire their full efficiency without a larger pipe than a 6-inch main in the street?

A. The question turns upon the size of pipe and the number of engines you are going to use in a given place. A 6-inch pipe would supply a single Lowry hydrant, if you were not drawing elsewhere.

Q. How would it be in case of a large fire?

A. As I understand it, there were forty engines. If they were on hydrants 200 feet apart, five to a hydrant, a 6-inch pipe would not begin to supply them.

Q. How large a pipe would, in your judgment?

A. I should have to go into a calculation to answer that. Those engines are said to throw a cubic foot in a minute. Five engines would make a velocity of five or six feet in a 12-inch pipe, which is going pretty fast.

Q. Would there not be a considerable advantage, in cases of great conflagrations, in connecting the high service with that part of the city which is burning?

A. No; because the high service would not be equal to the quantity of water required. The high service is supplying about a million of gallons a day; and with all those engines playing, it would draw it down very quick.

Q. Would it not be an auxiliary?

A. No, sir; it would not be of any good at all. It might be for five or ten minutes.

Q. You mean, you cannot use that in connection with your other supply?

A. No, sir. There is no reservoir connected with the high service; it is a stand-pipe; and the capacity of the engines playing on the fire would be more than that of the engines pumping into the stand-pipe, so you could not keep the head up more than ten minutes.

Q. It was not let on?

A. I suppose not.

Q. Is there any connection between the Beacon Hill reservoir and the pipes in the burnt district?

A. Yes, sir.

Q. Is it constantly open?

A. No, sir.

Q. Do you know whether it was used that night?

A. I don't know.

Q. If it had been used that night, would it have made any difference?

A. As long as the amount of water in the reservoir held out.

Q. Who would know whether it was in use or not?

A. Mr. Jones.

Q. Do you know if it was filled that night?

A. I do not. They can only fill it from the high service. That is to say, the head is such, that I understand, on the low service, it will only run in a little every night. It has water in it now, but whether it had at the time of the fire I don't know.

Q. Looking at all the advantages of the Lowry hydrant, as compared with the common hydrant in use, would you, or would you not, recommend its being placed over that burned district to-day?

A. I think the best system, so far as the delivery of water is concerned, would be a combination of the two. I don't think there is any use in putting Lowry hydrants every two hundred feet on a six-inch pipe. I don't see anything specially gained by concentrating five engines at one point. Perhaps it is a little disadvantage rather than otherwise, but at the same time, there is no hydrant in use that delivers that amount of water, if that is the desideratum.

Q. How would you use both?

A. I would put the Lowrys in at the street corners, and then the others two hundred or three hundred feet apart. What uses up the head is the hose on the engines themselves. They will use up more than several miles of pipe.

Q. Then would it be an advantage to have them nearer together?

A. Yes, sir, but it seems to me to be unnecessary to have five nozzles to every two hundred feet.

Q. Do you know anything about the Lockport hydrant?

A. No, sir. The chief thing an Engineer looks to is the quality of the manufacture of the hydrant. There are a great many Engineers who will not use them, because the valves get out of shape; but most any of them deliver water enough.

Q. You say the only objection to the Lowry is placing it in the streets on account of snow?

A. Yes, sir.

Q. Have you ever heard any objections made to it where it has been placed in the Highlands or East Boston?

A. No, sir, I am not in the way to hear. I have recently come to the city.

Q. Since you have been here you have not heard any complaints?

A. No, sir. I have been on the Lowell works, and there, when the question of hydrants came up, we went round to determine what we should have. The commissioners went with me, and after looking the matter over, they considered it was not advisable to put in the Lowry in Lowell. We put in a more capacious hydrant than we have here. It is a three-nozzle hydrant.

Q. As compared with these, how much more water will one of those deliver?

A. They are five-inches, and these are three; they will supply three nozzles, these are intended to supply one.

Q. How large are the mains there?

A. The main which comes from the reservoir is thirty-inch, and that is reduced down to six, which is the smallest pipe we used.

WILLIAM J. MOREY, *sworn.*

Q. (By Mr. Russell.) Did you give the alarm at the State-street-block fire?

A. Yes, sir.

Q. What time did you give it?

A. I think it was three minutes past ten.

Q. Did any one tell you about the fire, or did you discover it yourself?

A. I heard somebody hallo; I didn't know whether it was "murder," "fire," or "watch." I was on Oliver street at the time. I ran down through Broad street into India street, and there were three or four, probably half-a-dozen women and children at the corner, and they said there was a fire in that direction, pointing toward the State-street block. I looked up and saw the blaze from where I stood, on the corner of India and Wharf streets, and ran to box thirty-seven. I found officer Shea there. I asked him what the matter was that there was no alarm turned in. He said the box did not work. I told him I would run over to Faneuil Hall, and if I didn't hear the alarm by the time I got over, I would turn in the alarm there. Not hearing any by the time I arrived there, I opened the box and turned one in.

Q. What box was that?

A. 16.

Q. Do you know whether he tried any other box?

A. I am certain he did not, but between the time he arrived there and I arrived there, he sent another officer down to box forty-seven, which is down to Rowe's wharf, and I think that box was out of order, and didn't work.

Q. Who was that officer?

A. Officer Stuart.

HENRY MORSE, *sworn.*

Q. (By Mr. Russell.) What station are you connected with?

A. Ten.

Q. Did you time an engine that came in?

A. I did.

Q. What engine was it?

A. No. 12.

Q. Where does No. 12 start from?

A. It is located on the corner of Warren street, near Dudley, — facing Dudley.

Q. What time did it make?

A. I looked at my watch. It made about twenty minutes to the place where we first stopped. It was in Kingston street where we first stopped, and after that there was some one came and directed them up Columbia street.

Q. Was it at the corner of Kingston street where they stopped?

A. No, sir; I don't know what streets they went through, but they turned back a little and went through a cross street, and up, and where they stopped was Columbia street.

Q. What time did you start that night?

A. I helped them out of the house and we got round on to Harrison avenue, and then I looked at my watch, and it was fourteen minutes of seven. I made an allowance of one minute for getting out.

Q. You mean eight?

A. It might have been eight. I had got home, eaten my supper, and was reading the paper, when I heard the alarm and went up there.

Q. What time did you get in?

A. It was five minutes past.

Q. What was the point where you first stopped?

A. It was beyond Beach street, on Kingston street. I don't know exactly. I know when they turned to go into the other place, they came back a little and went up a little street, and they were about three minutes going from where they first stopped to where they finally stopped, and that was the corner of Columbia street.

Q. You came in by hand?

A. Yes, sir. I looked at my watch; I thought it was something out of the usual course, and that I would see just about how long we were coming.

GEO. B. PRAY, *sworn.*

Q. (By Mr. Russell.) What time did you come to the fire?

A. I was on the corner of Summer and Washington streets when the alarm was rung out.

Q. Did you go immediately?

A. I went as quick as I could get there.

Q. How soon did you see any engine there?

A. I should think the East-street engine, I think it was No. 7, — the one that is located in East street, — arrived there in three or four minutes after I was on the ground. No. 4 was the next one that I saw, and I think like enough it was somewhere in the vicinity of eight or ten minutes before she arrived. The rest I did not notice particularly.

Q. Did you see 4's hose come, or 7's ?

A. I saw a hose, but I did not notice particularly to see whose hose it was. I could not state.

Q. How soon was there a stream on the fire?

A. There were two hose companies that were about ready to get their streams on, — hydrant streams, — when I arrived there. I should not think it was over three minutes before there was one hydrant stream on; I am not positive but two. They were getting their hose out to get on a stream.

GEO. L. BURT, *sworn.*

Q. (By Mr. RUSSELL.) What time did you reach the great fire?

A. I did not come in until Sunday morning.

Q. Tell us anything you think the Commission ought to hear.

A. I went inside of the lines immediately after I got here. The reason I did not come in that night was there was not a horse to be had. I have four myself. Every horse that we had at that end of the city was sick. Our steamer came in by hand. I tried the stables and tried privately to get a horse to come in that night, but we hadn't a horse we could drive to Boston, and our steamer came in by hand, drawn by men and boys. By the way, I believe our steamer made as good time within ten minutes as she made at the State street and Rand & Avery fire. That ten minutes she lost at the Highland stables, expecting to get horses there. They told them they might have them, but when they went to get them, they came to the conclusion they had no authority to let them have them, and they didn't. After I got inside of the lines, I went to looking after the firemen as well as I could. I found by that time they were pretty thoroughly exhausted, and it was time they had something to eat.

Q. What time did you get in?

A. I walked in until I got the cars, I should say somewhere about nine o'clock, and then I was at City Hall and round among the firemen all the rest of the day, and during the day, I was put on the Relief Committee, and at night went round to look after them.

Q. Are you on the Committee on the Fire Department?

A. Yes, sir.

Q. How did the firemen behave that day?

A. As well as ever I saw them. They were all pretty thoroughly tired, but every one seemed to be willing to do the utmost he could.

Q. Since you have been on that committee, has Engineer Damrell ever called your attention to the exposed condition of this district and the want of steam fire apparatus there, or more water?

A. At the time of the Chicago fire, our committee thought it was best to send him on there, and we sent him to Chicago, and when he came back, one of the committee asked him if it was possible that such a fire could ever come to Boston. He told him it was, and this is one of the very places, among others, that he spoke of.

Q. What reason did he give?

A. From the height of the buildings, so much wood on the top of them, and the narrowness of the streets, that if they got on fire, they would make such a terrible heat it would melt everything before it. I will state right here that since I have been on that committee I have had a great many people say to me, "Why do you allow your Chief to go to every fire? Why do you allow him to run to every fire and make a show of himself?" I brought that to the Chief's attention and he said to me, "When certain boxes are struck, it seems as if I could not get there quick enough,"—while, he said, if he heard other boxes he did not feel such a terrible thrill.

Q. Did he ever speak of want of water and of proper apparatus in this part of the city?

A. We have always had the idea that our water-pipes were not so big as they should be, from him, in that district, and where we got a number of steamers located on one pipe, that one would take away from the others so they could not get the full force.

Q. Did he ever express any opinion about the location of the apparatus?

A. About a year ago, he wanted to put another steamer in town somewhere on the Fort-Hill district, but it was rather knocked on the head before the committee. I was in favor of it myself, and I believe there should be one there now. I believe the cheapest Fire Department is one so strong that we cannot have anything get ahead of us.

HON. WILLIAM GASTON, *sworn.*

Q. (By Mr. RUSSELL.) You are the Mayor of Boston?

A. Yes, sir.

Q. Will you state when you first became aware of the fire, and what action you took in regard to it?

A. I first became aware that there was an extensive fire between half-past nine and ten o'clock in the evening. I was then in Roxbury, and the first thing I did was to go to station house No. 10, with a view of ascertaining the locality of the fire, and all I could about its extent. I learned that it was in the vicinity of Summer street, but did not ascertain very much about the details of it, further than that it was a large fire. I was then in the vicinity of the depot of the Boston & Providence railroad, and the question was, what was the most speedy way of arriving here. I saw no horse-cars at that time. On inquiry, I found that a train of cars would be due at that depot at twenty or twenty-five minutes past ten, I think twenty-five minutes past, coming to the depot in Boston. I waited for that train, and started to come to the city in the immediate company of ex-Mayor Lewis of Roxbury, and Mr. Frederick M. Briggs. There were other gentlemen waiting for the train, a great many of whom I knew, but I was in the immediate company of those two gentlemen. We reached the depot in Boston not far from half-past ten; that is, assuming that the train was on time, and so far as I know, it was. We then went down Elliot street to Washington, thence down Essex, and (as near as I can remember) I went into the following streets: Essex, crossing over by some street from Essex to South, East, Federal, Broad, Congress, High, Pearl, Milk and Washington. At this time, the fire was raging with very great fury, and extending very rapidly. There was great excitement in the streets. They were filled with people moving merchandise and trying to save their effects; men connected with the Fire Department, and spectators; it was a scene of confusion. After going round the fire in that way, I came to the conclusion that I could render the best service by going to the City Hall. I accordingly went to the City Hall. I first went into the police office; there I think I met Alderman Jenks. I either met him there or soon after in the Mayor's office; I think in the police office. He told me that various messages had been sent to adjoining places for assistance, and gave me such information as he could about the progress of the fire. I then went up stairs, Alderman Jenks with me, and directed the officer to light my office; it was not then lighted. We remained there some time, and finally I went up to the fire-alarm office to see about the progress of the flames. While there, Mr. Minns came; we then went down to the Mayor's office, and some talk was had about what ought to be done, whether the blasting of any buildings was desirable. Finally, we all started to find the Chief Engineer and his assistants. We searched for him, and at length found him in Federal street, I think. He was there with several of his assistant Engineers. We told him that we wished him and his assistants to exercise their best judgment in this matter, and we would render them every assistance in our power. He then told me, I think it was at that time, that he had been considering the question of blowing up buildings, and with that view had sent some person, I think it was Capt. Quinn, to examine various points and to report to him the condition. He then, with several of his Engineers, went into a store that was close to the burning buildings; I am not sure whether that block was burning or not, but at any rate, the fire was burning very near by, and in the store the subject of the use of powder was discussed; I was present; and they then came to the conclusion to make the trial.

I told the Chief Engineer that in any trial which he or his officers might make, I hoped they would be very careful not to endanger human life. Amidst the excitement, I was afraid that they would not take the neeessary precautions, in case anything of that kind was done. I waited about there a considerable period of time, watching the progress of the flames, and watching the operations of the department. While there, however, the City Messenger told me there were some gentlemen at the City Hall who desired to see me. I soon after that returned, with the City Messenger, and went to my office. I found several gentlemen there. There was a talk about the fire. Of course, the parties were very much excited; the conversation I cannot give. After a while the Chief Engineer came in, and when he came in, talk was had between him and various persons about blowing up buildings. He gave written orders, as I supposed, — I did not read them, — to various persons, and after the orders were made, he went away, and a large portion of the gentlemen who were in there went away. My attention after that was directed largely to taking measures to preserve the public peace and assist persons in securing their property. A great many came there about that. At my request, Alderman Cutter went to the Adjutant General to ask him for military aid. He returned, having found the Adjutant General, and after awhile, I cannot give the hours now, because I did not watch the progress of the clock, the Adjutant General came, and I told him that in our confused and excited condition, we needed military strength to protect the city, and to protect the property and people. He asked how soon I wanted it. I told him as soon as it could be had. He asked what number. I told him as many as he could furnish. He told me he would take immediate measures. He did act very promptly, and the next day military aid came. Perhaps I might say here, that it remained in greater or less numbers for over a fortnight, and rendered very valuable service, extremely valuable service, in protecting the property and persons of the citizens. I found the State authorities very willing and anxious to give me aid. Aid came from the forts, and from the Navy Yard in Charlestown. During the night, of course, great numbers of people came in with various requests for me to give certain orders in respect to the blowing up of buildings. I told them,— or many of them, — that the power and responsibility belonged to the Chief Engineer and his Assistant Engineers; that I had no right to exercise the authority, and that if I undertook to usurp it, I thought it would produce disaster and confusion; but whatever the officers themselves determined upon, I would exercise all my power and influence to assist them in the execution and discharge of their duties. I remained in my office most of the time for four days and four nights, during which period I saw a very large number of people upon various errands, and I am willing to state, as far as I can state, what occurred, but all that occurred it would be impossible to remember.

I went again, perhaps I ought to say, to the fire on Sunday. I went to Congress street and Congress square, and watched the operations of the department, and the progress of the flames, and I saw that the department were acting with great industry, and, I thought, with great success, at that point. The hour on Sunday I should not be able to state, because, as I say, amid the excitement, I did not keep the distinction of the hours. I was constantly receiving reports during the entire progress of the flames, from various persons, but I think I went to the fire but three times. During the night and part of Sunday morning, I feared that the City Hall would be destroyed, and that the fire would extend beyond that. There were carts or vehicles provided ready to take away the records in case the danger there became imminent. There were also arrangements made with reference to the preservation of the books of the Registry of Deeds.

Q. Can you give the time or about the time when you were present at the meeting of the Engineers in Federal street?

A. My impression is, that when I first saw the Chief Engineer, it might have been between half-past eleven and twelve, but that is a mere impression.

Q. How many times did you see him that night while the fire was raging?

A. The first time I saw him was in Federal street. The next time I saw him was when he came to the Mayor's office, after that.

Q. Do you know how he happened to come?

A. No, sir, I do not. I have no recollection of sending for him myself.

Q. How did he appear that night?

A. He appeared, when I saw him in Federal street, to be quite collected and calm; earnest, but he talked very sensibly indeed, as I thought.

Q. Do you recollect then asking him what plans he had for staying the progress of the fire?

A. I remember his stating to me, I think it was at that point of time, what I have already stated, that he had requested Capt. Quinn to make an examination and report to him.

Q. Did he state anything else at that time except with regard to his proposed experiment with gunpowder?

A. I don't think any inquiries were made in regard to a general plan. My purpose was, and I suppose that of the Aldermen with me, to go and see him, and give him all the strength and encouragement our presence could give, and to do anything we could to assist him in the discharge of his duties.

Q. You say you thought the Chief Engineer, with two Assistants, was the party to give authority for the demolition of buildings. I will ask you, as an expert in law, if that is your opinion now?

A. Yes, sir.

Q. Did you give Gen. Burt authority to blow up buildings?

A. I have no recollection of giving him any such authority. I understood the authority to proceed from the Chief Engineer. There were a great number of things said that night; of course, I don't remember everything that was said; but my purpose was to let the responsibility rest where the law placed it, and so far as I can recollect, I endeavored to act consistently with that purpose. My impression is that the authority came in writing from the Chief Engineer to Gen. Burt. I did not intend to give Gen. Burt any authority; I did not have it to give.

Q. Do you recollect any conversation with Major Nichols, or anybody else, about the marines?

A. My impression is that Mr. Nichols made a suggestion to me about the marines. I told him I thought it was a good one, and asked him if he would do me the favor to go to the Navy Yard and ask the Commodore for assistance. He said he would, and started to execute the commission; and I have no doubt he did, because the marines came.

Q. You saw the Chief of Police personally during the night?

A. I saw the Chief of Police a great many times. He was very active. After I had been round to the fire I went to my office. Mr. Briggs and Alderman Jenks were with me, and I asked the officer in attendance there to light the office. He did so, and I left it lighted when I went away. I don't know that the lights were extinguished any time until the next morning after that. I found it lighted when I returned, and when I returned, I requested the messenger to light up the Aldermen's room, which he did.

Q. (By Mr. Greene.) Do you recollect how long it was after the building was lighted before you saw Gen. Burt?

A. I went up there and stayed some time talking over matters with Alderman Jenks and others who came in. Then I went in search of the Chief Engineer, found him in Federal street, and others with him, was present at the meeting with his Engineers, remained there a considerable period, and then returned to City Hall, and soon after that I saw Gen. Burt.

Q. He came in?

A. He came in.

Q. Was he there when you returned?

A. I don't remember seeing him when I first returned; there were quite a number there. In reference to the Chief of Police, I will say that I saw him several times, and he rendered me very valuable aid. He was very active during the entire period. The excitement, of course, continued. There was an exciting period for forty-eight hours, at least, and there was not much sleep to be obtained by anybody. The Chief of

Police was with me a great deal of the time; that is, up and down from his own office, aiding me by suggestions, aiding me by executing my orders. He was very faithful.

Q. (By Mr. PHILBRICK.) What do you think of providing for a more ready call of the military in case of a future contingency of the kind?

A. I think it would be very well, because this event shows that there may arise a sudden emergency where their presence would be very important. I presume the Commission have already heard the fact stated, but as I passed through the streets, I saw a great many people carrying goods and merchandise of various descriptions. It was hard to distinguish between those who were carrying their own goods, and those who were carrying somebody's else. I became convinced that there were a great many engaged in carrying off the goods of other people, and I saw, therefore, the very great need of having military aid at once, in order that the police might especially direct their attention to those who were engaged in plundering. It was also feared that the fire would attract from abroad — there was a great apprehension of that — knaves and scoundrels, who would engage in plundering, and the military relieved the apprehension of citizens in that regard veiy much. There was very great alarm. Delegations came to me in very great alarm, believing that the railroad trains would bring large numbers of these scamps, who would come here to plunder, and they did not feel any safety except in the presence of the military. I kept the military beyond the time when I thought there was any actual need of their presence from the danger of plundering, to allay the apprehensions of the people. I thought two things were important. In the first place, to preserve order, and in the next place, to inspire the citizens with confidence that they were secure; and the military stayed longer than I should have kept them, on account of preserving the public peace, in order that the people might be sure that they were to be protected.

Q. (By Mr. COBB.) Did you see Mr. Norcross?

A. I did. It is only justice to Mr. Norcross to say, that he came (my impression is that it was not far from one to two o'clock), and kindly offered to assist me in any way in his power. I told him his presence would be a very great pleasure to me, and I should like the aid of his counsel and advice. He accordingly stayed with me a great deal, and I had frequent conversations with him. He was very kind, and made, of course, wise suggestions, and gave me good counsel. I feel very much indebted to him for his kindness in that regard.

Q. Can you recollect when you first saw Gen. Benham that night?

A. No, sir, I cannot. I know he was there, but the time he first came I am unable to state. I saw so many that I cannot distinguish as to the time when I saw them.

Q. (By Mr. COBB.) Do you know whether he was authorized by the Chief Engineer to operate with powder?

A. Not to my knowledge. I understood that Gen. Benham wanted authority to blow up buildings. I referred him, as nearly as I can recollect, to the Chief Engineer for that. I said to him that he must understand the rules of subordination sufficiently to know that it would be improper for me to give him authority which I did not possess, and disarrange the plans of those who were entitled to exercise authority. Then I remember introducing him to the Chief Engineer on State street. Some of the gentlemen were very anxious that certain buildings should be blown up, and waited upon me Sunday, and were very urgent about it, saying that unless they were, State street would be in danger of burning, but I told them, as I had told others, that the authority belonged not to me, but to the Chief Engineer and his assistants, and if they could convince the Chief Engineer that the buildings should be blown up, and any assistance from me was needed, I should cheerfully render it. But at the request of several gentlemen, I went down to State street, and I remember bringing Gen. Benham and the Chief together. Gen. Benham wanted to put powder under some buildings in State street. The Chief Engineer told him that the buildings were not going to burn, and they had some further conversation; I don't know as I can give it. I know the Chief expressed to me, and I think he did to Gen. Benham, the opinion that there was no danger of those buildings burning at that point; that they were getting control of the fire, and I thought from the appearances they were.

Q. (By Mr. GREENE.) Can you recollect Mr. Burt's suggesting any general plan of operations, any comprehensive plan for combating the fire?

A. Mr. Burt was in the office and talked a great deal, but I don't remember any plans, sir.

Q. (By Mr. RUSSELL.) Do you recollect what buildings Gen. Benham wanted to mine?

A. My impression is, that at that particular point of time, he wanted to put the powder under the buildings this side of the Exchange. I may be incorrect about the precise buildings, but I think those are the ones he said he wanted to put the powder under at that time. I don't know that he proposed to blow them up, but he wanted to have the powder underneath them, and I went down, at the request of sundry gentlemen, in order to see the Chief Engineer, to enable Gen. Benham to have a conference with him. If Gen. Benham could give him any valuable suggestions, I was very glad to have him do so.

Q. (By Mr. RUSSELL.) Do you remember that among the buildings that were doomed, that is, that people were very anxious to blow up, were those between Spring lane and Water street? Did you have any applications about those?

A. Yes, sir; I had some applications about those. Many of the requests came from men under a very great degree of excitement, and, as I thought, some of them were very wild.

Q. (By Mr. PHILBRICK.) What do you think of the propriety of having attached to the Fire Department, ready for call, a small number of men who shall be expert in the use of explosives, for use in such exigencies?

A. I think such a body would be very useful. Of course, Mr. Philbrick understands better than I whether these men, expert in the use of explosives, would know how to apply the explosives to buildings; but I should think there would be a difficulty in having many experts whose knowledge was obtained from actual experience, because, probably a fire where their services would be needed does not occur once in a generation.

It may be that a knowledge of the explosive power of gunpowder and how to apply it might be useful, and such expert knowledge, no doubt, might be made useful on occasions of this kind. I should think it might be.

Q. I mean, whether it would not be prudent to provide beforehand. keep in view, a certain number of individuals, who might be called upon at such times?

A. I think it would. Then there is another reason for having a body of this kind, as it seems to me. My own belief is, that in the case of a fire of this kind, extending over sixty or seventy acres, it is impossible for the Chief Engineer and his assistants to be around all parts of the fire at the same time; and if it is necessary to blow up buildings, you cannot practically get an Engineer and two assistants to go and view each particular building, because the fire would be burning down all the rest of the city in the mean time. That is, practically the law could not have been carried out that night. I suppose it requires something in the nature of a judicial determination in regard to each particular building, "Shall that particular building be exploded or not?" While giving attention to that question, the fire is burning with great ferocity in all directions; so that it seems almost impossible, in a great fire, to go through that form. If they have to go through that form, they necessarily can do but little.

Q. Should you think it worth while to modify the law?

A. Yes, sir; if a body of this kind should be created, who should have particular charge of that matter, they might determine this question, leaving the general management of the fire to the Chief and his Assistant Engineers.

Q. (By Mr. Cobb.) Acting in conjunction with the Chief?

A. Yes, sir. Take this fire; in the first place, the Chief and his assistants were needed to direct the men in their operations on the fire. If their attention is to be withdrawn by the necessity of making this examination and determination in regard to blowing up buildings, of course their assistance is withdrawn from their men at the time when it is more especially needed, and the men then would not be under any control. That night, as the orders were given out, the question arose in my mind about the safety of giving them to various men; but, when I came to reflect, I did not suppose that there was anybody in the department who had any special skill in the service. I supposed that there was hardly an officer or man in the Fire Department who had special skill in the matter. They have no expert knowledge in that particular matter.

Q. (By Mr. Russell.) Did you hear from any expert that night the proper charge necessary to blow up a building? Did anybody mention the number of pounds that was sufficient?

A. I don't remember that I did.

Q. Did you give authority to any person to blow up the building on the corner of Milk and Washington streets, or Summer and Washington streets?

A. No, sir. I don't know what buildings were blown up, except from some rumors that I have heard.

Q. (By Mr. PHILBRICK.) Do you think the present statute calculated to operate efficiently in such cases?

A. No, sir, I don't think it is.

CHARLES H. STUART, *sworn.*

Q. (By Mr. RUSSELL.) Where do you live?

A. 50 Ridgeway lane.

Q. You are an officer of Station No. 2?

A. Yes, sir.

Q. What had you to do with giving the alarm when the State-street block caught fire?

A. The first knowledge I had of the fire was, I heard them crying fire on the avenue. I ran down as far as Broad and Atlantic avenue, where it comes round there, and saw smoke coming out of the second or third story window. I ran back to box 47, that is opposite Rowe's wharf, up in the alley-way, and there I turned the alarm in, and waited, I should think, some five minutes, and didn't get any answer from that box. Then I left the box, thinking I heard the bell strike, and ran right down to the fire. I didn't stop to count the alarm. I can't, in fact, tell where it did come from. I didn't get any answer from that box.

Q. (By Mr. COBB.) Did you count the number?

A. No, I did not. I heard the bell strike, and ran right to the fire.

Q. The only way you know that it didn't strike from your box is because there was no answer?

A. Yes, sir.

Q. (By Mr. RUSSELL.) That is the way you know?

A. Yes, sir, that is the way. I waited a sufficient time to know.

Q. Who do you understand gave the alarm?

A. I can't say as to that. I understand, though, that Mr. Morey went to box 16.

Q. How long after you saw the fire was the alarm given that night?

A. I should think it must have been some eight or ten minutes. No, it couldn't have been so long as that. I think it couldn't have been more than six or seven minutes. In fact, I heard the alarm before I left that box. I can't say how long I was at that box. It seemed longer than it was, but I should think five minutes; and when I first heard the alarm strike, I started right for the fire. Before I left my box, I heard the alarm.

JOHN SHEA, *sworn.*

Q. (By Mr. RUSSELL.) You are an officer of Station No. 2?

A. Yes, sir.

Q. Where did you first see or hear of the State-street fire? What was the first thing you knew about it?

A. I have not my book about me.

Q. Did you make a minute at the time?

A. I did, sir.

Q. Did you see the fire, or hear the cry of "Fire"?

A. I heard two men standing at the corner of Broad and Milk streets, halloing "Fire." I was then turning round the corner of State and Broad streets. I went towards them, and went down to box No. 37, corner of Central wharf and India street. I gave the alarm at that box and received no answer. I remained there five minutes exactly, and had no return. Another officer came up by the name of Morey. I told him to go to Faneuil Hall and try the box there, and so he did, and he got an answer from that box. I believe it was ten minutes of eight o'clock. I am not very particular, but I made a minute of it in my book.

Q. How long do you think it was from the time you heard the cry of "Fire" until the alarm was given?

A. It didn't take me a minute to run; I ran for it.

Q. (By Mr. Philbrick.) You had to send Mr. Morey over to Faneuil Hall?

A. Yes, sir. After I waited five minutes for an answer (the box was out of order, but I wasn't aware of it), when I found I got no return, I told Mr. Morey to try the Faneuil Hall box.

Q. (By Mr. Cobb.) Did you hear the bell in about five minutes after Mr. Morey left you?

A. I did before five minutes. It was five minutes from the time I gave the alarm at the box before the alarm was given.

CHARLES A. PRINCE, *sworn.*

Q. (By Mr. Russell.) Where were you when the fire broke out on the night of Nov. 9th?

A. When I first heard the alarm, I was at the corner of Charles and Beacon streets.

Q. Did you see the fire before you heard the alarm?

A. The alarm first called my attention to the fact, and I looked round, and then I saw it immediately.

Q. Did you go there immediately?

A. I went down there immediately.

Q. Was there any engine there when you got there?

A. When I got there, there was no engine there.

Q. How soon did any engine come?

A. When I left, no engine had come. I went down to Parker's, where I had an engagement, and ran right back again, and when I got there, there was an engine there; but when I was at the top of Beacon street, by the State House, I heard the Charles-street engine coming along, drawn by men.

Q. (By Mr. Cobb.) How fast was it moving?

A. I can't say. I didn't notice it.

Q. (By Mr. Philbrick.) When you arrived, are you sure there was no engine at the lower end of Bedford street?

A. I can't tell that, sir, but I didn't see any engine. I went right down Summer street.

Q. How far?

A. I went down, I should think, about to Hovey's.

Q. You couldn't see into Kingston street at all?

A. No, sir.

Q. (By Mr. RUSSELL.) Much later in the night, did you see Gen. Benham, who was engaged in blowing up buildings?

A. I did.

Q. Where was it?

A. It was on Lindall street, just a little below Kilby. I was standing there with my father, and a man came up with some fuses on his arm, and told the General that the train was lighted; the General asked him how long it was, and he said, "Eighteen minutes." My father happened to be there, and didn't catch it exactly. He said, "What?" The man says again, "Eighteen minutes." My father says, "Good God! why don't you have it a day long?" The building in question was somewhere near Mr. Smith's. My father asked the General why he didn't blow up the building on the south-west corner of Lindall and Kilby streets, and he said he couldn't get the men to do it.

Q. How near was the fire to the building they were blowing up?

A. Well, it was so near that the powder ultimately went off on account of the fire, not on account of the fuse.

Q. (By Mr. COBB.) The fire burned down to it?

A. The fire burned down to the powder.

Q. (By Mr. FIRTH.) Do you know how much powder there was?

A. No, sir. I recollect it was stated, but I can't tell how much it was now. I think he said five hundred pounds, but I don't know. It was a heavy charge.

Q. (By Mr. RUSSELL.) Did you remain there until the powder exploded?

A. No, sir. I went down street further. I know it took so long that the people kept going forwards and back, and finally said that there wouldn't be any explosion. It was quite dangerous in that way.

Q. Was this man acting under Gen. Benham's order, as you understood?

A. Yes, sir. He reported to him.

Q. (By Mr. PHILBRICK.) Did Gen. Benham express any surprise or disapprobation at the length of the fuse?

A. No, sir, I don't know that he did. He seemed to chime in with my father, I think.

Q. (By Mr. RUSSELL.) Did you retire with the General to a safe place?

A. I went part of the way.

Q. (By Mr. PHILBRICK.) You didn't go as far as he did?

A. No, sir, I did not.

Q. (By Mr. FIRTH.) Was the man you speak of a military man?

A. Oh, no. He was a man dressed in rather rough clothes. I think he had a little red beard. If I am not mistaken, part of his clothing was a Cardigan.

FREDERICK M. HINES, *sworn.*

Q. (By Mr. RUSSELL.) Are you in the Fire Department?

A. Yes, sir.

Q. Connected with what engine?

A. Foreman of Engine No. 3.

Q. How long did it take your engine to reach the fire?

A. About eight minutes.

Q. (By Mr. Cobb.) Where are you stationed?

A. Just south of Dover street, on Washington street.

Q. How soon after you reached the fire did you get a stream on?

A. In about four minutes, I should judge.

Q. Did that stream go through the engine from the hydrant, or did you have steam up?

A. No, sir; we had steam up.

Q. Did you have steam up in four minutes after you got there?

A. We had steam up before we got there.

Q. Was your water hot when you started?

A. No, sir, perfectly cold. We can get up steam in about four and a half or five minutes at the outside, travelling through the streets.

Q. Do you travel fast enough by hand-power to get it up?

A. Yes, sir.

Q. When you got there did you have the usual supply of coal?

A. We had a supply to last us about half an hour; probably a little more than that.

Q. Then did you get out of coal?

A. Yes, sir.

Q. Where did you get fuel?

A. Went into a house on Kingston street and got some wood.

Q. Did you lose steam at any time while you were getting that?

A. No, sir. The Engineer sent word to me he was out of fuel, and I went immediately into a house right opposite me and got some out.

Q. In getting up steam, did you use benzine or any other compound of that kind that night?

A. No, sir.

Q. How much faster do you think you should have gone if you had had horses? In how much shorter time should you have got there?

A. It might have made two minutes' difference in the time of getting there; not over that. I will state, that we were delayed in getting to work after we got to the fire by the crowd that was there. We had to drive them out of the way with sticks and anything we could get in order to get to work. We threatened them; we didn't strike any one, of course, but we threatened to if they didn't get out of the way.

Q. (By Mr. Philbrick.) You were located at the corner of Kingston and Bedford streets?

A. Yes, sir.

Q. How soon after you got there did you go for wood?

A. In about half an hour. The Engineer sent word to me he was out of fuel. We had two or three lumps in the tender when he sent word to me that he had got to have fuel or shut down on the water. I knew it would probably be some time before we could get coal, and I went into the first house I came to and got some wood.

SAMUEL ABBOTT, *sworn.*

Q. (By Mr. Russell.) You belong to Engine No. 3?

A. I do, sir.

Q. What is your post?
A. Hoseman.
Q. How soon after you got to the great fire did you get a stream on the fire?
A. I can't tell you exactly about that. We were bothered about getting to work at the hydrant on account of the crowd. It might have been eight or ten minutes.
Q. Did you have steam up when you got there?
A. Yes, sir.
Q. Did you have coal?
A. Yes, sir.
Q. Did you have the usual supply of coal?
A. Yes, sir.
Q. Later in the evening, did you get out of coal and have to use wood?
A. Yes, sir.
Q. How long after you began to play on the fire was that?
A. I can't tell you anything about that, sir; I was on the pipe.

SAMUEL ABBOTT, Jr., *sworn.*

Q. (By Mr. Russell.) Are you connected with Engine No. 3?
A. I am, sir.
Q. What is your position?
A. Hoseman.
Q. How soon after you got to the fire did you have a stream on the fire?
A. Well, in five minutes, I think.
Q. Was there any delay after you got there?
A. There was a delay in getting a connection with the hydrant on account of the number of persons on the sidewalk about the hydrant. We couldn't get to the hydrant as quick as we could if they hadn't been there, on account of the dense crowd.
Q. How did you get rid of them?
A. I took a lantern (we run with the old lanterns that they ran with in the hand-department), and I took it and held it over some of their heads and cleared them away from the hydrant.
Q. Was there any other cause of delay than that?
A. That is all.
Q. Was steam up?
A. Steam was up.
Q. Did you have the usual supply of coal?
A. The same that we always have.
Q. Did you get out of coal afterwards?
A. We did.
Q. How soon was that after you arrived?
A. I can't tell you that, because I was on the pipe.
Q. Do you know whether, when you first got there, any benzine or anything of that kind was used?
A. No, sir.

Q. Any burning fluid?
A. Not that I know of.
Q. Was there any unusual smoke about the fire?
A. Not that I know of.

WINFIELD S. LAWRENCE, *sworn.*

Q. (By Mr. Russell.) Do you belong to No. 3 engine?
A. I do, sir.
Q. What is your position?
A. Hoseman.
Q. On the night of the fire, how soon did you get a stream on after you got there?
A. That would be difficult for me to answer correctly. I should judge, though, that we got a stream on in from three to five minutes from the time the machine arrived.
Q. Was there any delay?
A. There was.
Q. From what cause?
A. Well, it was on account of the people congregated on the corner where the hydrant was that we took. We had to drive them back with wood that we took from the tender. That is, I had a stick in each hand, and talked pretty loud, and we had hard work to drive the crowd back.
Q. Did you move your hands with the wood in them?
A. I did, and struck one tall hat of a gentleman. I can't say who he was, but I had to do so.
Q. Was there any other cause of delay?
A. None that I know of.
Q. Was steam up when you got there?
A. Yes, sir. We had steam up when we got there, ready to go to work?
Q. Did you have the usual supply of coal?
A. Yes, sir, in the tender, we did.
Q. Did you get out of coal afterwards?
A. We did.
Q. Do you know how soon after you got there you got out of coal?
A. No, sir, I do not, but I should judge it was somewhere from fifteen to twenty minutes; it might have been longer than that, I can't say as to that, because I was attending to the business I was appointed to attend to.
Q. Was benzine or any burning fluid used to kindle the fire in the steamer when you first got there?
A. No, sir. The fire was lighted before we got anywhere near there. I met the machine on Beach street, living down that way, and when I got there, the machine came along, and then I hitched on to it, and I should judge the steam was up at that time.
Q. Did you see any peculiar smoke, as if they were burning fluid?
A. No, sir, I did not.

WILLIAM T. HINES, *sworn.*

Q. (By Mr. RUSSELL.) You belong to Engine No. 3?
A. Yes, sir.
Q. What is your position?
A. Hoseman.
Q. How soon after you got to the great fire did you get a stream on?
A. I should think in about four minutes.
Q. Was there any delay?
A. Yes, sir.
Q. On what account?
A. The great crowd in the street there. We had to break through it.
Q. Was there any other cause of delay?
A. No, sir.
Q. Was steam up?
A. Yes, sir.
Q. Did you have the usual supply of coal when you got there?
A. Yes, sir.
Q. How soon did you get out of coal, to the best of your judgment?
A. We got out of coal in about ten minutes, I should think.
Q. What did you do then?
A. We got wood out of two or three houses there, — blinds, casings, and one thing and another.
Q. Did they use benzine or any other burning fluid in kindling the fire?
A. No, sir.
Q. Did you see any strange smoke?
A. No, sir.

Adjourned to Thursday, three o'clock.

NINETEENTH DAY.

THURSDAY, December 26.

JULIUS L. CLARKE, *sworn.*

Q. (By Mr. RUSSELL.) What office do you hold?

A. Insurance Commissioner of the State of Massachusetts.

Q. When did you arrive here after your return from Europe?

A. I sailed from Liverpool on the 7th of November.

Q. Did you have any conversation while in England about what is now the burnt district?

A. The construction of the buildings in this district was a theme of common conversation between English underwriters and myself in London and Liverpool. Immediately after the Chicago fire, they sent over to this country their best underwriters, men who were experienced in the character of insurance risks. Their first purpose was to secure plans of American cities. They commenced that work immediately. Their first plans were at Chicago and San Francisco, next New York, and lastly Boston, and they are going on to secure plans of all our other cities. Immediately after receiving their plan of Chicago, and understanding the location of its streets, and the character of its buildings, some of the companies issued orders for the cancellation of large amounts of risks. While I was in Liverpool, a single company sent orders to cancel a large portion of its risks in Chicago, and in San Francisco, based upon information which they had obtained from the plans transmitted to them. These plans, by the way, are the most perfect plans you can imagine. Just before I visited Liverpool, the plan of Boston had been received, showing the location of all our streets, and many of the lanes and alleys, the construction of the buildings, their surroundings, their means of protection, and everything else appertaining to the character of risks; and in London and Liverpool, the character of risks in this burnt district of Boston was a theme of frequent reference. The feeling among underwriters was, that risks in that locality were of an extra hazardous character, and I was given to understand that it was their purpose to immediately make a thorough investigation, and issue directions for the cancellation of risks here. I have no doubt that if this fire had not occurred until six months later, instead of about four millions and a half which now comes to Boston for the payment of losses from English companies, the risks would have been cancelled to such an extent that probably not more than one-half of that amount would have been found within this burnt district. On the evening before I sailed, I had a conversation with some English underwriters upon the character of these risks, and one of the gentlemen present, who had a little while before received his plan of Boston, made this remark to me, as he came to bid me good-bye: "Mr. Clarke, we look upon your Boston, especially upon Franklin street and

Devonshire street, and that whole locality, as the next most likely place for a Chicago fire." I said, "What do you mean? Please explain why you think so." He referred to the plan which he had just received and said, "Our Directors have been looking it over, and we find that although your walls are comparatively thick, yet the great number of narrow streets which are located in that vicinity, and the great height of the buildings, and the tinder-boxes on their tops (using his own language), are reasons for looking upon risks in that locality as of such a hazardous character." And I was told by this gentleman, and by others, that very soon they should give orders for the cancellation of their risks, to a very large extent, wherever it could be done without wrong to the policy-holders. It was the general feeling among all those underwriters, that the construction of buildings in very many of our American cities was of such a character, that the writing of risks must be suspended, in a very great measure, by English companies. They had come to entertain a great deal of fear in that connection.

Q. Have you read the Building Act which passed this Legislature?

A. I have not read it carefully; I have not had time to look over the amendments.

Q. (By Mr. Cobb.) Was anything said by the English underwriters concerning our means of extinguishing fires?

A. Yes, sir; the general impression was, that our Fire Departments were not so efficiently organized as the English Fire Departments, and in connection with that subject, I was shown an illustration, at midnight, of the operation of what they term "The Salvage Corps." We have nothing like it in this country. The nearest organization to it is one existing in Philadelphia. The purpose of the organization is to save property from destruction by fire, and injury by water. This corps is provided with tarpaulins and other means of protection. Their duty is, on the first alarm to go to the place of the fire, go into the premises, see what property is within and what is most exposed, remove that which is necessary to be removed, and protect the remainder by covering it with their tarpaulins, and other means of covering, so as to prevent damage by water. The removal of property by that corps amounts to a very large sum.

Q. (By Mr. Russell.) Have we not something like that in Boston, in the Insurance Brigade?

A. There is something like it, but it is not organized with anything like the efficiency which exists in London, Liverpool, and other English cities.

Q. (By Mr. Cobb.) Is that sustained by the public?

A. No, sir; the companies do that. I will state one thing further. In connection with the Chicago, and other large fires, it appeared to me, from such information as I was able to glean, that the English companies had not been conversant with the character of the risks which their representatives had taken in this country. The moment the Chicago fire happened, they sent their best men over here to investigate, and they found such a state of things existing, that they are cancelling risks in all directions in this country, and it has become a question with them, whether it is advisable for them to continue writing risks in American cities. One very large company, and one of the best and strongest of the English companies, is to-day hesitating about coming to America for that reason.

Q. (By Mr. Cobb.) Is that a company that has never done business here?

A. Yes, sir. As I have said, I have not the slightest doubt, that, if this fire could have been postponed six months, Boston would have lost four millions that it gets now.

THEODORE HERSEY, *sworn.*

Q. (By Mr. Russell.) Are you a member of Engine No. 21?

A. Yes, sir.

Q. How long did it take you to come to the fire?

A. I can give you a little history about getting in to that fire that will probably be of some little benefit to you. I was at my place of business at Upham's Corner, in the Sixteenth Ward, when the first alarm of fire was turned in. I came out of doors as soon as I heard the alarm, and saw the fire; and the alarms came in pretty lively. When the third alarm struck, I went to the engine-house, and found they were all ready to start. The ropes were lengthened out, and plenty of men there. The moment the fourth alarm struck, which comes in first on the ticker in the house, we went out of the house, and we went very quick indeed. At Washington Village there were plenty of fresh men to take hold, and at No. 15's house, in South Boston (I think she had not gone out) there were men standing who wanted to take her out, and they all bent on to our engine. To-day is a pretty stormy day, but to make more sure of this thing, I started from 21's house, and timed myself from that point to Summer street, and I walked it in thirty-two minutes to-day, true time; and now I am confident in stating here, that to the best of my judgment, that engine came in inside of twenty-five minutes on the night of the fire.

Q. What was your opinion before?

A. Well, I have set it from twenty-five to thirty minutes; that was my opinion, judging from the distance. It is a road I have travelled a great many times.

Q. (By Mr. Cobb.) How much would you have saved if you had had horses?

A. Well, sir, we might have saved five minutes. I think on the night of the fire at Rand & Avery's we were not over twenty minutes coming to the hydrant in front of the Court House.

Q. They had horses then?

A. Yes, sir; I think the engine from Washington Village to Summer street, after we struck the railroad track, came just about as fast as it would with horses. You know how excited men get when they have hold of an engine rope, if they do not have a chance to run. I am a pretty good runner, and I had all I wanted to do to keep up.

B. F. PALMER, *sworn.*

Q. (By Mr. Russell.) Do you reside in East Boston?

A. Yes, sir.

Q. Did you come over to the fire on Sunday night, the 10th of November?

A. Yes, sir.

Q. With what engine?

A. Engine 11; I think that is the number.

Q. At what time did you start?

A. I cannot from memory tell you. I only remember generally that she was a long while getting to the fire.

Q. As near as you can state, how long was she coming?

A. From the time the alarm was given to the time she got to her place to work, it was about an hour and a half.

Q. Was there any delay at the ferry?

A. The engine did not arrive at the ferry until some time after I got there. Then from the ferry on this side, to the fire, we were good half an hour. I do not remember now, but I think it was about forty minutes from the time we arrived at the ferry until we got to the corner of Temple Place, where she went to work. We drew her up by hand. I found they were going to be a long while, and I took hold and helped pull her up.

Q. Did you look at your watch?

A. Yes, sir; I did at the time, and it is fixed in my mind that it was about an hour and a half from the time the alarm struck until she got on the ground to work.

Q. Do you think you used your watch in regard to the forty minutes?

A. I am not sure that I took it out then. I would not be positive about the forty minutes. I want to say that I find fault about the horses. They say that there are no horses provided except for East Boston, and she had no right over here, except by order of Mr. Barnes. He took the responsibility of ordering her over here, outside the general order of the full board.

I understood from what I heard that night that no engine or hose carriage can leave there unless by order of the engineer in charge. When I got to the ferry, there was a hose carriage standing there, and I asked the engineer why he didn't go over. He said he could not go over except by order of the Engineer. I went on board the boat, waited some few minutes, and Mr. Barnes, the Engineer, came along, and went into the cabin, and was adjusting his necktie. A fireman came in, and told him No. 11 had arrived, and said he, "Tell her to come on board;" so that she had waited half an hour. I have learned since, from some of the Engineers, that the engine had no business here, that there were no horses to bring her over; that horses were provided for her in case of a fire in East Boston only.

JOHN S. DAMRELL, *recalled.*

Q. (By Mr. RUSSELL.) I want to inquire what the practical effect of the order issued by you on the 26th of October was. I will read the order: —

"FIRE DEPARTMENT OFFICE, CITY HALL
BOSTON, Oct. 26, 1872, 5 o'clock, P.M.

"To the Chief of Police:

"DEAR SIR,—Will you cause the following instructions to be promulgated to the several police districts in the city proper:—

"On the discovery of fire by any of the officers, they will endeavor to locate the fire as near as possible, and if it appears to be below the third story, they will give an alarm from the nearest box; if above the third story, they will give an alarm and repeat the same as soon as the first alarm is done striking. This is necessary, in order to aid the Board of Engineers in carrying out the rules adopted to meet the present exigencies. Please instruct the officers to spring their rattles and cry 'Fire,' giving also the number of the box, in case of an alarm in the night time.

"I remain, yours, etc.,
"JOHN S. DAMRELL,
"*Chief Engineer.*"

A. The Board of Engineers districted the city of Boston into nine fire districts, and the apparatus is so arranged that the first, second and third alarms will call out certain pieces of apparatus. The first alarm being sounded, it is supposed that it will take the engines from five to eight minutes to get upon the ground. The matter of the horse disease coming before the Board at a special meeting, they considered all the difficulties that might arise, and in order that there should be no delay whatever in the summons, this communication was sent to the Chief of Police, asking that that authority be exercised by the officers, which has heretofore been exercised by the Engineer who first arrived upon the ground. When, in his judgment, the threatening appearance of the fire warranted a second alarm, he was instructed to give it at once, this being done to save the eight or ten minutes that would be lost without such an order. For instance, a police officer, under the old arrangement, after sounding the first alarm, would wait until an Engineer came upon the ground, before giving the second alarm, which would have consumed eight or ten minutes. By this arrangement, the apparatus called out by the second alarm would get to the fire eight or ten minutes sooner than under the old plan. Then, again, it works in a different way. For instance, the second alarm calls certain engines that do not respond on the first alarm. It gave us eight or ten minutes' advance on the engines coming in to the fire who would respond to the second alarm which did not respond to the first alarm. The third alarm brings in the engines that respond to that alarm certainly eight or ten minutes sooner than they would otherwise reach the fire.

Q. To make it clearer, suppose you tell us what engines would have come to this fire on the first alarm?

A. Nos. 3, 4, 6, 7, 8 and 10, go on the first alarm.

Q. Now, what engines go on the second alarm?

A. No. 1 is the only one that responds to the second alarm.

Q. What other apparatus would come on the second alarm?

A. On the second alarm would come Hose 4 and 5. On the first alarm come Hose 9 (at South Boston), Hose 8, Hose 3, Hose 2, and Hose 1, Hook-and-Ladder companies 1 and 3, with the two extinguisher wagons. We have to make arrangements so as not to leave uncovered certain sections of the city. For instance, we cannot bring, except by special call of an Engineer, certain apparatus from South Boston to the city proper, unless an alarm is sounded from South Boston, which would call a special alarm, and then sound that from that point. There is an impression abroad in the community that the third alarm might be sounded as indicating a great fire.

It is not so. For instance, an alarm of fire is sounded in the Highland district; a second alarm does not bring a single piece of apparatus; it simply notifies the engines further down in town that all that territory is uncovered, and they are obliged to respond to the first alarm, where by the rules they do not ordinarily respond until the second, thereby covering certain portions of our territory which are left uncovered by the apparatus going away.

Q. Will you repeat the order during the horse disease?

A. During the horse disease, the vote of the Board was, that the department be doubled, by the addition of five hundred men, to meet the exigency.

Q. Was there ever any order given as to not using horses?

A. Oh, no, sir. Allow me to say, right here, that each Engineer is made responsible for certain pieces of apparatus, to care for and look after, and he is left with full power, in case of emergency, to get horses, and levy upon them wherever he can. It would be impossible to issue an order that would cover all cases of emergency. We could not possibly do it. For instance, the Engineer in the Sixteenth District had full authority, and the authority was also conferred on the foremen, in case a special call was made, to get horses anywhere they could, and come in with them.

Q. When was that authority given?

A. That authority was given at the time we had our meeting.

Q. Have you a record of the votes passed at that meeting?

A. I have not, on this subject. You will see by the City Ordinance that it is not required. A good many people have the idea that the Chief can do all this, but he cannot. If you will allow me, I will read Section 4 of the Ordinance:—

"The Engineers shall, at such times as they may by their by-laws determine, hold such meetings as may be necessary for the prompt transaction of all business coming before them, and a majority of the whole Board shall be necessary to constitute a quorum. They may make such rules and orders for their government, as a Board of Engineers, as they may see fit, subject to the approval of the joint Committee of the City Council. They shall be responsible for the discipline, good order, and proper conduct of the whole Department, both officers and men, and for the care of all houses, engines, hose-carriages, hook and ladder carriages, horses, furniture, and apparatus thereto belonging. They shall have the superintendence and control of all the engine and other houses used for the purposes of the Fire Department and of all the horses, furniture, and apparatus thereto belonging, and of the engines and all other fire apparatus belonging to the city, and over the officers and members of the several companies attached to the Fire Department, and over all persons present at fires; and they may make such rules and regulations for the better government, discipline, and good order of the department, and for the extinguishment of fires, as they may from time to time think expedient; such rules and regulattions not being repugnant to the laws of the Commonwealth, nor to any ordinance of the city, and being subject to the approval of the joint committee of the City Council, and to alteration or revocation by them at any time."

It was under that provision that the Board of Engineers made the arrangement to meet the exigencies occasioned by the horse disease.

Q. Has your attention ever been called to the difficulty of giving alarms, in consequence of some defect in the boxes?

A. Quite often, sir.

Q. What is the trouble?

A. Well, we report to the Superintendent of Fire Alarms, and there our responsibility ends. We have nothing to do with it, except simply to notify him of the fact.

Q. To what committee does that belong?

A. To a separate committee from the Committee on the Fire Department — the Committee on Fire-Alarms. I believe that Alderman Cobb will bear testimony to the fact, that I asked to have the two committees united, believing that, as the fire-alarm system was a part of the Fire Department, it should be controlled by one committee.

Q. How often do you suppose that such reports have been made?

A. Constantly; every day.

Q. Do you know anything about the defects, or reported defects, on the night of the State-street fire?

A. I was not present at the fire, but I was immediately notified that the alarm was turned in from the proper box, and after waiting a sufficient time, and finding there was no alarm, they had to go from that place to Faneuil Hall to give the alarm.

Q. How were you notified of that?

A. By the Engineers.

Q. And upon that, what was your action?

A. Simply to notify Mr. Kennard, by word of mouth, that that was the case. He has always been prompt, as far as I know, to rectify any deficiency, or make any necessary repairs. There is constant complaint about the boxes being out of order.

Q. Has your attention ever been called to the question whether there cannot be some way of insuring an alarm, rather than leave it as a mere accident?

A. Well, sir, it is mere accident. My judgment is, that the City Hall is one of the proper lookouts, and should be made available for all purposes of that kind, and that any unusual smoke, or anything of that kind, indicating fire, should warrant the telegraph operators in striking an alarm in the closest proximity possible to that, without waiting for somebody to turn it in.

Q. Is there any practical way of having more persons furnished with keys to the boxes?

A. Well, sir, there are several amendments that ought to be made. I do not want to find fault with the course that has been adopted by a department over which I have no control, but rules have been made which have worked very detrimentally to our citizens; viz., the rules attached to the turning in of an alarm. For instance, this: "Be sure that there is a fire before sounding the alarm." One of the greatest difficulties that we have to encounter comes from that rule. To show you how it operates: suppose there is a fire in Harvard place; the watchman goes away round through Temple place, crying "Fire," through Tremont street, down School street, and into the station in Court square. When he gets there, he goes in and says, "There is a fire in Harvard place." The officer in the station says, "I must go out and see." He goes out and sees that there is a fire, and after that, turns in the alarm. At the time of the fire in Congress street, about a year ago, a man told a police officer there was a fire there, and he says, "I must go and see whether there is or not." He did not take the citizen's word, but had to go away back to the scene of the fire, and then go and give the alarm. I think that, while it may have been intended as a corrective, it really works very badly.

Q. (By Mr. Cobb.) You think it would be better to have four false alarms than to have any delay in reaching an actual fire?

A. Yes, sir. As I have said to some gentlemen who have asked me about it, "Give the alarm first, and then do your best to extinguish the fire. If you try to extinguish the fire, and fail, and give the alarm afterwards, the opportune time has gone by." "Never let the key go out of your possession, except called for by the Superintendent." That is all very well; but I have seen instances like this: A man who keeps an apothecary store has a key. A citizen comes to his store at night and gives an alarm of fire; he hesitates about giving the man the key to the box, because the rule says, "Never let it go out of your possession," and he must stop and dress himself before he gives the alarm.

Q. (By Mr. Russell.) Has the Chief Engineer any staff to carry messages?

A. I have a member of the fire alarm at the north section of the city, and a member at the south section, who reports to me as soon as possible upon the fire-ground, and waits any message I may have, for fire-alarm purposes. That is for that special department. I have no special messengers, any more than to detail this man and that man, hoseman, or whatever he may be, to do whatever may suggest itself to my mind for the time being.

Q. Do you know anything about scaffolds for raising pipes, so that they can play water without playing from the street?

A. Yes, sir; there is a hose-elevator in Chicago, and one which I approve of very much.

Q. How long have they had it?

A. About a year.

Q. Since the great fire?

A. They had it before the great fire. I went on to see it before the great fire, and saw it raised.

Q. How high does that carry the pipe?

A. About sixty feet.

Q. Is it constructed of iron or wood?

A. Of wood.

Q. (By Mr. Cobb.) Have you ever recommended its use here?

A. No, sir; from the fact that those streets where it would be of use to us here are not wide enough to bring the carriage in and use it. The carriage is something like fifteen feet wide between the wheels, and if it was put in one of our narrow streets, it would block up the passage. In our wide streets, such as Tremont street, it would not be necessary. That is the reason I do not recommend it.

Q. Do you use any hose-bridges, except for horse-railroads?

A. No, sir; only for horse-railroads.

Q. Is it not desirable to have them?

A. It would be desirable to have them, and I have no doubt they could be brought into practical use by establishing a company who should make that a specialty. I do not think it could be made available for use in any other way.

Q. Can you tell us now how many firemen were killed and how many were maimed on the night of the fire?

A. I can't say from memory; I have a record of them, which I will send you. I would like to make a statement here about one matter which I think should be investigated, and about which I have felt considerably aggrieved. At a very early period in the evening, I sent an officer to the Deputy Chief of Police, with the request that he would report to me with fifty men, and I would give them the necessary authority to open any store or dwelling-house and take from it carpets for the purpose of covering the roofs of the buildings in the range of the fire. I waited patiently, but no report came to me from the officer whom I sent; but subsequently I met the Deputy Chief of Police, and asked him the question where his men were, and why he did not report to me. He answered that he had no men, or he couldn't get any, or they were all engaged. Of course, I had no time to debate the matter then, but subsequently I was called to the City Hall, and a gentleman requested that a sufficient force of police should be detailed to aid certain persons in the work which they were undertaking, and the Chief of Police notified him then that he could have all the men he wanted. I thought then, as I think now, that it was very strange. If the men could be had at a later hour, they certainly could have been collected for so important a work at an earlier hour, and I do not know why it was not done. I think it should be inquired into, to say the least, because I have no knowledge of any police alarm being given which could call the entire force to the rescue. They should have been called by the police-alarm, for I am under the impression that there were many police officers at home and a-bed who might have been doing valiant service to the city of Boston, had the police-alarm been sounded and called them to the ground. But of course, I do not know anything about it. I felt then, as I feel now, that a request of that kind should have been answered, either with regular policemen, or policemen who could have been sworn in by the proper parties, within fifteen minutes, from our citizens, who would have aided very much in that work.

Q. Will you give us the regulations in regard to Steamer 11, at East Boston?

A. Steamers 9 and 11 are not allowed to come to the city proper only alternately, unless especially sent for. That is, for instance, if Engine No. 9 comes one month, Engine No. 11 may come the next month.

Q. How was it at the time of the fire on Sunday night?

A. No. 11 came, but against orders. Arrangements were made for horses to do the work at East Boston, in answer to all calls from the boxes there, but no arrangement was made to take them this side, because there was no reason to believe, with the large amount of force we had here, there would be any occasion to call them into service. We had some ten steam-fire engines on the ground from out of town, besides our own apparatus, and our five reserve engines, which were in active service.

Q. How did she happen to come over?

A. The engineer, Capt. Barnes, came down to the ferry and came over, and took No. 11 over with him.

Q. I suppose you cannot account for her coming so slowly?

A. No, sir; I had no knowledge that she was on the ground, for I did not expect her.

Q. You say Capt. Barnes came with her?

A. Yes, sir. That is to say, I so understood from the men. They said Capt. Barnes came with her.

Q. There has been some criticism in regard to the manner of playing on buildings where the water did not reach to the fire, and it has been said that a great deal of water was wasted in washing the windows and granite fronts of buildings, without any effect, the windows not being broken. Do you know anything about that?

A. I have no doubt that in many cases such was the fact. It was a matter that we could not possibly overcome. There was a large number of engines from out of town, and they were in the streets. If you got the men into a building, no sooner did you leave, than they were out. All the water that was played from the street that night was perfectly fruitless; it did not amount to anything. I mean, in the earlier stages of the night, when the fire was among the higher buildings.

Q. Take the earliest stages of the fire, when there was nothing here but Boston engines; did you see anything of the kind then?

A. Nothing of the kind, except this: We have twenty-one engines and ten hose companies. Those ten hose companies are independent of the engine companies, located in different sections of our city. When they get to a fire, where the fire is above the third story, they immediately connect with an engine, because the hydrants are not available, the engines being connected with the hydrants. We then take two streams, the engine company furnishing a line of hose for themselves, and the hose company, attaching to the engine, runs off another line; consequently, Engine No. 4, for instance, would play her own stream, and she would also play Hose 1's stream. Now, the hydrant supplying both lines through the engine, we get just as much water, but not so powerful streams as we should if there was only one line playing. Hose 1 may be in a very important position, and we are obliged to shut off 4's stream in order to supply them. That pipe may be some distance from the engine in the street, and the moment word should be passed to give Hose 1 all the water, you would see the water from No. 4's pipe come out on the street. There would be no use in keeping men in the smoke without an adequate stream. We had a good many feeble streams, occasioned by shutting off the water from one line in order to get as full force as possible on the other. Men are very anxious to do all they possibly can, and they would play when in fact good judgment would have dictated that the water should have been entirely shut off, if it could be done. But then, in many cases, they did not know the position of affairs. You cannot communicate immediately with the men holding the pipe. For instance, one stream is in the upper part of a building, and the other is in the second flat below; you cannot communicate from one to the other sufficiently quick to have them stop playing. I have been experimenting for two months with two devices designed to overcome that difficulty. One is what we call a water telegraph, by which to communicate instantaneously from the pipe to the engine. That is done by a swivelling nose-piece, which, being gradually turned, shuts the water off from the pipe, stops the stream entirely, and that opens the relief valve at the engine, and passes the water into the street, which the engineer notices at once, and knows the water is shut off. The moment it is opened again, the valve shuts, he sees no water, and knows the engine is playing. The other is a telegraphic signal, so arranged that by touching a knob on the pipe, a gong is struck on the engine, by which we can communicate with the engineer: We want more or less water, shut down, or stop. That has worked very satisfactorily, and I am in hopes to get it introduced through the department, but it takes time to bring about these improvements. That matter was referred by the Committee on Fire Alarms to the Superintendent of Fire Alarms, as an expert electrician, to report whether, in his opinion, it was practicable or not.

Q. (By Mr. COBB.) On the first alarm that night, was all the apparatus called out that is usually called by a first alarm, or more, or less?

A. On the first alarm, I think it is understood that the first five blows indicate that the hose is to be taken at once; the second calls for everything that always goes on the first alarm.

Q. In view of the then condition of the horses, don't you think it would have been better if you had made a different arrangement, whereby, on the first alarm coming from a bad box (which you call box fifty-two) you could have had everything there on the first alarm?

A. Well, sir, there are a good many points that, knowing what we know now, we probably should have changed; but from our past experience at that time, knowing the different localities of our city, and the vast number of tinder-boxes which are scattered all over the city, I do not know that I should not, without this present information, do just the same thing again. For instance: just look over the whole field. Engine No. 3 is located on Washington street, just beyond Dover. With this exception, we have not a single steam fire engine in that part of the city, where there are a great many high buildings, piano-forte factories, for instance, and those large family hotels, where hose companies would not be available. Now, if one of those hotels had caught fire, and any lives had been lost for the want of a steam engine, I should have regretted it all my life. Box fifty-two is considered to be one of the bad boxes. Why bad? Simply because in those buildings we have all the way from one hundred to five hundred thousand dollars' worth of property. That is why we call that a bad box, and then they are so contiguous to other property, by being built up so closely, that we are liable to a conflagration there; it is so understood.

Q. In view of the difficulty of moving your apparatus, by reason of this epidemic among the horses, don't you think it would have been better to have arranged to have had a larger force called out on the first alarm?

A. I will tell you, gentlemen, — I am entirely frank in this matter,— so far as regards the movement of the apparatus in the city proper, the emulation that exists among the several companies in the department will prevent any loss of time. Every inch of ground, I know, has been measured with a tape line over and over again, and the idea of letting one company get to that box four feet in advance of another would not be tolerated by the companies for a single moment. Now, during the horse disease, the companies were all in their houses, there was a large number of volunteers on hand, waiting to earn their dollar whenever an alarm should be struck, and we did not apprehend that the apparatus would be delayed one single moment during that time. Then we had cautioned the Engineers to be on the alert all the time. I tell you, we felt that our horses were getting well, they were convalescent, and we had made arrangements to double up our teams. We did not suppose that one minute or two minutes would make any essential difference; but had I known that a building was to be so quickly literally consumed (a sight I never before beheld), I certainly should have taken greater precautions. But I do not think any gentleman in this city had any reason to expect such a thing.

Q. (By Mr. Russell.) Was there ever any discussion among the Engineers, or in the Committee on the Fire Department, so far as you know, in regard to getting other horses to replace those that were sick?

A. Yes, sir, there was some, and we went to one or two places with a view to get horses, but we found they were in as bad condition as our own. As to taking green horses, that is one of the worst things in the world. If you harness green horses to an engine, they are sensitive to the flying cinders, the smoke, and the shouting in the streets, and it is not easy to control them. For instance, we have driven the horses up to a building on fire, and found that it was impossible to drive them through the smoke. Then again, we got into a tight place out in Cambridge, where we were hemmed in by the flames. An ordinary pair of horses would never have brought the engine out, but our trained horses came right through the flames.

Q. Would it not have been possible to supply the place of your horses?

A. I don't believe that, in the city proper, we could have gained much time by supplying the place of the horses. I should rather rely on the additional men to take the apparatus promptly to the fire, than on strange horses. I am very glad now that the Board of Engineers was discreet and wise enough to organize those five hundred men, because we had that large extra force on duty at the fire, to take the lines of hose to the upper parts of buildings, or wherever they were wanted. We had been reduced to our minimum strength, we increased to the maximum, by taking five hundred extra men. Whatever delay there might have been in getting in was more than made up by the extra men.

Q. How were they paid?

A. One dollar for going to the fire, and twenty-five cents an hour for all the time they served. In regard to the engines at a great distance, at Dorchester, for instance, I confess that the absence of horses would make considerable difference to them; but of course we did not contemplate having to call for them. We supposed that with the ordinary success that had always attended us, we should be able to extinguish any fire in the city proper without calling for them. In Roxbury, the Engineers, if they saw a light, were to move without waiting for the alarm, and get horses wherever they could.

Q. When was that order given?

A. That was an arrangement that was understood by talking it up in the Board of Engineers. For instance; a body of gentlemen looking the field all over, agreed to do certain things, to guard against certain contingencies; the whole Board a perfect unit, acting together upon one plan. And to show you that they meant business, I will say, that the Engineers having charge of the several companies travelled round Saturday night (which you recollect was a very rainy night) with the ropes on their backs, and delivered them to the several captains, so that they should be ready to move.

THOMAS C. SARGENT, *sworn.*

Q. (By Mr. Russell.) Are you a police officer?

A. Yes, sir.

Q. Where?

A. In Charlestown.

Q. How long have you been an officer?

A. Twelve years.

Q. Did you see any pilfering at the great fire?

A. Yes, sir; I was on Milk street at about half-past three P. M., on Sunday, and saw Goodyear's rubber store broken open. There was a promiscuous crowd of firemen, who smashed in the windows and doors. There was no fire there then, and no hose. They took gloves and small articles, and secreted them in their pockets. They put on three or four coats, and carried them away by the armfull. I went into the store, but had no authority. I took notes from their hats, and asked them where they belonged. The initials were "N. F. D." They said they belonged in Newton Centre. I saw a dozen of these men. Another party had letters, "M. L. D." There were eighteen or twenty of them. They said they belonged in Medford. Another small party had "Hancock S. L. W." on their belts. I asked Alderman Jenks what it meant. He said it was a Boston steamer. He said, "This grieves me more than all that has been burned." I did not hear the men make any reply; they did not stop, but kept on.

Q. Did you see any person giving the things away?

A. No, sir; I saw no person in the store in citizen's clothes. Alderman Jenks stood on the steps and spoke to the men inside. I think I could identify some of the men,—one "S. L. W." perhaps; but men change in appearance at such a time.

Q. Did you see any other instances of the kind?

A. No, sir.

Q. When did you first see or know of the fire?

A. I saw the fire at ten minutes past seven, at Charlestown, at the lower end of Austin street, at Prison Point Bridge, on the Eastern Railroad. It was very small, hardly perceptible. I looked at the clock in the depot and noticed the time. Wm. H. Brown was with me. His recollection is the same as mine. I was on duty in Charlestown till one A. M. I found a stream of people on the bridge with goods from the fire. I took them to the station, and kept at this until three o'clock, when other officers came. A great many goods were thrown overboard from the bridge. Some of the persons we discharged, and others we kept. I took from them furs and other goods; many of the articles were identified and taken away. A Boston officer was on Milk street, and saw part of the stealing to which I have referred. A gentleman said he should hold him responsible, but he was not to blame; he was powerless. The police could do nothing with the crowd.

WM. H. BROWN, *sworn.*

Q. (By Mr. RUSSELL.) Are you a police officer of Charlestown?

A. I am.

Q. At what time did you see the fire on the night of November 9th?

A. At ten minutes past seven, P. M.; I looked at the clock immediately after seeing it. This was the clock of the Eastern Railroad depot, at Prison Point Bridge. When I looked, it was about two minutes after first seeing the fire. It was then ten minutes past seven, exactly. We were then helping get a vessel through the draw in time for the ten minutes past seven train. I said to Officer Sargent, "There is a fire in Boston!" We could see quite a light, so that any one would notice it.

CHARLES R. MORSE, *sworn.*

Q. (By Mr. RUSSELL.) What is your business?

A. I am U. S. truckman, at the Custom House.

Q. On November 9, how many horses were you using?

A. We were using all our horses, twenty-one in number. We had lost five. They had all been sick.

Q. Was there any difficulty in getting horses at that time in Boston?

A. No, sir. As early as the 30th of October, horses could be had. I rode in the torchlight procession on that night; so did a hundred others, although there was no general cavalcade. By the 9th, horses could be had in any number.

Adjourned.

TWENTIETH DAY.

FRIDAY, December 27.

SAMUEL MAY, JR., *sworn.*

Q. (By Mr. RUSSELL.) At what time did you go to the store of May & Co., on the night of the fire?

A. It was almost quarter before ten Saturday night.

Q. Who was there besides you?

A. I saw only one there then. Afterwards, my partners, Mr. Holder, and Mr. Stoddard, came.

Q. At what time did the danger become imminent there?

A. The fire on the further side of Oliver street took in the rear, I should say, about six o'clock on Sunday morning, or a little after.

Q. What did you do to protect the building?

A. Early in the evening I filled all the tubs, buckets, etc., I could find, with water, and had them carried up stairs, so as to wet the roof if there was any danger of sparks coming there. Afterwards, I got a bale of cotton waste and saturated that with water, and we used that as swabs to brush the sides of the windows as they caught fire. The building caught first in the upper story.

Q. What time was that?

A. That was, I should think, about seven o'clock Sunday morning.

Q. Did it take fire first on the wood-work of the windows in the upper story?

A. The wood-work of the windows first.

Q. How did you put it out?

A. By thrashing it with a handful of wet waste. That was done at the suggestion of Mr. Frederick May, who had seen it done at fires before. In that story, we had crucibles which were packed in straw. The straw caught fire, and when the room was so filled with smoke that we were nearly suffocated, we had to give it up. We were then the only two persons in the building. The rest, after taking the books, had left two hours before, thinking there was no danger then, — that they were going to stop the fire in Pearl street.

Q. How long did you continue to fight the fire?

A. I should think an hour, perhaps. After we had given up the building and were coming out of the rear exit, I discovered a hose-company coming up the court leading from Sturgis street, and I got them to come into the building. In the first place, they insisted upon playing from the second or third story from the street, on to the buildings opposite. I told them it was no use to do that, as we were on fire above, but they might save our building, and probably stop the fire, as I knew that Briggs & Robinson's store had an immense amount of inflammable stuff in it, and so, after a while, they sent down and got an extra length of hose and attached it, and carried a line into the upper story.

Q. What company was that?

A. That was No. 7 hose.

Q. Did they play from a steamer?

A. Yes, sir.

Q. Was there any other fire apparatus throwing streams on your building that you know of?

A. Yes, sir. There were two steamers in front of the building; one of them was a Lynn engine, the other I don't know. I went out several times to get them to move further down the street to get a more direct stream on the building, but they seemed to have the insane idea of playing on the buildings on the other side of the street, which were pretty thoroughly gutted at that time. Then there was a line of hose on the roof, which Maj. Chadwick got through his store, which was next to ours.

Q. Is there anything further which you think of about the manner in which you fought the fire?

A. I should think the hose company were in the store perhaps three-quarters of an hour, and then they took their hose out. I don't know why. I never could ascertain why they did it, because the danger was not over then, but they insisted on going, and we couldn't keep them any longer. Then we put sheet-iron and copper up at the windows. The majority of the frames had been pushed out into the street, and we put up sheet-iron and copper.

Q. You and your uncle?

A. By that time we had assistance.

Q. Where did you put up the sheets of metal?

A. I think the sheets of copper were on the street floor, and the story above, nailed up against the windows. A great many of our clerks live out of town, and those who live in town had gone out to pass Sunday, so that we did not have so full a force at the store as we should on any ordinary evening.

Q. Did you supply any of the steamers with fuel that night?

A. I think we did not, but the Lynn engine, which was standing in Oliver street, was repeatedly out of fuel.

Q. So as to lose steam?

A. Yes, sir. It stopped several times. It would play for perhaps ten minutes, and then stop.

Q. How was it supplied? With what sort of fuel?

A. Shoe cases, mainly; and I saw the same thing down in Pearl street.

Q. At an earlier hour?

A. Yes, sir. I was travelling back and forwards from the store to the scene of the fire, speculating on the chances of its coming on. My partners, Mr. Holder and Mr. Stoddard had left. Mr. Stoddard took the books and went off, and Mr. Holder went off on other business, both convinced that the fire was going to be stopped at Pearl street.

Q. Is there any other fact that occurs to you which you think we ought to know?

A. No, I think of nothing else. I don't suppose my testimony is very important, but I certainly think if our store had gone, the fire would have gone to the water's edge. I don't think anything could have stopped it if it had got into this oil house.

Q. (By Mr. Cobb.) Did you see the Chief Engineer at your store?

A. No, sir.

Q. Did you see any Engineer?

A. I think the foreman of the hose company was the only officer I saw to speak with.

LEONARD R. CUTTER, *sworn.*

Q. (By Mr. Russell.) Are you an alderman of the city?

A. Yes, sir.

Q. At what time did you go to the City Hall on the night of the fire?

A. I didn't look at the time, but I should judge it was half-past eleven, or between that and twelve.

Q. Was the Mayor there?

A. Yes, sir.

Q. Did you have any conversation with the Mayor about the fire, and the plans for subduing it?

A. I passed up and went into the Mayor's office and spoke to him. I asked him if he knew how extensive the fire was. He was talking, I think, with Alderman Jenks. He said it was a very large fire. I said to him, "I suppose we can see it from the top of the building;" and I went immediately up to the top of City Hall, and was there half an hour, I think, looking at it. I thought then it would stop in Franklin street; but when it came across Franklin street, I went down and saw the Mayor, and told him I thought the City Hall would be in danger, and that we ought to have some more policemen there; that we ought to have them summoned to the Central Office. Mr. Damrell came in, and some citizens, Mr. Burt, Mr. Allen, and a few others, and had a sort of consultation. Mr. Burt said that water was insufficient; that they ought to resort to some other remedy, and recommended some other remedy. I think the remedy was in blowing up buildings. Mr. Damrell didn't approve of it, but the pressure seemed to be so strong from the citizens to have something resorted to different from water, that he yielded. The question then was, who could take charge of the powder? I think Mr. Burt inquired if there were any aldermen present, saying that he thought it would be proper to give each alderman a street to take charge of. I think Alderman Jenks took Milk street. The question was asked me what street I would take, and I remarked that I didn't think I was a proper person to take charge of powder; that I had had no experience, and might do more damage with it than good. I thought I could be more useful in aiding the Mayor around the City Hall. Mr. Damrell remarked to me that he thought I could aid him, if I would get some policemen for him, and I started for the Chief, and found him in Station 2. I requested him to summon all the officers he could to the Central Office. I then went up and had some conversation with the Mayor about the force being sufficient to control the thieves who would probably be stealing goods. I told him I knew where Gen. Cunningham was, and if he thought best, we would call out the militia; and he asked me if I wouldn't go at once, and have Gen. Cunningham come to his office. I immediately went up to where Gen. Cunningham lived (he is a tenant of mine), and called him out, and told him the Mayor desired to see him forthwith at the City Hall. He was down there in about twenty minutes. Then the Mayor gave him directions to call out the militia. Then Mr. Nutter came in. He thought the Registry of Deeds ought to be cared for; that we ought to be prepared to take care of the books of the Registry of Deeds, and the Registry of Probate. I thought also that we ought to have the different superintendents there in the City Hall, and I sent a messenger for Mr. Tracy, and the janitor of the Registry of Deeds office, and for Mr. McCleary, and the different heads of departments. I dispatched messengers to them to have them report at City Hall forthwith; and also to Mr. Forristall, to have some teams in the square that we could use. The question was raised, what we should do with our books and records. Some thought we must carry them over to East Boston, and some thought they ought to be carried to Cambridge. I told them I had a place where they would all agree they would be safe, and that was under the reservoir. They all agreed with me, and it was arranged that the records of the City Hall, the Registry of Deeds, and the Registry of Probate, should be carted to the reservoir. The only question was when we should commence. I sent word to have them get their teams ready, and also for the key of the reservoir. After getting everything ready, I went to the top of City Hall. I thought we had better not move anything until the fire crossed Washington street, and then we had better go to work. We watched the fire, and saw that it didn't cross Washington street, and therefore we didn't move. Some of the heads of departments moved a few things down to the lower part of City Hall. After I felt assured that the fire would not cross Washington street, I went out to see the fire; and as I went down by the Old South, I noticed that the firemen, or men with firemen's caps and badges on, were breaking into stores promiscuously. I saw two or three stores broken into — a ribbon shop, and a cigar shop.

Q. (By Mr. Cobb.) Were those stores on fire?

A. No, but the fire was coming towards them. It looked as if they would burn, and I believe they did burn afterwards. The firemen would load themselves up with boxes of goods and carry them off. I saw Mr. Chamberlain, who had an Engineer's cap on, and said to him, "You ought to control your firemen. They are loading themselves up with goods and carrying them home, and you won't have any men to take care of your hose." He came up to me and said, in a low tone, the firemen were out-of-town men and they couldn't control them. I went to one of our policemen, and asked him if he couldn't control them, and he said he was powerless. I then went over to some policemen on the other side of the street, who said they were Charlestown police. I asked them if they couldn't take hold and help our policemen prevent these men from breaking into the stores. They said they were not under our jurisdiction. I asked them what they were in there for, and they said they were in there to look at the fire. I told them their place was outside the line, unless they would take hold and help us and do us some good. Then I went up to the City Hall, and saw the Mayor and Chief of Police, and told them that law and order were being trampled on, that the firemen were breaking into the warehouses promiscuously and carrying off the goods in all directions, and we must have some police there or we should be in a state of chaos, we should have no law or order in the city. The Chief despatched some men with me, and we put a stop to the plundering by these fellows, who had firemen's hats on; they went off, and I didn't see them afterwards. The way they broke into the stores was, three or four of them would go up against the door and keep bumping their back-sides against it, until they broke it in. After that, I took a turn clear round the fire to see how things were going on, and I found, away down on the lower side, that there was a strong current of air, and I thought there was an east wind blowing, but when I got round so that I could see the vane on the Old South, I saw that it pointed west, so that the wind was west all the time. There was a very severe wind at the lower part of Water and Milk streets. I passed through Broad street, through Milk street, and clear round the fire. I was down in that locality, it may have been an hour, and when I got round again to City Hall the fire had been stopped at the Old South corner, and seemed to be progressing towards the Post Office; in fact, it had got in the rear part of it. I went on top of City Hall again, and after that I went home and got some breakfast, and came back again, and was attending to receiving the fire companies from out of town. Mr. Woolley, the chairman of the Committee on the Fire Department, had gone home, and there was no one there, and when telegraphs were received they were handed to me, and I provided places for the companies. I located a couple of Manchester companies at the American House, and a couple of companies from Fall River at the United States Hotel. Some question was raised whether we needed them or not. It was thought by Mr. Damrell that we should not need them, and that we might discharge them and let them go home. The Chief Engineer of Fall River told me they had but four companies there, and two of them were here. I told him I didn't want to give him directions to send any of his companies home, because we might have a large fire, but if he thought his city needed the force more than we did, he might exercise his judgment and send them home. I believe he afterwards did. I told Mr. Damrell we had better keep all the force we could, for if we had a fire that night, and it got the best of us, a great deal of fault would be found with us. It turned out that there was a fire at the head of Summer street, from the explosion of gas, at which I was not present. I stayed at the City Hall until about two o'clock, and having been up all the night before, I told Mr. Powers I would leave my duties to him, and go home and get some sleep. I didn't come down again until the next day. I believe that is about all I did, or the larger portion of it.

Q. (By Mr. Philbrick.) Are you on the Water Board?

A. Yes, sir.

Q. Are you also a member of the Committee on the Fire Department?

A. Yes, sir.

Q. Have you heard anything about the scarcity of water for fire purposes since you have been on the committee from the Chief Engineer?

A. No, sir.

Q. How long have you been on the committee?

A. This is my second year on the Water Board, my first year on the Fire Department Committee.

Q. Have you ever heard the question discussed as to a further supply of water for fire purposes?

A. No, sir.

Q. Have you ever been aware of any lack of water?

A. No, sir. I have heard of it since the fire. I am speaking now of up to the time of the fire.

Q. (By Mr. Cobb.) Neither the Chief Engineer nor any of the Fire Department, so far as you know, have ever made any request of the City Council to furnish any additional supply of water for fire uses?

A. No, sir, not to my knowledge.

Q. (By Mr. Philbrick.) Do you know anything about the actual supply in Boston, as compared with other cities, for fire purposes?

A. I have not visited other cities, and don't know. Since the fire, I have inquired in the Fire Department Committee whose duty it was to protect the water. It seems that when they put their engines on a reservoir or on a hydrant, if they were driven away, nobody turned it off. They left a number of hydrants and reservoirs running, which our Superintendent, Mr. Jones, said would amount to thirty-six hydrants. I understand that they found these running the day after the fire. I thought that it belonged to the men who turned on the water to turn it off. For instance, in these reservoirs there is a four-inch pipe, and they turn this four-inch pipe on to supply the reservoir, and that supplies two or three engines. I thought that the man who turned that four-inch pipe on should turn it off, if the fire drove the engine away; that he should see to it ten or fifteen minutes before he was obliged to leave, and shut off this water, because if the fire had continued to extend, I don't see how they would have got any water, if they let these reservoirs and hydrants flow full force. For instance, each building that burned would burn off a pipe, and there would be, of course, water wasted inside. I understand that when the fire was about checked, there was about twenty pounds' pressure, which I thought was rather a large pressure after the pipes had been tapped so many times as they were.

Q. At what point was that observed?

A. That was observed in the vicinity of the Post Office in State street.

Q. What means have they of gauging the pressure there?

A. That was told me, I think, by some member of the Fire Department, but it may have come from the Superintendent of the Water Works. It seems to me, that in a case like that, some provision should be made for shutting off the water, because, if the fire had crossed State street, and they had left the hydrants and reservoirs flowing, we should not have got any water at all, and should have been entirely powerless to put out the fire. It seems their rule is to carry these turning-off machines for the reservoirs on their Hook-and-Ladder Companies. The engines don't have them, but they have a machine to turn on the hydrants. A reservoir has a four-inch pipe, and a hydrant has either a two-inch or two-and-a-half-inch pipe, and they say that they can't unscrew the hose until they first turn off the water, because the water will flow all over them, but if the pressure is almost gone, I don't see any reason why they cannot. There is no rule, as I understand it, about turning the water off; it is not incumbent upon anybody, so far as I can find out.

Q. (By Mr. COBB.) Has this subject ever been brought before the Committee on the Fire Department?

A. Yes, I brought it up.

Q. Was any action taken upon it?

A. No, sir. The Chief Engineer is very sensitive if any fault is found with his department. He seemed to want to throw it on the Water Board. I told him I didn't care who it was, whether an agent of the Water Board, or an agent of the Fire Department, but certainly somebody should have the agency and should see to it. It is a very important item, because, if we lose our water, of course the fire will go over the whole city. If we do not keep our ammunition, I don't see how we can fight the enemy. The Engineers seem to think that the pipes are not large enough in the streets, but if you make the pipes ever so large, if you let all your force go, I don't see how you are going to get any more water. It is astonishing to me that they did not lose it all on the night of the fire. If they had shut off all these pipes at the reservoirs and the hydrants, I don't see but what they would have kept up their pressure, with the exception of what would have been lost by the waste of water in cellars from the burning off of the pipes in the houses; but if the pipes in the houses were burned off, and you let the hydrants and reservoirs run, you lose all the force of your water, no matter how large your pipes are.

Q. Since you have been on the committee, has the Chief ever called the attention of your committee to the lack of water supply in that district?

A. No, sir.

Q. Or in any district in Boston?

A. Not to my knowledge. The Fire Department say that the fire came on them so suddenly that they had to leave their hose, and they couldn't get at it after the building tumbled down; of course, that can't be helped.

Q. (By Mr. RUSSELL.) Is there any provision for going to fires now on runners?

A. I don't know of any. I thought this morning when I was coming down that I would go up into the Fire Committee and ask that question, and if we had not got any shoes to put on the engines, we should get them immediately. I think our Fire Department was well equipped for this fire. I had an idea, when I went into the Fire Department Committee, that it was an extravagant department, that it spent a good deal of money, and I thought if that was the course pursued in that department, the best way was to spend the money for a valuable consideration, and therefore I favored an additional supply of hose in the houses. My idea was to get an equivalent for the money we paid, and I also favored the purchase of two additional engines, and at our annual parade, I guess we showed more strength and had more hose in our houses than any year heretofore. That was my idea, to get an equivalent for this sum, $600,000, that it costs to run the Fire Department, because if we had it in our engines and hose, we had something to show for it, but if we expended it in junketing and travelling around the country, we had nothing to show for it.

Q. (By Mr. PHILBRICK.) Have you ever heard anything about any request from the Chief Engineer for the location of apparatus in that part of the city which was burned, or near there?

A. I think I have. I have heard him say that there should be some engine stationed in the vicinity of Franklin street. That was last year, when we located the engine up here in Bulfinch street. I have not heard him say anything about it this year. He has stated to me, since the fire, that the city ought to look out and get some land down there to locate an engine house.

Q. Have your committee ever taken it into consideration?

A. They have not, as yet.

Q. (By Mr. COBB.) Don't you think it is desirable to do it at an early day?

A. Yes, sir. I think we should do it right off, while we can get some land before they build upon it.

Adjourned to Thursday, January 2, 1873.

TWENTY-FIRST DAY.

THURSDAY, January 2.

JOHN QUINN, *sworn.*

Q. (By Mr. RUSSELL.) Did you own any buildings in Pearl place?

A. Yes, sir.

Q. Will you tell us anything that took place on the night of the fire, in regard to your property, which you think we ought to know?

A. There was a large building at the corner of Pearl place and Pearl street that was burned on Sunday morning and fell in. Between my building and this Pearl-street building, there was a fifteen-foot passage-way. There was a building on Sturgis street about ninety feet to the rear of my building, and that burned and fell in. There was a hose there in Sturgis street, and I asked the Captain if he wouldn't come into Pearl place and save my block. He said he would, for he could not do anything for anybody else; and he came in there, and stopped about two hours at my block; but about half-past five o'clock in the morning, Mr. Damrell came up and said: "Take that hose back." I could see him by daylight, and I judge it was half-past five o'clock. Then the Captain of the hose says: "Mr. Damrell, if you will allow me to remain here, I will save this block." Says he: "You do as I tell you." Then I went up and said: "I have had fifteen of my men here, helping these firemen save my building, and it is too bad to let it burn up when you can save it, when there are a hundred families homeless this morning." He says: "If you don't shut up your mouth, I will fix you d—d quick." That is all I can say about the affair. Afterwards, a neighbor of mine went up and influenced him to come down out of Milk street, and take the hose off of my buildings to cool down the buildings on Oliver street that were not on fire.

Q. (By Mr. PHILBRICK.) Did your building finally burn?

A. Yes, sir. After Mr. Damrell took the hose off, the building caught fire in one of the blinds next to Pearl street, and it took from that time in the morning until one o'clock before the eight buildings were burned. You may judge from that how much fire there was in the building when Mr. Damrell left. The last building fell then on the corner of Oliver street and Pearl place.

Q. What number was your block?

A. 7 and 8. The next house was Mr. Cronan's.

Q. How many families were there in your two houses?

A. In the house we occupied, No. 7, there were two other families besides my own; in No. 8 there were four families.

Q. (By Mr. RUSSELL.) When Mr. Damrell said if you did not shut up your mouth he would fix you d—d quick, did he take the whole of the hose away?

A. Yes, sir; he took the whole of it away.

Q. I understood you to say, that afterwards a neighbor went to him, and got him to move some of the hose to cool down some buildings on Oliver street?

A. I understood that Mr. Damrell came right down, and took the hose away.

Q. You mean, then, that your neighbor went up and saw Captain Damrell before he came down?

A. Yes, sir; he went up to the fire on Milk street, where he was, and took him down with him.

Q. Who is your neighbor?

A. I can't tell his name, but I can find him. A man told of it the next day, in the horse-cars, to let me know how smart he was in getting the hose away from us. I think he is connected with Chase's lozenge store and the Boston Lead Works. It was a neighbor of mine who owns property above me, who heard him make the boast of it the next day; and that is why we got so dissatisfied with it.

Q. (By Mr. Firth.) Did you at the time think that Capt. Damrell was doing you wrong?

A. Yes, sir; he was doing me wrong, because the Captain of his own hose told him, "Mr. Damrell, if you will allow me to remain, I can save the building." And after that the fire got into the building through the front blinds next Pearl street.

Q. (By Mr. Russell.) Can you tell who this man was who went to Capt. Damrell, and got him to come down there?

A. The man's name is Cushing.

Q. What is his first name?

A. I cannot say.

Q. Where does he live?

A. I can't tell you that, but I can find out all the particulars.

Q. Do you know what hose company it was?

A. It was Hose 5, of Salem. Capt. Pickering was the man who spoke to Mr. Damrell on the street, and told him, "I can save the block, if you will allow me to remain."

Q. Was there any other hose company there?

A. No, sir; none but Hose 6, of Salem. I had fifteen men of my own, besides Capt. Pickering's men. They got pretty well tired out, and we took the hose to let his men rest, and put the hose where he directed us.

Q. What is your business?

A. Stevedore business.

Q. Were the men you had there, the men whom you employ in your business?

A. Yes, sir. We took water in buckets and wet all our sheds down. We were ninety feet from the building on Sturgis street that was burned. That building burned down and caved in, and so did the building on Pearl street. I don't think Mr. Damrell could have saved the buildings on the opposite side of the street, for those were connected with stores, but ours wasn't. There was a fifteen foot passage-way between them. Capt. Pickering made the attempt to save the buildings on the opposite side, but he told the people: "I can't do anything more for you people; the best thing you can do will be to look out for yourselves.

The best I can do is to save this block on the other side." That was our side.

Q. Had you ever seen Capt. Pickering before?

A. No, sir; not until that morning, when he came to our assistance, when he could not do anything more on Pearl street.

Q. (By Mr. Firth.) Do you know that this man who said he would fix you, was Capt. Damrell?

A. Yes, sir, I know him. I did not know what he meant when he said he would fix me, unless he meant he would kill me. He said: "Who is running this fire, you or me?" I said: "The fire is running itself." All I was sorry for was that he did not keep away from our part. After I found I could not get any satisfaction, I used words that were not proper for me to use to any man, but after I had worked there all night with my men it would make any man mad.

JAMES R. KENDRICK, *sworn.*

Q. (By Mr. Russell.) Are you the Superintendent of the Old Colony Railroad?

A. Yes, sir.

Q. What time on Saturday night, Nov. 9, if at any time, did you receive any message from Mr. Damrell, about giving engines the road?

A. I did not receive any message from Mr. Damrell at all.

Q. Did you receive any message from any one?

A. Not during Saturday night.

Q. When did you?

A. My clerk received a message about noon on Sunday, I think, from Fall River, asking permission to come through with fire engines.

Q. What did he reply?

A. He gave the right of the road to come as soon as he could communicate through. The wires from our depot to the main office where the battery was were burned off, and no communication could be had except by the way of New York, I think.

Q. Was it not by the way of Providence?

A. I am not clear about that, but the impression I had was that they said at the Providence depot that they would have to send it by the way of New York to get to Fall River.

Q. Was that the first and only message you had?

A. That was the first message we had, and then we had others asking for the same permission from Newport; but at that time, there was no necessity, as I understood, for any more engines.

Q. (By Mr. Firth.) As I understand you, the requests came from the outside towns?

A. Yes, sir; they came from the extreme ends of the road.

Q. (By Mr. Russell.) Asking to come in?

A. Yes, sir.

Q. You had no request from any one in Boston to give them the road?

A. No, sir.

E. F. OLIVER, *sworn.*

Q. (By Mr. Russell.) Are you the Treasurer of the Lynn and Boston Horse Railroad?

A. Yes, sir.

Q. Just before the time of the great fire, Nov. 9th, were horses to be had in this neighborhood?

A. Well, our difficulty was that we were unable to run our road the full number of trips in consequence of the sickness which we experienced with our horses.

Q. Could you get other horses to take their places?

A. We didn't make any effort; we didn't try, for the reason that we were not buying them. The horses were generally sick.

Q. Do you know whether you could have bought them or not?

A. I can't state from actual investigation, because I did not make the effort. We had a full complement, but a great many were sick; otherwise we should have gone into the market and attempted to purchase, as we wished to increase our number just then, but on account of the sickness, we were prevented from doing so.

Q. (By Mr. Philbrick.) Can you tell me what proportion of the horses were on duty on the day of the fire, the 9th of November?

A. I should suppose, without making any careful estimate, that perhaps two-thirds of our horses were at work, but in double teams; that is to say, we ran four where we usually run two, and run a much less number of trips; but still, not all the horses.

Q. (By Mr. Philbrick.) Were they convalescent?

A. They were getting better fast, because we had suspended operations altogether, and had resumed them.

Q. You had passed the worst point?

A. Yes, sir.

WILLIAM HENDRY, *sworn.*

Q. (By Mr. Russell.) Are you connected with the Metropolitan Railroad?

A. Yes, sir.

Q. In what position?

A. Superintendent.

Q. On the 9th of November, and just before then, were you using your full number of horses on the road?

A. No, sir; I was running one hundred and sixteen cars; some of them with two horses, and some with four.

Q. How many were you using?

A. I can't tell you exactly, but probably about one thousand or eleven hundred.

Q. How large a proportion was that of your whole stock?

A. We had over thirteen hundred horses.

Q. Were horses to be had in this market at that time?

A. I don't know; we were not buying any at that time?

Q. Were you hiring them?

A. No, sir; we used our own horses.

Q. Have you any means of telling whether there were horses to be had at that time? Suppose you had wanted one hundred horses, could you have got them, or don't you know?

A. I don't know. I have no doubt I could have bought one hundred horses in two days, if I had wanted to, but I wasn't in the market buying.

Q. (By Mr. GREENE.) You say you think you could have bought one hundred horses in two days; do you think you could have bought one hundred well ones?

A. I don't think I could, sir. It was hard telling whether horses were well or not. We worked most of our horses more or less.

Q. (By Mr. FIRTH.) If you were using on that day, or on any special day, two horses on your cars, and doing your regular work with your regular force, what would be your inference?

A. I should consider the horses well. When a horse will eat, he is able to work, the same as a man or woman is. If he can't eat, we don't work him.

Q. But in regard to the work on any particular day, if you did your regular work with your horses, what would be your conclusion?

A. I should consider them nearly or quite well; we don't work them unless we consider them well.

Q. (By Mr. PHILBRICK.) Were the horses convalescent then?

A. Yes, sir, some of them. We had some horses that were not sick at all, but most of them had been more or less affected.

Q. Were they getting better at that time?

A. Yes, sir, they were getting better; some of them were well, and some of them were sick.

Q. (By Mr. COBB.) Do you mean, when you say that you could have bought one hundred horses, that you could have bought that number who would work?

A. I should think I might have bought horses at that time that would work, but I am not quite sure; I would not swear that I could, because I was not in the market, but I have no doubt there were horses here that could have been bought.

GEORGE H. VINCENT, *sworn.*

Q. (By Mr. RUSSELL.) Are you connected with the Metropolitan Railroad?

A. Yes, sir.

Q. Will you mention any fact you think we ought to know in relation to the fire on the 9th of November?

A. I will state that we were so well satisfied, on the night of the fire, that our horses would be called for and used, that on the Dorchester avenue line, a team of four horses for each of the two engines out in that vicinity was picked out by the Assistant Superintendent, and drivers detailed to drive them in case the engines stopped for them when they went by there.

Q. Were they used?

A. No, sir, they were not called for.

JOHN HENRY STUDLEY, *sworn.*

Q. (By Mr. Russell.) Are you connected with any horse-railroad?
A. Yes, sir; I am Superintendent of the Middlesex Horse-Railroad.
Q. On November 9th, how many horses were you using on that road?
A. The number of trips run on November 9th was one hundred and thirty in place of three hundred and sixty-five trips on our regular time-table. The trips were made with four horses attached to each car, and they were driven and used moderately. About fifty horses out of three hundred were not fit to be used on that day.
Q. Were the horses well, or nearly well, or what was their condition?
A. I think they were improving very fast.
Q. Had they all been sick?
A. Pretty much.
Q. Do you know whether horses were to be had then in the market?
A. I presume they were.
Q. Did you try to get any?
A. No, sir. I didn't hardly feel like buying just then.

HENRY L. HIGGINSON, *sworn.*

Q. (By Mr. Russell.) At what time did you reach the fire on the night of Nov. 9th?
A. Between half-past seven and a quarter of eight; I don't know exactly.
Q. Will you tell us anything which you saw which you think we ought to know?
A. The fire was in the corner store when I got there; it had not crossed Summer street. As far as I could see, there was no water from the top of Gray's building thrown down. It seemed to me at that time, that if they could wet the gutter and windows, and keep them wet, the fire would never cross Summer street, and I should say so now. The engine at the corner of Arch street and Summer street was whistling for coal before I had been there many minutes, and kept whistling for a considerable time.
Q. Was it working all the time or not?
A. I don't know, I am sure; I know it was part of the time, I don't know that it was all the time. Steamers arrived and kept arriving after I got there for an hour, I should suppose. After I had been there an hour, perhaps, I went round through Hawley street to Winthrop square, and through Winthrop place, and came down past where the church used to be, and went up very near the fire, and then I went round through Bedford street, and I didn't think the firemen were doing much.
Q. Do you mean over the whole route?
A. Well, they were working, but there were a good many who were not doing much. I know I made the remark to my companion: "It seems to me if there was anybody here to guide things these men would have something more to do; I should think they might find more." That was the gist of it. I went round through Bedford street into Kingston street a little way, and saw that the firemen were throwing

water from the steps and from the attics of some of these dwelling-houses in Kingston street, on the western side, and they were doing more, apparently, to put out the fire than any other men I saw; they were accomplishing more.

Q. How were they playing in the other portions of the district?

A. Throwing water up against the buildings from the street; against the house where Mr. John C. Gray used to live.

Q. With what effect?

A. It didn't seem to do any good at all.

Q. Did you see any hose carried on the roofs near Otis street?

A. No, sir, I did not; but then there might well have been at about that time, or later, hose carried up in Otis street and I not have seen it. I don't mean to convey the idea that the firemen were doing nothing, but there were a good many idle men, and they were not doing apparently as much as they might, and nobody seemed to guide anything. About eleven o'clock, I went down into Purchase street to the corner of what used to be Atkinson street; it is Congress street, I suppose now. There was almost nothing doing there at all.

Q. Was there any apparatus there?

A. There was an engine pretty near, but it was not producing any effect at all. The only firemen I saw were pulling the fence down in front of an old house which is standing now at the corner of Atkinson and Purchase streets.

Q. When you were there, had the main fire reached there, or was it fire caused by sparks and brands?

A. The fire was in full blast and coming very near there; the stores were going. I was at the corner of Franklin street and Federal street, very near to Channing street, about the same hour, or a little earlier, and there was but one engine there. That seemed to be all there was for that place. They were working well enough, but they were not accomplishing anything in the world.

Q. (By Mr. Firth.) How were they throwing their water?

A. Well enough, right on to the fire. It was well enough directed, and well enough thrown. There was energy enough about it, but there were not half enough men, and they were accomplishing absolutely nothing.

Q. (By Mr. Philbrick.) Do you think there was a lack of apparatus there?

A. Yes, sir. That was about eleven or twelve o'clock, I think.

Q. (By Mr. Cobb.) Did you see the Chief during the evening?

A. I never saw the Chief until eleven o'clock Sunday morning.

Q. Did you hear any order as coming from the Chief during the night at the different points you visited?

A. No, sir; but then there might have been such orders, and I not have known of them. A good deal of my time was spent between State street, where our office is, and on Devonshire street, about the Post Office, and I went up to the City Hall three or four times, I suppose, to see what they were doing there. I couldn't find out that they were trying to do much of anything. There were orders given to blow up buildings, but I couldn't learn that anybody in particular had it in charge except Mr. Burt. There were a dozen gentlemen, the Mayor said, who were ordered to blow up, but Mr. Burt was the only man named to me. I was told to go down to him, and call his attention to the fact that the buildings should be blown up from Washington street down to the water. That was my own suggestion, and the Mayor desired me to go and find Mr. Burt, and call his attention to the question whether it was not worth while to do it. That was when the fire was coming towards Milk street pretty fast.

Q. Did the Mayor tell you how Gen. Burt received his authority?

A. No; he did not say anything about that, except he said he had told him to do it.

Q. Did you find Gen. Burt?

A. No, sir. I looked for him all night, and didn't see him until eleven o'clock the next day.

Q. (By Mr. Cobb.) Did you see any gunpowder used?

A. I did, considerable.

Q. Where did you see it used first?

A. The first place was just back of the Post Office, on Congress street. It tumbled an old wooden building down on Water and Congress streets, just below the Post Office. That fell in, and of course it burned up, but it wasn't blown up until the fire reached it.

Q. What was the next building?

A. The next building was the old granite block in Congress street, where the "Evening Gazette" office was. Mr. Atkinson and Gen. Benham came down there, and the powder was put in, and that was blown up.

Q. Who superintended that?

A. Gen. Benham gave the directions.

Q. Did you hear him give any orders?

A. I heard him give these orders, — he gave them to me afterwards — about blowing up buildings. He said: "Every time you put your powder in, shove it down, put some heavy weights upon it, get it under an arch, if you can, and get your train all ready, but don't blow it up until the building catches fire. When the building catches fire, blow it up."

Q. Did he tell you what quantity of powder to use?

A. He did, sir; but my memory doesn't serve me as to the quantity. I should think it was about four hundred pounds. Mr. Atkinson came down with Gen. Benham, and Mr. Carpenter, who was down there, said Gen. Benham had been directed by the Mayor to do this thing. Gen. Benham seemed to be rather afraid of his authority, and Mr. Atkinson said he would stand by him in the matter. Then Gen. Benham gave those directions, and they were carried out by some men under Mr. Carpenter. Then powder was put down in Kilby street, in the building next to the express offices there, at the corner of Water street, and powder was put in the Revere Copper Company's cellar. But those directions of Gen. Benham struck me very decidedly. He repeated them several times, "Don't blow up the building until it catches fire."

Q. (By Mr. Russell.) Did he say that to you more than once?

A. He said that to me, and he gave those directions again and again. It seemed to me it only made it easier for the buildings to burn. I couldn't conceive what it meant.

Q. Do you know the length of the fuse, — how many minutes?

A. No, I do not. There seemed to be no head about it. There was no organization. There was nobody in particular to do anything. There was a man who undertook to put powder under the Revere Copper Company's office, and he didn't want to mind what was told him. He was ugly about it.

Q. (By Mr. FIRTH.) How did the powder work that was put under the Revere Copper Company's building?

A. It didn't amount to very much. It was not well put in. I carried part of the powder down into the cellar myself. Then we were ordered out, and afterwards, powder was placed there again. It was not well placed, and the explosion didn't amount to much.

Q. (By Mr. RUSSELL.) Do you know who ordered you out?

A. I do not. Afterwards, it must have been eight o'clock, Gen. Benham showed Mr. Atkinson and me a building in Kilby street which was next to the corner, I think, or very near there, one of the old buildings, and said, "That building must be mined; and you, gentlemen, can go and get some powder, and either of you who gets there first, put it in." We asked where we could get the powder, but he didn't know. Mr. Atkinson got some somewhere and put it in. I went down on Central wharf, where I heard there was powder, and found a powder-boat there, and got a wagon, and forty twenty-five pound kegs were rolled out to me, and put into this wagon, and the man drove up the wharf with me, and up State street to the corner of Kilby street. This was a covered wagon, open behind and in front. It was a wicked thing to do, I suppose. The powder was taken out, and half of it was carried up into Congress street, and the other half put in Kilby and State streets. Just then, Gen. Benham told me to mine the building in which Mr. Skillings had his office, the building this side of the Shoe and Leather Bank. He told me to put the powder in the cellar, and get my fuse ready and blow it up when the thing caught fire. I told Mr. Carpenter, who was still in Congress street, and who took part of the powder to use there, and he then said he didn't want it, and it was sent down, — one of the kegs open, covered, however, with a cloth,—and we went into that building, and just as we were putting the powder in there, Mr. Woolley came to me and the other men, and told us we must not put it in there at all. I told Mr. Woolley by whose orders it was put there; that it was by Gen. Benham's orders, and that Gen. Benham was instructed by the Mayor to attend to this thing. Mr. Woolley was as violent as he always is, I suppose, and said he would put me in jail if I didn't go away and mind my own business, and let the powder alone. He was very angry, and some of the firemen were very angry about it indeed. The consequence was, the powder was all taken and put into a store in State street and left there.

Q. (By Mr. PHILBRICK.) What become of that building, — was it burned?

A. No, sir, it was not. The instruction was, as I said, not to blow it up unless it caught fire.

Q. (By Mr. RUSSELL.) Where was that powder put? What became of it?

A. It was put in No. 80 State street, and left in the entry there. It is the building where Mr. Groom is. The bringing of that powder up

State street struck me as a horrible thing to do, but there was nothing else to be done. I was told to do it, and I did it. We drove by a couple of engines, and stopped about twenty feet from them, and took this powder out.

Q. Who superintended putting the powder in the Revere Copper Company's premises?

A. The work was begun under Gen. Benham's directions, but afterwards I think a man by the name of Hathaway had it in charge, one of the men in the Fire Department, who acted under Mr. Carpenter's directions.

There is one thing more about powder which I omitted to state. I bothered the Mayor almost to death, I suppose, that night. The last time I was there, it was about sunrise. I begged him to cut this path by blowing from Washington street to the Post Office, and then down to the water. We were right about the other side, but we were wrong as to this side. Then I went again when the Simmons building had burned, and I asked him to cut a path from Devonshire street to Congress street. I told him the buildings would be burned. He said he thought the fire would be stopped there, but I might go to Congress street, if I pleased, and represent the matter to Mr. Burt, if he was there, or to anybody else in charge, and call their attention to the fact that the buildings there had better be blown up to stop the thing. I went to Mr. Carpenter and told him what the Mayor said. He replied, "I will blow them up if the Mayor says so, but I think we can stop the fire here," which was what I had been hearing ever since eight o'clock the evening before. I didn't believe it, and he didn't stop the fire there, of course. If he had then blown up the "Evening Gazette" building, which was blown up later, the fire would not have gone any further. A building in Lindall street was blown out, either by powder or whiskey, I never knew which. It was a wine shop, and it was blown right out into the street, more completely than in any other case. At that time, when I went down there, Water street was not burning below Congress street, and none of the block opposite the Post Office, between Lindall and Water streets, was burning at all. Men were continually walking around there. There were not many engines there then; afterwards, they came with greater force.

Q. (By Mr. Cobb.) When you called upon the Mayor, did you hear him say anything about this matter of the use of gunpowder being in the hands of the Chief Engineer and his officers, rather than in the Mayor's?

A. Either the first or second time he stated that, and later, about ten o'clock the next morning, he read us the law on the subject.

Q. (By Mr. Firth.) To whom did he say the power belonged?

A. The Chief Engineer. The Mayor went down State street about eleven o'clock. It seemed to be so desperate at that time that I was afraid the Exchange would all go, and I went up to the City Hall with Mr. Appleton and somebody else, — three or four of us went up and asked him to go down, and he went down State street to Broad street, and looked at it, and then he got Gen. Benham and the Chief Engineer together, and having got them together, he went back to his office. They were to meet and decide whether they would blow up the row where the Merchant's Exchange is. It looked as if it was absolutely essential.

The fire was then burning in behind there; the Post Office was burning, and everything was burning up to the building of Mr. Gardner, right behind the Post Office. It looked as if the whole thing was gone, but the Chief Engineer said he had seen no good come from gunpowder, and finally refused to have the Boylston Bank building or the Columbian Bank building mined. He said he wouldn't have any powder put in there; he would beat the fire off there. He said he could, and would, and he did.

Q. (By Mr. Cobb.) Did you understand that the Mayor assumed any responsibility about the use of gunpowder in his official capacity?

A. I should say he did not assume any responsibility from the time the fire began until it was out. That is the way it looked to me.

Q. I mean particularly in regard to gunpowder?

A. I couldn't find that he exercised any responsibility in regard to that. We begged him, at ten o'clock, to give the order to have that row of buildings mined, and then he produced this law, and read it. He had told us of it before, and then he read it.

Q. (By Mr. Russell.) Was that row of which you speak from the Merchants' Exchange up?

A. Yes, from Kilby street to Congress street. It looked as if they would have to take the whole thing down. It struck me, who knew nothing about fires, of course, in comparison with firemen, that blowing buildings down did a great deal, for the moment they were flat, they were much more easily handled. But the uselessness of throwing water against a building, I saw in Milk street. I stood in the Post Office when the opposite side of Milk street was burning, and there was a stream of water thrown from Milk street across to a sign on one of the stores and they couldn't hit the sign; the water wouldn't go there. Afterwards, when the fire was burning in behind Congress square, against Mr. Freeland's building there, the City Exchange, the Mayor himself said he didn't see how they could save the City Exchange, and nobody would have supposed it could have been saved; but the water was poured down to such an extent that it was saved, which shows the advantage of pouring water down, which I suppose everybody knows.

Q. (By Mr. Firth.) Were there not a great many engines there at that time?

A. A great many were there. I think the larger part of the Fire Department had got around there at that time.

Q. (By Mr. Russell.) That path from Washington street to the water, which it was proposed to make, included the buildings between Spring lane and Water street, did it not?

A. I don't know. I don't think any one had it very clear in his mind what would be done, but I supposed it was going from this side of the old South to Water street, and going right down straight through. It is lucky it was not begun there at Washington street.

Q. (By Mr. Cobb.) Was there much time lost by the firemen in consequence of these explosions?

A. I shouldn't think there was.

Q. Were they fighting the fire while there was powder in the buildings?

A. There was only one engine, one pipe and hose, to withdraw in

Congress street (I don't think there was any more), when the "Evening Gazette" building was blown up. Those men fell back into Lindall street. There was not any hose at all in Kilby street. Everybody fell back for five or six minutes, but a part of the firemen went into Water street, where the fire was going on the same, and where they were of use. Part of them fell back for a few minutes.

Q. (By Mr. COBB.) Can you fix the length of time they ceased playing?

A. No, sir; but it was only a very few minutes.

Q. How long should you think it was?

A. Well, I should think it might have been four or five minutes.

Q. (By Mr. FIRTH.) Looking back upon it, what do you think now of the use of powder, as it was used that night?

A. I should think it helped the firemen to get at the fire and to extinguish it; but it seemed to me that it was as badly used as it could be. I may be quite wrong, but I can't see any point in letting a building catch fire, and then blowing it down. I had supposed, and do now, that the point of the whole thing was to throw the buildings down and make a path before the fire got there, and keep it back.

Q. Did you suggest that to Gen. Benham, or anybody you saw?

A. I told the Mayor. I didn't tell Gen. Benham, because he don't keep very quiet when there is any excitement. I knew him at the South. He gets a little worried. He ran round there, and seemed to have a worse time than anybody that morning.

Q. (By Mr. RUSSELL.) Do you know what time it was when you first saw him?

A. It was just about sunrise, or a little after, I should think. There is one thing about the fire that I will state. When I went home the first time, which was about half-past nine o'clock, it was quite evident, as I supposed, that powder had got to be used in order to stop the fire at Arch street and Franklin street, which I supposed would be the limit. I didn't think it would go the other side of Winthrop square. It was evident that they had got to use some powder. I so stated to somebody whom I met. I don't think it took any powers of observation beyond those of a child to see that, at the time. I wanted to say about the policemen, that I noticed three or four policemen who were round all night. I saw Deputy Chief Quinn about there, and in the Mayor's office, and it seemed to me that his head was kept all night; and there were two or three policemen who were terribly brave, I thought; always doing all they could, and always putting themselves in the post of danger.

Q. (By Mr. PHILBRICK.) I want to go back to about the time when you first arrived at the fire. When you saw the fire kindling on the north side of Summer street, did it appear to you a possible thing to extinguish it and stop it there?

A. I did think at the time that the fire would be stopped there. It seems to be an absurd thing to say, but I thought if there was only sufficient water, and if it had been carried into the upper part of the buildings, the fire could be stopped at that point.

Q. Was there apparatus enough there then to do that?

A. There was enough to throw streams from the street.

Q. How many did you see throwing streams from the street?

A. I can't tell. There were certainly two being thrown then.

Q. Without accomplishing anything?

A. I didn't see that they were doing anything in the world.

Q. (By Mr. FIRTH.) Did you observe anything in regard to the heat?

A. It was very great, but half an hour later, when I went round, I went up a considerable distance beyond where the church-yard extended, and the heat was not so great but that I could stand there and do anything I wanted to. The heat didn't trouble me at all. Up a little further, I have no doubt it was very hot. There were plenty of men, but they were down on the street. There was no one going into the buildings or on to the roofs.

Q. (By Mr. PHILBRICK.) Was there anything to prevent taking a line of hose on to the building on the corner of Otis and Summer streets, and playing on the other buildings from the windows?

A. I could not see that there was. It was not too hot to do that at all. If they could not have gone into that building, they could have gone into the one below, on Otis street, or into the one on Summer street above,—either one or the other. There was an enormous mass of human beings down there at first. There were plenty of firemen there.

Q. (By Mr. FIRTH.) When you went your round the first time, did you observe the Assistant Engineers anywhere?

A. I don't know just what the Assistant Engineers do. The engines were running and there was somebody looking after them. I didn't notice the Engineers at all. There was plenty of water, as I believe I told you, in the streets. I couldn't see that any engines lacked water at all, but the lack of fuel did strike me.

Q. (By Mr. PHILBRICK.) Did you see any engine failing for lack of fuel?

A. No, I did not; but I don't know enough about fire engines to testify as to that.

Adjourned to Monday, January 6.

TWENTY-SECOND DAY.

MONDAY, January 6, 1873.

HENRY A. PIPER, *sworn.*

Q. (By Mr. RUSSELL.) Of what firm are you a member?
A. Tebbetts, Baldwin & Davis.
Q. Have you any theory to account for the fire, or any clue to its origin?
A. No, sir, I have none at all; I do not live in town and was not here at the time of the fire. I have no theory. I suppose it originated up stairs; I see no good reason to believe it originated down stairs. The condition of the boiler-room, as we found it after it was excavated, did not show much evidence of anything being wrong on that floor. The safe fell into the basement, and when it was removed, the flooring was found to be perfectly sound. If the fire had originated down stairs, it would have been natural that the flooring would have been charred or burned, it seems to me.
Q. (By Mr. PHILBRICK.) Where was that floor?
A. In the basement, at the rear, next that passage-way.
Q. Near the elevator and boiler?
A. Yes, sir, right adjoining.
Q. (By Mr. RUSSELL.) Did you see the top of the boiler when there was no rubbish upon it?
A. No, sir; I think Mr. Tebbetts did.

WILLIAM C. TEBBETTS, *sworn.*

Q. (By Mr. RUSSELL.) Were you a member of the firm of Tebbetts, Baldwin & Davis?
A. Yes, sir.
Q. Have you any theory to account for the origin of this fire?
A. I have no theory about it. I have my impression, formed from the information I have got from people living in the immediate vicinity, and from one or two gentlemen who were passing by there at the moment of the fire, that it must have taken in the upper part of the building, somewhere on the third, fourth, or fifth floors. My impression would be that it took on the upper floor.
Q. When the excavation was made did you see the boiler?
A. Yes, sir.
Q. What was the condition of the boiler?
A. The condition of the boiler was just exactly as the Engineer says he left it. The doors were ajar, very nearly closed, but sufficiently open to stop the draught, and everything in the order that he reported to me before we excavated.

Q. Did you see the top of the boiler after it was cleared off?

A. Yes, sir; the rubbish was in about the same condition that it was when it fell. They excavated all around it, and cleared off the top of the boiler, but the rubbish and *debris* remain just the same as it was on the fall of the building; they haven't disturbed it at the present time.

Q. The boiler is in complete order?

A. The boiler is apparently in perfect order; the walls are plumb on the side and on the end. On the top edge of the wall, where some beam struck it, I presume, the top bricks are pushed over a little; that is all the injury there was done to the boiler; I don't suppose there was any more injury than that to the boiler; it has no appearance of it.

Q. Did you see the floor where the safe fell?

A. Yes, sir.

Q. What was the condition of that?

A. The floor was apparently as sound when we were taking the safe out, as it was the day before the fire.

Q. Was it charred?

A. I couldn't see that it was charred at all at the time. On getting our safe out, as soon as they commenced to clear the ruins, they got out a timber that was about half or two-thirds burned, and that left our safe on an incline. It was burned after we excavated the safe, but I attributed that to the great heat which appeared to be there after we got out our safe. After we got our books from the safe, the fire burned up very fiercely, so much so that the bricks were red-hot. There was a great deal of fire there, and when we got at two other safes which were there, we found that the contents, which were of but little value, were destroyed.

Q. When did you get out the first safe?

A. About five o'clock on Thursday afternoon.

Q. Was that a movable safe?

A. Yes, sir, resting on the street floor.

Q. (By Mr. FIRTH.) Did you say your books were destroyed?

A. No, sir, we saved all our books; but we had two other safes which belonged to some previous firms I was interested in, outside of the counting-room. There was nothing of any great value in them, and we thought it was not worth while to undertake to excavate them and get them out; they were simply old books.

Q. (By Mr. PHILBRICK.) Where was the safe found which had your books in it?

A. It was found just about in the position in which it stood, only tipped over on the doors.

Q. It was in the rear of the building?

A. Yes, sir; it tipped into the cellar about nine or ten feet, with the doors down.

Q. Was it about half-way between the Kingston street wall and the boiler?

A. It was a little nearer the boiler than the other side of the building.

Q. About in the centre of the building then?

A. It was near the centre of the building, I should judge. I would state that in front of the boiler, there was a brick ash-pit, and the Engineer stated that we should find when we got at that boiler, the door shut, that we should find everything clean there, as we did. I was there when the rubbish was cleared away, and I think there was an officer there also to examine the condition of that ash-pit, and we found that there were no burned coals there at all. On the contrary, we found there the coal which he had wheeled in from the bin in the afternoon, as he was accustomed to do to be ready for his fire on Monday morning, entirely unburned, and I had it all taken up, and have got it now in the cellar of my house, three barrels of it; there is no appearance of fire having been near it. The elevator floor, of course, was made of wood, and that was always left on the lower basement floor over night; it is there now, and I believe entirely unburned; possibly it may be charred a little on the top. It is partly covered now with bricks, but the floor of the elevator remains there now, and can be seen. They thought of removing it, but I told them they had better let it remain there. It would do no harm, and might be of use to examine.

Q. Do you remember anything about a brick fire-flue which extended from the top of the boiler to the chimney?

A. I know nothing about it specially. I have been in the engine-room very many times, but I don't know anything about that.

Q. Do you remember where it was?

A. I can't precisely locate it. I don't think I ever examined particularly enough to notice that.

Q. (By Mr. FIRTH.) The draft up that elevator must have been very strong when the fire got started?

A. Yes, sir.

Q. Would not that explain the non-burning of the wood at the bottom?

A. Yes, sir.

Q. (By Mr. PHILBRICK.) Have you seen any of the people who lived in the opposite houses?

A. Yes, sir; I have seen Mr. Hamilton, who is in the second or third house?

Q. Have you seen any of the people living in Mr. Pratt's house?

A. No, sir, I have not; I met a gentleman a fortnight after the fire, who keeps in Summer street, and he told me that one of his partners or employees (I can't say which) came from Chandler street to Kingston street and stood there, as he told me, ten minutes, and saw the fire burning in the upper part of the building, and says to himself, knowing some of the occupants below these gentlemen, "They will get nicely wet." He says he saw no fire anywhere about in the lower part of the building. If there was any fire in the lower part of the building, there is no question about a man's seeing it. The whole length of the store, which was 101 feet on Kingston street, and 51 feet on Summer street, was glass; the whole distance along the basement and lower end on the first floor, was nothing but glass and iron columns. No person going by or near there could possibly be mistaken about where there was a light.

Q. Were you there when the alarm was given?

A. No, sir; I started from my house in Walnut street immediately after the general alarm was sounded. I came down into Summer street, and finding I could not get through Summer street, I went round through Kingston street, and got into the rear of the building there. It might have been fifteen minutes after the first alarm sounded.

Q. How late were you in the basement that night?

A. I don't remember of being in the basement. I can't say whether I was there an hour before that, or half an hour. I was in the counting-room, and my partner, Mr. Piper, went below to wash his hands, in the dark. He came up into the counting-room, and I sat there talking with him. We came very near being there to know more about it, because I had just suggested to him, as he had been at work upon the books three or four days to find a few cents in his balance, that as I had nothing to do that evening, I would be very glad to stay with him for some little time and assist him; but he said he had been there some time, and had been at work three or four days, and he thought he would adjourn until Monday morning. If we had been there, we might have known more than we do now. We might have known enough to get the books out of our safe. The way I account for the very great flame immediately after the breaking out of the fire, is on account of the great amount of pine and light material, — the empty cases and the surplus hoop-skirt frames, which, when the fire got there, it was just like lighting shavings and kindling-wood in an oven; it would go very quickly. That accounts to me for the immense flame which seemed to be all over the building.

ALBERT DAVIS, *sworn.*

Q. (By Mr. RUSSELL.) You are a member of what firm?

A. Tebbetts, Baldwin & Davis.

Q. Were you in Boston at the time of the fire?

A. I was in town; I was not at the fire until after our building fell in.

Q. What time did you leave the building?

A. I left there at twenty minutes before six.

Q. Have you any theory about the origin of the fire?

A. Well, I have a theory, judging only from what I have heard. I know nothing personally about it, sir. I conversed with quite a number of gentlemen who live in Kingston street on the following day, and only know their theory about it. I helped to get out our safe. We found it on our basement floor, where our packing-room was, and the floor where we dug it out was not burned at all; it was as perfect as it was the day it was laid.

Q. (By Mr. PHILBRICK.) Was it not covered with rubbish which prevented its burning later?

A. It was burned later, but when we got out the safe, there was no appearance of fire there.

Q. (By Mr. RUSSELL.) Did you see the coal that Mr. Tebbetts has?

A. I did, sir; that had not been charred at all; it looked as bright and fresh as when they first put it in.

Q. (By Mr. PHILBRICK.) Have you ever seen Mr. Pratt or his son, who live directly opposite?

A. I saw a gentleman whom I supposed to be Mr. Pratt, Sunday morning; he was the only person I saw who had a different theory in regard to where the fire caught from the other gentlemen.

Q. What did you understand his theory to be?

A. His observation was, as I understood him, that he first saw the fire going up the elevator in the lower part of the building. Mr. Hamilton, who lives in the next house to him, told me he heard a cry of fire near his house, and went to the window, and saw the fire in the top of the building, and saw no fire except in the third or fourth story. Mr. John H. Rogers told me the very same thing. Then there was a young man, (I don't know his name, I know his face very well, he used to keep with a neighbor of ours in the dry goods business, and boarded with Mr. Pratt,) who corroborated all Mr. Hamilton told me.

ALBERT P. DAMON, *sworn.*

Q. (By Mr. Russell.) Were you an occupant of the building at the corner of Kingston and Summer streets?

A. Yes, sir.

Q. What was your firm?

A. Damon, Temple & Co.

Q. At what time did you reach the great fire?

A. I should think it was about a quarter to nine.

Q. What is your business?

A. Men's furnishing goods.

Q. How long had you been in that building?

A. We went in there the year before, — in March, I think it was.

Q. How long a lease did you have?

A. We had a lease of five years.

Q. On what terms?

A. It was $5,000, — taxes and steam extra.

Q. (By Mr. Firth.) What rooms did you have in the building?

A. The whole of the second story, up one flight.

Q. (By Mr. Russell.) What was the value of your stock at the time of the fire?

A. The value, as we have proved it, was $44,000, — in that neighborhood.

Q. What was your insurance?

A. The insurance was $25,000, on stock and fixtures.

Q. In Boston offices?

A. In New York offices and one Philadelphia office.

Q. Have you settled with the Insurance offices?

A. We have settled with one; our claims are adjusted with three.

Q. At what time did you leave the store Saturday afternoon?

A. It was about a quarter of five.

Q. Who of your firm left last?

A. I left last.

Q. (By Mr. Firth.) Have you any theory in regard to the origin of the fire?

A. Well, sir, I have a theory, but it is somewhat in conflict with some of the facts, or things which are reported as facts. I should say the upper part of the building was the most unsafe part of the concern; but if the fire originated in the upper part of the building, I don't see how it could have been so hot in the lower part at the time when the people got there.

Q. Why do you think the upper part was the most unsafe?

A. Because it was filled with the most combustible material.

Q. (By Mr. PHILBRICK.) You mean the goods themselves, the merchandise, not the building, was the most combustible?

A. The merchandise.

Q. (By Mr. FIRTH.) You say you think that the fact that the fire was very hot below indicated that it could not have originated above.

A. That would be a theory; but we have a man who boards right on the opposite side of the street who states that when he heard the alarm given he rushed out and saw the fire in the upper story; then the man who gave the alarm says he first saw the fire break into the elevator and rush up; so my theories don't amount to much. When I got there, the whole of Otis street was on fire. It was a quarter to nine, and my man says it was twenty minutes past seven when he ran down and telegraphed me, and that was immediately after the alarm was given.

Q. What is the name of your man?

A. Mr. George Pierce.

JOHN H. HATHORNE, *sworn*.

Q. (By Mr. RUSSELL.) How many horses do you employ on your omnibus line?

A. About two hundred and twenty.

Q. How many had you at work on the 9th of November,—the day of the great fire?

A. I had about one hundred and eighty of the two hundred and twenty. I think I may perhaps have used two hundred.

Q. Had they been sick?

A. They had.

Q. Were they convalescent then?

A. They were. The disease broke out with me about the 21st of October, on Monday. On Thursday, I took off all my stages, and laid still for seven days. On the seventh day, the 31st, I commenced to run, If think, three stages, four horses to each stage.

Q. Then how did you go on?

A. Then we increased from time to time as we found the horses were convalescent, got well, or able to work, and by the 9th of November, Saturday, we had thirty coaches running.

Q. Two horses each?

A. Two horses, pretty much; I can't say but we doubled up some of them.

Q. At that time could horses have been obtained in the market if you had wanted to buy or hire horses?

A. I can't answer in regard to that; I presume that at the sale stables most of the horses were affected. People were rather afraid to buy. I should have hesitated about buying any green horses from the country at that time.

WILLIAM H. JONES, *sworn*.

Q. (By Mr. RUSSELL.) Are you a member of the Committee on Fire Department of the city government?

A. I am.

Q. Did you ever have any conversation with Mr. Damrell with regard to a want of apparatus or want of water in this district which is now the burnt district?

A. Yes, sir.

Q. When was it?

A. I have had several talks with him previous to the fire and since then.

Q. Previous to the fire, what did he say?

A. He said the hydrants were not located near enough together. I really cannot give the conversation, except in general terms. He said the hydrants were too far apart altogether, and they were not suitable hydrants for the locality. I remember distinctly his telling about the Water Works taking out his Lowry hydrant in Winthrop square.

Q. How long was this before the fire?

A. Really, I can't tell that.

Q. Did you ever have more than one conversation with him about it?

A. I don't remember; it has very often been spoken of in talking the thing over in regard to the water supply.

Q. (By Mr. PHILBRICK.) Have your committee ever urged any action towards granting further apparatus or increasing the number of hydrants?

A. Not this year's committee.

Q. (By Mr. FIRTH.) You are speaking about the committee of 1872?

A. Yes, sir. You understand that the location of the hydrants, etc., does not lay with our committee.

Q. (By Mr. PHILBRICK.) The location and furnishing of engines does belong to your committee, does it not?

A. Yes, sir. Nothing has been done by our committee in regard to locating any apparatus in what is now the burned district.

Q. (By Mr. FIRTH.) Had your attention been called to the need of action on your part as the Committee on Fire Department during the year 1872, in this district?

A. No, sir; there has been talk in regard to the location of hydrants, and in regard to the water supply.

BENJAMIN P. PICKERING, *sworn.*

Q. (By Mr. RUSSELL.) Do you belong to any fire company?

A. Yes, sir.

Q. What one?

A. I am foreman of Lafayette Hose, Salem, No. 5.

Q. Do you recollect that you were throwing water on two dwelling-houses in Pearl place, leading out of Pearl street, and were called away to Oliver street?

A. I do, sir.

Q. At what time was it, as near as you can tell?

A. I should be rather poor on the time, for I had no way of telling it, but I should think it was along somewhere between seven and eight o'clock.

Q. Who asked you to leave there?

A. I was in the fourth story of the building with my men, and a man came to me and says, "The orders of the Chief Engineer are to come down out of there." I says, "Is it the order of the Chief?" The man says, "Yes." Our Engineer was with us, and I asked him what I should do. "Why," says he, "do as you are told," and I took the line out, and took the men round on the other side of the tenement house.

Q. (By Mr. PHILBRICK.) Where did you go with it?

A. There were two large brick houses. We were on the right-hand side going in. We came out with the hose, and went round up what they call, I think, Fort Hill, on the back side of the other tenement house, and played on that.

Q. Where did you go after that?

A. Well, we went from there down — I can't tell the street.

Q. On a street where there were stores?

A. Yes, sir.

Q. (By Mr. FIRTH.) Stone or brick?

A. Stone.

Q. (By Mr. RUSSELL.) Did you save the tenement-house you played on last?

A. No, sir.

Q. How did you happen to leave that?

A. I don't know from whom the orders came. I got my orders from the Engineer who came from Salem. He said he had orders to go down on this street. I know we lengthened out some two hundred feet of hose after we left.

Q. (By Mr. PHILBRICK.) Did you have to move the engine?

A. No, sir.

Q. Was it one of your Engineers who gave the second order?

A. It was one of our Engineers that gave me the order, but he said he got it from one of the Boston Engineers.

Q. You don't know who gave you the first order to come out of the building?

A. No. It was some of my men who came to the bottom of the stairs and halloed up.

Q. (By Mr. RUSSELL.) How long did you play on the second tenement-house before you changed?

A. I should think we were there an hour and a half.

Q. Could you have saved that if you had stayed there?

A. No, sir, nor any other one.

Q. (By Mr. FIRTH.) Could you have saved the first one?

A. That is rather a difficult question to answer. When we went into the building the fire was on the roof, and we went up stairs and got out on the roof, and put out all the fire there was. Then underneath, there were a number of woodsheds, lined all round the side, and we played from the window down on them, and when we left the building, there did not seem to be much fire in them. I thought that the object in ordering us round was to stop the fire from going further in that direction. About two hours after that, I saw the tenement-house we came out of, and the roof was all in a light blaze.

Q. (By Mr. RUSSELL.) Did you hear any quarreling or cursing about your leaving?

A. Yes, sir, I did.

Q. Was that when you left the first house or the second?

A. If you will allow me to go on and tell it, I can tell you best in that way. I think we must have been stationed on Pearl-street place, and we were ordered round on the back side of the house, and went to work on it. The man came who owned it, and asked, "Who are you?" I said, "I am foreman of Lafayette Hose, of Salem." Said he, "If you will take your hose round the building, you can save it." My Engineer stood there, and I said, "What do you say, Capt. Osborne?" He said, "I think you had better go round." I took the hose round, and the man who owned on the opposite side said that was partiality. I says, "Why?" He says, "You are saving that man's building, and letting mine burn." I said, "I can't take care of both, and I think I can save that building." The man said, "You can save my building, if you stay here." I said, I hadn't anything to do with that. "My duty always is to obey superior orders, and my orders are to go round and save the other building." The man cursed and swore considerably, but I didn't pay any attention to him, but I told the men to take the hose and go round, and they did. I don't think that any one stream could have taken care of any of the buildings there were there, they were so large.

Q. Was there any other stream in that place?

A. No, sir, there was not.

Q. (By Mr. PHILBRICK.) Are you sure this change was made, and you were ordered out of that building by daylight?

A. Yes, sir. It was about daylight.

Q. I understood you to say it was between seven and eight o'clock?

A. It was daylight. I recollect it was daylight; when we went round on the back side, some one said, "This is Fort Hill," and it was light enough to see all around.

Q. Wouldn't the fire have made it pretty light?

A. It was daylight. The fire was pretty well down around there then.

Q. (By Mr. RUSSELL.) When you went round on this other street, did you save the building?

A. The left-hand side was all down almost flat. On the right-hand side they did save most of them down on the end where we were. There they seemed to check it.

Q. (By Mr. PHILBRICK.) Did you see any sheet-iron put up over the windows, or anything of that kind?

A. No, sir, I didn't notice any.

Q. Were there any men in the building or on the roof?

A. No, sir. While we stood there, Chief Damrell came down, and the only man I saw go into the building was one of the men of a hook-and-ladder company. He ordered him up there with an axe. There were then three or four steamers and hose in that street.

[At this point, Capt. Damrell was invited to come into the room, and he was asked: —]

Q. (By Mr. RUSSELL.) Do you recollect giving any directions to Capt. Pickering in Pearl place?

A. I have a faint recollection of meeting this gentleman on Sunday morning about seven o'clock, but I wouldn't want to say positively.

Q. Do you recollect ordering the removal of any hose from Pearl place to Oliver street?

A. My impression is, that I did order a line of hose from some brick building, to take care of the front of the building on Oliver street, where the Boston Lead Works are.

Q. Do you recollect a Mr. Quinn having a lively conversation with you?

Mr. Pickering. — That is the man. I recollect the man's name when you mention it. That is the man who owned the first building. That is the man who made the most talk while I was there.

Capt. Damrell. — I don't recollect Mr. Quinn at all.

Q. Do you recollect a man who stated that that house might be saved, and was very earnest that you should allow his house to be saved?

A. Well, sir, there were so many such cases, that I really can't recollect any particular one. There was somebody, a stout, thick-set, dark-complected man, who called me all the damned scoundrels he could think of. I didn't know that I had given any directions to come in contact with him.

Mr. Pickering. — After we came out of the building, the men said, "The Chief is here," and Mr. Quinn came up and called him everything he could lay his tongue to. They said it was a wonder that he didn't knock him down or have him arrested.

Q. (By Mr. Russell.) Where did that hose go, Mr. Damrell?

A. I think it went round into Oliver street, and played on the front of Mr. May's building. I can't give the names. This much I know, that when I left this gentleman, I went into the store and met Mr. Chadwick, and he said that was his building, and I immediately had a stream brought into the rear under Capt. Munroe.

Mr. Pickering. — I recollect a remark made when we came round to this building. We had to take a ladder and got our stream right on to the fire. It seemed to be round the window-frames; and a man said, "I own this building; and that is the best thing that has been done for the last three hours."

Q. Did you say when you were directed to leave the other building, that you could save it if you were allowed to stay?

A. No, sir.

Q. Did you think at the time you went away that you could save it?

A. Well, at the time we went away, I don't know as I passed any opinion on it. There was so much fire around there, it would have been impossible to have passed any kind of an opinion.

Q. Did Mr. Damrell swear at this Mr. Quinn?

A. I never heard him.

Q. Did you hear him say he "would fix him damned quick"?

A. I never did.

Q. Did you say to Mr. Damrell that you could save that block if you were allowed to remain?

A. I never did.

Q. Did you say anything of the kind?

A. No, sir.

Q. Did you say it to anybody?

A. No, sir. I never made any talk with Mr. Damrell at all during the whole fire. He came to me once for some hose, and I gave it to him, and he came to me once for an axe, and I gave it to him.

Q. Did you make any objection to the order that was given to you to move your hose from that place to another?

A. No, sir, I did not.

JOHN S. DAMRELL, *recalled.*

Q. (By Mr. Russell.) Will you state what took place in Pearl street in regard to Mr. Quinn's house?

A. I really cannot. I simply passed on. This man was talking very violently to me. I did not know him; I had not come in contact with him; I did not know that I had trod upon his corns in any way, and consequently I paid no attention to him; but seeing this block on Oliver street, with the window-frames on fire, and this stream on the brick building in the rear, doing no possible good, I took it off and placed it there in conjunction with a stream under Capt. Munroe, to save that block, and keep the fire from working down further.

Q. How far was it from the building this hose was playing on to Oliver street?

A. It was really on Oliver street, only on the opposite side. Pearl place was a small place. I don't know that I can get it right, but I will make a little diagram to show you how it was. (Mr. Damrell made a sketch of the streets in that neighborhood, and pointed out the location of the building in question.) This stream was playing into that block of buildings leading from Oliver street into Pearl place. They were playing over some sheds, and I took them from that position, and brought them to this block of buildings on Oliver street, where the Lead Works were. That was on fire in front. The buildings on the opposite side of the street were on fire, and this stream that was playing on the rear of these other buildings was doing no possible good, and I regarded the merchandise in those stores as of forty times more value than one of those dwelling-houses, so that there was really no alternative, in my judgment, but to take the hose off and try to save that block in Oliver street, and so prevent the fire from going beyond, because, as I recollect it, there was an open space beyond that block.

Q. Did you hear the captain of the Salem hose say he could save that building if you would let him stay?

A. No, sir.

Q. Did he say anything of the kind?

A. No, sir.

Q. Did he make any objection to being removed?

A. Not the slightest.

Q. Did you swear at Mr. Quinn? Did you tell him you would "fix him damned quick"?

A. If I did, I must confess to a state of feeling that I never experienced before. I don't know that I ever used a profane word in my life, I should think it very strange, under the most trying circumstances. I think Mr. Quinn must be mistaken in the man. I really don't think it could have been me, because I had not come in contact with him. He commenced at me bull-terrier fashion, and I certainly made no reply to him whatever.

Q. Did the people there make any remarks about him, or about you?

A. I can't say one word as to that. I had just one point to make, and I never allowed any talk that might be made by outsiders at that time to divert me from the business I had in hand. If I should stop to listen, or argue any point, I certainly should be very reprehensible, in my judgment.

Q. Will you tell us how many firemen were killed and maimed at the fire?

A. We lost two from the Boston Fire Department.

Q. How many from out of town?

A. I think there were but three members of the Fire Departments. There were nine altogether, ex-members, and men who have been connected with the departments.

Q. How many Boston firemen were maimed?

A. I don't know of but one who was injured to any extent at that fire, Mr. Woodward.

Q. Were there any from out of town maimed?

A. Yes, sir. Mr. Jenness, of Cambridge, came in a well man, weighing one hundred and sixty-three pounds. I don't think he weighs a hundred pounds to-day. He is in a terrible plight.

Q. Where was he injured?

A. Some men were ordered under Captain Casey, of Cambridge, into a building, in order to cut off the fire from coming into the rear, and while there, a current of hot air, I call it, was formed, and it struck the rear wall of the building opposite, and it fell down and crushed the gable end of the building they were in, and in coming down stairs he fell, and got caught in the bight of the hose, and in the snap of the line his lungs were wrenched, or, as the doctor says, "He snapped the muscles connected with his lungs."

Q. What were the names of the Boston firemen who were killed?

A. One was William F. Farry, second foreman of hook-and-ladder company, No. 4, the other was Daniel Cochran, a member of the same company. Those gentlemen were lost on Washington street. They were away from their piece of apparatus. I don't know why they went away, but there is no question, from the information I have from members of the hook-and-ladder company, that they lost their lives in trying to save the lives of others who were caught in the building.

In regard to those from out of town, I will state, that I wrote to the Chiefs of the different towns, asking them to send me a list of those killed and injured, stating their name, age, the number of their families, and dependents upon them, and also to send me their photographs. I have received only two or three answers. I have the name of

George H. Smith, of Watertown, aged twenty-nine, single. He was injured, but not seriously. John Richardson, twenty-eight, married man; he fell from a roof on Monday morning, while putting a stream of water on Jordan & Marsh's store. He was injured quite seriously, and taken to the Massachusetts Hospital, and in about a fortnight we sent him to New Haven, where he belongs. He is a member of the New Haven Fire Department. Thomas Maloney, Worcester, aged twenty years and six months, single; he died from injuries received. He was not a member of the Fire Department, but came down as a volunteer. R. E. Extell, Worcester, injured in the back. James McCame, also of Worcester, injured. These are all the names I have recorded at present. Young L. Frank Olmstead, of Cambridge, was killed at the bazaar on Federal street, and Mr. Frazier, also of Cambridge. The case of the Abbotts of Charlestown, I suppose you are quite familiar with. I think the Abbott brothers were not members of the Charlestown Fire Department, but formerly were, and were at that time members of the Red Jacket Hose Company Association. One of them has not been recovered; the other had his back broken, and remained at the hospital until about a week ago, when he died, and his mother died of grief. The one whose body has not been found was Porter Abbott. The name of his brother who died in the hospital was Albert Abbott.

Q. (By Mr. Russell.) Were the out-of-town firemen paid for their attendance?

A. No, sir.

Q. Do they claim it?

A. Not to my knowledge.

Q. If any came and claimed pay, would they be paid?

A. I can't answer that question. I have no doubt the committee would very generously consider it.

Q. (By Mr. Firth.) When the department goes from Boston do they ever make a charge?

A. Oh, no, sir. I have made good their losses, furnished them with what hose they lost, etc. I have never presented any claim for anything our department has lost out of town. I have always done it gratuitously.

Q. You mean for lost material?

A. Yes, sir. I have always considered, that in case of a fire in Charlestown, for instance, the property was owned by Boston men, after all.

Q. (By Mr. Philbrick.) Did you find the loss considerable?

A. Oh, yes, sir; quite so. About nine thousand feet of country hose was lost.

Q. (By Mr. Russell). On the night of the fire, did you give notice to any superintendents of any of the railroads that you would want their tracks?

A. Only to the Boston & Albany; I sent there for an express train.

Q. When you telegraphed to Salem, or any other place for help, you left it to them to arrange for coming in?

A. I sent by telegraph and left the arrangement with the stations on the lines of the roads.

Q. (By Mr. FIRTH.) You did not communicate with the Eastern Railroad officials in Boston?

A. I sent to the Eastern Railroad by Mr. Allen, but what time it was, or the circumstances, I don't know. I sent to the Eastern Railroad, and the messenger found nobody there, and then Mr. Allen came to me, and asked me if he shouldn't go to the Superintendent of the Eastern Railroad, and make arrangements in regard to the transportation of engines over that road. I said if he would attend to that for me, he would do me a great favor. I think that was Mr. George Allen, Superintendent of Lamps.

Q. (By Mr. RUSSELL.) At what time did you first send to the Eastern Railroad?

A. I am not clear as to that.

Q. (By Mr. FIRTH.) Was it about the time when you sent to the others?

A. I think it must have been an hour or so after I sent to the Boston & Albany road. I sent a courier with dispatches to different towns, I suppose soon after eight o'clock, but I did not send for an express train from Worcester until I learned that the telegraph offices along the line were closed.

Q. (By Mr. PHILBRICK.) What is the regulation about shutting off the reservoir?

A. We always close our reservoirs the moment we disconnect our engine, but at this fire I was obliged to put the out-of-town companies at the reservoirs, and send my own to the different hydrants as far as I practically could, simply from the fact that the out-of-town companies had no connections to fit our hydrants. Thus when the engines were drawing from the hydrants, we could get no water from the reservoirs. This was the case with the Franklin-street reservoir, and near Church Green, and in one or two other places. But after we had ceased to draw on the hydrants on that line, of course the water came back again. I cannot conceive of any material detriment or damage to us on account of not shutting off the water, but generally it was to "get up and get" as quick as we could, and if the shutting off of the water was omitted sometimes, it would be no matter of wonderment to us, for the men stayed there just as long as it was in the power of men to stay.

Q. (By Mr. PHILBRICK.) Are there tools carried on every engine for opening and shutting those gates?

A. No, sir. On the ladder carriages we carry a long wrench made on purpose to reach the gates of our reservoirs; but the engine companies have no wrenches at all, only to disconnect with the hydrants. The wrench for the reservoirs is a long wrench, and we carry them on the ladder carriages. When we are obliged to resort to them, a ladder-man is detailed for the wrench to turn the water on the reservoir. He understands that. He has that particular duty to attend to, just the same as when a ladder is raised, a man who is called a "dog-man," arms himself with a hammer, and his duty is to dog the ladder, and make it secure. Then we have other men, who are called "axe-men," and their duty is to take axes from the carriage, and report themselves to the Engineer, and await orders. Then we have four men, who are called "rake-men," whose duty it is to go inside of the burning building, put in their rakes, and take the plaster off over head, so as to enable us to get at the ceiling as well as the walls. That is their special duty.

Q. (By Mr. Philbrick.) Is this man who carries the reservoir wrench ordered to attend to shutting off the water, as a general thing, after he opens it?

A. Certainly. He takes that back to his carriage.

Q. If they are obliged to leave the reservoir, is it his business to look after it and see that it is shut off?

A. Yes, sir. That is to say, if he can; but in some cases where we have a large amount of work to do, he might be sent immediately from that place to some more important point, and might be away. In the case of ordinary fires, to which we are accustomed to go, he would remain and take care of that; but where we have as much to contend with as we had on that night, he would answer any order given him by the Engineer.

Q. The chances are that on that night he would be absent at the time the engine left the reservoir?

A. I have no doubt about it, because we lost our wrenches.

Q. I want to ask you in regard to the practicability of attaching to your department a certain number of men, who are gas-fitters, who shall always accompany the engine to fires of any considerable size, with proper tools to shut off the gas at the meters or the inlet pipes?

A. We have men who are gas-fitters in each hook-and-ladder company now, who are supplied with a monkey wrench and other tools, and their duty is to report to me at once, and shut off the gas.

Q. They did not do any great amount of work that night, did they?

A. No, sir. The fact is, the ladder-men were detailed as quick as they came with small ladders to scale the roofs at the leeward of the fire to try to prevent, if possible, their taking fire.

Q. What means do they have, on scaling those roofs, for extinguishing the fire?

A. Simply by taking their hats or coats and beating it off, or throwing it off; getting up to the Lutheran windows, and getting behind the fire and brushing it out.

Q. What do you think of these little hand-pumps?

A. I think, in some instances, they serve very well. But you must have a bucket of water with them. You have got to carry a bucket of water in your hand. We have them in the department; we carry one on each carriage now, — Mr. Bird's pumps.

Q. I understand that they are a part of the London equipment, and are very well spoken of.

A. Yes, sir. I use, instead of them now, the Babcock Fire-extinguisher, and have three companies organized. They run to every fire. There are two men who make that a specialty. They take the extinguishers and start; and in ten seconds, can get up a pressure of sixty pounds to the square inch, which will throw a stream forty feet, by the power of its own effervescençe. Consequently, we find that they are much more effectual than the hand-pumps, where you have to carry a bucket of water, as it only throws a small stream. In the case of the extinguisher, you have only got to hold it; the power is behind it; it is automatic.

Q. Have you ever heard of one bursting?

A. No, sir, I have not, but I am apprehensive of it. I know it would be quite disastrous to the man who was behind it, should it explode, and I have some fears in that direction.

Q. (By Mr. FIRTH.) How have they operated in your experience?

A. Very successfully.

Q. They play only five or six minutes, do they?

A. No, sir; but you can charge them instantaneously. I have with each of these extinguisher-wagons, two-inch and inch-and-a-half rubber-lined linen hose, with the reducing couplings; so that if I am at the salt water and want to supply my boilers, I run this small line instead of taking a large line of hose to supply my engines. On the other hand, if I am running a long line of hose, I can slip the coupling and put on a branch hose, without stopping the other stream.

Q. How long have you used them?

A. It is about a year and a half since I introduced them.

Q. Are they used anywhere else?

A. I think not, sir, anywhere as a specialty, as I use them here. They carry them upon their ladder trucks in New York, and also in Chicago.

Q. (By Mr. PHILBRICK.) Do you ever put out fires with them without the help of heavier apparatus?

A. Yes, sir. For instance, we had a fire in Temple place which was in the ceiling, where we used only these extinguishers, and saved thirty-five or forty thousand dollars.

Q. Shouldn't you think it advisable to have permanent fire-escape ladders attached to some part of every block to enable the firemen to get off the roofs?

A. In every instance they should be obliged to bring them within certainly twenty-five or thirty feet of the ground.

Q. Would not that inspire the firemen with a great deal more confidence, in scaling a burning building, than they would otherwise have?

A. It would, indeed, and, in addition to that, some means of ready access to the roof from the inside, so that we could ventilate the building would be of great value to the department. Men hesitate to go unless they can find an exit somewhere.

Q. (By Mr. FIRTH.) You would not order them to go to the roof of a building unless there was some way of retreat?

A. No, sir; but the fact is, we do not order them to go; we generally lead them.

Q. (By Mr. PHILBRICK.) Have you ever had occasion to use any of the standing cast-iron mains in buildings?

A. No, sir, we have never had any that I know of. Jordan & Marsh have put in some since the fire.

Q. (By Mr. FIRTH.) Is that the only one you have heard of?

A. I think there was one put into Otis place some four or five years ago, — a perforated pipe. I have been consulted since the fire by a dozen different firms who are putting them in, — Mr. Sears, and others, who came up to ask my opinion about them.

Q. Did you know anything about there being any in the building occupied by John S. Wright, in Franklin street?

A. I knew nothing about it.

Q. Is there any practical difficulty in coupling on to them and using them?

A. I should say not.

Q. If they made them conform to your coupling, would it not save a great deal of time in getting the hose up, and save the risk of bursting the hose?

A. It would. It would save bursting the hose, and it would save a great deal of time in getting a line of hose up, if you could put it on the floor, and use the water there. That might be on the flight where the fire was, or on the roof.

Q. Don't you think it would be worth while for proprietors to keep hose coupled above?

A. Yes, sir. I think that every large warehouse should be obliged to put a hydrant in front of the building and run a standing pipe up to the top of its building, for its own security.

Q. (By Mr. Firth.) What should you think of having hose put in different parts of the city, easily accessible?

A. I hardly think I should approve of it, unless it belonged to private individuals. It would not do us any great amount of good. The fact of it is, the transportation of hose from one place to another is done as rapidly as we can possibly move round to do it. The great trouble in moving hose is in getting it up into a building. A building is on fire; of course it is full of smoke, and the difficulty is in working ourselves up in the heat and smoke. I do not know of any instance where we have experienced any great difficulty on account of having to wait for hose.

Q. (By Mr. Philbrick.) Suppose there was a certain amount of hose coiled round the hydrants, under the control of a policeman who might carry the key in his pocket, don't you think that would be of service?

A. I can conceive of a case where an immense amount of good might be accomplished in that way. If our police force was what, in my judgment, it ought to be, — that is, augmented in numbers, to make it efficient, — almost every fire might be stopped in its incipiency.

Q. (By Mr. Firth.) What do you think of the plan of offering a reward for the discovery of fires?

A. I think it would work very badly. I am of opinion that that was one of the disadvantages under which they suffered in Chicago. I understand that the underwriters offered a reward to any policeman for the discovery of fire after a certain time at night, and putting it out; and I was informed, and I suppose credibly, that fires did take place under very mysterious circumstances, and men claimed the reward for putting them out.

Q. (By Mr. Russell.) Can you think of any way in which the alarm can be secured more readily, except by having more boxes?

A. There ought to be a sufficient number of boxes, and there ought to be sufficient confidence in the citizens of Boston to trust them, when they say there is a fire, to commence with; and then, in the night, there ought to be a sufficient number of guardians of the public safety to give an alarm. This morning, for instance, we had a fire on Roby's wharf. The light was seen and we took it to be the gas house — the illumination from the gas retorts in opening the doors; but, on going down to the wharf and coming back, I saw cinders flying in the air, and, of course, I knew there must be a fire. I started off for the fire, and Mr. Garland, of the Insurance Brigade, went to the fire and then went back and gave the alarm himself, and we rolled in with our apparatus, certainly a quarter of a mile, and no alarm had been given by any officer. I don't know but it is all right. The officer may have been at the other end of his route. If he had too long a beat, then the safety of the city is at stake. Take it at the Mill Dam; there is but one officer, I understand, from the public Garden clear out to Parker street. Any one of those large dwelling-houses might take fire and half-a-dozen lives be lost, for the officer must go, I don't know how far, to give the alarm, and then it must take us fifteen or twenty minutes to get there with our apparatus. You can tell what the result would be.

Q. (By Mr. Philbrick.) I don't think I understood your opinion about the desirability of having hose attached to the hydrants, as they have in some of the western cities, under the control of the police. Do you think there would be any advantage in them?

A. I can conceive that if we could have hydrants, so arranged that they could be used by our police, it would be a great advantage, if we had a force sufficiently large to perform that service; but it is not adequate to it now. For instance, I furnished the police stations with Babcock Fire Extinguishers, some two years ago, or more, so that, in case they discovered a small fire, they could bring them into requisition before the department got there; but I did not hear of a single instance where one was used, and because they were not used, I took them out of the station-houses, and put them into requisition in my own department.

Q. (By Mr. Firth.) Do you see any other objection to supplying the hydrants with hose except the expense?

A. The cost don't amount to anything. Fifteen minutes of a fire would destroy an amount equal to the cost of the hose for five years, so that really it don't amount to anything. I see no other objection, except that a question might arise as to the discreetness with which it should be used. For instance, there are a hundred thousand dollars' worth of property to be destroyed by water, and if you allow the fire to burn for five minutes, only five thousand dollars would be destroyed. There is quite a consideration. Eighteen times out of twenty, when we have an alarm, we are promptly on the spot; and we know that we have a force sufficient to control the fire, and we hold our water until we can make a direct application, feeling that the amount of damage by the fire will be very much less than by water, and that we are justified in holding it as long as we have force enough to extinguish the fire at any rate.

Adjourned.

TWENTY-THIRD DAY.

Friday, January 10th.

WM. C. TEBBETTS, *recalled*,

Produced a plan and made the following statement: —

That is the Kingston-street plan. That is the store that is going up there now, but for size and position and everything you get just the same from this that you would from the original building.

Q. Is it a fac-simile of the original building?

A. No, sir, it is entirely unlike the other building in architecture, but the size is the same, and the style of the roof is the same, substantially, so it would give about the same idea of everything about the building. That is the Kingston-street elevation, and that is the Summer street. If you will recollect, all of these spaces here were clear glass. Those were the Hyatt lights. The door here had a window in it. All these spaces here were glass, clear glass; not dead glass but clear glass, and the same thing will apply to all the Kingston-street side. That was glass, the whole length of the building, so you could look into any part of the store or basement. They are all one room, except we had a glass partition, mostly all glass, running right straight through. The partition run through in the basement perhaps as far as that, four or five feet high of wood, then a glass sash all the way through, so you could have a view from this end of the store to the point. The partition was in the rear. The boiler was in front of the elevator. Then there was a space of six or eight feet for the ash-pit. It was brick, and in that corner was where I mentioned the other day we took out the fresh coal which was unburned. That is the elevator. A person coming from Otis street, approaching the store, if there was a light in any part of the basement, it would be the first thing that would strike him, if he was coming down the street, and he could not be mistaken.

Q. Suppose a man stood here?

A. A man standing there could not see anything there. That is a solid wall.

Q. Suppose he stood here in the first or second story of a building in Kingston street, what chance would there be to look down into the basement?

A. There are one or two houses which have a view of perhaps the second story. I don't think there is a house in the street below there that has any view of the rear.

Q. Were there no basement windows?

A. There were two small basement windows in the old building on the back passage. A person standing there could look right in.

Q. Who has the plan of the old building?

A. Mr. Klous has a photograph of it.

Q. Has Mr. Hall the plans?

A. I think Mr. Hall has the plans.

Q. Can you remember about where the fire-flue went from the boiler to the chimney?

A. I remember the pipe from the boiler came out in this direction somewhere, and entered, I think, as near as I can judge, about there on the wall.

Q. Didn't it run along that party-wall some six feet horizontally?

A. I should think it did.

Q. Wasn't it built out on a shelf or stone projection from the wall?

A. I could not say positively.

Q. I saw some North River stone sticking out from the wall.

A. That runs along for some distance. I don't know what it was for. I noticed there was some there broken off, but what it was in the wall for I don't know that I ever asked the question.

Q. You remember seeing the flue project from the wall there?

A. Yes, sir.

Q. How far below the ceiling?

A. I should say four feet.

Q. Was that wall bare brick or stone, or was it covered?

A. Brick.

Q. Bare?

A. Yes, sir.

Q. Not plastered?

A. Not at all

Q. I was going to ask you about your theory; whether you think there were any possibility of the fire originating in that flue?

A. I don't think there is a possibility of the fire having started there in any shape, manner, or form. I am very well conversant with that room, for I have been careful to examine the basement when I had been down to examine the plasterings along there. We had a partition wall along here which separated us from this boiler room. The Engineer had access to the engine-room here, by a door, at any time; and we were separated by a partition running along through here. There was a window there in the partition. There was a window there I think, and there was a door there, and a window there, and then a door here. We had access to the elevator by a large double door. Almost every night, I, and when I did not, somebody else did, if I was there last, went down there to examine the fastenings and see if they were all right. There were fastenings all along here at the entrances, and a window at this end of the partition, which was also fastened.

CLARENCE A. DORR, *recalled.*

That (indicating on plan) is where I observed it. I was thinking of going down this street to go to the station, and I looked at my watch to see if I had time to go that way, reckoning the time at about a minute's difference, or go by South street. I looked at my watch here, in Kingston street, and it was twenty minutes past seven. While I was there I heard a slight noise. It was very still indeed, and I looked up in the direction of the noise, and it was there at the end of this building, almost to the end. That is the relative position here, and I saw this steam escaping. As I said in my testimony it reminded me of passing by the "Post" building in Devonshire street. It was precisely the same as that.

Q. Was it a cracking noise like a fire?

A. No, sir, it sounded like a printing-press, just as a printing-press sounds in a still night, but not perhaps quite as loud as that. Immediately when I heard it my impression was it was a printing-press, and when I looked up and saw the steam, as it appeared to me, and as I thought it was when I looked at it, I made up my mind there was something or other in the way of printing going on there. It was perfectly still, and I did not see a living soul anywhere near me on the street. I wanted to say to some one, "Is anything the matter?" or "Is there a printing-press up there?" I did the same in going by the "Post" building once. In not perhaps more than half a minute I observed a jet-black smoke going up there, and then I knew the place was on fire. I looked up and down through all these windows. I stood about there, and I didn't see the least sign of fire there at all; neither was there the least sign of fire in these windows. Then I started and crossed the street into Summer street, and looked up and down the building and then I saw no sign of fire. Mr. Tebbetts' store was all black, and so it was all up and down in front. There was no sign of fire at all. I walked along and looked up, and I thought I saw the reflection of fire coming up from there. There was a slight reflection of red. Then I started and ran round as hard as I could, and by the time I got there some people were crying fire. Then I went into that yard, which was as near as I could get to it. I had forgotten about the passage-way. If I had remembered it I should have gone into it. I looked up, and there was the fire raging inside of the Mansard roof in the attic. I stood there some few minutes, and then came round to the front. Then it was all on fire here, although it hadn't got here. It seemed to confine itself there. It came down through here and melted the glass. Then I ran back again. Most of my observation was there; so that I didn't see the first engine, and the first thing I saw was this hose-carriage that came up South street. The impression I had was, and I made up my mind from the first, that it originated up there in that story. It seems to me I must have seen some sign of fire here if it had come up the elevator. It began up there, I am perfectly satisfied myself, although, of course, I could not swear to it, but I was perfectly satisfied as I stood there and talked with the people, that that fire originated in the upper story of that building.

Mr. PHILBRICK. I should like to ask Mr. Tebbetts if the elevator well was cased in all the way up?

Mr. TEBBETTS. Yes, sir, it was.

JOHN R. HALL, *sworn.*

Q. You were architect of this building — the building that was burned?

A. Yes, sir.

Q. Have you the ground plan of the basement?

A. No, sir, I have not. Mr. Klous had all the plans of the estate on the corner of Kingston and Summer streets. They were destroyed in his building when it was burned.

Q. You have no copies?

A. I have no copies of that building. I have of his other. I have the specifications of that building at my office, describing how it was built in every particular.

Q. Do you remember anything about the position of the fire-flue, running from the boiler to the chimney?

A. I remember it was a large flue 12×24, running straight up to the top of the building, surrounded on all sides by eight inches of brick wall.

Q. How far was it from the boiler?

A. I could not state exactly how far; it was very close to it.

Q. Was it within six feet of it?

A. I should think it was; I could not say for a certainty.

Q. Do you recollect how the fire draft was conveyed between the boiler and the flue?

A. No, sir.

Q. Was the party-wall in the basement story furred and plastered?

A. In the basement story it was sheathed with spruce sheathing.

Q. Sheathed on furring?

A. Yes, sir.

Q. Did that finish pass by the boiler?

A. No, sir; where the boiler was and the engine-room, it was a brick wall, white-washed.

Q. How was the elevator, — well lined?

A. Sheathed up with spruce sheathing and painted.

Q. Was the under side of the floor joist plastered over the boiler and engine-room?

A. Yes, sir.

Q. Was there a connected coat of plaster throughout the whole ceiling of the basement?

A. Yes, sir.

Q. Was there any drain-pipe passing down in that neighborhood, in that party-wall in the neighborhood of the engine? I saw a pipe in the ruins of the wall.

A. You mean a water-closet pipe, I presume.

Q. Yes, sir.

A. I think there was. I think that came down very close to it.

Q. Do you recollect about how far the top of the boiler-setting was below the ceiling?

A. About three feet.

Q. Was that an open space?

A. Yes, sir; the steam-pipes running over it were below the plastering immediately over the boiler; also the machinery that worked the elevator.

Q. Were you near the building at an early part of the fire?

A. Not nearer than the head of Summer street, on Washington.

Q. Was the elevator well cased in all the way up?

A. Yes, sir.

Q. With door-ways opening into every story?

A. Yes, sir, double doors.

Q. Both opening outward?

A. Both opening outward into the large rooms.

Q. There were no hatches in the elevator then?
A. No, sir.
Q. How far up did that elevator run?
A. To the attic story.
Q. To the attic floor?
A. Yes, sir; from the basement to the attic. I have the elevation and specifications of the building.
Q. Was the question of movable floors in the hatchway ever considered by you?
A. No, sir; you mean closing upon each story?
Q. Yes, sir.
A. No, sir; the machinery running those elevators at that time, run so that it was impossible to close the floors in each story. They may have made some improvements since, but at that time there was no chance to close them on each story.
Q. Have you ever seen the automatic elevator in operation at Wellington's store?
A. No, sir.
Q. In '66, this was built?
A. Yes, sir; somewhere in that neighborhood.
Q. What was the cornice?
A. Wood.
Q. Framed in?
A. Yes, sir. I built about twenty-seven stores down there during the four years after we commenced on Summer street, and put in the same kind of elevators, and sheathed in the same way.
Q. Were they with wooden cornices?
A. Yes, sir. The whole of the block opposite where the fire originated, called Everett Block. Mr. Rogers owned the centre, Wm. Gray owned fifty-four feet of it towards Arch street, and Faxon Bros. owned on the corner of Otis. I built both corners of Otis, the corner of Devonshire and the corner of Lincoln.
Q. Had every block a wooden cornice?
A. Yes, sir; all the stores that I built at that time were built with wooden cornices.
Q. Was that your choice or the choice of the owners?
A. It was to save expense more than anything else.

Mr. James H. McKay exhibited a model of the Wilson & Waring elevator attachment with automatic self-closing hatches, and said: —

"This invention is now in use in New York. 15 Whitehall street is the first one we put in. It was patented Oct. 23, 1872. It is manufactured by the Wilson & Waring Automatic Hatch Co. I have a report of a committee of the Fire Commissioners of New York, who have seen it in operation practically. This is a copy, and if you would like to have me read it to you, I will do so: —

"Head-quarters Fire Dep't., City of New York.
Office Board of Examiners, 127 & 129 Mercer St.
"New York, Jan. 3, 1873.

"At a meeting of the Board of Commissioners of the Fire Department of the city of New York, held this day, the Committee on Repairs and Supplies reported that they had seen the 'Wilson & Waring Automatic Hatch Cover' in operation at the store of Hoodless & Co., 15 Whitehall street, and from a careful examination of it deem it the best means of closing hatchways and elevator-openings that has come to our knowledge, and would earnestly recommend its adoption in all stores, warehouses, hotels and other places where hoistways and elevators are used, feeling satisfied, from its simplicity of construction and non-liability to derangement, that it certainly meets a want that has been long felt, in affording security to lives and property at all times.

"WILLIAM S. HITCHMAN,
"*President.*"

Q. At what speed can that be run with safety?

A. We have had two hundred feet a minute. It is hardly necessary to run them at that speed, but we have done it for the purpose of testing it.

Q. With any weight?

A. 7 boxes of tobacco, — 2,800 lbs.

Q. What is the cost of the patent for a warehouse of five stories?

A. It is for each floor $125, which includes everything, — hatchways and all the attachments of the elevator.

Q. Does your company furnish it?

A. Yes, sir; and put them up and warrant them for one year. The Board of Underwriters of New York have decided that they will reduce the rate five per cent. where the hatchways are put on.

Q. You mean with special reference to this?

A. Automatic hatchways. They do not refer to ours. The Superintendent of Buildings there also recommends it. I have a letter from him. The firemen are always certain that the hatchways are closed where this attachment is used. When we put one in we notify the firemen, and they know they can enter that building with perfect safety, and in case a fire originates in the basement, there is no draft to draw it up the hatchway. Whatever story it originates in, it will probably remain there until the firemen can get there. Most elevators run about 100 feet a minute; many of them less than that. 140 to 150 feet a minute is very rapid. It makes no difference how fast the elevator runs, the motion is positive. This is an elevator-attachment. The elevator itself has the same support and machinery that other elevators have.

EDWARD C. CABOT, *sworn.*

Q. (By Mr. PHILBRICK.) I would like to have you state what you think of the new building act.

A. In the first place, I think it is a little too comprehensive. It takes too much the character of specifications, goes too much into detail. I think if it could be condensed and simplified, it would be more likely to be useful. I don't know that it could be possible to avoid the fixing the dimensions of walls, or the strength of walls in certain ways, but there have been, from the various amendments which have been made to the original act, some features introduced, which seem to me very objectionable. One is in regard to substituting iron for stone in the bond of piers. There is a clause in the amendment, in which you will see they have substituted iron plates, which it is provided shall go through the wall in piers, supporting the floors, and also entirely across piers, supporting the floors in the basement story; and where iron is used it breaks the bond of the pier. It seems to me very objectionable. In the London act, and in most of the foreign acts, they use stone, common stone, corresponding to our blue stone. When that clause came up before the committee of the Legislature, somebody thought that would give a monopoly to the blue-stone quarries, and substituted iron; and it seems to me it is a great mistake.

Q. Does mortar form any permanent attachment to iron in building?

A. I think not.

Q. When a pier is heated, constructed in that way, what would be the effect?

A. I think the iron would have no value as a bond. I think it would be likely to break the bond by expansion.

Q. Would it not defeat its end entirely?

A. I think so; yes, sir; and it puts upon builders a very unnecessary expense. Two-inch plates of iron are very objectionable in every way. I think a thin piece of sheet-iron would be better, because there would be less expansion to it. It would be less liable to be injurious.

Q. Does not the general character of the act render it very difficult of execution?

A. I think it does.

Q. Would it be likely to be executed by the inspection which you would probably have?

A. I think not. There are so many things it would be almost impossible for any inspector to watch in detail.

Q. And too many details mentioned?

A. I think it would be inoperative in many ways. It is very difficult to draw any act which shall be sufficient in detail to protect the public, and at the same time simple enough to be easily administered.

Q. Did your Association have anything to do with drawing up this bill?

A. They were originally applied to by the city, and drew up an act.

Q. I mean during the special session?

A. Merely in a general way, as experts, to give their testimony before the legislative committee, and that was merely upon the amendments, not upon the original bill. The original bill was drawn by our society, and it was very carefully done.

Q. Do you mean the bill passed in 1870, or the one passed at this session?

A. In the first place, the city applied to the society of architects to give them a draft of a bill, which they did; they employed counsel, and were pretty careful in the preparation of the act.

Q. You mean for the special session?

A. No, sir, not for the special session; it was the one previous to that. That was very considerably changed by the city, and then submitted to the Legislature and still further changes made there. Very many of the provisions of the present act are very unlike the provisions of the original act.

Q. Were they concerned in drawing up this act passed at the last session?

A. No, sir, a few members went and examined the amendments and had some changes made in features that they saw were entirely objectionable, but did not go into very minute detail in regard to it; they didn't have an opportunity.

Q. Judging from your experience, do you think the code of penalties which are fixed by this recent statute are likely to be efficient in obliging people to conform to the act?

A. I should think not.

Q. Would it not require a large force of attorneys to prosecute delinquents?

A. I think very likely it would be a difficult thing to get through.

Q. How would it do, instead of fixing a penalty to be recovered in an action in court, to oblige the party putting up a structure not in accordance with the act to pull it down again?

A. I think it would be much better to arrest the work, to condemn it, and oblige it to be built as required by the act. I have the impression that is the case in some of the foreign acts.

Q. I notice this act provides penalties to be recovered by action in court?

A. There are so many technicalities that a case would find it hard work to get through.

Q. How are the foreign acts in relation to details?

A. They go into details very nearly as much.

Q. Is it possible to have legislation on the subject without this large amount of detail?

A. I think the introduction of these iron plates is a matter of detail which was put in, not by experts, but by ignorance.

Q. There may be mistakes about the details, but my question is whether it is not absolutely necessary that there should be a proper detail specified in the act?

A. There must be a very considerable amount of detail, but anything that is unnecessary to specify what is a safe building is of course a great injury to the bill, because it gives an opportunity for avoiding the provisions of it.

Q. What is your opinion about the desirableness of an entire revision of the present law?

A. I think it would be very desirable. I don't think the architects or builders are satisfied with the present bill. Mr. Bradley spoke of it a day or two ago as being very objectionable in some of its features. I didn't have time to talk with him about it, but I have met with that expression of opinion quite generally.

Q. That is the general impression in the profession?

A. Yes, sir. In putting in force the provisions of the bill now in these buildings that are just going up, they find they are obstructed by it. There is one very curious mistake. The bill intended to provide that the eaves of stores should not be over sixty feet, but as I understand the bill, the eaves may be on the back. It is not necessary to put the eaves on the front, and the front may be carried up seventy-four feet and the water carried to the rear. It is perfectly easy to do that, and it would be difficult to get over it. That makes it about as bad as it was before. It does not add any safety, certainly.

Q. Have not many of the objectionable features of this bill been introduced by amendments offered on the floor in the House and Senate by parties not experts?

A. I think they have. There is a clause of this amendment which I don't know the meaning of at all. It refers to bond timbers. I don't know what bond timbers are. I never used such a phrase in my specifications, and I asked Mr. Cummings, of Cummings & Sears, this morning, and he said he didn't know what it was. My impression is it was taken from the London act and applies to some construction they have, which is much more complicated than ours is in regard to timber framing. It is done a good deal in lobbying. The gentlemen are not familiar with the technical terms, and they do not get a clear idea of what is wanted by the persons whom they represent, and they make wild statements which are incorporated in the act and are of great disadvantage.

Q. Do you know whether there is an architect on the floor of the House this winter?

A. I don't think there is. I don't know of any. I know there was one attempt made to have a change in regard to corbelling out. It was objected to corbelling out with stone, and cutting off the gutters for party-walls, and they wanted to get rid of this corbelling out of the stone on the front and retain the wall above the roof; but as the amendment was passed at first, the corbelling out was left in and the party-wall above the roof was taken out. That was remedied, however, before the bill passed, by the parties themselves.

Q. Do you think it would be worth while to restrict the manner of constructing elevators, — hoistways? The clause that was first introduced in this bill was stricken out and did not become a law. There is nothing said about elevators in this recent act. Do you think it would be worth while to refer to that in the act?

A. It seems to be of the first importance to provide some means to cut off the draught through elevators, but whether that could be done I don't know. Of course it would be considered oppressive if people were obliged to put in any particular patent.

Q. Are there not several ways of overcoming that?

A. It would be desirable, it seems to me, to provide that the hatchways shall be closed by some automatic means, because if it is left as it was in the old bill, simply stating that hatchways shall be closed, people forget it.

Q. If left for private vigilance they would be left open?

A. I think they would, in a majority of cases. I think the firemen have a feeling of security when they enter a building where they know there is some automatic apparatus of that sort which is operated by the machinery itself.

Q. Do you think there would be any general objection among the architects to making iron fire-escapes on every block to enable the firemen to go on to roofs and get off of them, independent of portable ladders?

A. No, sir, I can conceive of no reason why they should make any objection.

Q. Should you not feel more hopeful of carrying the right bill through the present Legislature than any former one?

A. I should have more confidence in any recommendation that came from this committee than anything that came from any other source now.

Q. Has there not been a disposition among a good many of the members, especially the country ones, to undervalue the recommendations of architects?

A. I think the architect is rather a new creature in this part of the world, comparatively. I don't think, as a general thing, they are looked upon as very reliable by the majority of people.

Q. The country members consider the carpenter sufficient without the architect?

A. Yes, sir; they are the architects, in fact, to them. The society here took great pains about the preparation of the first bill, and spent five or six hundred dollars on their own account, which was never repaid them, in preparing it.

Q. And the more important of its features were stricken out?

A. Yes, sir.

Q. Are the architects generally members of your society?

A. There are about fifty, I think, out of those in the city.

Q. How many do you understand there are?

A. I have not looked into the directory lately, but I have the impression there are somewhere in the neighborhood of 100 who are represented in the directory as architects. There may be more now. I have not looked for several years. I believe almost all who have the largest practice in the city are members of the society.

Q. You are the president, I believe?

A. Yes, sir, I believe I am the oldest architect in town. I suppose that is the principal reason why I am president. I have been in practice longer than almost any architect here. I have been in practice since 1846; commenced practice in 1846.

Q. You were not the first professional architect in the city?

A. No, sir; Geo. Dexter, Mr. Young and Mr. Rogers, I think, were practising architects. I am not sure but that Mr. Billings was, at the time I commenced.

Q. Is there any objection to the Mansard roof constructed of proper materials?

A. No, sir.

Q. Is there any difficulty in constructing it of those materials?

A. No, sir, not any. I do not think the Mansard roofs burn up in Paris more than other roofs. They have the habit there of laying their slates mostly in mortar.

Q. Is there any reason why we should not on steep surfaces?

A. I think there is every reason why we should.

Q. Would not that prevent the roof boarding from being roasted into flames across the street?

A. I think it would. There is hardly any better non-conductor than mortar made with plaster of Paris.

Q. Does not plaster of Paris contain a great deal of water, and when it is heated does it not give out water?

A. Yes, sir, it has a great affinity for moisture. It does not throw off the material either.

Q. Plaster of Paris and all mortars contain a good deal of water in a solid form, and they give that water off when heated?

A. Yes, sir, and I think plaster of Paris is rather slower in giving off water than the common cements. It is used in Paris for filling up floors and filling in partitions and laying roof slates. In drawing a bill now there are many things that would occur, that did not occur then ; of course, the bill must be crude. It is difficult to draw a bill, taking foreign bills as the basis, for a state of society which is on an entirely different political basis.

Q. And the forms of construction are different here?

A. Yes, sir, and the materials are different.

Adjourned.

TWENTY-FOURTH DAY.

SATURDAY, January 11th.

GEN. HENRY W. BENHAM, *sworn.*

Q. (By Mr. RUSSELL.) At what time did you get to the scene of the great fire, what time of night?

A. It was not far from four o'clock, as I recollect. Soon after four.

Q. Where did you go first, — to the City Hall?

A. I went to the City Hall.

Q. Will you state in your own way what took place there?

A. I went to the City Hall, soon after four o'clock, and saw Mayor Gaston, and offered any service that I could render in the way of suggestion or of action. Is it desired that I should go through the detail of all I did? It will take a good deal of time to give it in detail.

Q. Give the important parts of it. We will leave that to your judgment.

A. Soon afterwards, nothing being asked of me, I proposed to the Mayor that the garrisons at the forts should be sent for, offering to write for them if he approved. I did write a note to the Commandant of each fort, and also to the Captain of my steamer at the wharf to fire up immediately, and suggested that some gentleman should carry the notes, and also get a steamer in case mine could not be fired up soon enough. Mr. Atkinson offered to take one, and some other gentleman whom I didn't know (I understood he was Assistant City Solicitor, I don't know his name), took the other. I don't know whether it is important, but I would say that as I was writing the notes for the troops, Collector Russell asked me about the amount of powder necessary for blowing up buildings, and I replied very hurriedly from my haste to write the notes. I did not give my advice as fully as I might, only mentioning one hundred, one hundred and fifty or two hundred pounds, according to the character of the building.

Q. Did you have occasion to change that opinion?

A. Not from the intention that I had at the time, I will say, which was, to use the powder effectually, by compressing or tamping it. I would mention in explanation, as to using larger charges, that where you do not compress them, more powder is necessary to have the same effect. And after waiting a few minutes I went out and reconnoitred round the fire to the northward, and came back and said to the Mayor that I recommended the mining at once of the "Evening Gazette" office (in Congress street, I think it was), and also, *immediately*, the Currier & Trott building, or the "Transcript" office; that they should be mined, but not then blown up, as yet. Nothing was done, that I know of, at that moment. I went, soon after, up to the dome of the City Hall, and after waiting a few minutes, being there five or ten minutes, I felt convinced the "Transcript" office was on fire, or the building in the rear of it. I came down immediately to the Mayor, and said I was prepared to recommend in the strongest manner that that building should be blown up at once.

Q. When you first proposed to mine it, did you indicate at what time it should be blown up?

A. No, sir, I did not indicate the time. I said they would have to blow it up very soon though. I recommended it should be mined to be blown up when necessary, but I said, "You will soon have to blow it up." "I recommend it to be mined at once," was the expression I used.

I gave the advice urgently to immediately blow up the "Transcript" building, and the Mayor crossed the room and went out, as I understood, to give the directions, and as he did so, I reminded him of my suggestion about the "Gazette" office; whether he ordered that or not, I don't know.

Q. Do you know what he went out for?

A. I understood him to be going out to give, and understood that he did give, the directions to mine the Currier & Trott building, on the corner of Milk and Washington; soon after that, Mr. Atkinson (it was still before light, as I recollect) asked me if I would go out, and, as I understood him, direct, or take action towards staying the conflagration, and I answered that I would with great pleasure, if I had authority to act.

Q. What followed that?

A. He said he would apply for authority for me immediately, and at once proposed to the Mayor that I should be invested with authority to act in staying the conflagration.

Q. What was done then?

A. The Mayor hesitated, or appeared to hesitate, and slowly replied, "I am afraid of a conflict of authority with Mr. Damrell." Mr. Atkinson was still there, and urged further, or spoke further in relation to it, and on the Mayor's repeating that expression, I said, "Mr. Gaston, as the citizens should select those who should have the charge of their property, I will say to you, if Mr. Damrell and myself differ in opinion, his opinion shall be carried out. Do you wish me, when I am not with him, or near him, to use my best judgment in the matter?" His reply, as I understood him distinctly, was, that he did so wish. I then went out with Mr. Atkinson and searched for Mr. Damrell in Congress street, I think in Devonshire and Congress streets, but I found there instead, Mr. Carpenter, and whenever we met we acted in entire accord after that, both Mr. Carpenter and myself.

Q. Did you act with any one besides Mr. Carpenter?

A. No, sir. I do not recollect that I acted with any one that I understood had the same authority that he or I had. He appeared to have authority to act. I don't recollect of acting with any other person, but I generally gave the directions that seemed to me best, alone, on my own authority; for in passing backwards and forwards four or five times from Congress street to Kilby street and back again, seeking for Mr. Damrell, I never was able to find, and did not see him until about eleven o'clock that day.

Q. On whose authority did Mr. Carpenter act, — the Mayor's or Chief's?

A. I don't know, but I understood the Mayor's. I did not understand that any one else had the supreme right to give authority until about eleven to twelve o'clock that day, except the Mayor. I mean to say, I supposed that no one had supreme authority except the Mayor. I supposed he had supreme authority.

Q. And then you learned he had not?

A. Yes, sir. I had been previously requested to remain opposite number 40 State street, and told that Mr. Gaston and Mr. Damrell would see me there. Mr. Gaston came first, and then told me that he had not the authority to order the destruction of buildings; that no one had it but Mr. Damrell, or, in his absence, the two senior magistrates present. I did not question him about it, or mention that he had given the authority to me, because my impression at the time was, that he had ascertained this power since the time of my leaving him.

Q. Did he say so?

A. No, sir, he did not. I had the impression so fully upon my mind that I did not question him about it. Ordinarily I should have asked him, "Did I not understand you that you had the authority when you gave it to me?" Ordinarily I should do that, but I was under the impression that he had learned it within this time. I told him briefly what I had tried to do, and especially that I had tried to find Mr. Damrell, and made the suggestion that it would be very important if Mr. Damrell had a position at the lower eastern balcony of the Old State House, and I offered to Mr. Gaston to go there with him, and remain there, and make suggestions, or act, as they might wish. Soon after this, Mr. Damrell came to me, accompanied by a young lawyer by the name of Barry, who had offered his assistance previously, and who I suspect, but do not know, asked him to come to me. Would you like the conversation that then ensued?

Mr. Russell. — We should like to have that conversation.

Witness. — Mr. Damrell came up and said, "Well, sir, what do you want?" His manner appeared somewhat excited or irritated. I answered him, and I took especial pains to answer courteously, "To aid you in any manner, Mr. Damrell, by suggestion or actions." He said, "Well, what do you suggest?" I replied, "I suggest the mining of the cellar of the Boylston Insurance Co., the poorest building, directly opposite us, which will give the best entrance into that block; and round the corner, back of the New England Bank, the cellar of the wing under Mr. Skillings' office should be mined." He said, "Well, you know you must have a very careful man at each of those places." My answer was, "I have not those men, Mr. Damrell. You have them, I suppose." He said, "Where is your powder?"

A gentleman had just told me there was some at 80 State street, and I knew there were two tons on board of my boat which I had sent for from Fort Independence, and I said, "There is powder at 80 State street, I am told." He said, turning to cross the street and looking over his shoulder, "Well, bring on your powder." I soon saw him, apparently engaged in fixing a ladder in the third story of the building opposite, west of the Boyston Insurance Co. I said to Dr. Nichols, who was standing near me, "I will not mine those buildings without his written authority." Dr. Nichols said, "I will go and get it for you." I had understood that I had the authority to do so, by his saying, "Bring on your powder," but, to be doubly sure, I made that remark, and Dr. Nichols went over, and returned in a few minutes. I will say before that, that I said to him, "Please get his authority on separate cards for each place, stating the building with the amount of powder that he wishes used." He came back in five minutes or more, saying, "He says he will not do it." I then said, "I am powerless of course," and I could not act further. I then went around, and reconnoitred the fire from Congress up to Devonshire street, and I came to the conclusion that it was then so far under control that no more buildings would need to be blown up. A few minutes after that Alderman Jenks (as I was told he was) came to where I was, and I was told that Mr. Damrell had given him authority to destroy buildings. He came to me, or where I was, and I said, "I have been examining the fire, and, as it is now, I feel that I can say I would not advise that any more buildings should be blown up, unless there is some change of wind. I think you will not need to destroy any more of the buildings." That is about the sum of what I said to him.

Q. Did you at any time send message to Mr. Damrell that you would "blow up State street, Damrell or no Damrell," or any words to that effect?

A. No, sir. I never heard such words used by any one before. I do not know whether it is of importance enough to mention, but I will say in regard to number 40 State street, that early in the morning it occurred to me as of the first importance that that building should be protected. I regarded it as the most important point for the people of New England. The immense amount of money there, I considered was of more importance to the people than the government money, and I asked them to open the door, and then said to the persons at the door, "There will soon be some regular troops passing up, and I want you to call upon the first officer that comes up and ask him for a non-commissioned officer and four or six men to guard your door." I watched for the troops as they came, and requested Lieut. Whistler, and afterwards Major Rawles, to send a guard there, which was done previous. And now as to your inquiry, I would say, that about ten or eleven o'clock, as I was passing there, the people at 40 called upon me, as I was passing, to blow up the whole of the opposite side. "If you don't blow that up," they said, "it will catch on this side of State street, and burn to the North end." I said, "I will do it;" but I looked out for the weakest buildings on that block, and I then ordered those two already mentioned to be mined ready to be blown up; but I said, "That treasury building is a protecting wall front of itself;" and it was in consequence of that conviction that I had looked after and picked out those weak buildings, the Boylston Insurance Co's building, next to the Exchange and Mr. Skillings' office.

When they called upon me to blow up that building opposite, I refused to do it,—the large building west of the Boylston Insurance office.

Q. Did you send any message to Mr. Damrell?

A. No, sir, not of any kind. I am positive I never sent a message to Mr. Damrell, except this last request by Dr. Nichols, for written authority to blow up those two buildings.

Q. Was anything done towards mining those buildings?

A. Not by me, after the message to Mr. Damrell. There had been this much done, previously, however; after ordering powder into different buildings in Kilby street, I was standing with Mr. Atkinson, perhaps somewhere near ten o'clock, at Central street, looking towards No. 19, near the Post Office, and the corner south was then on fire, the corner of the block on Lindall street, I think, and I said to Mr. Atkinson, "Those buildings should be mined at once, those two old buildings." He said, "If you say so, I will have it done." I said, "Yes, have them mined;" I think I said, "with two or three hundred pounds of powder." Afterwards, after selecting the Skillings building, I ordered two hundred pounds into the cellar, I think, and then I went away, and tried to find Mr. Damrell, to inform him, and when I came back I found the powder had been brought out of No. 19, and found the door of Mr. Skillings, which had been open, was shut, and found two policemen standing by the kegs of powder, which they said Alderman Woolley had forbidden to be put in there. I said, finally, "Open the doors and put this in." The Alderman came up and forbade it, and I said, "He is one of the magistrates, and I cannot give any further orders without written authority." This occurred after having ordered powder into several buildings. In some cases it was exploded; in other cases, it was ordered out; in these one or two cases by Alderman Woolley, as I was told. The Alderman gave as a reason that the people were knocking the powder barrels to pieces and scattering it on the floor. I told him I had, in every way I could, prohibited that, and had told them to have a single cask broken, but only at the right moment, and the fuse applied. I might mention this instance: The day after, as some gentlemen at the Post Office were removing the money, one of them said, "I had five casks broken in a building, and a fuse put in each." I asked the question, "How many sparks does it take to blow up a powder magazine?" He said, "I never thought of that."

Q. Who was that gentleman?

A. I don't know his name. He must have belonged either to the Post Office or the Treasury.

Q. It was not General Burt?

A. No, sir, it was a Mr. Bailey, or Bradley, or some such name, as far as I could learn. He was a man apparently attached to the Treasury, or the Post Office.

Q. What was the length of the fuse used that night?

A. I do not know. In sending down for the garrisons to come up, I requested the officers to bring the ordnance sergeants with fuses. I might mention an instance of a building that was mined, that was absolutely on fire, I may say, or the one adjacent to it, on the corner of Kilby and Water streets. Orders were given two or three times to mine it, but the foreman of the engine would not do it. He said, "That building is too good to blow up." Finally it was mined, and a man, a German, I think he was, said that he put in an eighteen-minute fuse. I said, "You can burn a whole block in eighteen minutes; you don't want more than a five minutes' fuse."

Q. Was he a soldier?

A. No, sir, he was a citizen, and of Teutonic extraction, as I judge. I had a very urgent contest with one very earnest person, who was as fully convinced he was right as I was, who wanted to mine in the second stories. He said, "I have blown up half-a-dozen buildings in this way." I said, "Put it in the cellar; then it will lift the building up, and drop everything down and bring the walls on top of it." I could not get him to do it, and finally I said, "Get your powder in in some way, at any rate; it must do some good." Those were the people I had to act with, so you may judge how efficient they were. He was determined to blow from the second story. That will blow it in every direction, while fifty pounds, weighted down under an arch in the cellar, will lift the building up, drop everything down, and the volume of air rushing down and in, will generally bring the walls on top of it, and it will be protected from the fire; and weeks after, instead of burning and smouldering, it is cold, and the property under it is not destroyed, although the boxes or furniture may be broken.

Q. How large charges were used that night?

A. I first ordered one to two hundred pounds, urging them to weight it down or stancheon it down. Afterwards, when I found they didn't do that, I told them they might double that, — three or four hundred pounds, — but what was done I can't say, because I had no trained subordinates. I only know that those were the directions I gave.

Q. What successful explosions did you see; I mean explosions that were successful in staying the flames?

A. I don't know that I could specify the different ones, more than to say that the Currier & Trott explosion was successful. I was with the Mayor at the time, and in a few minutes some one came in and said it had been exploded, but only with partial success; but I have been told it had complete success, for it broke the burning timbers in the "Transcript" building and dropped them down and put the fire out, while the walls sheltered the Old South. Another building was the one where I had the discussion with this man, — the corner of Lindall and Kilby streets. I think that aided a great deal in preventing it from getting to the one that Mr. Atkinson mined under my direction, and where Mr. Woolley had the powder taken out. Then there were one or two in Conlgress street. I ordered powder in there, and was running down Lindal-street when the explosion occurred. I did not go back soon enough to see what the effect was. I ordered two or three mined in Congress street, and I ordered mining in seven places in Kilby street, but as I did not remain to witness the explosions, I cannot speak definitely about them.

Q. Was the building where this interview with Mr. Woolley took place burned?

A. The interview with Mr. Woolley took place right in front of Mr. Skillings' office, on Kilby street and that, was not harmed.

Q. The powder was removed from Skillings' office?

A. I think so eventually, sir, as he would not allow it to go in. He also had the powder removed, as I understood, from this No. 19 to the Post-Office doorway in Kilby street. There were there two old buildings, and I said if they could find an opening in the wall of the cellar between the two buildings, to put it in this opening. But I ordered it not to be fired until the flames had led round from the granite building south into these; that was my theory, generally not to have a mine sprung until the next building was on fire. My orders were that the mine under Skillings' office was not to be exploded until the Shoe & Leather Bank building had gone, and the flames had lapped round it.

Q. Should you have acted on that theory if you had had supreme control?

A. If I had had supreme control, I would have mined for blocks around or beyond the fire; but I would not have exploded mines until we needed and could utilize the space which the powder makes.

Q. You would not have gone to a distance and made a break?

A. No, sir, I would not do that, for you cannot use the space to put the fire out or bring water until the fire is next adjacent. One of the most prominent gentlemen of the city said to me, "I would have blown up between Spring Lane and Water street hours ago." I said, "No, I would mine it, but not blow it up yet." That I think was the radical difference between my opinions and those of very many intelligent gentlemen.

Q. There was nothing offensive in Mr. Woolley's manner?

A. No, sir. He was earnest, but not offensive to me. I did not so take it. I felt he was earnest about it, and I was not offended. It was true I felt that I knew more about the use of powder, but I didn't tell him so.

.*Q.* He didn't want to use it at all?

A. He said, as I understood him, that he didn't want to use it, and when I was told that he had been a fireman, I could realize that feeling, because I could see how the firemen would be afraid of the use of powder by persons not accustomed to its use. I think if I had trained men who would obey me, to use powder as my feeling was, the firemen would wish it used. I would clear away the firemen before I set the fuse, as well as all others near.

Q. Was the Webster Bank building mined that night, — the corner of Congress and State; that tall freestone building?

A. I was told that Damrell mined it. It never was mined by any order of mine, because I didn't consider it necessary to mine that building or the other next east — those two large fine buildings. I said, "There is no use to mine those;" but the cheap buildings I was in favor of mining. By mining those it would give the whole side of the Treasury building, and open the space into the return passage-way in the rear. I wanted to strike into the heart without breaking the front surface of the block.

Q. Did you act in concert with Gen. Burt that night?

A. No, sir, I do not recollect of seeing him that night. I have not seen him often enough, so directly as to know him readily in the night.

Q. In case of another great conflagration, should you recommend the use of explosives?

A. Yes, sir.

Q. Should you use powder or some other?

A. We know better how to manage powder; there is so much danger in glycerine, and so few that are experienced in the use of it. I would not have either used by persons unfamiliar with them. If miners from Hoosac Tunnel could be brought with their explosives, that might be well, but without experience, I think powder is better understood and could be safer used, and is sufficiently effective. I believe 100 lbs. of powder properly placed in the Court House would tear a hole up through the building.

Q. Is there any other subject or any other fact to which you wish to call our attention?

A. I don't think of any. There is one point to which perhaps I have already referred sufficiently. I think in the future, as to the controlling head, the person with the full power to direct, that he should be an architectural engineer, with a knowledge of the construction of buildings, and of the strength of materials, and that it would be of the utmost importance that he should in time of fires have a position accessible and known to all, like a general on a battle-field. If a general has not a fixed position on the battle-field, he is of very little use. I look upon the position of the Chief Engineer as similar to that, and instead of being in the fire, or doing a private's duty, as I might say, or a fireman's duty, I think it is of the first importance that he should have a place where every foreman of an engine and every magistrate or other person could know where to go to consult him. If the fire was near the City Hall, he might have his head-quarters there. He might, of course, occasionally make a personal reconnoissance, but in that case he should have a person in his position to inform those who came for consultation or directions. On the march I always had a fixed position, about one-third of the way from the head of the column usually, and I never left it without leaving an Adjutant General to represent me, — as also in battle a fixed position when possible.

Q. Have you any other suggestions to make?

A. I don't think of any, unless this suggestion; that there should not be another month that your Fire Department should be without some few men added to it, trained in the use theoretically, at least, of explosives; either teaching those that are in it, taking some of the most intelligent, or adding others to it.

They may not be needed more than once in ten or twenty years, but the salary of a person for ten years is nothing to the good that a single word may do, a single five minutes of instruction, at such a time. My idea is, there should be anywhere from three to eight or ten persons trained theoretically as soon as possible, and connected with the Fire Department of every large city.

Q. Do you know anything of the blowing off the roof of the Merchants' Exchange?

A. I do not. I spoke of mining that building. I knew of the liquor store of Robinson's being directly in the rear, and I considered that very dangerous, — as dangerous almost as a magazine. There is another thing I might mention to object to, if you think it worth while, and that is the practice of knocking in the heads of barrels of spirits or oil. Let them stay until the last minute, and not scatter them to the fire. That was done repeatedly, I was told. Barrels of oil and spirits were rolled out and the heads knocked in. I should judge it was a very important thing that people should be instructed not to scatter the means of spreading the fire. As Sherman said about Columbia, they cut open the bales of cotton and scattered and threw them into the trees. It is charged that General Sherman burned Columbia, but when I saw him at City Point he said he didn't; that the rebels cut open the bales of cotton and set them on fire and scattered them on the trees through the city, and destroyed it in that way; and afterwards I met an ambulance of generals, — Lee, Ewell, Wise and others were among them, — when they were coming down as prisoners, and they told me that Wade Hampton fired his own house at Columbia, which is an additional proof of what Sherman said. That was the reason of the complete destruction of Columbia, and I look upon knocking in the heads of barrels of spirits and oil as a similar thing.

GEORGE W. BOYNTON, *sworn.*

Q. (By Mr. Russell.) What is your position?

A. I was appointed Chief Constable of the Commonwealth Nov. 20.

Q. Will you state what connection you had with the great fire?

A. There was no Chief on Nov. 9th. I arrived Nov. 10th, and all the officers in the vicinity were here, assisting in recovering goods. On Monday, all the officers in the State were called to Boston, and were divided into two details. I had charge of one detail. Capt. A. J. Gearey had charge of the other. When the fire was over, many merchants who had lost property, and who had money and other valuables in the ruins, asked for details of officers, and they were furnished.

Mr. Savage, Chief of Boston Police, issued orders to close liquor shops and beer shops. He issued a similar order as to liquor shops, and requested beer shops to close. Almost all complied with the order and the request, — all except some low places.

Other officers were detailed to watch various districts, with orders to arrest all persons violating the liquor law. They were relieved, and kept on duty day and night. The first day or two, they arrested thirty or forty, who were fined in the Municipal Court. After four or five days, we had occasion to arrest very few. When the excitement of the fire had abated, we procured search-warrants and recovered a large amount of stolen goods.

The city was as free from roughs as it usually is, and was as orderly as I ever knew it throughout the thirteen or fourteen days, and while our force was on duty. Our force amounts to one hundred men.

JAMES R. CARRET, *sworn.*

Q. (By Mr. Russell.) What position did you hold on Nov. 9th?

A. I was Mayor's clerk.

Q. State what took place at City Hall in relation to blowing up buildings that came within your knowledge.

A. Gen. Benham came in. After some conversation, he requested the Mayor to give him authority to blow up buildings. The Mayor said he had no power to do so, but asked him to give the Engineers the benefit of his experience.

About eight or nine A. M. Sunday, a young man came with a message from Gen. Burt, saying that the Chief Engineer had stopped him and

Benham from blowing up buildings, and asked him to overrule the Chief. The Mayor replied that he had not the power, but that it belonged to the Chief Engineer, and that it would make great confusion, if he, being at the City Hall, should give orders in conflict with the Chief. About 10 A. M. Gen. Burt in person repeated the complaint, and received a like answer.

Q. Did you hear the Mayor give any one authority to blow up buildings?

A. I was there all the time with the Mayor, and heard him give no one authority to blow up buildings. Gen. Benham repeated his request, and urged that he might receive authority from the Mayor, but was repeatedly refused.

APPENDIX TO EVIDENCE.

Statement (exact and estimated) of the several Companies, in relation to the time it took for them to get to the Fire on Saturday, November 9th, 1872, as per letters on file.

Company.	Location.	Time.	Letters signed by
Engine No. 1.	Cor. Fourth & Dorch. sts., S. B.	12 m.	John Ray, Engineer.
" " 2.	Fourth, bet. L and K sts., S. B.	25 m.	Geo. O. Twiss, "
" " 3.	Washington, near Dover.	8 or 10 m.	T. Hutchings, "
" " 4.	Brattle square.	6 or 7 m.	Dexter R. Dearing, "
" " 5.	Marion street, E. B.	20 or 25 m.	Josiah S. Battis, "
" " 6.	Wall street.	10 m.	J. C. Traver, "
" " 7.	East street.	1½ m.	Charles Riley, "
" " 8.	Salem street.	8 m.	B. S. Flanders, "
" " 9.	Paris street, E. B.	20 m.	Geo. W. Brown, "
" " 10.	Mt. Vernon and River streets.	12 or 15 m.	Gilman Tyng, "
" " 11.	Sumner street, E. B.	20 m.	W. H. Sturtevant, "
" " 12.	Warren & Dudley sts., Highlands.	20 m.	James T. Cole, "
" " 13.	Cabot street, Highlands.		
" " 14.	Centre street, Highlands.	25 m.	Thomas Nannery, "
" " 15.	Broadway Extension, S. B.	5 m.	David E. Gilman, "
" " 16.	Temple street, Ward 16.	55 m.	Eugene A. Freeman, "
" " 17.	Meeting House Hill, Ward 16.	30 m.	Chas. C. Lane, "
" " 18.	Harvard street, Ward 16.	55 m.	Lewis Briggs, "
" " 19.	Norfolk street, Ward 16.	1 h. 30 m.	E. B. Hebard, "
" " 20.	Walnut street, Ward 16.	35 m.	Franklin Muzzy, "
" " 21.	Boston street, Ward 16.	20 m.	J. R. Gilbert, "
Hose " 1.	Salem street.	8½ m.	A. L. Pearson, Driver.
" " 2.	Hudson street.	3½ m.	Frank Walker, "
" " 3.	North Grove street.	15 m.	H. Ely, "
" " 4.	Northampton street.	12 m.	B. F. Thayer, "
" " 5.	Shawmut avenue, near Canton.	10 m.	Silas Lovell, "
" " 6.	391 Chelsea street, E. B.	15 m.	Charles Brooks, "
" " 7.	Tremont streets, Highlands.	15 m.	Geo. W. Stimpson. "
" " 8.	Church street.	8 m.	William Blake, "
" " 9.	B street, South Boston.	8 m.	P. W. Gowen. "
" " 10.	Dorchester st., Wash. Village.	12 m.	A. P. Hawkins, "
Hook and Ladder No. 1.	Warren square.	6 m.	Geo. W. Thompson, "
" " " " 2.	Sumner and Orleans sts., E. B.	10 m.	J. E. Thayer, "
" " " " 3.	Harr. ave., cor. Wareham street.	8 m.	J. B. Prescott, "
" " " " 4.	Eustis street, Highlands.	15 m.	J. M. Huggins, Driver *pro tem*
" " " " 5.	Fourth and Dorch sts., S. B.	11 m.	B. F. Donnell, Driver.
" " " " 6.	Temple street, Ward 16.	Not taken	David S. Black, "
" " " " 7.	Meeting House Hill, Ward 16.	30 m.	Jason Gordon. "
Extinguisher " 1.	North Grove street.	7 m.	Thos. Merritt, Driver. *pro tem*
" " 2.	Wareham street, Harrison ave.	8 m.	W. A. Gaylord, Driver.

Steam Tug "Louis Osborn," from East Boston, having Blake's Fire Pump, 14-inch steam cylinder and 8-inch water cylinder, received orders at 9 : 30 o'clock, P. M., of Saturday, Nov. 9th, to proceed to the Hartford & Erie Bridge, and stay the fire at that point. The messenger was sent by the Chief Engineer, at 8 : 45 o'clock, P. M., and they received it at their wharf in East Boston, at the above time.

Statement of the different Companies, in relation to the time it took to get their apparatus to the "State Street Block Fire, Nov. 18th," and to "Rand & Avery's Fire, Nov. 20th," horses used.

Companies.	Nov. 18.	Nov. 20.	Remarks.
Engine Co. No. 1.	20 m.	20 m.	Horses used at the fire of Nov. 9th and 10th.
" " " 2.	20 m.	20 m.	Horses used at the fire of Nov. 9th and 10th.
" " " 3.	14 m.	14 m.	T. Hutchings, Engineer.
" " " 4.	4 m.		Were called out before the alarm was sounded.
" " " 5.	15 m.	15 m.	J. S. Battis, Engineer.
" " " 6.			Was in service on the burnt district of Nov. 9th.
" " " 7.	9 m.	10 m.	Charles Riley, Engineer.
" " " 8.	3¼ m.	3 m.	B. S. Flanders, "
" " " 9.	14 m.	18 m.	Geo. W. Brown, "
" " " 10.			
" " " 11.	25 m.	20 m.	W. H. Sturtevant, "
" " " 12.	25 m.	25 m.	J. T. Cole, "
" " " 13.	20 m.	25 m.	Francis Swift, "
" " " 14.	20 m.	20 m.	Horses used at the fire of Nov. 9th and 10th.
" " " 15.	15 m.	15 m.	D. E. Gilman, Engineer.
" " " 16.	44 m.	48 m.	Used horses at the fire of Nov. 9th and 10th.
" " " 17.	40 m.	35 m.	Charles C. Lane. Engineer.
" " " 18.	40 m.	40 m.	Letter signed by Lewis Briggs, Engineer.
" " " 19.	1 hour, 5 m.	55 m.	E. B. Hebard, Engineer.
" " " 20.	45 m.	35 m.	Horses were used at the fire of Nov. 9th and 10th.
" " " 21.		17 m.	J. R. Gilbert, Engineer.
Hose Co. No. 1.	4 m.	3½ m.	A. L. Pearson, Driver.
" " 2.	10 m.	8 m.	F. Walker, "
" " 3.	10 m.	5 m.	Thomas Merritt, " *pro tem.*
" " 4.	20 m.	18 m.	Benj. F. Thayer, "
" " 5.	17 m.	15 m.	Silas Lovell, "
" " 6.	w't to ferry.	w't to ferry.	Horse used at the fire of Nov. 9th and 10th.
" " 7.	20 m.	25 m.	George W. Stimpson, Driver.
" " 8.			
" " 9.	17 m.	12 m.	T. W. Gowen, the driver, states that it took as long as it would by hand.
" " 10.	14 m.	15 m.	Horse used at the fire of Nov. 9th.
Hook and Ladder No. 1.	5 m.	3 or 4 m.	George W. Thompson, Driver.
" " " " 2.	15 m.	20 m.	J. E. Thayer, "
" " " " 3.	17 m.	12 m.	J. B. Prescott, "
" " " " 4.	25 m.	20 m.	J. M. Huggins, " *pro tem.*
" " " " 5.	20 m.	25 m.	Horses used at the fire of Nov. 9th.
" " " " 6.	50 m.	47 m.	David S. Black, Driver.
" " " " 7.			Did not take the time.
Extinguisher Corps, 1.	10 m.	5 m.	Charles E. Wilson, Driver.
" " 2.	17 m.	15 m.	W. A. Gaylord, "

Statement of the number of Engines, Hose, and Hook & Ladder, Carriages, with the number of Men and amount of Hose that attended the great Fire of Nov. 9th, from out of town.

Chief Engineer.	City or Town.	Engines.	Hose Companies.	Hook & Ladder Companies.	Men.	Feet of Hose.
P. H. Raymond	Cambridge, Mass.	3	2	1	75	1,500
Wm. E. Delano	Charlestown, "	2	3	0	60	2,000
Samuel Hutchins . . .	Chelsea, "	1	2	0	85	1,000
W. W. Kimball	Lynn, "	2	2	0	27	1,400
D. B. Lord	Salem, "	2	1	0	67	2,000
Luther Ladd	Lawrence, "	1	1	0	11	700
Alfred Kenrick, jr. . .	Brookline, "	1 (hand)	1	1	69	1,100
C. A. Belford	W. Roxbury, "	2	1	0	21	1,200
James R. Hopkins . .	Somerville, "	1	3	0	60	1,200
A. D. Drew	Watertown, "	1	1	0	21	800
R. M. Lucas	Newton, "	2	2	0	51	1.750
S. E. Combs	Worcester, "	2	3	0	60	3,800
Thomas J. Borden . .	Fall River, "	2	4	0	60	2,200
Onslow Gilmore . . .	Stoneham, "	1	1	0	18	850
T. W. Hough	Malden, "	1	2	0	54	2,000
John R. Morton	Melrose, "	2	1	0	15	400
Benj. H. Sumner . . .	Medford, "	1	2	0	40	1,000
Chas. H. Davis	Wakefield, "	2 (hand)	0	0	88	750
Wm. H. Temple . . .	Reading, "	1 (hand)	1	0	105	500
A. H. Howland, jr. . .	New Bedford, "	1	1	0	26	700
Marshall Parks	Waltham, "	1	1	0	14	700
Oliver E. Green	Providence "	3	3	0	30	1,700
A. E. Hendrick	New Haven, "	1	1	0	22	900
Daniel A. Delamoy . .	Norwich, "	2	3	0	166	2,300
S. L. Marston	Portsmouth, N. H.	1	1	0	45	1,100
B. C. Kendall	Manchester, "	2	2	0	63	1.200
———	Biddeford, Maine. Started and got as far Portsmouth, N. H.	0	2	0	175	3,000
A. J. Cummings . . .	Portland, "	1	1	0	12	1,000
E. G. Parrott, Com'dant	Charlestown Navy Yard	2	2	1	81	1,000
T. T. S. Laidley, "	Watertown Arsenal,	1	2	0	25	1,100
E. P. Davis, Chief Eng.	Hyde Park,	1	1	0	55	1,200

THE RICHARDS FIRE ESCAPE AND HOSE ELVATOR.

This invention consists of a shaft put into or above the cornice of a building. On this shaft is a drum, and on the drum, which is 12 inches in diameter, is wound a pliable wire ladder, composed of 15 wire cables $\frac{1}{8}$-inch in diameter. The steps are composed of flat band-iron $\frac{1}{8}$-inch thick, $1\frac{1}{8}$ inch wide and 20 inchs long. Inside of the ladder drum, suspended from the shaft, is a sheave or pulley, through which passes a wire cable, one end having a hook and snatch-block, the other end a hook alone. These hooks are fastened to the bottom step of the ladder. The ladder and hose elevator are wound up together by means of gearing upon the roof. After they are wound up entirely out of sight and protected from the weather, a brake is applied, holding them in position. The brake is controlled from the sidewalk, in a box similar to the fire-alarm box, the same key fitting both.

On discovery of a fire by a policeman or a fireman, the box is unlocked, the lever pulled that releases the brake, and the ladder and hose elevator unroll and come to the ground, being ready for use in from twelve to fifteen seconds. The weight on the bottom of the ladder is sufficient to insure its coming down. On reaching the ground, the ladder is secured firmly to eye-bolts in the pavement. On the arrival of the firemen they find everything ready for work. The firemen first go to the roof or any story by the ladder, the hooks of the hose elevator are released from the bottom step of the ladder, and to one of them is attached the hose, while the other hook is fastened to the hose-cart. The horse is then driven off, and the hose rises to the desired height. The laborious work of elevating the hose by hand is entirely avoided. The ladders are always on hand, and can be made ready for use almost instantly.

The advantages of this plan are as follows: —

The ladders are always available, and may be ready for the firemen by the time they arrive upon the ground.

The safety of the firemen is provided for beyond a doubt, as the machinery cannot fall until the walls fall, and the men need not fear as to their escape being cut off, as is the case when they are dependent on the stairs for a retreat. With the present ladder system, firemen can neither ascend to nor escape from the top of a high building. Give the firemen a feeling of security and a sure means of retreat, and they will stay at their work with a determination to do something. A very important feature of this plan is, that it provides for the certain escape of the inmates of the burning building. In a hotel, each room may be provided with a stout web, or leather strap with a ring sewed into it. By means of this, a timid person, invalid or child may be lowered to the ground wieh perfect safety, simply by fastening this strap about the chest and attaching the ring to the hose elevator. By the same process, valuable trunks, pianos and other heavy articles of furniture may be taken from the building.

The present system of fighting fire often compels the firemen to open the lower doors of the building to carry their hose up the stairs, in order that the streams of water may be directed upon the fire. This action has the same effect on the fire as opening the register to a stove, giving an additional draught, and thus causing the fire to burn more fiercely. But by the proposed plan, the lower part of the building is kept entirely closed, as the fire is fought entirely from the outside. The water is applied only where it is needed, and the destruction of goods by water is avoided. The firemen are enabled to go to the roof, and by opening the roof they force the fire to burn directly up, and prevent its seeking the windows for vent, setting the whole house on fire and catching adjoining buildings.

The smoke is also allowed to pass out, which is the greatest enemy firemen have to contend with.

The whole body of the water is thrown on to the fire, which is not the case where it is thrown up from the street and only reaches the fire in the shape of a spray. The great waste of water is avoided, which is quite an item where the pipes are so small as they are in the thickly-settled parts of Boston. A stream of water has been taken to the roof of an 85-ft. building, by the Chicago Fire Department in 1½ minutes' time.

My plan in connection with my Fire Escape and Hose Elevator, for preventing general conflagrations, like those of Boston and Chicago, is looked upon favorably by the leading firemen of the United States. It consists of my ladders and hose elevators being placed upon the highest and most exposed buildings throughout the city, as shown in sketch, and marked with figures 1, 2, 3, etc.

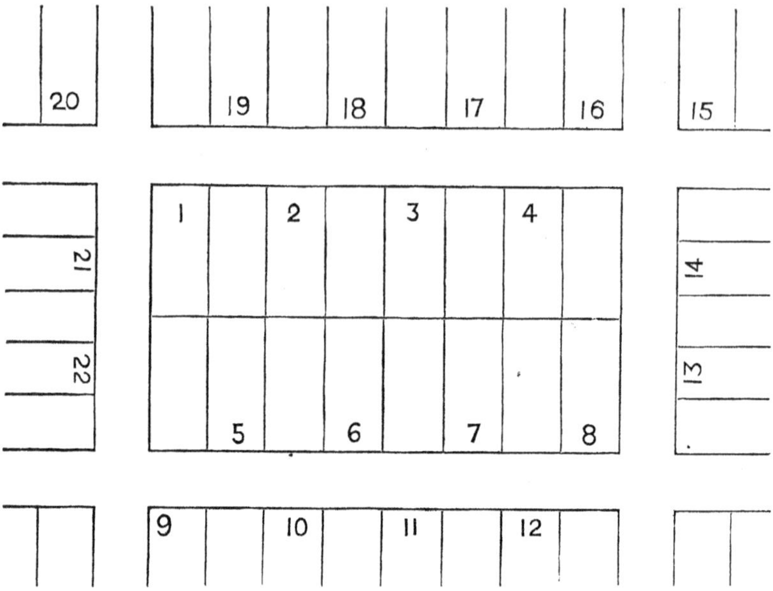

Suppose No. 1 to be the burning building, the ladder on No. 1 to be used, the fire would likely be stopped, with the assistance my ladder would give the firemen. If they were driven away, they could fall back and lower the ladders 2, 5, 19, 20, 21, which would enable them to take their hose to the roofs, and concentrate their streams upon the burning building, which would get the whole body of the water into it, instead of a spray, as if it were thrown from the street. A fire could not possibly get beyond the reach of the firemen where there is such a concentration of streams. If the city of Boston can sustain such a loss by fire on as calm a night as the 9th of November, surely something must be done to avert another such a calamity during the heavy winds and dry season. Another alarming thing is the small capacity of the water-pipes throughout the city. If a fire can be checked in its infancy, the pipes are large enough.

HENRY A. RICHARDS,
32 *Appleton street,*
Boston, Mass.

LETTER FROM CHIEF ENGINEER OF FALL RIVER.

FALL RIVER, Dec. 13, 1872.

THOS. RUSSELL, ESQ., *Chairman:* —

DEAR SIR, — Your telegram of 11th inst. came duly to hand, but my business engagements to-day are such that I am unable to comply with your request. I presume your object is to make inquiries in relation to the operations of the Fire Department on the occasion of your recent disastrous conflagration. — I will state briefly what knowledge I have of the matter : —

I did not reach your city until 5 o'clock, P. M. on Sunday, Nov. 10th, having been delayed several hours in procuring transportation, and therefore know nothing of the affair previous to that hour. Immediately on arrival I reported to Mayor Gaston, at City Hall, tendering him the use of two steam fire-engines, four hose reels, with 2,200 feet of hose, and sixty men. On consultation with the Mayor — the fire then being apparently under control — it was deemed expedient to allow one of the steamers, — viz. : "Metacomet No. 3,"— to return immediately to Fall River, for which I made arrangements at once (retaining for use steamer "Niagara No. 4," all of the hose and nearly all of the men) and then returned to the City Hall, where I then found Chief Engineer Damrell, who decided that we could best serve him by placing the steamer and hose reels in the house of your Steamer No. 7, and answering alarms, if any should be given. After seeing the apparatus properly stored in "No. 7's" house, I made the entire circuit of the "burnt district" twice. About three minutes after passing the corner of Washington street, — on my way back to "Steamer 7's" house, being then about twelve o'clock, — an alarm was sounded from Box 42, on Winter street. I hastened to the engine house, where I found the men sitting quietly, having no knowledge of the alarm, as the gong on that house did not strike, notified them of the alarm, and proceeded rapidly a little in advance of them to the corner of Washington and Summer streets, where I found a sharp fire raging in the buildings just east of one occupied by Shreve, Crump & Low. Deeming the rear or southerly side of the fire to be much the most critical point, I ordered the engine stationed at the corner of Avon place, and laid two lines of hose to the rear of the fire and on top of the low or rear part of the stores where the fire originated ; laid a third line from a hydrant, but with no effect, as there was not sufficient pressure to carry the stream twenty feet beyond the pipe. Afterwards laid a third line of hose from your steamer "No. 7," the hose and pipe being managed throughout by our men. Also supplied your "No. 2" with one line of hose. The two streams from our steamer "Niagara No. 4," and the stream from your "No. 7" maintained firmly at the original position, not moving more than fifty feet until the fire was nearly extinguished. All of them were powerful streams and did excellent service. The only assistance required by us from your department was a supply of fuel. Soon after our engine was well at work, I ascertained from one of your men the signal used by them to call for fuel, and then ordered our Engineer to sound it about once a minute until fuel was brought, which was soon done, and a good supply of excellent quality was furnished by your department throughout the night. Feeling that the vital point was to prevent the fire from spreading southerly and easterly, — the buildings in those directions being closely connected to those on fire, while at the north and west it was bounded by streets, — I did not leave that side of the fire until after daylight Monday morning, and therefore have no knowledge of the operations on the opposite side. One of your Assistant Engineers was with us frequently, and Chief Damrell several times, and their directions, I think, were very judicious. I reported to Chief

Damrell again at the City Hall, about nine A. M. Monday morning, when he relieved us from any further service, and we returned home with the apparatus and men at noon on Monday. The only weak points that I observed, were the absence of any provision for giving the alarm at Steamer 7's house,and the very low pressure in your hydrants, rendering them worthless except for supplying engines. If you desire to ask any questions which I am able to answer, I will answer them with pleasure; Tuesday afternoon next, between two and five o'clock, is the only time during the next four or five days, when it will be possible for me to appear before you, but I have no doubt the foregoing statement will answer your purpose.

Regretting that I am unable to comply literally with your request to-day,

Very respectfully yours,

(Signed,) THOMAS J. BORDEN,

Chief Eng. Fall River Fire Dep't.

SELF-PROPELLING STEAM FIRE ENGINE.

MANCHESTER, N. H. Dec. 18th, 1872.

HON. THOS. RUSSELL, Boston, Mass: —

MY DEAR SIR: — Your letter, of Dec. 17th, to our Mr. Bean, is just received and handed to me for answer.

The Self-Propelling Steam Fire Engine which was sent to Boston at the time of the great fire was built by the Amoskeag Manufacturing Company, with one other of a simliar pattern, in order to test the principle, and so far they seem to have been an entire success. The only objection we have known made to them, is their supposed liability to frighten horses when moving through the streets in the daytime. To this objection we give no weight, as our observation here in the country has shown that the Self-Propelling Engines are no more likely to frighten horses than Steam Fire Engines drawn by horses with the fires burning, as is usual when drawn through the streets; and as much the larger number of fires occur in the night, when there are no horses in the streets, this objection cannot lie with any force against the use of the Self-Propeller.

The mate to the one in Boston has been in use in the Fire Department of the City of New York since the First of November, and in one week run out to twenty-seven alarms and worked at eight fires. The Self-Propelling Engine there has proved a complete success, and no objection has been raised to its use. The engine is kept always ready to run out, with steam at about twenty to thirty pounds' pressure, which is done without substantially any extra cost. The Fire Commissioners are now contemplating the purchase of several more.

One has been ordered by the City of San Francisco, on account of its success in New York, and the Detroit Fire Commissioners have, I believe, decided to substitute a Self-Propellor for an engine which we are building for them.

The Self-Propeller in Boston is of the medium size; we have decided that it is preferable to make them of the largest size, as the trouble of moving them is not increased very much by their weight.

The Self-Propelling Steam Fire Engine costs from fifty-five hundred ($5,500) to six thousand ($6,000) dollars, being about $1,000 only more than the cost of the engine to be drawn by horses.

I do not wish you to understand that we consider this engine a perfect self-propelling machine, but so far as its use up to the present time goes, we consider it an entire success. Any alterations that may be needed will be very slight.

If desirable, our Mr. Bean will attend your committee and give you verbally any information you may desire on the subject.

Yours, very truly,

E. A. SHAW,

Per James A. Fracker.

Report from officers of United States Signal Service, in Boston, to the Chief of the Signal Service of the Army, at Washington: —

The wind at this station during the progress of the fire varied from north-west to north, with a velocity of five to nine miles per hour, the weather being cool, clear and pleasant.

"On approaching the fire on the north, or windward side, as close as the heat would allow, the in-draught of air through the burning streets assumed the character of a brisk wind, probably sixteen or eighteen miles per hour, while the heat was so intense as to cause smoke, steam, etc., to be carried up in spirals to a great elevation. On the south, or lee side, the induced currents of air were very strong — probably thirty or thirty-five miles per hour, carrying the fire bodily to windward. This state of affairs appears the reverse of the Chicago fire, where the strength of the wind was sufficient to overcome the induced currents, and the fire burned to leeward. It appears as if the high wind permitted the in-draught to rise at a considerable angle after reaching the fire, leaving a large space of rarefied air in its front, inducing stronger currents to flow, which, on meeting the in-draught, gave the spiral or whirlwind form to the ascending current.

"During the fire, a flock of ducks passed at a great height overhead; and the light reflected from their plumage made them appear as fire-balls, passing rapidly through the air. Many who saw them called them meteors, and likened them to the balls said to have been seen north-west during the great fires in that region. As an example of the great heat diffused, I would state, that, during the night, I exposed a thermometer in the observatory to the full glare of the fire, when it rose near five degrees, although placed upwards of two thousand feet from the burning district, and dead to windward of it. No other phenomena occurred, the barometer rising slightly, and the weather remaining unchanged."

H. E. COLE.

The "Traveller" newspaper observer, Mr. Q. T. Paine, of this city, reported the thermometer: —

	Sunrise.	*2 P. M.*	*10 P. M.*	*Weather.*
Nov'r 9.	41°	$51\frac{1}{2}$°	$41\frac{1}{2}$°	Very clear.
" 10.	36°	50°	40°	" "

Wind on the 9th throughout, W. N. W. (light); 10th, W. N. W., A. M; N. W., P. M.; N. N. W. evening (all light).

LETTER FROM W. W. GREENOUGH.

20 West Street, Boston, 20th Jan'y, 1873.

Hon. Thomas Russell: —

Dear Sir: — In answer to your inquiry of this date, relative to the supply of slide valves, since the time when I appeared before your committee, I will state generally and specifically.

1. Tihe district which was burned by the great fire was substantially the dangerous part of the city, so far as the distributing mains of the Gas Company were concerned. The mains are now separated from the rest of the city, either by an absolute cutting off or by iron slide valves. When the pipes are relaid in this district, they will be provided with all the iron valves necessary to protect each street in case of a similar or smaller catastrophe.

2. In the years 1870 and 1871 we introduced 136 slide valves at different points of our distribution. In 1872, 116 additional were put in, including those rendered necessary by the fire and for the protection of other neighborhoods.

3. We shall proceed during the present season to insert slide valves wherever throughout our distributing they appear to be most needed, — continuing the work from time to time, so long as deemed necessary. In this point the interest of the public is equally ours.

Yours respectfully,

W. W. GREENOUGH.

LETTER FROM GEO. GARDNER.

Hon. Thomas Russell: —

Dear Sir: — As you desired me to send you some details, omitted in giving my observations on the nights of the Great Fire, I would mention that Messrs. Hovey & Co., to aid in saving their store, had a large number of fire buckets to distribute where they might be wanted; that the gas light was an advantage; that there were plenty of hands, and, what was very fortunate, that there was an iron rod, about waist high, along the eaves of the building, put up for protection when clearing off snow; the security this gave added greatly to freedom of action in extinguishing the fire on the roof.

Sunday night there was danger on the upper side of the store, and had not the fire been checked before reaching it there would have been a less chance of successful resistance, for there was only the dim light of a few lanterns, and there were not many people in the store, the military having prevented those passing who had gathered to go there. It would have been better to have let them pass with a guard to verify their claim of connection with the building.

The gas explosions on Sunday night broke the drain in the stone, and gas was rising from it on Monday; I consequently called on the Mayor and suggested that, for the gas to escape, the street drain should be opened some distance above. He was prompt to require the proper persons to examine the suggestion; this, if an effectual mode, has advantages over shutting off the gas.

Respectfully yours,
GEORGE GARDNER.

HON THOMAS RUSSELL: —

DEAR SIR: — Mr. Tibbetts, of Salem, states that they received word there to furnish aid to the large fire at 10.15 o'clock, P. M. of Saturday, Nov. 9th.

Yours, etc.,
H. W. LONGLEY,
Secretary.

FIRE SURVEYS.

From a recent work on "Fire Surveys," by Capt. Shaw, the Chief of the London Fire Department, the Commission make the extracts below, and ask for their *carefnl* attention:—

Stone. — "In the whole range of building materials, there is perhaps none so unsuited for resisting fire as that most commonly used." p. 13.

"Stone is in no possible sense fire-proof, but, on the contrary, yields to the effects of a fire more rapidly than almost any other material commonly used for building."

Stone and other buiiding materials. — Serious and recent fires in large warehouses in London showed the following results: —

"Bricks, uninjured; wood, seriously damaged, but only partially consumed. Iron, fractured, and consequently worthless. Stone, shivered into fragments, and totally destroyed." p. 87.

There are instances of "worthlessness of stone and iron for resisting moderately high temperature, such as 600° or 700° Far." For supports of floors, "wood of any kind, but especially hard wood, is infinitely preferable to stone or iron." p. 42.

Cast-iron Columns. — "Iron at 212° Far., or boiling point, loses 15 per cent. of strength; at 612° has no strength at all; at 2787°, which is much below that of the centre of a large building on fire, it becomes liquid."

Introduction of steam power has undoubtedly increased the risk of fire to a very serious extent, in a fourfold manner. From "furnace, "friction," by "heating and dessicating buildings, so as to be more easily set on fire," and "vibration of buildings from machinery weakens the walls so that falling of roof, or floors," is "likely to bring the whole building down." p. 55.

Height of buildings. — "It is found that sixty feet is the greatest height at which a building can be quickly protected, and that the cube of 60, or 216,000 cubic feet, is the largest cubical capacity which can be protected with reasonable hope of success after a fire has once come to a head." p. 12.

Gas. — "Every building lighted with gas should have two command cocks to the main pipe, — one inside, and the other outside of the house, — and a meter should be placed so as to have free ventilation with the open air." p. 62.

Safety. — "For *safety of life*, all high buildings should be provided with external ladders of wrought iron." p. 10.

Risks of fire. — "With regard to risk of fire, the contents of a building are of much more importance than the building itself." p. 2.

Portable apparatus. — "Portable apparatus," among which he names: "Stand Pipes," "Hand Pumps, with Pails," and "Hand Pumps without Pails."

RESPIRATOR FOR FIREMEN.

COPY OF PART OF A PRIVATE LETTER FROM PROF. TYNDALL.

New York, Dec. 20, 1872.

I think you might readily get a fireman's respirator constructed by some skilful mechanician in Boston. The mouth-piece may be one of those employed for the inhalation of nitrous oxide gas. Of course it must be made to fit the mouth very well. Associated with this, you can have a cylinder of glass or tin, containing first a layer of an inch or so of cotton well moistened with glycerine, and well teazed, so as not to form a clot. On this a thin layer of dry cotton wool. On this a layer of an inch or so of small charcoal fragments, then a little more cotton wool to keep the charcoal in, and finally a cap of open wire gauze to hold all together.

With a little practice it will be easy to determine the proper density of the packing. Of course the breathing must be tolerably free. You can, if you like, have a hood associated with the respirator, and glass in the hood to see through, or the spectacles may be used separately.

With a respirator of this kind, a fireman could live for hours in an atmosphere, a single inhalation of which without the respirator would be intolerable. If carbonic acid be troublesome (but with the air circulating in fires I should think this was hardly ever the case), a layer of fragments of lime might be added. With such a respirator a young officer of Engineers at Chatham went some time ago into a cupboard with various animals, forced carbonic acid into the cupboard, and waited there till all the creatures had died around him!

Mr. Ladd, of Beak street, Regent street, London, undertook to construct these respirators. The subject was being experimented on by the London Fire Brigade when I came away.

(Signed,) JOHN TYNDALL.

INDEX.

INDEX TO WITNESSES.

INDEX TO EVIDENCE.

www.ingramcontent.com/pod-product-compliance
Lightning Source LLC
LaVergne TN
LVHW021048110826
845150LV00001B/16

* 9 7 8 1 4 2 5 5 6 8 3 4 4 *